The Annapolis
Book of Seamanship

by John Rousmaniere
Illustrated and Designed by Mark Smith

SIMON & SCHUSTER
New York London Toronto Sydney Tokyo Singapore

Simon and Schuster
Simon & Schuster Building
Rockefeller Center
1230 Avenue of the Americas
New York, New York 10020

SIMON AND SCHUSTER and colophon are registered trademarks
of Simon & Schuster, Inc.

Designed by Mark Smith
Manufactured in the United States of America

10

Library of Congress Cataloging-in-Publication Data
Rousmaniere, John.
     The Annapolis book of seamanship.

     Includes index.
     1. Sailing   2. Seamanship   I. Title.
GV811.5.R68 1989   623.88   89-6156
ISBN 0-671-67447-1

Dedicated to my father and
my sons:
James Ayer, William Pierce,
and Dana Starr Rousmaniere

By John Rousmaniere

Instructional Books

A Glossary of Modern Sailing Terms (1976, 1989)
The Annapolis Book of Seamanship (1983, 1989)
The Student and Instructor Workbook for The Annapolis Book of Seamanship (1984)
The Sailing Lifestyle (1985)
Desirable and Undesirable Characteristics of Offshore Yachts (editor, 1987)

History Books

The Luxury Yachts (1981)
America's Cup Book, 1851-1983 (1983)
The Golden Pastime: A New History of Yachting (1986)
The Low Black Schooner: Yacht America, 1851-1945 (1987)
A Picture History of the America's Cup (1989)

Other Books

No Excuse to Lose (with Dennis Conner, 1978)
The Enduring Great Lakes (editor, 1979)
"Fastnet, Force 10" (1980)
The Norton/Dolphin Book Club Sailor's Log (1987)

Videotapes

The Annapolis Book of Seamanship Video Series
    Volume 1, "Cruising Under Sail" (1987)
    Volume 2, "Heavy Weather Sailing" (1987)
    Volume 3, "Safety at Sea" (1987)
    Volume 4, "Sailboat Navigation" (1988)
    Volume 5, "Daysailers: Sailing and Racing" (1988)
Powerboat Navigation (1988)

Introduction to the Second Edition

Seamanship has been defined as "the art of sailing, maneuvering, and preserving a ship or a boat in all positions and under all reasonable circumstances." It encompasses the skills and equipment for safe sailing, accurate navigation, and general on-board self-sufficiency.

In other words, to be a good sailor in whatever type of boat is nothing more than to practice good seamanship. My purpose here is to describe those skills with thoroughness and clarity for beginning, intermediate, and advanced sailors of all types of boats.

Thoroughness and clarity receive equal emphasis here. While attention to detail is key to the success of any book like this one, it's just as important to present all those details so they will be understood and learned. With the help of Mark Smith's brilliant illustrations and design, this book has met both those goals.

This edition is a larger and considerably updated revision of the first edition, which was published in 1983. About 20 percent of the original 190,000-word text has been revised, and another 20,000 words have been added. There are two new chapters ("Personal Safety" and "Traditions and Courtesies") plus one new part devoted solely to safety issues. In addition, there are dozens of new or much-enlarged sections on such topics as heavy-weather sailing, celestial and electronic navigation, emergencies, racing, and sailing with children. Other additions include an index and review quizzes on navigation.

A summary of the contents begins where good seamanship always begins, with the helm and the sails. That is where we start in **Part I, "The Boat and Her Environment."** The first two chapters (directed toward novice and intermediate sailors) are about the basics of boat design and boat-handling. Chapter 3 tells how to trim and care for sails. The next two chapters in this part concern weather and working with ropes and other sail-handling gear.

Part II, "Safety," is new in this edition. It has been added in response to a widespread, healthy concern about the safety of sailors and their boats. Chapter 6, "The Sailor's Health," covers health-related issues of concern to all boaters, including seasickness, first aid, and clothing to keep the body dry and warm. The new chapter 7, "Personal Safety," has detailed descriptions of (among other things) the 1988 U.S. Coast Guard life jacket categories, crew overboard rescue techniques, and the proper use of safety harnesses. Chapter 9, "The Rules of the Road," tells how to avoid collisions with other boats.

Part III, "Navigation," includes the skills and equipment used to determine where you are and what course you should sail. The first two chapters are about the chart, compass, and other classic tools that will always be used wherever people navigate, and about the buoys and other aids to navigation that keep boats in safe water. In the next two chapters we see how to use these tools, with review quizzes that help pull everything together. At the end of chapter 12 there is a new introduction to celestial navigation. Chapter 13, on electronic devices, has been almost completely rewritten to keep readers up to date with the fast-changing wonders of Loran-C, radar, satellite navigation, and other instruments.

Part IV, "Self-Sufficiency," deals with the times when sailors are entirely on their own. Anchoring, heavy-weather sailing, emergencies, and boat maintenance are covered in separate chapters.

Completing the main body of the text is a new chapter called "Traditions and Courtesies." Here we cover flag etiquette, courtesies, uniforms, history, and language.

The appendix material includes summaries of regulations and duties of official agencies, plus practical introductions to cruising and racing. There is a new appendix on the pleasures and problems of sailing with children. "The Sailor's Library" is an annotated bibliography of helpful books and magazines. Finally, there is an index to facilitate reference to all the material between these two covers.

No place in the United States stands for seamanship better than Annapolis, Maryland, the home of one of the largest fleets of pleasure boats in the world as well as the United States Naval Academy, where I have sailed and lectured on seamanship. If there is one theme running through these pages that reflects the traditions of Annapolis it is the emphasis on developing clear and simple standard operating procedures for performing seamanship tasks.

In the first edition, the generic "he" and "his" were used to refer to a sailor. However, in all new material I have used the more inclusive "he or she" and "his or her" in respect for the many women who sail.

The introduction usually is the last part of a book to be written, since only at the end of the project does the author know what is in the finished manuscript. As I complete the demanding but enjoyable task of revising *The Annapolis Book of Seamanship* I repeat my parting words in the introduction to the first edition: may your days and nights afloat be as happy and interesting as mine have been, and may you never make the mistake of believing that you know all there is about sailing. Nobody can know it all, but here (I hope) you will learn at least a little.

John Rousmaniere

A Summary
of the Contents

An Amplified Table of Contents

Part II: Safety

Part III: Navigation

An Amplified Table of Contents

Part IV: Self-Sufficiency

Part I
THE BOAT
AND HER
ENVIRONMENT

Chapter 1
The Boat

The idea of sailing a pleasure boat upon the sea can seduce even the happiest farmer. There is something about boat and water that sends romance churning in our hearts, and simply the sight of a boat can inspire a reverie. She may be a 15-foot dinghy tied to the roof of a station wagon or a handy cruiser or an America's Cup yacht leaping off the cover of a boating magazine. Whatever she is, the boat gleams in our eye, and we find ourselves dreaming, "What if...?"

Limitless in her poetry, a sailboat is still restricted in reality. No matter how graceful her lines, tall her mast, strong her rigging, and snug her cabin, a sailboat is tied down (as poetry is not) by the harsh reality of wind and sea. There is simply no way to get around the water's friction and the wind's variability. Many beginning sailors have been disappointed, even injured, because they refused to face and learn about the realities of the boat's environment. Preferring to re-lax in their dreams, they suffered afloat, and while their souls gloried in their boats' beauty, their bodies ached because they neglected hard practicalities. Later in this chapter we'll look at some of those realities, at how wind and sea affect a boat and at how a well-handled boat responds. But first, let's build a foundation by describing the parts of the boat—fiberglass and metal and cloth that, working together, make a boat what she is. As a great seaman, John MacGregor, once wrote, "The perfection of a yacht's beauty is that nothing should be there for only beauty's sake."

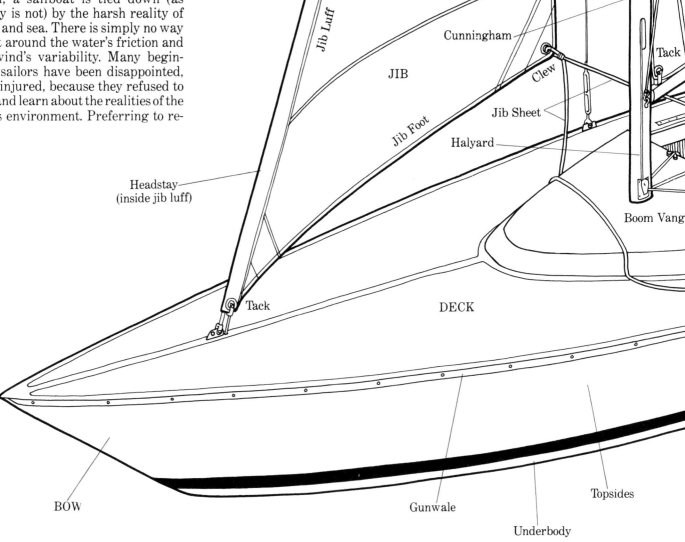

The Parts of a Boat

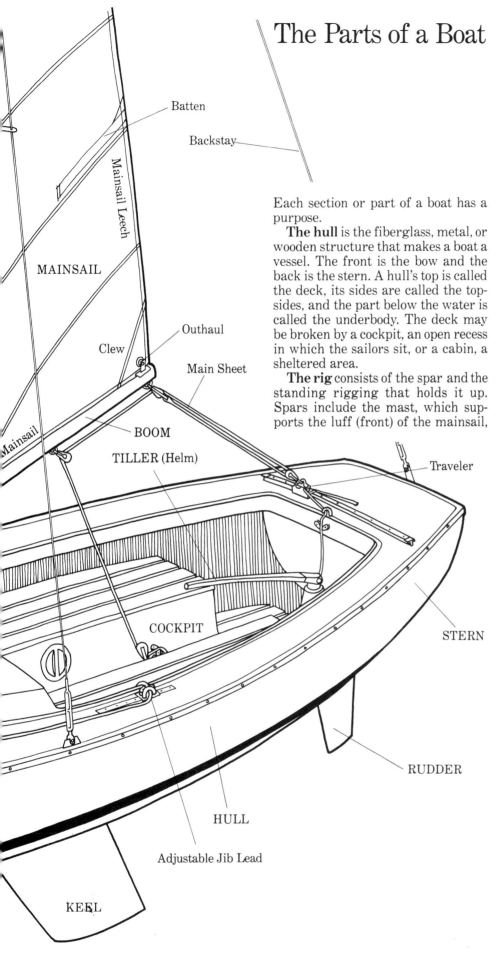

Batten

Backstay

Mainsail Leech

MAINSAIL

Outhaul

Clew

Main Sheet

Mainsail

BOOM

TILLER (Helm)

Traveler

COCKPIT

STERN

RUDDER

HULL

Adjustable Jib Lead

KEEL

Keel Daysailer

Each section or part of a boat has a purpose.

The hull is the fiberglass, metal, or wooden structure that makes a boat a vessel. The front is the bow and the back is the stern. A hull's top is called the deck, its sides are called the topsides, and the part below the water is called the underbody. The deck may be broken by a cockpit, an open recess in which the sailors sit, or a cabin, a sheltered area.

The rig consists of the spar and the standing rigging that holds it up. Spars include the mast, which supports the luff (front) of the mainsail, and the boom, which extends the mainsail's foot (bottom) from the mast. The standing rigging consists of wire stays and metal struts, called spreaders, that restrain the mast from falling or bending excessively. The headstay runs from the mast to the bow, the shrouds are stays running to the side decks, and the backstay runs to the stern. The mast is usually aluminum and the stays are usually stainless-steel wire. (A few boats have stayless masts that are allowed to bend.)

The sails are the boat's engine. The jib and the mainsail are the two types of sails found on most boats, although a vast variety of specialized sails is available for all kinds of sailing (we'll look at some of the sails later on). The jib is carried on the headstay. Some jibs, called genoas, are trimmed well aft so that they overlap the mast. Others, called working jibs, simply fill the foretriangle, the area between the headstay and the mast. Small boats usually carry only one size jib, but larger boats may carry a working jib plus one or more genoas, even though only one jib can be set at a time. The larger jibs are used in light winds, the smaller ones in strong winds. Only one mainsail is carried; its exposed area may be decreased by reefing, or lowering the halyard and tying the bottom part of the sail to the boom. Most sails are constructed of Dacron cloth.

The running rigging includes halyards that pull and hold the sails up and sheets that control the shape of the sails as well as the angle of attack at which they are set to the wind. In addition, other items of running rigging, called outhauls, Cunninghams, and boom vangs, are used to make small adjustments in a sail's shape. When they are tightened, a sail is made flatter; when they're loosened, the sail is made fuller. Running rigging is usually wire or Dacron rope.

The helm is the tiller or steering wheel with which the helmsman, or steerer, steers the boat.

The appendages are extensions from the hull's underbody. There are several types of appendage. The rudder, turned by the helm, changes the flow of water around the hull in order to turn the boat. The centerboard on a small boat provides a grip on the water and helps convert the side force of the wind on the sails into a forward force, keeping the boat from skidding sideways like a leaf. The skeg accomplishes the same aim and also helps the boat stay on course. On larger boats, a keel performs two important functions: it grips the water like the

The Parts of a Boat

centerboard does and because it contains a considerable weight in lead or iron ballast, it also provides a counterweight against the side force of the wind, which might make the boat capsize.

There are more than 500 types of sailboats in use today, and on each one the parts of the boat are arranged and used uniquely. Perhaps the best way to illustrate how they function is to describe two very different, very popular types of boats: the Laser dinghy and a 30-foot racer-cruiser. Then we'll examine the function of some important fittings by showing how to get a boat ready for sailing.

The Laser Dinghy

Only 14 feet long and weighing but 130 pounds, the Laser is one of the most popular boats in the world today. She is used for daysailing (casual sailing) and racing, and while she can support two adults or several children, the Laser is primarily sailed as a singlehander, meaning that only one person is on board. She is light enough to be hauled out of the water by two adults and placed on a car's roof rack. With her light weight and a sail area of 76 square feet in her mainsail (she has no jib), the Laser is capable of speeds as high as 15 knots in strong winds under capable skippers. Since her fiberglass hull is airtight and contains some blocks of foam, she'll float when capsized. If she does capsize, the sailor pulls down on the centerboard and leverages the hull back upright. Her small cockpit, which drains automatically, is designed not to sit in but to provide support for the skipper's legs and feet. Unlike a keel boat, this centerboarder carries no ballast as a counterweight against tipping. When the wind pipes up and she begins to heel (or tip), the skipper hooks his feet under a nylon strap in the cockpit called a hiking strap and leans backward to windward (toward the wind) in order to lever the boat back upright. Like almost all boats, the Laser sails fastest and most comfortably when she sails with little heel.

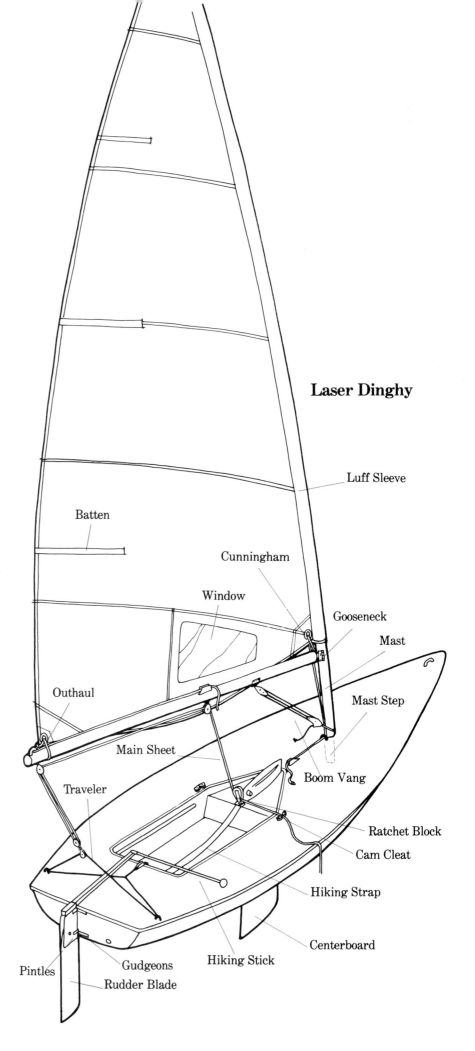

Laser Dinghy

Luff Sleeve

Batten

Cunningham

Window

Gooseneck

Mast

Outhaul

Mast Step

Main Sheet

Boom Vang

Traveler

Ratchet Block

Cam Cleat

Hiking Strap

Hiking Stick

Centerboard

Pintles

Gudgeons

Rudder Blade

remotely.

The Laser's rig is simple. Hers is one of those few masts that is left free-standing without stays. The mast consists of two aluminum tubes that connect together; the lower tube is stepped (installed) in a hole in the deck called the mast step. An aluminum boom is connected to the mast with a simple socket fitting called a gooseneck.

The single sail is installed without a halyard. A sock sewn into the luff, or front edge, is pulled over the mast. The lower forward corner of the sail— the tack—is held down by a short line called the Cunningham, which is one of those sail controls that is tightened to make a sail flat in fresh winds and loosened to make it full or baggy in light winds. Before the mast is stepped, plastic strips called battens are put in slots in the leech (back edge) of the sail to keep the leech from flapping.

Once the mast is stepped and the Cunningham is rigged (installed), the after (back) corner of the sail—the clew—is secured to the boom with a line called the outhaul. Like the Cunningham, the outhaul is tightened in fresh winds and loosened in light winds. A third small sail control is the boom vang, a short tackle that runs from the bottom of the mast to the boom. This restrains the boom from lifting.

The major piece of running rigging is the main sheet, a long Dacron line that runs from the boom's end to a block (pulley) on a sideways-running line called a traveler, back to the boom, and then forward to the sailor through two other blocks. Together, the traveler and the main sheet determine the angle of attack and general shape of the sail. The reason why the main sheet makes so many turns before it finally reaches the sailor is that the sail cannot be adjusted comfortably without adding to the pulling power of the sheet. Here the sheet is rigged so that it forms a tackle; when the sailor trims (pulls on) the sheet, the tackle multiplies his effort by a factor of 2½. Therefore if the sail has a pull of 100 pounds, the sailor can adjust it by pulling with a strength of 40 pounds. When he's not adjusting the sheet, the sailor may cleat (secure) it in a fitting called a cleat on the deck.

The Laser's two appendages are the centerboard and the rudder. The centerboard slips up and down through a slot in the hull called the centerboard trunk (this kind of centerboard is sometimes called a daggerboard because it retracts like a dagger from a sheath). When sailing across or before the wind on the points of sail called the reach and the run, the skipper retracts the centerboard in order to minimize the boat's resistance against the water.

But when sailing toward the wind's eye on a close-hauled course, the sailor leaves the centerboard fully lowered so that its whole area works effectively to resist side slippage. The other appendage, the rudder, is hooked onto the transom at the stern with pin and socket fittings called pintles and gudgeons. The sailor steers with a tiller. When he's hiked out in fresh winds, a connecting rod called a hiking stick allows him to adjust the tiller

Because they are very light, dinghies like the Laser are fast and require full concentration. On a reach, this Laser's centerboard is raised half-way and her boom vang holds the boom horizontal.

The Parts of a Boat

Racer-Cruiser

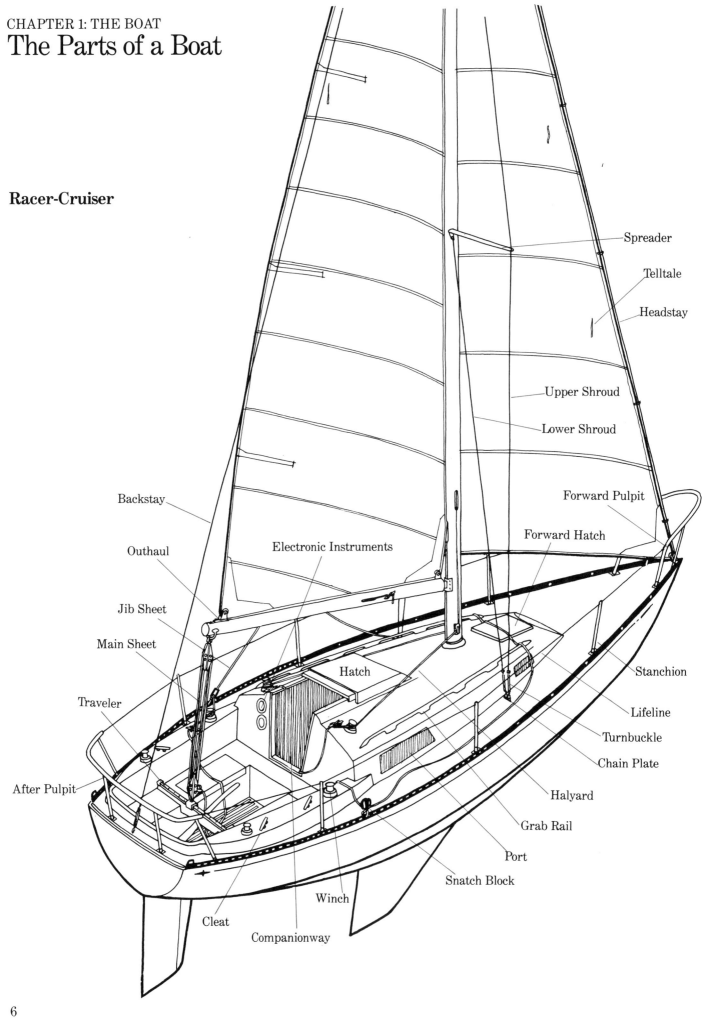

Spreader

Telltale

Headstay

Upper Shroud

Lower Shroud

Backstay

Forward Pulpit

Outhaul

Electronic Instruments

Forward Hatch

Jib Sheet

Main Sheet

Stanchion

Hatch

Lifeline

Traveler

Turnbuckle

Chain Plate

After Pulpit

Halyard

Grab Rail

Port

Snatch Block

Cleat

Winch

Companionway

The Racer-Cruiser

A 30-foot racer-cruiser sailboat is quite a bit more complex than the Laser. Weighing more than 8,000 pounds, she has a large, comfortable cabin in which several people can live for weeks at a time. To counterbalance her large sail area, she has a deep permanent keel which would sink her if she were ever to swamp (fill with water). But that's very unlikely since the keel offers superb protection against capsizing. Like the keel, her rudder is also permanently installed. It's adjusted by turning a long tiller or steering wheel on a pedestal in the boat's comfortable cockpit. The cockpit will drain automatically through drain holes in its sole (floor).

The tall aluminum mast is permanently stepped and supported by a network of stays and spreaders. The stays are adjusted with turnbuckles located at their ends near the deck. This boat has a masthead sloop rig, since the jib is hoisted through a block at the masthead, or very top of the mast.

Like the standing rigging, the running rigging is also fairly complicated. Because the crew of this boat can choose from several different size jibs, the blocks through which the jib sheets pass on deck are adjustable so that the jib lead (the angle the sheet makes to the sail) can be optimized. The strong pull of the sheets is too much for a single crew member. Since a tackle like the one on the Laser's main sheet would be too awkward to use on a jib sheet, the sheet is led to a winch. (A winch is a geared drum that is turned by a handle. The combined power of the gears and the handle greatly increases the sailor's pull.) The boat is equipped with winches for the jib sheets and also for the halyards. The main sheet may be a powerful tackle or it may be led to its own winch.

Most of the other important parts of the racer-cruiser are very similar to the Laser's. The main exception is that while the Laser has only one sail and no halyard, the larger boat carries a jib and a mainsail, both hoisted by wire halyards with rope tails (ends), which are easier on hands than stainless steel wire. Another difference is that the foot of the Laser's sail is loose and not attached to the boom except at the outhaul; the racer-cruiser's main-

Accommodations vary with boat size. In this 28-footer, the cabin is open. Aft are the galley and head. The strut supports the mast, which is stepped on deck.

sail, on the other hand, is attached all along the foot.

The racer-cruiser has an outhaul, a Cunningham, a traveler and a boom vang for adjusting sail shape, and since the forces on a 30-footer are much greater than those on a dinghy, these tackles have more parts and create more power than the simple tackles on the Laser. Both boats are equipped with cleats for securing sheets, halyards, and sail controls, although larger cleats are needed for the racer-cruiser's larger lines. Both boats are built of fiberglass reinforced by another material (wood in the case of the racer-cruiser, foam on the Laser).

Of course the racer-cruiser is a more demanding boat. Although she may be sailed singlehanded, it's much safer to take her out with a crew of three or more. And the complexity of her rig and running rigging requires many more fittings than a Laser needs — shackles and snap hooks and sail ties. To introduce them and the parts of the sail, let's look at how a crew rigs the sails on a racer-cruiser.

In a 40-footer, there's enough room for full separate cabins, plenty of bunks, and lots of storage space in lockers. Note the grab holes in the post and the many opening ports. The galley (foreground) has two sinks and faucets for both fresh and sea water.

How Boats Work

Bending on Sails

The mainsail is usually left furled (rolled) on the boom with a cover to protect it from the sun's ultraviolet rays, which degrade Dacron fibers. However, we'll show how a mainsail is bent on (rigged). First, make sure that the deck is clean so no grime gets on the sail. This may require hosing or swabbing (mopping) the deck and scrubbing the bottom of your shoes (use deck shoes or sneakers with white soles, please; hard-soled shoes provide no traction). Now dump the folded mainsail out of its bag and unfold it. Find the tack — the forward lower

(Above) The outhaul can be a simple permanent lashing, but rig a small block and tackle if you want to adjust it quickly.

(Right) The parts of a mainsail.

cringle

cringle

clew

corner, and the only one of the three corners that has a boltrope (rope or wire sewn into the sail's edge) on both edges. Next find the foot of the sail, which is the shorter of the two sides that meet at the tack. At the far end of the foot is the clew, which, like the tack, has a steel ring pressed into it. Between the tack and the clew, sewn into the boltrope of the sail's foot, are a dozen or more plastic cylinders called slugs. Starting with the slug nearest

head

leech

luff

battens

grommets

reef points

cringle

tack

the clew, insert the slugs one by one into the slot at the top of the boom, being careful that they are not twisted. (On some boats the boltrope itself is slid into the slot; on others, small slides go onto a track that runs down the boom.) When all the slugs are inserted, pull out the pin (called a clevis pin) from the gooseneck fitting at the forward end of the boom, insert the tack into the gooseneck fitting, and reinsert the pin. Always insert clevis pins from right to left on your boat. That way you'll be able to rig or unrig sails at night without having to inspect the pin to see which way it pulls out. Clevis pins can be secured in fittings in several ways. Sometimes a cotter pin, which looks like a bobby pin, is inserted through a hole in the clevis pin, and sometimes a lock on the clevis pin itself is extended.

Now walk aft pulling the clew of the sail with you. When the foot is stretched out, inspect it for twisted slugs. Then attach the outhaul shackle to the sail and tighten the outhaul until the foot is fully extended but not taut.

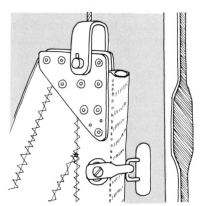

The mainsail's luff is connected to the mast by inserting slugs or the bolt rope into the slot or putting slides on a track.

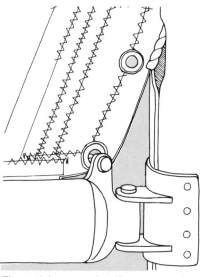

The tack is secured at the gooseneck, which may slide up and down the mast on a track. Always insert pins like the tack pin from right to left.

Return to the mast and, starting from the tack, work up the luff, making sure it's not twisted. At the head (the top corner), insert the top slug in the slot. (On boats without slugs on the sails, put the top slide on the track or guide the boltrope into the slot.) Gradually push the other slugs in behind the top one, and when the last slug is installed, close off the slot with the pin or gate provided. Inspect the luff to make sure that there are no twisted slugs. The sail is now secure on both boom and mast.

Insert the battens in their correct pockets—some are usually longer than others—and loosely furl the sail on the boom to keep it from blowing around as you finish bending on the sails. To furl a sail, first take the precaution of closing all the hatches on the cabin roof so you don't fall through. The famous principle "One hand for yourself and one for the ship" means that you should be careful as you do ship's work. Next, flop the whole mainsail over to one side (preferably the leeward, or downwind, side). Working

with another crew member, grab the leech in several places and pull it aft as far as possible. Then pull the sail away from the boom and shake it so the cloth falls loosely on itself in natural folds. Finally, roll these folds into a sausage and heave it onto the boom, leaning on it to keep it from unrolling. Take several sail ties or stops (6-foot lengths of webbing) and tie them tightly around the sail and boom, securing them with

bow knots. If you're alone you can do the forward part of the sail first, then move aft and go through the procedure again with the after part. When furling, be sure that the battens lie along the boom and not at an angle; otherwise they'll break and tear the sail.

Now you're ready to hank on the jib. Select the jib you want and bring it on deck. Smaller jibs are better on windy days or when you're sailing shorthanded (with a small crew). Pull the sail out of the bag; it should be folded. Find the tack; it will be the corner with a wide angle between a boltrope and hanks (snap hooks) on one side and an edge with no boltrope on the other side. Since the tack and the head often look alike, it's a good idea to mark each corner on the sail with an indelible pen, clearly indicating which corner and sail it is (for example, "storm jib tack" and "#1 genoa clew"). Now walk to the bow and, facing forward, pull the tack and the luff of the sail through your legs to the headstay. Shackle the tack fitting at the bottom of the headstay into the tack. This fitting may be a shackle or, like the gooseneck, it may be a clevis pin. Working up the luff, hank on (snap on) each of the hanks. They should all go on from the same side; if not, the sail is twisted. When all the hanks are on, tie up the forward part of the sail into a sausage, using a sail tie, and go aft, pulling the clew with you. With two or three other ties, secure the sail to the rail so it doesn't blow around. Remember to use bow knots that can be quickly untied.

Now locate the jib sheets and lead (pass) them through the appropriate blocks on deck. The lead should be marked with a piece of tape or an indelible marking. Tie the end of the sheets into the jib clew using bowline knots (see chapter 5; since shackles may open, we prefer the security of the bowline). Do not cleat the after ends of the jib sheets.

On some boats the jibs are not hanked on. Rather, the boltrope on the luff is fed into a special groove on the headstay that is much like the slot in the mast. There may be two grooves to allow quick changes of jibs while sailing; the new jib is hoisted in one groove before the old jib is lowered. While convenient, this system has one big drawback: until the sail is hoisted, it's secured only at the tack and clew. So if you use such a system, be sure to thoroughly tie down the jib with sail ties until you're ready to hoist.

Her sails furled and secured with sail ties and her jib halyard connected but kept tight with another tie led to the pulpit, this racer-cruiser can be got under way in minutes.

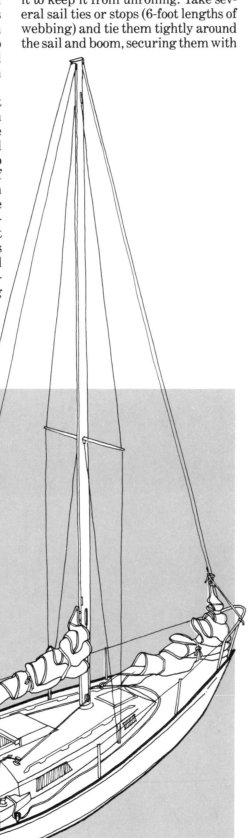

How Boats Work

Now your boat's rigged and you're ready to cast off and go sailing. Or are you?

It's a seafaring mistake to head out before you know anything about how or why a sailboat works the way she does. Generations of new sailors have figured that since they're perfectly sound, safe drivers despite their ignorance of automotive engineering, there's absolutely no reason why they should have to understand how a sail works or how a boat is steered. The difference that these people so conveniently ignore is that out at sea there's no state police or automobile association to tow you in when you get into trouble. They also are prisoners of the misguided belief that man can easily tame nature with a few modern gadgets.

Nonsense. If you want to enjoy sailing and survive any rough weather you stumble into, you should master some important theoretical principles, most of which are about as simple as the idea behind how the lever works. We're covering theory this early be-cause that's how important we think it is. If you'd prefer to start with some hands-on practicalities, skip on to chapter 2 and then come back. But this is information that you'll need. Some of our discussion will, of necessity, be simplified (if not oversimplified). At times we will use some extreme examples in order to make our points, and sometimes we'll suggest a "hands-on" teaching aid that might help you visualize the forces at play when a boat sails.

The Four Principles of Yacht Design

Yacht design is the art and science of designing pleasure boats. In layman's terms, the designer's problem is to produce an object that floats and sails with a minimum of rolling about and strain on the crew. These requirements can be grouped under four general headings: floatation, stability, propulsion, and balance.

The Laser and the typical racer-cruiser, which we looked at earlier, both satisfy these requirements quite

Representative of traditional heavy hulls that are ancestors of the modern racer-cruiser, the curragh is slow and cumbersome but an excellent, seaworthy load-carrier. A curragh is built of leather stretched over ash frames and has relatively primitive square sails, an offset rudder, and a hinged leeboard.

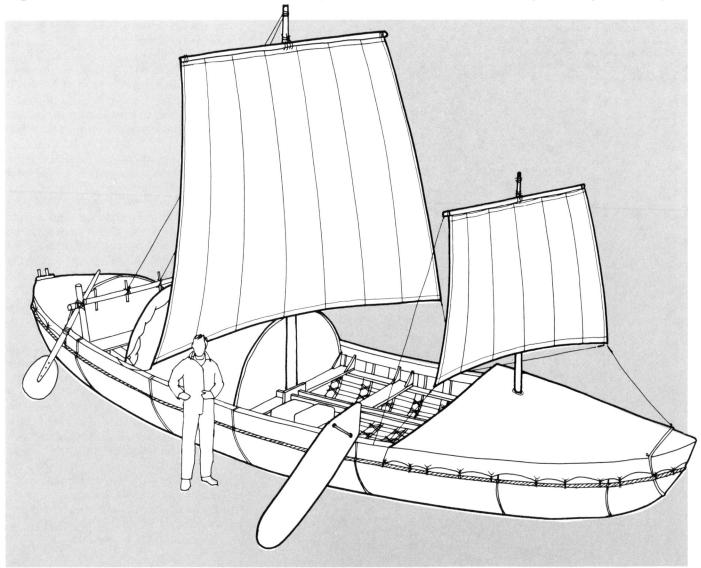

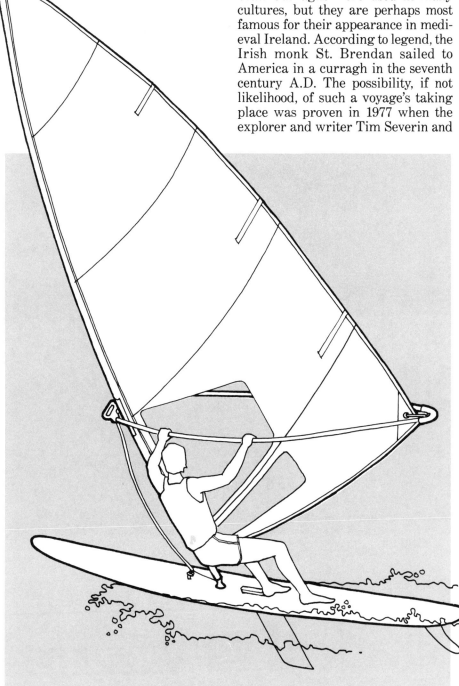

The quick, light sailboard was built to carry a small load — its athletic skipper — at very high speeds. The sail is a version of the fore-and-aft rig, and it is swung on a universal joint to steer the hull. A centerboard and skeg provide lateral resistance. Where the curragh provided relative comfort on long voyages, the sailboard supplies thrills on short outings.

well. But let's survey them using two boats that are even more unalike, on the assumption that extreme examples are often the most successful ones. These are the well-known sailing surfboard known as the sailboard and the medieval curragh, each of which is remarkably successful at satisfying the objectives of her designer.

The Curragh and the Sailboard

By far the oldest of the two is the curragh. An early form of this wood-and-leather boat appeared in ancient Mesopotamia some 5000 years ago; after the papyrus-reed raft, the curragh may well be the oldest type of boat. Curraghs were used in many cultures, but they are perhaps most famous for their appearance in medieval Ireland. According to legend, the Irish monk St. Brendan sailed to America in a curragh in the seventh century A.D. The possibility, if not likelihood, of such a voyage's taking place was proven in 1977 when the explorer and writer Tim Severin and

a crew of four men sailed a curragh from Ireland to Newfoundland. The trip was agonizingly slow, since *Brendan*, their curragh, rarely sailed faster than about 4 knots. But the tubby boat built like a washbasket kept her crew and their gear and food secure and reasonably dry through many icy storms.

Brendan was 36 feet in length overall, from bow to stern. She displaced, or weighed, 4 tons, and she was propelled by oars and about 400 square feet of sail. Cumbersome as she was, she was a superb load-carrier and seaworthy hull.

Where the curragh is ancient, bulky, and slow, the sailboard is modern, slim, and fast. Known also by various trade names (among them Windsurfer and Windglider), the sailboard was invented in the late 1960s in California by some surfers. In fact it looks like a surfboard with a sail attached. Just 12 feet long and weighing only about 40 pounds, it is built of plastic, foam, and fiberglass. The sail has about 70 square feet of cloth. A sailboard can sail rings about a curragh—one has been timed at 27 knots. A sailboard carries only one crew.

Despite their Mutt and Jeff dissimilarities, the two boats have an awful lot in common. They both have sails, although the curragh's rig consists of two square sails and the sailboard's has only one fore-and-aft sail. The older boat's sails are hung from horizontal spars, called yards, secured to two vertical masts. The sailboard's sail, on the other hand, is pulled over the mast like a sock and then held out by a horizontal spar called a wishbone boom. Both boats have appendages that stick down from the hull into the water. On the curragh these are a steering oar in the stern and a hinged leeboard on the side, which creates some side resistance. While the sailboard has no rudder (since it is steered by moving the rig), it has one fixed appendage near the stern called a skeg (which provides side resistance) and a centerboard like the Laser's.

Compared with the two boats we looked at earlier, the curragh is a tubbier version of the racer-cruiser and the sailboard is a tippier version of the Laser.

How Boats Work

Flotation: Buoyancy and Displacement

Obviously, an important characteristic that both boats share is that they float. The most basic principle of yacht design is that of flotation: a boat isn't a boat unless she floats. If an object is less dense than the fluid it sits in, it will float. In water, any object will float so long as its total volume (including hull, rig, equipment, crew, and the air between them all) weighs less than 64 pounds per cubic foot (if the water is saline) and 62.2 pounds per cubic foot (if it's fresh). If an object with a density of 32 pounds per cubic foot is put in salt water, it will float half in, half out of the water. If its density is 64 pounds per cubic foot, it will be suspended entirely below the water surface.

The weight of a boat is called her displacement because when she floats she displaces (pushes aside) a volume of water equal in weight to her own weight. As Archimedes discovered 2300 years ago, an object is buoyed up by a force equal to the weight of the water she displaces. The curragh *Brendan* displaces 4 tons, which means both that the boat weighs 4 tons and that when she is slid into the water she displaces 4 tons of water. Long tons of 2240 pounds are used when calculating displacement, so *Brendan* displaces 8960 pounds. Since she is quite heavy for her size and length, *Brendan* floats about half in and half out of the water, with 50 percent of her internal

The curragh must be big and buoyant if it is to safely carry as much as 2 tons of sailors and supplies. *Brendan* displaces 4 tons when loaded and floats half-in, half-out of the water.

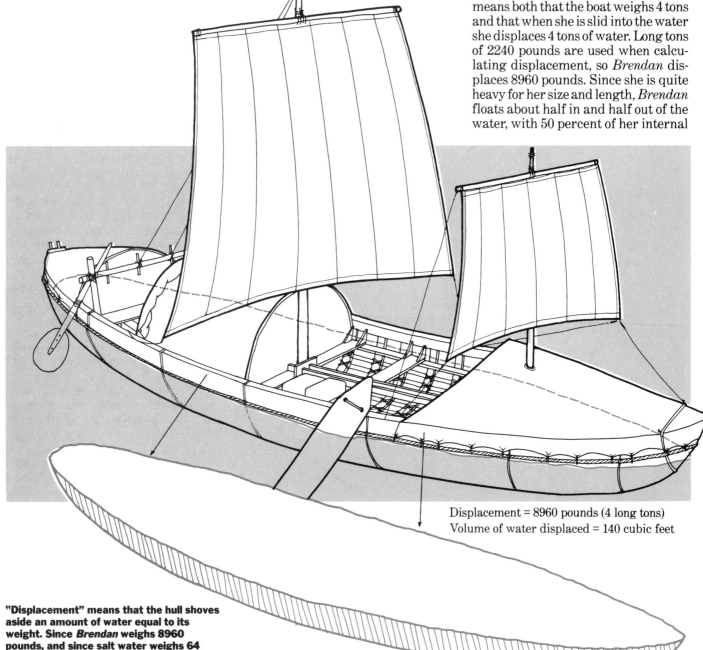

Displacement = 8960 pounds (4 long tons)
Volume of water displaced = 140 cubic feet

"Displacement" means that the hull shoves aside an amount of water equal to its weight. Since *Brendan* weighs 8960 pounds, and since salt water weighs 64 pounds per cubic foot, she displaces 140 (8960 ÷ 64) cubic feet of water. Therefore, her underbody — or hull below the water — has a volume of 140 cubic feet.

volume below the waterline and 50 percent above it. The sailboard, on the other hand, has an extremely light displacement for her length and sits on the water like a leaf. When her sailor comes aboard, she sinks down a couple of inches, but add the same weight to *Brendan* and the curragh seems not to notice it.

Which brings us around to boat-building materials. Wood is the classic material for boats partly because it's easy to work, strong, and easy to find. Wood also floats — or to be more exact, almost all kinds of wood float. A very few types are so dense that they sink. For example, lignum vitae has a density of 78 pounds per cubic foot and so is 25 percent denser than salt water. Hard enough to be used in propeller shaft bearings, lignum vitae is too heavy to be used as boat planks or frames. *Brendan* was built with frames of ash weighing 41 pounds per cubic foot and sides of leather whose density was 59 pounds per cubic foot — therefore unless she is overloaded with gear or crew, *Brendan* should float. On the other hand, the foam in a sail-board weighs less than 2 pounds per cubic foot. The key to a material's usefulness in boat building is its strength per pound. Wood is strong for its weight, and the load-carrier *Brendan* needs to be strong. Foam is less strong, but the sailboard must be lightweight, not muscular. Aluminum is almost 100 times more dense than foam and may be the best material there is for tough boats.

The vast majority of boats today are constructed of nonbuoyant materials such as aluminum, steel, and (especially) fiberglass. Aluminum sheets weigh 165 pounds per cubic foot, so are 2.5 times denser than salt water. Steel, weighing about 490 pounds per cubic foot, is even denser. Both materials have been used to build strong, expensive yachts for individual customers — what yacht designers call custom yachts. Much better adapted for building many versions of the same design — called stock or production boats — is fiberglass, a tough substance composed of glass fibers laid in hardened plastic. The chemical industry calls fiberglass "glass reinforced plastic" or "fiber reinforced plastic," both of which neatly summarize what the material is. Like most plastics, fiberglass can be easily shaped around molds and so is an excellent material for mass production. One of its drawbacks is that since it is derived from petrochemicals, its cost has skyrocketed since the 1973 Arab oil embargo. In addition it's not as strong as aluminum, although the use of foam or wood reinforcing usually makes fiberglass sturdier. Like the metals, fiberglass is nonbuoyant; it weighs about 96 pounds per cubic foot, so the Laser and other capsizeable fiberglass boats must have flotation compartments to keep them up if they go over, and larger fiberglass boats like our racer-cruiser must be carefully designed so that their total density is well under that of salt water.

With her rig in place and her crew on board, a sailboard displaces about 200 pounds as she skims across the water like a leaf. That's only 3 cubic feet of water spread out in a long, thin underbody.

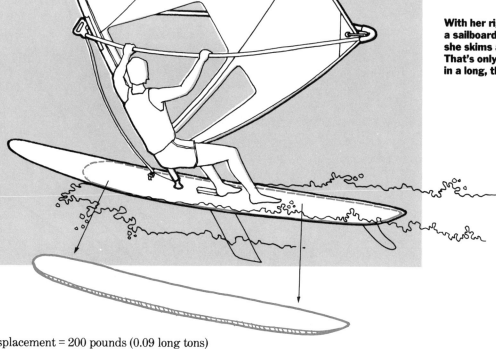

Displacement = 200 pounds (0.09 long tons)
Volume of water displaced = 3 cubic feet

CHAPTER 1: THE BOAT
How Boats Work

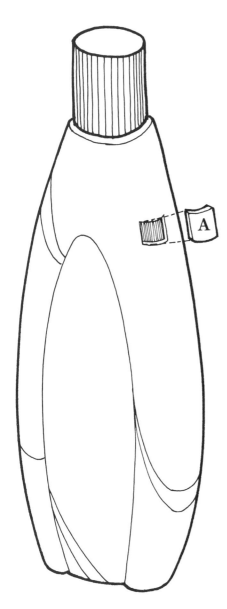

Even though a piece of its shell (A) is more dense than water and will sink, a bottle, like a hull, floats as long as its total density is less than that of water.

The buoyancy of the ends of a floating object depend on volume. The fine end of an oblong bottle is less buoyant — and will submerge deeper under the same downward pressure — than the full end of a round bottle. The fine end is like the narrow bow of a light-displacement boat such as the sailboard and Laser; the full one is like the blunt bow of the curragh *Brendan*.

Buoyancy, Shape, and Purpose

"The design in its entirety should be a frank, vigorous declaration of the use to which the boat is to be put." Those words, written by Norman L. Skene in his manual *Elements of Yacht Design*, summarize boat architecture in a nutshell. Just looking at our two examples, we can quickly determine what their use is. The tubby, sturdy curragh *Brendan* was built to carry men and their equipment long distances, not so much rapidly as safely. St. Brendan was not racing other monks to the new world; he simply wanted to stay dry while he explored the great ocean to the West. The light, flat sailboard, on the other hand, offers no protection whatsoever for her one-person crew — but she does offer thrilling, fast, risky sailing. While *Brendan* could be taken out in the harbor for an afternoon spin or the sailboard could be sailed far out into the ocean, most people would not buy either boat with those uses in mind. Of the two other, more conventional boats that we've looked at, the Laser is the closest to the sailboard: open, quick, and light. The racer-cruiser, however, shares characteristics with both types. She has a cabin in which she can accommodate several people for a while, and she has a sturdy, deep hull. But her sharp bow and tall mast suggest speed and maneuverability that, while not in the league of the sailboard and Laser, make her fun to take out on an afternoon sail. It's this combination of seaworthiness and liveliness that typlifies the modern stock racer-cruiser that so many sailors own.

Yacht designers, then, anticipate a boat's use by shaping her hull. Most hulls are derived from one of three shapes: flat-bottomed (like the sailboard and Laser), wedge-bottomed (like the racer-cruiser), and round-bottomed (like *Brendan*). A visit to a boatyard when boats are hauled out will give you an idea of these different shapes, but since you may have trouble interpreting the curves full-scale we suggest trying the following experi-

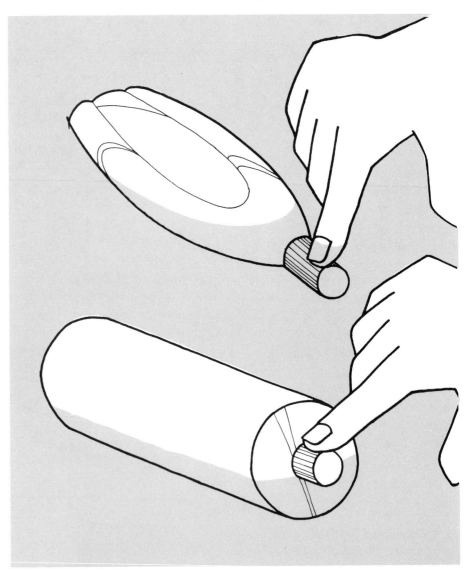

14

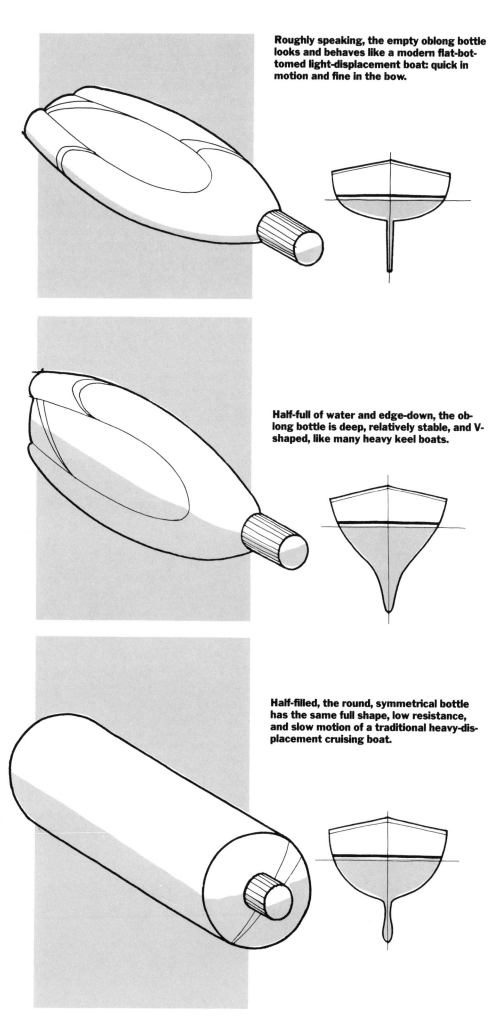

Roughly speaking, the empty oblong bottle looks and behaves like a modern flat-bottomed light-displacement boat: quick in motion and fine in the bow.

Half-full of water and edge-down, the oblong bottle is deep, relatively stable, and V-shaped, like many heavy keel boats.

Half-filled, the round, symmetrical bottle has the same full shape, low resistance, and slow motion of a traditional heavy-displacement cruising boat.

ment using simplified models. While no more sophisticated than figuring out how airplanes fly by observing flying squirrels, this exercise may concretize some of the principles we are introducing.

In a full bathtub or sink place two empty bottles: an oblong one like a baby-shampoo container and a round one like an adult-shampoo bottle. Leave their caps on. First compare the buoyancy of the two bottles. Press down in the middle until you find the spot that, when depressed, pulls the ends down equally. This is the bottle's center of buoyancy. Push down on the ends. The fine-ended oblong bottle, which has less volume at its end than in its middle, will pitch (bob) more readily than the full-ended round bottle. Notice how much more resistant and buoyant the center of the oblong bottle is than its ends. The oblong bottle behaves like a sailboard or Laser hull. It has little buoyancy in its end (or bow) because the sailor rarely goes that far forward; the designer makes the bow just buoyant enough so it doesn't dive under in waves. The middle is much more buoyant because that's where the sailor stands or sits. The round bottle is like the curragh and to some extent the racer-cruiser, which require considerable buoyancy in their bows to support the crew and equipment located forward.

Next, try to spin the bottles. The oblong bottle will spin less readily than the round one because its abrupt edges catch the water. Fill both bottles halfway and try to spin them again. There should be little difference. What this suggests is that the flat-bottomed Laser-type hull resists heeling forces better than the round-bottomed *Brendan*-type hull.

Finally, with moderate downward pressure slide the empty oblong bottle across the water surface on its flat side. Then fill it half-way, turn it on its edge, and slide it sideways again. On its side it provides very little grip on the water, behaving just like a sailboard or Laser with the centerboard retracted. But on its edge it presents a large lateral surface that resists the side forces like a centerboard or a keel on a wedge-shaped boat like the racer-cruiser. The lateral plane below the waterline resists the wind's side forces in the sails, and the larger the lateral plane and the more efficiently it is shaped, the greater the resistance will be. As we'll see later on, resistance to side forces is greatest when the boat is moving fast so that the appendage's airfoil shape is best exploited.

How Boats Work

Stability: Pitching, Heeling and Yawing

Stability is a boat's resistance to forces that threaten to throw her into violent motion (pitching), to lay her over on her side and capsize her (heeling), or to force her off course (yawing). Some boats are quite stable in all three ways, with full, bulbous bows that don't pitch and long heavy keels that lever them upright and work like railroad tracks to keep them on course. While good features to have in a boat in a few limited situations, such as sailing very long distances with a small crew who care little about reaching a destination quickly, such extreme stability may be counterproductive. Fast boats that are fun to sail inevitably pitch, heel, and yaw; the challenge for the designer is to match these instabilities to the boat's purpose. There are always trade-offs in yacht design, and "Different boats for different folks" is an excellent rule of thumb. Only you can determine how much instability your body and sailing skills can manage.

As we saw in our improvised bathtub experiments, the round-bottomed shape is more stable than the flat-bottomed one in one way: it is more buoyant in the ends and hence pitches less. Modern wedge-shaped racer-cruisers generally lie somewhere between these extremes. Some relatively heavy-displacement boats may be full-ended in order to accommodate a fairly large forward cabin in the bow; light-displacement boats with flattish bottoms may be quite fine-ended to the degree that the bow digs into waves and water is taken on deck. Very heavy boats with bluff bows, on the other hand, may be stopped by waves that a finer bow slices through.

Stability against heeling and rolling is created by two features, hull form and ballast. By hull form we mean the cross-sectional (across the hull) shape. As we've seen, a flat hull with a fairly tight angle between the sides and the bottom (or chine if the angle is sharp) should resist initial rolling better than a round hull. In general, given the same amount of wind and flying the same sails, a wide hull tips less than a narrow one. This is because the center of buoyancy (a locus through which all the buoyancy forces are summarized) has a larger area to travel with a beamy (wide) hull. When the boat is upright the center of buoyancy is in the middle of the hull, but as she heels her windward side lifts and her leeward side submerges, the underbody (hull below the water) changes shape, and there is a new center of buoyancy to leeward of the original one. If the center of gravity pulling the boat down is to wind-

"Different boats for different folks." The heavy long-keeled cruising boat (above) may not be fast, but she has plenty of volume for long-distance cruising. The racing dinghy (upper left) is physically challenging and fast. The racer-cruiser (left) is a compromise between the two extremes — roomy for a few people but, with her fin keel and light displacement, quick and demanding. Each type is excellent for its own purposes.

ward of the center of buoyancy, and the center of buoyancy doesn't run out of traveling room as it nears the leeward rail, the boat won't capsize. Obviously, then, a beamy boat provides a larger platform for the center of buoyancy than a narrow boat. This does not mean that beamy boats don't capsize, for the center of gravity plays an important role in this dynamic situation, as we shall see. It only means that wide beam often goes hand in

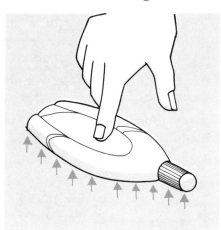

hand with resistance to heeling forces.

Two kinds of beam are important. One is the extreme beam, or the boat's beam on deck at the widest point. Extreme beam is related to a hull's latent stability, or her resistance to capsizing after she has already heeled quite far. As we'll see, ballast and the location of the center of gravity are even more important factors in latent stability. The other kind of beam is waterline beam, or her width at the water level. If the waterline beam is narrow, even a boat with wide extreme beam and tons of ballast will heel quickly in light winds — heel to the point, that is, when the stabilizing influence of the extreme beam and the ballast takes over. A home-grown example of the difference between the two beams is the relative ease of tipping a wide-brimmed, small-based salad bowl. A cooking pot whose brim has the same diameter but whose sides are straight will be much less wobbly.

On centerboarders hull shape plays an important role in keeping the hull upright, but perhaps more important

is moveable ballast that is shifted to windward to keep the center of gravity far out from the center of buoyancy. This moveable ballast is the crew, whose weight may well be greater than the boat's own displacement. Hiked out to windward or suspended on trapezes, with their feet against the windward rail, the human ballast levers against the side force on the sails. The heavier the crew and the farther out they hang, the greater is their leverage. On keel boats, however, the crew's weight is only a fraction of the displacement and the greatest effect on latent is made by the boat's fixed ballast in the keel or bilge. This lead or iron mass starts to work once the boat has heeled more than 10°; the heavier it is and the lower it lies, the greater is its effect. When the ballast is very heavy and deep, the boat does not require much form stability, or wide extreme beam, to keep from heeling. A good example is the 12-meter, which at 65 feet in overall length carries about 80 percent of her 60,000-pound displacement in ballast in her 9-foot-

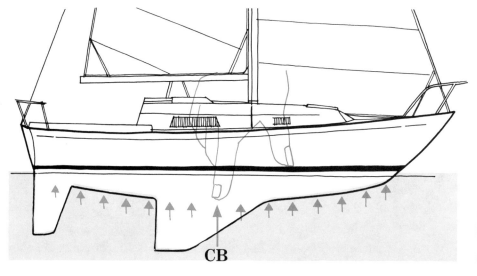

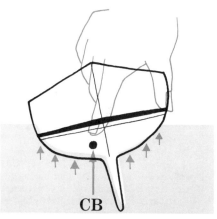

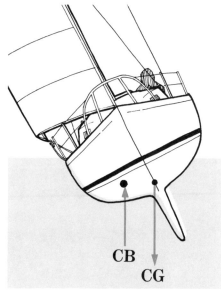

The center of buoyancy (CB) is a locus for all forces keeping the boat afloat. In the bottle, it's where pressing with a finger will push the ends down equally. As the boat heels and the underbody shape changes, the CB moves, and as long as the boat's center of gravity (CG) stays off to the side, the boat will not capsize. Keels keep the CG lower than the CB and provide stability even at large heel angles.

How Boats Work

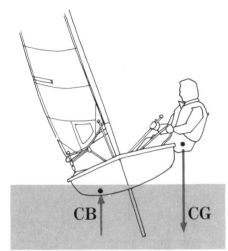

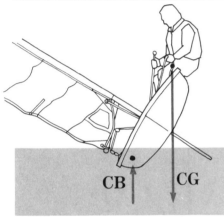

The center of buoyancy (CB) travels farther on beamy boats than on narrow ones, but when the center of gravity (CG) is well above the CB — as on a dinghy, whose crew is the only ballast — leverage against capsizing decreases. Note that as the boat heels, less of the appendage (here a centerboard) is exposed. Her draft shallower and her lateral plane smaller than when she is upright, the heeled boat will make more leeway (side-slippage). The winged keel found on some boats (below) makes up for loss of lateral plane when the boat heels. It also makes a shallow keel work more efficiently by cleaning up water flow along its bottom.

deep keel. Her extreme beam is 12 feet — the same as that of a 0-foot racer-cruiser displacing 13,000 pounds, only 40 percent of which is ballast.

While centerboarders like the Laser can always capsize in fresh winds or when overloaded or mishandled, keel racer-cruisers should have sufficient latent stability due to deep ballast to keep them from heeling much beyond about 50° in storms or when the crew is

The 32-foot long-distance cruiser *Sadalsuud* and the outrigger *Slingshot* show two extremes of boat design. The heavy keel boat is relatively stable and roomy but quite slow, while the outrigger (here kept on her lines by five men in the pod) has no reason for existence other than to sail fast. *Slingshot* has been timed at speeds of more than 35 knots; *Sadalsuud* will do well to make 7 knots.

tardy reefing or shortening sail in fresh wind. At that extreme angle of heel, no boat will sail even moderately fast; she'll be hard to steer and slide sideways — but she should not capsize. However, some light-displacement racing boats carry little ballast, and that high in the keel, and depend for stability on the weight of the crew on the windward rail. They have a narrow waterline beam and a very wide extreme beam (which extends the crew far to windward), but they lack reliable latent stability and may capsize in strong winds and rough seas much like centerboarders.

Multihulls (catamarans and trimarans) are exceptionally stable up to a point because their extreme beam across their two or three hulls is huge. A 25-foot racing catamaran may have the 12-foot beam of a 12-meter. The tremendous initial stability provided by this wide beam allows them to carry a cloud of sail much larger than the canvas a monohull can safely fly. Their extremely narrow, fine-ended, lightweight hulls slice through the

Trimarans like *Moxie* are among the fastest types of ocean racing (and cruising) boats. Their long hulls make little resistance and their exceptionally wide beams provide great stability under large sail areas. But because their centers of gravity are quite high, trimarans and catamarans have poor latent stability and can capsize.

water almost like an arrow through the air, but with an unarrowlike quick pitching motion. The main problem with multihulls is that, lacking keels, they have poor latent stability; like a centerboarder they may flip right over before the crew can let out the sheets and luff the sails in a hard puff of wind. The ultimate sailing machine when sailing near shore is the high-speed catamaran, but taking a catamaran or trimaran offshore, far from rescue services, may invite a capsize.

Yawing

When a boat is unstable directionally, she yaws, or does not stay on course. Flat, skitterish boats like the sailboard are constantly changing course because of the slap of waves or puffs of wind, and the skipper must pay careful attention to the course. The skeg and centerboard provide some directional stability, but the other forces are greater. A deep, heavy hull like the curragh's, on the other hand, tends to cut through the water more steadily; it takes a considerable side force to push her off course. The larger the lateral plane exposed by the underbody—the hull, keel, and other appendages below the water—the better the directional stability. Boats with good directional stability track well and require less attention by the helmsman, yet when you want to alter course, the tiller or wheel must be turned forcefully and the course alteration may be slow. Turning a boat that yaws slightly is like steering a truck, while turning a boat with poor directional stability is like driving a sportscar. A boat's directional stability may vary with the point of sail. When sailing close-hauled (as close to the wind as possible) the boat may track very well, but when she is turned off the wind onto a run she may yaw all over the ocean.

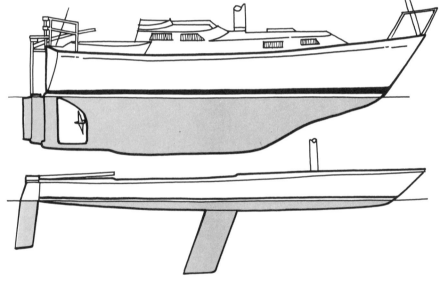

Directional stability depends mainly on the size of the lateral area. A long-keel cruiser will stay on course better than a flat-bottomed centerboarder like the Laser (upper left). The long, deep hulls of a multihull provide good directional stability, so while a catamaran or trimaran may be very fast it tacks and jibes slowly.

How Boats Work

Propulsion: Sails

When the wind is from behind, it works on the sails simply by pushing them and the boat's hull follows along. This is how the old-fashioned square rig on the curragh *Brendan* worked. When the wind is from ahead, square sails can be made to work, but nowhere near as efficiently as fore-and-aft sails like the one on the sailboard and other modern boats. While *Brendan* could sail no closer to the wind than about 70° (and very slowly at that), a modern boat can

sail closer than 45°. Here's how a modern sail works upwind:

As the wind passes over and is redirected by the curved sail, it goes to one side or the other. Air going to leeward, on the outside of the curve, speeds up and the air pressure on the leeward side decreases. Meanwhile on the windward side, on the inside of the curve, air moving more slowly creates a greater pressure on the sail. The end result is a force on the sail from the windward side

toward the leeward side. Some of this force aims aft and pushes the boat forward, and some of it is lost because of sail friction. But most of this force is sideways. The trick is to trim the sails and have well-shape appendages so as much side force as possible is directed forward, thereby sucking the boat upwind, and so as little force as possible goes into heeling and leeway (side-slippage to leeward).

Most boats have jibs, which work in somewhat the same way as mainsails but which also accelerate the flow of wind over the mainsail's leeward side, thereby decreasing pressure and increasing the side force. The large overlapping genoa jibs carried on cruising boats and America's Cup contenders work more efficiently than small, nonoverlapping jibs, partly because they are larger and catch more air and partly because they extend the gap of speeded-up air flow farther back into the mainsail.

Now how are the side forces translated into forward propulsion? The most important mechanism here is

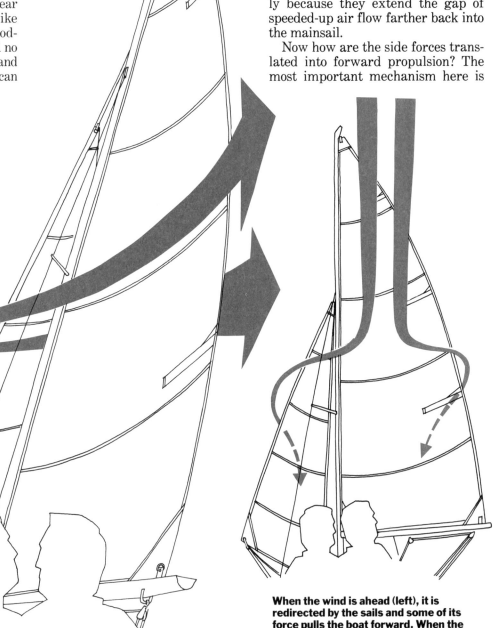

When the wind is ahead (left), it is redirected by the sails and some of its force pulls the boat forward. When the wind is behind (right), it pushes on the sails.

the appendage — the centerboard, keel, skeg, leeboard, and/or rudder — which keeps the boat from sliding sideways but which also creates forward thrust. In a well-trimmed sail the sum total of all those forces will not be directly to the side but slightly forward. Therefore a boat sailing without an appendage will slide mainly to leeward and also sail very slightly forward. If equipped with a well-shaped appendage, she will sail mainly for-ward while sliding slightly to leeward. The force works on the appendage like a thumb on an orange seed: when pressure is applied, the object squirts forward. A well-shaped appendage will look like an airfoil. It will have a fairly round leading (forward) edge and its widest point will be about one-third of the way back before the appendage tapers to a sharp edge Also like an airfoil, it works best when the fluid that surrounds it is moving over its surface rapidly and smoothly. At low speeds the appeandage provides little lift (or resistance to side forces), and at sharp angles of attack to the water or in turbulence (say when turning the rudder sharply) the water flow separates from the sruface and the appendage stalls (loses lift).

All this works very efficiently in light and moderate winds whenever the boat is sailing at an angle to the wind. Of course if the wind is directly astern and the boat is running, the sails work like the old square sails and are simply pushed along. The crew's job is to trim the sails so the forward force is maximized and the side force is minimized. If they trim (pull in) the sheets too far, the boat will heel and make little or no forward progress. If they ease (let out) the sheets too far, the sails won't catch enough wind to create any force. As the wind increases, the shape of the sail itself may have to be changed, because a baggy, full sail, while creating more forward force than a flat sail, also creates considerable heeling force that cannot be counterbalanced by the keel or by the hiking crew. (We'll look more closely at sail trim in chapter 3.)

You can get a feel for how these principles work by extending a hand outside the window of a moving car. Held palm open and flat to the wind, your hand will be forced directly back. This is what happens when a boat is running directly before the wind with her sail let all the way out: the wind pushes the sail along and the sail pulls the boat with it.

Now turn the side of your hand toward the front of the car and cup it, making it fuller. As you try different arcs of fullness (on a sail this would be called draft) and different angles of attack to the wind, be sensitive to how the strain on your arm changes. You'll probably feel more force on your palm than on the back of your hand until the hand has an angle of attack of about 45°. At that angle the pressure will begin to be equalized on both sides and you will have to work less hard to keep your arm from flying back. As the angle of attack to the wind continues to sharpen, note the gradual change in pressure on your hand and arm, until at one point your hand may actually lift up. That is the force that the appendages translate into forward drive. Flatten the arc and feel the pressure decrease, then gradually make the hand/sail smaller by folding fingers into your palm. This version of reefing (see chapter 15) should also decrease both backward and side pressure.

A hand extended in moving air acts much like a sail. The positive force on the palm and the negative one on the back of the hand combine to create a side force.

Most of the force on a sail is just forward of to the side. A well-shaped appendage — a keel, centerboard, skeg, and rudder — converts that side force into forward thrust.

How Boats Work

Balance

After flotation, stability and propulsion, balance is the fourth of the basic principles of yacht design. The degree to which the boat is in tune with wind and water, balance is usually measured by how well she sails herself with only a modest helping hand from the helmsman. A well-balanced boat steers more easily, sails faster and more comfortably, and is more seaworthy than a poorly balanced boat. Like trying to drive a car with weak shock absorbers or a misaligned front end, sailing a poorly balanced boat with bad weather helm or lee helm is tiring and potentially dangerous.

Unfortunately for their owners, some boats are unbalanced from the moment their designers set pencil to paper. Only major reconstruction can balance their helms and make them competent, seaworthy vessels. But the vast majority of boats are unbalanced only because their crews don't know any better and sail them that way. We'll cover balance in much greater detail in the next two chapters; here we'll look at the important aspects of the principle.

The Helm and Rudder

The helm is the tiller or wheel that turns the rudder and so changes the boat's course, and it also corrects imbalances in the boat and her rig. If the first place a driver notices an under-inflated automobile tire is in the tug of the steering wheel, a helmsman first senses that the sails are incorrectly trimmed through the pull of the tiller. Knowing how the car or boat should feel when everything is in balance, the driver or helmsman can quickly sense when something's awry. For the moment he can correct the imbalance by oversteering against the pull, but soon he'll have to attack the cause of the problem. As a rule, if a hull's or a rig's symmetry is destroyed, a boat in motion will tend to swerve from her straight-line course.

As the designer drew and the builder constructed her, the boat should be symmetrical. The starboard side has the same shape as the port side, she sits level in the water without a permanent list, and the water moves around her underbody the same way on both sides. If for some reason there is a built-in asymmetry, then the water will move around one side faster than it does around the other. Sometimes, for example, one side of a keel or centerboard may be flatter than the other side because the fiberglass shell was not carefully shaped. The side with the best airfoil shape will generate more forward thrust than the flat side, so the boat may make less leeway on one

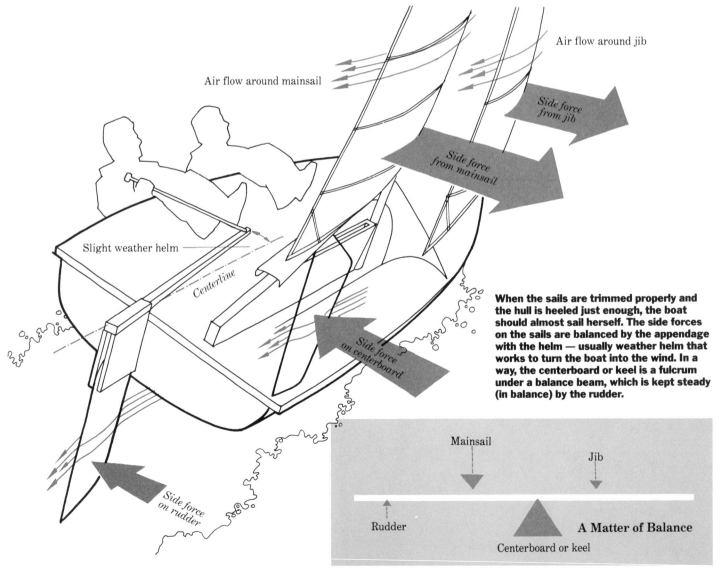

Air flow around mainsail

Air flow around jib

Side force from jib

Side force from mainsail

Slight weather helm

Centerline

Side force on centerboard

Side force on rudder

When the sails are trimmed properly and the hull is heeled just enough, the boat should almost sail herself. The side forces on the sails are balanced by the appendage with the helm — usually weather helm that works to turn the boat into the wind. In a way, the centerboard or keel is a fulcrum under a balance beam, which is kept steady (in balance) by the rudder.

Mainsail

Jib

Rudder

Centerboard or keel

A Matter of Balance

tack than on another. A more serious asymmetry results when the designer and builder miscalculate the weights of gear and fittings and the boat does not float on her lines. For instance, when the water tanks are full she may list to one side, which means that she'll heel more on one tack.

A list, or a heel, immerses one side and raises the other. The leeward side is the one that goes down as the windward side lifts. A level boat will steer straight with the rudder centered, but a heeled boat will tend to head in the direction of the windward, or raised, side. A boat heeled to port will head to starboard unless the helm is adjusted to compensate, and vice versa. Often sailors speak of "cranky" boats that "want" to head one way or the other. Like a wild horse with a bit in its teeth, a sailboat with powerful weather (windward) helm — a tendency to head toward the wind — can be a handful for a helmsman.

Adjusting the helm only compensates for the asymmetry — it doesn't fix it. Feeling the hard tug, the helmsman pulls on the helm — if it's a tiller he pulls opposite to the direction he wants to head; if a wheel, in the same direction. If he wants to head to port, he pulls the helm in the correct direction, which turns the rudder to port. The flaplike rudder impedes the flow of water going past, and shoving against the rudder the mass of moving water pushes the whole stern to starboard.

If he is simply compensating for an imbalance, the helmsman will pull the helm until the asymmetry of the swung rudder balances the asymmetry caused by the imbalance and the boat holds her course. But if he's actually changing course, he will hold the helm down or up until the bow has swung onto the new heading. As the stern swings one way; the bow swings the other. To stop the swing, the helmsman brings the helm back to center. Heavy boats and boats with long keels will have greater directional stability than light boats with short keels, meaning that turns will be slow to start and stop. Large rudders are more efficient than small rudders.

Helm, Rake, and Heel

Weather helm is the boat's tendency to head up and point her bow into the wind or to windward (also called "to weather"). Lee helm is the tendency to bear off and point the bow away from the wind or to leeward ("to the lee"). Lee helm should never be tolerated, but a slight amount of weather helm is good

since it both improves water flow over the rudder and urges the steerer to keep sailing closer to the wind. As a rule of thumb, when the boat is sailing close-hauled (with the wind at about 40° off the bow) in about 10 knots of wind, and is heeled about 15°, there should be a slight tug on the tiller or steering wheel and the rudder should be cocked about 3°. Much more weather helm is a reliable indication that something is wrong.

If the boat is designed properly, weather or lee helm should not be built-in. However, they can be induced or removed by adjusting mast rake, which is the mast's fore-or-aft tilt. When the mast is raked aft, or tilted with its top back, weather helm is induced and the boat tends to head up. When it's raked forward, lee helm is induced. Most boats are extremely sensitive to rake. Weather helm usually can be increased simply by letting off the headstay turnbuckle three or four turns so the mast rakes back less than 1 inch; tighten the permanent backstay if there is one. Decrease weather helm by winding down on the headstay turnbuckle and letting off on the backstay. The helm may also be adjusted by moving the mast in its step, or its support in the bilge or on deck. Move the mast aft to increase weather helm and forward to decrease weather helm.

Weather helm increases as the boat heels to leeward, partly because of the increased asymmetry of the hull in the water and partly because the sails tilted to leeward tend to twist the rig and boat upwind. If the boat is allowed to heel too far, weather helm will exceed the optimum slight tug.

Steerageway

An important point to make about rudders is that they're useless if there is no water flowing over them. If a boat isn't moving, she can't be steered any better than an airplane wing lifts a 747 parked at an airport loading bay. Before trying to steer, build up at least a couple of knots of speed. Once you have steerageway (enough speed to steer with), you can alter course. While waiting for steerageway to build up, keep the helm and rudder centered; otherwise the rudder will grab the slowly moving water and only slow the boat down. Try to alter course only when the boat has built up sufficient speed for the rudder to work.

Self-Steering Devices

When the boat is reasonably well balanced so that she'll stay on a straight course with the helm centered

Self-steering devices such as this windpowered vane system are often used by long distance and shorthanded cruisers and racers. Electronic autopilots, either built into the steering system internally or added, are also popular.

or near centered, you may rig a self-steering system. The simplest is made by connecting the jib sheet to the tiller (it doesn't work well on a wheel): when the sail luffs, the strain comes off the sheet and the tiller is pulled to windward by a length of shock cord; the boat heads off and when the strain of the full jib balances the pull on the shock cord, she holds course.

The most popular kind of self-steerer is the electric automatic pilot running off the ship's battery and connected to the steering wheel or tiller with a cable, belt, or rod. The desired heading is set on the instrument, which has an internal compass that keeps the boat on or near course. Since this self-steerer depends on the boat's electrical power, the battery must be charged periodically by running the engine or by connecting it to a trickle charger powered by solar panels, a windmill, or a propeller towed astern.

Another kind of self-steerer, the wind vane, does not need electricity. It orients the boat to the wind, not the compass. A small sail-like vane on a post over the stern is adjusted to the desired wind angle. It's connected to the helm, a flap (called a trim tab) on the trailing edge of the rudder, or a small separate rudder. When the boat swings off the desired wind angle, the vane turns the helm, tab, or rudder and brings the boat back on course.

Any crew using a self-steerer must still satisfy Rule 5 of the Navigation Rules (Rules of the Road): "Every vessel shall at all times maintain a proper lookout by sight and hearing."

How Boats Work

Hull Speed and Planing

A boat's speed potential is not unlimited. For one thing, because a strong wind provides as much heeling force as propelling power, a point is finally reached where no amount of lead in the keel or hiking by the crew will keep her sailing fast. Second, as the wind increases, it creates ever-larger waves whose resistance will slow any boat. While an owner can improve his boat's speed potential by giving her a smooth bottom and well-shaped appendages and sails, and by sailing her well, he will in-evitably be restricted by those and other limitations.

More important, keel boats and heavy centerboarders have a built-in maximum speed called hull speed. These boats are called displacement boats because as they move they are perpetually displacing a new patch of water. The opposite to a displacement boat is a planing boat, which can sail on top of the water. A curragh is a displacement boat while a sailboard is a planing boat.

Displacement Boats. As a displacement boat sails, she creates waves, which move along at about the same speed as the boat herself. Generally speaking, the heavier the boat, the deeper the trough of the waves she creates. Now the faster a wave travels, the longer is its period, or distance between crests. So as the boat's speed increases, the number of waves that she pulls along decreases until a point is reached where she's sitting in the trough of a single wave, with one crest at her bow and the other at her stern. She is, in fact, a prisoner of the wave that she herself has created.

After considerable research, scientists concluded that the speed of a wave is equal to 1.34 times the square root of its length, or:

$$\text{Speed} = 1.34 \times \sqrt{\text{distance between crests}}$$

So a 40-foot wave travels at a speed of 8.48 knots, a 50-foot wave at 9.48 knots, and a 100-foot wave at 13.4 knots. Since the wave-making resistance of a boat is created by her underbody, or the part below the waterline, the speed at which this single trough is created can also be predicted using the boat's waterline length (sometimes called L.W.L., or length on waterline). So a boat with a 40-foot waterline sailing at 8.48 knots will create a wave going the same speed. Since most displacement boats are unable to escape that wave, this speed is called the hull speed. It is the maximum theoretical speed of a displacement hull, and it is calculated with this formula:

$$\text{Hull Speed} = 1.34 \times \sqrt{\text{waterline length in feet}}$$

Some displacement boats are able to

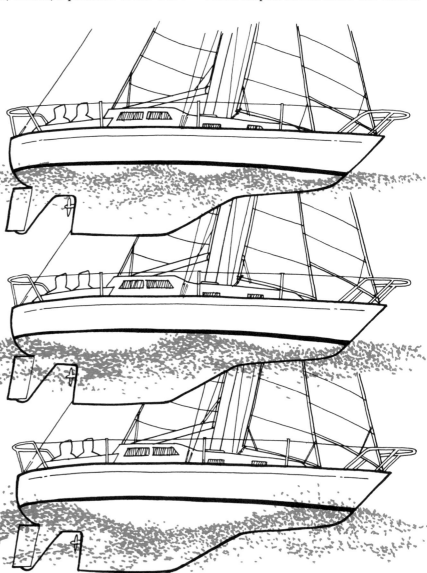

At about 1/3 hull speed, there will be three waves formed along the windward side.

As the boat accelerates to 1/2 hull speed, the waves speed up, lengthen, and decrease in number to two.

At hull speed, the boat is creating a wave slightly longer than her waterline length that, if she is too heavy, she can't escape.

go up and over the forward crest, escape the single-trough wave, and sail faster than the theoretical hull speed. These boats may be especially light and have very large sail areas or especially fair hulls. In addition, almost all displacement boats will occasionally beat their hull speed when surging down the face of a large wave. But it's fair to say that the vast majority of today's fiberglass stock keel sailboats designed for general-purpose cruising are limited by their hull speed.

If the single-trough wave appears at hull speed, then lower speeds create fewer, smaller waves in rough proportion to hull speed. You can reliably judge present speed by counting the waves on a boat's windward side between the bow and the stern and dividing that number into the hull speed.

Just because a displacement boat has a hull speed doesn't necessarily mean that she will automatically reach it, even in optimum conditions of smooth water and a moderate 12- to 15-knot wind. An overloaded boat that is very tender (heels readily) may drag

her heels and dig a big hole in the water well before she reaches hull speed, and a boat with barnacles on her bottom may create so much resistance that no matter how well she is sailed she never creeps above dead slow.

Multihulls. Although technically a displacement boat, a multihull is able to escape the restriction of hull speed because her pencil-like hulls create very little wave resistance as they

With half her hull flying clear of the water, this International 14 dinghy planes at 12 knots — more than twice her hull speed.

glide through the water. The great sail-carrying power of a wide, stable catamaran can push her to speeds two or three times her theoretical hull speed so long as she stays upright.

Planing Boats. Other than multihulls, most high-speed-sailing is done in planing boats. The simplest of these is the sailboard and the most complicated is the 38-foot Inland Lake A-Scow. In between are hundreds of dinghies that can get up and go at speeds far beyond their theoretical hull speeds. Many of these boats are so light that the total weight of their crews is greater than that of the hull and rig. When those sailors hike on the windward rail, they provide considerable righting moment to counter the heeling force on the sails, some of which are quite large.

In order to get planing, a boat must break out of her wave and skip over the crest at the bow. In a way, all planing boats start as displacement hulls when they sail at slow speeds through the water; given sufficient power by a gust of wind, they snap over the bow wave and then, freed from the confinement of the wave, accelerate off on a plane with the first half of the hull often out of the water. It's an exhilerating experience.

Why Speed Is Important

Our emphasis on speed may seem surprising. Going fast in a boat may be fun, but most people would not regard it as seamanlike. Yet experienced seamen know that a good turn of speed can be an important safety ingredient. As Colin Mudie, who designed many boats including *Brendan,* the curragh we have mentioned, once wrote: "Speed is not only a sensible part of seamanship, it is to a certain extent a satisfactory substitute for some of it." While excessive, hotrodding speed can certainly get you into trouble, quick acceleration and maneuverability can almost always be counted on to get you out of it. Many novice sailors mistakenly buy heavy, slow clunkers because of their apparent seaworthiness. Not only are these boats not much fun to sail — and enjoyment is what we're after on the water — but they cannot be relied on to make much progress against a strong current or a fresh wind. A Swedish sailor once spoke of a certain underrigged yacht that would "go a loooooooong vay an' take a looooooong time a-gettin' dere, too." Even world voyagers know the pleasures of taking a relatively short while to reach the next port, no matter how looooooong the mileage.

Planing boats behave just like displacement, non-planing boats in light winds, creating waves they cannot escape.

Pushed by a wave or a wind gust, the light boat quickly accelerates and her bow lifts clear of the hull-speed wave.

Once her hull has broken loose of the wave, a planing boat stabilizes on her flat after underbody and planes off.

Boat Dimensions

Boats are described by length, construction material, rig, and type. For instance, a "22-foot aluminum outboard" is an open boat powered by an outboard engine. The motor might be an "85-H.P. Johnson," or an 85-horsepower engine made by the Johnson engine company. Sailboats require a longer description because they are more complicated than powerboats. For example, the "Sabre 30" shown on this page is a class, or identical group, of fi-berglass cruising sloops built by Sabre Yachts in South Casco, Maine. But if you were interested in a Sabre 30, you'd also want to know her waterline length (which indicates her ultimate speed), her beam (a measure of her roominess and stability), her displacement (which suggests her hull shape, light boats being flatter than heavy boats), her ballast (yet another indicator of stability), her draft (as a measure both of the amount of water she needs and her ultimate stability), her sail area (an indication of her relative speed and ease of handling), and her sail plan (which tells how the sail area is divided up). As shown in the builder's literature and boating magazines, the Sabre 30 has these dimensions:

L.O.A. (overall length), 30′ 7″

L.W.L. (waterline length), 25′ 6″ (theoretical hull speed 7 knots)

Bm. (extreme beam), 10′ 6″

Disp. (displacement or weight in pounds), 9400# (lb.)

Ballast (weight in the keel or bilge), 3800#

Dr. (deepest draft), 5′ 3″

The published plans of a racer-cruiser or cruising boat show its profile, sail plan, and overhead views of the interior accommodations and deck.

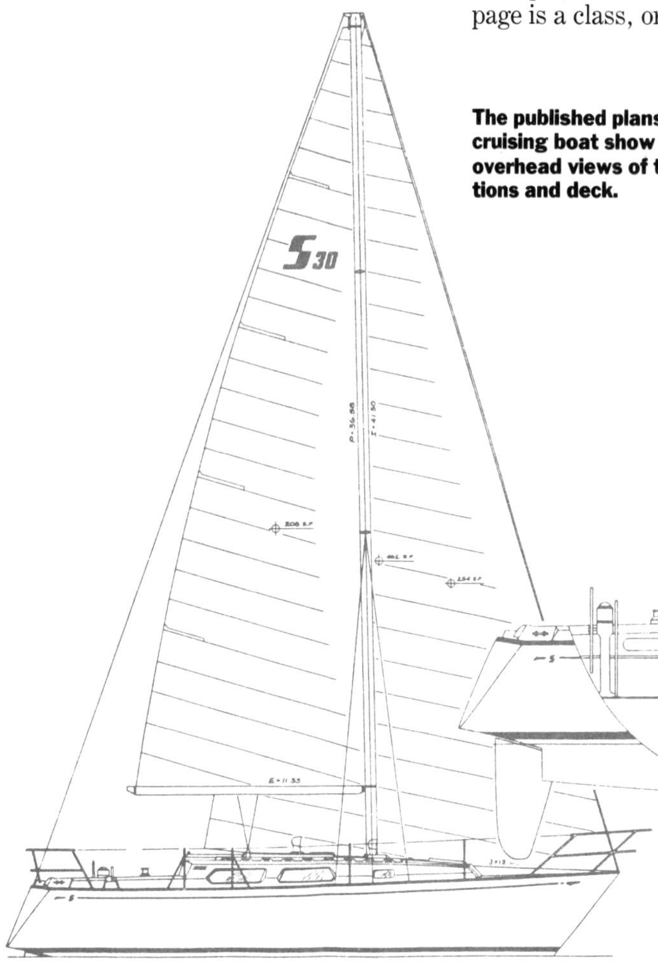

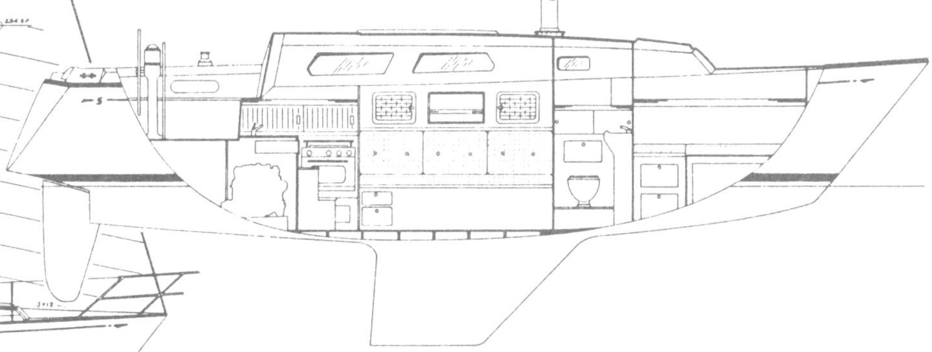

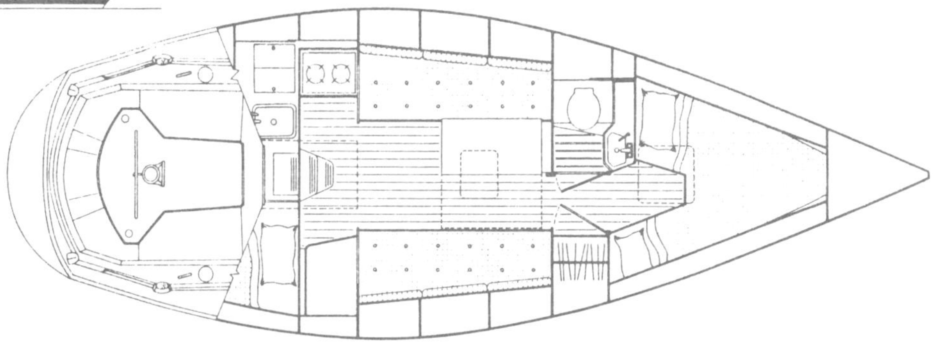

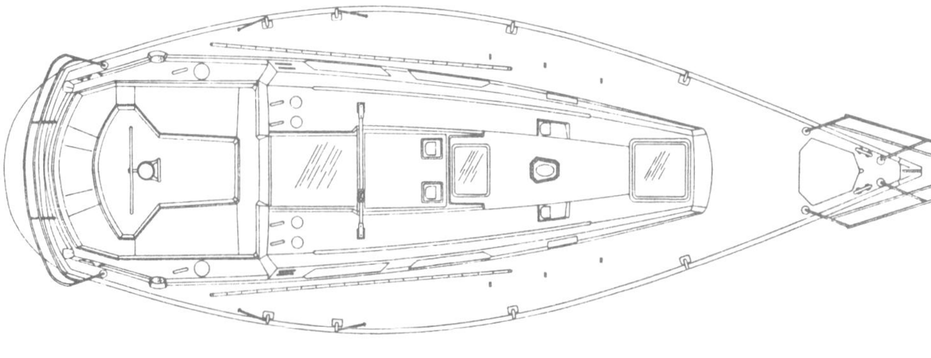

S.A. (sail area, mainsail plus foretriangle, or the area between the headstay, mast, and foredeck), 462 sq. ft.

We'll discuss the type of rig later.

To a beginner, these numbers mean very little, but to an experienced sailor they are vital statistics. First off, the expert will be able to compare the Sabre 30 with other boats around her size using a few mathematical ratios that can be run off on most electronic calculators.

The *displacement/length ratio* (abbreviated D/L) is a good indicator of a boat's weight for her size. If her displacement is light for her length, you can tell without looking at her that she's probably at the sailboard end of the spectrum rather than at the curragh end. She's probably fast, bouncy, and tricky to sail, with limited directional stability. "L" in this formula is L.W.L. Here is the formula:

$$D/L = \frac{\text{displacement in long tons}}{(.01 \times \text{L.W.L.})^3}$$

The length is cubed to put it in the same dimensional context as displacement,

which is a volume (a cubic dimension). Long tons (2240 lb. per ton) and the constant of .01 make the final product manageable, somewhere between 30 and about 350.

Boats with a D/L ratio of 325 and over are generally considered to be heavy cruisers. A ratio of 200-325 indicates the boat is a light- to moderate-displacement cruiser or moderate-displacement racer. Anything less than 200 is either a very light-displacement cruiser or a light-displacement racer. A ratio lower than about 125 puts a boat in the ultra light-displacement boat (ULDB) category.

The D/L for the Sabre 30 works out as follows:

$$D/L = \frac{\text{displacement in long tons}}{(.01 \times \text{L.W.L.})^3}$$

$$\frac{9400/2240}{(.01 \times 25.5)^3} = \frac{4.20}{.017} = 247$$

With a D/L ratio of 247, the Sabre 30 is in the area of lightish displacement, though she certainly is heavier than many other cruisers. For example, the

J/30, whose dimensions are given on this page, has a D/L of 186.

Another ratio, the *sail area/displacement ratio* (abbreviated SA/D), allows you to compare sail areas of different boats. It assumes that displacement is the only limitation on speed. This is an over-simplification since an unfair, rough, crudely built, light-displacement hull under a veritable cloud of sail will probably be slower than a well constructed, smooth, heavy-displacement boat with a small rig. Still, the SA/D ratio does provide a reliable ballpark comparison between boats, especially when it is used in conjunction with the D/L ratio.

Here's the formula:

$$SA/D = \frac{\text{sail area}}{(\text{displacement in cubic feet})^{2/3}} =$$

It's simpler than it looks. To find displacement in cubic feet, divide it by 64 (62.2 if you sail in fresh water). Then, to find the number to the 2/3 function, square it and then find its cube root either by trial and error on a simple calculator or by consulting an engineering manual.

For the Sabre 30:

$$SA/D = \frac{\text{sail area}}{(\text{displacement in cubic feet})^{2/3}} =$$

$$\frac{462}{(9400/64)^{2/3}} = \frac{462}{27.9} = 17$$

A SA/D ratio of 17 puts the Sabre 30 toward the upper range, though not as high as many boats designed for racing in light winds. Motorsailers (boats that depend on large engines as much as on their sails) have ratios of 8-13, while many sailing cruisers are in the 14-16 range. The J/30's SA/D is 20, putting her well into the high-performance area of racing boats.

All this suggests that the Sabre 30 is lighter and carries more sail than many other cruisers, but is still fairly moderate compared with the J/30. With her large sail area she would probably sail well and fast in light to moderate winds, yet with her moderately light displacement she probably would be a bit more comfortable and easy to handle in rough weather than a ULDB. This does not say anything one way or the other about seaworthiness; very light boats sailed by competent sailors have gone long distances.

What else do these dimensions tell us? With a draft of 5' 3", the Sabre 30 may be a bit too deep for shallow areas like Chesapeake Bay, but she may also have plenty of stability. A potential owner should ask the builder or de-

J/30

L.O.A.	L.W.L.	Bm.	Dr.	Disp.	Ballast	S.A.
29'10"	25'	11'2"	5'3"	6500#	2100#	443 sq.ft.

With a long waterline, wide beam, and light displacement the J/30 should be roomy, fast, and quick in her motion as well as a challenge to steer well.

Tartan 3000

L.O.A.	L.W.L.	Bm.	Dr.	Disp.	Ballast	S.A.
29'11"	25'3"	10'1"	5'2" (4'1")	7950#	3830#	441 sq.ft.

With a D/L ratio of 220, it has a more conservative hull shape than the ultra-light J/30, and should be both slower and easier to sail well. An optional shallow keel will facilitate cruising in shoal water.

Mariner 32

L.O.A.	L.W.L.	Bm.	Dr.	Disp.	Ballast	S.A.
31'10"	25'8"	10'	3'8"	12,400#	4000#	468 sq.ft.

The only non-sloop in the group, the Mariner 32 differs significantly in other ways. It weighs almost twice as much as the J/30 and has a D/L ratio of 315, which definitely puts it in the heavy cruiser range. Despite having relatively little ballast, it is quite narrow — suggesting that it is tender (heels easily).

A study of the key dimensions of different boats of about the same size should give you an idea of their strengths and weaknesses. Here, two sloops and a ketch of almost the exact same waterline length — and, therefore, the same theoretical hull speed — are strikingly different in other dimensions. One is a light-displacement racer-cruiser with the emphasis on "racer." Another is a moderate-displacement cruiser-racer with the stress on "cruiser." And the third is an out-and-out heavy-displacement cruiser. From here the buyer would look carefully at the boats themselves, talk to other owners, and finally choose the class that best meets his needs.

The Lines Plan

signer for a graph showing the range of positive stability, which is the angle at which the boat will capsize. For sailing in windy areas, the range should be no less than about 100 degrees.

The Lines Plan

Once the yacht designer has a good idea of the client's needs and how a proposed boat will be used, he or she establishes desired mathematical ratios between length, displacement, and sail area based on experience and sailing theory. These calculations determine the boat's approximate shape in the water, for instance whether she will be full- or sharp-ended, and how wide she will be at the waterline. Around this time the designer sketches the midship section, or the boat's cross-sectional shape from keel to deck at her widest point.

Now the designer can start drawing the two-dimensional lines plan, which is a set of detailed scaled drawings that show the boat's outlines as well as her shape in cross-sections. He or she must also make accurate estimates of the weights of the various components, such as the construction material, the mast, the furniture, the engine, and the crew that will be sailing. If the weights are wrong, the boat will float high or low of her designed waterline, or she may sail bow-down or stern-down. Computers speed up making calculations and drawing the lines.

The finished lines usually come in four major parts. One is the section plan, showing cross-sections taken from each side to the middle of the boat, looking down the length of the boat

The sail plan shows the boat from the side with all the sails she might carry. This boat, a Morris 36 designed by Chuck Paine, has a traditional appearance, with a transom (aft-cocked) stern, squared-off cabin, and gradually curving sheer (deck edge). She has a masthead double-headsail cutter rig on which two jibs can be set, one on the headstay at the bow and the other on the forestay partway back. Her dimensions are L.O.A., 36′ 3″; L.W.L., 29′ 6″; Bm. 11′ 7″; Disp. 16,602#; Ballast, 6000#; Dr. 5′ 6″; S.A., 627 sq. ft.

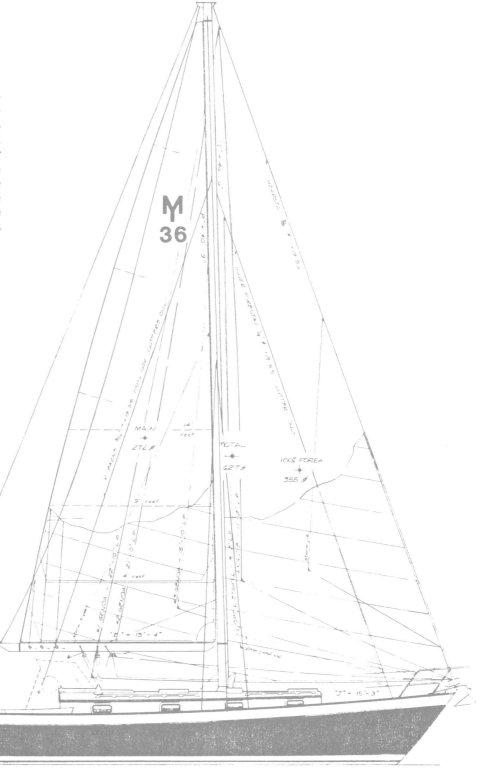

from the bow and stern. Another is the profile plan, showing cross-sections (called buttocks) taken vertically from the deck to the water. A third is the overhead plan, showing cross-sections (called waterlines) taken horizontally parallel to the water's surface from one side to the other. And the fourth is the sail plan, which shows the right placement of the masts, booms, and sails so the boat will balance properly without lee helm or weather helm.

These plans are a boat's fingerprint. The designer hands them over to the builder with other plans showing deck and interior arrangements plus lists of equipment to be installed and construction standards to be met. Also included is a table of offsets that allows the builder to scale up the plans to full-size. From there, the builder proceeds with construction of either one boat or a plug that will be used to build a series of fiberglass boats.

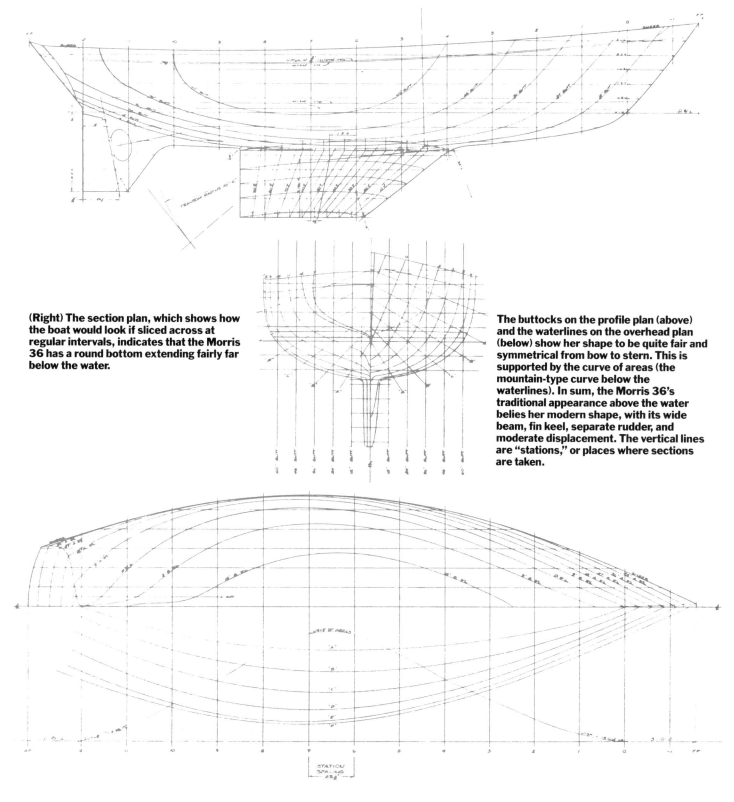

(Right) The section plan, which shows how the boat would look if sliced across at regular intervals, indicates that the Morris 36 has a round bottom extending fairly far below the water.

The buttocks on the profile plan (above) and the waterlines on the overhead plan (below) show her shape to be quite fair and symmetrical from bow to stern. This is supported by the curve of areas (the mountain-type curve below the waterlines). In sum, the Morris 36's traditional appearance above the water belies her modern shape, with its wide beam, fin keel, separate rudder, and moderate displacement. The vertical lines are "stations," or places where sections are taken.

29

The Rig

Besides their dimensions, boats are distinguished from one another by the type of rig they carry — the way they set their sails. The main components of a rig are the mast (supporting the halyards and the front edge of the mainsail), the boom (supporting the bottom edge of the mainsail), the stays (supporting the mast and the jibs), and the sails themselves. There are six rigs for sailboats, each with its own special characteristics.

The sloop is by far the most popular rig. On a sloop, there is a mast, a boom, a jib, and a mainsail. If the jib is hoisted from the top of the mast — and this is the case in most cruising boats — the rig is called *mastheaded*. However, if the jib is hoisted from anywhere below the top of the mast, the rig is called *fractional*. Most daysailers and some cruising boats have fractional rigs. On most mastheaded rigs, the jibs are large overlapping genoas, trimmed far aft and in square footage usually larger than the mainsails. The jibs on fractional rigged boats, on the other hand, are usually smaller than the mainsails, even if they extend abaft the foretriangle (the area bounded by the mast, the headstay, and the foredeck).

The cutter is a single-masted rig whose mast is stepped almost near the center of the boat. Since a cutter's foretriangle is larger than a sloop's, it is filled by two relatively small jibs

rather than one big one — an advantage for small crews. The inner jib is called the staysail and is set on a lower stay called the forestay, and the outer jib is simply called the jib.

The yawl probably is the most popular type of *divided rig* — or rig with two masts. Divided rigs are used on larger boats to break up the sail plan into small, manageable components. The largest sail that can be handled by a normal sailor contains 500-600

square feet of cloth. In the yawl rig, a jib and a mainsail are hung off the larger, forward mast, called the mainmast, and a small sail, called the mizzen, is hung off a small mast stepped way aft. This after mast is called the mizzenmast. In addition, large, light, jiblike sails called mizzen staysails may be hung off the mizzenmast to increase the sail area when reaching, or sailing across the wind. A yawl (or any other divided rig, for that matter)

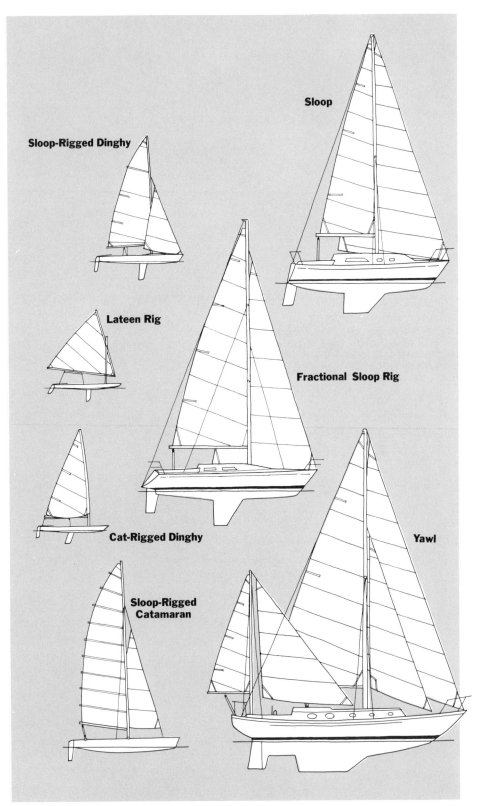

Sloop-Rigged Dinghy

Sloop

Lateen Rig

Fractional Sloop Rig

Cat-Rigged Dinghy

Yawl

Sloop-Rigged Catamaran

may have either a mastheaded or a fractional rig forward of the main-mast.

The ketch has the same general appearance as the yawl — tall main-mast forward and small mizzenmast aft — except that the mizzenmast is quite a bit larger in proportion to the mainmast. Therefore the mizzen is much larger than a yawl's mizzen; on some ketches the mizzen and the main-sail are about the same size. The miz-zenmast is stepped fairly far forward, usually forward of the steering wheel or tiller. The ketch can carry mizzen staysails. Because it breaks down the sail area into three roughly equal areas, the ketch rig has been a favorite for people sailing long distances in large boats.

The schooner is the reverse of the ketch. With the forward mast (called the foremast) shorter than the main-mast, the schooner carries her small sails forward and her large sails aft. Because this rig is fairly complicated, it is rarely seen on modern boats, but until World War I it was the standard rig used on yachts.

The cat rig looks like a sloop or ketch without a jib. The mast on a single-masted cat boat is stepped way forward (the sailboard has a cat rig). On a cat ketch the larger mainmast is stepped on the bow and the mizzen-mast is stepped in the cockpit; a cat ketch normally carries two sails — the mainsail and the mizzen — but may also carry mizzen staysails when reach-ing. Although the sail or sails on a cat rig are very large, they are set on eas-ily manageable booms. The most diffi-cult sail to use on a boat usually is the large genoa jib, and since the cat rig dispenses with jibs it's a good choice for sailing shorthanded (with small crews) or sailing with children.

Rigs may also be categorized by the shape of the mainsail. The *Marconi rig* is the three-sided mainsail or mizzen seen on almost all modern boats. Just after World War I the Marconi rig re-placed the classic *gaff rig*, in which the mainsail has four sides and is sup-ported at its top by a short boom called a gaff. The gaff rig is still used on some traditional boats. The Marconi rig de-rives its name from its great height (compared with the gaff rig) and from the complexity of stays needed to keep it upright — when it appeared, many people thought it looked like one of the tall radio towers built by Guglielmo Marconi. Another type of mainsail that is still seen is the *lateen rig*, used on the Sunfish and other small board-boats. This is a three-sided sail sup-ported at the bottom by a boom and at the top by a lateen, or long gaff, all pivoting around the mast. The *wish-bone rig*, used on sailboards and some cat rigs, is a pair of curved slats that hold the clew out from the mast.

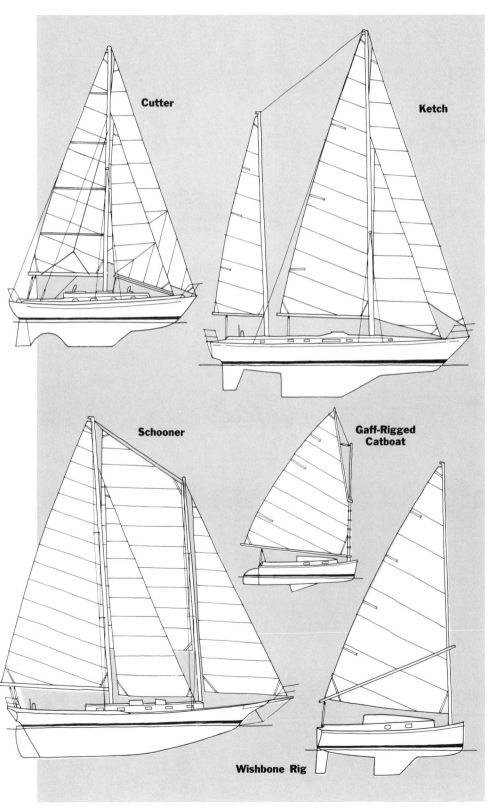

Cutter

Ketch

Schooner

Gaff-Rigged Catboat

Wishbone Rig

Sail Furling

Sails are furled, or put away, in different ways. Many sails are doused, or lowered, onto the boom or deck, where they are flaked in large folds, rolled up, tied down, or put away in bags. Jibs and mainsails may also be rolled up on stays with *roller-furlers* controlled by lines from the cockpit. Roller-furlers (which we'll say more about in chapter 3) are a blessing for the sailor for whom it is physically difficult to go on deck and handle sails.

Most mainsails and some jibs have *battens*, wooden or fiberglass slats inserted in pockets in the leech, or after edge of the sail, to support the roach

(the curved part of the leech) and keep the sail from flapping shapelessly. Most boats have short battens whose length is about one-quarter the sail's width. However, a growing number of boats have full-length battens running from leech to luff. On racing boats, the pressure of the battens in their pockets can be increased in order to make the sail more full, but on cruising boats, full-length battens are left untensioned and serve mainly to control luffing. Wild luffing is very noisy and can destroy the sail's shape.

Full-length battens also help the sail stack neatly on the boom when it's lowered. On many boats, lines called *lazy jacks* are led from the boom up to the mast to cradle the sail as it comes down.

Convenient furling systems include the nearly ubiquitous roller-furlers (top) and full-length battened sails that nestle between lazy jacks.

Boat Selection

Boats are successful or unsuccessful, loved or ignored, more for how well they meet the needs of their owners than for any other reason. "Different boats for different folks" is a reliable rule of thumb. Anybody who wants to own a boat should carefully examine those types in light of his or her own needs before making a purchase.

Small Boats

A person who is happy sailing alone will like a sailboard, catamaran, or dinghy smaller than about 14 feet from bow to stern (overall length, or length on deck). Two or three people will want a dinghy, catamaran, or centerboard daysailer between 14 and 20 feet. Keel daysailers for two to five people range from 18 to 30 feet. While more expensive than centerboard boats and more difficult to haul out of the water, keel boats have one big advantage over centerboarders and small catamarans: since stability against heeling and capsizing is provided by keels, not human weight on the windward rail, the crew does not have to throw itself athletically from side to side to keep the boat upright.

Most of these boats provide little or no shelter for their crews and should always be sailed on protected waters near shore, where the waves are not large and hospitable ports are close at hand.

Boat Selection

Cruising Boats

A cruising boat, which can range from 18 to more than 100 feet, is a boat with living accommodations in a shelter. Smaller, lighter boats may be very suitable for protected waters, where some of them sail very fast, but their ability to sail comfortably and safely offshore in rough weather may be questionable. Larger, heavier boats may be slower but more seaworthy in rough weather. This means that if you want to cruise out into deep water with the confidence that your boat can handle the roughest weather, you will want to concentrate less on speed than on seaworthiness and seakindliness, or the ability to go through big waves in relative comfort. This does not automatically mean that all fast boats are unseaworthy and all heavy boats are seaworthy. Just because a boat's heavy, it doesn't mean that she is well built.

Offshore Design Features

Size and displacement are factors in seaworthiness. A heavy 30-footer may be as seaworthy as a 40-footer of moderate displacement or a light-displacement 50-footer. In addition, a relatively heavy boat will be able to carry more crew, food, fittings, and other weights with less effect on her sailing ability and trim than a relatively light boat of the same waterline length. One sensible rule of thumb is that for sailing far from shore in rough conditions, a typical moderate-displacement cruiser with a displacement/length ratio of 250-325 should have an overall length of at least 35 feet.

Keel length has become something of a shibboleth in conversations about cruising boat design. This is partly because many light-displacement racing boats with very short fin keels have proven to be unseaworthy. However, seaworthiness is not a function solely of keel length. A boat is not safe just because she has a full-length keel and an attached rudder. Very many good, seaworthy boats have fin keels and separate rudders. Still, extremely small keels and rudders don't belong on boats cruising offshore.

Stability, or resistance to heeling and (ultimately) capsizing, is an important concern when choosing a boat to sail offshore and in rough weather. A reliable indicator of a boat's capsizability is a number that indicates range of positive stability. This is the angle of heel up to which she is safe from capsizing. For example, if the range of positive stability is 120°, when she heels from 1 to 120° she will come back up; but when she tips to 121°, she will keep going over and eventually lie upside down.

The positive stability range is determined by a complicated formula that takes many design and construction factors into account. It can be calcu-lated by a naval architect or by having the boat measured by a racing handicap rule called the International Measurement System (IMS).

An easier way to estimate a boat's resistance to capsize is to use the Capsize Screening Formula developed in the mid 1980s by the Joint Committee on Safety from Capsizing of the United States Yacht Racing Union and the Society of Naval Architects and Marine Engineers. Here is the formula, taken

The ultra light-displacement (ULDB) sloop (above) is suitable for short outings in smooth water, while the moderate-displacement cruisers (below) may be suitable for somewhat longer cruises in normal weather.

from the book *Desirable and Undesirable Characteristics of Offshore Yachts*, written by the Technical Committee of the Cruising Club of America and edited by myself. Take the boat's total weight in pounds and divide it by 64 to find the boat's volume in cubic feet in salt water (divide by 62.2 to find volume in fresh water). Divide the cube root of that figure into the boat's beam. If the result is less than 2, then the boat is relatively safe from capsizing in very rough conditions. If it is more than 2, she is relatively vulnerable to capsizing in those conditions. The higher the number, the more vulnerable she is. This is a guideline, not an absolute test, for estimating a boat's ability to cross large bodies of water when properly sailed.

Buoyancy when capsized or holed is not inherent in most keel boats but it is a characteristic of dinghies, catamarans, and trimarans with built-in watertight buoyancy compartments. Some keel monohulls that have watertight bulkheads or large expanses of foam will float when flooded. While ultimate buoyancy is a definite benefit for people heading out into the ocean (where boats have been sunk by whales and floating containers lost from freighters), the boatbuyer should balance its advantages against its accompanying disadvantages. Compared with heavier monohulls, multihulls may be difficult to slow down in order to sail safely in rough weather. As for monohulls with built-in buoyancy, living space can be greatly limited.

With her small cockpit and sturdy feel, this Fast Passage 39, drawn by the distinguished yacht designer Bill Garden, has the characteristics of a good ocean-going boat. Her large keel testifies to fairly heavy displacement. It's balanced by a large sail plan in a cutter rig. Her full pointed stern gives her a shippy appearance and adds somewhat to her seaworthiness by providing plenty of buoyancy aft. However, just having these (or any other) special features does not guarantee that a boat is suitable for going to sea; they must be properly designed and built, and the rest of the boat must come together as a whole. The accommodation plan shows a functional interior with plenty of privacy in three cabins.

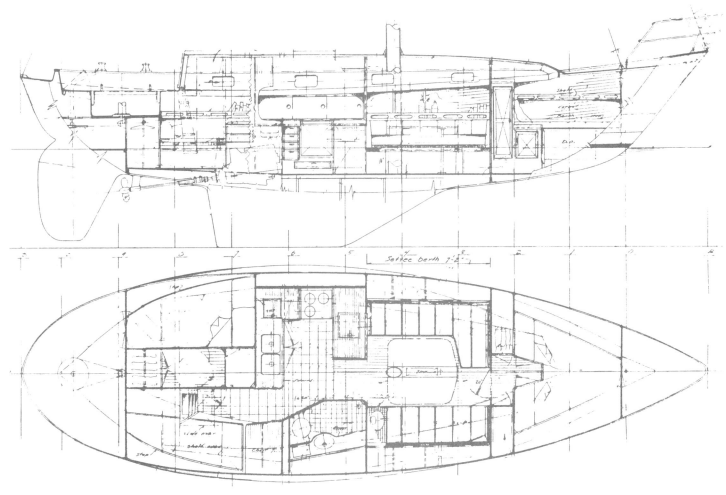

Traditional Rigs

Most of what we have said concerns the Marconi or Bermudian rig, which has a three-sided mainsail contained within a horizontal boom and vertical mast. While it is by far the most popular rig, it is a relative newcomer on the block, having been developed in Bermuda in the late 19th century and becoming popular only since the 1920s. The gaff and lateen rigs date back much further, and the wishbone rig was developed just before the Marconi rig became popular. The Marconi rig triumphed because it is faster. In the long history of pleasure-boat design, racing success has been the most important cause of changes. Yet each of these alternative rigs has its advantages, and while the Marconi rig is used on most boats, the traditional rigs still have their place.

Gaff Rig

Nothing on the water says "tradition" quite so eloquently as a gaff-rigged sailboat. The sail has four sides and is set between three spars: the boom, mast, and gaff, whose forward end slides up and down on the mast. Two halyards are needed, one at the forward end of the gaff to pull up the sail's luff, the other at the aft end of the gaff to pull up the leech. The first is called the throat halyard, the second the peak halyard. The luff may be attached to the mast with slides or with rings, called parrels, slipped over the mast. The gaff mainsail can be set alone in the cat rig or with jibs and other sails. The mainsail generally is left on throughout the sailing season; it should be covered when not in use to prevent deterioration caused by ultraviolet rays.

To hoist the sail, pull on both halyards at once until the luff is taut, with slight vertical tension wrinkles. At this point the gaff will be horizontal and the

This work-boat type, called the Cornish Crabber, flies a topsail over her gaff mainsail. Having the sail area in several small parts makes it easy to shorten sail.

sail will be only partially filled. In the language of the gaff rig, it is *scandalized*. You can sit comfortably like this until time to get under way. Then haul on the peak halyard until the gaff is cocked up and there are slight diagonal tension wrinkles across the sail from the peak (the end of the gaff) to the tack.

When the boat is sailing, the gaff falls off to leeward. To decrease the gaff's sag and the mainsail's twist, tighten the peak halyard. You can also rig a vang, which (on the gaff rig) is an adjustable line or tackle leading from the peak down to the windward deck. Tighten the vang to reduce twist in light air and ease it to increase twist in a gust of wind. To depower the sail altogether, scandalize it by easing the peak halyard until the gaff falls off and the top of the sail hangs useless.

To douse a gaff-rigged mainsail, scandalize it and then ease the peak and throat halyards down together, making sure the gaff and sail are nestled between the lazy jacks that usually are carried on gaff-rigged boats. The sail

On the gaff rig, the gaff is supported near the mast by the throat halyard and at the end by the peak halyard. To depower the sail, scandalize it by dropping the peak. Lazy jacks running from the mast to the middle of the boom will hold the boom up and secure the sail when the halyards are let go.

should fall neatly into natural folds, which will be held down by the gaff. Tie a couple of sail stops around the boom, gaff, and sail to keep everything secure.

An advantage of the gaff rig is that the boat can be gotten under way and put away very quickly. Another advantage is that the mast can be quite a bit shorter than the mast on a Marconi rig and the center of effort is low, which means that heeling forces are less (this probably is why most gaff-rigged boats are found in windy areas like San Francisco and Buzzards Bay in Southern Massachusetts).

There also are disadvantages. Since a sail with a high aspect ratio (long luff and short foot) provides more drive than one with a low aspect ratio (short luff and long foot), the gaff rig is less efficient than the Marconi rig. To provide equal driving power on the same boat, a gaff mainsail needs at least 20 percent more sail area than a Marconi mainsail. To increase sail area, many gaff-rigged boats fly large sails called topsails above the gaff. And because the rig is

Because it's so short, the Sunfish's lateen rig is easily stowed and handled, but like the gaff rig it's not as powerful as a long-luffed Bermudian (or Marconi) rig.

low and squat, the boom overhangs the stern and the jibs are set on a bowsprit projecting well forward of the bow.

Because of these and other restrictions, the gaff rig is rarely used except on schooners, cat boats, Friendship sloops, and other classic boats. But of all sailboat rigs, it probably is the most loved. After all, speed is not everything. If it were, would there be any sailboats other than high-speed catamarans and trimarans?

Lateen Rig

Found today mainly on Sunfish, the popular little daysailer, this rig is like the gaff rig except that the gaff and boom are extended forward of the mast to connect with each other at the sail's tack. A plus is that the spars are shorter than the hull, so the boat is easily rigged, put away, stowed, and transported with the spars lying on deck. In light air, raise the gaff and boom as far as possible on the mast to catch wind off the water. In fresh air, lower them to drop the center of effort and decrease heeling forces.

Wishbone Rig

Developed by the great Rhode Island yacht designer and builder Nathanael Herreshoff (1848-1938), without question the most creative person ever to mess around with boats, this rig is found on sailboards, cat-rigged Nonsuch cruising boats, and some boats in the Freedom line of cat-ketches. The wishbone rig uses a triangular sail whose clew is held out from the mast by two curved booms (which look like a chicken's wishbone) on either side of the sail. Sometimes a single boom is rigged. An advantage of this rig is that the downward thrust of the booms on the sail's clew automatically keeps the leech firm. This means that the main sheet only pulls the sail in and doesn't have to hold it down, so the tug on the sheet is relatively slight. On most wishbone-rigged boats, the mast is left freestanding without stays. In a gust, the mast bends to leeward and depowers the sail by spilling wind aloft. On cruising boats, light lines draped under the foot cradle the sail when it is doused.

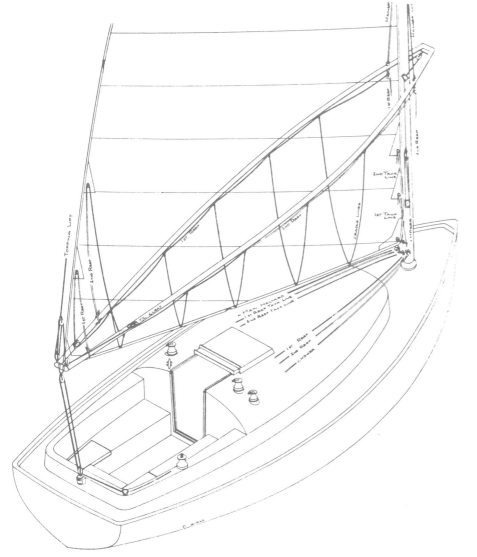

The wishbone rig (here on a Nonsuch cat boat) has a long luff. Because the wishbone pushes down, there is no need for a boom vang or for a large tackle on the main sheet. Loose lines between the wishbones gather the sail when it's doused. The sail is reefed much like a Bermudian mainsail.

Construction Materials

Fiberglass is by far the most popular material for building boats because it's easy to work around molds, and so can be used to build many sisterships of the same hull. A fiberglass boat starts with a plug, which is a wooden, plastic, or metal hull built to the designer's lines after careful calculations and sometimes testing with prototypes. Plastic female molds of the hull and deck are made from the plug. Sheets of fiberglass strands are laid into the molds in gluelike resin, with a releasing agent between the sheets and the molds. Wood or foam blocks are sometimes laid onto the fiberglass to form a reinforcing sandwich (fiberglass tends to flex and requires reinforcement in large flat areas). When the resin has cured, the hull is broken from the mold. The outside layer of the hull, called the gel coat, provides a shiny, attractive surface. Sometimes the hull is built in one piece, but many cruising boats are built in two pieces, and the starboard and port halves are bonded together after they cure. Any interior fittings such as bunks are installed along with transverse structural members, called bulkheads and floors, which stiffen the floppy hull. The deck, which was made in its own mold, is then laid over the hull. How well the deck and the hull are bonded together at the rail usually determines the quality of the boat. Some cheap builders only bond the deck and hull with resin, but the clamp (the point at which the attachment is made) should also be secured with bolts. If the attachment is weak, the boat will leak at the clamp, or much worse, come apart there under the strain of rough weather.

Other points to be attentive to when inspecting a fiberglass boat include the way the engine is secured in the hull (it should be strongly bolted in), the strength of the joint between bulkheads and the hull (unless it is heavily fiberglassed, the joint may break and the hull will flex), and the general appearance of fiberglassed areas (if loose strands or extra resin are lying about, the hull may not have been built with care). Few seamen know boats well

Fiberglass racer-cruisers at different stages of construction show (left to right) stiffening with a bulkhead, a deck mold, a deck being dropped on a hull, and a two-part hull mold.

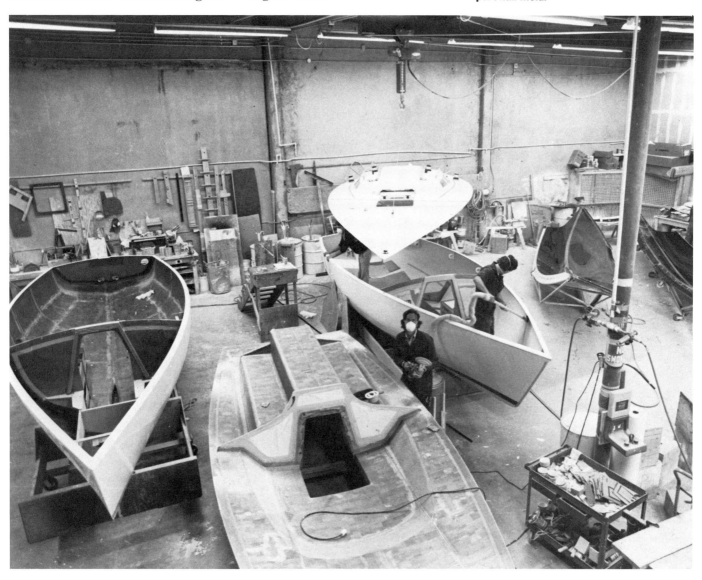

enough to inspect them properly. Specialists called marine surveyors are available to go over boats in search of structural flaws. Their advice is well worth their fees, especially if they save you from buying a boat that's on the verge of self-destruction.

Ironically, fiberglass is not the best boat-building material. Wood is. Wood is lighter, stronger, and more beautiful, but it also rots, must be painted or varnished, and dents easily in its softer grades. If you enjoy working with your hands and looking at the end product of all that labor, then you may be suited for a wooden boat. But if you enjoy sailing and prefer to spend your off-season weekends following other pursuits, then you should own a fiberglass boat.

Some large custom yachts (built for individual customers) are aluminum or steel, and many small powerboats are built of aluminum, which can be shaped in molds. Both metals require special preparation for use in salt water. Aluminum is usually considered to have the best strength-to-weight ratio of all building materials, other than such highly sophisticated and expensive space-age materials as carbon fiber and Kevlar.

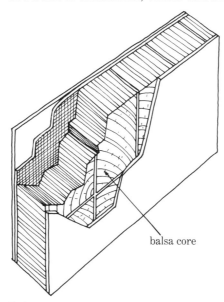

Standard fiberglass construction consists of layers of different types of material chosen for strength and compatibility with resin: (left to right) mat, cloth, woven roving, cloth, and mat. They are laid up in resin one layer at a time.

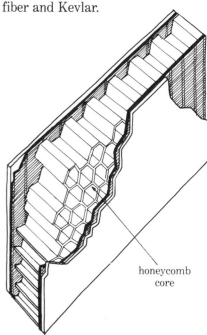

End-grain balsa wood is often used as a core to stiffen fiberglass, which can flex in flat surfaces.

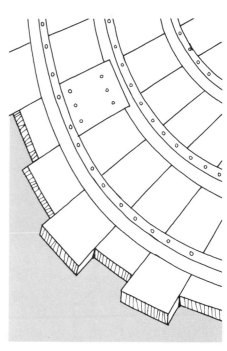

Other cores used in fiberglass sandwiches are Airex foam and Nomex honeycombs which may be laminated with fiberglass that has been pre-impregnated ("pre-preg") with resin and cured in special ovens. Builders may also combine plywood and fiberglass with "exotic" materials such as carbon fiber, Kevlar or aluminum in order to achieve high strength to weight ratios.

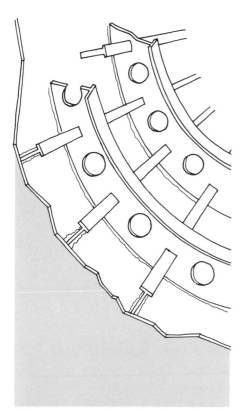

Aluminum construction consists of shaped and welded plates reinforced by frames (here shown with lightening holes that save weight without affecting strength).

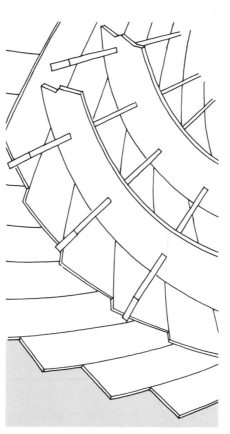

Molded plywood is used in many different types of boats, and many home-built boats are constructed with plywood sheets.

Traditional wood construction, with planks fastened to wooden or metal frames and seams filled with calking, is both light and strong. Many builders now seal wood with space-age resins.

Hints on Buying a Boat

Since seamanship in its broadest sense means to enjoy and safely use boats, nothing is more important than having the right boat to begin with and using her in a way that is compatible with your skills, resources, and ambitions. All too many people get in financial and, eventually, on-the-water trouble because they bought boats that they are not competent to use. If you must spend most of your free time maintaining a big or complicated boat, you won't have time to use her and learn from her. If you have little free time because the financial demands of boat ownership require you to put more days into your job, then a boat can be your downfall. Boat ownership is demanding.

Before you go shopping for a new boat, thoroughly erase every romantic notion you have about the sea from your memory. After heaving *Moby Dick* into the garbage can, sit down

When purchasing a used boat, many people are blinded by their passion to get sailing as soon as possible and forget to look for faults. Here are some problems that may lead to serious trouble.

☐ Illegal Marine Toilet
☐ Bent or Corroded Anchor
☐ Poorly Maintained Engine
☐ Corroded, Loose, or
   Insufficient Ballast
☐ Malfunctioning Electronics
☐ Scratched Compass
☐ Bubble in Compass

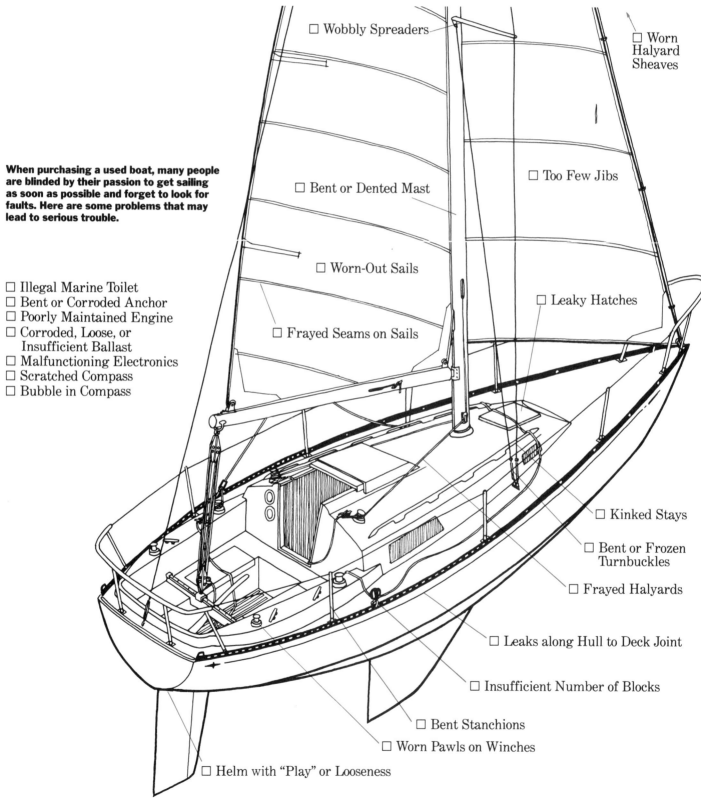

☐ Wobbly Spreaders
☐ Worn Halyard Sheaves
☐ Bent or Dented Mast
☐ Too Few Jibs
☐ Worn-Out Sails
☐ Leaky Hatches
☐ Frayed Seams on Sails
☐ Kinked Stays
☐ Bent or Frozen Turnbuckles
☐ Frayed Halyards
☐ Leaks along Hull to Deck Joint
☐ Insufficient Number of Blocks
☐ Bent Stanchions
☐ Worn Pawls on Winches
☐ Helm with "Play" or Looseness

and have an honest conversation with yourself and your family about what you want out of boating. Make a list of your objectives: fishing (deep-sea or river?); cruising (overnight or around the world?); entertaining (your best friend or your boss?); racing (informal or blood and guts?). If you're interested in cruising, try to anticipate how many berths you'll need. Find out where you'll be able to store your boat. In some areas waterfront storage is available only for trailerable boats and every marina slip has a 6-year waiting list. Will you normally be out in rough weather or calms? On weekends or for months at a time? Singlehanded or with your six sons and their football team?

Next, the tough question: How much boat can you afford? *Be realistic.* Unlike real estate, boats are not investments. The value of a well-built, well-maintained little yacht *may* keep up with inflation, but don't count on it. Few people make money on boats, so be sure to relegate your boating plans to your discretionary and not your investment bank account. Before you go shopping, check around with banks and other financial institutions to see what boat loans are available, and at what price. Draw up a preliminary budget based on a hypothetical boat of about the size you're considering, checking with marinas and boatyards to see what their charges may be. If you walk into the boat dealer's showroom with that budget in hand (and firmly anchored in your mind), you'll be well prepared to resist the temptation of a boat larger than you can afford — and probably need.

When you have finally decided exactly what kind and size of boat fits your needs and finances, before you make your down payment on a new model, look around to see if a used boat will be satisfactory. Boats normally depreciate at a rate of about 20 percent in their first year, and one year's wear and tear shouldn't make all that much difference on a boat's finish. Very often extremely sound boats are available at bargain-basement prices because the owner did everything that we've been counseling against. Finding himself with too much boat and making monthly payments that he can't afford, this unhappy soul will do anything to get the burden off his back.

Listings of used boats are carried in boating magazines and at many new-boat sales offices. Before making your deposit, familiarize yourself as thoroughly as possible with the type of boat you're looking at. If several are on the market, check them all out — and find out why, in fact, several *are* on the market (perhaps they all began to fall apart at the same age). If you do eventually decide to purchase a used boat, have a surveyor examine her thoroughly before you sign the papers.

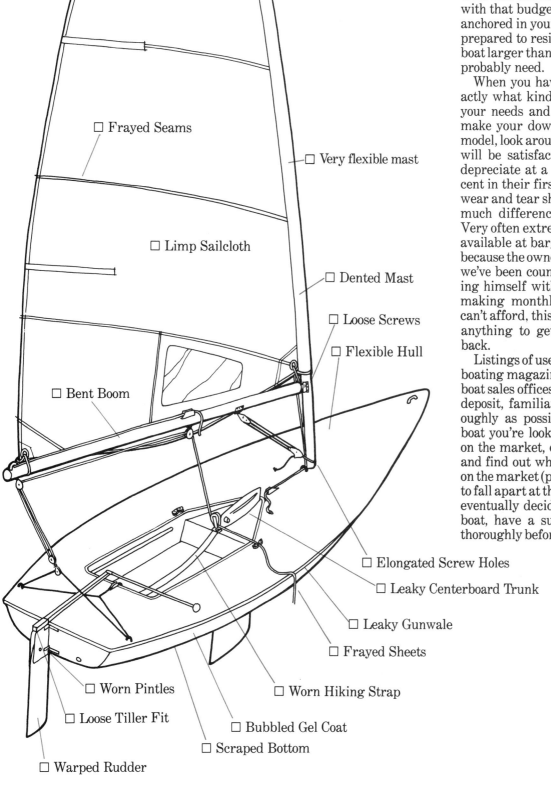

□ Frayed Seams

□ Very flexible mast

□ Limp Sailcloth

□ Dented Mast

□ Loose Screws

□ Flexible Hull

□ Bent Boom

□ Elongated Screw Holes

□ Leaky Centerboard Trunk

□ Leaky Gunwale

□ Frayed Sheets

□ Worn Pintles

□ Worn Hiking Strap

□ Loose Tiller Fit

□ Bubbled Gel Coat

□ Scraped Bottom

□ Warped Rudder

Chapter 2
Getting Under Way

"Boat handling" includes the basic skills of sailing in normal conditions: getting under way, trimming the sails properly, and getting back. "Seamanship," on the other hand, includes more advanced techniques that build on the foundation of boat handling — skills like sailing in rough weather and anchoring. Seamanship skills are described in part IV, but in this chapter and in chapter 3 we'll examine the all important techniques of boat handling.

Before we get to these techniques, we should learn a little more theory and terminology about how the boat and the wind relate to each other. We'll start with a concept called "the points of sail" and then move on to "apparent wind" — the wind that the boat helps to create as she moves through the water, and the wind that the skipper and crew trim their sails to.

The Points of Sail

The wind hits a moving sailboat from any one of three general directions: from ahead, from abeam (the side), and from astern. Over the centuries sailors have come to describe these wind angles as the points of sail, and have divided them into three categories: beating (also called close-hauled sailing), reaching, and running. In addition, several other terms describe sailing angles between the three points of sail.

The points of sail can be shown in an abstract overhead drawing, a pie diagram with a wind arrow at the very top and boat models around the edge of the pie. While this diagram does not accurately represent the forces involved, it does show the geometric relationship between wind and boat.

Running is shown at the bottom of the pie, with the boat's stern turned toward the wind in a small slice that

The points of sail — running, reaching, and beating — are the most basic concepts in boat handling.

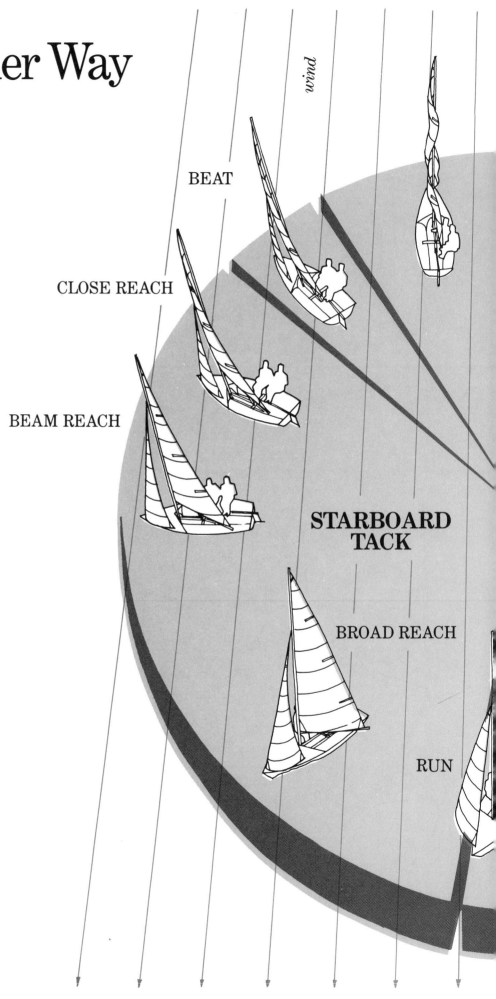

wind

BEAT

CLOSE REACH

BEAM REACH

STARBOARD TACK

BROAD REACH

RUN

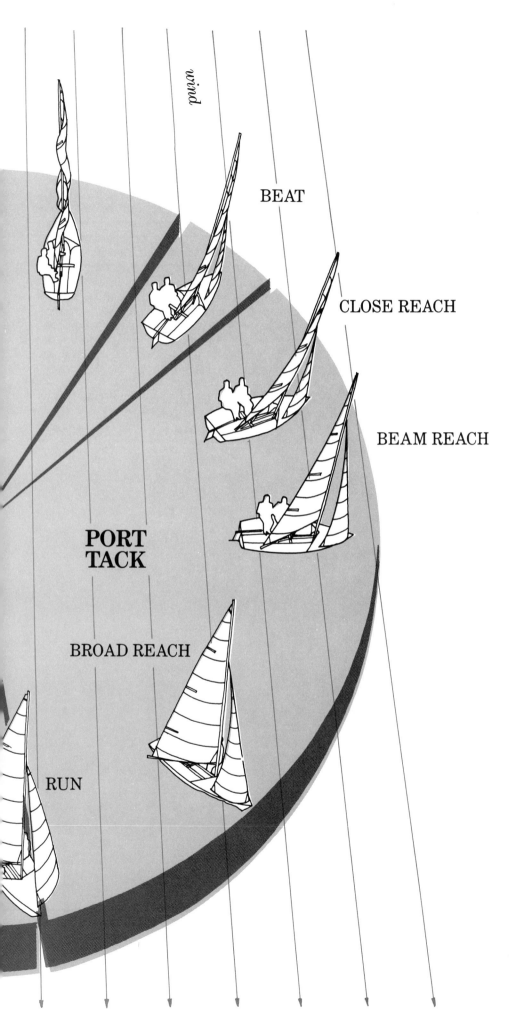

wind

BEAT

CLOSE REACH

BEAM REACH

PORT
TACK

BROAD REACH

RUN

takes up only 10° of the pie either side of the very bottom. On the right side of the slice, the boat is running on the port tack; on the left side, the starboard tack.

Reaching takes up a 120° slice on each side of the pie, between running and 50° from the top. At exactly 90°, when she is sailing at a right angle to the running course, the boat is on a beam reach with the wind coming directly over her beam, or side. Below that, she's sailing on a broad reach; above that, she's on a close reach. The reach is the fastest point of sail, with the close reach being the fastest reach.

Beating takes up another thin slice of the pie, between the close reach and 40° from the top, although some very close-winded boats may be able to sail as high as 30°. On this point of sail the boat is literally beating her way against the wind and waves with her sails trimmed in tightly — or close-hauled. Above the beating slice is a wide no man's land where sails do not fill completely. If headed dead (directly) into the eye of the wind, the boat will make no forward motion as her sails luff (flag). One side or the other of dead into the wind, she may be able to fill her sails partly and make some headway (forward motion). If so, she is forereaching.

When they aren't referring to the points of sail and the intermediate angles, sailors often speak of two broad categories of sailing: "on the wind," or beating; and "off the wind," or reaching and running.

Any boat can run, reach, beat, sail on the wind, and sail off the wind on either of the two tacks, starboard and port. A boat is always on one tack or the other. On starboard tack, the wind comes from over the starboard side (right side when facing forward), the boat heels to the port side, and the sails are trimmed to the port side. On port tack, the wind comes from port (left side, facing forward), heel is to starboard, and sails are trimmed to starboard. Later we'll describe the two ways that boats change from one tack to the other.

True Wind and Apparent Wind

The relationship between true wind and apparent wind is neatly illustrated by a bicyclist, whose forward motion (gray vector) redirects, decreases, or increases the true wind (dark blue vector) to create a wind that only he feels — the apparent wind (light blue vector). The only time when there is no apparent wind is when the true wind blows in the same direction and with the same velocity as the cyclist's progress.

There are two types of wind. The true wind is the wind that blows across the water, the wind a sailor feels when standing on the pier. However, when the boat sails, her motion alters the direction and force of the true wind to create the apparent wind. It is the apparent wind, not the true wind, that governs how we trim the sails and, sometimes, what course we sail. This phenomenon is familiar to anybody who has pedaled a bicycle in a crosswind. A bicyclist making 10 miles per hour in a 10-knot crosswind will feel the wind not on the side, but from forward of the side. And the felt wind will be slightly greater than the actual wind because the bike's own speed is augmenting it. If, however, the bike were heading directly into a 10-knot wind, not only would the cyclist have to work harder to keep up his 10-M.P.H. speed, but he would also feel 20 knots of wind in his face. If the bike were running with the wind, the effort would be less, and because the bike's speed and the wind's speed were the same, the cyclist would feel no wind at all.

The same phenomenon occurs on a moving boat. Using tables or a technique called vector analysis, we can even predict the exact direction and force of the apparent wind so long as we can estimate the boat's speed and heading and the strength and direction of the true wind. It is also possible to solve this simple geometric problem using an electronic calculator programmed with trigonometric functions. (Of course, if you know the apparent wind you can use the same techniques to work backward to find the true wind.) Yet precise prediction of apparent wind speed and direction is much less important to the average sailor than a simple understanding of how forces involved affect the boat on different points of sail. With some experience you'll find that you can predict the angle and velocity to within about 5° and 3 knots. Here are some helpful rules of thumb:

1. The apparent wind is the wind that the boat sails in.
2. On a reach or a beat, when a

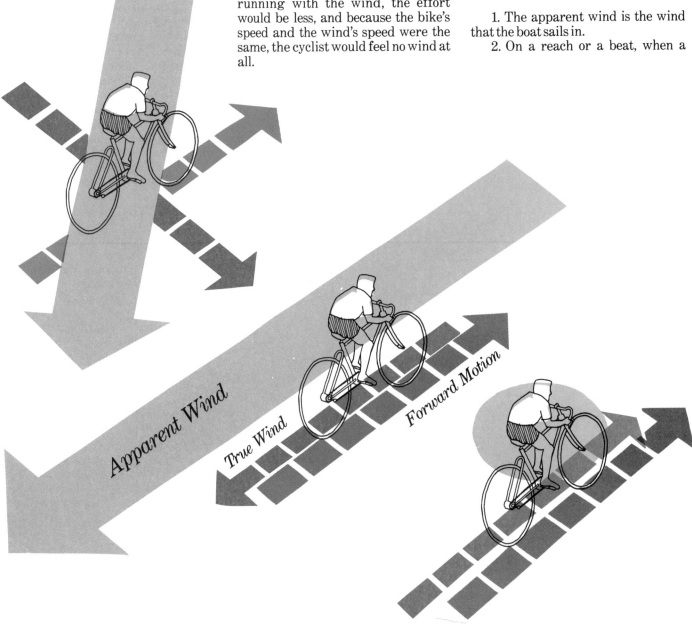

Apparent Wind

True Wind

Forward Motion

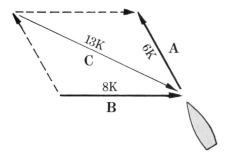

Using vectors (force arrows) you can determine the apparent wind. Line A is the boat's speed and course and line B (in the same units of measurement) is the true wind speed and direction. Line C is the apparent wind. Here a boat sailing at 6 knots in an 8-knot true beam wind has a 13-knot apparent wind on a close reach.

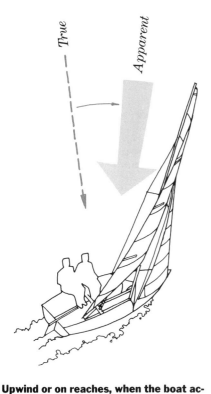

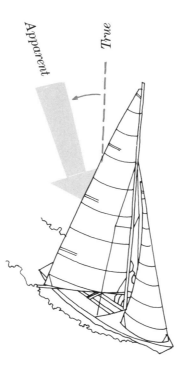

Upwind or on reaches, when the boat accelerates or there is a lull in the true wind, her apparent wind draws forward and she is headed.

When the boat decelerates or there is a puff, her apparent wind pulls aft and she is lifted. On a run, when she accelerates her apparent wind decreases.

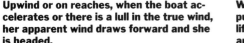

boat accelerates, the apparent wind will increase and draw forward.

3. On a run, when a boat accelerates the apparent wind will decrease and stay in the same direction.

4. While the apparent wind is the wind the boat sails in, it is the true wind that makes the waves. Often the waves will come at an acute angle to the apparent wind.

5. The farther forward the apparent wind draws, the greater are the side forces on the sail that cause heeling and leeway (side slippage).

6. The sails work best when the wind flows over them from the luff (front edge) to the leech (back edge) at an apparent wind angle of about 80°. Therefore, of the points of sail, a close reach is the fastest and a run is usually the slowest. Instead of sailing on a run, with the wind just slapping against the sails, head up to a reach and allow the wind to flow over the sails.

7. When the difference between the boat's speed and the true wind's velocity is great, the apparent wind will not differ much from the true wind. That is, slow boats don't change fresh winds very much.

8. When the boat's speed and the true wind's velocity are close, the apparent wind will be very different from the true wind. In light conditions, even slow boats can have a big effect on the true wind, and fast boats may have radically different apparent winds. (For example, iceboats are so fast that they're almost always sailing close-hauled, even when the true wind is way aft. Iceboats and other fast sailboats can "make their own wind" in some optimum conditions: the apparent wind is greater than the true wind.)

9. Unless it is also a shift in direction, a puff of wind always pulls the apparent wind aft. (This is because the puff increases the difference between the boat's speed and the true wind's velocity.)

10. Unless it is also a shift in direction, a lull in the wind always pulls the apparent wind forward. (This is due to the fact that a lull decreases the difference between boat and wind speeds.)

Even thought the true wind is only a 10-knot broad reach, these fast Tornado catamarans are making at least 12 knots in an apparent close reach of 20 knots. They are literally making their own wind.

Basic Sail Trimming

The key to making good use of the wind is to allow it to flow properly across the sails. When sailing off the wind on a reach or run, this is fairly simple.

First, get on a steady course, either by aiming at a stationary object like a buoy or a lighthouse or by sticking to a compass course. Keeping a careful eye on the luff of the sail about halfway up, ease (let out) or trim (pull in) the sheet until the cloth is just beginning to luff (or bubble). On a sloop or a boat with a divided rig, accurately trim the forwardmost sail first, then trim the after sail or sails. This is because the air

flowing off the forward sails affects the ones farther aft.

In small, light boats like the Laser dinghy, cleat the sheet only if the wind is light. In gusty or strong winds, a cleated sheet may quickly lead to a capsize since you won't be able to ease it out quickly to spill the wind from the puff. Sheets may be safely cleated on keel boats in almost all conditions, the exception being a strong, puffy offshore wind with violent shifts.

On a reach, the sail or sails will be between about halfway to three-quarters of the way out. As you ease the sheets, tighten the boom vang to keep the boom approximately horizontal, with the mainsail's leech curving off slightly to leeward. If the leech is straight, the vang is too tight; if the leech billows to leeward, the vang is too loose. The greater the apparent wind, the tighter the vang should be — which means that it must be loosened

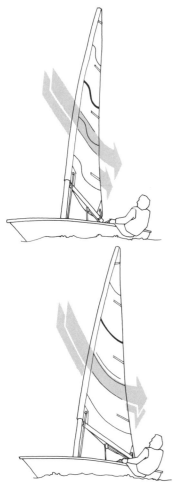

Off the wind on a reach or run, steer a steady course and adjust the angle of attack of the sail to the wind by playing the sheets. Ease the sheets until the sails begin to bubble at their luffs (top), then trim back in slightly until the luff disappears (bottom).

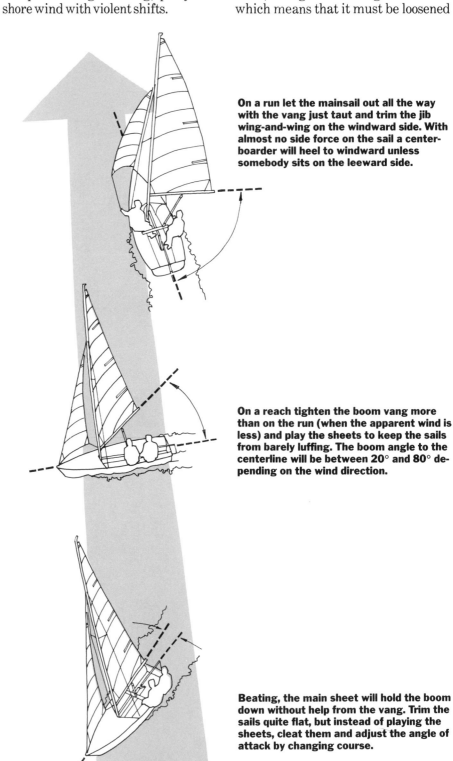

On a run let the mainsail out all the way with the vang just taut and trim the jib wing-and-wing on the windward side. With almost no side force on the sail a centerboarder will heel to windward unless somebody sits on the leeward side.

On a reach tighten the boom vang more than on the run (when the apparent wind is less) and play the sheets to keep the sails from barely luffing. The boom angle to the centerline will be between 20° and 80° depending on the wind direction.

Beating, the main sheet will hold the boom down without help from the vang. Trim the sails quite flat, but instead of playing the sheets, cleat them and adjust the angle of attack by changing course.

wind

as you head off from a reach to a run. On a run, the mainsail will be all the way out with the boom almost against the leeward shrouds (side stays); be careful, though, to keep the upper part of the sail from chafing (rubbing) against the shrouds and spreaders — eventually it will rip.

In the next chapter we'll look at sail trim in considerably more detail, but the simple technique of easing the sheet until the sail luffs will be enough to help you get under way and sail around. This technique is called "playing the sheet." If the boat heels uncomfortably far, ease the sheets until she comes back upright, even if the sails are luffing quite a bit.

Basic Close-Hauled Sailing

A different technique is used to keep the wind flowing properly over the sails on a close-hauled course. Instead of sailing a steady course toward a stationary object and playing the sails as the apparent wind shifts, you alter course using the luff of the forward-most sail as a guide. Cleat all sheets

(except in gusty winds and in dinghies) with the sails pulled in almost all the way and the boom vang loose. The helmsman sits in a position where he can see the sail luff and tries to keep a very slight bubble in the sail. When the bubble becomes large and the sail luffs a few inches back, he heads off (turns the bow away from the wind). And when the bubble disappears and the sail is not luffing at all, he heads up (turns the bow toward the wind).

This Laser skipper carefully sails by the luff of the sail as he sails on a beat with the sheet cleated.

These course alterations will be very small — in most cases no more than about 3°.

A wind change that forces the skipper to head off, called a header, may be caused either by a shift in the direction or a *decrease* in the velocity of the true wind. On the other hand a lift, which allows the skipper to head up, is caused by a shift in direction or by an *increase* in velocity.

The helmsman may also use the feel of the wind to help sail close-hauled. Sitting facing forward on the windward side, he will feel the wind on his windward cheekbone when the boat is properly oriented to the apparent wind. If he feels the wind on his mouth, he should head off; if on his ear, he should head up. We'll have more to say about close-hauled sailing in the next chapter.

A lift (A) is a wind shift allowing the crew to ease sheets or head up. A header (B) forces them to trim sheets or head off.

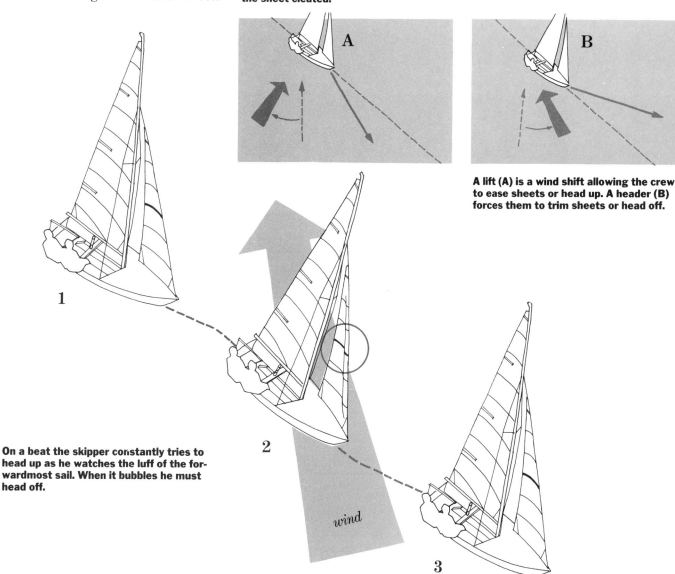

On a beat the skipper constantly tries to head up as he watches the luff of the forwardmost sail. When it bubbles he must head off.

47

Changing Tacks

Sometimes the wind shifts so far that the boat must change from one tack to the other in order to stay on or near course. At other times a major course alteration may require a tack change. There are two ways to change tacks: tacking, or coming about, by heading up; and jibing by heading off.

Tacking (Coming About)

Tacking occurs when a boat close-hauled on one tack swings her bow through the eye of the wind and ends up beating on the other tack. The first step is to head up with a strong, fluid shove of the helm. The sails luff partially and then entirely. The bow passes through the wind, and with the helm still over, falls off with the wind on the new side until the sails fill. What carries the boat through the maneuver is her momentum from her old tack. Heavy boats carry considerable momentum and so lose little speed as they tack. Light boats, if they're not tacked properly, may stop dead head-to-wind, or "go into irons."

Don't shove the helm over too hard. An abrupt motion will slow the boat drastically as water piles up on the rudder. More important, the water flow may actually separate from the rudder and cause it to stall like the wing of an airplane in too steep a climb. Keel boats should be tacked more gently than light centerboarders, with a gradually increasing shove. During the tack, ease the mainsheet slightly — about 3 inches on a light centerboarder and more on a keel boat — so that when the boat ends up close-hauled on the new side the sail is fairly full, allowing her to accelerate back to speed. Since heavy boats accelerate more slowly than light boats, be careful not to trim the mainsail back too tightly and too quickly. When there are waves, acceleration may be extremely slow.

One common error is to shove the helm over for too long and sail beyond the new course. During a tack from one close-hauled course to the other, the boat will change course about 80°. You can precalculate the compass course on the new tack. Better yet, as the boat completes the tack, keep your eye on the luff of the forwardmost sail and be sensitive to the changing feel of the wind on your face.

It's important that the skipper and crew communicate clearly during a tack. Here are the orders and responses they should use:

Helmsman: "Ready about." The crew prepares for the tack by coiling sheets so they are ready to run out through blocks, uncleating sheets (but holding them), and making sure no loose gear will get in the way. When ready, they reply:

Crew: "Ready."

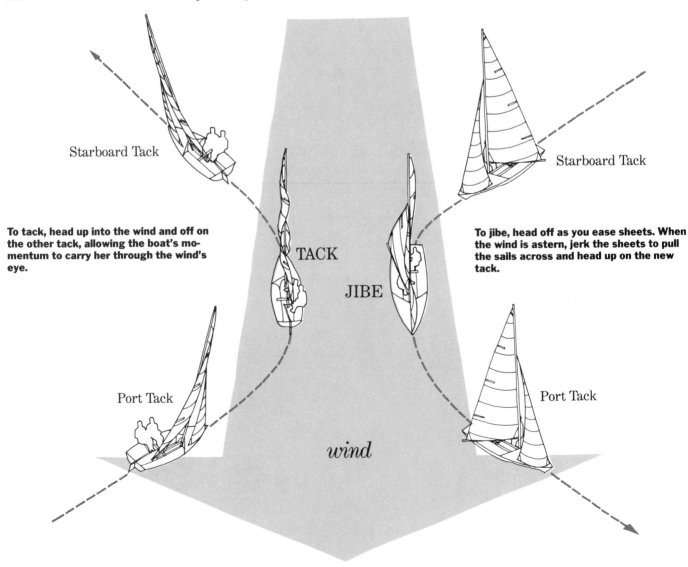

Starboard Tack

To tack, head up into the wind and off on the other tack, allowing the boat's momentum to carry her through the wind's eye.

Port Tack

TACK

JIBE

wind

Starboard Tack

To jibe, head off as you ease sheets. When the wind is astern, jerk the sheets to pull the sails across and head up on the new tack.

Port Tack

The helmsman looks around for any obstructions, such as other boats, then pushes the tiller down (or pulls the wheel up) saying:

Helmsman: "Hard a-lee." This ancient command means that the boat is being tacked as her helm is pushed to leeward. As the bow swings up toward the wind, a crew member uncleats and prepares to cast off (free) the leeward jib sheet. When the forward half of the jib is luffing, he casts off (this may require pulling the sheet off a winch) and carefully lets the sheet run out through his hands to remove any kinks. Meanwhile another crew member (or on a small boat, the same man or woman) pulls in the slack in the other jib sheet and takes one turn clockwise around a winch.

The jib swings through the foretriangle, the bow passes through the eye of the wind, and the sail flops over on the new leeward side as the jib sheet is trimmed. The crew pulls on it, taking two or more turns around the winch to snub it against the wind's force and, if needed, grinding the sail in on the winch by turning the winch handle. If the new course is close-hauled, the sheet should be trimmed a few inches shy. The full sail will help her to accelerate. Meanwhile the helmsman has stopped the bow's swing when it has reached about 40° off the wind. As the boat accelerates, he tells the crew to trim the jib some more and then to cleat the sheet. How tight the jib should be trimmed depends on the boat, the size of the sail, and the wind strength. Generally, there should be a slight arc in the foot of the sail. If it's trimmed too tightly, the boat will have a lee helm; if too loosely, a weather helm.

If a tack is sloppy, it's usually because the old, windward sheet jammed in a block as it ran out. Be sure to remove any kinks first.

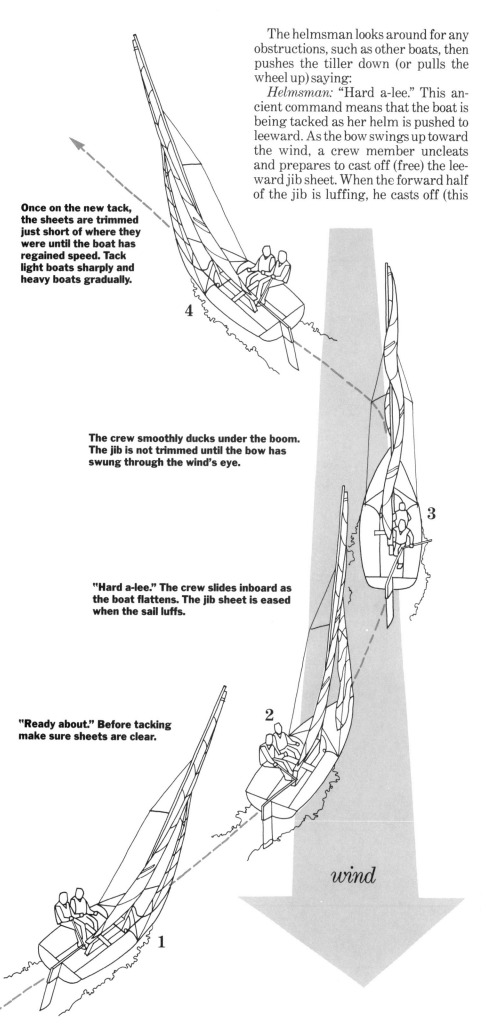

Once on the new tack, the sheets are trimmed just short of where they were until the boat has regained speed. Tack light boats sharply and heavy boats gradually.

The crew smoothly ducks under the boom. The jib is not trimmed until the bow has swung through the wind's eye.

"Hard a-lee." The crew slides inboard as the boat flattens. The jib sheet is eased when the sail luffs.

"Ready about." Before tacking make sure sheets are clear.

wind

Genoa jibs must be helped through the foretriangle. Steer a keel boat through a tack with a gradually increasing rudder angle so that momentum is not lost.

Changing Tacks

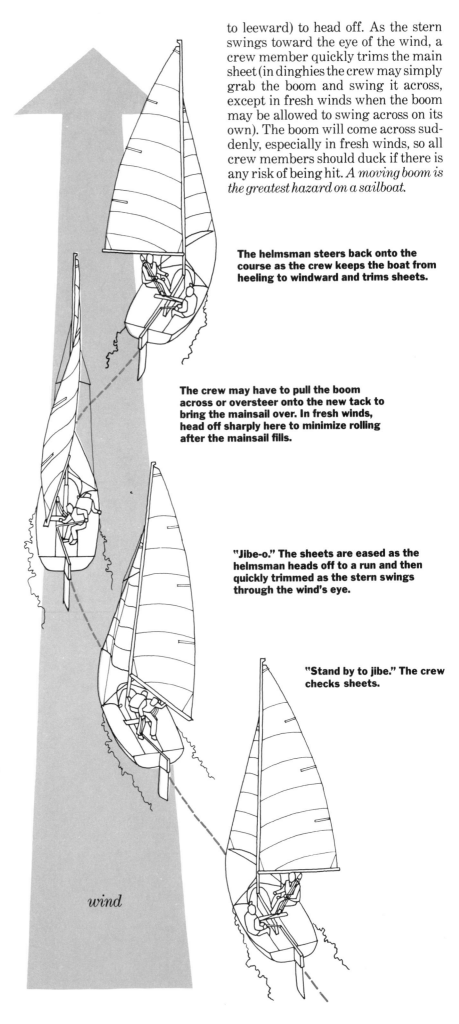

Jibing

The other way to change tacks is to jibe, by swinging the stern through the eye of the wind as the boat changes course from a run on one tack to a run on the other. Here are the orders and replies:

Helmsman: "Stand by to jibe." The crew clears and uncleats the sheets and checks for loose gear. The helmsman makes sure he can jibe without risk of a collision.

Crew: "Ready."

Helmsman: "Jibe-o." He pulls the tiller to windward (or turns the wheel to leeward) to head off. As the stern swings toward the eye of the wind, a crew member quickly trims the main sheet (in dinghies the crew may simply grab the boom and swing it across, except in fresh winds when the boom may be allowed to swing across on its own). The boom will come across suddenly, especially in fresh winds, so all crew members should duck if there is any risk of being hit. *A moving boom is the greatest hazard on a sailboat.*

The helmsman steers back onto the course as the crew keeps the boat from heeling to windward and trims sheets.

The crew may have to pull the boom across or oversteer onto the new tack to bring the mainsail over. In fresh winds, head off sharply here to minimize rolling after the mainsail fills.

"Jibe-o." The sheets are eased as the helmsman heads off to a run and then quickly trimmed as the stern swings through the wind's eye.

"Stand by to jibe." The crew checks sheets.

Sailing by the lee happens when the boat heads off too far and the wind comes slightly from leeward.

wind

The mainsail may stay full and not jibe even though the stern has swung through the eye of the wind. Called "sailing by the lee," this situation can be rectified by oversteering beyond the course on the new tack until the boom finally comes across. Otherwise, the jibe should be timed so the boom is trimmed amidships (over the boat's center) just as the stern crosses the wind. Ease the main sheet quickly on the new tack. Meanwhile the jib is let go and trimmed, much as during a tack.

In fresh winds and in waves, small boats are very unstable as they come out of jibes, and the momentum built up as they swing rapidly from one tack to the other may carry them right over into capsizes. For this reason, cautious sailors may tack instead of jibe in heavy weather. But experienced small-boat sailors have developed a way to stabilize the boat on her bottom. Just as the boom swings over the centerline and the crew eases the sheet, pull the tiller sharply to windward, heading the boat directly downwind for a moment. She will level off, any rolling will stop, and she will soon be able to head up on the new course.

Recovering from a Bad Tack or Jibe

Sometimes a tack or jibe will leave a boat at her most vulnerable, without any way on and with her beam to the wind. If she isn't moving, she of course can't be steered. The first step out of this fix is to gain steerageway. Put the tiller amidships and trim both sails carefully. If you trim the mainsail too far, she'll just head up into the wind, spinning on her centerboard or keel. And if the jib is overtrimmed she'll round off and surprise you with a jibe. Remember also that a boat will make more leeway if she's stopped than if she's moving. A boat that is not moving is like a boxer staggering up from the mat. Neither is sturdy enough to withstand a blow, whether a right hook to the jaw or a strong, unexpected gust of wind. The sailor's equivalent of a boxer's low, square crouch is steerageway. As long as she's going fast enough to be steered, the boat and her rig will absorb much of the wind's blow by translating it into forward drive, but if she's sitting still, the punch will be converted into heeling force.

A bad tack may leave a boat in irons, or lying head-to-wind (with the bow in the wind's eye), and she may gather stern way (start to sail backward). If so, steer her stern by pushing the tiller in the opposite direction that you want it to aim (or the wheel in the same direction) while also pushing the main boom out to the opposite side. If you want to back down to starboard, push the tiller and boom to port. Once the bow has fallen off, trim the jib to get her moving, and then trim the mainsail.

The stages of a jibe as demonstrated by these Lasers. The skipper nearest the camera should be sitting to windward to heel the boat in that direction and induce leeward helm to help him head off without a sharp (and speed-diminishing) turn of the rudder. Though safe in a dinghy, don't let the boom swing across uncontrolled in a larger boat.

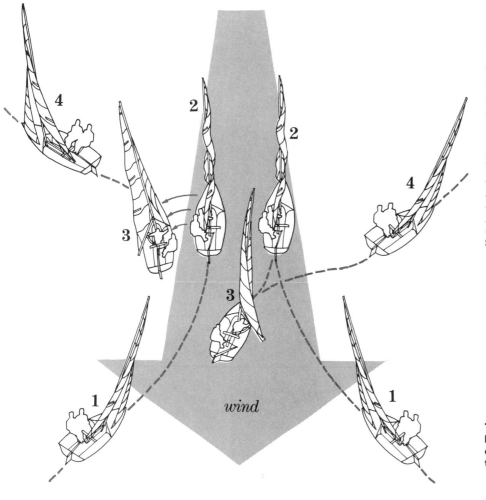

wind

To get out of irons in a bad tack either back the jib to windward to pull the bow off or steer backward to expose her side to the wind.

Climbing Aboard

We've had an overview of how a boat shapes the wind and uses it to sail. Now let's look at the steps a crew takes to get a boat under way.

For some people, simply getting aboard the boat may be the most difficult part of the day. Even when climbing aboard from a marina pier you must make a long step that, if not taken carefully, could turn into an awkward lunge. The best way to get aboard a large, high-sided boat is first to pass up all your baggage and then, with both hands free, put your dignity aside and clamber up as expeditiously as possible on your knees. Plant yourself firmly on the deck before trying to stand, otherwise you may topple backward. Of course you should be wearing boat shoes or sneakers with non-slip soles so you don't slip when you finally stand up.

Going aboard a dinghy is a double problem: not only must you step down from a pier or another boat, but when you get into the dinghy there is little room or stability. When stepping into a dinghy, your foot must immediately go onto the centerline. Stepping onto a rail or on either side of the centerline may skid the dinghy out from under you. If nobody else is aboard, make this first step right into the middle of the boat. If one or more people are aboard and seated, aim for a spot that balances their weight. Step aft if somebody is forward, forward if somebody is aft — but *always* step onto the centerline. Don't let go of the pier or other boat unless you're absolutely sure of your footing. As you bring the second foot down, grab the dinghy's rails and sit down, again on the centerline.

Be careful, too, when climbing out of a dinghy. Remember that when someone gets out of one end, the other end will drop suddenly. The best way to unload a dinghy so she stays in trim is first to take cargo or crew from the bow and then to take it from the stern, which (because it's wider) is more buoyant than the bow. Dinghies swamp more quickly when bow-down than when bow-up. Finally, unload the middle. Never make a sudden or unconsidered move in a dinghy.

While a dinghy is being loaded or unloaded, her painter (bow line) should by held by somebody or cleated on the float or the bigger boat. Many dinghy painters are made from polypropylene rope which, becuase it is buoyant, will not sink and foul propellers. Unfortunately, this rope is also very hard and slippery and does not hold well in knots or on cleats, so double-check after you secure it. Anybody holding a polypropylene line that is under a load should not wrap it around the wrist or hand because it may cut deeply.

A sailor successfully boards a dinghy from a float, crouching low and stepping into the middle.

Getting Going

Getting under way from a mooring, a trailer, a dock, or a marina slip can be either a snap or a disaster, depending on the wind and sea conditions and the crew's skill. Often it's somewhere in between: a frantic, loud, barely controlled exhibition of bad tempers and clumsy seamanship. It need not be that way.

Leaving a Mooring

The easiest of the four maneuvers is leaving a mooring, which is a small buoy connected to an anchor or heavy weight (such as an old engine block) permanently set in the harbor bottom. The boat is secured to the anchor rode (line) with a mooring pendant (a short line) cleated on the bow.

The crew goes out to their moored boat in a rowboat, a launch, or a shore boat, climbs aboard, and stows their personal gear. They then pump out the bilge and make sure that all the equipment they'll need is aboard. If they plan to get under way under power, they carefully sniff around below to check that no gasoline fumes have settled in the bilge, and they run the engine blower for at least 4 minutes to vent all fumes from the engine compartment (these two steps are not necessary with diesel engines or with outboards in open boats). The engine is started and the instruments are studied for a few moments to be sure that oil and water pressures are not too low or too high.

The crew looks overboard on both sides and astern for loose lines, which might foul the propeller. One crew member walks or crawls onto the foredeck, uncleats the mooring line (usually by slipping a spliced eye off the cleat), and drops it over the bow, shouting "She's off!" to the helmsman, who slowly backs the boat clear and then puts the engine in slow forward gear to power out of the mooring area.

If there's a rowboat, she can either be left behind tied to the mooring buoy or towed along behind with the painter (bow line) kept short so the bow almost touches the yacht's stern. Later, when clear of the mooring area, buoys, and

other boats, the speed may be increased and the painter let out until the dinghy rides on the crest of the yacht's stern wave, which can be anywhere between 6 and 20 feet astern depending on the speed.

If you're leaving the mooring under sail, the crew goes through almost all the same steps. They will pay special attention to stowing (putting away) personal gear, food, and equipment, since heeling will cause anything that isn't secured to fly around the cabin and cockpit. Then they bend on the sails (as we described in chapter 1) and hoist them "after sail first" — starting with the mizzen if she's a yawl or ketch, then raising the mainsail, and finally the jib just as they are about to drop the mooring. The "after sail first" rule is important because while a hoisted mizzen or mainsail tends to aim a boat dead into the eye of the wind, the jib will pull her bow off on one tack or the other and the boat will sail around the mooring, perhaps careening into nearby moored boats.

Hoisting a sail is simple. Remove any sail covers and then untie sail ties or stops. Inspect all fittings to be sure that there are no twists and that shackles are securely shut. Make sure the battens are inserted. Tighten the outhaul until there are strain lines along the foot of the mainsail. Attach the halyards and look aloft to make sure they don't foul (wrap around) the spreaders or any other fittings. Uncleat the mainsail and the boom vang, so the boom can rise, but cleat the trav-

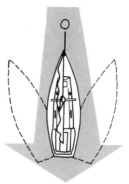

To avoid sailing around the mooring hoist the sails only when the bow is directly into the wind.

eler control lines so the sliding part, called the car, won't bang back and forth. Now pull the halyard with a strong, steady motion while looking aloft to check for tangles. If the halyard is wire with a rope tail (end), wrap the wire around the winch. The boat should be hanging off the mooring head-to-wind (with her bow pointed into the wind), so the sail will go up easily without filling on either side. Sometimes, however, the tidal or river current may not run parallel to the wind direction and the boat may lie with her bow into the current and the wind on one side or another. If this happens, the sail will fill on one side, making hoisting difficult and (more important) creating a forward force exactly when you don't want to be making way. If this occurs, stop hoisting and steer her into the wind. When the sail luffs completely, quickly pull it all the way up. Its resistance should now keep the boat head-to-wind. Cleat the halyard and coil it carefully (as described in chapter 5) so there are no loose lines lying about. (Always neaten up immediately after doing a job; you may not have time later.) If the sail has a boom that is held up by a topping lift off the mast or the backstay, uncleat or unfasten it after hoisting the sail so you can trim the sail tight once you get under way.

Now is the time to pull on sweaters or foul-weather gear if there is any chance that you'll need them. You can always take them off later. Now if you're ready to cast off, hoist the jib looking aloft, being careful that the sheets are loose so it doesn't fill. The skipper should take the helm and look around to plan his best route out of the mooring area. If the clearest path is to port, he says, "We'll go off on starboard tack. Cast off to starboard." The crew must acknowledge this order so there is no misunderstanding. One crew member goes onto the foredeck and uncleats the mooring pendant. On a big boat or in a fresh wind it may be pulling hard, so he might have to

By hoisting the mainsail first, you'll keep the bow into the wind until you're ready to get under way. However, don't leave sails luffing for long since flapping damages the sail cloth. Watch out for the swinging boom.

Getting Going

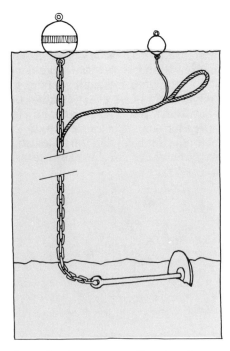

A mooring is a permanently set anchor whose rode (line) is buoyed. The pendant, which is cleated on deck, has its own small buoy.

heave on it to gain the few inches needed to pull it off. When the pendant is uncleated, the crew member snubs it (takes a half-turn) around the bow cleat to decrease the strain on his arms.

The next step can be tricky. The mooring pendant cannot be let go until the boat is on a tack with some steerageway on. If the desired course is to port, she must be got onto starboard tack; if to starboard, onto port tack. In fresh winds the boat may be sailing around the mooring anyway, so the crew waits to cast off the mooring when the boat is on the desired tack. But in light to moderate winds she'll need some help. First, back the jib while easing the main sheet all the way out. To back the jib, trim it to the side that will be to windward either by pulling the sheet on that side or by grabbing the clew or (if it's an overlapping genoa jib) the foot about halfway back and pulling it to the new windward side. For example, if you want to head off to port on starboard tack, back the jib to starboard. The backed jib will pull the bow off in the opposite direction, and, because it is luffing, the mainsail will not work against the jib. As the bow swings off, the crew member on the foredeck frees the mooring pendant from the cleat and the chock (a metal slot on the bow), and pulls it aft along the windward side. Except with large boats, this should shoot her forward to provide a bit of steerageway.

As soon as the bow has fallen off about 40°, trim the jib sheet on the new leeward side and trim the main sheet. With her sails full, the boat will accelerate and can be steered out of the mooring area on a close-hauled course or on a reach. Highly maneuverable boats may be turned completely around to a run by keeping the jib backed after dropping the mooring. In all cases, however, don't try to make any big course alterations until you have steerageway.

Whenever possible, let the mooring go on the windward side so that the bow doesn't swing down onto it.

Leaving a mooring under sail alone is an exercise in seamanship that teaches plenty about boat handling and gives great satisfaction. But if the mooring area is crowded with boats or you feel uncomfortable, use the engine. Power forward a couple of feet to take the strain off the mooring pendant so it can be taken off the cleat. Carefully drop the buoy and pendant overboard. Once the person on the foredeck signals that the pendant is clear, back down to keep the propeller away from the pendant.

The skipper should closely supervise all these steps and be ready to stop the process if something goes wrong. For example if the route out of the mooring area is blocked by other boats, tie up and wait until the way is clear.

Launching from a Trailer

Getting a dinghy or other small boat into the water from a trailer is not difficult in normal, moderate conditions. If you're using a hoist, just make sure that the boat's weight is within its capacity. Push the trailer directly under the hook and have competent

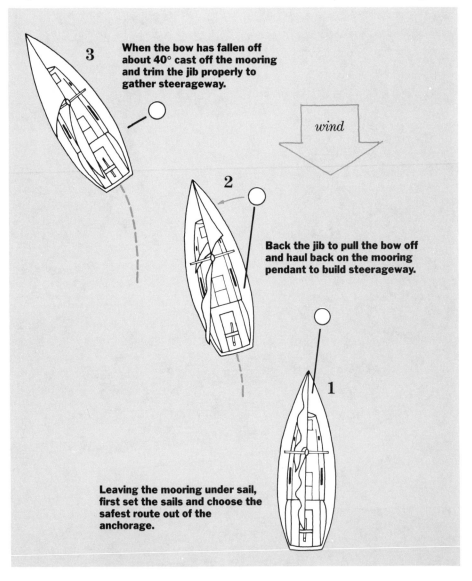

3 When the bow has fallen off about 40° cast off the mooring and trim the jib properly to gather steerageway.

wind

2 Back the jib to pull the bow off and haul back on the mooring pendant to build steerageway.

1 Leaving the mooring under sail, first set the sails and choose the safest route out of the anchorage.

people handling the lift-drop controls and the guy ropes. Check carefully for overheard electrical wires, which can be lethal if the mast touches them.

If you're launching on a ramp, rig the boat, bend on the sails, and if you have one, install the outboard engine. Take off the tie-downs but leave the bow restraint secured. Place aboard any equipment that you'll need after the launch. Then slowly back down the ramp with one crew member guiding the driver with hand signals. Many ramps are built at angles steep enough so that a shallow boat like a dinghy floats off before the car tires touch the water. If you usually are not so lucky, equip your trailer with a tongue extender. This is a metal rod that, when extended, pushes the trailer several feet farther away from the car so that a deep boat can be launched in shallow water without immersing the car's wheels or axle. This is particularly important around salt water, which can corrode like a harsh acid, but even lake and river water have their impurities.

Once the boat becomes buoyant, unhook the bow restraint and push her off. A single person should be able to maneuver a small boat in all but the roughest weather while standing in the water. When the boat is clear of the trailer, either jump aboard and paddle out or pull the bow up on the beach so you can drive the car back up the ramp.

Sailboats launched from a trailer are usually paddled to a nearby pier before sails are hoisted. Small boats, however, may be sailed off a beach in light winds, but be careful not to drop the rudder or centerboard until the water is deep enough. An onshore wind (blowing from the water to the land) is the worst for trailer launching. The oldtimers' fear of a lee shore is as justified as it was in clipper-ship days, when gales blew huge square-riggers right up onto beaches. Most launching ramps are well protected from the wind and sea, but even they usually have a vulnerable point.

Leaving a Dock

Of course, once you've paddled out to the pier, you have another problem. A pier is a narrow platform sticking out from the land on posts. Connected to a pier by ramps are floats, which rise and fall with the water level. It is to the floats off the piers that a boat usually ties up. The area of water that the boat occupies is called a dock, so the tying-up maneuver is called docking. Given a choice, you want to dock with the

boat's bow dead into the wind so that getting under way is as simple as leaving a mooring. When this is not feasible, the best you can do is avoid docking on the windward side of the pier or float, with the wind banging your boat against the float. Small boats can be walked from one side of a float to another in any except the strongest winds. Just grab their rails or shrouds (side stays) and pull them around. But any boat larger than about 25 feet is

When rigging or launching a boat on shore, be very careful to stay away from overhead power lines. If the mast hits or gets near a line, electrical shock can kill or injure sailors working below. A tongue extender on the trailer allows launching without the car's rear axle getting wet.

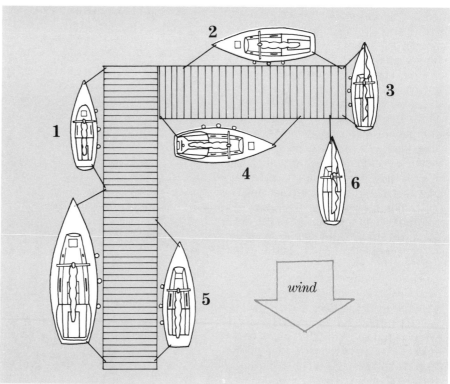

The best way to dock is to lie with the bow into the wind (1, 3, and 5) or on the leeward side of the float (4). On the windward side (2) the boat will be blown onto the float. You can also hang off the float on a bow line (6).

Getting Going

Docking Lines

Almost all boats eventually spend some time docked at a float or pier. Boats smaller than 20 feet can be secured temporarily with only a bow line and a stern line running forward and aft at 45° angles at moderate tension. The spread of the line will restrain the boat from sliding back and forth against the dock. But more docking lines are needed if you want to lie at a float in a larger boat or if you plan to stay for a while in a small boat.

Docking lines should be cut from nylon rope, which provides both strength and stretch, and they should be sturdy — no smaller than ⅜-inch diameter for 20-footers, and up to ⅞-inch diameter for 50-footers and above. Docking lines should be at least 20 feet long. There are no fittings on a proper docking line, for it's secured to cleats and eyes with wraps and knots (see chapter 5). Docking lines can be used in one of two ways: by dead-ending (securing one end) on the float, cleating on board, and leaving the excess on board for easy adjustment by

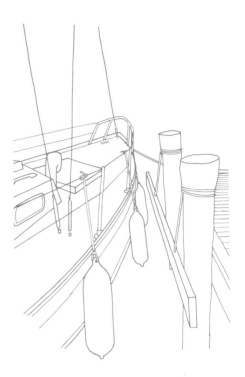

Rubber fenders protect the topsides. A fender board (above) provides a flat bearing surface if the float's side has supporting pilings.

too heavy to be manhandled like this, and you may have to power or sail off from an unfavorable position.

Whenever a boat is lying at (tied to) a float or pier, her topsides should be protected with fenders. These are rubber bumpers hung by lines between the boat's sides and the float. Some floats may have canvas-covered pads but often these pads are abrasive so it's better to use the boat's own fenders.

The ease with which a boat leaves a dock depends on the conditions and, mostly, on how the boat is lying at the float or pier.

If she's lying along the float's windward side with the wind coming over the side, you might be able to sail directly off, but leeway, heeling, and waves may force the boat against the float and create so much friction that she cannot develop steerageway. In this situation, small boats should be walked to the edge of the float and shoved off before the sails are hoisted. Larger boats may be taken off under power, or an anchor may be set upwind and the boat pulled up to the anchor so she hangs head-to-wind. Then sails may be safely hoisted, the anchor retrieved, and the boat sailed away.

If she's lying along the leeward side of the float, you can sail away by casting off all dock lines except the bow line and allowing the boat to hang head-to-wind, then hoisting sails, casting off the bow line, and sailing away, much as you would leave a mooring.

If she's lying with the wind over her stern, you could either leave the dock on a run under jib alone or turn the boat around until she's head-to-wind and then hoist sails.

These techniques for leaving a pier will work if the crew knows what they are doing, if the dock isn't crowded, and if the wind is light or moderate. In rough conditions, do the best you can to get as far away from the pier as soon as possible, even if this means leaving the dock under power or under tow. Otherwise your boat may be badly holed by the float while you're hoisting sails.

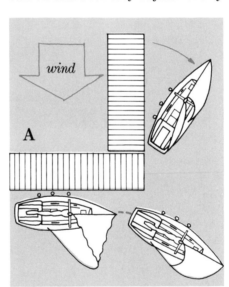

When sailing out of a dock the most important priority is to get away from the float as soon as possible. (A) Use the jib to pull the bow away. (B) Pull the boat along the windward side until her bow is clear, then set the jib. (C) You may have to set an anchor and pull her away from the windward side.

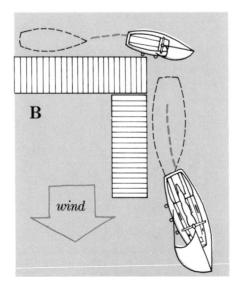

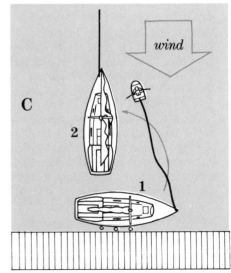

the crew; or by doubling (turning back) around a cleat or other fitting on the float and securing both ends on board. The advantage of doubling is that the line may be cast off without going on the float, yet it may tangle around itself or the cleat as one end is pulled around.

To tie a boat up properly you need the bow and stern lines plus two spring lines, which are intermediate lines that literally spring the boat against fore and aft surges. They are laid out in an X arrangement. The *forward spring line* runs *forward* from a point about one-fourth of the boat's length forward of the stern, where it is securely cleated or tied to a sturdy fitting, such as a winch. From that point the forward spring runs to a cleat or other attachment point on the float or pier about one-fourth of the boat's length aft of the bow. The *after spring line* runs *aft* from a point on deck opposite where the forward spring is cleated on the float, to another cleat on the float opposite where the forward spring is cleated on deck.

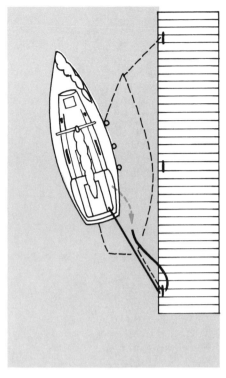

By doubling a docking line you can cast it off from the boat and pull it back around the cleat on the float.

The forward spring runs forward, but keeps the boat from surging aft. The after spring runs aft, but keeps the boat from surging forward. When they are equally tensioned, the center-line of the boat will be parallel to the float. If the after spring is tighter, the bow will be held in closer than the stern; if the forward spring is tighter, the stern will pull into the float. When properly rigged, spring lines take almost all the boat's load at the float and the bow and stern lines just restrain the ends from swinging out. In rough weather, additional bow and stern springs should be rigged to reduce the surge back and forth along the float. These run forward from the after spring's deck attachment point, and aft from the forward spring's deck attachment point.

An additional docking line that is helpful temporarily is the breast line, which passes from the boat to an attachment point on the float directly alongside. A breast line gives no fore-and-aft support but only provides point-to-point attachment.

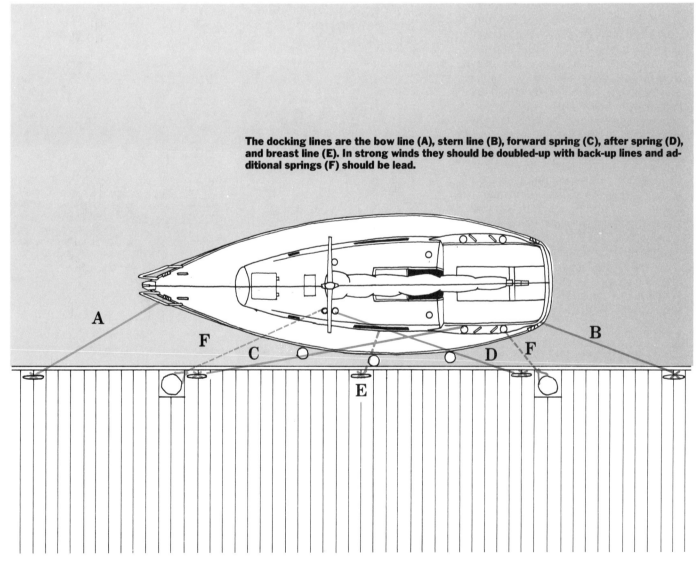

The docking lines are the bow line (A), stern line (B), forward spring (C), after spring (D), and breast line (E). In strong winds they should be doubled-up with back-up lines and additional springs (F) should be lead.

Getting Going

Springs can be a great help when leaving a float. Because sailing auxiliaries both accelerate slowly and steer poorly at low speeds, aiming the bow or stern out from the float often cannot be accomplished solely under power. Instead of turning out from the float, the boat typically scrapes along, meanwhile banging into other docked boats, until she has gained steerageway. Of course, a crew member can jump ashore and shove the bow or stern out, but he may need seven-league boots to get back aboard. Instead, lines may be used to lever the bow or stern away from the float.

The basic principle is that as a boat pulls against line secured to one end of her hull, the other end swings out. Therefore powering forward with the after spring attached will force the bow into the float and the stern away from it. The farther forward the spring is attached, the closer the bow will approach the float. With only the forward spring attached —that's the one running from the after part of the boat forward to the float —if the boat goes into reverse, the stern will swing in and the bow will swing out. Using the spring line this way in reverse gear is a major advantage, since most boats steer very poorly when going backward.

Once the bow or stern is aimed away from the float, the spring line is cast off, the gears are changed, and the boat can be powered out from the float with the rudder centered.

Procedures

The order of proceeding is:

A. **To Back Out:**

1. Cast off the stern line (being sure it's clear of the propeller).

2. Cast off the bow line.

3. Double the after spring (pass it around the float cleat and back to the deck cleat; cleat it there).

4. Check that no lines are dragging.

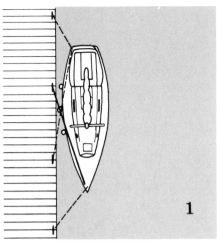

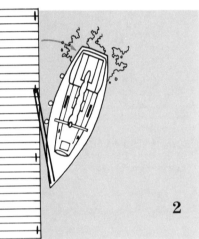

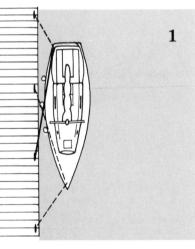

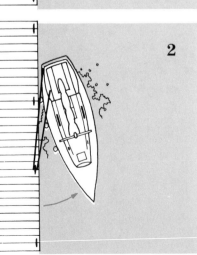

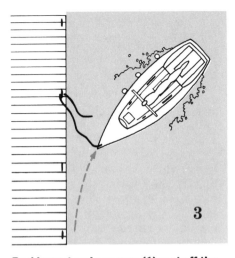

Backing out under power, (1) cast off the stern and bow lines; (2) double the after spring, cast off the forward spring, and power forward slowly; (3) when the stern has swung out back away from the float and recover the after spring.

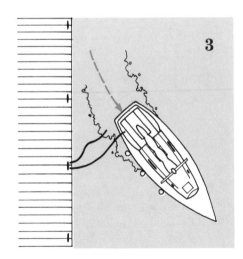

Powering away forward, (1) cast off the stern and bow lines; (2) double the forward spring, cast off the after spring, and back down; (3) when the bow has swung out, shift to forward gear and recover the forward spring.

5. Cast off the forward spring.

6. Go into forward gear, slowly with helm centered.

7. When the bow has swung into the float and the stern has swung out, shift into reverse gear and cast off the after spring by uncleating one end and pulling on the other end (or by lifting the bight of the spring off the float cleat).

8. With the helm centered, back straight away until completely clear of the float.

B. To Leave a Dock Forward:

1. Cast off the stern line.

2. Cast off the bow line.

3. Double the forward spring.

4. Check for dragging lines.

5. Cast off the after spring.

6. Go into slow reverse with the helm centered.

7. When the stern has swung into the float and the bow has swung out, shift into forward gear and cast off the forward spring.

8. Head out with the helm centered.

Leaving a Slip

Leaving a marina slip is a bit like departing a float, except that a slip has three sides. Since boats usually enter slips bow-first, they must back out. It's often helpful for a crew member or two to stand on the float alongside the boat and push her out; most sailboats reverse gears need all the help they can get. Sailboats up to 20 feet L.O.A. may be pushed out of a slip, and when they are in the waterway the crew may hoist a sail. If the wind is strong or from a difficult direction, this tricky maneuver demands considerable strength and finesse. A good crew commanded by a helmsman with a good feel for his boat can do it — usually to the applause of his neighbors.

Backing out of a slip, either leave the stern line attached until you're ready to head out into the harbor (A) or use the after spring to swing her stern out (B). Leaving forward, spring out the bow (C and D). As when leaving a dock, try to get away from the float as soon as possible.

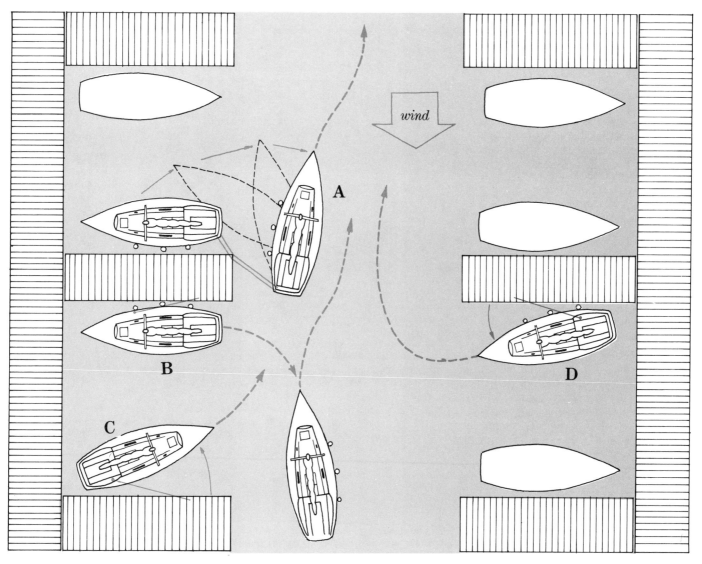

Coming Back In

All right, you're under way. Early on in this chapter we described the basic techniques of using the true and apparent wind to make your boat sail in the direction you want to go — sail trimming, steering on a close-hauled course, changing tacks — and in the next chapter we'll show how to optimize those skills to make your boat sail fast and in balance too. Right now, though, let's assume that you're returning to the mooring, shore, dock, or slip. In most cases it's no more difficult than leaving.

Picking Up a Mooring

Picking up a mooring under power is relatively simple. From dead downwind of the buoy, head slowly toward the mooring. The wind's resistance will help you slow down when you reach it. A crew member goes forward, with a boat hook (a rod with a hook on the end) if the boat is high sided, and with hand signals tells the helmsman where the buoy is as the boat approaches it. He should point at the buoy, and when the bow is just over it, hold his hand up in the air to indicate "stop." The helmsman puts the engine into neutral or slow reverse gear to hold the bow right over the mooring as the crew reaches down to retrieve the buoy. When he has the buoy and pendant on deck, the engine should be in neutral. He cleats the line and then passes it through the bow chock. When the line is secure, he shouts, "Made!" (meaning "secure"), and the helmsman may turn off the engine. The worst thing that can happen during this maneuver is for the boat to run over the buoy and tangle it or the mooring line in her propeller. That's why the helmsman must know the buoy's exact location as he approaches it, and why the boat should be moving as slowly as possible while retaining steerageway.

Picking up a mooring under sail is more complicated. It should be done under mainsail alone, unless the jib is small. Large overlapping genoa jibs can take charge of a boat extremely quickly, and may also obstruct the helmsman's vision as he sails through a crowded mooring area. A genoa should be doused and securely tied down or bagged before reaching the mooring area.

The boat should approach the buoy from dead (directly) downwind, her sails luffing. This is called "shooting into the wind," and the distance that a boat shoots, or "carries her way," depends on her displacement (heavier boats take longer to slow down than light boats) and the wind and sea conditions. A boat will shoot longer in flat water and a calm than in 2-foot waves and a fresh wind. There is no formula here; only experience will tell you how far your boat will shoot. If you think you're going too fast, to slow down swing the helm back and forth several times. The resistance of the rudder will brake her momentum. Be sure, though, that the main sheet is completely free so the sail doesn't fill as you snake toward the buoy. You may also stop the boat right at the buoy by backing the mainsail: push the main boom out until the wind catches on the wrong side; the boat will stop and begin to back down. This method of stopping is not safe in fresh winds or with small, weak crews, since main booms can be extremely dangerous weapons.

The final approach should be coordinated between the helmsman and the foredeck crew. It is very important that the boat be stopped, or at worst be moving slowly, and headed dead into the wind when the buoy is brought on deck and the pendant is cleated. Otherwise she'll charge off on one tack or the other and perhaps ram other boats. Don't try to pick up the buoy if she's moving faster than 1 knot. If the foredeck crew is having a lot of trouble, tell him to drop the mooring; then circle around and try again.

As soon as the line is cleated and the crew has shouted "Made!" quickly lower the sails, forward sail first. Then neaten up by furling or bagging the sails, replacing sail covers, coiling sheets, and double-checking the mooring. Using shock cord led from the shrouds, tie the halyards as far away

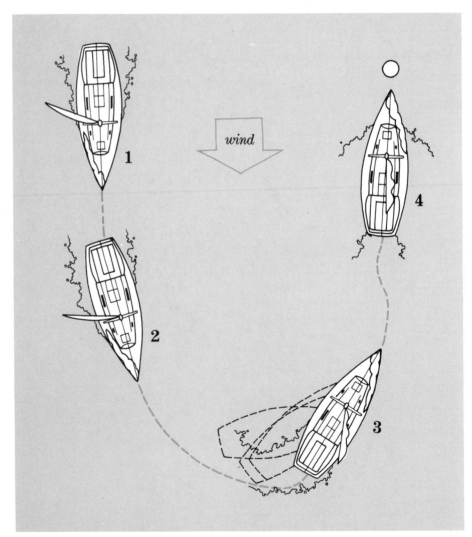

Picking up a mooring, shoot into the wind's eye from downwind of the buoy. If you're going too fast, slow down by swinging the helm back and forth or backing sails.

from the mast as possible so they don't slap and annoy neighbors, either ashore or in nearby boats. Secure the tiller or wheel so the rudder is centered under the hull, turn off any electrical switches, fuel valves, and sea cocks (valves fitted in pipes leading overboard) and lock the hatches. Then you can go ashore.

Returning to a Launching Ramp

The major mistakes that people make when sailing back to the launching ramp are forgetting to retract the centerboard and rudder (or outboard engine) when the water gets shallow and trying to stop the boat by sailing onto the beach. Damage to the appendages and hull can be avoided by dousing the sails relatively far offshore (or letting them luff in light winds), pulling up the appendages, and walking ashore pulling the boat. While one crew member holds her in a couple of feet of water, another can be getting the car and trailer. Of course, there's no great risk in nudging the bow onto a sandy beach, but only after you've inspected it for rocks. When the trailer has been backed down into the water, pull the boat on (making sure she's centered), secure the bow, and drive up the ramp. Be sure to hose both the trailer and boat off if they've been exposed to salt water.

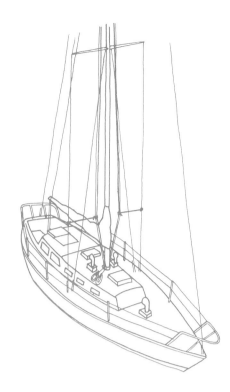

Tie off the halyards with gilguys to keep them from clanking against the mast.

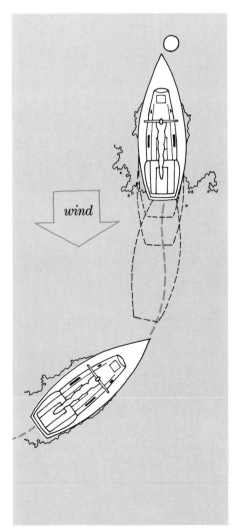

Pick up a mooring under power by heading upwind slowly and stopping with the bow right over the buoy.

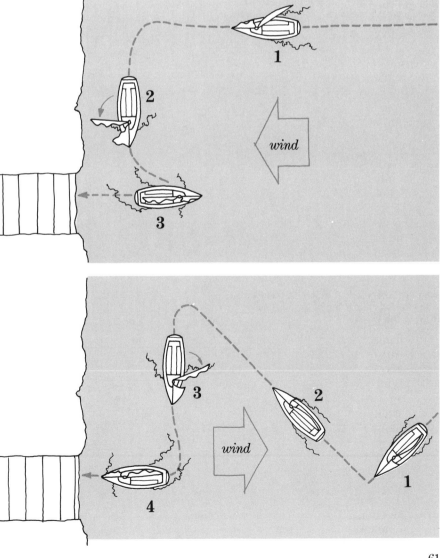

Returning to a launching ramp, raise the centerboard and stop the boat by heading into the wind as close to shore as possible. While somebody in the water steadies her, lower the sails before pulling or paddling her to the ramp.

Coming Back In

Docking

Docking is the departure from a float or pier played in reverse. Approach the docking area slowly, but with steerageway, at as shallow an angle as possible to the float. If you're coming in under power, don't count on reverse gear (which is notoriously inefficient in most sailing auxiliaries) to stop you. Neither should you anticipate that your crew or any bystanders on the float will be able to stop the boat by pulling on the shrouds and deck fittings. The best way to stop is to approach slowly and have docking lines ready to throw over cleats on the float.

The bow, stern, and spring lines should be ready to use on deck, and the after spring line — the line that will stop the boat better than any of the other three — should already be cleated with several feet ready to hand to someone on the float. The fenders should be dropped over the side, with the largest ones near the boat's widest point. Tie the fender lines to the rail or the lifelines with clove hitches (see chapter 5) and lower them until they're at the float's level.

As the boat snuggles up against the float, either pass or carry the after spring line to a cleat and snub it with a turn. As the boat pulls against the line, her bow will spring in, so rig the stern line to restrain the stern from swinging out. Next come the bow line and the forward spring. The stern and bow lines should run aft and forward at about 45° angles. Each docking line should have a fair lead from its cleat on deck to the float — meaning that it should not chafe (rub abrasively) against a sharp object. If you run out of deck cleats, you can always lead the

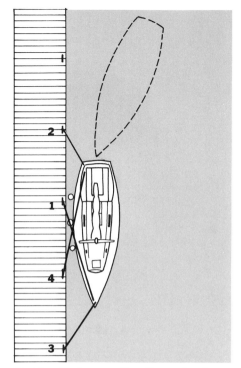

Docking, first secure the after spring line to stop her (1), then the stern line to restrain the stern (2), then the bow line (3) and forward spring (4).

Approaching in an offshore wind, come in head to wind to slow her, then turn sharply.

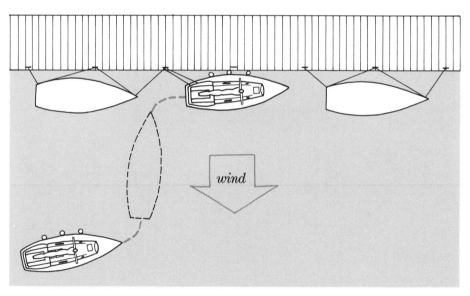

In an onshore wind, stop just to windward of the dock to allow the boat to be blown down to the float.

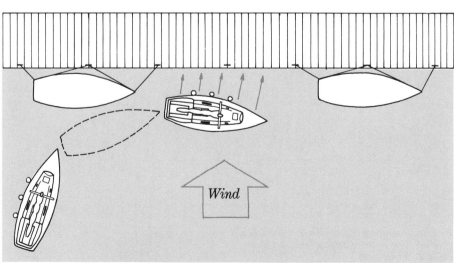

spring lines to winches. Adjust the springs until she lies with the centerline about parallel to the edge of the float, although on some boats one end may have to be pulled closer than the other to make it easier to step ashore. Then take tension on the bow and stern lines to keep the ends from swinging in and out.

Sailing into a dock should not be tried with boats larger than about 30 feet unless you're *absolutely* confident of your ability to stop her where you want. This may be impossible if the approach is a run or a reach. Even under power you can use the wind to help your docking maneuver. A crosswind onto the float will push you into the dock and one away from the float will push you away from it. At slow speeds, a high-sided boat will be blown about considerably by crosswinds, and a sailboat's rigging always makes her vulnerable to any wind. Don't underestimate the momentum of a moving boat. Don't put hands or feet between the boat and the float. When fendingoff (pushing off), put a fender between the hull and the float.

Entering a Slip

Returning to a marina slip is easier than leaving it because the return usually is bow-first. Except in a dinghy or other small boat, enter under power or by carrying your way (sustaining your momentum) after dousing (lowering) the sails. Use the after spring line to stop her just as you would when docking.

Returning to a slip, use minimum steerageway and, if necessary, tie up to the end of the float before spinning around into the slip (A and D). Use appropriate docking lines to stop her and keep ends from swinging out. As when docking all boats larger than centerboarders and small keel boats, resist the temptation to stop her and fend off floats and other boats with your legs and arms. Let the docking lines do the work.

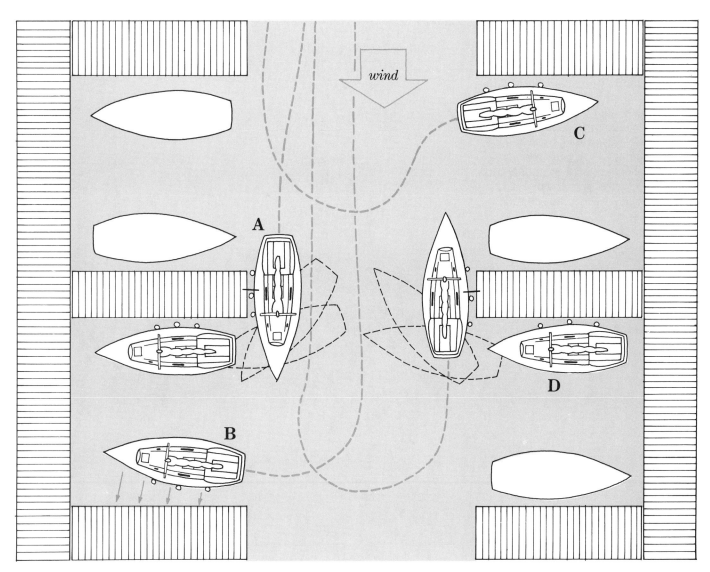

Maneuvering Under Power

If your boat has an engine, you should be aware of the special handling characteristics that apply under power.

The Propeller

A propeller is sometimes called a "screw" because it seems literally to screw itself through the water, pulling the boat along with it. Yet its main force is forward thrust as its blades grab the water and redirect it aft. Depending on the weight of the boat and the horsepower of the engine, propellers vary in blade number, blade diameter, and pitch or blade angle. Pitch is measured in inches — the distance the propeller would travel forward during a single revolution. Outboards and other light, fast boats with engines that turn at high revolutions per minute tend to have small-diameter two- or three-bladed propellers with high pitch. On the other hand, low R.P.M., heavy, slow boats like the typical sailing auxiliary usually have large-diameter, low-pitch propellers with two or three blades. In order to reduce resistance when the boat is under sail, many auxiliaries are equipped with special propellers that automatically

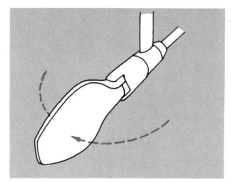

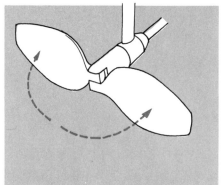

A propeller that folds when not in use reduces water resistance. Some propellers automatically feather for the same reason.

fold up, or feather, when the engine is off.

Propellers work most efficiently when entirely submerged. Air bubbles pulled down from the surface may cause water to detach from the blades. Called cavitation, this will decrease the propeller's thrust. Make sure that the stern is sitting low enough so the propeller is several inches under water.

Propeller Thrust

A clockwise-turning right-handed propeller slightly pushes (or "walks") the stern to starboard; a counterclockwise-turning left-handed prop pushes it to port. In reverse gear, this side force is to the opposite side and is usually more noticeable than in forward gear, which is why an auxiliary is hard to steer backward. You can always use this force to help pull the boat into the pier when docking. For example, if your boat has a right-handed propeller, give a quick burst with the throttle in reverse as you slide into the dock to push the stern to port.

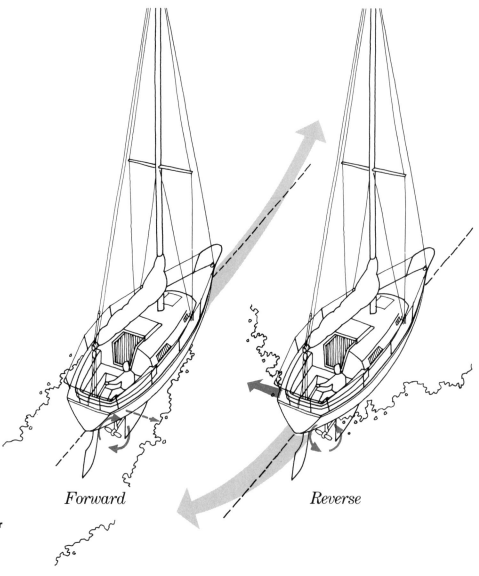

Forward

Reverse

A right-handed, clockwise-turning propeller walks the stern slightly to starboard in forward gear but walks it to port more noticeably in reverse.

Hints for Better Boat Handling

Once under way, you'll be facing plenty of challenges — trimming sails, finding your position, avoiding other boats, and coping with an ever-changing environment. All these problems are important and will be the subject of several chapters later in this book. But while you're dealing with them, keep in mind these five basic guidelines for better boat handling:

1. **Keep the boat moving.** Steerageway is an absolute necessity for avoiding obstructions or just changing course. Know your boat well enough so you're certain when she has or doesn't have steerageway. When planning a maneuver, make sure you allow enough time and room for developing steerageway and for using it once you have it.

2. **Be especially careful near land.** Almost any boat can survive a storm in open water, but few boats can survive running into land. If you're unsure of your boat-handling capabilities or if the weather is dangerous, stay as far as possible from floats, piers, shallow water, and the land itself.

3. **Take nothing for granted.** Life aboard a boat is always changing, and you must constantly anticipate new wind and sea conditions, equipment breakdowns, crew errors, and the approach of other boats. Develop a standard operating procedure (S.O.P.) for handling sails, for piloting, and for reporting changed conditions. As skipper you don't have to be a martinet, but you should be alert to everything that's going on near or on your boat, and also feel confident that your crew is doing their best to avoid trouble. While every sailor should concentrate on the job he is performing — whether it's steering or rigging docking lines or hoisting a sail — he should be sensitive to what's going on elsewhere on deck.

4. **One hand for yourself, one for the ship.** This old-time sailor's adage means that the seaman should always watch out for his own safety while he does his job. If unsure of your footing, walk on deck with a hand on the lifelines. When pulling a line that's under load, snub it on a cleat with a single turn or wrap it clockwise around a winch. In rough weather, wear a safety harness to avoid falling overboard, or a life jacket so you won't drown if you do. Remember that your shipmates depend on you not only to perform certain tasks but also to be healthy and ready to pull your own weight.

5. **Stay with the boat.** On larger boats, this means not disappearing ashore after docking until she's secure. On dinghies, it means hanging on if you capsize or swamp. While she probably won't sink, you almost certainly will if you try to swim for it — especially in cold water, where body heat and strength are quickly lost. Under way, the sailor's main job is to help the boat sail through the water. When *you* are in the water, let your boat help you.

6. **Stay alert.** Many accidents occur when sailors stop paying attention because they are distracted, tired, or intoxicated. According to federal and state laws, recreational sailors can be arrested, fined, and/or imprisoned for being caught with an alcohol content in the blood of .10 percent, or for behaving in an intoxicated manner. In addition, there are large penalties for negligent boating. For more information on boating laws, see appendix II.

Relaxed but alert and secure, this young crew obviously is in command of its boat and the situation.

Safety Equipment

Every time you head out in a boat, you must assume that you are on your own. Even if you should get into serious trouble, you can't count on the U.S. Coast Guard or some other agency or individual to come to your rescue. Therefore, you have a responsibility to yourself and your crew to carry clothing and equipment that will promote safety on board. We will outline safety equipment here and go into greater detail in other chapters.

Clothing and Personal Gear

In order to prevent slipping and stubbed toes, sailors on boats big enough to walk on should wear boating shoes with non-skid soles. However, there are some brands of general-purpose sneakers that can grip wet decks; if they have white soles they won't scuff the deck.

A warm body functions better than a chilled one, so except in hot, dry weather carry along a sweatshirt, sweater, or pullover. The best materials are wool and synthetic bunting or pile, which retain body heat exceptionally well when wet. Take along a hat to keep heat from escaping through your head.

Since water conducts heat 25 times faster than air, a basic requirement for staying warm is to stay dry. A simple water + resistant warm-up jacket keeps light spray off, but for heavy rain and spray you'll need foul-weather gear, which is a fairly heavy waterproof jacket and trousers. Sometimes called a "slicker," it should be yellow, orange, or red so a sailor who has fallen overboard will be quickly spotted in the water. A hat or hood will keep the water off your head and retain heat. Waterproof sea boots with nonskid soles will keep your feet and lower legs dry.

Other valuable personal gear includes a sharp pocket or sheath knife, sunglasses, suntan lotion with a sun protection factor (S.P.F.) of 15 or greater, and, if you are subject to motion sickness, antiseasickness medication in patch or pill form (whichever works best for you with the least side effects). For more on health and clothing, see chapter 6.

Required Equipment

By law, certain safety equipment must be on board. If the Coast Guard finds that any of this gear is missing from a boat, her owner is subject to a fine. Here is a general overview of this equipment. For detailed discussions, see chapter 7 (life jackets), chapter 8 (navigation lights), and chapter 16 (fire extinguishers and distress signals). Appendix I is a summary of required equipment.

Life Jackets (PFDs)

The generic term "life jacket" includes buoyant throwable devices and wearable vests that support people in the water. Until 1988, the Coast Guard used the term "Personal Flotation Device (PFD)" to refer to them, and categorized them in approved types from Type I to Type IV. (There was also a Type V for experimental and specialized PFDs.) The official terminology has been changed to more descriptive language, but because the old "type" terms will linger on for a while, we'll use both the old and new terminology.

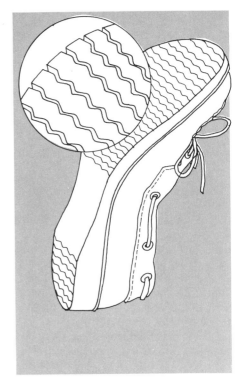

(Above) A non-skid shoe or boot sole has slits that spread to allow the rubber to grip the deck with a squeegee effect.

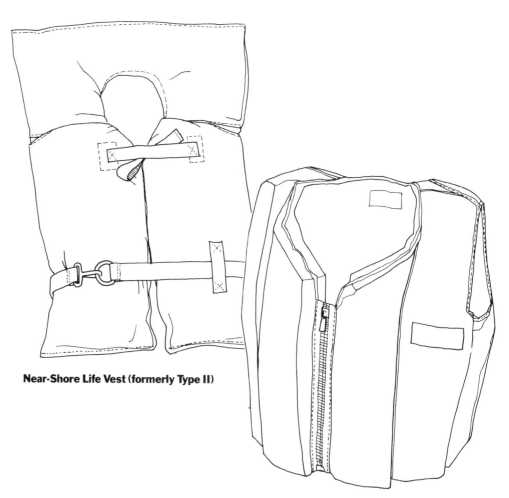

Near-Shore Life Vest (formerly Type II)

The Flotation Aid (formerly Type III PFD) is usually used by sailors because it's comfortable and allows quick movements. However, it won't keep an unconscious person's face clear of the water.

The general rule is that there must be one U.S. Coast Guard-approved life jacket (PFD) for each person on every boat (except kayaks, sailboards, and other special craft). There are different specific rules for boats smaller than 16 feet and larger than 16 feet. Boats 16 feet long or shorter must have one approved wearable *or* throwable device for each person. Boats longer than 16 feet must have one approved wearable device for each person plus one throwable device.

Approved wearable life jackets (PFDs) come in three categories. The most buoyant is the Off-Shore Life Jacket (formerly Type I PFD), which has at least 20 pounds of buoyancy, generally enough to float an unconscious person high enough so the face is clear of the water. However, since different body types behave differently in the water, some people may not float face-up. Less buoyant is the Near-Shore Life Vest (formerly Type II), with at least 15.5 pounds of buoyancy, which should be enough to float a face clear of the water (dependent on body type).

The Flotation Aid (formerly Type III), which is less bulky than the other two, has the same amount of buoyancy as the Near-Shore Life Vest, but since the buoyancy is distributed around the body instead of near the neck this device does not automatically keep the face clear of the water.

Approved throwable devices (formerly Type IV) have at least 16.5 pounds of buoyancy and are designed to be leaned on but not worn. Seat cushions and life rings fall into this category.

Coast Guard approval is shown on a special label on the life jacket. If there is no such label, the device is not approved and may not be used to meet the regulations.

Fire Extinguishers

Boats with engines must carry one or more fire extinguishers, depending on boat length. These extinguishers must be Coast Guard approved and must also be charged. Type B extinguishers, intended to extinguish fires in flammable liquids, are specified for marine use.

Flame Arrestors and Vents

Inboard gasoline engines must have flame arrestors, which control flames caused by backfires and exhaust blowers. All gas-powered boats (except open boats) must have at least two ventilation ducts for every engine and fuel tank compartment. These regulations were written in response to a number of fatal explosions of gasoline-powered boats after fumes settled in the bilge and were ignited.

Distress Signals

Visual distress signals (flares) and sound distress signals (whistles) are required on most boats.

Navigation Lights

To indicate her type and course when sailing at night, each boat must carry navigation lights of a particular kind. These are described in chapter 8, "The Rules of the Road."

Recommended Equipment

The above covers required equipment. The following is highly recommended:

1. An accurate compass that is or can be secured in front of the helmsman.

2. One large-capacity portable bilge pump, or a permanently mounted manual bilge pump for boats larger than 20 feet plus a large bucket.

3. A nautical chart covering your normal boating area.

4. For salt-water areas, a tide table.

5. An oar or paddle.

6. A large flashlight with extra batteries, stored in a waterproof container.

7. A simple tool kit, including a pair of pliers, a screwdriver (Phillips-head or slotted-head to match the screws on board), a crescent wrench, a hammer, a sharp knife, and a roll of waterproof tape.

8. A basic first-aid kit, including a packet of over-the-counter seasickness pills.

9. For auxiliaries, spare sparkplugs (and a tool for installing them) plus a spare propeller.

10. Three fenders of a size suitable for the boat.

11. At least one suitable anchor and at least 100 feet of ⅜-inch (or larger) nylon anchor rode.

12. Four 20-foot (or longer) lengths of ⅜-inch (or larger) nylon line for docking, towing, and emergencies.

13. At least one sharp knife.

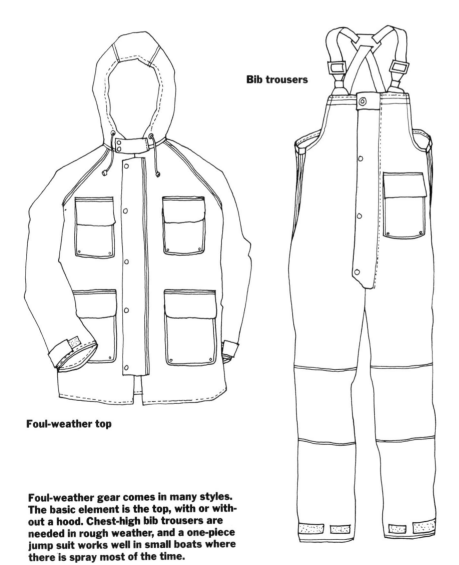

Bib trousers

Foul-weather top

Foul-weather gear comes in many styles. The basic element is the top, with or without a hood. Chest-high bib trousers are needed in rough weather, and a one-piece jump suit works well in small boats where there is spray most of the time.

Chapter 3
Sail Trim

A sailboat's engine is her sails and her throttle is her running rigging. In chapter 2 we provided an overview of how they work in order to get you and your boat under way. Now we'll look more closely at the skills of trimming sails properly. Getting the most out of your rig requires some knowledge and considerable attention, and at first the job may seem confusing to the point of distraction. But when you finally learn how to use the sheets and other sail controls, and how to meld them to the feel of the helm, you'll have the satisfaction of knowing that you have accomplished a small miracle by harnessing the forces of wind, hull, and sail.

Sail-trimming must satisfy two goals:

1. To keep the boat sailing fast.
2. To keep the boat sailing in balance.

If the wind, waves, and point of sail never changed, meeting these aims would be simple. All you would do is cut sails out of metal to a scientifically predetermined shape, stick them onto the hull, and get going. These big air-foils would push the boat forward through the unchanging air and water with a predictable force. But, of course, the wind and waves are never steady, and a boat rarely stays on one point of sail for more than a few hours. As the conditions change, so does the optimum sail shape (and size too). A good crew is constantly aware of lulls and puffs, wind shifts, and changed headings — and they're always trying to keep the sails properly shaped to match the new conditions.

Depending on the conditions, a crew tries either to make the sails more powerful or to make them less powerful. Powering — making sails more powerful — happens in light to moderate winds of 2 to about 15 knots (apparent), although the upper range may be about 12 knots in dinghies and centerboarders with large sails. Because most boats heel less than about

15° in these lightish winds, the sails may be set quite full, or baggy.

However, as the wind increases, its impact builds rapidly (the wind's force increases with the square of its velocity), and most boats begin to heel at an angle of over 20° unless the sails are depowered or made less full. Large heel angles throw a boat out of balance by creating bad weather helm.

Later we'll look more closely at this all-important question of balance. But now let's review sail controls and then examine how to use them in light to moderate winds, in powering conditions.

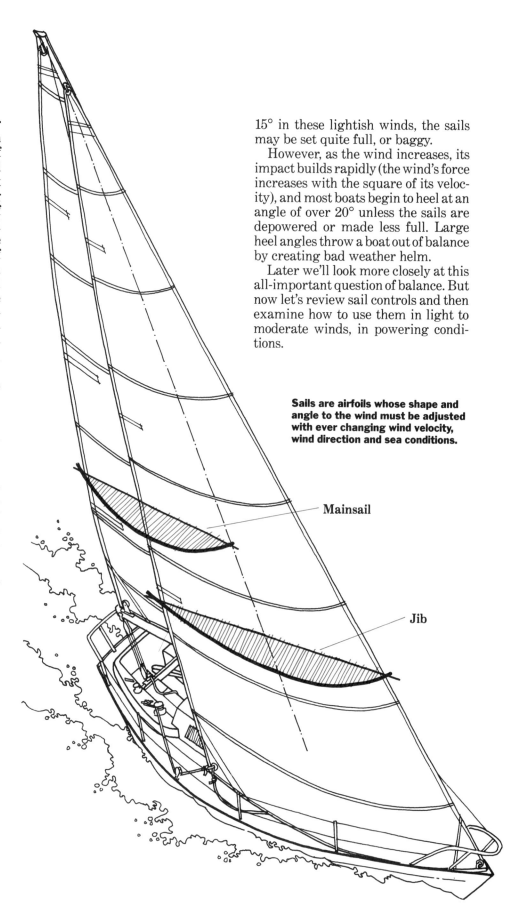

Sails are airfoils whose shape and angle to the wind must be adjusted with ever changing wind velocity, wind direction and sea conditions.

Mainsail

Jib

Sail Controls

There are two interrelated parts of sail trim: the sail's shape and the sail's angle of attack to the apparent wind. Some sail controls affect only one or the other, and some affect both.

The main sheet pulls both down and sideways on the boom, therefore affecting both shape and angle of attack. As the boom is pulled down, the sail's leech becomes increasingly tight or cupped, eventually hindering the clear flow of air along both the leeward and the windward side. The tight leech far aft also creates some weather helm. Ideally, the leech should not be tight or cupped but should

curve to leeward about 5° as it ascends toward the top of the mast. Sailmakers call this curve "twist," and it's important because it allows a clear flow of air across the sail. In addition, because the apparent wind is slightly farther aft aloft than it is on deck since the velocity is greater up high, the sail must be trimmed at two angles of attack — one up high, which is fairly broad, and one below, which is about 5° tighter. The main sheet also pulls

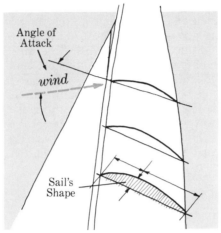

Angle of Attack

wind

Sail's Shape

the boom in and out, narrowing and broadening the angle of attack down low. A helpful indicator for mainsail trim is a 10-inch telltale (length of yarn) sewn into the leech about two-thirds of the way up — near the top batten in a three-batten sail, and near the second batten in a four-batten sail. When the telltale is barely streaming aft on all points of sail except a run, the sail is trimmed and twisted correctly. If it is stalled (hanging slack or making circles), there isn't enough twist and the sheet is trimmed too tightly. Another indicator is the top batten, which should be about parallel to the boom when sailing close-hauled in 5-12 knots of true wind in smooth water, and cocked slightly to leeward in lighter or stronger wind or rough water. Batten angle and leech telltales are guides. Ultimately, the best indicators are weather helm, which should be a slight tug, and the boat's speed.

The jib sheet more directly affects the jib's shape than the main sheet controls the mainsail's shape. The jib sheet pulls the sail aft to flatten it.

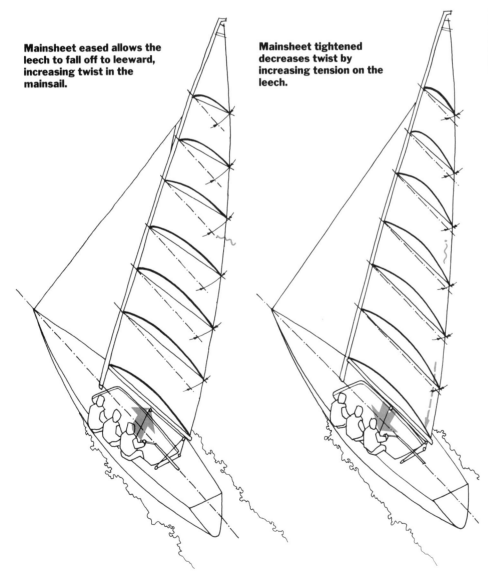

Mainsheet eased allows the leech to fall off to leeward, increasing twist in the mainsail.

Mainsheet tightened decreases twist by increasing tension on the leech.

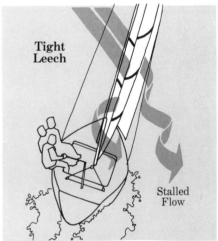

Tight Leech

Stalled Flow

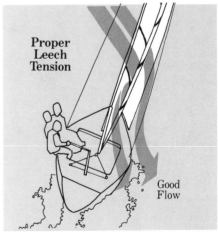

Proper Leech Tension

Good Flow

Too much mainsheet tension can cause a "tight leech," which hinders the flow of air as it leaves the sail.

Sail Controls

When the sheet is eased, the sail becomes fuller. The jib sheet also pulls down on the leech of the sail.

Finding the right angle for the sheet so it does both jobs equally well is extremely important. First, sew or tape three sets of telltales to the luff of the jib. The telltales should be spaced evenly along the luff's length. For example, on a jib with a 30-foot luff length the telltales will be located every 7′6″, beginning 7′6″ above the tack. Most sailors use wool or acrylic yarn, which may be pushed through the sail with a sewing needle and knotted on either side. The telltales should be 3-12 inches

behind the luff — shorter distances for boats smaller than about 16 feet, longer distances for larger boats. They should be long enough to be seen clearly by the helmsman. Bright red or green yarn is more visible than blue or brown; use red on the port side and green to starboard. The telltales should be trimmed so they do not touch the headstay; otherwise they may tangle around the stay and be useless.

The jib sheet lead is the block on a track on deck through which the jib sheet passes on the way to a cleat, or on a larger boat, to a winch. The fore-and-aft position of the jib sheet lead determines how effectively the sheet pulls both down *and* aft on the jib. If the lead is too far aft, trimming the sheet will stretch the foot but let the leech sag off uselessly; if too far forward, the leech will be too tight and the foot will bag.

To find the right position for the lead, get sailing on a close-hauled course with the mainsail and jib trimmed so you are moving fast at an angle

of attack to the apparent wind of about 35°. Now slowly head up until the luff of the jib begins to luff (or bubble). The windward luff telltales should all lift at the same time and at the same angle — that is, the wind should be striking them all at exactly the same angle of attack. If the top windward telltale lifts before the bottom telltale, the angle of attack is narrower up top than it is near the tack. Move the jib lead slightly forward and try again. If the bottom windward telltale lifts first, move the lead slightly aft. After some trial and error you'll find the right lead for the sail so that it works most efficiently from foot to head. Mark the lead on deck with a marking pen or a piece of plastic or duct tape, and duplicate it on the other side. Go through this routine for each jib you have on board. Since the sail's shape may change with the wind velocity, be prepared to move the lead as the conditions alter.

The jib sheet lead often can be moved inboard and outboard (sideways in and out) as well as fore and aft,

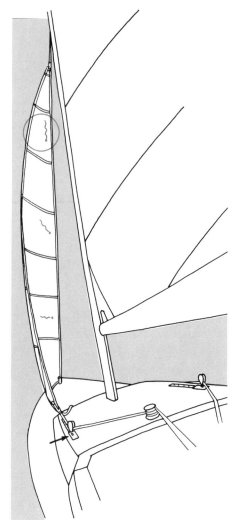 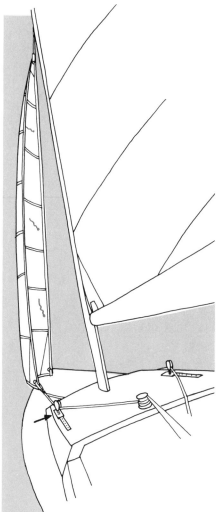 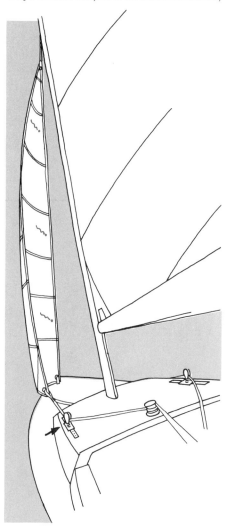

If the top jib telltale lifts first (left) the lead must be moved forward to tighten the leech and make the foot more full. If the bottom telltale lifts first (center) move the lead aft. When all telltales lift at the same time (right) the shape should be right.

either on athwartships tracks or by releading the sheet through another block, in order to change the jib's angle of attack to the wind. When the lead is far inboard, the jib's leech is close under the mainsail's luff and the air flowing aft from the jib may harmfully backwind (blow into) the mainsail. In addition, trimming the jib sheet far inboard may cup the leech to windward and create excessive lee helm. While every boat seems to have her own optimum jib lead angle, we can say that on close-hauled courses, small, nonoverlapping jibs should be trimmed no closer than about 8° off the centerline and overlapping jibs should be trimmed no closer than about 10°. As the wind increases, the lead is let outboard, for while an inboard lead may allow a boat to point well (sail very close to the wind), it may cause excessive heeling force. Easing the lead outboard on a track or by moving the sheet from one block to another uncups the leech and increases forward thrust while it marginally decreases pointing ability and greatly

decreases heeling thrust. On reaches the lead should be as far outboard as possible, since pointing ability is not desired when sailing off the wind.

The main sheet traveler is used to adjust the mainsail's angle of attack to the wind. This athwartships track sits under the main boom, either in the cockpit or on deck. On it slides an adjustable car on roller bearings, and the main sheet runs through blocks on the car. The car can be pulled to windward of the centerline or let down to leeward — the first narrows the angle of attack of the sail, the second widens it. Narrowing the angle of attack improves pointing ability, increases side thrust, and causes weather helm; widening it increases forward thrust and decreases weather helm. The traveler is used primarily when sailing close-hauled and is adjusted in tandem with the athwartships jib lead; when one is let outboard, so is the other. When beating in light to moderate conditions, the traveler usually is set so that the main boom is just above the centerline; this may mean that the traveler car has to

be pulled to windward. When the jib lead and traveler car are at a narrow angle of attack in light winds, the sheets should be fairly slack to allow the leeches to twist off. As the wind builds, trim the sheets to control twist and, as the leads are moved outboard to leeward, trim the sheets further.

The boom vang controls the main boom's vertical rise and the mainsail's twist when the sheet exerts no downward pull on reaches and runs. On small boats the vang is a tackle running from the boom to the mast, but on larger boats it may run to the deck or may be a hydraulic-powered ram between the boom and mast. A tackle simply holds the boom down, while a hydraulic ram supports the boom in a chosen vertical plane, thereby keeping it from dropping as well as lifting. This is an advantage on a cruising boat, whose heavy, potentially dangerous boom would otherwise be supported by a wire called a topping lift running from the top of the mast to the end of the boom. But since hydraulics can malfunction or leak on deck, they usually are found only on boats that are scrupulously maintained, like ocean racers. When the vang is set properly, the mainsail should still have a twist of about 5° from foot to head.

The outhaul pulls the mainsail aft to flatten it and lets it forward to increase the amount of draft, or fullness. The outhaul is effective only on the bottom one-third to one-half of the sail. This sail control is a tackle attached to the mainsail clew, which it pulls out to the end of the boom.

The Cunningham stretches the mainsail or the jib luff to change the fore-and-aft position of the point of deepest draft (fullness). To pull the draft forward, tighten the Cunningham; to ease it aft, let the Cunningham out. Most Cunninghams are short tackles led to a cringle (hole) in the luff 6 inches to 1 foot above the tack. (On jibs, the draft position may also be adjusted by tightening or loosening the halyard.) Sails are cut with a rope luff that, when stretched, pulls the attached cloth forward, thereby also pulling the point of deepest draft forward. On some older boats, mainsail luff tension is adjusted by moving the boom's gooseneck up and down on a track under the control of a line called the downhaul, but most boats now have fixed goosenecks and Cunningham lines.

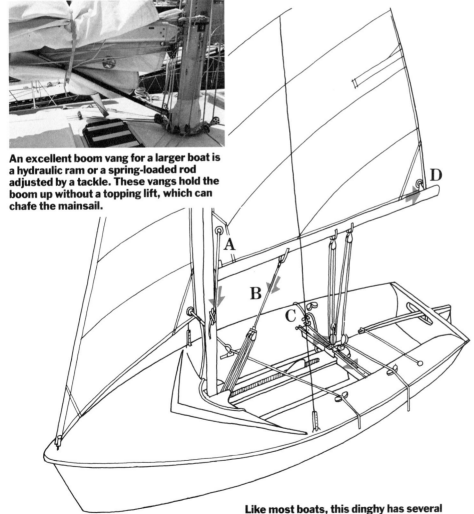

An excellent boom vang for a larger boat is a hydraulic ram or a spring-loaded rod adjusted by a tackle. These vangs hold the boom up without a topping lift, which can chafe the mainsail.

Like most boats, this dinghy has several sail controls besides the sheets: (left to right) the Cunningham (A), boom vang (B), traveler (C), and outhaul (D).

Sail Materials
Sail Size

Sailmakers build mainsails, jibs, and other sails much the same way that clothes designers make suits and dresses. In sailmaking, as in dressmaking, the materials are sewn together with tapered seams to produce a desired shape. Unlike dresses, however, sails can be misshapen, or stretched, and must be pulled back into the desired shape with the sail controls.

Most mainsails and jibs are made of Dacron cloth specially woven for boating use. Cruising boats usually use sails made of soft, easily handled Dacron that can be furled and bagged without too much effort. Boats that are raced, however, usually use a cloth with a resinated finish that helps reduce stretch. This cloth is stiff and hard to hold; to avoid creases, resinated sails must be carefully folded before they are bagged. Dacron cloth of both types comes in a wide variety of weights identified by a number that indicates weight per sailmaker's 36 by 28½-inch "yard." Heavier cloth stretches less than light cloth. The higher the loads, the heavier the cloth. A dinghy like the Laser uses a mainsail made of 3.8-ounce cloth, while a 30-foot racer-cruiser may have a 6-ounce mainsail, a 3-ounce genoa jib, and a 5-ounce smaller jib. Sailcloth weights as high as 12 ounces are common on very large racing boats. By carefully aligning the sail panels so that the strains are along the lines of the warp and woof threads running at right angles to each other, the sailmaker can minimize stretch. In the early 1980s Dacron began to be replaced as the primary fabric for racing boats' sails by Mylar, which, while more expensive and slippery to handle, is less stretchy. Sophisticated racing sails are made of Mylar and Kevlar,

an extremely low-stretch brown cloth. While Kevlar is very strong (it has been used in bulletproof vests) it is also very brittle, and Kevlar sails tend to have short lives if not treated with great care. Spinnakers are made out of nylon, whose stretch is often reduced with a resin finish.

Careful handling is required for modern sails made of high-tech materials if they are to stay together and keep their original shape. The governing rule is to avoid crinkling them by allowing them to flap excessively or by stepping on them. Once the finish and fibers are bent, they will break. If they must luff, flatten them by tightening the boom vang, outhaul, and Cunningham. Some sailmakers recommend that high-tech sails (like the cotton sails of two generations ago) be slowly broken-in in light winds to allow the seams to stretch gradually.

When not in use, sails should be covered or kept in bags in order to prevent degradation by the sun's ultraviolet rays.

Sailmaking is part art and part science, for while they use space-age materials like Mylar and cut it with computers, sailmakers must rely on traditional handworking skills to assemble the sail. Strong stainless-steel, bronze, and aluminum eyes are inserted in the clew, head, and tack, and the boltropes that run along a mainsail's foot and luff and a jib's luff must be carefully sewn to the cloth. Sails undergo considerable chafe, and reinforcing patches must be sewn on where the spreader touches an overlapping jib.

Dinghy and daysailer sails are quite simple: a mainsail, a jib, and perhaps a spinnaker (described later in this chapter). The sail inventory on larger boats may include anywhere from 3 to 20 sails, with the greatest variety among the jibs. The reason for this is that large, overlapping genoa jibs suitable for light and moderate winds of less than 15 knots are too big for stronger winds, when they develop more side force than forward force. So as the wind increases, the crew changes down to a smaller jib.

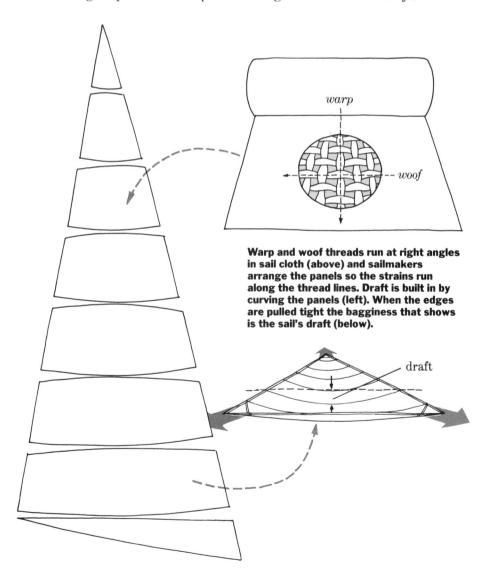

warp

woof

Warp and woof threads run at right angles in sail cloth (above) and sailmakers arrange the panels so the strains run along the thread lines. Draft is built in by curving the panels (left). When the edges are pulled tight the bagginess that shows is the sail's draft (below).

draft

For ease of identification, these jibs are numbered, with the number 1 being the largest, the number 2 being the next largest, and so on. On a racer-cruiser, the number 1 is trimmed about halfway back along the deck, the number 2 is trimmed a couple of feet forward of that, the number 3 (or working jib) is trimmed just at the leeward shrouds, and the number 4 is trimmed so it doesn't overlap the shrouds. There is usually a tiny storm jib too. Ocean racing yachts may carry two number 1 genoas of different sail cloth weight, the lighter, fuller sail being used in light winds and the heavier, flatter one in moderate winds. Also in a racing boat's sail inventory will be special reaching jibs, some staysails (small jibs carried under reaching sails and spinnakers), and many spinnakers. Since large, skilled racing crews can change sails very quickly using twin-grooved headstays and two halyards, this sail inventory can usually be exploited to match the weather conditions.

The normal cruising boat, however, will probably carry only two or three jibs. The largest will correspond to the racing boat's number 2 (the number 1 being too big for small crews), and the others might be the number 3 or the working jib, plus a small storm jib.

Besides exposed area, jibs also differ in profile shape. Racing sails are usually cut (made) so their bottom edges, or feet, hug the deck to keep wind from escaping. While efficient aerodynamically, these decksweeping jibs cut off almost all visibility to leeward. In crowded waters a lookout must be posted in the bow to warn the helmsman of approaching obstructions, such as other boats. This obviously is impractical for shorthanded cruising crews; thus cruising sails are cut with a high clew so there is a large area of visibility between the foot and the deck. The problem is solved on dinghies and daysailers by inserting clear plastic windows in the mainsail and jib.

Cutters carry two small jibs at once, one set from the headstay and the other, called the forestaysail, set from the forestay running from partway up the mast to the middle of the foredeck. While less efficient than a big genoa jib, these two sails are physically easier to trim, set, and douse. This is called the double-headsail rig, with headsail a synonym for jib.

Ketches and yawls may carry a large inventory as well as special light sails called mizzen staysails that are set from the mizzenmast on downwind legs.

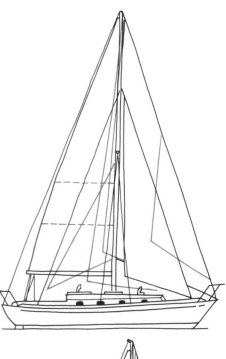

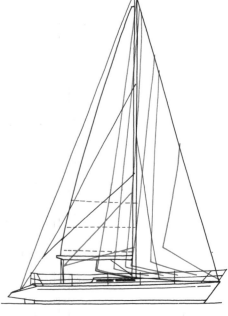

(Top) With the addition of a storm jib and perhaps a cruising spinnaker, this is the sail inventory of the average cruising cutter. (Above) Ocean racers have a much larger inventory, with each jib designed for use in a narrow range of wind conditions.

Low-stretch Mylar is used in templates for making sails as well as a sail cloth.

73

Sail Shape

What should a sail look like? How powerful, or full, should it be, and where should the deepest draft be located? While every boat's sails are unique, sailmakers have been able to establish an envelope that surrounds most optimum shapes.

Mainsail Shape

When sailing close-hauled, the mainsail should have its point of deepest draft between 40 and 60 percent of the distance between the luff and the leech. The best position depends on whether the boat also carries a jib, and if she does, on the size of the jib. On a cat-rigged, mainsail-only boat like a Laser, the deepest draft should be about 40 percent abaft the luff. That is, if the sail is 10 feet wide, the draft should be 4 feet behind the luff. A boat with a small working jib that does not overlap should have the point of deepest draft between 40 and 50 percent aft in her mainsail — 40 percent near the top batten and 50 percent near the bottom batten. If the jib overlaps but is fractionally rigged (set from partway up the mast), the draft should be about 40 percent abaft the luff up top and 55 percent abaft the luff down low. And a masthead-rigged boat carrying a large overlapping genoa jib should carry the mainsail draft well aft — 50 percent back near the top and 60 percent back near the bottom.

Taken from Wallace Ross's excellent book about sails, *Sail Power*, these figures are approximate. You can estimate draft position while sailing close-hauled by looking up from under the foot of the sail, adjusting the Cunningham control, and watching to see when the sail luffs. As you tighten the control and pull the draft forward, the sail will luff more forward; as you ease it to let the draft slide back, the sail will luff less forward.

In general, the mainsail luff should carry slight pucker marks or wrinkles when the Cunningham is properly adjusted, and seen from below the sail should look like the arc of a circle. If the luff has deep tension wrinkles and the sail is almost flat over its after two-thirds, then the Cunningham is too tight. But if the luff carries hundreds of shallow wrinkles, if the forward two-thirds is flat, and if the leech is abruptly cupped to windward, the Cunningham is too loose.

The *amount* of draft in the mainsail is independent of the *position* of deepest draft. Draft is built in by the sailmaker when he tapers the panels' seams, but you can also adjust it by tightening or loosening the outhaul. Like draft position, draft amount varies from the foot to the head. It is generally greatest about halfway up. Sailmakers refer to draft in terms of camber, a ratio that converts to a per-

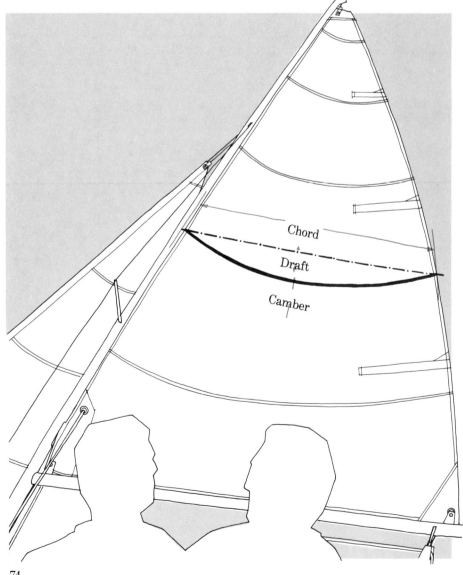

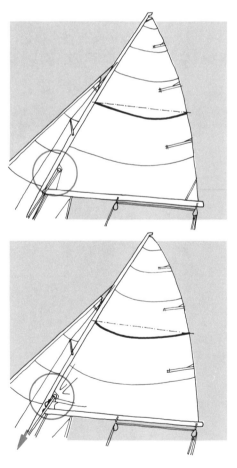

(Left) This well-trimmed, rather full mainsail has a camber of 14 percent and its draft 45 percent aft along the chord. **(Top)** The draft is too far aft with the Cunningham eased, **(above)** too far forward with it tightened. Pulling the draft forward flattens the leech.

centage. The ratio is between the sail's depth and the sail's chord length — the distance from the luff to the leech. If the depth is 1 foot and the chord is 10 feet long, the camber ratio is 1:10, or 10 percent. Camber ratio can be measured by taking a photograph of the sail and then drawing chord and depth lines on the print, or it may be estimated when the sails are hoisted by using a ruler and a tape measure.

A mainsail camber of 10 percent is about right for close-hauled sailing in light to moderate winds in the average racer-cruiser and cruising boat. Heavier, wider keel boats that make more resistance may need a more powerful sail with a camber of about 12½ percent (1 foot of draft for every 8 feet of chord). So, too, will centerboarders. As camber increases, the sail becomes more powerful. But while the greater draft increases power, it limits the boat's pointing ability. Therefore narrow boats like 12-meters, which make very little resistance, can use flat sails both to go fast and to point close to the wind. Their sails may have a camber

of about 7 percent, or 1 foot of draft for every 14 feet of chord length. The camber for effective sails ranges between about 18 percent (1:5.5) at the fullest and 5 percent (1:20) at the flattest. Cruising boat mainsails are generally on the flat side, since they can-

not be changed when the wind pipes up. Racing daysailers often carry two mainsails in their sail inventories: a full one for lightish conditions and a flat one for fresh air (winds).

(Above) Since their great stability allows considerable power aloft, these catamarans carry full mainsails on a reach. (Left) Flatter sails are necessary on this close-hauled, well-sailed ocean racer. The slot —the gap between the mainsail and the genoa jib — is even up and down, the boom is on the centerline with the traveler car to windward, and the crew concentrates on sail trim. Not surprisingly, *Scaramouche* compiled an enviable racing record.

Sail Shape

Mast Bend

When the sailmaker constructs a mainsail, he anticipates the amount that the mast will be bent by building in luff curve, a convex curve of extra cloth. When the mast is bent, this extra cloth is sucked up and the sail is effectively flattened. On dinghies and small boats, the mast is bent simply by trimming the main sheet. As the boom comes down, two things happen: the leech tightens, pulling the top of the mast back; and the gooseneck is thrust forward, bowing the bottom of the mast forward. Only the stiffness of the mast and any standing rigging keep

mast bend within safe limits; when a spar is bent too far, it goes out of column and collapses.

In larger racing keel boats, mast bend is effected almost exclusively by shortening the backstay — the wire stay that runs from the masthead (top of the mast) to the stern — with a hydraulic ram or a block and tackle. Again, the standing rigging should limit the amount of bend to keep the mast from breaking. Make sure your sailmaker knows if your boat is equipped with mast-bending devices and if you plan to use them. Otherwise he'll probably assume that the mast won't be bent and will build in very little luff curve. You should bend the mast only as far as the amount of luff curve permits, for otherwise you'll simply suck all the draft out of the sail and distort it.

Since the average boat usually does not have mast-bending equipment, this point is moot for most readers of this book. But if you do plan to bend your mast, and have the right equipment and the mainsail to go with

(Above) Leech tension and the boom's forward thrust bend the mast and flatten the sail on the stayless Laser. (Right) Masts with standing rigging are bent by shortening the backstay with a block and tackle or hydraulic ram.

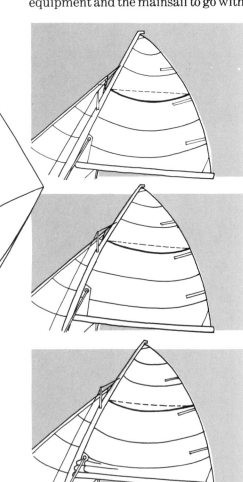

When the sail and mast are well matched, the sail is full if the spar is straight (top) and gradually flattened as it is bent. Mast bend throws the draft aft (middle), so tighten the Cunningham to pull the draft forward (bottom).

it, here are a few pointers:

First, mast bend throws the point of deepest draft aft in the sail. So as the mast is bent, the Cunningham should be tightened.

Second, bendy masts should be rigged with great care. The spreaders — which are the primary limits on mast bend — must be especially strong and securely fastened to the mast. The shrouds should be tightened in such a way that the mast is perfectly straight athwartships, with no side bend, when the boat is close-hauled in moderate winds; otherwise the aft bow in the bent mast may throw the spar severely out of column and break it. The lower stays providing fore-and-aft support take immense loads when the mast is bent and must be especially reliable. These are the after and forward lower shrouds, running from the base of the lower spreader to the deck on either side. (Sometimes the forward lowers are replaced by a single lower stay called the jackstay, which runs from the mast to the foredeck.) All shrouds, headstays, and backstays should have

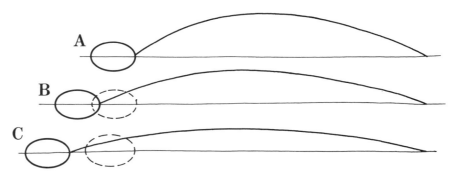

This cross-sectional view shows how mast bend extends the mainsail's luff and flattens the sail from a camber of 16 percent (A) to one of 13 percent (B). Overbending the mast beyond the extent of the luff curve removes almost all draft (C).

high safety factors — at least twice the anticipated load on the mast — and be equipped with sufficiently large turn-buckles and eyes. Frequent inspection for corrosion is a must. In addition to these fixed stays, some boats carry running backstays, which are set up only on the windward side to limit mast bend or to counter the pull of the headstay on a fractional rig.

Third, moderate or eliminate mast bend in rough seas. Already slightly out of column, a bent mast may be snapped by the added moment of inertia created when the boat lurches off a wave. (For more on masts and standing rigging, see chapter 17.)

The towering mast on the 79-foot ocean racer *Bumblebee IV* is bent aft at the top by the backstay and forward in the middle by the babystay and forestay, leading to the foredeck. Running backstays leading from the stern to part way up the spar control bend. Hold a straight edge along the mast to see the result, which would be impossible without a thin, limber mast, powerful hydraulic systems, and the crew's assiduous attention.

Mast bend can throw the spar out of column and impose huge loads on fittings, especially when the sea is rough and the spar pumps fore and aft. Light, bendy spars are more prone to failure than heavy, stiff ones.

Sail Shape

Jib Shape

Because the jib is unaffected by air flow off another sail, its draft can be farther forward and slightly deeper than a mainsail's. The draft position should be about 40 percent of the way between the luff and the leech. When working with soft Dacron, which stretches readily, the sailmaker usually designs the draft about 33 percent back, anticipating that it will be blown aft as the wind increases. In racing jibs built of low-stretch, hard-finished Dacron or Mylar, the draft usually stays where it was built. A jib's camber should be somewhere between

10 percent (1:10) and 15 percent (1:7). In cross section, a good jib looks something like a fat airplane wing, with a round area forward and a flat surface tapering off aft.

Working jibs are usually equipped with battens, which keep the long leech from flopping about, but battens are impractical on genoas since they would break during tacks and jibes. Genoa leeches, then, are prone to cupping and noisy chattering, especially as the wind freshens. Usually, these annoyances (which can absorb some of the sail's driving force) can be controlled by adjusting the leech line — a small line that runs inside the leech from the clew to the head. If the leech line doesn't correct them, the sail should be returned to the sailmaker for recutting.

Sailmakers build a luff curve into jibs as well as into mainsails, but it's a negative, concave curve since the free-standing wire headstay can never be as straight as a mast. If you can straighten the headstay, however, you can flatten the jib and generally im-

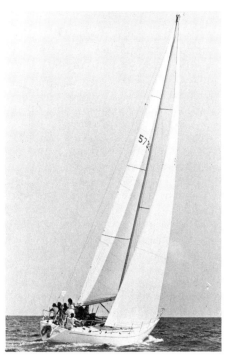

The slot is ideal on *High Roler,* sailing close-hauled in moderate air with Dennis Conner at the wheel. Black tape on the mainsail and jib help the crew observe camber and draft position.

Another view of a good slot, this photo shows how the mainsail's draft moves forward as the genoa's leech is hollowed out aloft. The headstay sags off perceptibly. Like all ocean racers and many racer-cruisers, this boat carries her jib luff in a groove in the aluminum rod headstay instead of hanked onto the stay. Besides minimizing turbulence, this system permits quick sail changes since another sail can be hoisted in an adjoining groove before the old sail is doused. The black dot on the jib is a window for telltales.

prove pointing ability. The headstay can be straightened by shortening the backstay or the windward running backstay (if your boat has one). When you order new sails, be sure that the sailmaker knows how straight you can make the headstay; he'll shape the jib's negative luff curve to match.

Since a jib automatically becomes fuller as the sheet is eased, letting out the sheet is almost all you have to do to shape it properly for a reach or run. But also move the jib lead outboard and forward, so the three luff telltales continue to mimic each other as we described earlier, and cast off the Cunningham and let the headstay sag a bit (though not so much that it whips around).

To make the jib more full, lengthen the backstay and let the headstay sag off; to flatten it, straighten the headstay.

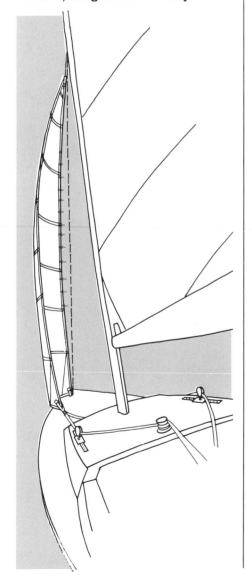

Determining Wind Direction

You can't trim sails properly if you don't know which way the wind is blowing. Of course, you can feel it on your neck or face, but a visual reference point is a great help too. So there should be some wind indicators on board.

We've already described one set of wind indicators — the yarn telltales taped or sewn to the luff of the jib and the leech of the mainsail. Not only do they help determine the correct angle of attack and twist when sailing close-hauled, but they can also help when playing the sails. If you read the jib telltales, you'll be able to anticipate a luff before the sail itself bubbles or flaps. (This is especially true when using resinated Dacron sails or Mylar sails, whose stiff surface reacts very slowly to wind shifts.) When playing the jib, look at the middle telltale. Some sailors put telltales on the luff of the mainsail, but because the mast greatly disturbs the air flow over the front 10 percent of the main, these don't help very much. The leech telltale usually is the best possible indicator of mainsail trim other than luffing in the sail itself.

Telltales in the rigging indicate apparent wind direction. Tie 6-inch lengths of yarn to the shrouds at a place where the helmsman can easily see them while also looking at the jib, and a 10-inch telltale to the backstay to show apparent wind while running.

Even more reliable than rigging telltales is a masthead fly — a balanced wind arrow screwed to the top of the mast above the air flow off the sails. Several good masthead flies are on the market; some of them are even connected to electronic instruments that provide a readout on a dial in the cockpit or are connected to small computers that will figure the true wind direction and optimum angles of attack. Unfortunately the mass of antennas and other gear that sits at the masthead of many racer-cruisers often gets in the way of a masthead fly. Some skippers get around this problem by securing the masthead fly to the headboard at the top of the main-

sail so that it is clear of the other equipment when the sail is hoisted.

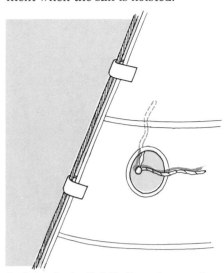

A window in the jib luff allows the crew to see the windward and leeward telltales simultaneously. To avoid confusion, use green yarn on the starboard side and red yarn to port.

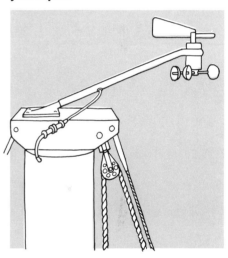

A masthead fly is a wind direction arrow either secured to the top of the mast above the wind velocity cups and other electronics (above) or taped to the head of a dinghy's mast (bottom).

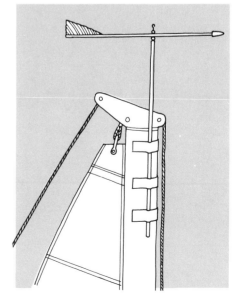

Sail Trim in Light to Moderate Conditions

In powering conditions, when the wind is lighter than about 15 knots, here's what you should do to trim your sails for good speed and balance.

Drifting Conditions (0-4 Knots)

The biggest problem in really light winds is developing steerageway, so don't trim the sails too tight when sailing close-hauled. If possible, heel the boat by sitting to leeward in order to allow the sails to flop into shape and induce weather helm. Trim the jib fairly far outboard and carry the boom about halfway to the rail in order to maximize any forward force. Tighten the outhaul more than might seem appropriate; by flattening the sail, you'll make it easier for the wind to stay attached to the cloth. Move around in the boat gently, and avoid making jerky motions with the tiller or steering wheel. In puffs, be careful not to overtrim the jib, thereby creating harmful lee helm — the genoa affects the heading more than the rudder when the wind is this light. And above all, don't be greedy about pointing too close to the wind. Sail for speed. Runs and broad reaches are very slow in these conditions and slightly above, so increase the apparent wind by heading up to a beam reach, if possible.

Light Air (5-8 Knots)

Now that there's enough wind to give good steerageway, move the jib lead inboard and pull the traveler up until the boom is about over the centerline. However, if the water is rough you may have to sacrifice pointing ability to keep her moving by carrying the sails farther outboard. The outhaul should be fairly loose, with slight wrinkles along the foot, and the Cunninghams should not be tensioned, since there's not enough wind to blow the draft aft. Beating, you should be able to sail about 35° from the apparent wind, heading off a couple of degrees (footing) only in lulls or waves. But be careful not to overtrim the sails. Off the wind, let the sails bag and keep the boom vang fairly slack.

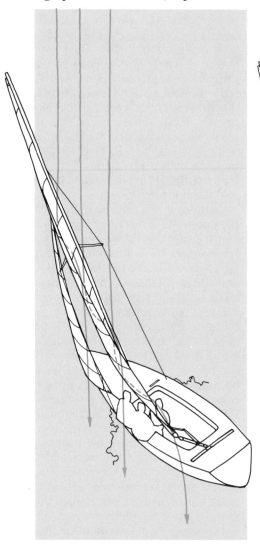

Don't try to point too high in drifting conditions.

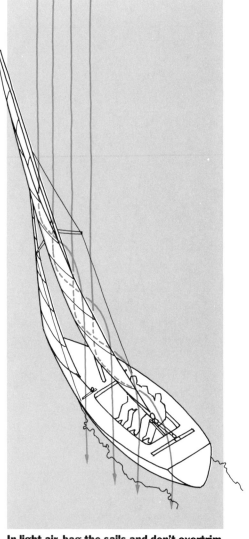

In light air, bag the sails and don't overtrim the sheets.

Moderate Air (9-15 Knots)

This is when most boats spring to life. Upwind, sails are carried fairly full with moderate outhaul tension and the sheets trimmed a few inches short of all the way. The jib lead and main boom should be slightly to leeward of where they were in light air, and eased down gradually as the wind increases or the waves become larger. Tighten the Cunninghams in order to keep the draft position optimum (as described earlier), and bend the mast slightly, if possible. Watch the angle of heel and be sensitive to the helm. If weather helm increases dramatically, let the traveler down even if the mainsail begins to be backwinded by air flow off the jib. Because the forward part of the mainsail isn't very effective on a beat, this backwind is not harmful. Off the wind, the vang should be snug to keep the boom from lifting.

"When in Doubt, Let It Out"

The most common mistake sailors make when trimming sails is to pull them in too far, both on the sheets and on the athwartships leads. This is especially harmful after tacks, when all boats need some time to accelerate with eased sails before they're brought back on a close-hauled course. If the boat's speedometer is reading lower than you think is right, or if the boat feels sluggish and is heeling over too far, let the traveler out a few inches and ease the jib sheet slightly. You won't be able to point quite as high, but she'll be making much better use of the wind and sailing faster.

Pinching

When sailing close-hauled, some helmsmen like to think that they can sail right up into the wind's eye. Sailing with the jib light, with the jib's windward telltales pointing straight up to the sky, is called pinching. In smooth water and moderate air you might be able to get away with pinching, but as soon as the wind dies or the waves build, it's extremely inefficient. The boat speed will plummet, and because the water flow is slowed, the appendages won't resist the sails' side forces as well as they should and the boat will make more leeway. Pinching is especially self-defeating in drifting conditions and light air, when boat speed is painfully acquired and easily lost, and in rough water, when a single wave can slap a boat's speed down to half what it could be.

Yet there is one situation in which pinching can be helpful. When sailing in gusty winds, you may be overpowered so suddenly that you don't have time to ease a sheet or the traveler. When that happens, make the sails less efficient with a quick pinch. Once the first blast of the gust has passed, you can head off to an efficient close-hauled course.

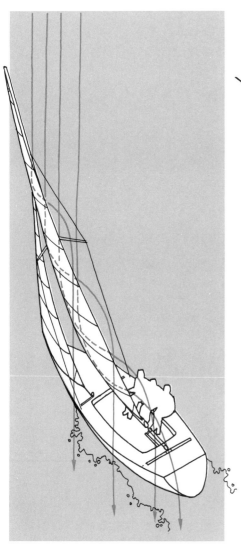

Flatten sails in moderate air but ease sheets slightly if the water gets rough.

Gust

When you feel a gust, pinch quickly until the telltale is straight up. This is called feathering. Try to keep the angles of heel and weather helm constant before, during, and after the gust, easing down the traveler car if necessary. When the gust passes, head off to close-hauled.

81

Depowering in Fresh and Strong Winds

No matter how good the sails look, no boat sails well when they are pulling her over at extreme angles of heel. When a dinghy heels more than 15°, a beamy keel boat heels more than 25°, or a narrow keel boat heels more than 30°, she slows down, develops severe weather helm, and wallows sluggishly through the water. She must be brought back upright by depowering the sails. If powering in light and moderate winds means to make sails full at narrow angles of attack, depowering in winds stronger than about 15 knots (apparent) means to flatten sails and trim them wider.

Going one by one through the list of sail controls, this is how you depower a sailboat:

The main sheet works quickest. When a gust hits and the boat begins to flop over, quickly ease out one or more feet of main sheet and keep it eased until she rights herself. This works both on the wind and off the wind. Either the helmsman or a crew member can cast the sheet off — the former when he first feels the drastic weather helm through the tiller or wheel, the latter when he sees the helmsman begin to fight the helm. Even though the wildly luffing mainsail may seem to be wasted, the boat is sailing better because she's sailing on her bottom.

The jib sheet may also be eased quickly in fresh winds to spill air from the jib.

The jib sheet lead should be moved outboard in fresh and strong winds to decrease side force and increase forward force. It may also be moved aft to increase the amount of twist in the upper part of the sail, effectively spilling wind up high, where it exerts the greatest heeling leverage over the hull. When the lead is moved aft, the upper of the three jib luff telltales will flutter before the lower two do.

The main sheet traveler should be carried down to leeward of the centerline when sailing close-hauled in fresh winds. Just how far is determined by the helm, for the two have a direct relationship. Drop the traveler car down until there is about 3° of weather helm (later in this chapter we'll show how to measure this). When the helm becomes neutral in a lull, pull the car back up to windward; if weather helm increases uncomfortably, drop the car farther. On many boats, the helmsman can adjust the traveler himself, but sometimes another crew member will have to do it for him. When sailing off the wind, on a reach or a run, pull the traveler car up to the centerline in order to eliminate downward pull on the boom by the main sheet.

The boom vang is used to depower the mainsail when sailing off the wind. With the traveler car centered, the

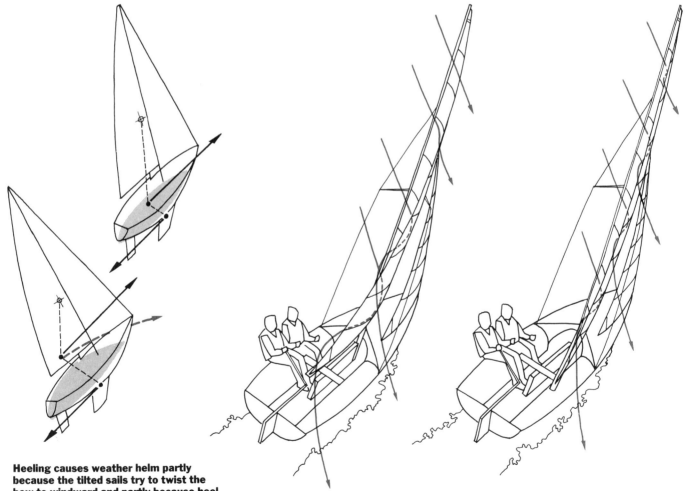

Heeling causes weather helm partly because the tilted sails try to twist the bow to windward and partly because heel makes the underbody (shaded area) asymmetrical. Since their underwater shape changes more drastically when they heel, beamy boats induce more weather helm than narrow boats.

To depower the sails with twist, move the jib lead aft and let the boom rise by easing the main sheet or boom vang.

To depower by narrowing the angle of attack to the wind, move the jib lead outboard and let the traveler car down to leeward.

main sheet does not pull down on the boom, so the boom's rise and fall — and with it the mainsail's twist — can be adjusted easily by easing and tightening the vang. When the upper part of the mainsail twists off, wind is spilled up where its leverage on the hull is greatest. When sailing off the wind in fresh to strong winds, lead the boom vang control aft to the helmsman so he can throw it off, spill wind, and counter the heeling force with the flick of a wrist. Unfortunately this quick-release system works better on a reach than it does on a run, when letting the boom rise will allow the mainsail to plaster itself all over the leeward shrouds and spreaders. The resulting chafe may cause the sail to rip. So when running in fresh or strong winds, overtrim the mainsheet so the boom is well in from the leeward shrouds, or tie in a reef to decrease the sail area.

The outhaul flattens the bottom part of the mainsail when it's tightened. Since flat sails create less sideways heeling force than full sails, pull the outhaul out as tightly as you can in

On a reach, depower by easing the sheets or twisting the mainsail by easing the boom vang.

fresh and strong winds.

The Cunningham control does not actually flatten the sail, but tightening it pulls the draft forward and eases (uncups) the leech. Since a cupped leech on either the mainsail or the jib creates bad helm, the Cunninghams should be pulled down hard in fresh and strong winds.

Mast bend flattens a mainsail that has been designed for it. At the same time it also increases a mast's chances of breaking. In fresh winds and relatively smooth waves, you can bend the mast to flatten the mainsail, but as the wind strengthens into the mid to high 20s and the seas build, you should not bend the mast far. In a cruising boat, you will have reefed by this time anyway, effectively flattening the mainsail without mast bend. As you bend the mast, the headstay usually is straightened, which flattens the jib.

Changing Down

In chapter 15 we'll look carefully at reefing and sail changing in rough conditions. Here, in the context of winds between 15 and 30 knots, we can say that a very effective way to depower a cruising boat or a racer-cruiser is to change to a smaller jib. When changing down, be sure to secure the old jib on deck (using sail ties) or below before hanking on the new one.

When daysailing or cruising, most boats can be depowered simply by lowering a sail. A sloop can sail under mainsail alone; when beating, let the traveler car all the way to leeward in order to decrease weather helm. A sloop may also be sailed under jib alone except in very rough seas. This limitation is important, because without the fore-and-aft support provided by her mainsail, the mast may whip around and break. A ketch or a yawl can be sailed comfortably under "jib and jigger" — with the mizzen and the jib set and the mainsail furled — but with the same warning about rough weather.

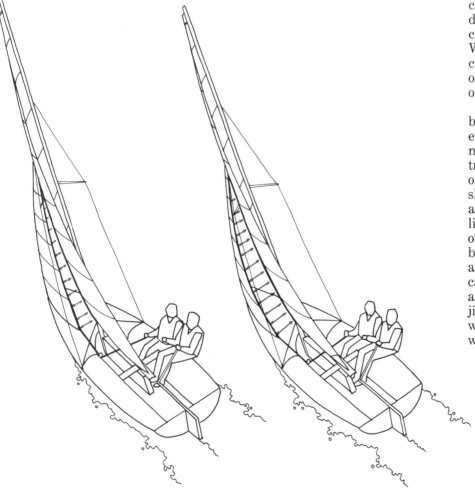

Avoid constricting the slot. As the jib lead goes outboard move it forward to keep the telltales symmetrical.

An open slot keeps the wind from jamming up behind the mainsail. Keep sailing at a steady angle of heel.

How Boats Balance

We have seen how boats are balanced in practice by adjusting sail controls. Now let's look at the theory behind it all. As we saw in chapter 1, an unbalanced boat wants to turn one way or the other off her course, and the helm must be adjusted to compensate. This may be because she is heeled; when heeled to one side, a hull automatically tries to turn toward the other side. Or it may be because the rig and the hull are not the way the designer intended.

There are two "areas" that a yacht designer includes on his drawings and tries to balance against each other. One is the sail area spread around the mast or masts. The effective center or balance point of this area is called the center of effort (C.E.). The other area is the lateral area of the underbody (the hull under water), and its center is called the center of lateral resistance (C.L.R.). The designer calculates the C.E. geometrically by drawing lines from each corner of each sail to the middle of the opposite edge. Where those lines cross is the C.E. for the sail. He then marks the C.E. for the entire sail plan by finding the balance point along the line between the two (or three) centers of effort. To find the C.L.R., he may cut out a drawing of the underbody and balance it on a point. The relationship between these two centers determines how the boat will balance, assuming she floats the way the designer intended. Ideally the C.E. should be just aft of the C.L.R. in order to create the desired 3° of weath-

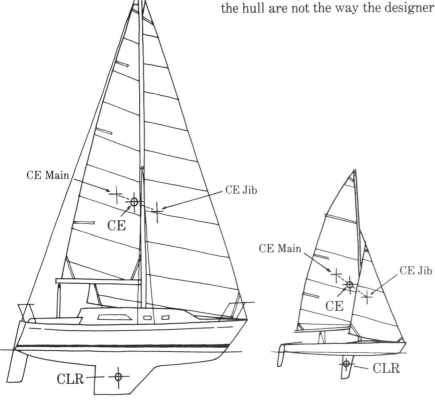

The sail area's center of effort is just forward of the underbody's center of lateral resistance, which can be moved aft by raising a centerboard but which is fixed in a keel boat.

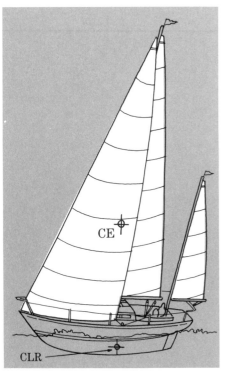

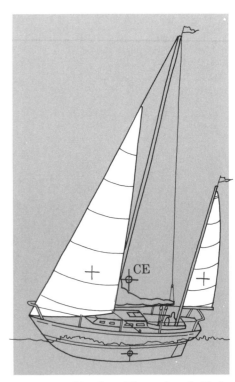

An advantage of the divided yawl or ketch rig is that the boat can be balanced well under several sail combinations. The center of effort is in the same place whether the boat is under full sail in light air (left), under mainsail and jib in fresh air (center), or under "jib and jigger" in heavy air (right).

er helm that makes the rudder work most effectively — that is, the pressure of the sails on the after end of the boat makes the bow swing to windward around the fulcrum of her C.L.R. But because of certain inefficiencies in the sails (for instance, turbulence caused by the mast), and because when the boat heels she automatically develops weather helm, the designer arranges the two areas on paper so the C.E. is "led" slightly forward of the C.L.R. As she sails, the effective C.E. moves aft.

Correcting Imbalances

What if the boat doesn't float the way her designer intended? How do you bring her back into balance? One common problem is that the boat floats bow-down because she's too heavy in her bow. This moves the C.L.R. forward, and thus increases weather helm, since the C.E.'s "lead" forward of the C.L.R. has been eliminated. A solution to this problem is to move weight aft so the boat floats on her lines as the designer intended. You can move anchors or some other heavy

weight back from the bow to the stern or lockers under the cockpit, or you can relocate any lead pigs that the builder put as ballast in her bilge. By bringing the C.L.R. aft, you are effectively decreasing weather helm.

Sometimes, however, the C.L.R. is too far aft and the boat has lee helm even when she's heeled. To induce weather helm, rake (tilt) the mast aft by lengthening the headstay, or slide the mast step (bottom) aft. Moving the C.E. aft like this narrows the "lead" between it and the C.L.R., effectively increasing weather helm.

Neither solution is very practical when you're underway. Previously we saw how you can cut back on weather helm by decreasing the amount of heel through depowering the sails. Here are some other ways:

Since a boat can usually heel an equal amount under a number of possible sail combinations, you might be able to increase weather helm by increasing the sail area aft and decreasing it forward, and decrease weather helm by decreasing the sail area aft and

increasing it forward. The mainsail can be reefed or unreefed, different size jibs may be set, or the mizzen (on a yawl or ketch) can be set or doused. The important requirement is to keep in your mind's eye a clear picture of the location of the C.L.R. of the underbody and that of the C.E. of each combination of sails you set.

A centerboard may be raised or lowered to change the helm. Raising the centerboard moves the C.L.R. aft, which decreases weather helm. In dinghies, raising the centerboard or daggerboard has another effect that decreases weather helm. As the board is retracted, the amount of exposed lateral area is decreased — which means that the boat skids sideways. Therefore the sideways force of the wind on the sail is translated less into heeling and more into leeway. So while she slides more to leeward, she heels less and has less weather helm.

The Sailboard Example

The best example of the way that the center of lateral resistance and the center of effort interact is the sailboard, or Windsurfer. Rather than turning a rudder, the sailor steers by tilting the sail fore and aft over the hull. Forward rake creates leeward helm and heads her off to jibe; aft rake creates weather helm and heads her up to tack. When a boardsailor tacks, he makes the following motions:

1. He rakes the mast way aft until the boom drags in the water. The boat heads up into the wind's eye.

2. Then he walks around the front of the mast, grabs the boom, and rakes the mast way forward. The sail's C.E. pulls the bow downwind as the boat pivots around her C.L.R.

3. Finally, when the boat is at an angle of attack of about 45° to the wind, he pulls the mast erect and sails off on the new tack.

While a normal boat appears to handle more simply, the only difference between her and a sailboard is that her rudder speeds the process up slightly by carrying her through the eye of the wind without an adjustment of the rig. Otherwise it's the same procedure; the C.E. rotates around the C.L.R.

On a straight course this Windsurfer's rig is held about upright.

Rudderless sailboards are steered by shifting the center of effort fore and aft over the center of lateral resistance.

To head up, the sailor tilts the mast aft. During the tack he steps around the spar.

To head off on the new tack, he tilts the mast far forward.

Boat-Handling Drills

Nothing teaches boat-handling techniques as effectively as a few quick drills conducted in a variety of wind conditions, both with and without rudders. Try them out in your boat in a body of water free of obstructions.

The Standing Start

Come to a dead stop, head-to-wind, and let the sheets all the way out. Before the boat gathers stern way (starts to sail backward), get under way, first under mainsail alone and then under jib alone. Finally, remove the rudder (or lash the helm amidships with the rudder centered) and try to get underway without steering.

The Serpentine

Once you've developed steerageway, alter course in a serpentine fashion, first with the helm alone and then also easing and trimming sheets as you change course. Notice how much easier it is when the sails help the helm. Finally, remove the rudder (or lash the helm) and steer solely by trimming the mainsail and easing the jib (to head up) and easing the mainsail and trimming the jib (to head off). On a dinghy or other small boat, try steering by shifting crew weight to create heel: heel to leeward causes her to head up; heel to windward causes her to head off.

Steering Backward

From a dead stop, gather stern way and steer backward using the rudder and backed sails. Then steer backward using the sails and heel alone. (Don't try this drill in fresh winds; the rudder may swing hard and break.)

Finding Neutral Helm

Sail on beating, reaching, and running courses, adjusting the sail controls and angle of heel until the helm is absolutely neutral with no weather or lee helm. Then make adjustments until you have a comfortable amount of weather helm. Concentrate on making small adjustments to the Cunningham and traveler.

Shooting a Mooring

Under a variety of sail combinations, practice shooting (heading at and picking up) an upwind mooring or some other buoyant object, like a cushion. Try to slow down using sharp alterations in the helm or by backing the sails.

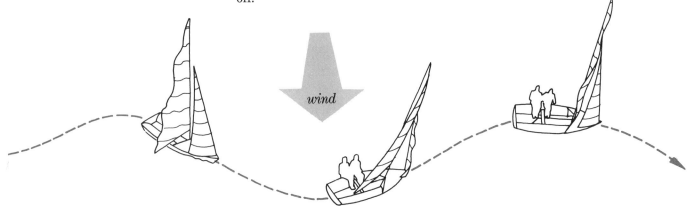

A good way to learn how your boat balances is to sail a serpentine course steering by trimming and easing sails rather than with the helm. Trim the jib to head off and the mainsail to head up. Small boats can be steered by shifting weight and changing heel angles. You can do this drill either alone or in a line of boats playing follow-the-leader.

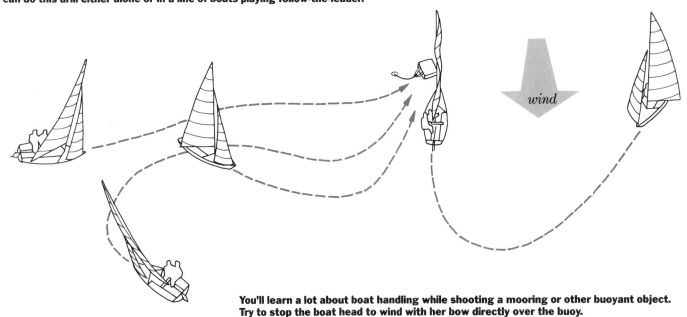

You'll learn a lot about boat handling while shooting a mooring or other buoyant object. Try to stop the boat head to wind with her bow directly over the buoy.

Reefing

If your boat can be reefed, shorten sail (described in chapter 14) and see how it affects balance and speed.

Heaving-To

You can balance the windward-turning force of the mainsail against the leeward-turning force of the jib to slow your boat down to a near-stop and let her lie comfortably, even in rough seas. This tactic is called heaving-to.

To heave-to, first put the boat on a course about 60° off the wind, on a close reach. Then back the jib (trim it to windward) so the clew is near the windward shrouds and trim the mainsail so it is mostly full. Push the helm to leeward and tie it there. Adjust the main sheet or traveler until she jogs slowly along at a 60° apparent wind angle. Because the backed jib creates no forward drive and the turned rudder acts as a brake, the mainsail pushes her along at about 2 knots in a series of gradual swoops — without anybody at the helm.

You can also heave-to without a jib, with the mainsail traveler car all the way to leeward, the main sheet trimmed so the sail is half-full, and the helm lashed where she sails herself at a 60° angle to the wind.

Many boats have survived gales and storms while hove-to under small storm sails, with the jib backed and the helm lashed to leeward, but even if you're in fine weather, you can use this simple tactic to stop for a bite to eat.

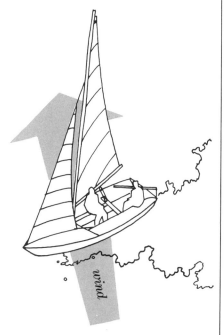

Heaving-to by backing the jib and securing the helm is a good way to stop for a while as well as a sound tactic for dealing with storms, as long as the waves are not breaking.

How to Measure Weather Helm

We have said that you should carry 3° of weather helm when sailing close-hauled to improve the leeway-resisting characteristics of the rudder and to make the helmsman's job a little easier by providing a slight tug as a frame of reference. Anything much more than 3° will create a braking action; anything less may cause the boat to wander all over the ocean or lake without any "feel" to alert the helmsman.

You can calculate exactly how far the tiller or wheel has to be pushed to have 3° of helm, and then mark it for easy reference while you're sailing. The boat must be out of the water so the rudder and helm angles can be measured at the same time. With one crew member standing under the rudder, center it exactly so it aims fore and aft. The helm should also be centered, but if the tiller is cocked to one side, or the center wheel spoke, called the king spoke, is not vertical, adjust the linkage between the helm and the rudder post (the rod that turns the rudder). Then mark the centered position by drawing a line under the tiller or wrapping a piece of tape around the king spoke. The mark should be clear so it can be seen or felt even at night.

Turn the helm until the rudder is angled 3° to one side. A large protractor held under the rudder will help here. Mark the tiller position or the top of the wheel with a different type of marking than the one you used when it was centered. Repeat this process on the other side. You now have 3° reference points for both tacks.

Control is often difficult when reaching under spinnaker but here, Dennis Conner's well-balanced *Stinger* carries only a few degrees of weather helm in her tiller. Easing the main sheet or the hydraulic boom vang would depower the mainsail in a gust. A staysail is set forward of the mast and a reaching strut (behind standing man) increases the after guy's leverage on the spinnaker pole.

Upwind Sailing Techniques

The main requirement for successful upwind sailing is concentration: the helmsman must focus his eyes on the behavior of the jib's telltales (always keeping the windward telltales barely lifting) while tuning his other senses to the feel of the helm and the angle of heel. Steering at a good narrow angle of attack to the wind isn't enough, for the boat must also be balanced. Try to keep the weather helm at about 3°. About 5° may not be too harmful for short periods of time, but 8° is always too much. Ease the traveler car down to cut your helm, and pull it back up to increase it.

If your boat is equipped with a speedometer, find the closest angle of attack that produces the best trade-off in speed. Usually this is about 40° to the true wind or about 35° to the apparent wind, although the optimum angle of attack varies from boat to boat. Very fast boats not limited by hull speed, like catamarans and planing dinghies, usually sail at wide angles of attack, as do relatively slow boats like heavy cruisers. Narrow keel boats like 12-

meters generally sail closest of all. The average centerboard daysailer or racer-cruiser should not be sailed too close to the wind. Remember that pinching slows a boat and can increase leeway.

In smooth water, keel boats should be sailed in a series of long scallops, at first heading off slightly (with the jib's windward telltales streaming aft) to foot and gain speed, then heading up 2° or 3° (with the telltales lifting) to use that momentum to climb to windward a little, and then, when the momentum is expended, footing off again.

In waves, all boats should be steered around breakers or especially large lumps whenever possible. You'll be able to point a little higher when sailing up the crest of a wave, since the decrease in boat speed effectively pulls the apparent wind aft. But when you accelerate down into the trough, there will be a header because the wind is pulled back forward.

When tacking in rough weather, always wait for a flat spot. Big waves tend to come in groups of three, so you

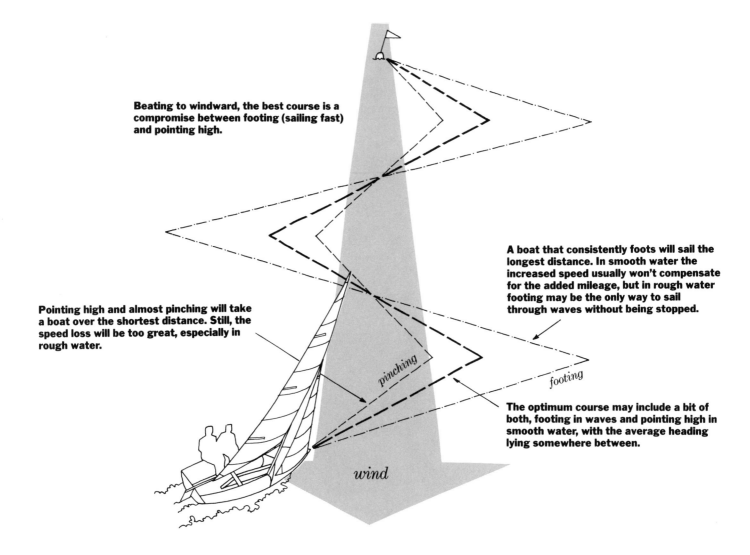

Beating to windward, the best course is a compromise between footing (sailing fast) and pointing high.

A boat that consistently foots will sail the longest distance. In smooth water the increased speed usually won't compensate for the added mileage, but in rough water footing may be the only way to sail through waves without being stopped.

Pointing high and almost pinching will take a boat over the shortest distance. Still, the speed loss will be too great, especially in rough water.

The optimum course may include a bit of both, footing in waves and pointing high in smooth water, with the average heading lying somewhere between.

pinching

footing

wind

Starboard Tack Header

Resist the temptation to pinch toward the destination even if it's just a few degrees upwind. The odds are that you'll be headed again.

Stay near the middle of the course — the rhumb line between your departure point and destination — so you'll be in a position to take advantage of every wind shift.

Direct Upwind Course

Port Tack Header

The favored tack is the one that takes you closest to your destination. If headed at least 5° for 30 seconds or more, tack if the other heading is favored.

The wind is always shifting and if you can take advantage of the shifts by tacking on headers you'll spend less time on windward legs.

can usually tack safely just after confronting a trio of waves.

Tacking on Headers

You'll sail a shorter, faster course if you always sail on the tack that aims you closest to your destination. This is easy when the wind is off to one side: sail one long leg and, if necessary, tack and sail a short leg when you're near the destination. Always sail the longest leg first. However, if the upwind destination is in or near the eye of the wind and neither tack seems to be favored, first sail on the tack that takes you into the most favorable current and the fewest obstructions. The chances are that the wind will shift and head you, forcing you to head off a few degrees. When you are headed, tack; the other tack will now take you closest to your destination. When you're headed again, tack again. Tack only on substantial shifts of 5° of more, and don't change course until you've sailed into the header for 30 seconds, or the tack will take you right out of it. By tacking on headers, you will always be sailing on the lifted, favored tack closest to the destination.

Downwind Sailing Techniques

Since a boat generally sails on a compass course or toward a buoy or landmark when on a reach or run, downwind sailing is usually less difficult than upwind sailing. Once the sails are trimmed right for the apparent wind, with the jib luff telltales just lifting and the mainsail barely luffing, the helmsman just grabs the tiller or wheel and aims. But downwind sailing can be as challenging as sailing close-hauled.

In drifting conditions or light air, a run or broad reach will be very slow because the wind is merely pushing on the sails. To increase speed between puffs, trim sheets and head up to a beam reach to get the wind flowing aerodynamically across the sails. As the boat accelerates, slowly head off. Keep the apparent wind just on the beam; when the boat slows and the apparent wind dies and starts to haul aft, head up and trim sheets again. This series of swoops will cover more distance than a straight-line broad-reaching or running course, but it will be much faster. "Head up in the

lulls and off in the puffs" is a good rule of thumb for light-air running and reaching.

To get to a destination directly downwind in light air, instead of sailing on a slow dead run, take a series of faster legs on a near-beam reach, jibing periodically. Because this course looks like a beat to windward, the tactic is called "tacking downwind." In moderate to fresh winds a dead run may be just as fast as a reach, so tacking downwind may actually take longer than sailing right toward your destination.

Many boats roll badly on windy dead runs because there is no force pushing one side of the hull down. When this happens, head up to a broad reach and trim the mainsail to increase lateral pressure and steady the boat.

In waves, try to get surfing by turning the transom square to the crest and then riding down the face. Centerboarders and some light keel boats will get planing with the assistance of waves and sometimes if the crew gives two or three hard tugs on the sheets (this is called "pumping the sheets").

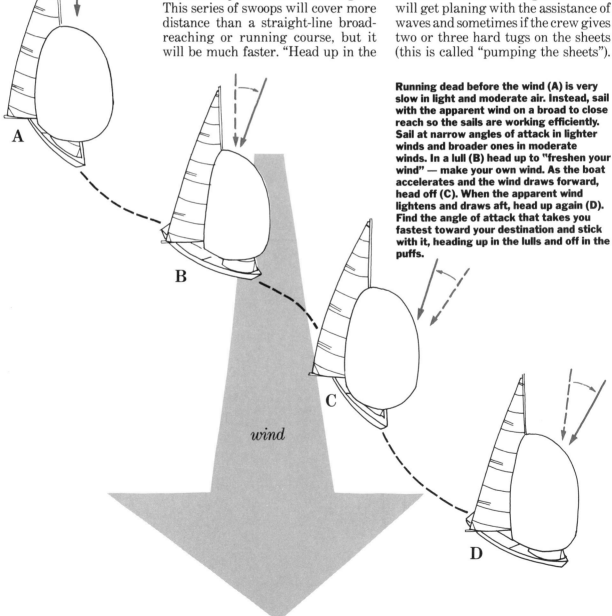

Running dead before the wind (A) is very slow in light and moderate air. Instead, sail with the apparent wind on a broad to close reach so the sails are working efficiently. Sail at narrow angles of attack in lighter winds and broader ones in moderate winds. In a lull (B) head up to "freshen your wind" — make your own wind. As the boat accelerates and the wind draws forward, head off (C). When the apparent wind lightens and draws aft, head up again (D). Find the angle of attack that takes you fastest toward your destination and stick with it, heading up in the lulls and off in the puffs.

A

B

C

wind

D

The apparent wind will quickly move forward as a boat accelerates on a surf or a plane, so be prepared either to head off or to trim the sheets.

When jibing in moderate winds and above, wait for a wave and then jibe as you surf down its face. With your increased speed, the apparent wind will decrease and the main boom will swing across with less force. Remember to head off slightly as the boom comes across in order to decrease the chances of capsize.

On a centerboarder, retract the board about one-third on a close reach, about one-half on a beam reach, about two-thirds on a broad reach, and almost all the way on a run — leaving just enough to provide some directional stability. In strong winds, retracting the board even more will decrease heeling on reaches, but leaving it down slightly more will increase directional stability on a run.

Jibing on Lifts

The principle that governs tacking on headers applies equally to course changes when running with the wind. If the wind lifts you at least 5°, instead of holding your course and easing sheets, jibe. The new course should be the one closest to your destination. By sailing the shortest course, you will reach your destination quicker.

Running Wing-and-Wing

The jib isn't much use in its normal position on a run or a broad reach because it's blanketed by the mainsail.

With her boom vang tight, centerboard half-way up, and skipper hiking hard as he steers down a wave, this Laser is broad-reaching very fast.

But you can catch the wind with it by setting it wing-and-wing. Pull it to windward and let it billow out, either by holding the sheet with your hand or, more permanently, by supporting it with a spinnaker pole rigged out from the mast. Lead the jib sheet through the end of the pole and, with the topping lift, adjust the pole height so the jib's leech is fairly straight. The sheet must be led outside the shrouds to a block fairly far aft. This sail trim can be used on broad reaches as well as runs.

Many long-distance cruising boats carry jibs hung on both sides with the mainsail doused. The equal pull of the two jibs tends to keep the boat from rolling very badly, and there is very little chafe.

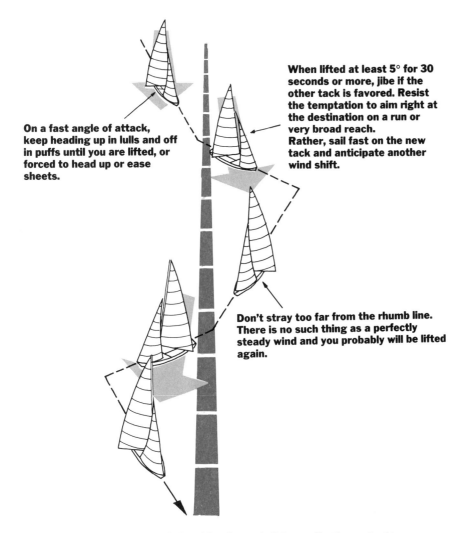

On a fast angle of attack, keep heading up in lulls and off in puffs until you are lifted, or forced to head up or ease sheets.

When lifted at least 5° for 30 seconds or more, jibe if the other tack is favored. Resist the temptation to aim right at the destination on a run or very broad reach.
Rather, sail fast on the new tack and anticipate another wind shift.

Don't stray too far from the rhumb line. There is no such thing as a perfectly steady wind and you probably will be lifted again.

Off the wind, jibing on lifts (also called tacking downwind) is as effective as tacking on headers upwind. Again the idea is to sail as fast as possible on the course that takes you closest to the destination.

The Spinnaker

The spinnaker is a big full, light-weight sail set on downwind legs to increase sail area and speed. Usually considered a racing sail, it can nonetheless be extremely useful if handled carefully aboard cruising boats and daysailers. This sail looks very different from the working sails — the mainsail and jib. First off, it is symmetrical; it has a foot and two equilength leeches. And it is made of extremely light cloth — sometimes as light as ½ ounce. Nylon is used in spinnakers because it is more stretchy, and therefore more resistant to rips, than Dacron.

A spinnaker may be larger than the mainsail and jib combined, and because of this and because it's attached to the boat at only three points (instead of along a spar or stay), it must be set, carried, and doused with care. The crew must be particularly cautious about allowing it to fill before it's hoisted all the way and while it's being doused. For these two reasons the spinnaker should be hoisted and doused in the blanketing zone of the mainsail or jib.

Spinnaker Gear

Equipment used to handle spinnakers includes a halyard led through a block just above the jib halyard, a sheet led to each clew through blocks aft on the deck, and a spar called the spinnaker pole, which is secured at one end to the mast and at the other end to the windward clew (called the tack). The spinnaker pole is held up by the topping lift running down from the mast, and kept from rising by the fore guy running up from the deck (the fore guy is sometimes called the pole downhaul). The sheet led to the pole is called the after guy; the other sheet is simply called the spinnaker sheet. All these lines are secured to the sail and the pole with snap shackles.

Preparing the Spinnaker

Before setting, the spinnaker is bunched in a container, which might be a sail bag, a sack, or a plastic bucket. First the crew locates the head and

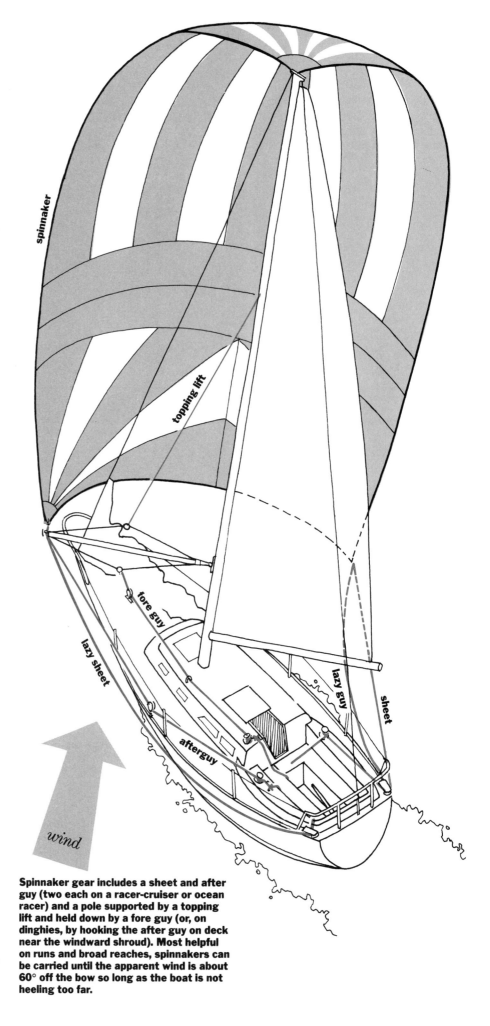

Spinnaker gear includes a sheet and after guy (two each on a racer-cruiser or ocean racer) and a pole supported by a topping lift and held down by a fore guy (or, on dinghies, by hooking the after guy on deck near the windward shroud). Most helpful on runs and broad reaches, spinnakers can be carried until the apparent wind is about 60° off the bow so long as the boat is not heeling too far.

Rig the pole with the after guy led through the outboard fitting and pull the tack to the headstay. Hoist a big spinnaker behind the jib to keep it from filling prematurely. Assign a crewmember to the fore guy to keep the pole from skying up after the sail fills.

then, with their hands, runs down the two leeches to make sure they aren't tangled. The middle of the sail is then stuffed into the container and the three corners are left exposed. To keep it from filling prematurely, the spinnaker may be bunched every few feet by rubber bands or light twine. Before setting the spinnaker, the container is secured to the leeward side — on a racer-cruiser, along the lifelines; on a small racing boat, near the leeward

shrouds. The container should be snapped to a fitting with its own special snap shackle to keep it from lifting while the halyard is pulled up.

Then the spinnaker pole is hooked onto the mast with the outboard end "cup-up" — so that a line can be inserted in its fitting from the top down. The topping lift and fore guy are clipped on. Finally, the pole is lifted to windward of the headstay until it is perpendicular to the mast at an appropriate height. On small boats this height is determined by the fixed fitting on the inboard end. But on larger boats the inboard end slides up and down on the mast, and predicting how high the pole should be may be difficult. Only experience will tell.

Hook on the sheets and halyard and make sure they run fair from the spinnaker container to their blocks. The after guy is led around the headstay, and after being snapped to the tack, it is dropped into the outboard end of the pole. The sheet runs straight aft from the container. Check for tangles around life lines, jib sheets, and fittings.

Only when you are about to hoist the spinnaker should you hook the halyard into the head. Check aloft for snarls.

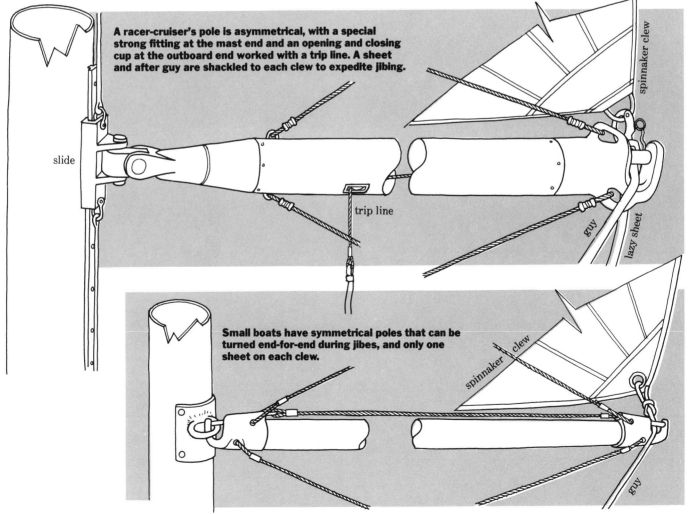

A racer-cruiser's pole is asymmetrical, with a special strong fitting at the mast end and an opening and closing cup at the outboard end worked with a trip line. A sheet and after guy are shackled to each clew to expedite jibing.

slide

trip line

spinnaker clew

guy

lazy sheet

Small boats have symmetrical poles that can be turned end-for-end during jibes, and only one sheet on each clew.

spinnaker clew

guy

The Spinnaker

Setting the Spinnaker

On your first few sets, sail on a broad reach in light to moderate winds. Later, once you've gained your confidence, move on to sets on a beam reach (where the loads are higher) or on a run (where the chances of the sail's tangling in the standing rigging are greater).

The crew should first "talk through" the set by taking responsibilities. One crew member each should be on the halyard, the sheet, the after guy, and the fore guy. On small boats the sailors may have to take several jobs each. On big boats you may need more than one person for jobs requiring a lot of hauling, such as the halyard and the after guy, and you may also need a person forward to help pull the spinnaker out of its container. The helmsman should be left as free as possible to concentrate solely on steering. If the helm is not tended carefully, the boat may broach (round up) in the middle of a spinnaker set and cause frightful problems as the big sail flies out of control.

The sail *must* be hauled up to leeward of the mainsail or jib. Once the helmsman gives the command to hoist, the halyard is pulled smartly while the sheet and guy are trimmed about 3 feet in order to spread the leeches away from each other. When the spinnaker halyard is two-blocked (hoisted all the way), the halyard man yells "Hoisted." Then the crew trims the after guy. When the tack reaches the pole end, it pulls the pole back until stopped by the fore guy. Trimming the after guy is called "squaring the pole." *The fore guy must be taut during the set.* Otherwise, when the sail fills, the pole will sky (lift) and the spinnaker will go out of control and cause a broach. The pole is squared until it is at about a right angle to the apparent wind — this is where a telltale on the shroud or a masthead fly is a great help.

Meanwhile the spinnaker sheet is trimmed or eased to get the sail full, while the halyard is coiled neatly. The sheet is then played (trimmed and eased) as the trimmer looks at the sail's luff (edge above the pole). When the

Partially trim the guy and sheet to spread the leeches as the sail is hoisted. When the spinnaker is two blocked (hoisted all the way) square the pole (pull it aft) and trim the sheet. Keep the jib well eased so it doesn't suck wind out of the spinnaker, and lower it after the set. Here, the windward jib sheet is led over the pole and topping lift so the boat can be quickly tacked when the pole is dropped on deck after the spinnaker is doused.

luff curls badly, it is light and the sheet is trimmed. Ideally there should be a slight curl or twitch in the luff.

On dinghies and other boats with small jibs, the jib may usually be left up when the spinnaker is carried, but overlapping jibs should be doused and secured to the deck with sail ties. If you leave the jib set, undertrim it (trim it less than optimum), with the luff telltales standing straight up. Otherwise the sail may suck air out of the spinnaker and make it collapse. Ocean racing boats carry special downwind jibs called staysails under the spinnakers.

Pole Height

The location of the curl or twitch is a guide for determining optimum pole height. The curl should appear first at the shoulder, just above the widest point. If it starts lower, the pole is too high; if it starts higher, the pole is too low. Another helpful guide is the relative height of the clews, which should be at the same level.

Whenever you adjust the height of

the outboard end, if possible also adjust the inboard end so the pole is perpendicular to the mast. This guarantees that the tack is extended as far as possible from the mast.

Trimming Hints

As you play the spinnaker, try to picture its chord — the imaginary straight line between the leeches. The chord should be at right angles to the apparent wind in order to maximize forward drive.

On a beam or close reach, let the pole forward until it's almost touching the headstay. If it touches the stay, the pole may be thrown out of column and break.

Undertrimming the spinnaker sheet will cause a collapse starting at the luff. To get it full again, trim the sheet. Overtrimming the spinnaker, on the other hand, will pull the leech way around to leeward and magnify the wind's side force to increase heeling and perhaps cause a broach. You can guard against overtrimming by keeping the spinnaker luff just curling or

twitching. Remember to keep the pole about square to the apparent wind.

The trimmer and the helmsman must communicate with each other while the spinnaker is up. In moderate winds and above, the spinnaker controls the boat's progress and heading, and if the helmsman senses that the boat is about to broach he must tell the trimmer to ease the sheet and let the sail luff. The sheet may be overtrimmed, causing weather helm. The helm should be as neutral as possible; most often, there's slight weather helm that can quickly develop into uncontrollable weather helm and a broach.

In light winds, the sheet and guy may be cleated and the helmsman can "steer the spinnaker full" by sailing by the sail's luff, much as he steers on a close-hauled course.

With its clews level and the pole squared just right, *High Roler*'s spinnaker not only looks beautiful but is pulling hard too. If the spinnaker sheet were led over the boom the leech would be too slack.

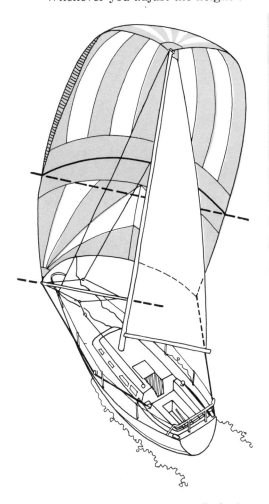

The pole should be about perpendicular to the apparent wind, as should the chord running between the two leeches so most of the sail's force is forward. Adjust the pole height until the luff curls first near its shoulder.

95

The Spinnaker

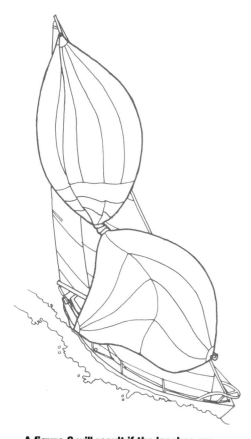

A figure-8 will result if the leeches are twisted while the spinnaker is being packed or if the clews are not spread during the hoist.

Spinnaker Problems

Most problems with the spinnaker are caused by letting the fore guy loose. The pole must be held down at all times. Of course the fore guy has to be eased when the pole is being squared with the after guy, but a crew member must let it run out through his hands slowly and be ready to pull it down hard.

Sometimes the spinnaker goes up in a figure-8, with a twist in its middle, because it was packed wrong. If this happens on a small boat, pull down and back on the leeward leech and the twist may come out. This trick can work with a large spinnaker in light air, but in moderate winds and above it's safer to pull the spinnaker right down as soon as you see the twist, untangle it, and haul it back up again. A twist may also result when the spinnaker sheet is let loose during the set. There should be just enough strain on the sheet and guy to spread the leeches while the sail is hoisted — but not so much that the sail fills before it's two-blocked.

On a run or broad reach in fresh and strong winds, the spinnaker may oscillate wildly and cause the boat to roll. Steady it by choking it down: trim the sheet way forward through a block near the leeward shrouds, and lower and oversquare the pole slightly as you trim the sheet to keep the sail from collapsing. The wide, flat, stable surface presented by the sail should stop the rolling.

Jibing the Spinnaker

You'll have to jibe the spinnaker as well as the mainsail when tacking downwind or making large course alterations, like rounding a buoy. Jibing a spinnaker means that you move the spinnaker pole from one side to the other. The procedure is different on small and big boats.

On small boats like dinghies and daysailers the spinnaker pole is double-ended: both ends have the same fittings. The topping lift and fore guy are led to the middle of the pole, allowing it to be jibed end-for-end. Unhook the inboard end from the mast and hook it

To jibe the spinnaker on a small boat like this Lightning, unclip the pole from the mast and the after guy, then clip it to the sheet and the mast. Keep the sail full; if it collapses it may wrap around the headstay.

on the sheet to leeward, which is now the new guy. Then unhook the other end from the old guy and secure it to the mast. This may be done before, while, or after the mainsail is jibed. During the spinnaker jibe, another crew member plays the sheets to keep the sail pulling and the skipper steers slowly through the jibe, keeping the spinnaker balanced over the bow like a seal juggling a ball.

The jibe is more complicated on larger boats because the spinnaker poles are asymmetrical. The strains imposed by very big spinnakers are so great that the poles must be secured to the mast with special fittings that do not accept the after guy. Therefore the pole changes sides by having its outboard end dropped, dipped, and swung through the foretriangle. The topping lift and fore guy lead to the outboard end.

These spinnakers require an extra set of sheets on each clew. Between jibes, only one sheet is under strain; the other is lazy (unused) until the jibe. These are the steps of a twin-sheet, dip-pole jibe:

One crew member takes the slack leeward sheet forward to the bow. Because this will be the new guy, it's called the lazy guy. The outboard end of the spinnaker pole is opened by pulling a trigger (with a line led through the pole), allowing the old guy to float up and out (this is why the pole is arranged cup-up). A crew member eases the topping lift to lower the pole to the foredeck crew. When the outboard end reaches the foredeck crew, he clips the new guy (the old lazy guy) into the fitting, which he then closes. As the pole swings to the new windward side and is raised with the topping lift, a crew member aft trims the new guy. When the pole fitting comes up snug against the sail's clew, the old sheet is released. Presto! The spinnaker has been jibed under perfect control.

The dip-pole jibe can be performed without twin guys, but only in light wind. After the pole is dropped from the old guy, a crew member pulls the new guy (under strain) down to the foredeck where it is wrestled into the pole fitting.

What do you do with the mainsail during a spinnaker jibe? In small boats it will swing across as it is trimmed and eased by the helmsman. On larger boats the helmsman will have his hands full with the tiller or wheel, keeping her under control as her stern swings slowly through the wind. One crew member may be delegated to trim and ease the main sheet through the jibe, or if you're shorthanded you can trim the mainsail amidships before the jibe, leave it there while the spinnaker pole is dipped and reconnected, and then ease the sheet out after the jibe. Never allow the main boom to swing across out of control — a fractured skull or a broken mast may result — and don't head up drastically on the new course until the crew is ready to trim both the mainsail and the spinnaker. If you swing up fast with the sails trimmed too tightly, you may be knocked right over on your side and round up in a sudden broach.

In heavy weather, many larger boats are jibed with two spinnaker poles, running out a new pole on the new side and clipping it up to the lazy guy before the jibe, and then removing the old pole after the jibe, thereby providing excellent control on both sides of the sail. This twin-pole system requires two sets of topping lifts and fore guys.

On a large boat with a twin-guy system, the pole is dipped during the jibe after being unclipped from the after guy. Clip it to the lazy guy on the new side and raise the topping lift. The mainsail on this boat, skippered by Ted Turner (in the cap), is allowed to swing across freely since the wind is light.

The Spinnaker

Dousing the Spinnaker

Plan the spinnaker douse as carefully as you did the hoist, with a crew member assigned to each task. Although the sail will almost always be pulled down behind the mainsail, there are exceptions.

On a small boat, raise the jib (if necessary) and trim it properly for the course. One crew member then moves to leeward and grabs the sheet as another frees the after guy, which runs out through the pole fitting. The sheet and leech are pulled in behind the mainsail, and as the halyard is eased quickly but under control, into the cockpit. Afterward the pole is removed and the lines and spinnaker are neatened up.

Alternatively, in a race the spinnaker may be doused to windward. After trimming the jib, remove and stow the pole. Then pull back on the after guy as the halyard is eased off and haul the spinnaker into the cockpit on the windward side. The main advantage of this system is that nobody has to go to leeward, so heel can be controlled.

On larger boats, hoist and trim the jib and then lower the pole until the outboard end can be reached from deck. The foredeck crew trips (opens) the after guy's shackle, and as the spinnaker blows behind the jib, one or more crew members gather the leeward leech behind the mainsail or jib. They can let the freed leech fly to leeward because, without a sheet, it won't fill. Only when they have complete control over the sail is the halyard eased slowly and the spinnaker brought down on deck. Don't try to douse the spinnaker if it's filled aloft. Once the sail is below, lower and stow the spinnaker pole on deck.

When the after guy is tripped, the pole will snap back violently as the guy rebounds from stretch. The foredeck crew therefore should stand to leeward of the pole when he trips.

A big-boat spinnaker can be doused like a small boat's by letting the after guy run out through the pole end, but the considerable friction of sheet against pole may well allow the sail to fill far out to leeward of the jib's blanketing zone. Just in case you must douse this way, be sure not to tie knots in the ends of the spinnaker sheets and guys. But don't use this system on a large boat unless you are forced to douse extremely quickly, or unless the crew cannot reach the pole end from the foredeck.

The spinnaker may also be doused using a special light retrieving line that leads down to the deck from its middle. During a retrieving-line douse, the spinnaker sheet is trimmed hard and the jib is overtrimmed until it sucks so much air out of the spinnaker that the light sail collapses. Then the halyard is let go completely as the retrieving line is pulled in. Instead of dropping into the water, the sail will fly out like a sheet on a laundry line. The guy isn't touched until the sail is completely on deck. Used primarily on ocean-racing boats, the retrieving-line douse works best on a reach and is least effective on a run.

Some big racing boats douse spinnakers to windward on a run, much as we described earlier for small boats. Be careful to keep the sail well away from spreaders during this and any other douse, for the sail may rip.

Special Spinnakers

Racing boats have several spinnakers of different shapes and cloth weights for specialized conditions, carrying ½-ounce big, full spinnakers in light air and 2-ounce small, flat ones in strong winds. In addition, cruising boats sometimes carry a special type of asymmetrical spinnaker that, instead of being set from a pole, is tacked down near the stem like a jib and trimmed with a normal spinnaker sheet. While it doesn't project as much area as a regular spinnaker, this sail has one important plus for shorthanded cruising crews: they needn't rig the complicated, and sometimes dangerous, spinnaker pole. A sail called a blooper, looking much like the cruising spinnaker, may be carried when racing, along with a big spinnaker on a pole.

Dousing the spinnaker behind the mainsail or jib keeps it from filling (left and left below). Don't worry if it gets a little wet, but avoid catching a clew in the water. (Below) If you can't douse the spinnaker immediately, just let the after guy out all the way (this is why you don't tie knots in spinnaker sheets) and allow the sail to flag to leeward. This crew should trim the sheet tighter so the sail is right under the mainsail.

Sail Care and Repair

Modern hard-finish sailcloth will lose its resistance to stretch if it's heavily creased, so carefully furl or fold your sails after each use. To fold a jib, stretch its foot out on the foredeck, pier, or ground, and with one person at each end, make 2- to 3-foot flakes. Then take three or four folds toward the luff and insert the sail in the bag with the tack clearly visible on top. Heavily resinated Dacron or Mylar jibs may be too stiff to be placed in a sailbag, so they are zippered-up into long sausage-shaped "turtles" after the initial folding.

The two main causes of sail damage are the sun's ultraviolet rays and chafe. To protect against the former, which eventually will destroy stitching, always cover or bag the sails when they're not hoisted. A roller-furled jib should have a dark bolt of cloth down its leech to cover the rest of the sail when it's rolled up. When the dark cloth becomes worn, it can readily be replaced by the sailmaker at a fraction of the cost of a whole new sail.

Chafe is most likely where the sail bears against the standing rigging. When the mainsail is eased all the way out on a run and the boom vang is not tight, its belly rubs against the leeward spreader and shrouds. Genoa jibs are likely to rip if they are trimmed too hard against the tip of the leeward spreaders. Reinforcements called spreader patches must be sewn or taped on the sails at the point of chafe; the sailmaker usually delays installing spreader patches until the sail has been set and he's been told exactly where they should go. The stanchions supporting the lifelines may also puncture a jib. Nylon, which is stronger and stretchier than Dacron, chafes through very rarely, but a nylon spinnaker can be ripped on a fitting.

Small rips and punctures in sails can be repaired with tape. Lightweight Rip-Stop tape is used on spinnakers and Mylar jibs, and silver duct tape works fine on Dacron. Stretch the sail over a flat surface and press the tape down hard. Use enough tape to extend several inches beyond the rip.

Carry with you a sailmaker's sewing kit consisting of special needles and twine, and a palm — a small glove with a hard center used to shove needles through cloth (or line, if you're whipping an end or sewing a sail back onto a boltrope). Using this equipment you can sew a Dacron or tape patch over a large rip or sew up a ripped seam. A simple over-and-under stitch works best, six stitches per inch and taken quite loosely, since the sail will stretch around your seam once it fills. Patches should extend at least 1½ inches beyond the rip.

If you sail on salt water, give your sails a thorough hosing off with fresh water every now and then. While they won't damage the sail's integrity, salt crystals absorb moisture, which increases the sail's weight and may lead to mildew. *Never* wash your sails in automatic clothes washers, dry them in dryers, or iron them. The tumbling and heat will take the life out of them.

Sails that have been used for more than 50 hours should receive an annual checkup at the sailmaker's loft. There, any necessary repairs will be done by professionals and the sails will be carefully washed.

Battens can break when sails luff violently in heavy weather, and their sharp ends may cut through the sail. Keep luffing down to a minimum and carry a spare set of battens.

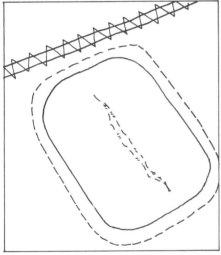

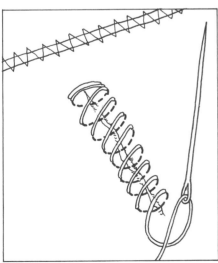

Tape over sail rips using a large overlap (top) and sew broken seams with a loose over-and-under stitch (above).

Keeping battens parallel to creases, fold mainsails and jibs in large flakes and stow them in sailbags. Long sausage-shaped bags work best, but you can also use large sack-type or (for small sails) briefcase-type ones. Extremely stiff sails should be rolled tightly and stowed in cloth tubes.

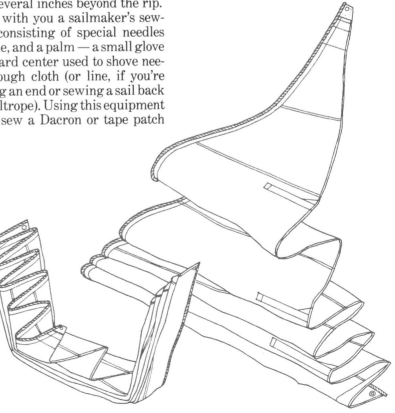

Furling Systems

the wind usually is strong, the sail will be relatively small; in a light-air area, it will be fairly large. Jibs can be changed on some furlers, but when the sail comes down and its luff pulls out of the rod, be sure it doesn't fill with wind and get away from you.

When a roller-furler misbehaves, there can be big trouble because the sail probably will jam in a partly unrolled condition. Repairing the system or lowering the sail could be very diffi-

Roller-furling jibs provide great convenience but, because they can be tricky to change, should be handled with care. The sail should be cut specifically for the furler, the boat, and the average local conditions.

Hardware manufacturers and sail-makers have developed ingenious ways of taking much of the burden out of setting sails and putting them away.

The Roller-Furler

The roller-furler is most often used on jibs, but some mainsails have it, too. The main item in this piece of gear is a stay, rod, or tube rigged to support the luff of the jib or mainsail. It is attached to the mast, deck, and/or boom with swivels at both ends, and it is rotated by a line led to the cockpit. For a jib, the furler replaces (or sits over) the headstay or forestay. For the mainsail, it is positioned on or in the after side of the mast. The sail's luff rope is inserted into a groove in the rod and the sail is hoisted by the halyard (on less expensive systems, the halyard is built into the furler).

To set the sail, uncleat the control line and trim the sheet. The sail will unroll. To furl it, ease the sheet until the sail luffs and pull the control line. The rod rotates and the sail rolls up around it. Keep pulling the line until the sail is completely rolled up pretty tight with a couple of wraps of sheet around it. All this work is done in the cockpit, so there is no reason to go onto the foredeck to set or lower sails.

Sails designed to be used on roller-furlers should be cut more flat than normal sails. The flat shape makes them versatile in a wide range of winds. While a sail can be reefed by partially rolling it up, it will be baggy unless there is a system for taking in the relatively full middle faster than the relatively flat head and foot. This is why some sailmakers sew foam pads into the luff at the middle. As the sail is reefed, the sheet's lead block must be moved forward.

Do not expect a roller-furler system to work equally well across your entire sail inventory. The jib on the roller-furler should be the sail that you would most often carry in your sailing area's average conditions. In an area where

(Left) The swivels on deck and aloft must be carefully aligned. If the control line is flattened out, the system may be malfunctioning. (Below left and below) A roller-furler in the mast or boom will get rid of large mainsails without risk of injury to an on-deck crewmember from a swinging boom.

cult. The typical jam-up is caused by the halyard's twisting around the stay or rod because the sail is hoisted too far and the upper swivel cannot turn. The sail's luff should be exactly the correct length for the system and the halyard should not be pulled too high.

If the system jams, resist the temptation to put the control line on a winch to try to grind the jam out. That could seriously damage the system. The best response is to lower the halyard slightly and start rolling again while a crew member looks at the head and halyard through binoculars. Reliable indicators that the system isn't working right are a frayed halyard, wear on the swivels, jerky rolling, and a control line that has flattened out due to excessive loads.

Mainsail Furlers

While roller-furlers have been installed on many mainsails, the price that must be paid is that the sail can't have battens, which means that the leech must be hollowed out with a resulting loss of sail area.

There have been some ingenious ideas for semi-automatic mainsail furling without the use of roller devices. Most of these systems are based on old-fashioned lazy jacks. Lazy jacks are two sets of lines, one on either side of the sail, that run from about half-way up the mast to the middle of the boom. As the sail drops, the lazy jacks automatically guide it onto the top of the boom and cradle it there. The job is neater if the mainsail has full-length battens running from luff to leech. When

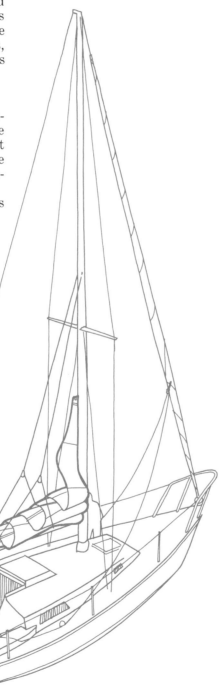

Lazy jacks provide a simple, time-tested way to control a doused mainsail. Carefully position the lines' attachments and adjust the tension so the sail is under control as it drops. The job is neater if the sail has full-length battens.

hoisting the sail, be sure to avoid fouling its head and battens in the lazy jacks.

There also are some patented mainsail furling systems that use more complicated developments of lazy jacks. They rely on additional gear on the boom and sail to guide the mainsail into a neat package as it drops.

Spinnaker Furlers

Spinnakers can get out of control if they fill with wind while being set or doused. That's why a spinnaker should be raised and lowered in the blanketed area behind the mainsail and jib. But that's not always possible, and experienced sailors often set the spinnaker in stops, which are rubber bands or lengths of light string bundled around the sail every couple of feet. Once the sail is hoisted all the way, the sheet and guy are pulled to break the stops, and the sail opens its leeches to the wind.

There is no way to re-stop the spinnaker before lowering it. However, there are devices that keep the spinnaker rolled up as it is hoisted and then roll it up before dousing. One of these devices is a long sock with a zipper, which is opened when setting and pulled shut over the sail when lowering. Another is a series of plastic or wooden rings around the sail and connected to each other with a long continuous line reaching down to the deck. After the spinnaker is hoisted, pull the rings up to the head to free the sail. When dousing, pull the rings down over the spinnaker to roll it up.

Chapter 4
Weather

"Weather" means something more to sailors than it does to landspeople. It's not simply the day's local temperature, visibility, and precipitation, but a process. In the Northern Hemisphere, packets of warm and cool air flow from West to East, driven by huge whirlpools of wind located over the centers of the oceans and pulled along by the earth's spin. Within and around each air packet, weather is reasonably predictable. Accurate weather forecasting requires more than a memory of the morning's or previous evening's conditions. Among the factors that forecasters and mariners consider are local geography (which can funnel air packets and change wind direction), the season (for weather follows seasonal cycles), the time of day (winds generally shift as the land heats up in the afternoon), weather patterns stretching hundreds of miles both to the West and to the East (for tomorrow's weather is partially a product of yesterday's), and most important of all, the wind direction and barometer reading (which indicate where and when the next air packet will arrive). As Rear Admiral William J. Kotsch writes in his excellent book, *Weather for the Mariner*, "Air, moisture, and heat — these are the basic ingredients of earth's weather."

When describing winds, we use the direction *from* which they come. Therefore, a "Westerly" is a wind blowing from the West.

As it does in most sailing areas, the afternoon sea breeze dominates San Francisco Bay's summer weather pattern. By mid-afternoon the wind pouring through the Golden Gate (opposite) reaches Force 6 (22-27 knots) and the sky is clear. A fog bank (below) heralds the late afternoon cooling of the land and the death of the sea breeze.

The Daily Weather Cycle

Before looking at storms and large-scale weather, let's see how local conditions can affect wind and visibility. Our example is a typical summer day at San Francisco, California, but the forces that affect weather over that cool, windy city apply almost everywhere else where a harbor fronts on an ocean or a large lake. In some other places the wind blows from the East, contrary to the general flow of weather; in still other places it may blow from the South. In few places does the wind blow as hard as it does in San Francisco Bay, where almost every summer afternoon is swept by a cool,

wet Southwesterly whistling through the Golden Gate at 25 knots.

But the afternoon Southwesterly is simply one act in San Francisco Bay's daily summer drama. At dawn the bay is overcast, calm, and foggy. What wind there is comes from the South Southwest (202°). By late morning the sky has started to clear and the breeze begins to pick up a bit as it veers (shifts clockwise) toward Southwest (225°). By 2 P.M. the sky is blue and the wind is whipping up steep, short waves. By 4 P.M. it may be blowing 30 knots, but an hour or so later the sun dropping beyond the Golden Gate becomes hazy behind great balls of cottony fog rolling in from the Pacific, and the wind fades in velocity as it sharpens in chill. At sunset, all that remains of the afternoon wind is a jumble of leftover waves harmlessly spurting over and around each other. As the wind dies, it backs (shifts counterclockwise) into the South Southwest. It has followed the sun all day by veering; now that the sun has set, it returns to its night direction. By midnight only a

light wind wafts through the bay's fogbanks.

The weather changes on San Francisco Bay follow universally applicable principles. First, the Westerly component to the wind is due to massive geographical and atmospheric conditions. Sitting about 900 miles out in the Pacific is a mountain of cool air called the Pacific high, or high-pressure system. This is one of a series of highs lying in a belt North of the Equator (another belt of highs lies South of the Equator). This air is relatively stable and dense because it sits above a huge expanse of relatively cool water whose temperature changes very little during the day. On the other hand, air over land is both warm and unstable because the earth under it changes temperature rapidly.

Now, warm air tends to expand and become less dense than cool air. Another way to say this is that a given volume of cool air weighs more than an equal volume of warm air. And yet *another* way to explain the difference is that areas of cool air have relatively high atmospheric pressure, compared with areas of warm air. As you know, atmospheric pressure is measured on a barometer. A barometer in the middle of the Pacific high (or Atlantic high, in mid-Atlantic Ocean) may read 30.5 inches (or 1034 millibars), while one toward the edge of the high, nearer land, may read as low as 30.0 inches (1016 millibars). On weather maps these pressure levels are shown as lines, much the same way that elevations are shown on contour maps. These are lines of equal atmospheric pressure in inches or millibars, and are called isobars.

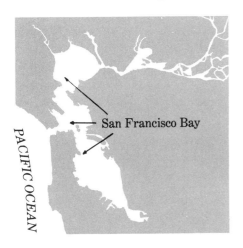

PACIFIC OCEAN

San Francisco Bay

(Left) Fronting on the Pacific, San Francisco Bay is a good example of a sailing area whose winds are governed by the daily cycle of changing land, sea, and air temperatures.

The Prevailing Southwest Wind

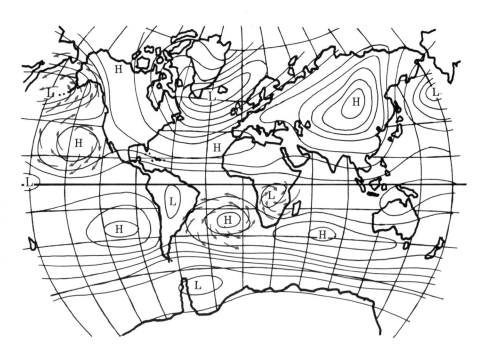

Like water flowing down a hill, air rushes from the peaks of the high-pressure "mountains" over the cool oceans to the low-pressure "valleys." This rushing air is wind, and the greater the difference between atmospheric pressures, the steeper the slope and the harder the wind will blow. Thus there is a natural tendency for wind to blow from the Pacific high toward land, like California. But the wind does not blow directly from the peak of the high toward land because it is curved by the atmospheric effects of the earth's spin. This curving tendency, called the coriolis effect, pulls

Air flows down the slopes between high-pressure "mountains" and low-pressure "valleys" in great swirling patterns. In the Northern Hemisphere, air circulates clockwise and outward from a high and counter-clockwise and inward to a low. South of the Equator the directions are reversed.

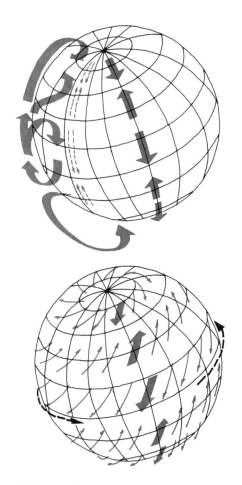

If the earth were stationary, cold dense air would flow directly from the poles to the great low-pressure "valley" at the Equator. But the earth's spin and the resulting coriolis effect redirects flow to the right in the Northern Hemisphere and creates vortexes of moving air.

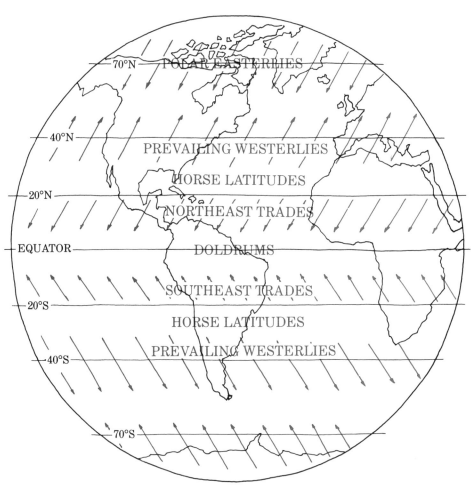

The vortexes of air are distributed in belts, and the flow between belts of highs and lows is remarkably predictable. Between the belts of prevailing (or trade) winds lie belts of calm called doldrums. The patterns change seasonally and during temporary fluctuations in land and sea temperatures.

104

the wind to the right in the Northern Hemisphere. A high, then, behaves like a great pinwheel throwing wind out to the right as it rotates clockwise. South of the high, the prevailing (normal) wind will blow from the North and East. North of the high, the wind will prevail from the South and West.

Now the belt of highs girds the globe at approximately 30° North latitude, which passes through northern Florida. Sometimes the highs are farther North, sometimes they're farther South. But almost all the time, most of North America lies above the belt of highs. That's why Southwesterlies usually blow across North America. Later we'll see how other factors may cause the wind to shift into the North or East.

Low-pressure air packets, or lows, work opposite to highs. Where highs spin air outward in a clockwise direction, lows pull in air in a counterclockwise direction as wind follows its curved downhill course across the isobars. When they're tangent, winds around a high and a low spin much like two interlocking gears.

How Geography Affects Prevailing Winds

When the Pacific high's prevailing winds finally reach San Francisco, they are Westerlies, but the land deflects them into the South Southwest. Early in the morning, before the sun has been up sufficiently long to warm the land, this wind brings cold, damp

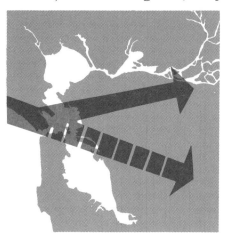

air off the ocean into the bay and city. Across the bay in Marin County, where there is a larger landmass than on the peninsula, the land and air heat more quickly than in the city and the sky is relatively clear. But over in the city, people make their way to work in a clammy, gray morning. Ten miles out to sea at the barren Farralone Islands there is little landmass to moderate and back the wind. There a fresh Westerly may be blowing at 20 knots.

When wind blows onto a shore like the San Francisco peninsula at an acute angle, it is deflected so it hits land at a right angle. If it blows at a shallow angle, it is deflected until it is parallel to the shoreline.

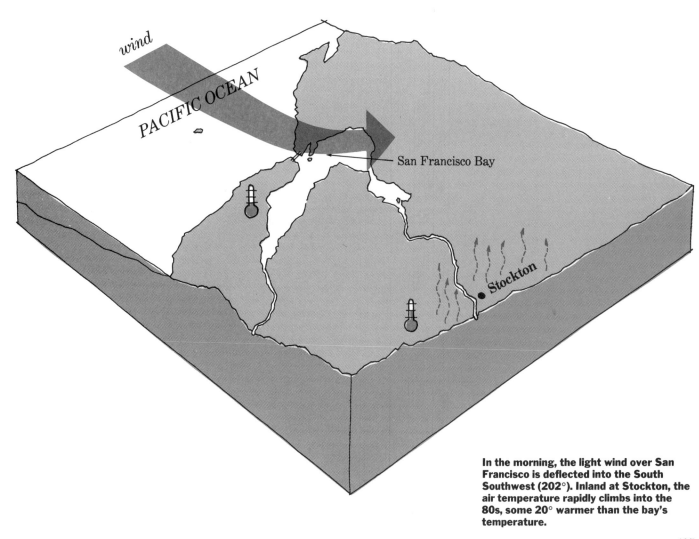

In the morning, the light wind over San Francisco is deflected into the South Southwest (202°). Inland at Stockton, the air temperature rapidly climbs into the 80s, some 20° warmer than the bay's temperature.

The Thermal Effect, or Sea Breeze

Meanwhile, the star of the San Francisco weather drama is just getting out of bed. Some 50 miles inland from the bay, the dry semidesert of the San Joaquin River Valley is beginning to heat up under the morning sun. The night before, the temperature at Stockton, the major city in the valley, may have dropped into the 60s as the land cooled under a cloudless sky. Now Stockton's temperature is quickly climbing; by noon it's in the high 80s, 10-20° higher than the air and water temperature over at San Francisco. This hot dry air expands and rises like a thermal mushroom cloud to create a local low-pressure system that literally sucks in the denser, cooler air over the bay and the ocean. The valley sucks in air like a great vacuum cleaner, and tumbling down the intake hose that is the steep gradient between the two pressure systems come the cool, dense air particles of the Pacific high. As the temperature rises at Stockton, the wind increases on the bay until it rushes through the Golden Gate at over 20 knots. As the wind

builds, it veers into the Southwest, since the intake of the thermal vacuum cleaner has moderated the land's effect. The sun gradually breaks through the cloud cover, and by 2 P.M. the bay is a glory of sparkling white caps. In late afternoon the San Joaquin Valley starts to cool and the air over it settles. With its mainspring winding down, the great San Francisco Bay wind machine begins to slow. The wind dies as the air cools, and by sunset the breeze is less than 12 knots and gradually backing into the South Southwest as the fog rolls back into the bay from the Pacific. By midnight the city is damp and still, the silence broken only by foghorns.

Especially dramatic on San Francisco Bay, this diurnal three-act play is acted out throughout the world wherever warm land fronts on a large body of water. When hot air rises, cool air is sucked in under it. This is called a sea breeze or lake breeze, an onshore wind created by the temperature differential between water and land. The larger the difference (up to a point),

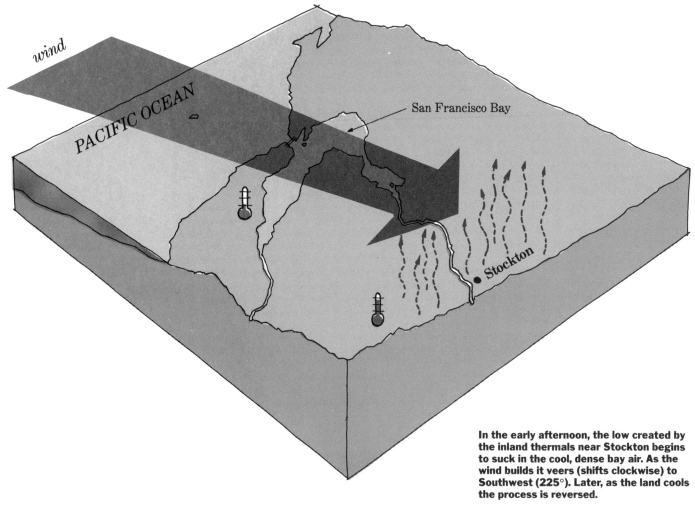

In the early afternoon, the low created by the inland thermals near Stockton begins to suck in the cool, dense bay air. As the wind builds it veers (shifts clockwise) to Southwest (225°). Later, as the land cools the process is reversed.

the stronger the wind. If the land cools rapidly, there may be a nighttime land breeze in which the air rushes from the relatively cold land to the relatively warm water, whose temperature is more stable.

Often these breezes are called thermals, but a thermal actually is a rising column of warm air caused by the uneven heating of the land or sea. The invisible cloud of hot air rising over California's San Joaquin River Valley is a thermal, not the wind that it sucks in. If the landmass fronts on a water mass to the East, the temperature difference will cause Easterly winds; to the south, Southerly winds; to the North, Northerly winds. Since the high-pressure systems that hang relatively stationary along the latitude of North America create prevailing Westerly winds, any sea breeze from the East will be weaker than a sea breeze from the West. San Francisco's Southwest sea breeze is augmented by the prevailing Westerly.

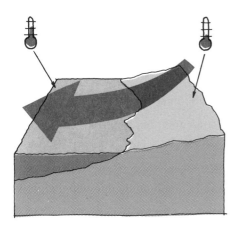 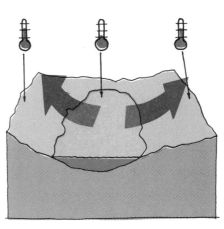

Land temperature is more unstable than the temperature of large bodies of water, so when the land cools at night an offshore land breeze may develop (left), to be replaced by the daytime onshore sea or lake breeze (right).

If the local sea breeze and the prevailing wind are from the same direction, like the Southwesterlies of San Francisco, they augment each other and create relatively strong winds. But if the two winds are contrary, the resulting wind will be relatively light. A shore facing the East may have an Easterly sea breeze.

Trade Winds

Highs and Lows

Oldtime commercial seamen called the offshore prevailing winds trade winds. Blowing in great highways from pressure system to pressure system and untouched by land, they were mapped and exploited as thoroughly (and as secretly) as a commuter traces a shortcut between his home and job. The North Atlantic Northeast trades blew explorers from Spain to the Caribbean, and the Southeast trades of the South Atlantic carried slave ships from Africa to America. Pursued by the great Westerlies of the Southern latitudes were grain ships racing to and from Australia. Between the trade winds lie narrow belts of calm called the doldrums. Sometimes the belts are wider than predicted; sometimes the trades are tardy or weak. The seasonal shifting of the earth under the sun has its effects, weakening or strengthening pressure systems or moving them, but those effects are generally predictable.

The prevailing (trade) wind patterns change seasonally as the land, sea, and air temperatures are affected by alterations in the earth's tilt — and hence the angle at which the sun's rays strike. The upper chart shows April-June patterns, the lower July-September ones.

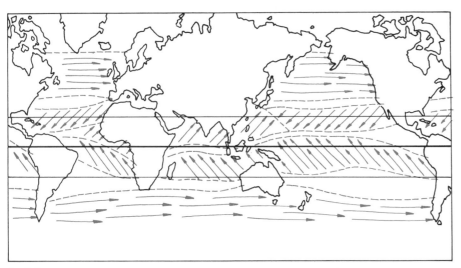

April-June

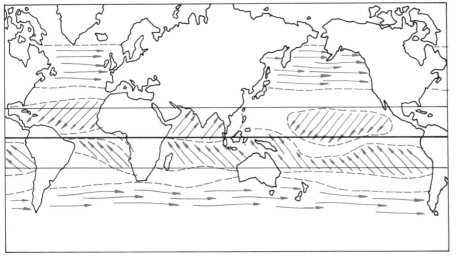

July-September

The passage of small pressure systems will change the pattern of prevailing winds. By small we mean no larger than about 300 miles in diameter; most are much smaller than that. A stationary pressure system like the Pacific high is much larger and very stable, but a small high or low may march across the North American continent in four or five days, pick up speed over the Atlantic, and three or four days later cut across England and Europe. These battalions are pockets of hot or cold, dry or wet air usually riding on the prevailing winds of the stationary pressure systems. They are like eddies and whirlpools formed at shallow points or edges of streams. Sometimes the vortex is weak and carries for only a few feet; sometimes it is powerful and charges off on its own course. Likewise, a low-pressure system may build up and die with no more consequence than a rain shower or two, or it may become a destructive tornado or hurricane, with a swirling column of tightly packed air ranging across land or water on an erratic path. Meteorologists are not totally sure what causes storms. They know that pressure systems are created by irregular differences in air temperature and humidity — and therefore in air pressure. Apparently, if the differences are very great (even within the system itself) an immense amount of energy is released. In human psychological terms this is like the violence unleashed by a split personality. If the earth were smooth with no valleys or mountains, if the sun's rays struck each square foot of land and sea for the same length of time at the same angle, if the earth's surface were of equal density everywhere — then there probably would be no differences in air temperature or pressure, and no storms. But that's not the case, and pressure systems of varying intensity and danger bounce across the continents and seas, sometimes spawning other systems. Only rarely is the atmosphere stable.

These air masses are named after their origins: maritime (air coming from the sea), continental (from large landmasses), polar (from the polar regions), and tropical (from the Equator). Continental polar air sweeping down from Canada is cold and dry; continental tropical air coming up from Mexico is hot and dry. Maritime polar air moving South from Alaska or Greenland is cold and wet; maritime tropical air from the Caribbean is warm and wet (Another air mass, arctic, has extremely cold air but has little effect on summer weather.).

Air masses are known by their areas of origin: maritime (wet), continental (dry), polar (cold), and tropical (hot), and can combine in several variations.

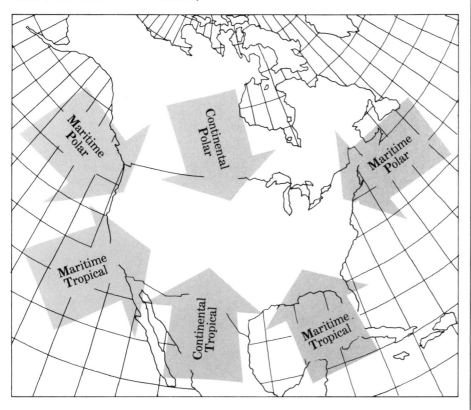

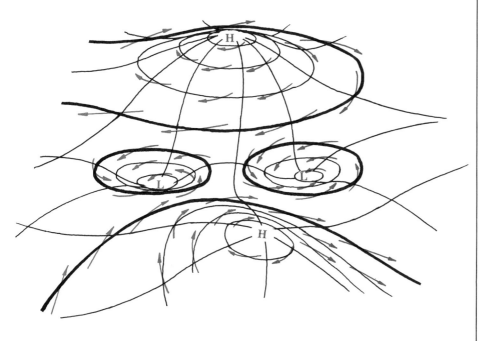

The coriolis effect, changes in air pressure and temperature, and other factors combine to create chains of low- and high-pressure systems that interlock like gears.

Fronts

When one air packet confronts a different one, there is a front line. For example, a mass of continental polar air lumbering over the Canadian border on the jet stream — the West wind in the upper atmosphere — brings cold, dry, high-pressure air to the midwestern United States. If it collides with a packet of maritime tropical air that has wandered North from the Gulf of Mexico, bringing hot, damp air in a low-pressure system, sparks will fly. That is literally true, since one outlet of the energy created by the two masses is lightning. Another is wind and a third is rain. The weather is most unstable and dangerous along the front line where the two masses meet. If it's a cold front, with continental polar air following maritime tropical air, the temperature will drop quickly and the damp clouds of the maritime tropical air will be blown away by gusty, cool Northwest winds rushing down the steep gradient of the "mountain" of cold high-pressure air toward the "valley" of warm low-pressure air.

We all recognize a summer cold front. One day may be hot and humid, sometimes under a suffocating layer of clouds. That afternoon black clouds filter in among the gray ones, thin currents of cool air pierce the thick blanket of humidity, and the atmosphere seems charged with the promise of change. The Western sky darkens, the wind races from a languid yawn to a shout, lightning flashes, rain whips horizontally. Sometime in the middle of the night you awaken in a chill and dig the blankets out of the closet. Hours later the sun rises on a clear, blue, cool day swept dry by a fresh Northwest wind, "the clearing Northwester." Inland and on the East Coast, the clearing Northwester is gusty and shifting because it arrives after a long journey across a continent of irregular land shapes and an atmosphere of warm and cold valleys and mountains.

Although they're drawn as lines on weather maps, fronts actually are thick zones of transition between 5

Fronts

and 60 miles wide in which are mixed the characteristics of both air masses. On either side of the front the weather is relatively stable from hour to hour, but within it the weather is dynamic and sometimes dramatic.

There are four types of front:

Cold Front. Colder (usually polar) air replaces warmer (usually tropical) air.

Warm Front. Warmer air replaces colder air.

Occluded Front. A cold front overtakes a stationary or slow-moving warm front and pushes the warmer, less dense air aloft.

Stationary Front. The front does not move, and air is not replaced or displaced.

The Cold Front

The cold front may often be the most dangerous. As continental polar air passes over warmer land, it is heated and becomes unstable. This means that its component air masses never really settle down. A cold front's calling card usually is a mass of dense towering cumulus clouds indicating vertical instability. Other signs are thunder squalls, lightning storms, and gusty winds. Cold fronts move very fast, about 600 miles a day in winter, but slower in summer, so they often take people by surprise.

As a cold front passes, the wind veers (shifts clockwise). If you stand with your back to the wind the wind will shift to your left as the front passes — more likely than not settling down around Northwest and becoming extremely gusty.

Another herald of the front is a rapid drop in the barometer. As the front swings through, however, the cold, dense air of the new system brings the barometer up again. The steeper and more prolonged the drop in the barometer, the more intense the frontal storm will be.

A cross-section drawing of a cold front shows the new, heavier air forcing its way under the old, lighter air like a wedge. A cold front's passage is usually sharp and violent, as when a lever is forced under a stable, heavy

A cold front is a fast-moving wedge of dense cool air prying up the warm air it meets in a tower of cumulus clouds, followed by squalls and strong wind.

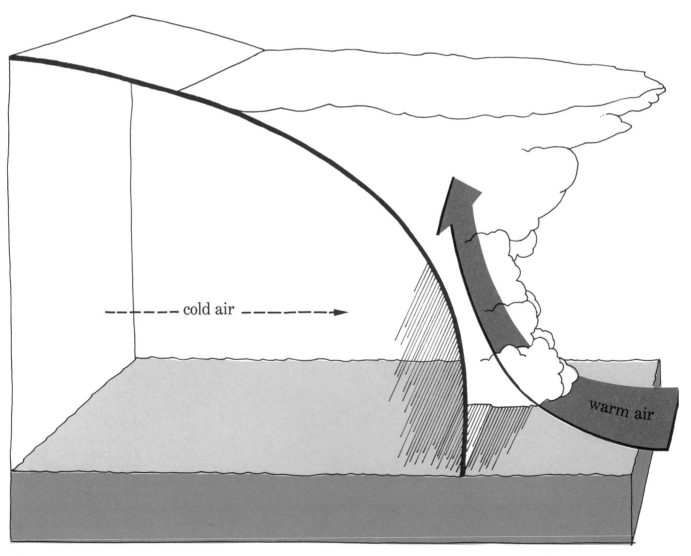

cold air ⟶

warm air

object to pry it up.

The Warm Front

A warm front is less dramatic. Because warm fronts usually originate over water (often the Gulf of Mexico), they are more stable than cold fronts. The advancing warm, moist air slides East over the cooler air ahead in a blanket of filmy high cirrus clouds. The cloud section may be 600 miles wide and 1200 miles across as it spreads over the retreating wedge of cold air. On the second or third day of the warm front's gradual approach, the clouds lower and become dense. Rain starts to fall and continues unabated. The barometer falls too; the steeper and quicker the drop, the stronger the wind will be. If there is a confused mix of air in the front, there may be local instability, with thunderstorms and rapidly building winds. Once the front finally passes, the rain stops or becomes a drizzle, the wind veers, and the barometer steadies.

Warm fronts move at a speed of about 360 miles a day during winter

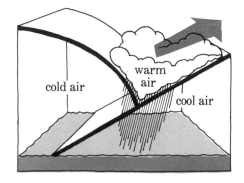

An occluded front can occur in several ways when cool air heaves up large packets of warm air, often when two low-pressure systems collide.

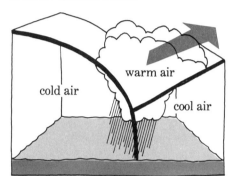

and less than 180 miles a day in summer.

The Occluded Front

The occluded front sees the faster moving cold front shoving the entire warm front up into the atmosphere — not simply wedging under it as the cold front does. The warm air rises in high cumulus clouds. If the temperature and humidity differences between the two systems are not great, an occluded front may lead to stable weather, but stormy, unpredictible weather results if the air packets are radically different.

The Stationary Front

The fourth type of front is the stationary front, in which two different air masses lie on either side of a distinct frontal line with no interaction — much like the ingredients of the oil-and-vinegar dressing. Usually this happens because neither air mass is particularly well defined. A change in their characteristics, or the arrival of another air mass, may transform this neutral front into either a warm or a cold front.

A warm front is preceeded by a long layer of cirrus clouds and rain. It moves more slowly and is less violent than the typical cold front.

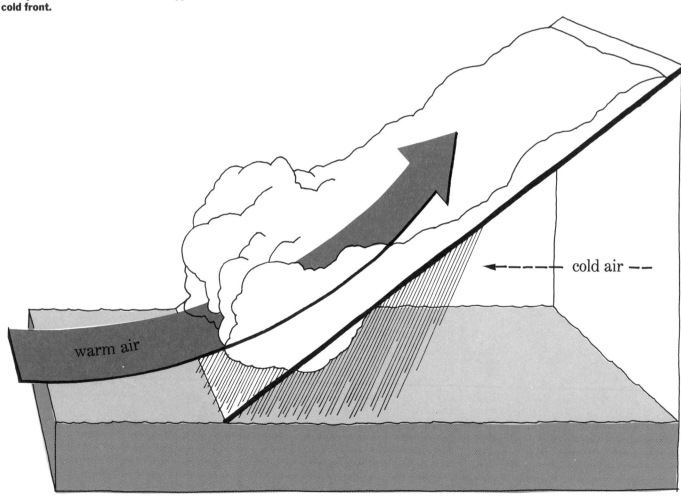

Low-Pressure Systems (Depressions)

More dangerous and less well understood than fronts are depressions, the tight, volatile, low-pressure systems that seem to appear out of nowhere and move so rapidly that normal weather prediction systems cannot keep up with them. Depressions are created by instability, whether on earth or in the atmosphere. Sometimes the instability is caused by local anomalies in air or water temperature. The depressions that have helped give Cape Hatteras, North Carolina, the gloomy nickname, "the graveyard of ships," are so destructive because the cape is an intersection of cold, dry air swinging down from the North and warm, damp air flowing up from the South above the 80° waters of the Gulf Stream, which passes just offshore. In many parts of North America some of the year's worst storms occur around the spring and autumn equinoxes, when there are equal amounts of daylight and warm air, and nighttime and cool air.

Depressions may be generated by waves of warm air pushed ahead by an advancing cold front. Meteorologists think that these waves spiral outward in the upper atmosphere as they are propelled by outward-blowing winds of the high-pressure system behind the cold front. To feed this vortex, air is sucked in at the earth's surface. The center of a spiral becomes the center of a depression. As the upper-air spiral moves along, it pulls the bottom of the vortex along with it. A tornado is an extremely small, localized depression, as is a waterspout. In each case warm air is sucked into the column at its base and feeds it. A hurricane or a typhoon is the most powerful kind of depression. Scientists believe that they are formed over warm, tropical waters when a small, deep depression with abnormally low atmospheric pressure is charged by strong winds blowing far above the earth's surface. These three conditions, plus some unknown factors, combine to start the depression on its erratic, destructive course, much the way a boy pulls on a string to get a top moving.

As it pinwheels across the Gulf of Mexico, Hurricane Allen shows the shape of a classic depression in this satellite photo taken on August 7, 1980. Clouds swirl toward its center from as far away as Puerto Rico. Another depression has formed off the West coast of Mexico.

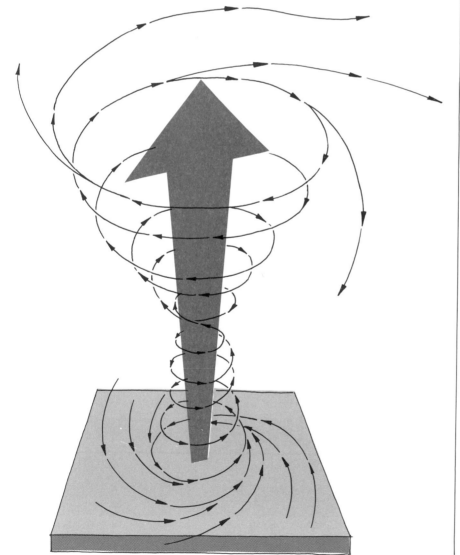

Depressions may be caused when air packets near cold fronts spin off on their own, fed by warm air sucked in at their bases. Meteorologists believe that especially violent depressions may form over abnormally warm water.

A Classic Storm

The most famous storm in the history of yachting was a deep depression that on August 14, 1979, battered the 303 ocean racing yachts sailing in the Fastnet Race off England, killing 15 sailors and sinking five boats. It started life six days earlier and 6000 miles to the West in the great corn and wheat fields on the Midwestern border between the United States and Canada, a historic birthplace of destructive tornados and depressions where cold continental polar air mates with hot thermals rising from millions of acres of farmland. The depression was small, but it had an unseasonal force. It dropped almost 2 inches of rain on Minneapolis, Minnesota, on August 9, then sped East across Lake Michigan, upstate New York, and northern New England. Its greatest effects were to the South, where the gusty Westerlies spinning counterclockwise around its center blew the roof off a toll booth on the New Jersey Turnpike, tore a limb off a tree in New York's Central Park, killing a passerby, and capsized boats and caused many boats to drag their anchors all along the coast of southern New England. One sailor, safely ashore in Newport, Rhode Island, mistook the black, savage low for a hurricane. With this trail of destruction behind it, the de-

113

A Classic Storm

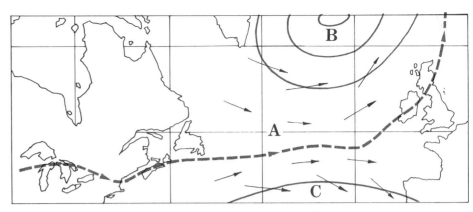

The 1979 Fastnet Race depression was re-energized by a patch of unusually warm water (A) and then rode across the Atlantic on a highway of Westerly winds circulating around the low to the North (B) and the high to the South (C).

pression bolted into the Atlantic on August 11 and charged off toward Europe at a speed of 50 knots (1200 miles a day), so compact that it was missed by many weather forecasters on both continents.

A day later it was East of Newfoundland. The dynamic chemistry of cold and hot ingredients that had blasted the depression East from the Dakotas was now made more explosive by two factors. One was an enormous, 1000-mile low-pressure system far to the North, moving slowly from Greenland to Iceland. Its own counterclockwise circulation pushed cold air South and

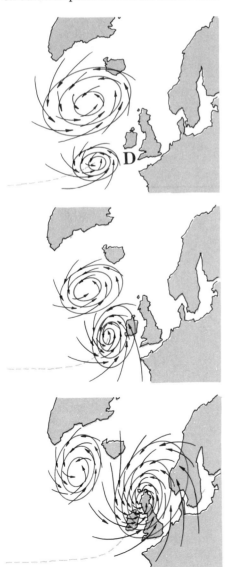

Overtaking the Northern low, the Fastnet storm changed course to Northeast and swept up and across Britain and a fleet of 303 ocean-racing yachts (D). The storm's front edge was a sharp scythe of clouds, as the satellite photo above shows.

into the path of the depression. The other was a large patch of exceptionally warm air created by water that had been heated to 5° above normal by a storm that had passed this way two days earlier. The new mix of cold and warm air reinvigorated the depression, which otherwise might have fallen apart in mid-Atlantic. As it was being energized, the depression slipped into an Eastbound superhighway created by the big low to the North and the huge mid-Atlantic high-pressure system to the South. The low, with its counterclockwise circulation, created Westerlies in its Southern extremes; the high, spinning clockwise, created Westerlies to its North. So on August 13 the depression sped up.

It would have ended up in the Bay of Biscay, off France's West Coast, if the corridor between the Northern low and the Southern high had remained straight. But on the morning of August 13 the low stopped moving and stalled off the West Coast of Iceland. Overtaking it at about noon on the 13th, the depression soon moved into the area where the wind blew not from the West but from the Southwest, and therefore redirected the depression straight for Ireland. It passed quickly across Ireland, and the 60- to 70-knot Westerly winds in its southern half screamed across the Western Approaches, the 170-mile-wide body of water between the Southwest corners of England and Ireland. And halfway across the Western Approaches at that very moment were 2600 men and women sailing 303 small yachts in the Fastnet Race. For more than half a day they were battered by hurricane-strength winds and breaking waves as high as 40 feet. Those of us who survived the Fastnet storm will not soon forget its violence.

The Fastnet storm was dangerous partly because it never lost energy but rather seemed to gain it, and partly because it moved so fast. In retrospect we can see that its fate was laid out almost from the moment of its birth. It would be hard to find a gale that so well illustrates how local and large-scale forces can create and direct depressions.

Meteorologists describe violent storms like the 1979 Fastnet gale as "bombs." Technically a bomb is a depression in which the barometer drops at a rate of 1 millibar an hour for 24 hours, or about three-quarters of an inch of mercury a day. The faster the drop, the steeper the "hill" between the high's "peak" and the nearby low's "valley," and the stronger the wind.

Squalls

A thunder squall may be the herald of an approaching cold front (sometimes traveling along a front line with other squalls) or it may simply be an extremely local storm caused when hot air rises over a baking summer landscape and becomes unstable when it encounters cool air aloft. Rain forms and creates electrical charges and lightning. Some cool air may drop back to the ground and the rapid rise and fall of air may heighten the storm. Winds may build to strengths of 60 knots or more, from any direction.

Because they are not always caused by long- or even moderate-term patterns, squalls are unpredictable, and thus may be even more dangerous than cold fronts or major depressions. Thunder squalls are usually preceded by extremely hot, humid weather, and are announced by swift-moving black (or sometimes green-black) cumulus clouds. The distance to a squall may be determined by timing the difference in seconds between a lightning flash and its thunderclap, and dividing that time by five. If the time difference is 25 seconds, the storm is 5 miles away. Since a squall may move faster than 20 knots, precautions for shortening sail (described in chapter 15) should be taken as soon as black clouds appear.

The towering dark cumulus clouds of this approaching squall should encourage any skipper to head to harbor or shorten sail.

Fog

Like pressure systems and wind, fog is caused by differences in air temperature. Every parcel of air has a temperature called the dew point at which the air becomes saturated with water. If the parcel of air already has a humidity of 100 percent and is entirely saturated with water, it is at its dew point. The lower the humidity, the more the air must be cooled to reach the dew point; the higher the humidity, the less the air must be cooled to reach its dew point.

The term "dew point" is derived from the moisture that forms on clear, cool summer nights, when the land chills low-lying humid air to the point that it can no longer hold the moisture and so deposits the tiny raindrops we call dew. Dew will not form if the temperature does not drop sufficiently (for instance, because a cloud cover insulates the land and keeps warm air from escaping at night).

Fog forms because local conditions cool the air below the dew point. For example, a warm onshore wind may blow across an upwelling of cooler

When the air reaches its dew point, it becomes completely saturated with moisture, much like a sponge that has been left in a dish of water. Cooling the air further compresses the air and, like the sponge, moisture is released.

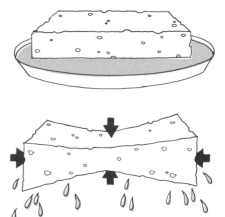

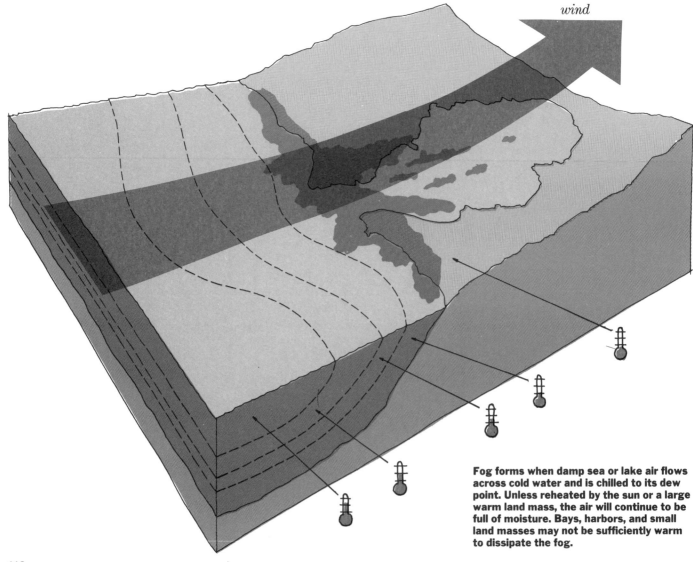

wind

Fog forms when damp sea or lake air flows across cold water and is chilled to its dew point. Unless reheated by the sun or a large warm land mass, the air will continue to be full of moisture. Bays, harbors, and small land masses may not be sufficiently warm to dissipate the fog.

water and be chilled to its dew point. Or an area that is fog-free on clear days becomes choked with the stuff on an overcast day heralding the arrival of a warm front, simply because the sun isn't available to keep the air temperature above its dew point. In both cases the absolute amount of water in the air remains constant, whether or not there is fog.

How to Predict Fog

To predict fog, you must first know the dew point of the air. A device called a hygrometer compares the temperature shown on a dry, normal thermometer with that shown on a thermometer whose bulb is wrapped in a wet cloth. As water evaporates from the cloth, heat is drawn from the wet bulb. Water ceases to evaporate when the cloth's saturation is equivalent to the air humidity. When the wet-bulb temperature stabilizes, subtract it from the dry-bulb temperature, then enter the difference into Table 1.

A more portable instrument for predicting fog is the sling psychrometer, which measures relative humidity and dew point more quickly than the hygrometer. This also has two thermometers, one wet and one dry. To speed up water evaporation, the instrument is twirled (slung) around in the air on the end of a rope. When the wet-bulb temperature ceases to drop, take the difference between it and the dry-bulb temperature and enter it into the table. (If the temperatures are the same, the air is completely saturated with water, the dew point has been reached, and you should be surrounded by fog.)

In fog, distances to other boats and hazards to navigation are extremely difficult to gauge, so proceed slowly and keep careful track of your position.

Table 1. Predicting Fog

Dry-Bulb minus Wet-Bulb	Air Temperature (Dry-Bulb Thermometer)												
	35	40	45	50	55	60	65	70	75	80	85	90	95
1	2	2	2	2	2	2	2	1	1	1	1	1	1
2	5	5	4	4	4	3	3	3	3	3	3	3	2
3	7	7	7	6	5	5	5	4	4	4	4	4	4
4	10	10	9	8	7	7	6	6	6	6	5	5	5
5	14	12	11	10	10	9	8	8	7	7	7	7	6
6	18	15	14	13	12	11	10	9	9	8	8	8	8
7	22	19	17	16	14	13	12	11	11	10	10	9	9
8	28	22	20	18	17	15	14	13	12	12	11	11	10
9	35	27	23	21	19	17	16	15	14	13	13	12	12
10	—	33	27	24	22	20	18	17	16	15	14	14	13
11	—	40	32	28	25	22	20	19	18	17	16	15	15
12	—	—	38	32	28	25	23	21	20	18	17	17	16
13	—	—	45	37	31	28	25	23	21	20	19	18	17
14	—	—	—	42	35	31	28	26	24	22	21	20	19
15	—	—	—	50	40	35	31	28	26	24	23	21	21

Using this table, dry-bulb and wet-bulb thermometer hygrometer readings can be converted into a dew point, at which fog will occur. First subtract the wet-bulb temperature from the dry-bulb temperature and locate the difference in the left-hand column. Then read across to the column under the temperature nearest to the dry bulb's. Subtract the number at the intersection of the line and the column from the exisitng dry-bulb temperature to find the dew point. For example, if the dry-bulb temperature is 76° and the wet-bulb temperature is 66°, the difference is 10°. Reading across to the column under 75°, we come to 16°. The dew point therefore is 60°. If the air temperature drops to 60°, there will be fog.

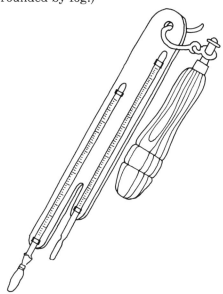

Using a sling psychrometer (above) or a gyrometer and Table 1 (right), you can determine the dew point and thus predict the likelihood of fog.

Fog

Fog Types

There are six important types of fog:

Advection fog occurs day or night when warm air flows over colder water or land. The warm air is cooled to its dew point, and fog results. Advection fogs usually do not occur over land in winds stronger than 15 knots, which, because of land's rough texture, cause vertical mixing of air currents that is too unstable for even cooling; layered stratus or stratocumulus clouds form instead. But over water, which is much smoother than land, advection fog can form in strong winds. Southerly winds blowing over cold water near shore can cause the most persistent and thick advection fogs.

Frontal fog occurs ahead of warm and occluded fronts. Rain falls from the upper, warmer air into the cooler air of the retreating air mass, increasing the water content of the air. With the higher humidity, the air temperature must drop less to reach its dew point (the greater the water content, the higher the dew point). A slight drop in air temperature brings fog. Likewise, frontal fog may occur behind cold fronts as rain falls from the warm air aloft into the cooler air of the advancing system.

Inversion fog is caused by warm air blowing over upwellings of cold water, as happens off the entrance to San Francisco Bay or on lakes undergoing seasonal thermal turnovers in spring and fall.

Radiation fog occurs over land on calm nights, when air at peak humidity near sunset is brought rapidly to its dew point by the cooling land. (Since water cools more slowly than land, radiation fogs are not seen offshore.) A very light wind helps the formation of a dense radiation fog by mixing cool lower-air particles with warm upper-air ones, but a wind stronger than about 12 knots creates too much turbulence. In a flat calm with no wind whatsoever, the cool lower-air particles remain near ground, so the fog may be only a few feet thick. This ground fog is favored by makers of horror movies. A clear night is required for a radiation fog (as well as for dew), since insulating cloud cover keeps the earth and the air above it from cooling to the dew point.

Sea fog, as the name indicates, occurs at sea when warm air and cold water meet. There are often sea fogs in the Atlantic where the warm Gulf Stream flows near the cold Labrador Current.

Steam fog is often seen over rivers and small lakes. It is formed early in the morning by cool air sinking down hills and valleys onto warm waters. The sinking cold air meets the warm air over the water to produce low rising columns of mist. (In polar regions, very cold air blowing over warmer water causes a similar type of fog called Arctic sea smoke.)

Fog is more likely over cold waters than over warm waters, particularly where the prevailing wind is from the warm South. The foggiest sections of the United States' major boating areas are: on the Pacific Coast, Northern California; the Great Lakes, Lake Superior and Northern Lake Michigan; and the Atlantic Coast, New England, and especially Maine (where July may be fogged in one-third to one-half the time). Because the Pacific Ocean is colder than the Atlantic, Southern California South of Santa Barbara can experience about three times as much fog as the South Atlantic states on the same latitude from September through February. Fog peak frequency in other areas follows these seasonal patterns: Northern California, Oregon, and Washington —July-October; New England — June-August; Middle Atlantic states — December-May; South Atlantic and Gulf of Mexico — very rarely, and then December-March; Southern Great Lakes — March-September; and Northern Great Lakes —May-September.

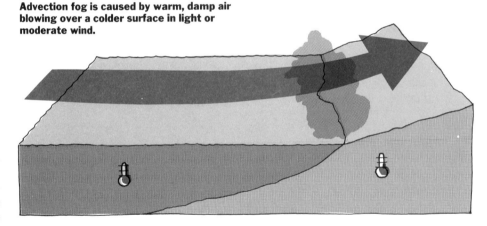

Advection fog is caused by warm, damp air blowing over a colder surface in light or moderate wind.

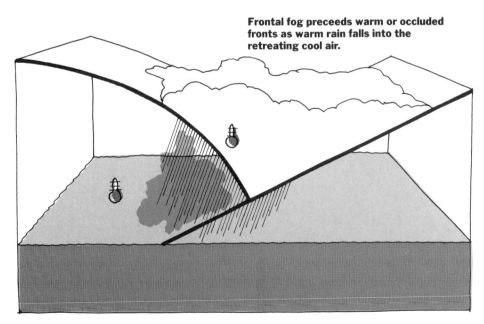

Frontal fog preceeds warm or occluded fronts as warm rain falls into the retreating cool air.

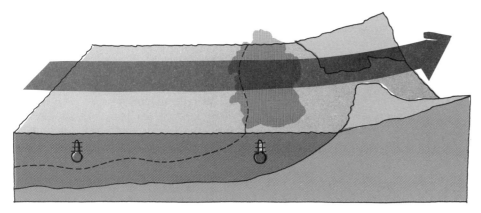

Inversion fog results when warm air blows over upwellings of cold water, either near or far from land.

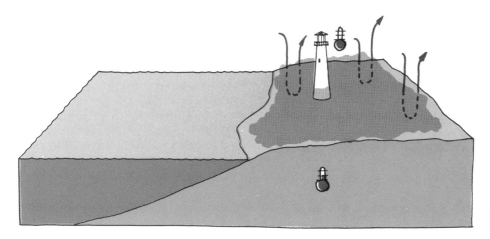

Radiation fog occurs on land when the air is suddenly cooled at sunset. A light wind increases its likelihood.

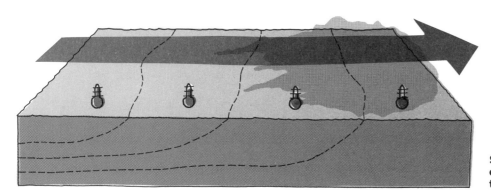

Sea fog appears when cold water currents confront warm, moist air (like that over the Gulf Stream) out in the ocean.

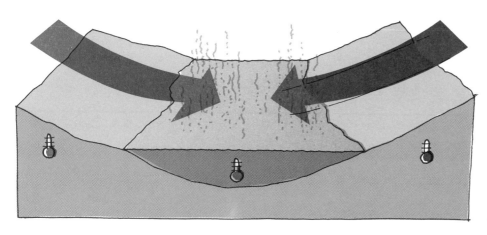

Steam fog occurs in the morning when cold air sinks and cools the air over a river or lake to its dew point.

Weather Forecasting

The most experienced seamen, fishermen and others who make their living on the water can read weather changes by looking at the sky above them and to the West and drawing on their years of experience. Later we'll look at some of their rules of thumb. Yet any wise seaman also uses barometers, radio broadcasts, and weather maps to help forecast short- and long-range patterns.

Barometric Pressure

The simplest of these aids is the standard aneroid barometer, which indicates air pressure in both inches and millibars of mercury, and which has an adjustable hand to be used as a reference point against which changes are measured. On many barometers the words "fair," "changing," "rainy," and "stormy" indicate pressure readings that might cause those conditions, but these labels usually are not very helpful when predicting changes. Rapid rising or falling of air pressure, at a rate of about 1 millibar (0.03 inches) every 3 hours or less, is the best indication that the weather is about to change radically. A good procedure is to line up the reference hand with the pressure indicator when you wake in the morning, and then keep track of the changes in air pressure during the day. If there is any reason to be concerned about the weather — dense clouds appearing to the West, gusty winds, or changeable air temperatures — you should regularly enter the barometer reading in the log book. If it rises or falls quickly, prepare for strong winds and possible storms, and head to shore. A special type of barometer called a barograph traces atmospheric pressure historically from hour to hour on a paper tape, providing a graphic display of barometric trends.

Often, barometric levels and trends and wind direction together indicate changes in weather. Table 2 summar-

izes some predictions, starting with high pressure. In general, the lower the barometer level, the worse the weather; the faster it falls, the stronger the wind. The atmospheric pressure at the center of the 1979 Fastnet Race storm was less than 28.8 inches (980 millibars), the third-lowest barometric reading in an English August since 1900. Equally significant was the very narrow interval between the isobars clustered around the center of the depression, over which the wind poured like water down a cliff.

In addition, deep depressions typically drag along on their southern side a long, narrow occlusion situated between a warm front and a cold front. It's the close proximity of warm and cold air that provides the depression with its energy and created the depression in the first place. This is why the air temperature and humidity change so rapidly before, during, and after the passage of intense depressions, whereas the climate variations are more gradual around a slow-moving warm front. In Table 2, notice the

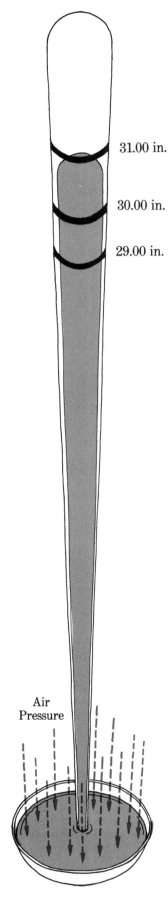

31.00 in.

30.00 in.

29.00 in.

Air Pressure

The mercury barometer is the most accurate indicator of atmospheric pressure. Mercury in a glass tube open at one end rises when the atmospheric pressure increases and drops when it decreases. The tube is graduated in inches or millibars for easy reference.

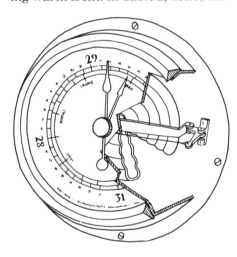

The aneroid barometer, though less accurate than the mercury barometer, is handier for sailors. Changes in atmospheric pressure are felt by a vacuumized metal container connected to a dial graduated in inches or millibars. (Below) On a weather map, isobars — lines of equal atmospheric pressure — define areas of high and low pressure. The relative steepness of the slope between a high and a low is called the gradient. If the isobars are close, the gradient is steep; if distant, shallow.

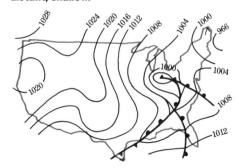

Table 2. Weather Forecasts Based on Barometric Pressure and Wind Direction

Pressure in Inches (Millibars)	Wind Direction	Forecast
30.2 (1023) and higher. Steady	SW-NW	Continued fair with little temperature change.
30.2 (1023) and higher. Falling slowly	SW-NW	Fair for 2 days with slowly rising temperature.
30.1 (1019) and higher. Falling slowly	NE-E	In summer in light winds, rain within 3 days. In winter, rain within 24 hours. Weak warm front approaching.
30.1 (1019) and higher. Falling rapidly	NE-E	In summer, rain within 12-24 hours. In winter, increasing rain or snow within 12 hours. Deep warm front approaching.
30.1-30.2 (1019-1023). Steady	SW-NW	Fair for 1 or 2 days with little temperature change.
30.1-30.2 (1019-1023). Rising rapidly	SW-NW	Fair, but rain within 2 days. Cold front approaching.
30.1-30.2 (1019-1023). Falling slowly	SE-S	Rain within 24 hours. Weak warm front approaching.
	NE-SE	Wind and rain increasing within 12-18 hours.
30.1-30.2 (1019-1023). Falling rapidly	SE-S	Wind and rain increasing within 12-18 hours.
	NE-SE	Wind and rain increasing within 12 hours.
30.0 (1016) and lower. Falling slowly	NE-SE	Rain for 1-3 days and perhaps longer. Weak warm front.
30.0 (1016) and lower. Falling rapidly	NE-SE	Rain and strong winds within a few hours, then clearing within 36 hours and lower temperatures in winter. Deep cold front.
30.0 (1016) and lower. Rising slowly	S-SW	Clearing within a few hours and then fair for several days. Weak cold front passes.
29.8 (1009) and lower. Falling rapidly	N-E	Severe storm and heavy rain within a few hours. In winter, snow followed by a cold wave. The typical New England "Nor'easter" caused by a deep depression.
	E-S	Severe storm within a few hours, then clearing within 24 hours with lower temperatures in winter.
29.8 (1009) and lower. Rising rapidly	Veering to W or NW	Storm ending followed by clearing and lower temperatures. Passage of cold front or depression. Expect high winds with clearing, gusty and shifting if they come from over land or steady if they come from over sea.

quick, sudden changes whenever the barometer falls or rises rapidly as the different air masses race through on each other's heels.

A barograph tape of a depression like the Fastnet storm shows readings in a sharp V shape — a rapid drop, a momentary pause at a deep low, and a rapid rise. The passage of a less dramatic depression or a weak front is marked by a long, shallow slide in pressure, shown on a barograph as a wide bowl.

Official Forecasts

Weather forecasts are available from government agencies. The most accessible are those broadcast over radio and television, although forecasts on commercial stations sometimes are too vague and short-term to be of much help to sailors. The United States National Weather Service broadcasts much more detailed weather forecasts over Very High Frequency radio frequencies 162.40 megahertz (MHz), 162.475 MHz, and 162.55 MHz. The frequencies are found on Very High Frequency (VHF) radiotelephones, many multiband portable radios on the "marine band," many radio direction finders, and special radios that receive only those signals. The broadcasts are continuous, running about 5 minutes and containing both local observations and short- and long-range forecasts. They are interrupted and changed as required to report alterations in conditions and forecasts. The language used by the announcers is relatively non-technical. Since VHF broadcasts have a "line of sight" range of approximately 40 miles, the weather radio reports cover limited areas, the 80-mile-diameter circles of coverage overlap, and adjoining broadcasts are made on different frequencies so that sailors may learn about weather beyond their local area. Of course no forecast can accurately cover every cove and island. While tuning your ear to the VHF weather broadcasts, keep your eyes and senses alert to the Western sky and the local environment.

Weather Forecasting

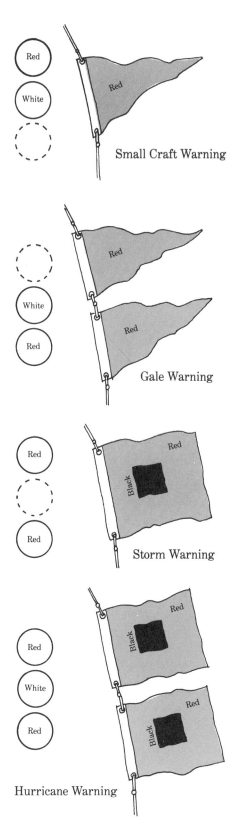

The National Weather Service also broadcasts weather information over single-sideband (SSB) frequencies, which have a range of hundreds of miles. These reports and forecasts provide more data than the VHF broadcasts, including enough information to allow the listener to draw a weather map. Even more detail is sent out in Morse Code. Special transmissions are received by weather facsimile machines that actually draw detailed weather maps. Becoming increasingly compact and inexpensive, these machines may soon be found on many small cruising boats.

Formerly, all U.S. Coast Guard stations displayed visual weather warnings, such as a single red flag (small craft should stay off the water), two red flags (gale warning), a red flag enclosing a black square (storm warning), and two red flags enclosing black squares (hurricane warning). Lights used for night warnings are, respectively, red light over white light, white light over red light, red light over red light, and red light over white light over red light. These visual signals may be displayed unofficially at yacht clubs, marinas, and other private shoreside facilities, although the U.S. Coast Guard itself no longer uses them, preferring to use marine weather radio broadcasts for weather warnings.

Synoptic Weather Maps

If you don't carry a weather facsimile machine, the most convenient weather map may be the one published in your daily newspaper. These maps are derived from extremely detailed synoptic (overview) maps sent out by the National Weather Service every 6 hours (and more frequently in threatening weather). Local newspapers often eliminate just the details that sailors need to know, such as locations of front lines, and may actually include only air temperature and areas where there is precipitation, but large-city papers may print more detailed maps as well as satellite photographs on their weather pages. Television weathermen often illustrate their presentations with satellite photos and

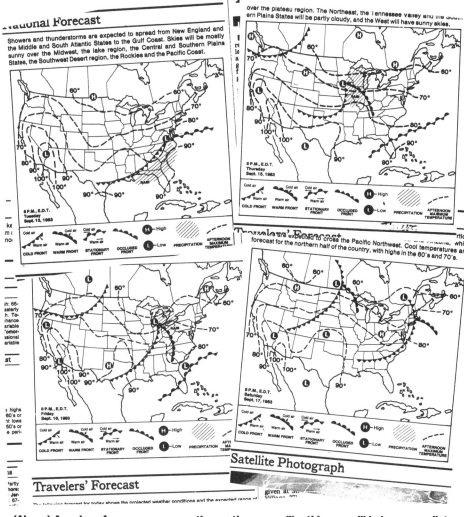

(Above) A series of newspaper synoptic weather maps like this one will help you predict weather changes. **(Left)** The visual signals for bad weather, from top to bottom: small craft warning, gale warning, storm warning, and hurricane warning.

radar pictures that show approaching storms.

No matter how thorough it is, a weather map is not very helpful when studied in isolation — yesterday's weather map will tell you little about tomorrow's weather unless you know trends. Experienced sailors who have developed an intuitive feel and memory for weather developments usually don't study synoptic weather maps unless they're heading out of range of National Weather Service broadcasts or sailing in predictably stormy times of year. But if you're unsure of your own weather senses and want to learn something about the environment, you'll enjoy studying synoptic maps for the three or four days before you head out. Most newspaper weather maps are based on National Weather Service synoptic maps. NWS maps are marvels of information and compression, and tell much more about our climate than the average newspaper or television map will provide.

The National Weather Service publishes 15 Marine Weather Service charts that include lists of NWS offices and NWS and commercial weather broadcasts. These charts are available for a small fee from Distribution Branch (N/CG33), National Ocean Service, Riverdale, MD 20737.

Airport Weather Broadcasts

Many commercial airports provide information about wind direction and strength, either over the telephone or in broadcasts. These data usually are for an altitude of several thousand feet. If you know how to convert this information to sea-level readings, you may be able to predict wind shifts. The trick is to understand how the coriolis effect, or the effect of the earth's rotation, works at different altitudes.

At an altitude of 3000 feet the wind direction is parallel to the isobars of the prevailing weather system. If the isobars on the weather map run North and South, the wind aloft will blow from either the North or the South, depending on whether the system is a low or a high and whether it is approaching from the West or passing to the East.

Once you know the wind direction and velocity aloft, you can determine them for land and sea using these rules of thumb:

1. On the ocean or a large body of water, the wind is two-thirds the velocity of the high-altitude wind and blows at a 15° angle to it (blowing 15° outward in a high and 15° inward in a low).

2. On land, the wind is one-third the velocity of the high-altitude wind and blows at a 30° angle to it (outward in a high and inward in a low.

Obviously, the greater friction of land affects wind speed and direction more than the comparative smoothness of water.

Remember: wind circulates clockwise around a high and counterclockwise and inward around a low.

A weather facsimile machine (or "weather-fax") will receive weather transmissions sent over special radio frequencies and draw reliable synoptic maps.

Clouds

Clouds are the faces of weather. Created by differences in temperature and humidity, just like fog, clouds usually foretell weather changes. The Latin names for clouds describe their appearances: *cirrus* means "curl" or "tendril"; *stratus* means "blanket"; *cumulus* is a "heap" or a "swelling"; *alto* is derived from the Latin *altus*, or "high"; and *nimbus* means "violent rain." The important cloud types, described below from the highest to the lowest, use one or more of these words and characteristics.

Cloud Types

Cirrus clouds are the highest and the least substantial. Composed of ice crystals, cirrus clouds lie at altitudes close to 45,000 feet. Wispy and lying at oblique angles, these clouds may herald the approach of a warm front.

Cirrostratus clouds (wispy clouds lying in sheets) may form slightly lower than cirrus clouds as a warm front nears and layers of cold air mix with upper warm air. Cirrostratus may drape the entire sky in a gray haze and cause halos around the sun or moon — a traditional indication of a nearing storm.

Cirrocumulus clouds (barely defined puffy balls), like cirrostratus, lie at altitudes of 16,500-40,000 feet, usually in large clumps. From below, these clouds may look like fishscales. The saying "Mackerel sky, mackerel sky/ Not long wet, not long dry" indicates that cirrocumulus is a sign of changeable weather.

Altostratus clouds are sheets lying between about 6,000 and 23,000 feet above the earth. Thicker, darker, and more claustrophobic than the higher cirrostratus clouds, they promise rain.

Altocumulus clouds indicate fair weather, particularly at lower levels. These are the cottony puffs that are so beautiful against the deep blue of a fine midsummer sky. But if they begin to darken or to enlarge, squalls may follow.

Cumulonimbus

Cumulus

Stratocumulus clouds are puffy balls occurring in more compressed layers at altitudes below about 6,500 feet.

Cumulonimbus clouds are dark, tightly packed balls, which may churn and tower as thunderheads at about 6,000 feet. If a cumulonimbus is broader above than below, it's called an "anvil head." This shape is due to violent updrafts through a wide range of temperatures; as the updraft hits cold air, more of it condenses as a cloud. Winds are strong around these threatening clouds.

Cumulus clouds are much less ominous than cumulonimbus thunderheads. They're puffy and white and lie at about 6,000 feet. Like the altocumulus, the cumulus promises fair weather. But cumulus clouds may begin to darken and be transformed into stratocumulus or cumulonimbus clouds. Cumulus clouds over land indicate rising thermals and promise a good sea breeze.

Nimbostratus clouds are the rain-laden, heavy, low-lying, dark-gray blankets that come with warm fronts and wet Northeasters. Their soggy bases may lie just above the earth's surface and be indistinguishable from heavy fog, and they may rise to over 10,000 feet.

Stratus clouds are less ominous than nimbostratus; if they bring any rain it's usually in the form of drizzle. Lower and flatter than nimbostratus, they are not dangerous in themselves but may disguise approaching storm clouds.

How to Read Clouds

Here are some hints for predicting weather by reading clouds:

1. Isolated, wispy, white, and/or very high clouds are indications of fine weather. Among these are cirrus, altocumulus, and cumulus clouds.

2. Crowded, dense, dark, and towering clouds indicate changing or worsening weather. Cirrostratus, altostratus, stratus, nimbostratus, stratocumulus, and darkening cumulus clouds announce rain and squalls.

3. The sharper the edge of a thundercloud and the darker its color, the more violence it contains.

4. The weather will change if cloud color, shape, and size change.

5. Warm fronts are preceded by stratus clouds.

6. As cumulus clouds darken and enlarge and become cumulonimbus clouds, expect squalls within 60-90 minutes.

Traditional mariners often used easily remembered jingles to help predict weather. One of these is:

Trace the sky the painter's brush,
The winds around you soon will
*   rush.*

That is a concise summary of the rule that bad weather is dramatic. Striking contrasts of color and shape usually indicate worsening weather.

Clouds are often given colloquial names. High cirrus clouds are called "chicken scratches" after their fine lines and "mare's tails" for their filmy quality. Since they often precede a storm by a day or two,

Mare's tails, mare's tails
Make lofty ships carry low sails.

The changeable, puffy weather under fishscaley cirrocumulus clouds inspired the line "Mackerel scales, furl your sails."

Altostratus

Cirrus

Altocumulus

How to Read The Wind

North winds send hail,
*   South winds bring rain;*
East winds we bewail,
*   West winds blow amain;*
Northeast is too cold,
*   Southeast not too warm;*
Northwest is too bold,
*   Southwest blows no harm.*

This is an accurate catalog of the winds of America's Atlantic coast, where the prevailing Southwest wind is the fair-weather reliable.

Wind direction indicates the location of pressure systems. According to Buys-Ballot's Law (derived in the mid-19th century), if the wind is on your back, low pressure will be to your left and high pressure to your right. This is because of the contrary circulation patterns of wind around low- and high-pressure systems. An English meterorologist and sailor named Alan Watts has developed the following rule for predicting weather in the short range: Stand with your back to the surface wind and look aloft for indications of wind direction at high altitudes. If the flow of clouds or flight path of birds is from your left, the weather probably will deteriorate in the next few hours. (The wind is veering, so a depression is approaching.) If the wind aloft is blowing from your right, the weather probably will improve. (The wind is backing, so a high is approaching or a low is passing through.) If the wind above you is from the same direction or from the opposite direction as the surface wind, the weather probably will not change.

"In by day, out by night" describes the sequence of daytime onshore sea or lake breezes (as the land heats) followed by nighttime offshore land breezes (as the land cools).

A Westerly or Southwesterly sea or lake breeze is often said to "follow the sun," meaning that it veers (shifts clockwise, in a Westerly direction) during the afternoon as the land heats up and the thermal effect increases.

Predicting Squalls and Storms

Oldtime sailors made up many short poems to guide them through squalls and storms:

The sharper the blast,
The sooner it's past.

When the wind before the rain
Let your topsails draw again;
When the rain before the wind,
Topsail sheets and halyards mind.

These two reflect the fact that a small, relatively shallow front passes quickly, with rain only on the backside. Larger, deeper fronts and intense depressions are surrounded by bad weather whose precipitation may precede the strongest wind. Square-rigger crews would be wary about setting large, almost inaccessible topsails if they thought the wind would rise.

Rain long foretold, long last;
Short notice, soon will pass.

Warm fronts move slowly, preceded by several hundred miles of gradually lowering cirrus clouds and a day or more of rain. Faster moving cold fronts, on the other hand, pass through quickly and dramatically. After a sudden storm, the weather clears rapidly.

Visibility and Cloud Cover

When the dew is on the grass
Rain will never come to pass.
When grass is dry at morning light
Look for rain before the night.

Dew forms only if the air is cooled to its dew point. At night this can happen only in clear weather, which allows the day's heat to escape into the atmosphere. Cloud cover insulates the earth. If the grass is dry on a rainless summer morning, there is cloud cover.

A heavy dew usually promises a fresh sea breeze that afternoon. The cool, clear night lowers the water temperature, and the following hot, clear day raises the land temperature and creates thermal updrafts that suck in the cool sea air.

Red sky in morning,
  sailor take warning.
Red sky at night,
  sailor delight.

This is probably the most famous of all weather sayings, and it may be the oldest. St. Matthew tells us that when the Pharisees asked Jesus for a sign from heaven, they were told, "When it is evening ye say, it will be fair weather, for the sky is red. And in the morning it will be foul weather today for the sky is red and lowering." A sharply defined red sunset or dawn is caused by the sun's rays shining through a cloud of dust particles in the air in clear, dry weather. Since in the evening the clear red sunset is to the West of the observer, good weather is on the way. But the red sun of dawn is weather that has passed to the East. Given the 3-day cycle of weather systems, the odds are that wet weather is overhead or imminent.

Humidity washes the air of dust particles and thus improves visibility, as the saying "The farther the sight, the nearer the rain" suggests. And since low, dense, rainy stratus and nimbostratus clouds keep sounds as well as heat from escaping into the atmosphere,

Sound traveling far and wide
A stormy day will betide.

Many of these and other weather indications are neatly summarized in a single six-line poem:

When the glass falls low,
Prepare for a blow.
When it rises high,
Let all your kites fly.
The hollow winds begin to blow,
The clouds look black,
  the glass is low.

Weather and air pressure are inextricably related. The "glass", or barometer, when low foretells ominous winds and black clouds; when high, fair weather for flying every sail. The old seamen's weather sayings are not infallible, but the barometer almost always is.

Waves and Tides

Strictly speaking, waves are not weather, but they are caused by weather and may be as dangerous as the 60-knot winds of a strong gale. Their force should never be underestimated. Since salt water weighs 64 pounds per cubic foot and fresh water 62.2 pounds per cubic foot, a large breaking wave can hurl as much as 12 tons of water at a velocity as high as 30 knots.

Tides

Almost all waves are wind-driven. The most important exception is the tide, that great wave of water that flows around the world, generally on a semidiurnal (twice-daily) schedule. Tides are caused mainly by the gravitational forces of the sun and moon, with the moon having the greatest effect because it is closest. Tide levels and changes can be predicted with reasonable accuracy based on the positions of the sun and moon and the known effects of land masses. A very broad area of high water flows around the world following the moon, and a similar mound of water moves along on the other side of the earth. Since the moon's "day" as it rotates around the earth is 24.8 hours long, tides normally cycle at an interval of about 12.4 hours, with semidiurnal changes every 6.2 hours — or every 6 hours, 12 minutes. Tide levels change from day to day for several reasons. One is that the sun, which also exerts a gravitational force, has a 24-hour "day" and the relative positions of the two heavenly bodies change. When the sun and moon are either in the same direction (new moon) or in opposite directions (full moon), the highest and lowest tides occur because their gravitational pulls are augmenting each other. These levels are about 20 percent higher and lower than average and are called *spring tides*. When the sun and moon lie at right angles to each other, relatively low tidal ranges called *neap tides* occur.

If the moon is passing substantially North or South of the Equator, then one of the semidiurnal tides in a given location will be about 10 percent

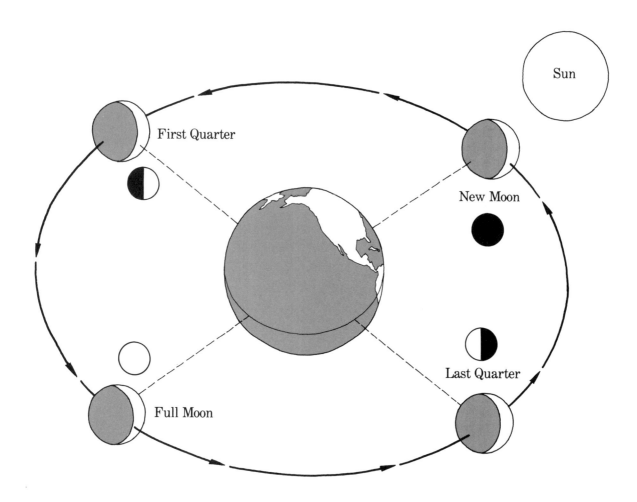

The main cause of tides is the gravitational pull of the moon, although the more distant sun also has some effect. Tide times and levels are predicted using the astronomical positions of these bodies as well as the known effects of land formations and ocean size and shape. The tides are highest at full and new moons (spring tide), when the bodies are aligned, and lowest at first and third quarters (neap tide).

higher than the other. And if the moon is at its perigee — when it is closest to the earth — its pull will be greater and the tides will be even higher. For example, according to tide tables the average rise and fall of the tide at Boston, Massachusetts, is 9.5 feet, which means that the mean (average) level at high tide is 9.5 feet above the mean level at low tide. When the moon was full on February 8, 1982, the spring tide was 11.2 feet. Ten days later, when the moon was in its third quarter, the neap tide level was 7.6 feet. Four months later, on June 21, the new moon and the perigee coincided at 8 A.M. and the spring tide that evening was 12 feet, or 26 percent higher than normal.

The moon's gravitational pull is the greatest force acting on the wave called the tide, but there are others. High atmospheric pressure tends to hold water levels down and low pressure allows them to rise. A strong on-shore wind blowing into a bay or an enclosed body of water like Long Island Sound may alter tide changes or

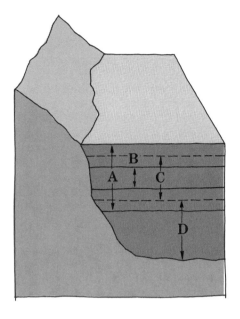

Spring tide (A) is the depth and range between high and low tides when the moon is full and new. Neap tide (B) is the depth and range at first and third quarters. Mean tide (C) is the average depth and range. Mean low water (D) is the average most shallow level (the water will be shallower at spring tide).

increase the level of high tide. If the wind is caused by a hurricane or a depression, the high winds and low pressure of the storm may cause flooding, especially at spring tide. Similarly, strong offshore winds blowing out of bays may cause low, delayed tides.

Tidal Current

Tide and tidal current are two different things, although one causes the other. As the gravitational pull of the moon tugs on a point on the earth (and a point exactly opposite it on the other side of the globe), and creates a "tidal wave," water flows "uphill" toward it. The point is constantly changing, so all tidal waters are everywhere in motion on the surface (and possibly below the surface as well). The tidal current flows strongest in constricted channels, such as narrow entrances to bays or sounds where large quantities of water flood and ebb in a tumult in the roughly 6 hours 12 minutes allowed to each tide in a semidiurnal system. Government and private tide tables

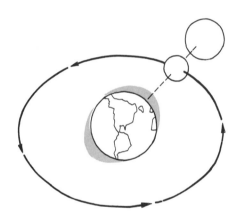

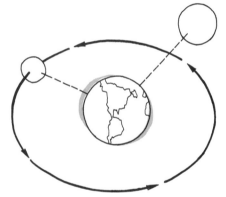

At spring tide, the moon and sun are aligned either at full moon (above) or new moon (below), and the mounds of water under the moon and on the opposite side of the earth are 20 percent higher than the mean.

At neap tide, the moon and sun are at a right angle and their gravitational pulls conflict, so the mounds are 20 percent lower than the mean. (Below) If the moon swings far above or below the Equator or is at its perigee, tide ranges will be greater.

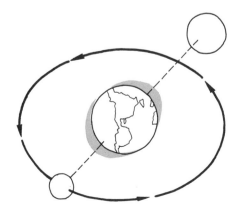

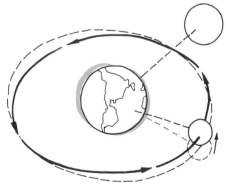

129

Waves and Tides

provide convenient schedules for times of high and low water, and current charts show direction and velocity of tidal currents. Since tidal currents can flow as fast as 12 knots, and velocities of 4 or 5 knots are common, knowing the time and characteristics of a tide is vital. This great wave of water can either stop you or help speed you along. Here it's enough to say that the saying "still waters run deep" is wrong, at least when the waters are tidal. Current runs fastest (though it may not seem that way) in deep water, and slowest in shallow water. Where currents clash, there may be steep waves and whirlpools in tidal "races." And where tidal currents meet wind-driven waves, natural forces augment each other in powerful ways. Oceanographers estimate that when a current as slow as 1 knot runs against wind-driven waves, the waves may double in size. This is a massive increase in an already-massive force.

Wave Shape

Wind-driven waves have a natural rhythm, like the pulsing of a long rope whose ends are held by two people who swing them up and down steadily. The greater the arc through which they swing their ends, the longer are the waves up and down the rope. These waves are called "sine waves," since they look like the fair, symmetrical arcs of sine curves. While the rope seems to be moving, its fibers actually are stationary on the horizontal plane as the waves snake through it from one end to the other. If one of the rope-holders changes the rhythm, the fair sine waves are broken up into a jumble of irregular waves, but after a while a new pattern takes over and either larger or smaller sine waves are formed. This is what happens when a new wind increases over calm water. The wind causes ripples, which gradually build into wavelets, which become waves. At first there were thousands of ripples, then hundreds of wavelets, then tens of regular waves. The larger the waves, the fewer there are of them. And the longer the wind blows, the larger the waves. If the

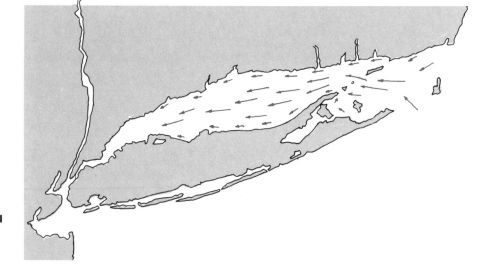

As the current vectors (force arrows) on this chart of Long Island Sound show, tidal current flows fastest in deep water (long vectors) and slowest in shallow water (short vectors).

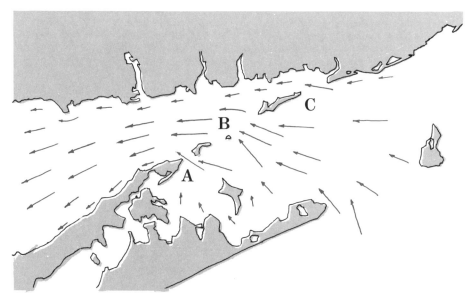

Tidal current flows fastest of all in constricted deep channels between large bodies of water. Here, the flood (incoming) current races into the sound at almost 5 knots in the deep channels at A and B, but flows at only 2 knots in shallow channel C.

wind were to shift suddenly, an entirely new group of ripples, wavelets, and waves would come in from the new angle, breaking up the regular pattern of the original waves. The water would be broken by clashing sets of waves until, after a while, the first set would die down and a new regular pattern would take over. Just as with the swinging rope's fibers, the actual molecules in the water do not travel with the waves (although they are subject to local stresses and tensions and may move slightly).

Wave Size

Wave size is measured in length (the distance from crest to crest), height (the distance from trough to crest), and period (the time interval between crests). Their size is determined by several factors. Foremost among these is wind strength. The harder the wind blows, the bigger the waves will be, although, in very shallow and narrow water, there are limits on wave size and speed: in 30 knots of wind a small lake will be broken by many more and smaller waves than the ocean or a large lake. The longer and steadier the wind blows, the larger and faster will be the waves. On the ocean there is a continuous wave train (pattern) called a swell which runs with the prevailing wind. Only storms with winds from other directions will eliminate these immense, rapid waves, which are so long that they're almost unnoticeable. When these swells approach a shoal (shallow water) or an island, they become steeper and eventually break.

A breaking wave is one whose base cannot support its top. Sometimes the wind will blow the top off the base; at other times the wave is so steep that the base simply is not wide enough and the crest falls off. If the wind builds very rapidly, the base may not grow as quickly as it should and breakers may form prematurely. If there is a strong contrary tidal current, or a pattern of waves from another direction, the wave may become extremely unstable and break, with thousands of pounds of foaming water dropping off its top at great, destructive speeds. And if large waves created in deep water cross a shoal, they will become dangerous breakers. Breakers have smashed in lighthouses and decks, torn masts and people out of yachts, and turned 60-footers upside-down with the insouciance of a 5-year-old capsizing a toy boat in the bathtub.

Every body of water is vulnerable to the so-called rogue wave, which unlike the waves we've been describing cannot be predicted with mathematical precision. An oceanographer has estimated that 1 out of 20 offshore waves is a rogue. This may be a thundering breaker that appears out of nowhere on a relatively quiet night, or a sequence of two or three big, safe rollers twice the size of every other wave in the neighborhood. Rogue waves may be caused by the collision of two or more waves from distant weather patterns — the remnants of gales thousands of miles apart that meet somewhere in mid-ocean, join forces, and redoubled in strength, roll on in a new direction. Most of these end their lives relatively harmlessly on a barren coastline. Some, unfortunately, sweep an unlucky boat or two before them.

For sailors concerned about safety and comfort, it's not enough to know the wind speed. A 15-knot Northwesterly blowing over waters churned up by the previous 3 days' Northeasterly will create an extremely rough, irregular seaway. Fortunately, the Northeast waves probably will die within a few hours, but until then the boat's motion will be hellish. An offshore wind will create waves much smaller than those churned up by an onshore wind of the same strength. Only good judgment, experience, and caution will tell you whether to go out in difficult conditions.

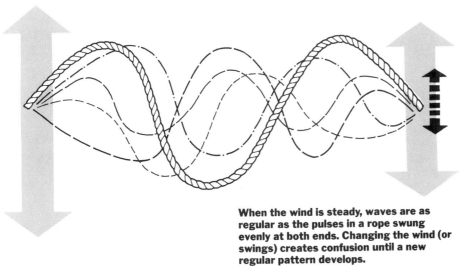

When the wind is steady, waves are as regular as the pulses in a rope swung evenly at both ends. Changing the wind (or swings) creates confusion until a new regular pattern develops.

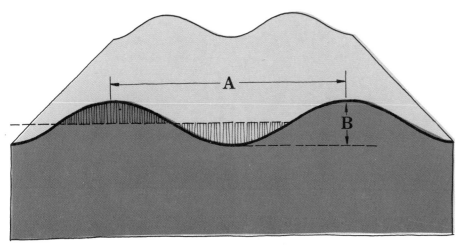

A wave's length (A) is the distance from crest to crest and its period is the time between two crests. Its height (B) is the distance from trough to crest.

How Hard Is It Really Blowing?

Table 3. The Beaufort Scale of Wind Forces

Force	Wind Speed (Knots)	Wind Description	Sea Conditions	Probable Wave Height
0	0	Calm	Smooth, like a mirror.	0
1	1-3	Light air	Small ripples like fish scales.	$\frac{1}{4}$-$\frac{1}{2}$ foot
2	4-6	Light breeze	Short, small pronounced wavelets with no crests.	$\frac{1}{4}$-$\frac{1}{2}$ foot
3	7-10	Gentle breeze	Large wavelets with some crests.	2 feet
4	11-16	Moderate breeze	Increasingly longer small waves, some with white caps (foam crests).	4 feet
5	17-21	Fresh breeze	Moderate lengthening waves, with many white caps and some spray.	6 feet
6	22-27	Strong breeze	Large waves, extensive white caps, some spray.	10 feet
7	28-33	Near gale	Heaps of waves, with some breakers whose foam is blown downwind in streaks.	14 feet
8	34-40	Gale	Moderately high waves of increasing length, and edges of crests breaking into spindrift (heavy spray). Foam is blown downwind in well-marked streaks.	18 feet
9	41-47	Strong gale	High waves with dense foam streaks and some crests rolling over. Spray reduces visibility.	23 feet
10	48-55	Storm	Very high waves with long, overhanging crests. The sea looks white, visibility is greatly reduced, and waves tumble with force.	29 feet
11	56-63	Violent storm	Exceptionally high waves that may obscure medium-size ships. All wave edges are blown into froth, and the sea is covered with patches of foam.	37 feet
12	64-71	Hurricane	The air is filled with foam and spray, and the sea is completely white.	45 feet

The combined effect of wind and wave is so important that offshore sailors and seamen usually refer to sailing conditions not by wind strength alone but by a number that reflects both wind strength and sea conditions. They take this number from the Beaufort Scale of wind force. Developed in 1805 by Admiral Sir Francis Beaufort of the British navy, the scale divides wind and sea conditions into 12 "forces," ranging from calm to hurricane. It describes typical conditions offshore in large bodies of water, so is not of special relevance to people who knock about in small harbors where a fresh breeze does not always build up white caps (waves with foam tops). Most people overestimate wind strength, converting moderate breezes into small gales, as well as the size and period of waves. For restricted, protected waters such as rivers, small lakes, and bays, the Beaufort Scale might be modified by reading sea conditions one force higher and ignoring wave height. For instance, at sea white caps form in Force 4 winds, but in protected waters they may not appear until the wind is blowing about 18 knots, or Force 5. Note that the wind speed is in knots. Since 1 knot equals 1.15 statute miles per hour, multiply these figures by 1.15 to convert to M.P.H. To convert back to knots, multiply by 0.87.

The Beaufort Scale is summarized in Table 3.

The Beaufort Scale and Boat Handling

Like "beginner," "intermediate," and "expert" signs on ski trails, the forces on the Beaufort Scale indicate the difficulty of sailing conditions. Sailors should be careful not to be caught in wind and sea conditions far beyond the limits of their experience, knowledge, and physical ability. This does not mean that new, challenging conditions should be avoided out of timidity, because skills improve with experience. But nobody should recklessly charge out into conditions that he's totally unprepared for.

Forces 0-3 (0-10 knots of wind and smooth seas) are light conditions and should be safe for all sailors, assuming that the body of water is not too crowded, the boat is properly equipped, and there are a sufficient number of crew members.

Force 4 (11-16 knots and moderate seas) is a moderate condition that will challenge beginning and novice sailors, particularly if they're sailing small, capsizable boats.

Force 5 (17-21 knots and white-capped waves) is a fresh condition in which beginners and novices may lose control of their boats and generally feel overwhelmed.

Force 6 (22-27 knots and large waves) is a strong condition and no place for a beginner or novice. Very experienced sailors will feel challenged and sometimes overpowered in a strong wind, particularly if the wind is gusting in sudden puffs. As an indication of the possible danger of a strong wind, many sailboat races are automatically called off if the strength reaches 25 knots.

Forces 7-9 (28-47 knots and foaming seas) are gale conditions. In the lower range, large cruising boats that are well handled can make progress to windward, but when the wind gusts up into the 40s, most boats must heave-to or run with it. Small boats should not leave shore.

Forces 10-12 (48-71 knots and breaking seas) are survival conditions and no place for any boat.

Experienced seamen know that there are only two ways to survive a storm: hide way up a secure creek; or sail far offshore into open water in order to minimize the risk of being blown onto land.

Most people overestimate both wind strength and wave size, so to provide some standards of measurement here are some boats in Forces 2-9. Since waves tend to be flattened by photos, the seas are slightly larger then they appear.

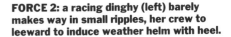

FORCE 2: a racing dinghy (left) barely makes way in small ripples, her crew to leeward to induce weather helm with heel.

FORCE 4: an ocean-racing sloop approaches Bermuda in a moderate wind and short waves, almost making hull speed under spinnaker.

FORCE 5: a cruising cutter making knots on an ideal reach as white caps just begin to appear.

FORCE 6: a 6-Meter slices into a strong wind. Though sailing in a sheltered part of San Francisco Bay, she meets steep, high waves.

FORCE 9: a dismasted ocean racer is taken under tow in a gale's breaking waves.

133

Chapter 5
Sail-Handling Gear and Knots

Almost all sail controls are lines running through blocks — short lengths of rope in pulleys, as a landsman might put it. Lines are also used to connect the boat to her anchor or a float, and sometimes to connect the helm to the rudder. Without the woven synthetic and steel strands that make up ropes and line, and without the blocks through which they are led, a boat would be but a leaf drifting helplessly with the wind.

If lines and blocks are the primary sail-handling equipment, fittings such as shackles, cleats, and winches perform highly important secondary roles. In this chapter we'll look at all this gear and how it is used, as well as at how line is secured with knots and splices.

On this well rigged stock racer-cruiser the jib sheet is led through the adjustable block on deck, back through the angled black foot block, and to a cockpit winch. On reaches the sheet is moved outboard to a snatch block on the rail (not shown). The main halyard is raised on a reel halyard winch (starboard side of mast), the two jib and two spinnaker halyards — for back-up and sail changes — on deck winches, which in rough weather are easier to grind than mast winches. On the mast are two sliding black cups for the inboard ends of the spinnaker poles, which are stowed clear of feet and sheets in deck recesses. Dorade vents (white cowls) and a prism (near port shrouds) let air and light below. The jackstay (aft of forward hatch) prevents the middle of the mast from bending back. Way aft behind the large cockpit compass is a chimney for a cabin heater. High double lifelines surround the deck, whose teak surface provides excellent traction. The shroud turnbuckles are properly taped, but the Flemish coil in the bow line invites kinking.

Line

While rope is the stuff produced by manufacturers and delivered to chandleries (marine hardware stores) on large drums, a line is a length of rope used for a specific purpose. A sheet is a line, and so is a halyard. Even a boltrope on the edge of a sail is a line. A 500-foot length of ½-inch-diameter nylon rope can be cut into several lines — say, six 20-foot docking lines and two 190-foot anchor lines (technically called rodes). The most common ropes are made of synthetic polyester fibers (although, as we shall see, some are made of wire). Polyester has almost completely replaced natural fibers

like manila and cotton, which rot and are relatively weak. Of the synthetic ropes, Dacron (Terylene in Britain) is used for sail controls, nylon is most prevalent as anchor rodes or docking lines, and polypropylene serves in tow lines or painters. Each of these ropes has a special chemistry and set of characteristics that make it most appropriate for its use, but before looking at them in greater detail, we should describe the two forms in which rope is woven — laid and braided.

Laid Rope

In laid rope, the yarns are twisted into strands and three strands are then twisted around each other, usually in a clockwise direction. Because of the clockwise torque woven into laid rope, it must be taken off a drum by pulling the bitter end (the very end) from the inside of the drum. If the outside end is pulled, the rope will come off the drum in a mass of kinks that can be removed only by recoiling it clockwise or dragging it astern of a moving boat so it untwists itself.

Coiling Laid Line

The best way to store an unused line is to coil it in loops. Coil "with the lay." Since most laid line is constructed with the strands twisted left to right, this means coiling in the same direction to compensate for the torque of the "lay." To coil a light laid line that is not in use, first pick up an end in your left hand, then begin making equidiameter clockwise loops about 2 feet long with the right hand. As each loop is laid in the open palm of the left hand, make a quarter turn to the right with your right hand. If the loop or the twist is made in a counterclockwise direction, or if the loops are made without the twist, severe kinks will result. When all but the last 2 feet of the line has been coiled, finish the coil off by wrapping half the remaining line around the middle of the loops three times, forming a figure-8. Then push the bight (middle) of the remainder through the top hole in the "8," pull the bight over the top, and slide it to the middle again. Tighten it and hang the coil up with the remaining bit of line. When coiling the tail (leftover part) of a cleated line, go through the same steps starting the coil near the cleat, but don't finish it off with the figure-8, which would delay uncleating and easing the line. Instead, reach through the coil and grab

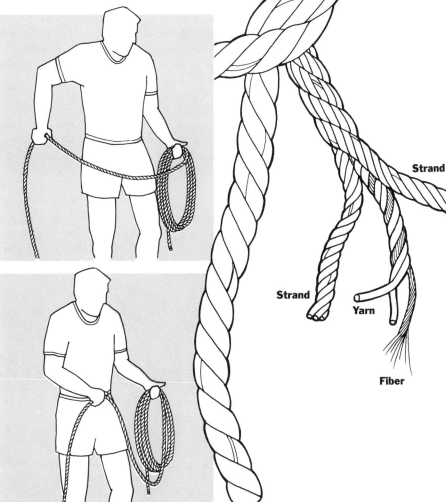

Coiling laid rope, twist your wrist a quarter turn clockwise with each loop to compensate for torque.

Laid rope is made up of synthetic fibers, yarns, and strands twisted tightly around each other.

Cable

Strand

Strand

Yarn

Fiber

Line

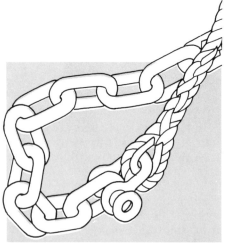

Because it is permanent and weakens line less than a knot, an eye splice is often used at the end of an anchor rode or a docking line.

a few inches of line near the cleat. Pull out this bight and twist it to form a loop. Hang the loop over the cleat and the coil will be secure.

Heavy or extremely long laid lines, such as anchor rodes, should be coiled on deck since they're too awkward to hold in one hand. To coil a line on deck, stand over a clear area and pay out the line in 3-foot clockwise loops, making sure to twist the line a quarter-turn clockwise with each loop. To finish off the coil, tie four or more short lengths of light line, such as marline, around it at equal intervals using a bow knot so it can be undone quickly. Or tape the coil in four corners; you'll need a knife to cut the tape when you want to use the line, but until then the coil won't undo itself.

When preparing a halyard, sheet, anchor rode, or heaving line to run out, undo the coil and then, starting at the fixed end (near the cleat for a sheet or halyard), fake it (lay it on deck with long loops). This will get any kinks out and minimize the chance of snagging on a fitting or your own arm or leg.

Splicing Laid Line

Laid rope has one major advantage over its cousin, braided rope: it can be easily spliced. A splice is an interweaving of strands that either joins two lines of the same diameter or forms an eye or a stopper in the end of a line. Long and short splices, which join two lines, are about 15 percent weaker than the line itself. An eye splice, which forms a permanent loop in the end of a line, is about 10 percent weaker than the line it is made from, yet considerably stronger than a knot used for the same purpose. The strength of a splice depends on the friction between the interwoven strands of the line. The strands are tucked under one another in a set pattern, with three to six sets of tucks being the norm.

To make an eye splice — which is more common than the short or long splice — unravel the three strands about 6 inches, then form the eye, or loop, with the desired diameter. Lay the unraveled end over the standing

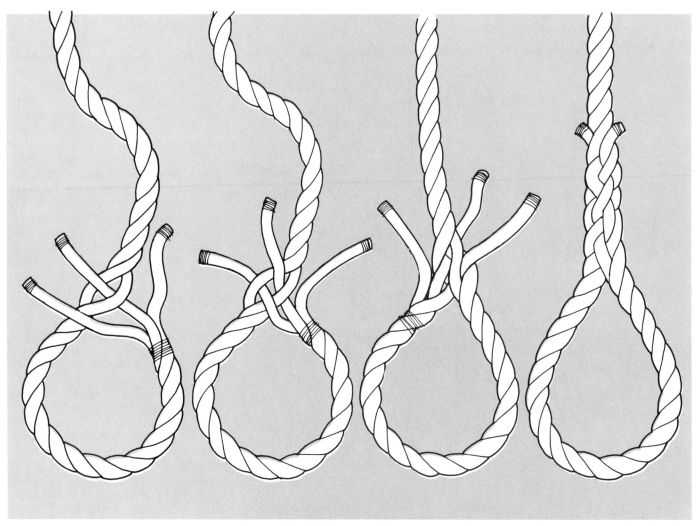

To eye splice laid line, unravel the strands and take tucks, over one strand and under one, in a center-left-right sequence. Take several tucks pulling them tight as you go and trim the excess.

part (main portion) of the line with the strands lying naturally. Tuck the center strand under a strand on the standing part, then tuck the left-hand strand under the next strand up. Now take the right-hand strand partway around the standing part to the right and tuck it under the remaining strand. Pull on the three strand ends to smooth out the tucks and then take three to six more tucks (over one strand and under the next one) in a

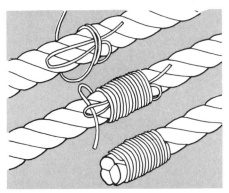

Whip a laid line's end by wrapping twine around it (above) or passing a needle and twine through it and making wraps.

center-left-right sequence, smoothing out the splice as you go along. When finished, rub the splice hard between your two palms to seat the strands more deeply and cut off the ends of the strands. When splicing large lines, the strand ends may become fuzzy or unravel. To guard against this, wrap them tightly with a turn of plastic electrician's tape.

Since an eye splice is permanent, it should be made in lines that you don't intend to knot — for example, in the end of an anchor rode where the eye will be shackled to the anchor, or in the ends of docking lines. Where it will chafe against a metal fitting like a shackle, put a metal or plastic loop called a thimble inside the eye.

Whipping Laid Line

A line will unravel unless it is whipped. To whip a line, tightly wind several turns of waxed string called sailmaker's twine around it counterclockwise, and tie the ends with a secure square knot. A more permanent whipping can be made with a strong

sewing needle and sailmaker's twine. To start the whipping, pass the needle through the line and pull the twine until the knot at its end stops against the line. Then make several tight wraps before finishing the whipping off with two or three more passes through the line. The whipping's length should equal the line's diameter. The whipping will be neater if you do it before cutting the line.

The line's bitter end may also be locked temporarily with a tight wrapping of plastic tape, or if the diameter is small, by burning it with a match or blowtorch after it has been wrapped with cellophane tape. The melted cellophane will seal the end for a while.

Braided Rope

The alternative to laid rope is braided rope, in which fibers are interwoven along the length of the rope with clockwise and counterclockwise torques balancing each other out. From a near distance, the fibers in braided rope seem to be running in the same direction (although they actually

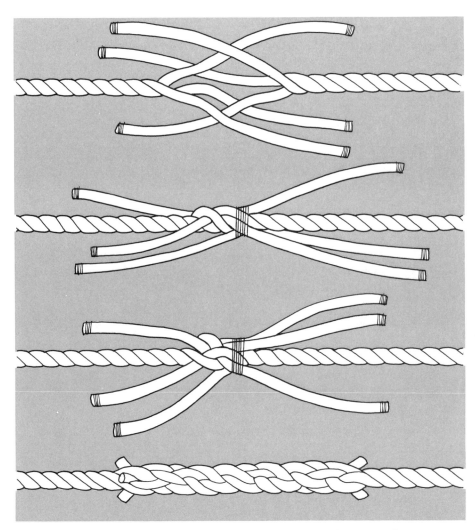

A short splice, done much like an eye splice, joins two laid lines of the same diameter. Before starting, whip or tape the bases of splices to forestall unraveling. A short splice may not render through blocks, so use a long splice if size is important.

Braided rope, more common on boats than laid rope, has a strong, hard core inside a soft cover.

Line

vary by a few degrees), whereas the fibers in laid line run distinctly on the bias. Braided line usually has two parts: a hard, strong core, and around the core, a softer cover. Some braided line can be spliced into eyes by removing the core from the bitter end and doubling it back into the cover.

Because of its relatively complex construction, braided rope is usually more expensive than laid rope of the same size. Since Dacron braid is usually less stretchy and easier on the hands than Dacron laid line, the extra cost is often worthwhile. In nylon, braid and laid line may be comparable in strength, but, again, braid is not as rough on hands.

While it can be whipped, a braided end can be securely sealed by applying a blowtorch's flame or a very hot knife blade to melt the fibers.

Another advantage of braid is that it may be coiled without using a clockwise quarter-turn of the wrist. Since no torque is woven into the line, there is none to be removed. But braid can kink badly. It should be coiled in long loops and faked on deck before it's allowed to run out. A proper coil will hang in large figure-8s; it should be finished off the same way as a laid line's coil.

The anchor rode and docking and mooring lines should stretch to absorb heavy strains and ease the load on the cleats, anchor, and other gear. They should be made of nylon, which stretches more than Dacron. For these purposes, laid construction (rope with three large strands) is preferred because it is less subject to chafing than braid.

Halyards and sheets should stretch very little, otherwise you will have to adjust them constantly. Dacron rope works well for sheets in most boats and in halyards in many boats smaller than about 50 feet. Larger boats (and small racing boats, where stretch can hurt speed) need halyards and sometimes sheets made of wire or special low-stretch Kevlar rope. Kevlar is a brown synthetic fiber that stretches

even less than stainless-steel wire. Since Kevlar fibers have almost no give, they fracture when making sharp bends, so the sheaves on blocks must be especially large and Kevlar lines should not have knots.

Nylon Rope

Of the ropes available, nylon is one of the strongest as well as the stretchiest. It is best used when stretch is either helpful (as in anchor rodes, where a stretchy rode will absorb shocks on the boat without pulling the anchor out of the bottom) or at least not harmful (as in docking and mooring lines, which do not have to be kept drum-tight). Nylon can stretch up to one-half again its length and then rebound without permanent damage to its fibers or construction. Nylon also resists chafe extremely well, so it can be led around fittings without excessive cause for concern about breakage. Nylon fibers are rough and can irritate hands, so a crew member with soft hands may want to wear gloves when handling the anchor rode.

Dacron Rope

Size for size, Dacron is about 10 percent weaker than nylon — but Dacron stretches much less than its synthetic cousin. (Dacron, by the way, is always capitalized because it's a trademark.) From a distance, nylon and Dacron look much alike, but Dacron is smoother and easier to handle than nylon. Dacron is much preferred for halyards, sheets, and other lines that should not stretch or that are adjusted frequently. Dacron can be chafed through more quickly than nylon, so it must be led carefully away from obstructions. If two Dacron lines under tension are touching, the larger one may saw through the smaller like the proverbial hot knife through butter.

Polypropylene Rope

Neither nylon nor Dacron is buoyant. When getting under way, always check to see that docking and mooring lines, the anchor rode, sheets, and other lines are not dragging overboard, where they may foul the propeller or rudder. The Gordian Knot is

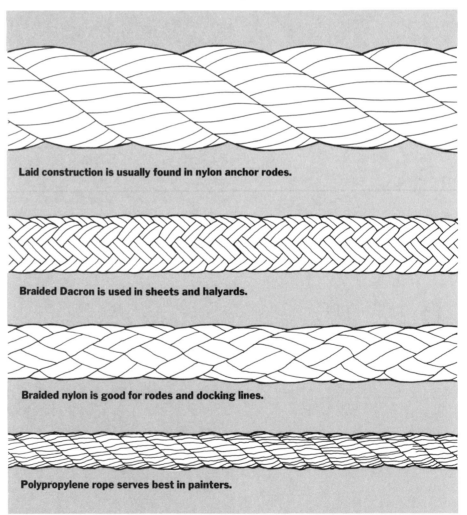

Laid construction is usually found in nylon anchor rodes.

Braided Dacron is used in sheets and halyards.

Braided nylon is good for rodes and docking lines.

Polypropylene rope serves best in painters.

Each type of rope has characteristics that suit it for specific jobs: strong, stretchy nylon for anchor rodes and docking lines; buoyant polypropylene for painters; low-stretch Dacron for sheets and halyards. Whichever you use, make it large enough to handle comfortably — at least 3/8-inch diameter for most jobs on boats larger than 20 feet.

child's play compared with a dozen wraps of Dacron line around a seized-up propeller shaft. The only solution to the problem is to dive overboard and slice away at the tangle with a sharp knife or cut it with a hacksaw.

It's best, then, to use buoyant polypropylene line for jobs near the propeller, for instance, in the painter (bow line) of the dinghy that's towed astern, or in waterskiing lines. Polypropylene floats, comes in a variety of bright, highly visible colors, and (though it's 40 percent weaker than nylon) is strong enough for these duties. Its major drawback is its extremely hard texture; it will slip on cleats and in a crew's hands. Under load, it can cut into fingers and palms. Since polypropylene comes in both laid and braided form, it can be spliced. Still, it is best suited for relatively low-load jobs in which its buoyancy is a major asset and not merely a small bonus.

Selecting a Line

Lines should be chosen for their use-

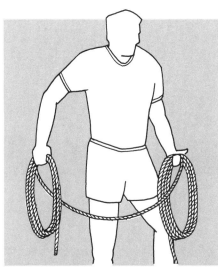

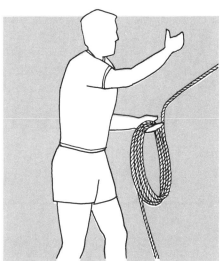

Heaving a line, throw three coils while letting the rest run off the other hand. Aim upwind of your target.

fulness for specific jobs. In chapter 14 we'll have a lot to say about selecting the right size nylon for an anchor rode based on the anticipated loads. Dacron, too, should be chosen with the load in mind, but also with some consideration toward its ease of handling. The loads on a sail vary with its size, the apparent wind velocity, and the air's temperature. For a given sail, as the air temperature drops the load increases gradually, but as the wind velocity increases the load is squared. The load on a large boat's genoa jib in a fresh wind may be over 5,000 pounds, but on a 30-footer's genoa in moderate air, it may be only 500 pounds. As the loads increase, use larger line.

Very small Dacron — 3/16-inch or 1/4-inch diameter — may be suitable for some jobs on dinghies, but its light weight and low friction are more than counterbalanced by its handling problems. The human hand has trouble holding onto line smaller than about 3/8-inch diameter, so use large lines on sheets and halyards. (If your hands are soft, wear leather sailing gloves to improve your grip.) Two other benefits of choosing a line larger than required are that large line stretches less under a given pull than a smaller line and also holds on a winch with fewer turns. Of course, large line costs more and requires larger blocks, cleats, and shackles.

Heaving a Line

You may sometimes have to pass a line from your boat to a pier or another boat over a long distance. Ideally you would have a special heaving line aboard. This is a long, skinny line with a handsome, heavy piece of ropework called a monkey's fist at the bitter end. The monkey's fist is whirled and thrown across, and the other crew hauls in the heaving line and the heavier tow line or docking line tied to it.

But if you don't have a proper heaving line, here's how you can get your line across. First, fake the line on deck and pull off enough to cover the distance, plus 6 feet. Coil this amount carefully and hold the coils loosely in your nonthrowing hand. Take three coils in your throwing hand. Move as far as you can from obstructions, such as the mast and rigging. Open your nonthrowing hand so the line will pull off smoothly, then heave the line with a sweep of your other hand, ending with a flick of the wrist (like throwing a Frisbee underhanded). Aim just upwind of your target, who should have an arm extended to grab the line. As the three coils fly out from your right

(Above) The right way to neaten up a line in use, this coil can be quickly undone. (Below) A more permanent coil is made before stowing an unused line.

hand, extend your left arm so the remaining line follows behind with little resistance. Don't take a strain on the line until your target has a good grasp on it.

A line is heaved so rarely these days that somebody who can do it well usually gets considerable acclaim. Beyond that, it may be a lifesaver someday.

Wire Rope

Besides synthetic fiber rope, there is also wire rope, made from either stainless steel or galvanized steel. Wire rope is either flexible 7 x 19 wire used in most halyards and some boats' sheets and sail controls or stiff 1 x 19 wire used in stays. The first number represents the number of strands in the wire, and the second number indicates the number of individual wires in each strand.

The main advantage that wire rope has over synthetic rope is its strength. Size for size, wire rope is about 25 percent stronger than nylon rope and 35 percent stronger than Dacron rope. It stretches considerably less than either, and (because a smaller diameter is required for a given load) 7 x 19 wire runs through blocks more efficiently. Wire rope is more resistant to chafe, although its strands can break and stick out of the rope where it passes through blocks. These breaks are called "meat hooks" because the sharp wires can snag hands or clothing as efficiently as a butcher's hook. You must be extremely vigilant about keeping wire rope free of meat hooks, which, besides damaging sailors, can rip sails. Tape a meat hook, or better yet, snap it off with wire cutters or break it off with a marlinspike (spike on a sailor's knife) rubbed vigorously against it.

Breaking load for breaking load, wire rope is more expensive than synthetic rope, and it's heavier per running foot too. Although it can be spliced using special tools, it's usually attached to fittings with swaged clamps. (Professional riggers are best qualified to splice or swage wire.) Handling wire can be uncomfortable, so Dacron tails generally are long-spliced into flexible wire to facilitate handling.

Galvanized steel wire is less expensive than stainless-steel wire — but it's also weaker and stretchier, and when the galvanizing eventually wears off, the wire may rust. Galvanized wire rope is more flexible than stainless, so it's less likely to develop meat hooks. Whatever the type, wire rope should be inspected periodically for meat hooks, wear, and rust. It should be replaced if kinks develop or when you see rust between the strands. When wire breaks, it generally goes suddenly, with little or no notice, and since most wire rope is used aloft in stays and halyards or below deck in steering cables, a break can be more disastrous than the snapping of an easily replaceable jib sheet.

Because it is so much smaller than synthetic rope, 7 x 19 wire requires special sheaves in blocks, with deep, narrow grooves that capture the halyard and keep it from jumping out and jamming. This accident is called jumping the sheave.

The weakest part of a wire halyard is the wire-to-rope splice, which can reduce strength by more than 10 percent. The splice itself should carry as small a load as possible. The best way to guarantee this is to wrap at least six turns of wire around the halyard winch, leaving the splice between the winch and the cleat, so the winch and not the splice absorbs any shock loads. Since jibs have different length luffs, to meet this requirement you may have to rig wire pendants from their heads to the optimum position for the halyard shackle.

Meat hooks — broken wire strands — rip hands and sails. Clip them off with wire cutters.

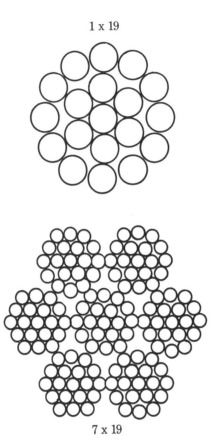

1 x 19

7 x 19

Stiff 1 x 19 wire (top) is used in stays, flexible 7 x 19 wire rope in halyards. The first number is the number of strands and the second is the number of wires in each strand. Wire can be spliced by professional riggers.

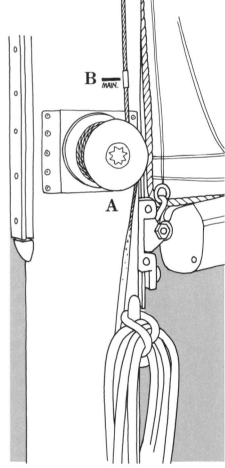

B —
MAIN.

A

With the sail hoisted, the splice between the wire halyard and the rope tail should lie between the winch and cleat when at least six turns of wire are on the winch drum (A). Mark the halyard over a reference point on the mast (B).

On the mainsail halyard, leave enough wire so there are six turns on the winch even when the sail is deeply reefed, with the halyard lowered several feet. This requires a lot of surplus wire when the sail is fully hoisted — to get it out of the way, you can wrap it in loops around the winch and the cleat. Or you can use an all-wire halyard on a reel halyard winch, which works much like a fishing reel. When the sail is fully hoisted and the wire is wound up on the drum, a friction brake is applied to keep the reel from backing off. Unfortunately the brakes on these winches are not entirely foolproof; sailors have been injured by the backlash of wire and by the spinning winch handles.

Coiling Wire Rope

Coil wire rope "with the lay" — in large clockwise loops with a right twist of the wrist if it is laid to the right, and vice-versa. If it has a rope tail, coil the wire first, secure the coil with tape at three places, and then coil the tail.

Protecting Line Against Chafe

All lines can be chafed (abraded) either by fittings or by another line. The best way to deal with chafe is to avoid it in the first place. Lines should lead fair (without chafe); if this is impossible, rig turning blocks to redirect the line away from sharp edges. Narrow redirections will add very slight friction to the line, but if you change the line angle by more than 60°, hauling will be much more difficult. If the block redirects a line by 100° or more, the load on the block will be as high as twice the load on the line. Therefore turning blocks must be installed strongly.

When hoisting a sail, be sure that the halyard is not wrapped around itself, another halyard, or a stay. Due to the increased friction, the halyard will suffer abrasion, denting, or breakage. Sheets can be easily misled around lifelines, shrouds, or stanchions, which can saw rapidly through synthetic fiber. The anchor rode should be led through a chock (open slotted fairlead) at the bow, but if the chock is too small or has sharp edges, the rode will chafe. You may have to relead the rode through a block shackled to the jib tack fitting at the base of the headstay.

Chafe sometimes is unavoidable, and then the best you can do is minimize it. You can wrap a heavy cloth, a piece of leather, or a split piece of garden hose around the line. Or you can let out or pull in the line every hour or so in order that the chafe is not concentrated on one spot.

The lines most liable to chafe are the jib sheets and the docking lines. If one end is chafed badly, simply end-for-end the line to put the abraded part where the load is least. This is a good reason to make sheets and docking lines much longer than you would first think is necessary, for as the ends are chafed you can cut them off and still have plenty of line left for the job.

A good sailmaker will anticipate chafe by wrapping the tack, head, and clew with sacrificial leather that can be readily replaced. Likewise, jib halyard shackles that abrade in the narrow notch between the headstay and the mast should also be protected with leather, particularly around their splices or clamps.

Halyard and Sheet Marks

A frequent cause of chafe is hauling a halyard too high so the shackle or the head of the sail jams in the halyard sheave, or trimming a sheet too far in so the sail rubs against the standing rigging. The best way to prevent these mishaps is to mark the halyards and sheets at a clearly visible spot so the hauler or trimmer knows when to stop pulling. Sometimes you may have to mark the deck or mast under the line to provide a reference point. You may also mark the sheets to indicate proper trim for certain wind strengths. Use indelible pens on synthetic rope. Wire rope can be marked with plastic tape or by weaving a piece of light wire between the strands. It's a good idea to mark the main halyard to show proper heights for the reefs; this will save time and guesswork in rough weather.

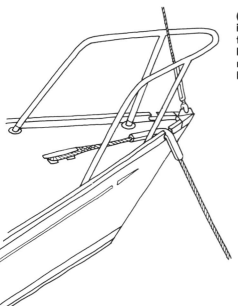

(Above) A foot (turning) block isn't needed if the lead from the block to the winch is fair and properly angled. (Left) A short length of hose, piece of leather, or even a rag protects the anchor rode and docking line from chafe.

Knots, Bends, and Hitches

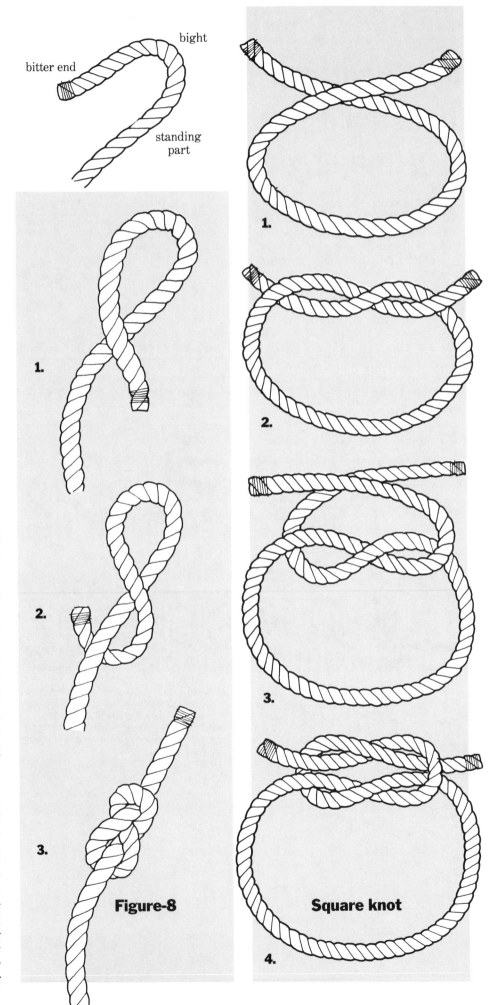

Synthetic lines are tied to fittings with a hitch and to other lines with a bend. While a knot, technically speaking, is an alteration in one line not affecting other objects, the word "knot" has come to include the definitions of "hitch" and "bend" as well. No matter what you call it, a knot, bend, or hitch works because of the friction created by turns in the line. This friction also weakens the line, and sometimes it's so great that the knot can't be untied. Of the thousands of knots that have been invented over the ages, the following eight are most applicable to normal sailing use because they're strong and easy to tie and untie.

First, some terminology: the *bitter end* of a line is its very end, the *standing part* is the main section, a *bight* is a U-shaped portion of the standing part, and a *loop* is a small circle in the standing part.

The Essential Eight Knots

The figure-8 is tied in the ends of lines to stop them from running out through blocks. Because it's easier to untie than the simple overhand knot, the figure-8 can be used in the ends of lines that will have to be rerigged frequently (jib sheets, for example). But for the same reason, the figure-8 should not be used in the ends of lines that are rarely rerigged or that will shake or vibrate. The overhand knot, which cinches very tight, is best for these lines. Whichever knot you use, tie it at least four inches from the bitter end so it has room to slip. Do not tie these knots in the ends of spinnaker sheets. If you lose control of the spinnaker, you may want to let the sheets run.

The square knot is the best-known sailors' knot. Used to tie two lines of the same diameter together, it's nothing more than two overhand knots. The first is tied "right over left" by passing the right-hand bitter end over and under the left-hand standing part. Next, go "left over right" by passing the new left-hand bitter end over and under the new right-hand standing part. You know you've tied it correctly if the two bitter ends come out of their loops on the same side of the standing

142

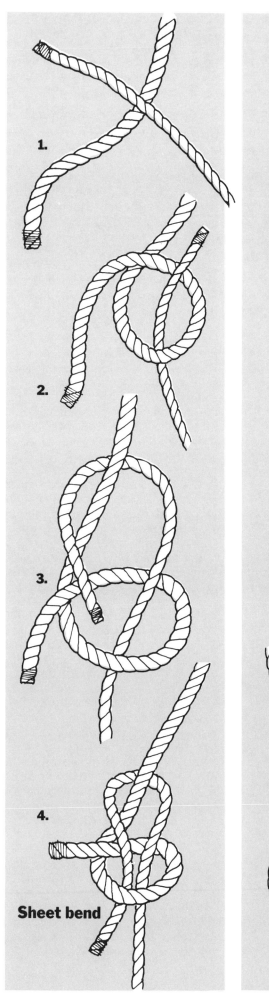

Sheet bend

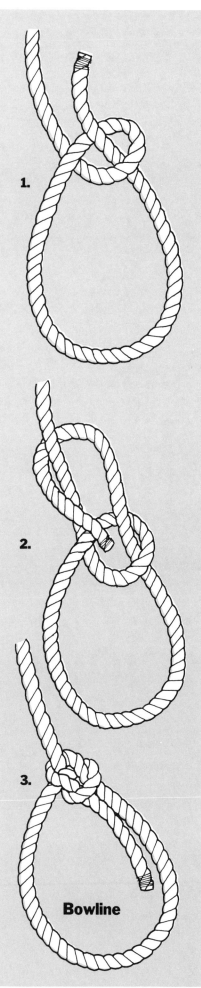

Bowline

parts or when, if you push the two ends toward the middle, there are two symmetrical bights. Otherwise you've tied a granny knot, which will come undone very quickly. The advantage of the square knot is that it's easy to tie and untie, except when it's wet under heavy strain. The disadvantage is that because the turns are abrupt, it's 50 percent weaker than the lines themselves, so is not a knot to stake your life or rig on. A version of the square knot is the reef knot, used to secure the middle of a reefed sail to the boom. Here, the second overhand knot —"left over right" — is not completed but left with a bow, which allows the knot to be untied by simply pulling the bow out.

The sheet bend is used instead of the square knot to tie lines of different diameters together. Form a loop with the end of the larger line, with the bitter end lying on top of the standing part. Pass the smaller line's bitter end up through the loop, around the standing part, and back through the loop. Be sure to slide the smaller line down hard onto the loop. Easily untied, the sheet bend is almost 50 percent the strength of the smaller line.

Bowlines are one of the most reliable knots for making loops, and are used to tie jib sheets to the clew and lines to fittings. It usually is the most common knot seen aboard sailboats. Tie it by forming a small loop in the standing part, leaving hanging a length of line to the bitter end equal to twice the size of the large loop you want to make. This part of the line should lie over the standing part. Pass the bitter end up through the small loop, around the standing part, and back through the small loop. Cinch the knot tightly. Generations of sailors have learned how to tie the bowline by remembering, "The rabbit goes up through the hole, around the tree, and back down into the hole." To tie a bowline quickly, lay the bitter end over the standing part and then twist the standing part up and away from you, forming a loop with the bitter end sticking up through it. Pass the bitter end around the standing part above the loop and pull it back through the loop. The bowline very rarely jams even when it's wet, since the standing part can be "capsized," or pulled up by hand or by prying it up with a marlinspike or screwdriver. The bowline is about 40 percent weaker than the line and 30 percent weaker than an eye splice.

Knots, Bends, and Hitches

The clove hitch, two loops side by side, is used to make a docking line fast to a bollard (a post on a pier), or to tie a fender to a lifeline. It can be tied two ways. One is to loop the bitter end around the object twice, each time with the end on the same side of the standing part. If the clove hitch is properly tied, the two ends of the line should end up going in opposite directions. The other way is to "throw a clove hitch" by forming the loops first in your hands and then dropping them over the bollard or post. While simple to tie and untie, the clove hitch can loosen itself. The best prevention is to secure it with a half hitch (overhand knot) tied around the standing part and pulled down hard against the object. A clove hitch is about 40 percent weaker than the line.

A double half-hitch is just that: two half-hitches (or a clove hitch) tied around the standing part to form a loop that can be adjusted by sliding the double half-hitch up and down. To increase its security, take a round turn (a full turn) around the object to absorb some of the strain. Also called two half-hitches, the double half-hitch is about 30 percent weaker than its line. While a double half-hitch is quicker to tie, a bowline makes a safer loop.

The fisherman's bend, or anchor bend, makes a more secure loop than the bowline, which can shake loose. When used to tie a rode to an anchor, it is formed by twice passing the bitter end through the fitting, then passing the end around the standing part and back under the two round turns, and finishing off with a double half-hitch around the standing part. With laid line, tuck the bitter end under a strand in the standing part to prevent an accidental untying. Because it's only 25 percent weaker than the line it's often preferred to a bowline, but it may be hard to untie.

The rolling hitch has many uses. With it you can tie one line around the middle of another or around a mast in such a way that it won't slide when under strain. It is especially useful to take the strain off another line, such as a jib sheet, while the end of that line is untied or repositioned. To tie this hitch, make three loops with the bitter end around the object. It is essentially a clove hitch with a third turn. The second turn must overlap the first to cinch it down. To jam the rolling hitch, pull the line in the direction of the overlapped turn; to slide it, pull the line the other way. The rolling hitch slightly weakens the line to which it is secured.

Learning to tie these knots shouldn't be hard. Three feet of light line, a table leg, and a little time are all you need. Keep practicing until you can tie each in less than 10 seconds. You should be able to tie the bowline, the clove hitch, and the rolling hitch — the most valuable of the eight — in the dark. Someday, one of those three knots may save your boat, even your life.

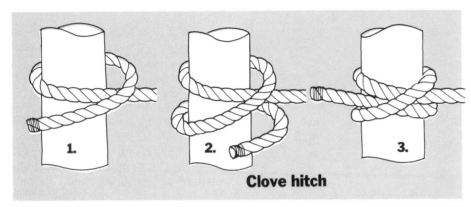

Clove hitch

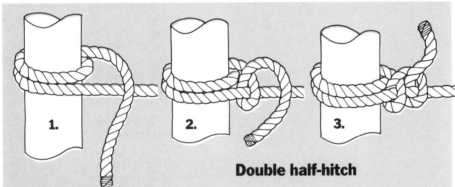

Double half-hitch

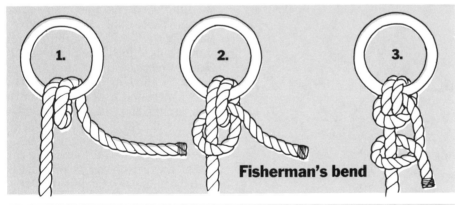

Fisherman's bend

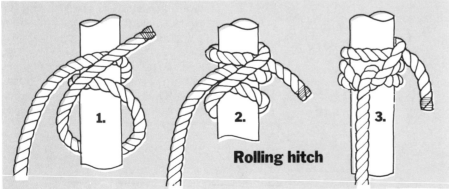

Rolling hitch

Winches

A winch is a mechanical aid that increases a sailor's pull on a sheet, halyard, or other loaded line. It consists of a revolving drum mounted on a secure base. The drum rotates clockwise when it is turned by a metal arm, called a winch handle, inserted in its top. (Some winches are turned by electric motors.) The handle usually works through gears that increase the mechanical advantage already provided by its own lever effect. The simplest winches have only one gear; more complicated ones have as many as four gears that are changed by revolving the winch handle the other way or by activating switches.

The sheet or halyard led to the winch should come up at it at a slight angle (or the winch should be cocked slightly); otherwise, if the sheet is led down or at a right angle to the drum, the turns of the line on the drum will overlap each other and jam. Called a riding turn, this jam-up can be removed in light air by heaving back on the sheet, and in fresh air by taking the strain off the sheet with another line using a rolling hitch and unwrapping it.

How to Use a Winch

To operate a winch, wrap the sheet or halyard clockwise around the drum. If you're just taking in slack — say, when tacking — use only one turn, but increase the number of turns as the pull builds. With large-diameter line, which creates excellent friction on the drum, you'll need fewer turns than with skinny line. Four turns should be all you need when using synthetic line, and six or more turns with wire rope.

To trim the line, insert the winch handle in the top of the winch and turn it with one hand while tailing (pulling on the tail of the line behind the winch) with the other. Use more powerful gears if you need them, or turn the handle with both hands while somebody else tails. The best position for grinding the winch handle with both hands is to stoop or lean over it, facing down, so you get your arms, shoulders, and back into the turns. When trimming short lengths of line, sit or stoop

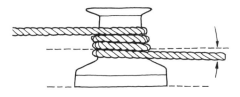

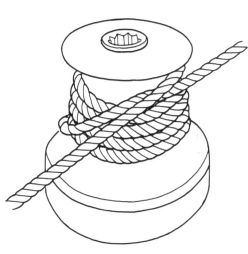

(Top) Leading the line up to the winch at a slight angle will prevent riding turns. (Bottom) Unwind a riding turn by pulling the sheet out counterclockwise or taking the load off with another line and loosening the wraps.

On this 46-foot ocean racer halyards, sheets, and sail controls are handled by 12 winches and many Clam and jam cleats. A self-tailing winch is used for the main sheet (lower left) and the big jib sheet winches are cross-connected so the leeward drum can be turned by a total of four men, two at each station. The average 30-foot cruising boat should have a winch for each halyard, two for the jib sheets, and if the mainsail is big, one for the main sheet.

Winches

facing the sail or other object that you're adjusting and pull the handle toward you. Always remove handles when they're not in use, since they can snag sheets or legs.

To ease the line, hold the tail with one hand and push the palm of the other hand against the turns on the drum. Then ease out the tail and your braking hand simultaneously, letting out about 2 inches at a time. To cast off a line when tacking or lowering a halyard, pull it directly off the drum and let it run out through your hands.

Be extremely careful not to let fingers, long hair, or clothing catch in

turns around a winch. It can be awkward and painful.

When you're using a winch and there isn't a free cleat, secure the line to the winch using a knot called the "towboat hitch" or "tugboatman's hitch." To tie it, first make a bight or small loop in the tail. Second, pass the bight under the standing part between the winch and the sail and snug it up tight to the drum. Third, to lock the hitch, take the loop back and over the winch. Most of the work is done at the standing part at the second step. The loop on the winch should not be so tight that you can't get it off quickly.

Special Gear

Some winch handles have a lock worked with a button that secures them when they are inserted. These lock-in handles should always be used when working a vertically mounted winch on a mast, for otherwise the handle will slip out and go overboard — or worse, injure a crew member.

A few winches are equipped with special cleats that hold the line as it is

trimmed, so a tailer is not necessary. These self-tailing winches are more expensive than regular winches but are well worth the added cost, particularly for shorthanded sailing with small crews.

We described reel halyard winches earlier in this chapter. Other specialized winches include coffee grinders and windlasses. A coffee grinder is an extremely powerful deck-mounted winch consisting of a large drum and one or two sets of vertical handles at which two or four grinders can work. These elaborate winches are standard equipment on ocean racers and America's Cup yachts.

A windlass is used to handle anchor rodes. Some electrically powered windlasses are actually large winches run off the yacht's batteries; others are operated mechanically, with a handle. Most windlasses have a drum for rope rodes as well as a wildcat — or notched drum — for chain rodes. The links and the notches in the wildcat must match up; otherwise the chain will not hold. Windlasses should be inspected and cleaned out more frequently than winches, if only because their location on the foredeck is wetter than a winch's position back in the cockpit. Mud and weed that come up with the chain will foul the windlass and its cat unless they're scrubbed off. Large yachts are equipped with special deck pumps that carry sea or lake water through a hull fitting and up to a hose on deck for washing down dirty anchors.

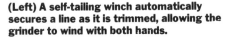

(Left) A self-tailing winch automatically secures a line as it is trimmed, allowing the grinder to wind with both hands.

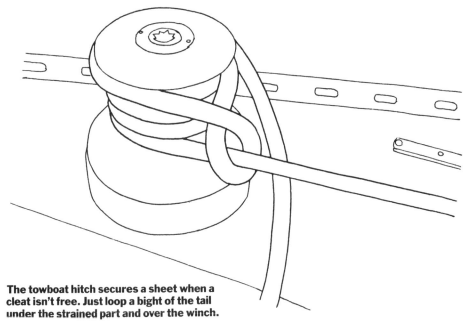

(Top) Have at least three turns on the winch when pulling a loaded sheet or halyard. (Above) Release a sheet or halyard by pulling the wraps up and off the drum.

The towboat hitch secures a sheet when a cleat isn't free. Just loop a bight of the tail under the strained part and over the winch.

Cleats

Except in small racing dinghies, most lines are cleated when they aren't being eased or trimmed. Several types of cleats are available besides the self-tailers on winches. The most reliable is the metal or wooden horn cleat — little more than a short bar supported by legs an inch or two above the deck or spar. The cleat should be securely screwed on, or even through-bolted if there's any chance that it will take a vertical strain. Screws will withstand normal sideways sheet strain. The cleat bar should be angled 10° to the left of the line leading to it to allow the line to be passed completely around

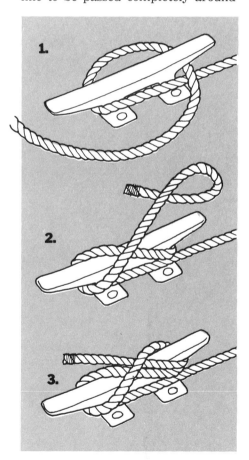

To cleat a line start by snubbing it with a turn (top) and finish with a half-hitch.

the cleat without jamming in itself. The line should not be too big for the cleat.

Using the Horn Cleat

To cleat a line, first pass it around the back horn, then around the forward horn. This usually creates enough resistance to snub the line against heavy strains, so long as a light pull is kept on the tail.

To secure the line completely, pass it around the back horn in the opposite direction from the way you originally

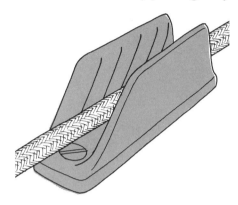

A plastic or aluminum Clam Cleat must fit its line.

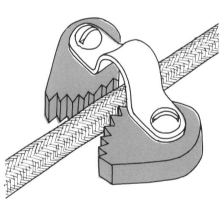

Cam cleats release lines quickly but their moving parts may break.

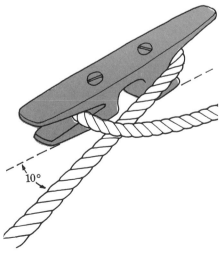

Jam cleats, like horn cleats, should be angled 10° to the line.

led it, so it crosses the top of the horn. Then pull it to the front horn and loop it in a half-hitch. You've done it correctly if the line comes out directly over the first loop you made.

The half-hitch locks the line so it won't fall off the cleat. With thin line that is too small for the cleat, that may not be a threat, and the half-hitch may actually jam. But if the line and the cleat are correctly mated, the cleating system that we've just described — one round turn, a loop, and a half-hitch — is the most secure, and you shouldn't have any trouble uncleating quickly.

Once the line is cleated, you can coil or fake it. Some well-thought-out boats are equipped with small sacks for the tails of sheets and halyards. On other boats, small lengths of line or shockcord are used to secure coils of line so they don't get loose and drag overboard. More than one person has compared a sailboat with an unruly spaghetti factory; try to keep all that pasta in the pot.

Quick-Action Cleats

Besides the traditional horn cleat, there are several types of quick-action jam cleats. The most popular is called the **Clam Cleat** (it's a trademark), a notched channel of hardened plastic or aluminum into which the line is dropped. The notches dig into the sides of the line to hold it. To let the line go, trim it some more and lift it out. Although the Clam Cleat works quickly and has no moving parts, it has two disadvantages that apply more to cruising boats than to small daysailers and dinghies. First of all, since the line must be trimmed to be released, it may take a while to cast off a heavily loaded sheet — which is exactly the sort of thing you should be able to do easily in dangerous, gusty winds. And an open Clam Cleat may sometimes suck up and capture lines that aren't meant for it, like a jib sheet that's flying around during a tack.

The **cam cleat**, on the other hand, has two moving jaws that spring tight on any line that's dropped between them. It won't suck up loose lines, but neither does it have the strength of a Clam Cleat. Its moving parts can create a maintenance problem. Like the Clam Cleat, the cam cleat is best suited for small boats.

The **jam cleat** looks much like the horn cleat except that there is a sharp notch in the front horn that can grab lines securely with only one wrap. As with the Clam Cleat, however, freeing a heavily loaded line from a jam cleat may be difficult.

Blocks and Tackles

Blocks

A block is a nautical pulley. It consists of a sheave suspended between cheeks (sides) either on a pin or on two ball-bearing races. The block is attached to the deck, a spar, or other fittings with a shackle (which we'll say more about later). There are several types of blocks:

A **single block** has a single sheave and shackle and is used primarily to redirect lines, like sheets or halyards. A **double block** has two sheaves, side by side, and a **triple block** has three sheaves. In a **sister block**, two sheaves are arranged end to end.

A **becket block** may have one, two, or three sheaves plus a stationary eye to which a line is dead-ended (tied at its end).

A **snatch block** has a side gate that opens and closes, allowing a line to be inserted at its standing part, rather than working all the way to the bitter end and threading it in.

A **halyard sheave**, while not a true block, is a sheave inserted in the mast to carry halyards.

A **foot block** is a single or double block whose side is screwed or bolted to the deck and through which sheets are led.

A **cheek block** is a single or double block whose side is secured to a spar and through which halyards and sail controls are led.

Blocks come in many different sizes to meet most sail-handling needs, and are made of plastic, metal, or wood. When buying a new block, be sure you know how it will be used. Wire rope requires special grooved sheaves which, because wire is brittle, must be larger in diameter than sheaves for synthetic rope. Some jobs impose especially heavy loads and therefore require especially large blocks — turning blocks, fore guys, and boom vangs come under sharper, more intense strains than jib sheet leads and Cunninghams. Manufacturers' catalogs specify safe load limits, including large safety factors. By matching these specifications to the anticipated

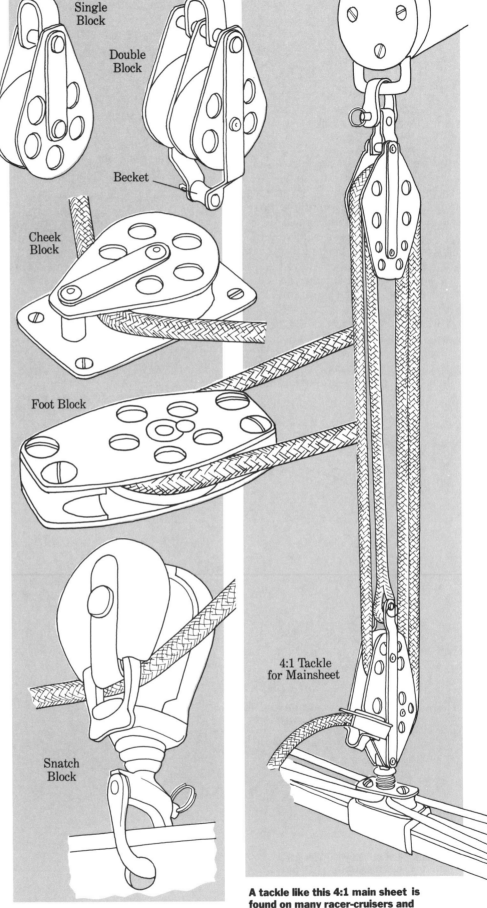

Single Block

Double Block

Becket

Cheek Block

Foot Block

Snatch Block

4:1 Tackle for Mainsheet

A wide variety of blocks are found on even the smallest boats. Some provide power; others simply direct lines so the leads are fair.

A tackle like this 4:1 main sheet is found on many racer-cruisers and daysailers. The integral cam cleat holding the main sheet is angled up slightly so the line can be quickly released with a downward snap of the wrist.

loads and the line's breaking strength (also supplied in catalogs), you'll be able to make a safe choice. Take a sample of the line to the store to guarantee that you'll buy the correct size sheave.

Tackles

Tackles are systems of blocks and lines that increase pulling power. Where winches work best on long hauls, like on a sheet or halyard, tackles provide excellent power for short pulls, like on the Cunningham or traveler control. Tackles also lessen the load on the line so small rope can be used for a job that, if performed without a tackle, would require larger rope. And since the blocks in a tackle can be spread, there's less risk of damage to the object being hauled. For example, a main sheet tackle pulls safely on two or three points spread over several feet on the boom; a single-point load might break the spar.

The power of a tackle, called the mechanical advantage, can be easily calculated by counting its parts — the number of short lengths of line in the tackle. In a three-part tackle, a single block and a single block with a becket divide the line into three parts to make a mechanical advantage of 3:1 (technically, a little less due to friction in the sheaves). What this means is that you can haul a 90-pound load by exerting 30 pounds of pull on the line. As parts are added, the mechanical advantage increases; in fact on some tough jobs a tackle may be pulling on another tackle.

The main limit on a tackle's utility is its friction. Even ball-bearing sheaves have some friction, and in most tackles the line chafes against itself. The larger the tackle is, the more friction there must be. This imposes a practical limit on the use of high-power tackles, since there is a direct correlation between mechanical advantage and the amount of line that must be pulled. For example, using a 3:1 tackle, you must pull 3 feet of line to haul the object 1 foot — which means that you'll require 30 feet of line to move an object only 10 feet.

With the advent of strong winches and, more recently, sophisticated, accurate hydraulic devices, the old-fashioned tackle has gone somewhat out of fashion on boats. But for an inexpensive way to pull objects a short distance, you probably should look no further. Figure out the load on a job and divide it by your strength. The quotient is the required number of parts.

Shackles

To a great extent shackles hold rigs together. They link halyards to sails, spinnaker sheets to clews, main sheet blocks to the boom — and do so in a wide variety of forms and ways. Most shackles are made entirely of stainless steel, which is strong but somewhat brittle. When a stainless-steel shackle is bent or dented, it cannot be repaired without losing some of its strength, unlike a fitting made of softer bronze. Manufacturers specify safe working loads for sound shackles; the gear should be used on loads one-half that number to provide a safety factor of two. An exception to this is the use of a relatively small shackle as a "weak-link" sacrifice to keep more valuable equipment intact. For example, the main boom may break if allowed to drag in the water on a reach in windy weather. So you might install a weak-link shackle between the boom vang and the spar so the boom will lift if a crew member can't release the vang control in time.

The most widely used shackles are these:

Screw shackles have U-shaped structures with a gap closed by a threaded clevis pin. Though slow to open and shut, a screw shackle is the most secure shackle available. It's used on the main halyard and the anchor, and to secure blocks permanently to fittings. To doubly secure a screw shackle, wire, lash, or tape its pin after it's been screwed in tightly. A version of the screw shackle, the *twist shackle*, used on small boats, is closed by pushing a pin through a hole and twisting it.

Snap shackles open and close around a manually operated, spring-

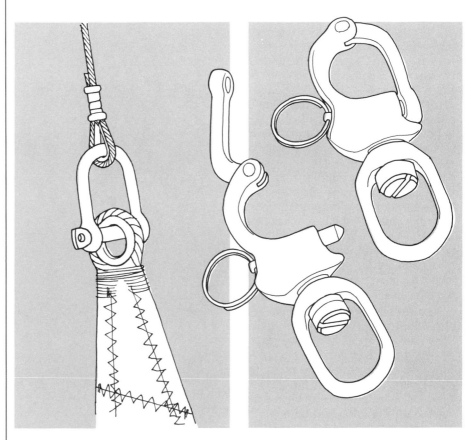

A screw tackle is used when security is more important than quick opening and closing, for example on a halyard.

A snap shackle is used when a sheet or halyard is frequently changed. For added security wrap tape around the pin when closed.

Shackles

Sail-Handling Safety Guidelines

loaded pin or latch. Because they work quickly, they are used on jib and spinnaker halyards and spinnaker sheets. Most snap shackles include swivels to keep the line from twisting. While these swivels decrease the fittings' strength, the main weakness in a snap shackle is the spring that holds the pin shut and the shackle closed. For added security, they may be wrapped in tape. These pins should be inspected periodically for wear and corrosion. The trip lines to the pins are liable to catch in rigging and open the shackles while a sail is being hoisted so trim them as short as possible. Snap shackles may open on a flogging sail; more ominously, they're dangerous to anybody standing nearby. Snatch blocks are secured to the deck with snap shackles.

Cotter pin shackles are used in permanent connections between fittings. U-shaped, they have an unthreaded clevis pin that is held shut by a metal cotter pin, which looks like a bobby pin. (Cotter pins must be inserted with care; for instructions on their use, see chapter 17.)

Snap hooks are smaller than snap shackles, but also are spring-loaded. When used to hook jibs onto the headstay they are called hanks. Most snap hooks are made of bronze or brass, which eventually will be sawn through by a headstay. Swap badly worn hanks near the head and tack with lightly worn hanks from the center of the luff.

Brummel Hooks are lightweight aluminum shackles used in pairs. When the slot of one hook engages the slot on the other, they are secured. Since there are no moving parts, the only problem to look out for is corrosion. These trademarked shackles are used mainly on small racing boats for securing the sheets to the spinnaker (although many dinghy racers simply tie the sheets to the sail with short bowlines).

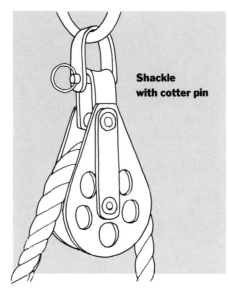

Shackle with cotter pin

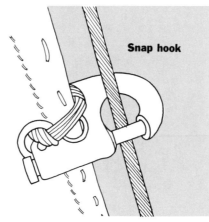

Snap hook

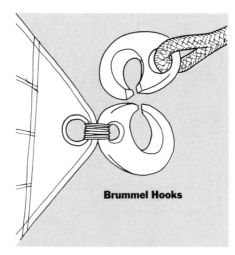

Brummel Hooks

Special shackles are used in certain situations because they are very secure (top), easy to operate (middle); or lightweight (bottom).

While sailing is one of the safest sports around, nobody should underestimate the force of a sailboat and her rig in moderate to strong winds. As we have already said in this chapter, people have been hurt by rigging, some of them severely. Having once seen a shipmate clobbered by a spinning winch handle — he suffered a concussion and a broken wrist — we know this from personal experience. Here are a few essential guidelines that should be observed on any boat, and particularly on larger boats in rough weather.

1. Inspect every screw, bolt, clevis pin, and cotter pin. Are they securely installed? Will they rip a sail or your skin?

2. Don't try to perform a two-person job alone. When doing a multihanded job, never assume that the other person is doing his or her work.

3. Use clear oral instructions. Helpful announcements: "boom coming across" (when jibing), "pole coming down" (when lowering the spinnaker pole), "halyard free" (when dousing a sail), "made" (when a shackle is made fast or a fitting is installed).

4. Use hand signals when it's noisy. Point toward somebody holding a line ("trim"), point away from her or him ("ease"), point down ("douse the sail"), point up ("hoist the sail"), open palm ("stop temporarily"), circle with index finger and thumb ("stop and cleat the line").

5. When handling a line with a load on it, snub it around a winch or cleat with one or more wraps.

6. When hauling on a halyard or trimming a sheet, always keep an eye on the sail it's attached to so you don't pull it too far.

7. Unless you have to work on an object that is moving or may soon move, stay away from it. This includes booms, spinnaker poles, jib clews, traveler cars, blocks, and winch handles. Don't sit where a line or block may hit you if something breaks.

8. One hand for yourself, one for the ship. What this means is that while you do your job, take care of yourself.

Part II
SAFETY

Chapter 6
The Sailor's Health

Seamanship in its broadest sense means to enjoy and safely use boats in all kinds of situations and weather conditions. A good seaman has mastered the principles and techniques of basic boat handling and piloting, and while continuing to learn new skills, can move on to confident self-sufficiency afloat. Anchoring, heavy-weather sailing, handling emergencies, and maintaining the boat and her equipment are all within the realm of proper seamanship, and each will be given due attention in subsequent chapters. First, though, let's look at the human factor in seamanship, at the psychological and physical aspects of sailing. How a skipper can best command and how a crew can best follow, and how to prevent and treat hypothermia, seasickness, sunburn, and serious injury — these are important considerations for anybody who wants to follow the sailor's life.

When well-led, assigned to specific tasks, and properly outfitted with warm clothing, a good crew has the confidence not only to survive rough weather but also to enjoy it.

Roles on Board

The Skipper

Somebody has to be in charge. The crew may vote on where to sail to, what to eat for dinner, or when to get under way in the morning, but there must be a commander. This man or woman should be a knowledgeable mariner who is able to steer, manage the motor and sails, anchor, pilot, and do all the big and little chores that are required to get the boat and her crew safely through the day. The skipper should also be a leader, skilled at delegating authority, willing to teach and learn, and (most of all) able to take responsibility. Like all commanders, a skipper must walk the fine line between leadership and tyranny. This is especially challenging on a pleasure boat, which unlike an army platoon or a division of a corporation, is a purely voluntary organization. People go sailing for fun, and many will get off the boat if they're not having any. Captain William Bligh of the *Bounty* may have been an excellent seaman and an extraordinary leader in emergencies, but the mere mention of his last name evokes images of a petty, cruel autocrat more interested in his ship than in his men. A skipper must indeed care for his vessel, but he should also command with the attitude of being first among equals rather than God Almighty.

As tactfully as possible, the skipper should from the beginning of the day's sail or the week's cruise establish a clear routine. The first thing he must do is make sure that the crew knows how to use all vital equipment, such as the marine toilet, the engine, the radiotelephone, the bilge pumps, and the stove. Here he may have less trouble instructing landlubbers than changing the habits of experienced sailors familiar with other systems on different boats. Next the skipper should point out the location of emergency equipment such as fire extinguishers, life jackets, and safety harnesses. Then there should be a calm discussion about emergency procedures. For trips longer than a day, a second-in-command should be appointed — somebody whom the skipper trusts both as a sailor and as a leader.

Next comes the delegation of authority, which can be difficult. All seamen are proud of their skills, but a ship with only one performer is an unhappy one. When new crewmembers come aboard for their first sail, they hope they'll be allowed to help out so they'll learn some skills by the end of the day. At first they'll be clumsy. The skipper should respect their eagerness and try to ignore their clumsiness by giving them jobs to do. Obviously the job should not be a vital one, like steering through a crowded anchorage in a 30-knot wind, but casting off the mooring or dock lines, hauling up sails, trimming sheets, and dropping anchor are all chores that are important, simple, and easy to learn. Anybody doing them, whether a 6-year-old child or a 60-year-old grandmother, will be satisfied that he is making a contribution. Later on, in open water, allow anybody who wants to a chance to steer.

There are a few jobs that are always challenging and sometimes very tricky. One is anchoring; another is steering up a crowded channel. A confident skipper should not feel like a Bligh if he takes charge at such times if he thinks it important. Inevitably a novice on board may bristle when he or she is relieved at the helm or the chart table by a skipper who seems to doubt his or her ability. Feelings inevitably will be hurt. But feelings inevitably will be patched up again if the crew member sees the situation from the captain's point of view.

There are right and wrong ways to accomplish just about every important task on a boat. The skipper should tactfully but firmly make clear how and why he wants jobs done, demonstrating both correct and incorrect techniques. Among the key tasks where a mistake could lead to disaster are cleating a halyard incorrectly, taking a bearing carelessly, steering by the wrong lubber's line on the compass, walking on deck in rough weather without holding lifelines, and lighting a gas stove the wrong way. Somebody on board might be used to different equipment; if so, explain why you use your procedures. If the other person comes up with a better way, don't let command ego get between you and effectiveness.

As in many other areas, women have only recently begun to be skippers if not co-skippers and equal partners on boats. Yet there are still wives who know almost nothing about piloting and seamanship despite having sailed with their husbands over thou-

Captain Bligh or Queeg a skipper should not emulate, yet he or she should still be a decisive, competent sailor who knows the limits of the crew, the boat, and him- or herself.

Roles on Board

Beginners must start somewhere so when the situation allows, let young and inexperienced sailors take a trick at the helm.

sands of miles and many years. The "first mate in the galley" ideology is both unfair and dangerous. If the male skipper is suddenly incapacitated, the female cook may be the only person on board to call for aid or sail back to the harbor. Barring strength limitations (which are as inevitable with small, unathletic men as with small, unathletic women), there are few jobs on board even a big sailboat that the moderately fit woman cannot perform. To keep women from commanding, steering, navigating, and other arts of the mariner is to shut them off from many of the glories of sailing.

The Crew

A crew member on a boat has a responsibility to himself and everybody else who is aboard, and he should frankly admit any physical or other limitation on his ability to perform that responsibility. Don't give a misleading or false answer exaggerating your abilities if the skipper asks about your sailing, swimming, or other athletic experiences. If you have a tendency to get seasick, bring your own pills and take them before you get under way. Try to help out, but don't get in the way during difficult maneuvers. Many skippers get excited when they're tense; try not to take their comments personally. If you don't know how to do a chore that you have volunteered for or that has been assigned to you, *ask* — nobody will think less of you for wanting to do a job right, but the wrath of Poseidon will descend on you if your claims of competence prove to be false. At first you may be annoyed by a skipper's seemingly militaristic procedures, such as asking you to repeat orders after they're given or to coil lines in a specific way. You can respond by simply ignoring them, but such passive-aggressive behavior may lead to even more hassles. Better yet, take the edge off your frustration by asking (at the right moment, please), "Why do you do it this way, Skipper?" A truly militaristic captain will answer such a reasonable question with a cold, withering stare, convincing you that perhaps you might enjoy yourself more on somebody else's boat. But a skipper with a sense of fair play will answer your question politely and thoroughly.

The old adage "One hand for yourself, one for the ship" means to take care of yourself while you take care of the vessel. This is literally true in rough weather, when you must hold on with one hand while doing even the most menial jobs, but the saying's

deepest meaning is that you should always be alert to what is going on, both on deck and below. Don't assume that the skipper is on top of every maintenance job; inspect gear as you use it, and if it's broken, ask for tools and fix it yourself. On cruises and long daysails, your "one hand for the ship" might be a small donation to the boat's provisions — some beer, a bottle of wine, a pound of cheese. A good skipper should have made it clear who is responsible for food and other provisions, either by announcing that he or she is buying everything or by charging a *per diem* fee, yet it's still good sailor's manners to help provide some entertainment.

On long sails people can easily get on each other's nerves. Try to understand and minimize your own eccentricities just as you attempt to tolerate your crewmate's. Whistling, constant talking, and repeated humming of the same song are among the otherwise petty annoyances that have led to discord, but worst of all is sloppy seamanship. Do your job right and you'll be respected.

Sailing with Children

Children can be very enjoyable company on boats — for some people. So warn your guests ahead of time that your or somebody else's kids might be joining the cruise. The age of the child plays an important role in his accommodation to boating. Very young children get along well just about everywhere as long as they're in good health. A young child's playfullness and eagerness to learn can be a joy on board if the parents and other crew are willing to tolerate the constant anxiety about his falling overboard. In the later years a child usually is old enough to learn a few basic safety rules — among them, "always do what the skipper says" — and may be helpful with small tasks that tolerate a short attention span. But even when they are 11 or 12 you should not consider children to be working crew members, although they can enjoy steering, helping with the anchor, and even doing elementary piloting. The novelty of living in the semi-outdoors might even encourage kids to help with the dishes. Most important when sailing with children, make sure they know by the tone of your voice when they must follow orders. The world of children is so benign that they are not attuned to the kind of quick-rising dangers that can occur on the water.

For more on children and boats, see appendix IV.

Clothing

Whether skipper or crew, you must bring appropriate clothing when you come aboard. A wet, cold sailor will inevitably make careless errors, endangering himself, his shipmates, and the vessel herself. In chapter 2 we described the shoes and foul-weather gear available for sailors. Going barefoot may seem salty, but the inevitable torn toenails, broken toes, scrapes, and tumbles on wet decks are a great price to pay for that transitory self-image. Wear either deck shoes with special nonskid soles or ribbed-sole sneakers when working on deck. If the water is cold, or even if it's warm and you like

to keep your feet dry, wear sea boots over cotton or wool socks. Be realistic about your resistance to cold and go aboard overprepared, with foul-weather gear, a wool sweater or thick sweatshirt, and a towel to wrap around your neck to keep water from trickling down. Carry this gear and anything else that you take aboard in a small duffel bag that on boats is called a sea bag. A hard suitcase can mar a boat's finish, and since it holds its shape, takes up considerable space when empty. Good sea bags have waterproof pouches for wet clothing; otherwise take along a plastic garbage bag for your damp laundry.

Shoes

Except on very small boats, going barefoot is asking for slips, falls, stubbed toes, torn toenails, and cut feet. Some general-purpose sneakers (with white soles so they don't mark up the deck) may provide good footing, but if you plan to do a lot of sailing buy some special boating shoes called "deck shoes" or "Topsiders" (the trademark of one of the first boating shoes). Their slitted soles will hold even on wet decks. Don't wear them ashore, where their soles will pick up dirt and oil.

For sailing in spray and rain, nothing beats rubber sea boots, knee-high for ocean sailing, calf-high for calmer waters, or ankle-high for small-boat sailing. Since the fit varies widely from manufacturer to manufacturer, try different styles before you make your choice.

Expect the worst when you pack your sea bag. Include a thick towel to keep water from dripping down your neck.

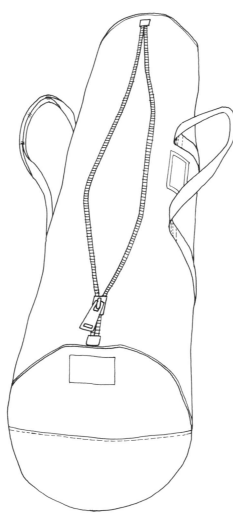

The soles of boating shoes grip decks with a squeegee effect. Sneaker-type shoes provide better arch and ankle support and dry out more quickly than moccasins.

Sea boots — either shin or knee high — will prevent the discomfort of soggy socks.

Moccasin-type deck shoes are both fashionable and safe on a wet deck. Some sneakers also grip well.

Foul-Weather Gear

A dry body is a warm body. Here are some tips for selecting foul-weather gear.

First, consider styles. A one-piece jumpsuit is fine in cool, damp weather when you will always want to wear pants and a jacket at the same time; it may be too confining the rest of the time. For sailors in the tropics and other warm areas, a knee-length smock provides protection from head to knees. The most versatile outfit is the classic two-piece suit, with a jacket and chest-high bib pants; you can wear the jacket alone in light spray, the pants alone when the deck is wet, and both the jacket and pants when heavy spray is flying.

Second, look for good construction: heavily reinforced seat and crotch; sturdy, large zippers (the jacket zipper should open from the bottom as well as the top to allow ventilation); no seams on such vulnerable spots as the seat and shoulders, where they may leak; and plenty of reinforcement on the seams, seat, knees, and cuffs. A nylon liner provides an air space that cuts uncomfortable condensation on the inside. Some jackets have insulation for cold-weather sailing. Well-designed elastic cuffs and a tight fit around the neck keep out large amounts of water. Small drips through openings are inevitable, but you can stop some of them by wearing a small towel around your neck under the jacket. The trousers should have strong suspenders and snaps. Both top and bottom should have sturdy pockets for a knife and other items. A good hood has a short bill to keep water off the eyes and should be capable of being rolled up out of the way.

Third, examine the material. If it's very slick on the outside, it's PVC, which is sturdy, very waterproof, relatively inexpensive, pretty heavy, and potentially hot inside. In a PVC suit on a warm day, you won't take in much water but you may perspire heavily unless you vent the suit by opening zippers. If the fabric is slick on the inside and textured on the outside, it's either sturdy, expensive neoprene or less expensive, less sturdy urethane (PTFE). Both materials are less heavy and hot than PVC, and often less waterproof too. If the fabric is slick or textured on both sides, it's probably a water-resistant (not waterproof) material that will provide enough protection for light spray or rain but won't be much help in rough weather or heavy rain.

Be suspicious of any advertising claims about fabric "miracles." In the early 1980s, the outdoor clothing industry came up with fabrics that it claimed kept out moisture while "breathing out" condensation. Though "breathable" fabrics have served the needs of hikers nicely, they have often failed the

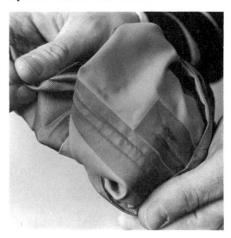

The insides of seams should be heavily taped so there is less chance of leaks.

The two-piece foul-weather gear suit is more versatile than other outfits. A jacket belt allows a tight fit. The pants should have sturdy suspenders and be chest-high, with no scoops under the armpits to catch water. Note the large flap to go across the neck, the reinforcements at the pants knees, the deep pockets, and the special slits for warming hands.

tougher requirements of sailors. Sailors discovered that when they sat in puddles or were pelted by sheets of spray or rain, these new fabrics sometimes leaked badly. Perhaps these fabrics will be improved, but it may well be that perspiration is the price of a reliably waterproof material.

Buy only red, orange, or yellow jackets so you'll be visible if you accidentally fall into the water. White, green, and blue make a swimmer all but invisible.

When buying foul-weather gear, be sure to try it on over all the clothing you may wear in cool weather. Touch your toes and grind an imaginary winch to see if you have the right size. If in doubt, get a size too big.

As a guide for choosing from the wide variety of styles and materials, perhaps my experience will be helpful. I sail mainly in warm weather, although I sometimes go out in cold climates (for example, in 1987 I cruised off the Alaska coast). Therefore, I require versatility in my foul-weather gear. On top, I have two choices. For very wet weather I have a moderateweight red

A spray-resistant jacket lined with bunting may provide sufficient protection in cool weather unless there's heavy spray or rain. As with all outer clothing, make sure the fit is loose to allow physical activity.

urethane jacket, and for light spray I wear a water-resistant windbreaker with a lining. In cold weather I wear the windbreaker under the jacket, thus saving the cost of a heavy parka. For trousers, which take a greater beating than a jacket, I use a pair of very sturdy PVC foul-weather pants.

Warm Clothing

While wool has long been regarded as the best material for cold-weather clothing, it now has a competitor in the synthetic materials known generally as bunting (short fibers) and pile (long fibers). Like wool fibers, synthetic fibers trap air and provide insulation; the longer the fibers, the better the protection. Also like wool (but unlike cotton), these synthetics provide good insulation when wet. Unlike wool, synthetics are light in weight and hold their shape when wet. Bunting and pile go in shirts, pullovers, gloves, socks, pants, and hats. One synthetic, polypropylene, is an effective insulator when used in long underwear and sock and glove liners (silk is also used in those three areas).

Body heat escapes especially rapidly through the head, feet, hands, crotch, and armpits, so make sure these areas are well insulated. A watch cap made of bunting or wool works like a heating vent. Put the cap on if you're cold, and take it off if you get overheated.

Dry Suits

A dry suit is a one-piece waterproof jump suit made of light material with strong waterproof seals at the neck and cuffs. Access is through a flap on the back. Most dry suits are worn by dinghy racers and sailboard sailors.

Wet Suits

Board and dinghy sailors and others who expect to get wet while boating often use wet suits in place of foul-weather gear. A wet suit is a synthetic, tight pullover that traps water between its surface and the wearer's skin. The body quickly heats the water layer to form a thin liquid insulator. Wet suits come in many different thicknesses for a variety of water temperatures and in several styles: full-length, half-length, top only, short-sleeve, long-sleeve, hooded, hoodless, and so on. Wet-suit gloves and boots are also available. Although they provide considerable buoyancy, wet suits must not be used in place of life jackets because they will not always float a swimmer head up. The major problem with wet suits is that putting them on and removing them is extremely

Jump suit

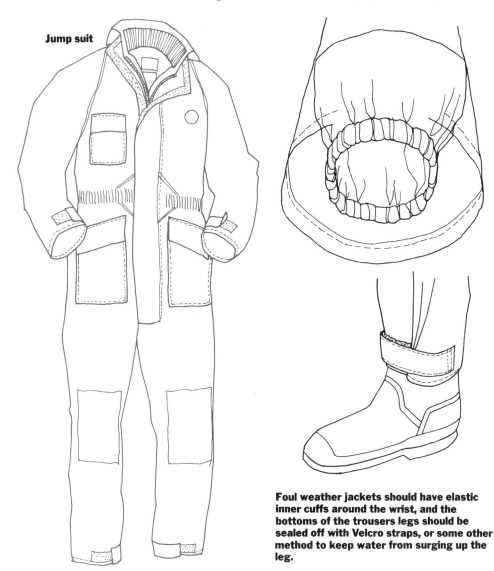

Foul weather jackets should have elastic inner cuffs around the wrist, and the bottoms of the trousers legs should be sealed off with Velcro straps, or some other method to keep water from surging up the leg.

Foul-Weather Gear

awkward, so they're not recommended for use except on short passages when they won't be taken off.

Survival Suits

Developed for military use in extreme climates, survival suits are exactly what the name suggests. They'll float a swimmer while protecting him from cold and wet for long lengths of time. However, many are so bulky that the quick movements so important on a boat are almost impossible when they're worn. Boats heading far offshore in cold weather should be equipped with at least one survival

suit in case of emergency.

Keeping Warm and Dry

Most sailing is a mix of energetic activity and patient waiting. You may exert yourself strenuously for a few minutes while tacking or changing sails, then sit quietly for an hour. In warm weather, bathing suits, shorts, and T-shirts are all the clothing you need for both periods; but in cool weather, if you get overheated your sweat will soak the clothing you need for warmth, causing discomfort and possibly a cold. The answer is to wear several layers of insulating clothing rather than one thick layer, and to discard layers and replace them to fit the circumstances. Starting on the inside, fishnet underwear provides air pockets between the skin and the next layer of clothing in which sweat evaporates before soaking a shirt, long-john underwear, or trousers. Even if it does get wet, if the next layer is made of wool it will continue to insulate and warm the body — wool shirts and sweaters work superbly. Other good

insulators include polyester pile jackets, polyester quilted vests, down jackets (which, unfortunately, lose their insulating qualities when wet), thick foul-weather gear, and "float coat" parkas.

Sometimes all you have to do to ventilate is open up the cuffs, neck, and front zipper of the foul-weather jacket. Since most body heat escapes through the head, putting on and removing a wool watch cap, Sou'wester hat, or hood can be an excellent thermostat. At other extremities, wool socks will breathe and still insulate even when they're wet under sea boots, and wool, rubber, or pile gloves warm hands and fingers.

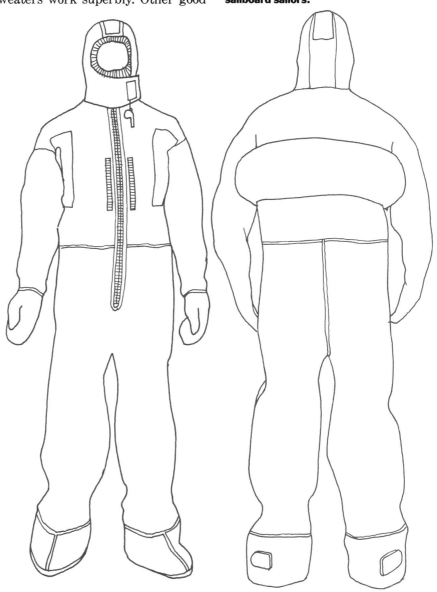

A survival suit provides buoyancy and, with rubber gaskets around cuffs and the face, near complete protection from the elements. A cousin of the survival suit is the thin dry suit used by dinghy and sailboard sailors.

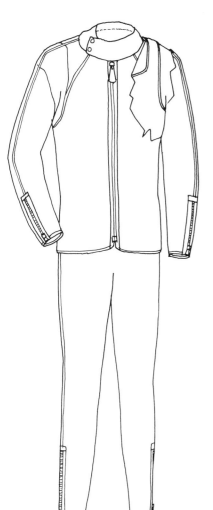

Small-boat sailors should expect to get wet and cold. Wet suits provide excellent insulation with little bulk.

Medical Problems

Hypothermia

Why worry so much about staying warm, dry, and comfortable? One obvious reason is that it's no fun at all to be cold and wet, no matter what you're doing. But more important for seamanship, your body and mind will function much more efficiently if you're warm. The medical term for loss of body heat is hypothermia. If you are hypothermic, not only will you feel chilled but your agility, strength, endurance, and mental acuity will decline rapidly. You'll make careless mistakes, like cleating a line wrong or forgetting simple rules like "Red Right

Returning," and put your vessel and shipmates at risk.

Here is how hypothermia affects the human body. As its temperature drops from 98.6°, the body's natural urge to preserve the vital organs in the trunk leads to a cutting off of blood circulation in the extremities — first the fingers and toes, then hands and feet, then as it drops into the low 90s, the head. This is why we first feel cold at the end of our limbs, and why our mental functioning slows down as we get colder. For a while the body tries to warm itself up with activity — shivering and chattering teeth — but when the temperature reaches about 93° the muscles become rigid and mental disorientation intensifies. In a way, shivering is a healthy symptom; when it stops the victim is rapidly on the way to severe hypothermia. He may become unconscious when the body temperature reaches about 87°, and his heart may stop at approximately 85°.

A major problem with hypothermia is that the victim may be so disoriented that he's unaware of his dangerous condition. If he appears unnaturally vague, clumsy, and quiet, even while claiming that he's "all right," consider him to be hypothermic and treat him as described below. Extreme hypothermia may seem like death.

The U.S. Coast Guard has a rule of thumb about hypothermia that it calls "50/50/50." This means that a person immersed in 50° water for 50 minutes has a 50 percent chance of survival. Few pleasure sailors ever venture out in water as cold as 50°, but even water temperatures in the 70s can cause hypothermia in bony ectomorphs who aren't properly dressed.

How to Treat Hypothermia

Almost all cases of hypothermia can be treated successfully. Unfortunately the common wisdom handed down to us from our grandparents is exactly the *wrong* treatment. Recent studies and experience decisively conclude that the most important rule is to *warm the body gradually.* Over rapid warming will quickly stimulate blood flow in the extremities and pump cold blood from fingers and toes back into the trunk and its organs. Anything that stimulates blood flow rapidly is a potential killer. Among the *dangerous stimulants* (all of which have traditionally been considered healthy) are hot drinks, caffeine, alcohol, rubbing the hands, feet, or head, and exercise. Any one of these — a cup of hot soup or coffee, a shot of brandy, a fast walk on deck — may stop the heart with a charge of cold blood streaming from the frigid extremities.

The *correct* way to treat a hypothermic person is to *bring his body temperature back gradually.* He can't do it himself, so you must do it for him. First, remove all his wet clothes and lay him down in a protected space well insulated from cold surfaces — placing him in a sleeping bag in a bunk is an excellent technique. Then apply warmth. Another person's warm body, warmed blankets, or warm water bottles work well (with "warm" meaning roughly body temperature), as do towels wet with water that is warm to the touch applied to the groin, chest, neck, head, and sides. Reapply the warming object as often and as long as necessary, keeping the patient still and periodically checking his pulse rate (which should increase gradually). You may give him a warm (*not hot*) non-caffeine drink. This recovery process is both safe and gradual. After a while the patient should once again be able to generate his own body heat

Symptoms of Hypothermia

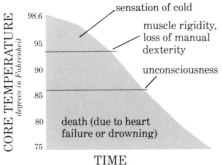

CORE TEMPERATURE *degrees in Fahrenheit*

- 98.6 — sensation of cold
- 95 — muscle rigidity, loss of manual dexterity
- 90
- 85 — unconsciousness
- 80 — death (due to heart failure or drowning)
- 75

TIME

(Left) Blood circulation decreases as body temperature drops. (Below) On a boat, the best way to bring a hypothermic crewmember's temperature back up is to put him in a sleeping bag with warm towels or, even better, a healthy shipmate.

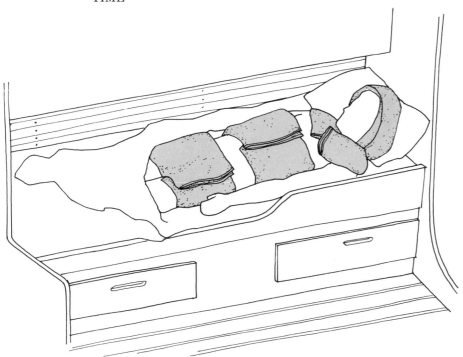

Medical Problems

inside a sleeping bag or under blankets.

If the victim is unconscious or shows no vital signs, apply cardiopulmonary resuscitation (CPR, described later), especially mouth-to-mouth resuscitation, which pushes warm air into the body. When vital signs return, warm the victim as we have just described.

Since water conducts heat 25 times faster than air, hypothermia is a very big risk for swimmers or for sailors who fall overboard. For instructions about what to do to avoid hypothermia when in the water, see chapter 7.

Seasickness

The symptoms of seasickness are more obvious than those of hypothermia, and it's more likely to afflict a sailor in normal weather and conditions. But in extreme cases seasickness can be just as dangerous; a fairly mild case can be more or less incapacitating; and even a slight dose can ruin an afternoon's pleasure. Some people, of course, are more prone to motion sickness than others. Since bad experiences in cars or airplanes probably have made this known early in their lives, they should come aboard well prepared with medication. Over the counter anti-seasickness pills may work, but they may have unpleasant side effects that include drowsiness, dry mouth, and psychological disorientation. Many sailors swear by the prescription drug Scopolamine, which is released into the body through a patch worn behind the ear and which has limited side effects for many people.

For some lucky ones, seasickness comes and passes quickly (if messily). But most sufferers endure its miseries for hours at the very least, although their systems may quiet down in calm water or after a day or so at sea. The extreme results of seasickness include dehydration and exhaustion. Not much can be done for a victim at this stage other than providing fluids, rest, and encouragement.

Even if invulnerable to manifest seasickness, every sailor has felt queasy at one time or another, and the following recommendations for anticipating and minimizing seasickness probably apply to anybody who sets foot on a boat:

Before going aboard, watch your diet: a greasy dinner the night before, or even worse, too much alcohol (even *any* alcohol) may make it hard to adjust to the boat's motion. Take your pills before leaving home.

Early in a cruise, before your metabolism has settled into its new routine on a platform that is constantly in motion, you may begin to feel queasy. A slight headache and constipation often accompany the feeling of unsettledness. If the constipation is allowed to continue, your stomach may never calm down. Fresh fruit, grains, a daily walk ashore, and if necessary a laxative will eventually return your bowels to their normal schedule.

If you begin to feel queasy or seasick, immediately go on deck and focus your eyes on the horizon or get busy. Somehow, fresh air, a steady reference point, and distraction help to stabilize both the inner ear and the stomach.

Finally, don't be ashamed to admit that you're seasick; hiding and resisting it only make it worse. It's not a sign of weakness — almost every sailor has suffered from it at one time or another, and it has affected some great seamen throughout triumphant careers afloat.

Sunburn

Besides hypothermia and seasickness, sunburn is the sailor's third most important health worry. The body's

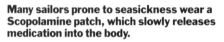

Many sailors prone to seasickness wear a Scopolamine patch, which slowly releases medication into the body.

largest and most sensitive organ, the skin can be dried out, reddened, or badly burned by the sun's rays. Prolonged exposure to the sun can lead to skin cancer. Water only increases the sun's power through reflection, and a misty haze or even fog may further intensify its capacity to burn. Fair-haired people who are particularly vulnerable to burns should expose their bodies with caution, being sure to wear shirts during the most glaring hours around noon.

Recently, pharmaceutical companies have devised a whole new family of sun lotions based around a scale called the Sun Protection Factor (S.P.F.). An S.P.F. of 2 provides minimum sun screen and a factor above 30 provides the maximum. Fair people will choose lotions in the 12-20 S.P.F. range. These products will not necessarily hasten a good tan, but they will block out most of the sun's damaging rays. People with dark complexions who tan easily without bad burning will use lotions whose S.P.F. is in the 6-12 range. Even an S.P.F. 20 lotion may not be enough for noses, lips, and ears, which are the most exposed parts of the body. Special products are available for these vulnerable spots, but the best is plain white zinc oxide ointment. Not only is it relatively inexpensive and a versatile salve for cuts and burns, but its glossy whiteness while not glamorous always advertises its presence so you can tell if your nose needs another coat.

Rope Burns

The calluses on a sailor's hands take a long time to build up. Until they appear, you may want to protect your palms and fingers from rope burn and cuts with leather gloves available at chandleries. The tips of the fingers on these gloves are cut off to aid manipulation of shackles, tools, and other objects. Even if your hands are well callused, you'll probably have to wear gloves when working with lines smaller than 5/16-inch diameter.

Eye Strain

Especially on hazy days, the sun's glare can be intolerable, cause painful eye strain and headaches, and eventually lead to bad judgment. Of the many kinds of sunglasses available, those with polarized lenses seem best for sailing. They absorb glare well and provide sharp contrast, making it easier to identify puffs of wind on the water and shallow spots. Glasses should be secured around your head with a length of string or elastic.

First Aid

Your boat should be equipped with a standard Red Cross first-aid manual to guide you when dealing with injuries. Here we will summarize the four basic principles of first aid and make some suggestions for your boat's first-aid kit.

The Four Principles of First Aid

As established by the American Red Cross, these are the basic principles of first aid:
1. Check and clear the airway.
2. Stop the bleeding.
3. Protect the wound.
4. Treat for shock.

Clearing the Airway

This means resuscitation through artificial respiration plus external heart massage, which combine in cardiopulmonary resuscitation procedures — otherwise known as CPR.

Artificial Respiration

Start with mouth-to-mouth breathing.
1. Place the victim on his back.
2. Kneel beside his shoulder.
3. Clear his mouth and air passages of foreign objects such as vomit, chewing gum, seaweed, or dentures.
4. Place a hand under his neck.
5. Place the other hand on his forehead so you can close his nose with the thumb and forefinger.
6. Raise the neck gently and close the nose. This will open the other air passages in most cases.
7. Breathe quickly four times into the victim's mouth without interruption, then take a very deep breath and, with your mouth wide, place your mouth over the victim's and blow.
8. When the victim's chest rises, remove your mouth to allow him to exhale naturally.
9. Repeat this process 12-14 times per minute for adults and 18-20 times per minute for children.
10. If the victim's chest does not rise, check to see if your mouth is entirely over his with an airtight seal and that there is no foreign matter in his mouth.

He may be choking. If so, have him try to cough up the matter. If he is a child or an unconscious adult, strike him sharply with the heel of your hand between the shoulder blades. Otherwise use the **Heimlich Technique:** Stand behind the victim with both of your arms around him just above the beltline. Allow his head, arms, and upper torso to hang forward. Grasp your right wrist with your left hand and

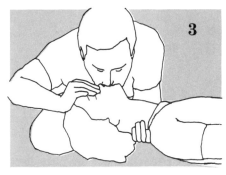

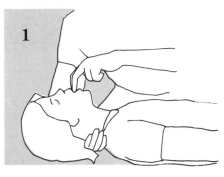

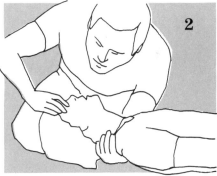

Begin artificial respiration by clearing the throat (1). Then lift the neck (2) and, closing the victim's nose, breath into his mouth (3).

161

First Aid

pull up quickly into his abdomen, forcing his diaphragm up to compress his lungs and expel any residual air and any foreign object in his windpipe. If the victim is lying on his stomach, sit astride his buttocks and perform the hug and thrust. If he's on his back, sit astride his pelvis, place one hand on top of the other, and thrust into the abdomen as a second rescuer waits to remove the foreign matter from the victim's mouth.

11. If the chest still does not rise, remove your hand from behind the victim's neck, insert your thumb into his mouth, and grab the lower jawbone between the thumb and forefinger. Lift the jawbone up as you continue to perform mouth-to-mouth breathing.

12. Mouth-to-nose breathing may be carried out using much the same technique with the victim's mouth shut.

External Heart Massage

If artificial respiration doesn't start the heart, if the victim does not have a pulse (check the large carotid artery near the adam's apple), and/or his pupils are dilated and do not constrict — start external heart massage.

1. Lay the victim on his back on a hard surface.

2. Locate the notch at the top of his breastbone.

3. Locate the lower end of the breastbone and measure two fingerwidths up from there.

4. Place the heel of one hand over the lower one-third of the breastbone and the other hand on top of the first hand.

5. Bring your shoulders directly over the victim's breastbone. With your arms straight, rock back and forth slightly from the hip joints exerting pressure vertically downward to depress the lower breastbone, then release pressure without lifting your hand from his chest. Compression and relaxation must be of equal duration.

6. For adults, compress and release the breastbone 1½-2 inches.

7. For small children, compress with only one hand. For infants, use only the index and middle fingers. In small children and infants, the heart lies higher in the chest than it does in adults.

8. Repeat the cycle in a smooth, rhythmic fashion 60-80 times per minute for adults and 80-100 times per minute for children. Keep your fingers away from the victim's ribs to avoid fractures.

9. Check the pulse frequently to see if the heart has restarted.

Combined: CPR

1. A single rescuer can administer CPR — both artificial respiration and

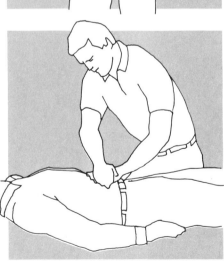

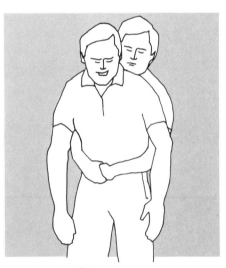

A choking victim should be treated with the Heimlich Technique by pulling in on his diaphragm (top) or pushing onto his abdomen (above).

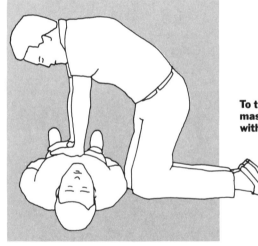

To try to restart the heart, continuously massage the victim's lower breastbone with the heel of one hand.

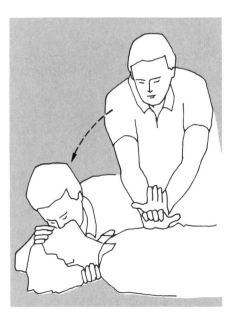

CPR includes heart massage and artificial respiration alternated by one or two rescuers.

external heart massage — by rapidly massaging the chest for 15 beats, then giving two deep-lung inflations (not allowing full exhalations), then massaging the chest, and so on.

2. Two rescuers can divide their work, one giving artificial respiration and monitoring the carotid artery on one side of the victim and the other performing external heart massage on the other side. For every five chest compressions there should be one full lung inflation.

3. Continue CPR until spontaneous breathing and heartbeat occur or until a doctor takes over. Under no circumstances should CPR be interrupted for longer than 5 seconds.

Stopping the Bleeding

Once the airway is clear and the victim is breathing, stop any bleeding by applying direct pressure to the wound with a thick wad of cloth — preferably sterile — or even the hand alone. Do not remove blood-soaked material but rather continue to add layers of cloth. Raise the affected area

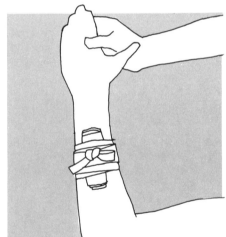

above the level of the victim's heart. A pressure bandage may also be used; this is a bandage secured over the wound by strips of cloth that are attached to it.

If direct pressure does not stop the bleeding, apply pressure to one of two pressure points on either side of the body while continuing the steps described in the first paragraph of this section.

The **brachial artery** — midway be-

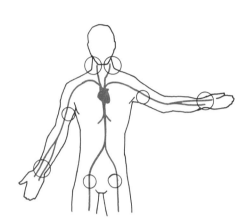

When treating a bleeding wound, first apply a pressure bandage directly (left) and keep it elevated above the heart. If the bleeding continues, locate a pressure point over one of the arteries (above) and apply pressure there (below). Don't remove bloody clothing or bandages; keep adding more layers of cloth until the bleeding is under control.

tween the armpit and the elbow on the inside of the arm in the groove between the biceps and the triceps — controls arterial bleeding in the lower arm. Grab the arm with your thumb on the outside and your fingers on the inside, using the flat inside surface of the fingers and not the fingertips.

The **femoral artery** controls arterial bleeding in the leg. This pressure point is on the front center part of the "hinge" of the leg, in the crease of the groin area and over the pelvic bone. Apply pressure with the heel of your hand.

A tourniquet should be used only in cases of life-threatening arm and leg bleeding that cannot be controlled otherwise. Use a band of cloth wrapped twice around the limb just above the wound edges or directly above a joint if the wound is below a joint. Tighten the band with a stick, screwdriver, or similar object, and secure the stick in place. Treat the victim for shock.

Protecting the Wound

After breathing and the heartbeat have resumed and bleeding has been controlled, any open wound must be protected from aggravation, infection, or injury. The most common kind of on-board wound is a burn, ranging in degrees from first to third, all of which must be treated promptly and carefully.

A **first degree burn** is red, with mild swelling and some pain to the victim. This kind of burn may be a bad

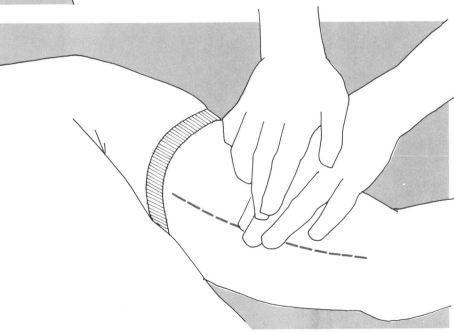

First Aid

sunburn or be caused by contact with the side of a cooking pot that is on a burner. The treatment for a first-degree burn is to relieve the pain with cloths soaked with ice water or with cold running water over the affected area. A dry, sterile dressing may then be applied to protect the burned skin.

A **second degree burn** is more serious. The skin is more deeply burned and there may be blisters. Again, cold running water (but not ice water) or applying cold cloths will help to relieve pain. Then blot the wound dry with a sterile or clean cloth and apply another sterile or clean cloth as a protective dressing. Do not break the blis-

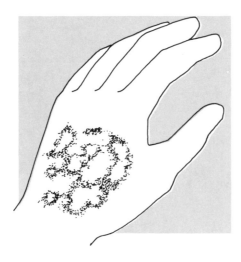

Treat a first degree burn (above) with ice water and a dry dressing, a second degree burn (above right) with cold water and dry dressings, and a third degree burn (right) with a clean cloth and elevation. Only a doctor should break blisters and apply medication to burns. Treat for shock.

ters or remove shreds of skin tissue. Also, do not apply home medications — *only a doctor should apply medicine.* Treat the victim for shock, as described in the next section.

A **third degree burn** is the most serious of the three. This is a very deep burn with a complete loss of all layers of skin. Cover the burn with a sterile or clean cloth — a freshly laundered shirt or sheet may do — and treat the victim for shock. Elevate the affected parts of the body. Obtain medical attention as quickly as possible. *Do not* remove charred clothing from the wound or apply ice water or home medications to the burn.

Chemical burns to the skin should be washed with large amounts of water for at least 5 minutes in order to flush away the chemical. If a chemical is in an eye, flush the eye out for at least 5 minutes, then cover both eyes with a clean bandage, seek medical attention, and treat for shock.

Treating for Shock

Injury-related traumatic shock is a state of circulatory deficiency that results in a depressed state of many vital body functions. Even though the related injuries many not be fatal, the shock may threaten life. A victim of an accident may go into shock immediately or not for hours after rescue and administration of first aid, so rescuers must be alert to the symptoms of shock syndrome. These symptoms do not appear together in every casualty and they are not equally noticeable.

The symptoms of shock include:

1. The eyes may be glassy or lackluster, and the pupils may be dilated or suggest fear and apprehension.

2. Breathing may be rapid or labored.

3. The lips may be pale or bluish-gray.

4. The skin may be extremely pale or ashen-gray.

5. The skin may be cold to the touch and be covered with a clammy sweat.

6. The pulse may be rapid or weak.

7. The victim may be nauseous or may retch, vomit, or have hiccups. He may have dryness in the mouth, tongue, and lips.

8. The victim will feel restless or apprehensive.

9. Normally visible veins at the front of the elbow or forearm and on the backs of the hands may collapse and become invisible.

10. The victim may frequently complain of thirst rather than pain even when he is badly injured.

A group of some of these symptoms indicates that the victim of an accident is in shock. Recognizing that a victim is *about to go into shock* is more difficult, however, so a rescuer should always be alert and anticipate the likelihood of shock with any serious injury or when the victim is hypothermic.

To prevent shock, or to treat for shock:

1. Keep the patient lying down.

2. Maintain the victim's normal body temperature.

3. Get medical care as soon as possible.

Have the victim lie down on his back, with these variations and exceptions:

a. If the injury is to his back or neck, do not move him from his original position.

b. If he has a wound to his face or jaw, have him sit up, leaning forward.

c. If he is bleeding from his mouth, place him on his side with knees bent and head on his arm, and watch him carefully to see that he keeps breathing.

d. If he is unconscious, place him on

his side.

e. If he has a head injury, have him lie flat on his back or propped up with his head level with or higher than his trunk.

f. If he is experiencing breathing difficulty, have him lie down with his head and shoulders elevated.

g. If none of the above applies and if he can breathe well, have him lie on his back with his feet elevated 6-8 inches.

To keep the body at normal temperature (98.6°), protect him from cold or damp with blankets or additional clothing and from the heat of the sun with shade.

Unless the victim is unconscious, having convulsions, vomiting, or nauseated, or if surgery is likely, give him 4 ounces of water every 15 minutes (2 ounces for a child, 1 ounce for an infant) if medical care is delayed for an hour or more. If possible, give him a solution of ½ level teaspoon of baking soda and ½ level teaspoon of salt per quart of water.

Other Injuries

Broken bones may be recognized by pain, swelling and discoloration, and a deformity of the injured part. If a fracture is suspected — and assume that an injury is a fracture unless proven otherwise — protect and immobilize the victim and treat him gently. Apply any splint before moving the victim. ("Splint them where they lie" is a good rule of thumb.) Any splint should be well padded, snug but not so tight as to cut off circulation, and long enough to immobilize the joints above and below the injury. Leave the victim's toes or fingertips exposed to check for adequate circulation. Treat the victim for shock.

A **heart attack** may be recognized by shortness of breath, chest pains, a bluish color of the lips and about the fingernails, a chronic cough, and swelling of the ankles — one or the other usually is most noticeable. If necessary, administer CPR to the victim.

Heat exhaustion may cause fainting, pounding of the heart, nausea, vomiting, headaches, or restlessness. Another symptom is sweating. To treat for heat exhaustion, move the victim to a cool place, keep him lying down, and treat for shock.

Heatstroke is much more serious than heat exhaustion and is characterized by an extremely high body temperature and *no sweating*. A victim of heatstroke may also have a headache, be dizzy, urinate frequently, be irritable, and have disturbed vision,

seeing objects through a red or purplish tint. His skin is hot and dry, his pupils are constricted, his pulse is strong if not bounding, and he may have convulsions and suddenly fall unconscious. His body temperature may be between 105° and 109° F. Heatstroke can prove fatal and the body temperature must be lowered immediately. The victim should be placed in a cool spot. Remove the victim's clothing and lay him down with head and shoulders slightly elevated. Pour cold water over his body, rub him with ice and place ice in his armpits, cover him with sheets soaked in ice water, or place him in an ice-water bath. Give him cool (not iced) drinks, but do not give him stimulants such as tea, coffee, or liquor.

Heat cramps are caused by depletion of salt from body fluids through excessive sweating. They may be recognized by severe pain and be treated by drinking cool water with ½ teaspoon of salt per glass. *Do not drink sea water!* (In extreme survival conditions sea water may be used when

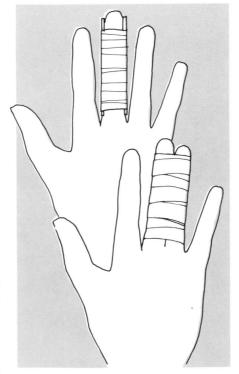

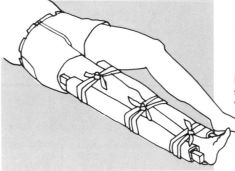

mixed with fresh water or food, but only with risk.) Do not apply hot packs to heat cramps: they will increase the cramping.

A **stroke** may cause unconsciousness and paralysis of the limbs, or it may cause only a bad headache and dizziness. Treat for shock.

Poisoning should be treated, first, by having the victim drink milk or water in order to dilute the poison, and second, by inducing vomiting (although instructions on the material's container may specify other treatment). Find a doctor as soon as possible.

Fish bites and stings should first be treated by stopping any bleeding. To treat for the sting of a jellyfish, Portuguese man-of-war, or similar stinging fish, remove the tentacles and wash the affected skin with alcohol. Then apply ammonia water or calamine lotion, or provide a hot-water soak. Application of meat tenderizer (monosodium glutamate) will help relieve pain. The victim may go into shock and require CPR treatment.

A First-Aid Kit

When assembling a first-aid kit for your boat, do not automatically buy the same materials you have on your home's emergency shelf. You should have a complete set of bandages of different sizes, gauze, tape, scissors, and a thermometer and aspirin. But you also may require seasickness pills, meat tenderizer for jellyfish stings, sun lotions with Sun Protecting Factors for sensitive as well as hearty skin, a small knife and tweezers for removing fish hooks from skin, small splints to help with broken bones, and other special items for all possible emergencies. The longer your voyage, the more complete should be your first-aid kit; transoceanic cruisers routinely stock a small supply of morphine or other painkillers on a doctor's prescription, and one crew member may be asked to undergo training in its administration. The first-aid kit should be stowed in a dry, secure compartment with a list of the contents taped to the door for quick reference.

For specific guidance on assembling a first-aid kit, consult your doctor or the American Red Cross.

Broken bones should be treated with splints before moving the victim. Treat the victim for shock.

Chapter 7
Personal Safety

There is nothing crazy about feeling unsafe in a boat, and especially about fearing that you might fall overboard and drown. According to Coast Guard statistics, more than 2000 people died by falling overboard from 1981 to 1986. While that's a very small proportion of the number of people who go out in boats, it is still a significant reminder that personal safety is a concern every time we go sailing. Unfortunately, many people seem to think that planning for life-threatening situations only invites trouble. That is the voice of superstition, not reason. This chapter is about reasonable safety concerns that

affect the well-being of individual sailors, including life jackets, avoiding falling overboard, and rescuing someone who has gone over. In chapter 16 we will describe how to handle emergencies that affect the entire boat.

Think of these safety devices and skills the way you would a major medical insurance policy. You may never use them, but knowing they are on call provides a sense of security that allows you to take the prudent risks that sometimes are a necessary part of good seamanship.

If there is one essential rule of thumb in emergency situations, it is *stay with*

the boat. This rule applies whether the boat is an ocean cruiser, a capsized dinghy, or a life raft. Do not try to swim more than very short distances for help. If safety records prove anything, it is that even expert swimmers in calm water will quickly tire and drown when attempting to swim without life jackets. Experiments have proven this point. In tests at the U.S. Naval Academy at Annapolis, midshipmen wearing foul-weather gear and sea boots were asked to swim in an indoor swimming pool. Despite their excellent physical condition, these people could swim no farther than 25 yards without

Many modern dinghies are self-rescuing; after a capsize the crew can bring the boat back upright and sail away. With any kind of boat, the universal rule of thumb is stay with the boat after a capsize. Never try to swim to shore.

becoming exhausted.

Small Boats and Dinghies

The art of keeping small, unballasted boats upright and their crews out of the water can be summarized in two rules. First, keep your weight concentrated on the windward side or (if wind is not a factor) in the center. Second, keep your weight as low as possible so the boat does not roll about; don't stand up.

In boats like these, each crew member should be wearing a life jacket of the right size so if your boat does capsize you will have buoyancy assistance. If the boat capsizes, don't panic. Almost all dinghies and many centerboarders smaller than 20 feet float when capsized. Most are self-righting. Many are self-rescuing, which means that the water can be drained out through sluices in the bilge called self-bailers once the boat is upright and sailing again (otherwise the crew must bail the water out with buckets).

If there are two or more crew, cast off the sheets, swim the bow of the capsized boat into the wind, and right her by pulling down on the centerboard and the elevated rail. Once the boat is upright and stable, climb back into the cockpit on the windward side (or with a crew member on either side) to keep the hull from flipping over again. Retrieve any equipment that has floated away.

If the boat is self-rescuing, open the self-bailers and sail as fast as possible on a reach until suction through the bailers pulls the water out. If the boat is not self-rescuing, bail her out with buckets (you may have to lower the sails to stabilize her).

If the boat is not self-righting or you are too tired to right her, hang on to the hull and attract the attention of a nearby boat by waving your arms. Don't panic; the boat should not sink.

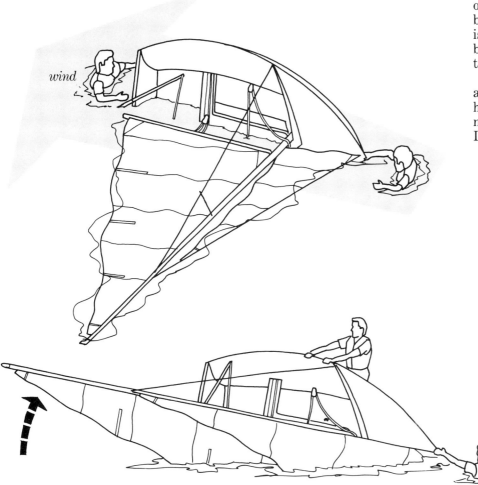

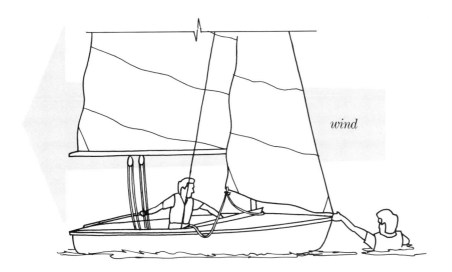

The most common method for re-righting a capsized dinghy is to first turn the bow into the wind and then stand on the centerboard until the boat swings back upright. After one crew climbs back on board, the crew at the bow swims around to the windward side of the stern and is hauled back onboard.

167

Life Jackets

The primary personal safety item is the object known as a life jacket, life vest, or PFD. When worn or leaned on, it increases a swimmer's natural buoyancy in the water in order to keep his or her head clear and prevent drowning. As we will see, there are different types of life jackets providing varying amounts of buoyancy. Some are suitable for smooth water, while others are best used in rough water.

Let's begin with a note about terminology. Until 1988 the Coast Guard used the term "Personal Flotation Device (PFD)" to refer to what most people called a "life jacket" or "life vest."

The Coast Guard categorized PFDs in approved types from Type I to Type IV, adding a Type V for experimental or specialized use. The Coast Guard has now changed to more functional terminology, but since "PFD" and "type" have been in use for many years, we will use both the old and the new terminology interchangeably.

The best life jackets are made of tough fabric with the internal flotation material sealed in waterproof plastic bags. On every boat, life jackets must be stowed where they are dry and clear of sharp edges that might cause tears. The crew must know where they are located and how they are used. The best-organized boats have occasional drills to see that everyone can get into a life jacket quickly.

Regulations

Federal regulations specify how many and what kinds of Coast Guard-approved life jackets must be carried. Here are the rules. Later on, we'll look at the approved types in some detail.

1. **Boats 16 feet long or shorter:** for each person who is on board, one approved wearable or throwable device chosen from the first four types described below.

2. **Boats longer than 16 feet:** for each person on board, one approved wearable device chosen from the first three types described below, plus one throwable device chosen from the fourth type.

The only exceptions to these rules are a few small, highly buoyant specialized craft such as sailboards, canoes, and kayaks. However, some states do not recognize these exceptions.

Life Jacket Types

The Coast Guard approves devices of five distinct types distinguished by buoyancy and design. The approval label on the device indicates its type and the weight it was designed to float. Some jackets have crotch straps to keep the jacket in place. Never cut off a strap; without one, the swimmer must struggle to keep the life jacket on at just the time when she or he should be conserving energy and body heat by

The Off-Shore Life Jacket (formerly Type I PFD) provides more than 20 pounds of buoyancy. It should float most wearers very high with their faces safely clear of the water.

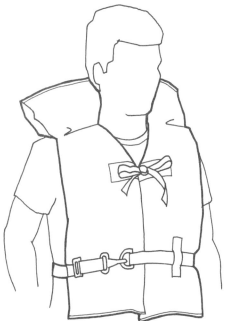

The less bulky Near-Shore Life Vest (Formerly Type II) has 15.5 or more pounds of buoyancy. With much of it under the neck, wearers' faces may float clear of the water.

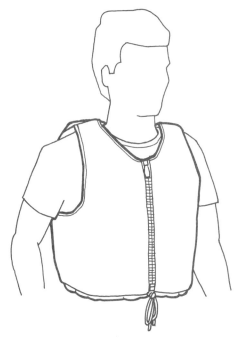

Popular among sailors because it is the least bulky is the Flotation Aid (formerly Type III). The problem is that wearers may have to tread water to keep their faces clear.

staying still.

Note that Coast Guard regulations do provide some choice of type. Too many boatowners interpret this as an invitation to purchase the least expensive, most compact PFD available. That is a mistake. Select your boat's life jackets with an eye to their possible use. Concerning wearable life jackets (those in PFD Types I-III), the rule of thumb is this: the farther from shore and the more demanding the environment, the lower the type number. High-buoyancy Off-Shore Life Jackets (Type I) should be carried when far from land. Lower buoyancy Flotation Aids (Type III) may be carried or worn near shore.

Off-Shore Life Jacket (formerly Type I) provides the greatest buoyancy, more than 20 pounds. This jacket is designed to turn an unconscious person's face clear of the water. This is the type to put aboard a boat that may sail well away from possible rescuers or in cool or cold water, which can quickly cause hypothermia and unconsciousness. Unfortunately, this jacket's bulk can inhibit the quick movements often required of sailors.

Near-Shore Life Vest (formerly Type II) provides at least 15.5 pounds of buoyancy and is less bulky than the Type I. Its yoke-type design, with buoyancy around the neck, may float the swimmer's face clear of the water, but since it has less buoyancy than the Off-Shore Jacket it is not the life jacket of choice for people far from help.

Flotation Aid (formerly Type III) also has at least 15.5 pounds of buoyancy but since the buoyancy is evenly distributed around the trunk rather than around the neck, the Aid will not automatically keep a swimmer's face clear of the water. An unconscious person may well drown wearing this life jacket. A conscious person may have to tread water in order to keep his or her face clear, which means that survival will depend on the swimmer's endurance. This jacket may not suffice for use far away from potential rescuers. Less bulky than the first two types, it is often used in such activities as water skiing and dinghy sailing where rescue is near, the activity requires that a life jacket, be worn, and bulk is obstructive.

Throwable Device (formerly Type IV) is easily thrown and has at least 16.5 pounds of flotation. Examples are seat cushions and life rings. Cushions should never be worn on the back because they will force the wearer's head into the water. Horseshoe-shaped life rings usually are stowed on the decks or lifelines of larger boats. Cushions and life rings may become waterlogged by rain, so they should be stowed below when the boat is not in use.

Special Use Device (formerly Type V) includes buoyancy devices intended for specific purposes. Among the devices here are sailboard harnesses, some special devices for rescue and commercial work, and the only Coast Guard-approved inflatable life jacket, the "hybrid vest" with 7.5 pounds of permanent buoyancy when uninflated and 20 pounds or more when inflated. Devices in this category do not meet the Coast Guard rules described above.

Inflatable Devices

One of the requirements for approval in the four types required by the rules is that buoyancy be provided by foam or some other buoyant material, but not by air. Despite the widespread use of inflatable life jackets in foreign countries, the Coast Guard for many years has refused to approve inflatable PFDs on the ground that they require a level of maintenance average boatowners can't be expected to meet. Still, several types of inflatable devices are becoming increasingly popular because of their extreme compactness when uninflated, which means that they may be more likely to be worn than bulkier jackets. Of course, every boat is required by law to carry a full complement of approved life jackets in the categories formerly covered by Types I-IV.

Many inflatable devices provide more than 20 pounds of buoyancy when inflated by carbon dioxide cartridge or by mouth. A valuable device is an inflatable life ring carried uninflated in a compact pouch either in the cockpit or on the sailor's belt. When the swimmer goes into the water, the first type is thrown and automatically inflates, or the second type is inflated by the swimmer by pulling a tab on the pouch.

Inflatables must be maintained assiduously. A small puncture caused by a cotter pin or shackle may render an inflatable useless. Inflatables should be inflated and tested for leaks regularly, and a backup stock of carbon dioxide cartridges should be on hand.

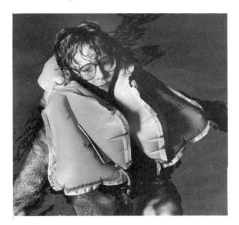

Though not officially approved by the Coast Guard, inflatable life jackets are gaining in popularity because of their compactness when uninflated. Coast Guard approved Type I-IV life jackets still must be carried onboard.

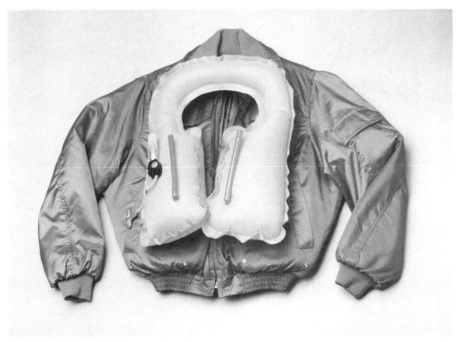

Staying on Board

Even a swimmer wearing a high-buoyancy life jacket is at risk in the water. Since water conducts heat away from the body 25 times faster than air, hypothermia (which can lead quickly to drowning) is a major threat. Although the swimmer must try to conserve energy by avoiding all unnecessary exercise, some body movements will be required. Here are some tips.

1. If you are wearing a life jacket, try to get it to fit as snugly as possible using the crotch strap and other adjustments.

2. Do not pull off clothing, shoes, or boots. Since they have neutral buoyancy in the water, they won't weigh you down and they will provide some insulation for conserving body heat. Putting on a hood or hat will lower heat loss through the head and also improve your chances of being spotted in the water. Trap or breathe air under the foul-weather jacket to provide some buoyancy.

3. Get rid of objects with negative buoyancy, such as tools. However, don't dispose of a flashlight (which may attract rescue) or a knife (which may be needed to cut away obstructions).

4. Do not swim unless certain rescue is very close nearby.

5. If you are alone, get in the fetal-type heat escape lessening posture (HELP position) in order to conserve heat. In this position, you cover the groin and armpits, from which heat escapes the most quickly. If you are with others, huddle together to conserve heat.

According to the National Transportation Safety Association, in 60° water a swimmer will survive for 3 hours without flotation (treading water), for 4.1 hours with flotation (lying still), for 6 hours with flotation (HELP position), and for 6.2 hours with flotation (huddle position). In 50° water, survival times are approximately two-thirds these times.

Staying on Board

The best way to avoid drowning is not to fall overboard in the first place. We have already covered staying on board a small boat. On a large boat work hard to keep your footing, and wear a safety harness in case your footing fails. While working on deck, remember the traditional mariner's rule, "One hand for yourself, one hand for the ship."

Footing

Even the most experienced, talented sailors lose their balance, especially during the first day or so after they come aboard. You'll see these women and men unembarrassedly holding on tight and wearing safety harnesses while novices are trying (and usually failing) to swing around like Tarzan. Once you've got your sea legs, your se-

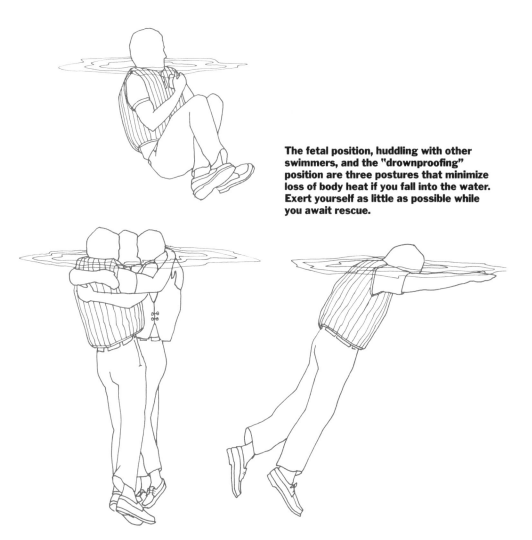

The fetal position, huddling with other swimmers, and the "drownproofing" position are three postures that minimize loss of body heat if you fall into the water. Exert yourself as little as possible while you await rescue.

cure footing depends first of all on good nonskid surfaces on the deck and the soles of shoes. But even they won't hold your feet in place when the boat is heeling, rolling, and pitching. In those conditions, shuffle along in a boxer's crouch with your legs far apart. Face the direction in which you are moving, with your body weight centered over a spot halfway between your feet, and keep a grasp on lifelines, grab rails, and other handholds. If you're still unstable, don't be proud: slide along on your butt, or crawl on your hands and knees or stomach.

A word of caution about lifelines. Since they may rust under their plastic covers and weaken where they bend through stanchions, they should be used less as sturdy banisters than as boundaries for the deck. Do not put all your weight on them without a backup support like another sailor's arms or a safety harness hooked to a sturdy through-bolted attachment point. If you must lean outboard, put your weight directly against a stanchion, not the lifelines (but first check that the

Most offshore cruising and racing boats have grabrails along the cabintop and on the overhead down below to aid crew movement on an unsteady boat.

stanchion is secure in its base with a tight set screw).

On the foredeck, while working with jibs or the anchor, sit down and keep your feet braced against cleats or the toerail around the deck. In the cockpit and on the after deck, make grab straps from sail stop material and tie them to the stern pulpit, cleats, or other sturdy objects. You should be able to stand securely in the middle of the cockpit or on the center of the after deck with a grab strap in either hand. When sitting in the cockpit, lean against the windward (uphill) back rest and brace your feet against the leeward (downhill) seat.

Men often urinate off the afterdeck so they don't have to go below to the head. This can be very dangerous as hands that should be holding on are busy with buttons and zippers. In an ocean race off Florida in 1979, a man peeing off the afterdeck fell overboard and drowned. In rough weather there should be a policy that nobody urinates off the after deck unless he is kneeling and hooked on with a safety harness. Otherwise, men must go below.

Another dangerous location is the companionway or hatch on a cruising boat, where you may be caught off balance while leaving or coming on deck. In very rough weather, the best way to negotiate these openings is to get down on your knees or belly and snake along, with your safety harness hooked on at all times.

When a boat is pitching or rolling, experienced sailors learn to move with their center of gravity low, always with a sure grip on lifelines, grabrail or other handholds.

Safety Harnesses

Besides the life jacket, the most important piece of personal safety equipment on a larger boat is a safety harness hooked to a sturdy attachment. The harness will brace you when you need to stand, keep you on board if you're knocked off your feet, and serve as a "third hand" to hold on with when your own two hands are busy with a job. There should be one harness for each crew member so everybody can be on deck at the same time. In 1988 a good harness cost about $70, which isn't much for the best insurance policy a sailor will ever have. To put that into perspective, an individual sailor's personal harness costs less than six charts, and a boat's inventory of four harnesses costs about the same as one suit of good foul-weather gear.

The best safety harnesses have a tested strength of at least 3000 pounds, are made of 2-inch webbing with heavily stitched seams, and have a 6-foot tether with a stainless steel snap hook at the end. The design should be simple enough to allow the harness to be easily put on without assistance in the dark and in rough conditions. Otherwise, people will have excuses for not wearing harnesses. Homemade and inexpensive harnesses are too weak to take the heavy loads of a falling body, and usually are too complicated to be put on quickly.

Good harnesses are available in several sizes. Some are adjustable to allow a close fit no matter how many layers of clothes are being worn. Other options include a snap shackle between the tether and the harness to permit the wearer to disengage quickly from a sinking boat, and a second snap hook halfway down the tether that allows the wearer to move from attachment point to attachment point while always staying hooked on (sometimes two distinct tethers are rigged). While these options are attractive, if they make the harness heavy and complicated the sailor may be discouraged from wearing it.

An excellent option that does not add too much weight is an emergency light sewn into the harness or stored in an attached pocket. If you go into the water at night, this light will help lead the boat back to you.

Some foul-weather jackets and parkas have built-in safety harnesses. While this option is a good investment for a sailor who frequents wet, cold, windy areas, it is not a good idea for people who will often need the harness in warm weather and who may not want to wear foul-weather gear.

Jacklines and Other Attachments

A harness is only as strong as its attachment points. Good attachment points usually include: through-bolted padeyes, cleats, and winches; stays; the mast; and stainless steel eyes on the base of stanchions and pulpits. Unreliable and even dangerous attachments include: sheets; the grab rail over the cockpit compass; cockpit dodgers; pulpits and stanchions (which may bend); and lifelines (which may break).

The best attachment is a trolley consisting of a line or wire onto which the harness tether is hooked. It allows you to move unrestricted between the ends of the trolley without unhooking. An excellent, simple, and easily assembled trolley system is a jackline or jackwire (sometimes "trolley line" or "jackstay"; "jack" is a prefix meaning "useful"). This is a length of strong rope, webbing, or wire securely connected at its ends to through-bolted padeyes, cleats, or other fittings. The primary jacklines run between the bow and stern on the side decks. They should lead as far aft as possible so the crew in the cockpit can hook on before climbing on deck, and as far forward as possible so the crew doesn't have to unhook while going forward to work with the jibs or anchor.

While every boat's deck arrangement will determine how the jackline or jackwire will be laid out, a few general rules of thumb apply. First, run the line in such a way that anybody who uses it is not obstructed or entangled by jib sheets and the shrouds. Second, leave enough slack in the jackline so you can work on the leeward side while hooked on to the windward line. If you don't

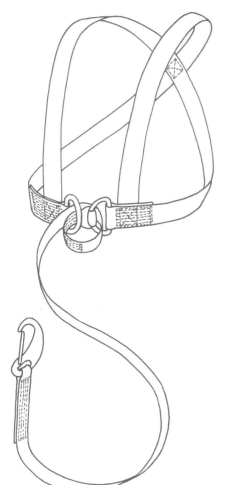

A simple, sturdy safety harness is an invaluable piece of safety gear. It should have a tested strength of at least 3000 lbs. to withstand the shock loading of a crew dragging in the water.

have to unhook to go from one side of the boat to the other, that's one less chance of being caught unprotected. Third, make the line or wire strong.

Nylon rope and webbing are excellent for jacklines because they are strong, resist chafe, and stretch to absorb sharp loads before they are transmitted to the harness. The diameter should be just small enough for the harness hook. Jacklines should be secured with the fisherman's bend with the bitter end seized or taped to the standing part of the line. Rope may be confused with jib sheets and other lines on deck. Wire, while easy to spot, has no stretch, acts like a ball bearing underfoot, and may corrode out of sight under its plastic cover. If you use wire, put eyes in the ends about 1 foot short of each attachment point and secure them with some passes of medium-size nylon line to act as a shock-absorber and allow for adjustment.

Another trolley is a patented device called the Latchway system. On each side of the boat, a wire is run from stem to stern inside and low on the stanchions. The harness tether is hooked into a car that slides on the wire and skips across the stanchion attachments. The advantage of this ingenious system is that the car, elevated above the deck, is easier to locate than a jackline. Its disadvantages include cost, complication, and the risk that the wire and stanchions may not take the heavy load of a person thrown a long distance by a wave or rolling deck.

Through-bolted padeyes, grab

With the Latchway system, the safety harness tether is attached to a car that rides on a wire from bow to stern along each gunwhale, skipping across attachments at the stanchions.

straps, or jacklines inside the cockpit allow people to hook on as they come up and go down the main companionway. Some sailors like to stay hooked on to a deck fitting when they go below, and then unsnap the tether from the harness so the tether hangs through the companionway. They wear the harnesses when below, even while sleeping. If they must go on deck quickly, all they have to do is reattach the tether and climb up through the companionway.

Hints on Safety Harness Use

1. Hook on whenever you begin to feel unstable. Nobody should have to apologize for using a harness in calm weather.

2. Hook on whenever you are on your own. This includes sailing single-handed, at night, and whenever a shipmate cannot see or help you (for example when working on the foredeck and the afterdeck out of sight of the crew in the cockpit).

3. Hook on when steering in rough weather. A spinning or tugging wheel or tiller has a lot of force.

4. Put on the harness before going on deck.

5. Hook on only to through-bolted fittings and strong lines or wires between them.

6. Always hook on to the windward (uphill) side. This is because if you are thrown it will be to leeward (downhill). If you are hooked on to windward, you will fall the length of the tether and fetch up on deck with relatively little force. But if you are hooked on to the center of the boat, you may fall from the windward side all the way across the boat, or twice the length of the tether until you smash heavily onto the leeward side. This type of fall may cause injury. Finally, if you are hooked on to the leeward (downhill) side, you probably will be thrown overboard and towed through the water.

7. Keep the tether as short as possible. Short tethers mean short falls, which mean less risk of physical injury.

8. Don't depend entirely on the harness. The harness is an insurance policy to keep you on board should you fall.

9. Take care of your harness. Stow it and its gear in dry places, and frequently inspect them for wear.

All this may sound melodramatic to somebody who has never been to sea in rough weather, but any sailor who has experienced a gale or two knows the violent power of waves and the wild rolling of a boat. At those times you will be thankful for the "third hand" provided by a safety harness hooked to a strong attachment point.

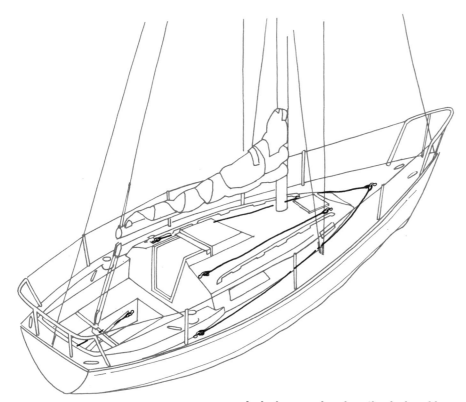

Jackwires running along the deck, cabin top, or cockpit provide a place to attach a safety harness tether while allowing fore and aft movement. Always snap onto the windward jackwire, avoid snapping onto lifelines or stays, and keep the tether as short as possible.

Crew-Overboard Rescue

Over the years much thought has gone into solving the frightening problem traditionally known as "man overboard" (MOB) but accurately called "crew overboard" (COB). Until the mid-1980s, thinking on the COB problem produced some awkward gear and elaborate techniques that were impractical for the average small cruising crew. However, thanks to the energetic efforts of sailors and researchers working under the umbrellas of nonprofit and commercial organizations, we now have simpler, more efficient equipment and doctrines that will help save many sailors' lives.

The problems inherent in COB rescue are: first, stopping the boat's forward progress; second, getting buoyancy to the victim; third, quickly and accurately getting the boat alongside; fourth, connecting the victim to the boat; and fifth, recovering the victim.

The Quick-Stop Method

A key factor in COB rescue is to keep the boat near the victim so he or she stays in sight of the crew on deck. Once he or she disappears, the odds of finding and recovering him or her are extremely low. The importance of stopping the boat as soon as possible to stay near the swimmer has been proven in actual experience as well as in on-the-water testing by the Naval Academy Sailing Squadron in Annapolis and the Sailing Foundation of Seattle, Washington. This research shows that traditional boat-handling doctrines (including Williamson turns, sailing reciprocal courses, and jibing and reaching back) take the boat too far away from the COB.

Stop the boat's forward progress by immediately heading into the wind and tacking back toward the swimmer. This is called the quick-stop method. You don't have to tack the jib; let it back and pull the boat off on the new tack. Don't worry about neatness or whether the sail will rip or the mast will stay in; modern sails and rigs can take enormous loads. While the quick-stop may seem unseamanlike, it is reliable even with crews that have not practiced it (although practice will speed up the maneuver).

A boat can do a quick-stop even under spinnaker. Head up until the bow is almost in the wind's eye. Ease the spinnaker pole forward to the headstay and tighten the foreguy (spinnaker pole downhaul). Then let go the spinnaker halyard without checking it as the crew retrieves the sail under the main boom with the sheet. The spinnaker will get wet, but it will come down quickly. (The halyard should be coiled, and there should be a knife handy in case you have to cut it.) When running wing-and-wing with a jib poled out, you won't be able to do a quick-stop unless the jib

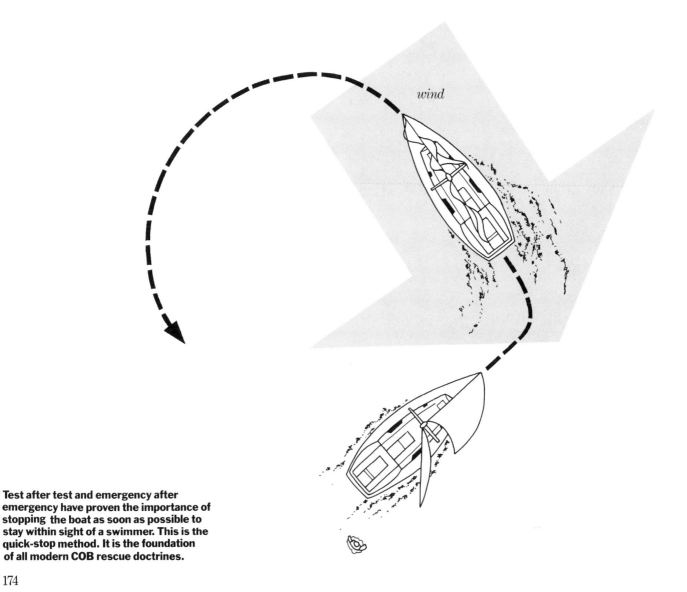

wind

Test after test and emergency after emergency have proven the importance of stopping the boat as soon as possible to stay within sight of a swimmer. This is the quick-stop method. It is the foundation of all modern COB rescue doctrines.

sheet can be eased out through the end of the spinnaker pole.

This system of returning works entirely under sail except in very calm weather, when the engine may be needed. A spinning propeller can tangle in lines or (worse) chew up the swimmer. The Sailing Foundation reports that in eight COB cases where the engine was engaged, there were five fouled propellers, one fatality, and no rescues.

Getting Buoyancy to the COB

Many tests have shown that the quickest way to get flotation to the victim is to throw a cockpit cushion, which can be deployed faster and more accurately than a life ring stored on the stern (unless the life ring can be let go by a remote control system). This is a good reason why cockpit cushions should be of high-visibility colors like red and orange, and why they should not be allowed to become waterlogged. Throw cushions or life rings slightly upwind of the swimmer so they will be blown down to her or him.

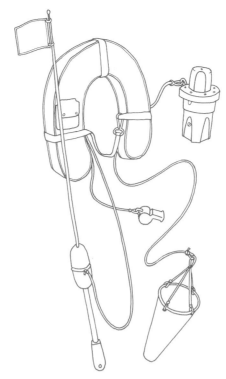

Many life rings are attached to poles, strobe lights and whistles to help crew locate the victim. A drogue helps slow down drift.

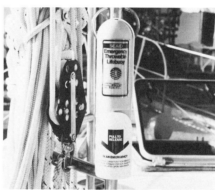

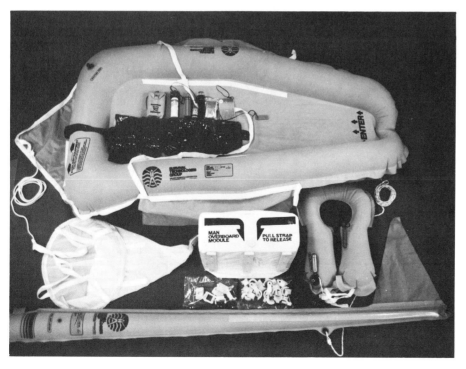

However, one advantage of a life ring is that it may be tied to a tall, buoyant bamboo or plastic pole (called a crew-overboard pole or man-overboard pole) visible from a distance. Tied to this gear should be a drogue to resist downwind drift, a bright strobe light whose flashes are visible even in daylight, and dye marker to attract aircraft and big ships. Stowing a crew-overboard pole so it is both secure and easy to deploy can be a problem. On many boats, the pole is tied to the permanent backstay or lifelines using light cordage that can be broken by hand or cut with a pocket knife. A few practice exercises will tell you how and where the pole should be stowed.

A more compact version of the COB pole and ring is a patented device called the Man Overboard Module (MOM), manufactured by the Survival Technologies Group. When triggered by a crew member, it drops overboard from a container on the stern pulpit and automatically inflates into a life ring and high-visibility pylon. Options include a strobe light, an emergency pack, and a one-person life raft. A more compact inflatable rescue device (mentioned earlier in this chapter) is a throwable canister that opens when it hits the water and expels a life ring. This device (also made by Survival Technologies) would be good to have within reach of the steerer in case somebody goes over the side. Inflatables must be maintained with care, and backup carbon dioxide cartridges should be carried.

As you return to the COB, shout encouragement to assure her or him that you are coming back. People who have survived falling overboard report that such assurances forestalled panic and pessimism. After completing the rescue, try to recover all the gear in the water so that another crew won't worry if they come across it.

A more modern version of the life ring is the Man Overboard Module (MOM), which is released from a container on the stern pulpit and automatically inflates into a life ring and pylon. Options include a strobe, emergency pack and a small life raft. Another modern safety device is a throwable cannister that inflates into a life ring on contact with the water.

Crew-Overboard Rescue

Immediately after the person goes over the side, a crew member must be posted to look for and point at the COB. Even in calm weather and broad daylight, finding the person can be very difficult, since a human head in the water is about the size, shape, and color of a half-submerged coconut. Just in case the swimmer is lost from view and the boat has to return to the accident location to begin a sweep of the area, the navigator should fix the boat's position; many Loran-C instruments have emergency buttons that, when pushed, record and store the boat's position.

Finding the swimmer at night is a big problem. Lights are the answer. On many boats, crews on deck at night are required to carry small strobe lights. Strobes may also be sewn onto safety harnesses, life jackets, and foul-weather jackets. A pocket flashlight won't be as bright as a strobe light, but it's better than no light at all. The boat should carry easily accessible waterproof buoyant flashlights that can be thrown after the victim goes over.

Once the COB has been spotted and you are sailing back to him or her, plan the recovery as you continue to shout encouragement. The first step is to stop or greatly slow the boat either alongside the victim or a short distance away in order to pull her or him to the boat with a heaving line.

One way to stop the boat is to get rid of the sails by dropping them or rolling them up. While this system truly stops the boat except for drift caused by wind, it has three disadvantages: the sails and lines on deck obstruct crew activity and may drag overboard and foul the propeller should the engine be used; the boat has no maneuverability; and

without the steadying force of sails, the boat may roll violently.

You can't stop the boat until you're next to the COB, and to get there you'll have to sail there. On a close reach under mainsail alone, slowly aim just to windward of the swimmer, cutting speed by heading up a little and increasing it by heading off. This calls for delicate steering and a quick hand on the sheet to luff and trim the mainsail. You must keep steerage way until the swimmer is directly alongside the boat, yet at the same time you must avoid going so fast that the swimmer can't hold on to the boat or a line thrown from the boat. Practice this approach by sailing up to a small anchored buoy or a cushion thrown in the water.

When the victim is almost alongside, stop the boat with the mainsail still hoisted by either heaving-to or doing a Rod-stop, both of which are described in the following paragraphs. Throw a heavy line with a large loop in the end and tell the swimmer to put the loop under her or his armpits.

Heaving-to and the Rod-stop don't

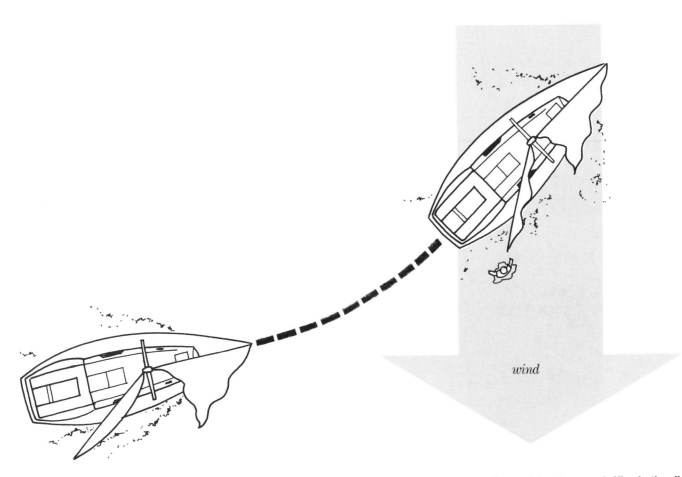

wind

When approaching the victim, maintain just enough speed for steerage, luffing both sails as you come alongside. If you are moving too fast, the victim will not be able to hold onto the boat or a thrown line. Once alongside, stop the boat by heaving-to or doing a Rod-stop (see next page).

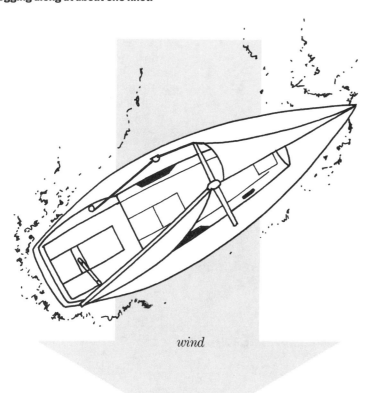

When heaving-to, trim the jib to windward and the mainsail to leeward to keep the boat jogging along at about one knot.

wind

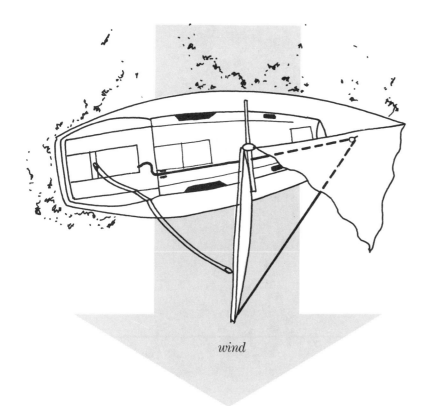

With the Rod-stop, the boom is trimmed forward against the leeward shrouds and vanged down to flatten it. The jib is luffed, lowered or furled.

wind

stop the boat completely. But they do keep the deck steady, allow the boat to steer herself without someone at the helm, and permit getting under way quickly. The boat will jog along very slowly and make some leeway (slide sideways) until the COB is ready to be hauled on deck, when the boat can be completely stopped by luffing the sails.

To **heave-to** sail closehauled or on a close reach (40° to 60° off the wind) with the jib backed (trimmed flat to windward) either by hauling it up with the windward sheet or by tacking and not casting off the old sheet. (This system does not work well with large overlapping genoa jibs.) Adjust the main sheet and traveler so the boat steers herself as she jogs along at about 1 knot. Heaving-to under small storm sails is also a standard technique for handling storms when waves are not breaking (see chapter 15, "Sailing in Heavy Weather").

The **Rod-stop method** gets its name from the great sailor man and yacht designer Rod Stephens, who first publicized it. Sail on a close reach and dowse, roll up, or luff the jib. Then cast off the main sheet and pull the boom forward to the leeward shrouds, securing it there with a line led from the boom to the foredeck (for example the preventer or the spinnaker pole foreguy). This line should be controlled from the cockpit so you can get going quickly. Hold the boom down and flatten the sail by tightening the boom vang, outhaul, and Cunningham. Held out with almost no shape, the mainsail will flag back and forth, alternately filling on one side, then the other. The boat should jog along with no one at the helm. Anytime you want to get going again, just trim the sails.

Besides being an excellent technique for staying near a COB, stopping the boat while keeping her under control is also an excellent seamanship technique in all conditions for taking a break in order to rest, repair damage, or do navigation.

Crew Overboard Rescue

The next problem is to get the COB to the boat. The swimmer may swim to the boat, but only if the boat is very near. The record of people who have drowned while attempting to swim to rescue is long and grim.

An excellent recovery device is a heaving line made of about 100 feet of buoyant polypropylene line with a weight on the end. The weight can be a softball or a pouch filled with sand or water. Good heaving lines are sold by marine hardware stores and mail-order outfits. On board, keep the heaving line close at hand in the cockpit. Don't throw the heaving line until you are

A heaving line with a padded weight at the end is an excellent means of throwing a recovery line to a victim in the water.

stopped dead in the water upwind of the COB. Luff the sails and wait until the boat has lost almost all her speed. You won't be able to make the recovery if you have to tow the swimmer. Tell the swimmer what you intend to do. Throw the line over him or her, wait until he or she has a good grasp on it, and slowly pull the swimmer in. If you miss, recoil or repack the line and try again.

Without a heaving line, you will have to stop the boat right alongside the COB.

Hauling the Swimmer on Deck

Getting an exhausted person who is weighed down by soaking wet clothes up and over the high topsides of a modern sailboat is very difficult, and many rescuers have reached this stage only to fail with tragic results. Several types of rescue systems are available; they break down into two categories, active and passive.

In an **active recovery**, the swimmer is able to assist in the rescue, usually by climbing up a swimming ladder temporarily hung on the topsides or perma-

Getting a helpless, exhausted, and soaking wet victim back aboard is difficult for several strong people and may be impossible for one or two. The victim probably won't even be able to use a ladder.

nently mounted on the transom. The first may be easier to grab because it's hung near the middle of the boat, where the deck is lowest and the hull is most steady, but the ladder may be wobbly and its mountings weak. A transom-hung ladder may have a stronger installation, but since the stern can pitch wildly in waves it may be hard to grab and may also lure the swimmer under the stern. If there is no swimming ladder, you may be able to improvise one by hanging loops of heavy line over the side.

Active recovery is impossible if the COB is exhausted, hypothermic, or injured. After even a few minutes in cool water, swimmers may not have the strength and agility needed to pull themselves up a few feet. In this case, passive rescue is the only solution.

One **passive rescue system** is to have several people grab the COB by the arms and belt and haul her or him on deck. But while this may work with a large team of strong and agile rescuers or with a victim who is a child, two or three average-size people cannot haul in an adult swimmer whose weight may have been doubled by waterlogged clothes.

What's needed is a sling. An improvised sling made of sail stops or rope may be hung from a halyard or from a tackle hooked to the boom. The boom must be cocked up at least 20 degrees so the victim clears the lifelines when swinging in.

Another passive system is to lift the swimmer in the belly of the jib; however, people who have been recovered this way report that they felt extreme claustrophobia.

It is generally not good seamanship to send a crew member over the side to help the victim, who may panic and pull the rescuer down. However, this may be necessary if the victim's life is in danger. The rescuer must wear a life jacket and be attached to the boat with a retrieval line.

A passive recovery system can be improvised using a rope sling dropped from the boom, which must be steadied with a preventer and cocked up so the victim clears the lifelines. The rope sling may cause considerable pain and loss of circulation.

The Lifesling System

One COB rescue system combines buoyancy for the swimmer, attachment to the boat, and a hoisting sling for passive recovery. Developed by the Sailing Foundation in Seattle, Washington, this is the patented device called the Lifesling (nicknamed "Seattle sling"). It was designed specifically to solve the problems faced by one person of limited strength who must singlehandedly recover one or more other persons.

The equipment is a buoyant yoke that

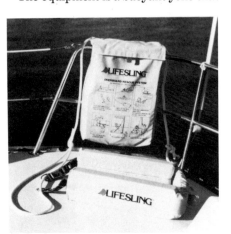

looks like a life ring but is larger and more flexible. It's tied with a large bowline to the end of a long length of polypropylene line whose other end is tied to a strong fitting on the boat's stern (for example a docking cleat). The yoke and line are stored ready for use in a protective pouch hung inside the after pulpit. An option is a tackle, also stored in the pouch.

The Lifesling is simple enough to use that the directions are printed in large letters on the storage pouch. Recovery with the device begins with the quick-stop maneuver described above. The jib is left backed on the windward side to spin the boat and also to make boat handling easier for the crew.

At the same time as the boat is turned back, the crew on deck pulls the buoyant yoke and line out of the pouch and heaves them over. (A singlehander must briefly leave the helm to get to the pouch before or after turning back.) The line pays out until the yoke is towed well behind the boat.

Without touching the sheets, the crew then sails in circles around the

The Lifesling system is deployed as the boat does a quick stop. The boat sails around the victim until he or she reaches the line or yoke. The sails are lowered. The victim climbs in the yoke and is pulled to the boat.

COB until the line or yoke swings into his or her grasp. This usually happens within three circles. The crew then heads the boat into the wind to stop her. The COB climbs into the yoke. The crew drops or rolls up the sails. (Secure the main boom to keep it from flopping around dangerously.)

With the boat now dead in the water, the crew pulls the swimmer to the boat's side and hauls the bowline that secures the polypropylene line to the yoke up and over a winch or cleat so the swimmer's head is clear of the water and he or she is not under the stern.

The crew connects the bowline to the main, jib, or spinnaker halyard. If the crew is strong, shackle the halyard directly to the line and winch the COB out of the water. Otherwise, rig the optional tackle (or another tackle) between the halyard shackle and the bowline, raise the halyard and the top block in the tackle about 15 feet above the deck, and lead the pulling end of the tackle to a winch (using a block to provide a fair lead).

Every boat has slightly different re-quirements, so crews should practice with the sling before an accident requires them to use it. The goal is to pull the person aboard about amidships, well away from the mast and shrouds.

For night rescues, there should be a light on the yoke so the crew can see it.

COB Drills

It should be clear by now that crew-overboard rescues won't happen if crews don't know how to do them. Start out practicing on a calm day with a cushion as your "victim," sailing up to it until you can stop the boat right along-side. When you feel confident, practice with a crew member wearing a life jacket or wet suit as a friend in another boat stands by.

Pay special attention to mastering the sailing skills and sail-handling re-quirements. It's a good idea to write out a standard operating procedure (SOP) that takes into account your boat's and crew's unique characteristics, weaknesses, and strengths. When out for a sail, occasionally pull out the SOP and walk through it, and then heave a cushion over for more practice. Since there's no way to predict who's going to fall overboard, make sure that everybody in your crew knows how to steer the boat back to the victim and how to rig and use the rescue gear.

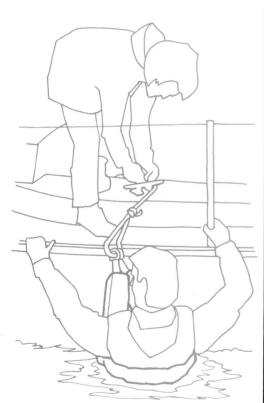

The crew cleats the line to keep the victim's head clear of the water, then attaches a tackle led to a halyard (or the halyard itself) and winches the victim on deck. Lifesling rescues should be rehearsed so each sailor knows what to do.

Chapter 8
The Rules of the Road

Every time boats come near each other there is a risk of collision. The Navigation Rules (commonly known as the Rules of the Road) lay out specific requirements enforceable by the Coast Guard, state and local maritime police, and courts of law. Some of this is pretty dry, but it is not irrelevant. There will come a day when you will have to know at least one of these rules in order to avoid running into somebody else. The Rules of the Road for typical boats and situations are summarized below. The complete rules are contained in the U.S. Coast Guard booklet *Navigation Rules: International-Inland*, available at many marine stores and from Coast Guard district headquarters.

Early seamen devised local rules of thumb in order to keep out of each other's way. As the sea was internationalized, so were these rules, and as of 1982, one set of Rules of the Road applies (with a few local variations) everywhere that a boat sails in and near the United States. What had been a confusing mix of regulations for international, inland, Great Lakes, and Western Rivers waters has been reduced to two sets of rules that almost entirely duplicate each other. These are the International Regulations for Preventing Collisions at Sea — also known as the International Rules of the Road or COLREGS — and the Inland Navigational Rules of the United States, authorized by the Inland Navigational Rules Act of 1980 — known as the Inland Rules. The Inland Rules and COLREGS use the same numbering system and arrangement, but differ (usually unimportantly) in wording in several places. *Most of us sail under the Inland Rules, which apply to lakes, rivers, and near coastal waters.* COLREGS, on the other hand, applies to outer coastal waters and the high seas. The boundary between the two is the purple line of demarcation printed on NOS charts. Before 1982 this line was extremely important due to the fact that the two rules differed in several important ways. Now that they are all but the same, the demarcation line is less significant.

The purpose of these rules is to enable seamen to avoid collisions. The rules apply to *all* craft — whether a sailboard or an aircraft carrier — and violators of the Inland Rules are liable for fines and penalties. The rules require timely action and good seamanship on the part of skippers and pilots. For example, Rule 8(e) says, "If necessary to avoid collision or allow more time to assess the situation, a vessel shall slacken her speed or take all way off by stopping or reversing her means of propulsion." That is to say, when in doubt about a situation, slow down or stop until it is clarified. Too many sail-

The give-way vessel, here on port tack, is the one required by the rules to alter course to avoid the stand-on vessel, here on starboard tack.

Give-Way Vessel

Stand-On Vessel

ors barge into trouble with a bravado that they would never exercise in their automobiles.

Give-Way and Stand-On Vessels

Under the rules, when two or more boats are in situations that might lead to collisions, at least one of them has to stay out of the way by altering course, speed, or both. A boat that must stay out of another vessel's way is called the *give-way vessel*. A boat that does not have to get out of the way is called the *stand-on vessel*. (These terms replace the old "burdened vessel" and "privileged vessel.")

Sometimes all the boats are give-way vessels, which means that every boat involved must alter course. But most of the time there is at least one give-way vessel *and* at least one stand-on vessel. The give-way vessel must get out of the other vessel's way by altering course and/or speed. The stand-on vessel must continue on her course at her current rate of speed in order not to mislead the give-way vessel. Of course, if the give-way vessel does not get out of the way, then the stand-on vessel must alter course, change speed, or both.

According to rule 8 in the Navigation Rules, the action taken by the give-way vessel should be made in ample time, should be substantial enough to be seen clearly by the other boat either visually or on radar, should be steady (one big turn is favored over a series of small ones), and should allow a safe margin.

Here is a summary of rule 8 by commercial pilot Captain John W. Trimmer in his eye-opening little book of advice to pleasure boaters, *How to Avoid Huge Ships*: "Make one sensible and substantial course change early to clear the ship. The key word here is *early*."

The preferred course alteration is to starboard (the right). However, if a turn to starboard will take you directly into the path of the other vessel, you may turn to port (the left), or you may stop or back down.

Signals

In many situations, one or more

boats must signal their intentions or actions with blasts from a whistle or horn. On very large boats (bigger than 66 feet), the horn must be audible at least 1 mile away. The range requirement for boats between 39 and 65 feet is ½ mile; it often can be met with a hand-held freon horn. While boats smaller than 39 feet do not have a range requirement, they should carry freon horns or whistles.

The rules specify certain patterns of short, loud horn blasts. Each horn blast should be about 1 second in duration. At night, boats may also use light signals in the same patterns.

If turning to starboard, sound one short blast with the whistle or horn. If you must turn to port, signal your intention by sounding two short blasts. If you must back down, sound three blasts to announce that your engine is in reverse. If a collision seems imminent, or if the other crew seems unresponsive to your signals and actions, make the danger signal of five or more blasts or flashes.

Under the Inland Rules (in lakes, rivers, and other American waters inside the demarcation lines shown on charts), a horn (and light) signal is made before your turn to show your *intention*. Once you have given the signal, don't turn until you hear or see the other boat make the same signal as a sign of *agreement* with your intention.

In international waters, where COLREGS applies, the horn (and light) signal reports *rudder action*. Make the turn when you make the signal. (This difference between intent-agreement and rudder action sound signals is one of the few disagreements between the Inland Rules and COLREGS.)

If you have doubts about safety and you have a VHF/FM radiotelephone, call the other vessel on channel 6 or 16 (13 if the other vessel is a ship) and talk over the situation. If her crew shows no awareness either of the danger in the situation or of what to do to avoid collision, make the danger signal and get away from her.

Size Ranges

The rules sometimes specify different requirements for different size boats. The demarcation is the overall length in meters: 7 meters (23.1 feet), 12 meters (39.6 feet), 20 meters (66 feet), and 50 meters (164 feet). Since the metric system is not widely used in the United States, we'll use the next smallest whole foot of overall length: 23 feet, 39 feet, 66 feet, and 164 feet, respectively.

The Rules in Summary

The Rules of the Road are summarized below. The complete rules are available in the Coast Guard publication *Navigation Rules, International-Inland*, which all powered boats 39 feet and longer must carry.

General Rules

The following five rules are generally applicable. Since almost all of them involve vessels under sail, they are the basic rules for sailors.

When an auxiliary sailboat's engine is in gear, she is a powerboat under the Rules of the Road. Listed after the five basic rules are rules that determine

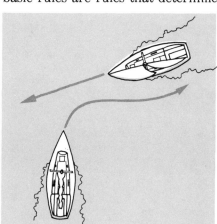

right of way when powerboats are near each other and signals that both sailboats and powerboats must make in certain situations.

A Moving Boat and a Boat Not Underway

Moving boats must stay out of the way of an anchored, stopped, moored, docked, or otherwise not moving vessel.

In Narrow Channels

Boats smaller than 66 feet, boats engaged in fishing, and all sailboats must not impede passage of a vessel that can safely navigate *only* in a narrow channel or fairway. Large, relatively unmaneuverable vessels — such as big power yachts, ferryboats, tugs with barges, tows, and tankers — have the right-of-way in tight channels. If they're obstructed by a small boat, a sailboat, or a boat with fishing lines or nets out, they will sound the danger signal.

In Traffic Separation Zones

Boats smaller than 66 feet, boats

(Left) An auxiliary sailboat under power is considered a powerboat and must give way to a sailboat. (Below) In a traffic separation zone, smaller boats (including sailboats) give way to large vessels. Cross zones as quickly as possible and at a right angle.

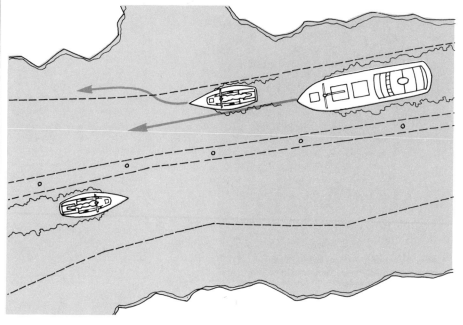

The Rules in Summary

engaged in fishing, and sailboats must also give way in traffic separation lanes and zones. Any boat obligated to cross a traffic separation lane should do so at a right angle to the flow of traffic.

Sailboat and Powerboat

In almost all circumstances power vessels must give way to sailboats. As soon as the auxiliary engine of a sailboat is turned on and put into gear, the boat becomes a powerboat under the rules. However, sailboats must give way to large powerboats in channels and traffic separation zones, to vessels engaged in fishing or trawling, to vessels not under command, to vessels restricted in their ability to maneuver such as tows, dredges, and ferries, and to vessels engaged in minesweeping. The rules assume that *in open water* powerboats are more maneuverable than sailboats and sailboats are more maneuverable than fishing boats or boats that for some reason do not have a helmsman. *In narrow channels,* large vessels are presumed to be less maneuverable than sailboats. The old tradition of "power gives way to sail" has thus been changed to "power usually gives way to sail."

Sailboat and Sailboat

When boats are on different tacks, the port-tack boat gives way to the starboard-tack boat. When boats are on the same tack, the windward boat (the boat upwind of the other) gives way to the leeward boat. (These two rules are the foundation of the yacht racing rules, summarized in appendix · III.)

Powerboats Overtaking (COLREGS Differs from Inland Rules)

An overtaking vessel is one that approaches a vessel ahead from greater than 22.5° abaft the leading vessel's beam — or aft of roughly 4 and 8 o'clock. If you're passing a boat on a parallel course and are not quite dead abeam (exactly alongside) her, you are overtaking and just give way unless one of the general rules listed above applies.

Under the INTERNATIONAL RULES (COLREGS):

1. **In open water (not in a channel)** an overtaking power vessel sounds one short blast to indicate that she is altering course to starboard and intends to pass to starboard; two short blasts to indicate that she is altering course to port and intends to pass to port; or three short blasts to indicate that she is in reverse and backing away from the leading boat. At night, one, two, or three short white-light

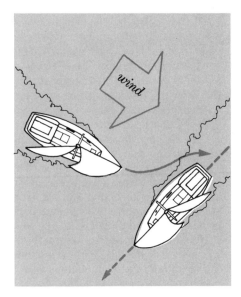

Sailboats on port tack must give way to ones on starboard tack either by altering course to one side (above left) or by passing astern (above).

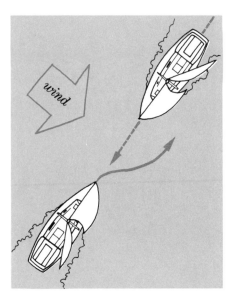

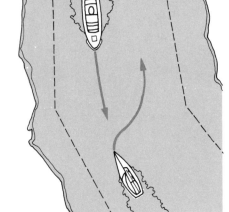

Sailboats must give way to relatively unmaneuverable power vessels in constricted channels.

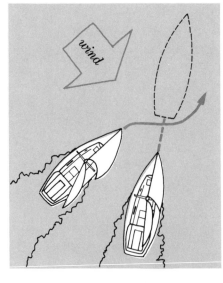

When sailboats are on the same tack, the windward boat is the give-way vessel and must avoid the leeward one.

flashes may be used to supplement the whistle blasts, using a 360° light. The leading vessel does not acknowledge these signals, which are "rudder-action" signals made as the helm is altered. If the leading, stand-on vessel doubts that the overtaking, give-way vessel can avoid a collision, she should sound the danger signal. Note that sailboats do not signal when overtaking in open water under COLREGS.

2. **In a narrow channel or fairway,** if the leading vessel, power or sail, must alter course to make way for the overtaking vessel to pass, an overtaking power or sail vessel sounds two long blasts followed by one short blast to indicate that she plans to pass to starboard; or two long blasts followed by two short blasts to indicate that she plans to pass to port. The leading vessel must acknowledge this signal. If the leading vessel agrees with the overtaking vessel's intentions, she sounds one long, one short, and one long, which is the International Code signal for "Charlie" or "affirmative." She must then make way for the over-

taking boat. But if the leading vessel disagrees with the overtaking boat's plan, she sounds the danger signal of five or more short blasts. The overtaking vessel must not attempt to pass until the leading vessel agrees. This exchange of signals is called "intent-agreement." Unlike a "rudder-action" signal, it cannot be acted upon if there are cross-signals; the two parties *must agree* that the first boat's intent does not risk collision.

Under the INLAND RULES, only powerboats signal when overtaking — and then only if both or all boats are powerboats. "Intent-agreement" signals are made on inland waters regardless of whether the boats are in open water or in channels. (In other words, power vessels *always* exchange signals *before* changing course. Remember that a sailboat under auxiliary power is considered a power vessel.) The overtaking, give-way boat sounds one short blast if she intends to pass to starboard, or two short blasts if she intends to pass to port. If the leading, stand-on vessel agrees, she re-

peats the overtaking vessel's signal, one blast meaning "Pass to starboard" and two blasts meaning "Pass to port." But if she disagrees, the leading boat sounds the danger signal. If the leading vessel's response is a cross-signal (for example, one blast answering the overtaking boat's two blasts), the overtaking vessel should not attempt to pass, but should repeat her signal. If the leading vessel sounds the danger signal, the overtaking vessel should not attempt to pass until the leading vessel signals that passage is safe by sounding the correct agreement to the overtaking boat's original intent signal.

To summarize the rules on overtaking:

In international waters in open water, overtaking powerboats only make signals, and then only to signal rudder action. There is no acknowledgment.

In international waters in channels, all overtaking boats and leading boats make "intent-agreement" signals.

In inland waters, overtaking and leading powerboats only make "intent-agreement" signals.

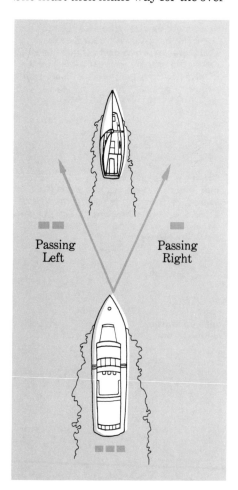

A boat is overtaking if she is more than 22.5° abaft the leading boat's beam (shaded area). Under the Inland Rules, sound one short blast if you intend to pass to starboard and two if to port. Await the leading boat's agreement signal. Three short blasts signal backing away.

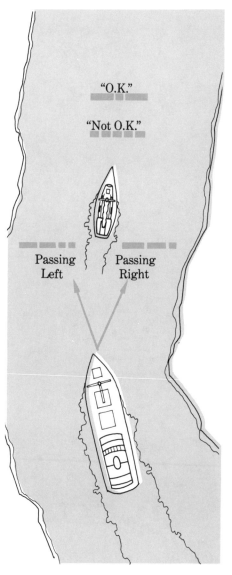

Different signals are used under COLREGS when passing in a narrow channel, but the leading boat must still agree or otherwise use the danger signal to show her non-agreement.

The Rules in Summary

Powerboats Meeting (COLREGS Differs from Inland Rules)

Vessels are meeting head-on when they approach each other on reciprocal or nearly reciprocal courses. If you see another boat approaching you from ahead, you're in a meeting situation. *Both* vessels here are give-way vessels. If collision is possible, both must alter course, preferably to starboard so that they pass port side to port side (although the rules make a provision for starboard side to starboard side passage).

Under COLREGS, if port side to port side passage can be safely made, no signals are required. But if a collision is possible, each vessel must make a rudder-action signal *as she turns*: one short blast for turning to starboard or two short blasts for turning to port. If a vessel is forced to back down, she makes the backing-down signal of three short blasts.

Under the Inland Rules, intent-agreement signals must be made if two powerboats are to pass within ½ mile of each other. These signals are the same as those used under COLREGS: one short blast for course alteration to starboard, two short blasts for course alteration to port, or three short blasts for backing down. When one vessel hears the other vessel's signal, she either sounds the same signal to indicate agreement or sounds the danger signal (five or more short blasts) to indicate disagreement. If there is disagreement, both vessels "shall take appropriate precautionary action until a safe passing agreement is made." Slowing down or stopping is usually the correct "precautionary" action. If they agree, the vessels turn to starboard or to port, or back down, in order to make safe passage. If the signals cross — for example, if one boat sounds three blasts and the other sounds one blast — both boats should sound the danger signal and take appropriate precautionary action. While the Inland Rules make provisions for starboard side to starboard side pas-

sage, they specifically *authorize* it only in the following situation: on the Great Lakes or the Mississippi River or other Western Rivers, a vessel running downstream with the current has right-of-way over a vessel proceeding up-current, and *may* propose a starboard side to starboard side passage in a narrow channel — say, around a river bend. At all other times the Inland Rules (like COLREGS) assume a port side to port side passage. "Stay to the right and you'll be right."

Under both rules, in international and inland waters, common sense and caution should prevail when deciding whether or not you are in a meeting situation, whether or not a meeting situation requires an alteration of course, and whether or not you should pass port side to port side. If you have any doubts about the safety of a situation:

1. Assume that you are meeting the other vessel.
2. Sound one blast ½ mile from the other vessel.
3. Listen carefully for his response.

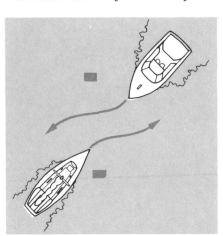

4. If there is agreement, turn to starboard well to the side of the other vessel.
5. If there is disagreement, sound the danger signal and stop.

Remember that this rule applies only when powerboats meet. When sailboats meet or when a sailboat and a powerboat meet, the general rules apply. Except in narrow channels, the powerboat must give way to the sailboat. The tack or relative position determines which sailboat gives way to the other.

Powerboats Crossing (COLREGS Differs from Inland Rules)

Boats that approach each other without either meeting or overtaking are crossing. That is, if the vessels are not approaching each other on reciprocal or nearly reciprocal courses, or if one vessel is not passing the other from astern, they are crossing. Both COLREGS and the Inland Rules say that when two boats cross, "the vessel

Powerboats meeting head-on sound one short (for a turn to starboard) or two shorts (for a turn to port). Under the Inland Rules, the other boat must agree; under COLREGS, the signals only indicate rudder action.

Crossing, the give-way powerboat is the one to port and sounds one short (turn to starboard), two shorts (turn to port), or three shorts (backing away). The stand-on powerboat must signal agreement under the Inland Rules.

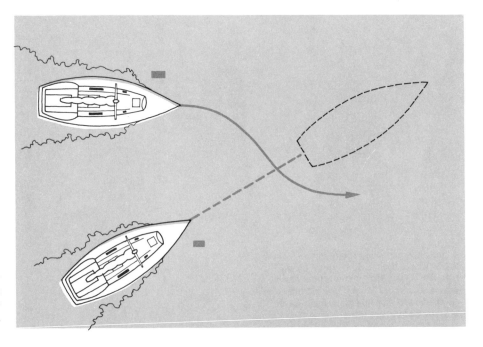

which has the other on her starboard side shall keep out of the way and shall, if the circumstances of the case admit, avoid crossing ahead of the other vessel." Therefore the boat to the *left* is the *give-way vessel* and the boat to the *right* is the *stand-on vessel*.

If there is doubt as to the definition of the situation, assume that it is *not* a crossing. For example, one vessel may be approaching from an angle of about 22.5° abaft the other vessel's beam. Since she could be either overtaking or crossing, assume that it's an overtaking situation.

The two rules require different signals in crossing situations. Under **COLREGS**, the left-side, give-way vessel sounds one short blast if she intends to turn to starboard (toward and astern of the stand-on vessel), two short blasts if she intends to turn to port (but not into the stand-on vessel's projected course), or three short blasts if she intends to back down to allow the stand-on vessel to pass ahead. But if the give-way vessel intends to slow down or stop, she makes no signal. The right-side, stand-on vessel neither signals nor alters course unless a collision is imminent. She must provide a constant standard against which the give-way vessel measures the effect of her actions. If a collision threatens, the stand-on vessel sounds the danger signal (five or more short blasts) and takes appropriate action, usually by stopping, backing down, or turning to starboard, making the appropriate signals.

Under the **Inland Rules**, intent-agreement signals are *always* exchanged by vessels in a crossing situation. If the left-side, give-way vessel intends to turn to starboard and go astern of the right-side, stand-on vessel, she sounds one short blast. When the stand-on vessel indicates her agreement with one short blast, the give-way vessel makes her turn (usually slowing down as well). The give-way vessel may make two short blasts to indicate that she intends to turn to port. Thoughtless skippers sometimes do this not to allow the stand-on vessel to pass but to announce that they are barging across the stand-on vessel's bow, regardless of the Rules of the Road. This dangerous practice is so prevalent that the real significance of two blasts — "I'm altering course to port to enable you to pass to my starboard" — has been widely forgotten. It's always safer for the give-way vessel — the one to the port of the other vessel — to sound one short blast, and when the stand-on boat echoes it, to

turn *hard to starboard* and pass well astern. We say "hard to starboard" because a drastic course alteration of 20° or more clearly shows the stand-on vessel how the give-way vessel will fulfill her obligations under the rules. A minor course change may be interpreted as a small steering error, confusing the stand-on vessel. As with overtaking and meeting under the Inland Rules, crossing situations lead to collisions if signals are crossed. If the give-way vessel signals an intent that the stand-on vessel does not agree with, the stand-on vessel should make the danger signal, not the signal of the crossing she would prefer.

Fog and Restricted Visibility

COLREGS and the Inland Rules are the same, with minor wording differences, concerning safe navigation in fog and restricted visibility. They require that every vessel "at all times proceed at a safe speed so that she can take proper and effective action to avoid collision and be stopped within a distance appropriate to the prevailing circumstances and conditions." In other words, the more restricted the visibility, the slower the speed. Each vessel is *required* to maintain a lookout for lights and sounds such as foghorns or the wash of other vessels — no matter what the visibility. Lookouts must be especially attentive to the bearings on approaching vessels. If the bearings do not change as the boats converge, there will be a collision. If the bearings do change, one boat will pass astern of the other.

In poor visibility, vessels are required to reduce speed to a minimum when their lookouts hear another vessel's fog signal from forward of the beam. This is an indication that the boats are approaching each other, and such an approach should be made at the lowest possible speed until all are certain that there is no danger of a collision. There are several required fog signals, each for a different situation. The signals must be made with bells or whistles by vessels 39 feet or longer. Smaller boats are not required to, but should, sound fog signals in periods of restricted visibility.

Sound Signals in Fog

Types of whistles and bells used as fog and other signals are specified in Annex III of both COLREGS and the Inland Rules. Below is a summary.

On vessels that are underway, the following whistle or horn signals are made at intervals of 2 minutes or less:

1. Sailboats, vessels engaged in fishing, towing, or pushing, and vessels either not under command or restricted in their maneuverability: one long blast followed by two short blasts (long-short-short).

2. Powerboats making way through the water: one long blast (long).

3. Powerboats under way but stopped: two long blasts (long-long).

4. A vessel being towed: one long blast followed by three short blasts (long-short-short-short).

5. (Under COLREGS only) A powerboat whose room to maneuver is constrained by her deep draft: one long blast followed by two short blasts (long-short-short).

On vessels that are *not* underway, these signals are made in periods of limited visibility:

1. Vessel at anchor: if shorter than 328 feet, a bell forward is rung rapidly for 5 seconds every minute; if longer, a bell forward and a gong aft are rung rapidly for 5 seconds every minute; in addition, an anchored vessel may sound her horn in a pattern of one

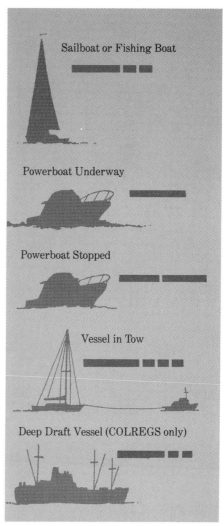

Special sound signals identify different types of boats in fog.

The Rules in Summary

short blast, one long blast, and one short blast (short-long-short) at intervals necessary to alert approaching vessels.

2. Vessel aground: if shorter than 328 feet, three distinct bell strokes, then rapid sounding of a bell forward for 5 seconds, then three distinct bell strokes, at an interval of 1 minute; if longer, that bell sequence followed by the rapid sounding of a gong aft for 5 seconds, all at 1-minute intervals; in addition, a vessel aground may sound the whistle signals "F" (short-short-long-short, meaning "I am disabled; communicate with me"), "U" (short-short-long, "You are running into danger"), or "V" (short-short-short-long, "I require assistance") at necessary intervals.

3. (Under the Inland Rules only) An anchored vessel that is engaged in fishing or is restricted in her ability to maneuver: one long blast followed by two short blasts (long-short-short) at an interval of 2 minutes.

4. Vessel moored at the end of a pier: any noise with a horn, bell, or gong. (While not a rule, this requirement has been suggested by some courts.)

Under the Inland Rules only, a powerboat leaving a berth or dock must sound one long blast, even if she is visible to all nearby vessels.

A vessel about to round a bend in a river or channel where the other side of the bend is obstructed must sound one long blast, to be echoed by any vessels approaching the bend on the other side.

The signal for requesting the opening of a drawbridge is one long blast followed by one short blast (long-short), to be echoed by the bridge tender within 30 seconds if the draw is to be opened immediately. If there is a delay, the response is five short blasts — the danger signal. If the skipper, for reasons of emergency, must pass immediately, he then makes the danger signal. When approaching an open bridge, the vessel should make the long-short signal. The bridge tender will not respond unless he plans to close the span before the vessel passes through. Contiguous bridges must be signaled individually. Bridge tenders will acknowledge each opening request from boats on both sides of the bridge. If the skipper requests an opening over his vessel's radiotelephone, he should not make a horn signal.

Special Circumstances

Both COLREGS and the Inland Rules allow for special circumstances — situations when for one reason or another the rules don't quite cover all possibilities. In those cases there is no stand-on vessel, and all boats involved are to consider themselves give-way vessels regardless of their original evaluation of the situation. There may, for example, be a third vessel that due to damage cannot comply with the rules or that has been thrust into the scene. Or a stand-on vessel in a crossing situation suddenly realizes that the give-way vessel to port is attempting to inch across her bow regardless of the signal she gave.

Seamanship

Rule 2(a) makes it clear that the Rules of the Road are no substitute for good seamanship. A good seaman knows his own and his boat's capabilities; is aware of the effects of wind, tide, and waves; knows his location; is alert to nearby vessels, landmarks, and aids to navigation; carefully regulates his boat's speed; posts a full-time lookout in periods of restricted visibility; does not depend entirely on any one navigational aid; and most important *is always looking ahead*, anticipating trouble.

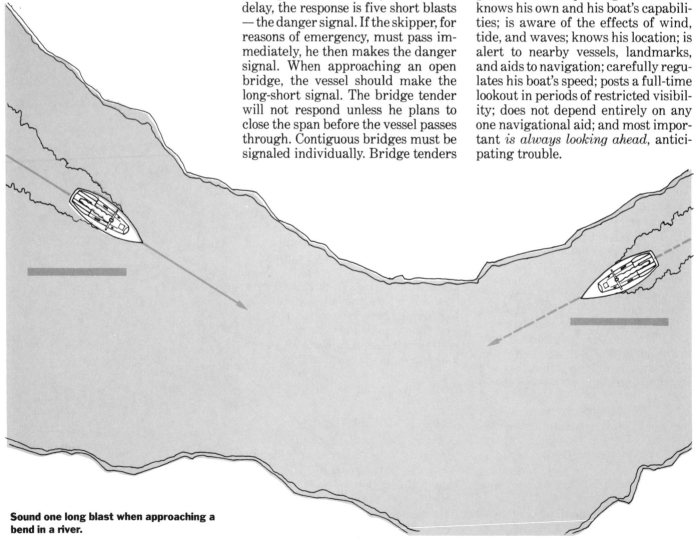

Sound one long blast when approaching a bend in a river.

Navigation Lights

There is a choice of three lights to carry at the top of a sailboat's mast. (1) The tricolor light combines the red and green side lights and the white stern light. It may be lit only when the boat is under sail. It is legal only on boats shorter than 66 feet. (2) A white all-round light, which is lit when the boat is at anchor. (3) A flashing all-round emergency strobe light, which may be lit only to signal distress.

All vessels that are under way or at anchor must show (or be prepared to show) at least one navigation light at night, from sunset to sunrise. Each type of vessel carries a specified combination of navigation lights in order to make it easier for other boats to identify her. Here are the lights that most boats must carry (and some day signals, called dayshapes, as well):

1. **Sidelights**, red for the port side and green for the starboard side, showing from dead ahead to 112.5° off the bow (or from 12 o'clock to almost 4 and 8 o'clock). If you don't see the other boat's sidelights, you are astern and may be overtaking. If you see both, she's headed at you. If you see her red light, her port side is turned toward you; if you see her green light, her starboard side. Boats smaller than 66 feet may carry sidelights on either side of the bow, in the shrouds, or in a single lantern on the bow or at or near the top of the mast (the last is legal only when under sail and has the greatest range of visibility).

2. **The masthead light** is a white light located not at the top of the mast, as the name suggests, but partway down (although on small power vessels it may be placed at the top of a short spar). On most sailboats it's about a third of the way down from the actual masthead. The masthead light must be above the sidelights. Showing over the same arc as the sidelights, it is turned on only when the boat is under power. This light is commonly called the steaming light or the bow light. When lit, it must be the highest light on the boat in order to indicate clearly that the boat is under power and not under sail.

3. **The sternlight** is a white light showing aft from the stern through 67.5° on either side, or an arc of 135°.

4. **An all-round light** is any light shining through 360°.

The light requirements for pleasure boats vary with type and size.

The white steaming or bow light (technically known as the masthead light) is lit only when the boat is under power. It shines to 22.5° abaft the beam on either side so it is visible to overtaking as well as oncoming vessels.

Required on sailboats larger than 23 feet, the white sternlight shows through an arc of 135° and is always lit at night.

Red (port) and green (starboard) sidelights shine to 22.5° abaft the beam and are always lit at night.

Navigation Lights

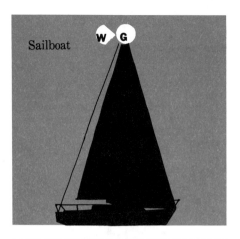

Sailboat

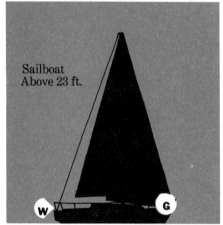

Sailboat
Above 23 ft.

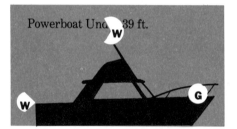

Powerboat Under 39 ft.

Navigation lights help mariners identify the type, size, and heading of vessels they see at night. This helps crews understand the situation and determine the course of action they should take. Here is a brief summary of the rules on navigation lights, which must be shown between sunset and dawn and at other times of restricted visibility. The complete rules are contained in the Coast Guard booklet *Navigation Rules: International-Inland.*

Under Sail

A boat *longer than 23* feet that is under sail or being rowed must display red and green sidelights and a white sternlight. A boat under sail between 23 feet and 66 feet may show these lights in a tricolor combined light at the top of the mast.

A boat *shorter than 23 feet* that is under sail or being rowed should display sidelights and a stern light. But if these lights are not displayed, a boat in this category must carry a flashlight or lantern that can be quickly lit and displayed in time to prevent a collision.

Under Power

An auxiliary sailboat that is under power must observe the same rules all powerboats observe except that during the day a sailboat under sail and being propelled by her engine must display a black cone point down (the Inland Rules do not require this of boats smaller than 39 feet). The basic rule for powerboats is that only the steaming ("masthead") light, the sidelights, and the sternlight must be lit, with the steaming light above the sidelights. An option for a power-driven boat shorter than 39 feet is a pattern of sidelights and an all-round white light. If this optional pattern is displayed, the sternlight and steaming ("masthead") light must not be lit.

A vessel longer than 164 feet must show a second masthead (steaming) light abaft of and higher than the forward one.

Under COLREGS only, a power-driven boat shorter than 23 feet that has a maximum speed of 7 knots or less may show only an all-round light.

Large Vessels and Tows

Other types of lights are specified for larger powerboats and for fishing boats, tow boats and tows, and other vessels with limited maneuverability.

1. **A range light** is "a second masthead light abaft of and higher than the forward one" in the Rules of the Road. It is a white, forward-facing light shining through 225°, located on a mast directly behind the forward mast. When the two lights are in line and form a range, you know that the vessels shorter than 164 feet, a pair of masthead lights, one behind and above the other, is required on larger vessels. the Great Lakes, range lights are required on larger powerboats.

2. **A yellow towing light** is a yellow, aft-facing, 135° light placed just above the sternlight.

3. **Towing masthead lights** are two or three white lights with the same characteristics as masthead lights.

4. **Towing range lights** are used on inland waters only, in groups of two or three. They have the same character-

To help crews identify other boats so they can make the correct maneuvers and avoid collision, each type of vessel carries a unique combination of navigation lights. Sailboats shorter than 66 feet under sail may carry sidelights and the sternlight in a tricolor combination light at the top of the mast (upper left).

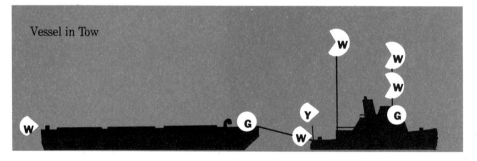

Vessel in Tow

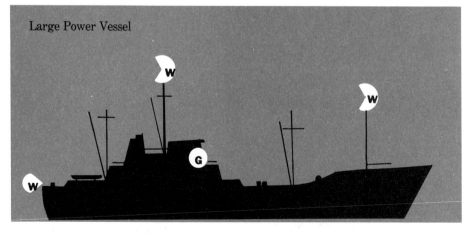

Large Power Vessel

istics as range lights.

5. **Yellow flashing lights** are used on the forward end of a tow being pushed ahead in Inland waters only. Showing through 90°-112.5° on each side, they flash 50-70 times per minute.

Power Vessels Longer than 164 Feet

All large power vessels must carry sidelights, a masthead light, a range light, and a sternlight.

Tows

Tugs and other vessels pulling a tow shorter than 657 feet must carry sidelights, a sternlight, a yellow towing light, a range light, and two towing masthead lights (one above the other on the same mast). With a longer tow, the tow boat carries the same lights except that she shows three towing masthead lights. During the day a diamond shape is carried on both the tow boat and the tow only if the total length is more than 657 feet. No shape is carried if the tow is shorter.

If the tow is severely restricted in its ability to change course, and is longer than 657 feet, both COLREGS and the Inland Rules require that a vertical sequence of all-round white light, red light, white light be displayed where it's most visible, in addition to the lights described in the previous paragraph.

During the day, limited maneuverability of a long tow is signaled by a black diamond dayshape and a ball-diamond-ball dayshape sequence hung vertically where best seen. Shorter tows that are severely restricted in their ability to alter course are, under the Inland Rules only, identified with the red-white-red light line or the ball-diamond-ball dayshape line in addition to the other lights included in the two-towing-range-lights option described above.

Vessels Pushing Ahead or Towing Alongside

Under COLREGS only, the pushing vessel shows sidelights, a sternlight, a range light, and two masthead towing lights. The Inland Rules offer two options, each of which requires sidelights and two yellow towing lights. Under one option, two towing masthead lights and one range light are carried. Under the other option, the combination is two towing range lights and a masthead light.

If a pushing or alongside tow is severely restricted in its ability to change course, COLREGS and Inland Rules require sidelights, a range light, two masthead towing lights, the vertical line of red-white-red all-round lights, and either a sternlight (COLREGS only) or two yellow towing lights (Inland only).

Vessels Being Towed or Pushed

Barges being towed show sidelights and sternlights, each barge being considered a separate vessel. The dayshape for a towed vessel is a black diamond.

Barges being pushed are treated as one vessel. Sidelights are shown at the forward end along with a yellow flashing light.

Barges towed alongside are also considered to be one vessel. Sidelights are shown forward and a sternlight is shown aft.

Fishing Vessels

Only when they are making way through the water are fishing vessels required to show sidelights and sternlights. While stationary and fishing, they show an all-round red-over-white light at the masthead, and if their gear extends more than 492 feet to one side, an all-round white light that indicates the direction of the nets or other gear. Dayshapes for fishing boats are two black cones with their points together or, for vessels shorter than 66 feet, a basket plus a black cone whose point aims toward outlying gear.

Trawlers dragging nets also do not show sidelights and sternlights when they're underway, but while stationary and fishing they show a range light and, under it, a green-over-white all-round light. Trawlers show the same dayshapes as fishing boats, but do not have indicators of outlying gear.

Vessels Not Under Command

In the circumstance that she cannot be steered or make way, a vessel shows two all-round red-over-red lights in a vertical line where they are best seen, and if she's underway, sidelights and a sternlight. Her dayshape is two black balls in vertical line.

Vessel Pushing Ahead

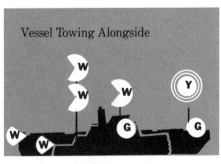

Vessel Towing Alongside

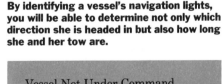

By identifying a vessel's navigation lights, you will be able to determine not only which direction she is headed in but also how long she and her tow are.

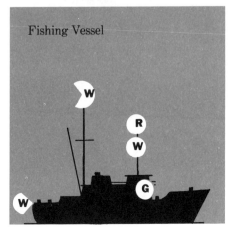

Fishing Vessel

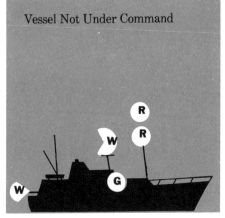

Vessel Not Under Command

Navigation Lights

Vessels Engaged in Minesweeping

Minesweepers carry sidelights, a sternlight, a masthead light, and three all-round green lights — one at the top of the foremast and one at each end of the yard on the foremast. Three black balls are the dayshape. *On minesweepers or any other vessel, these lights and shapes indicate danger within 1000 meters astern or 500 meters to either side.*

Vessels Restricted in Their Ability to Maneuver

On vessels whose maneuverability is limited, other than minesweepers and dredges, the night signal is all-round red-white-red lights in line, and if the vessel is underway, sidelights, sternlight, masthead light, and range light. At anchor they keep the red-white-red lights displayed along with the required anchor light (see below). During the day, they carry a ball-diamond-ball dayshape sequence.

Vessels engaged in dredging or other underwater work carry those lights too, with the addition of an all-round red-over-red light on the obstructed side and an all-round green-over-green light on the clear side. Their dayshape is also the same, but two balls (obstructed side) and two diamonds (clear side) are added. The code flag "Alpha" (blue with white vertical stripe) indicates that a diver is below.

Pilot Vessels

Vessels that carry pilots out to arriving ships display sidelights, sternlights, and an all-round white-over-red light at the masthead when they are underway. At anchor they light the white-over-red lights and the proper anchor lights; during the day they show one black ball for their dayshape.

All Vessels at Anchor or Aground

When anchored, a boat smaller than 164 feet shows an all-round white light

where it is best seen unless she is anchored in a Coast Guard-approved special anchorage (see chapter 15), when she need not display an anchor light. The 360° light at the top of a sailboat's mast serves as an anchor light unless it is a strobe, which indicates distress; so does a lantern hung off the headstay. Large vessels show two anchor lights, one forward and the other aft. The dayshape for an anchored vessel is a ball. If aground, the vessel shows her anchor light or lights plus an all-round red-over-red light where it is best seen.

Other Lights

Law enforcement vessels usually show a flashing blue light. Moored barges carry two white lights. Partially submerged vessels or objects under tow in Inland waters carry an all-round white light at each end if less than 82 feet wide, four all-round white lights if wider, and, if very large, all-round white lights no more than 328 feet apart. Submarines in the United States Navy carry normal navigation

lights plus a flashing yellow light that flashes once per second for 3 seconds and then is off for 3 seconds.

Distress Signals

Rule 36 allows any vessel to attract another's attention with light or sound signals "that cannot be mistaken for any signal authorized elsewhere in these Rules" — many blasts on the whistle is one example; a flashing strobe light is another. Rule 36 also permits a boat to aim a searchlight at a danger.

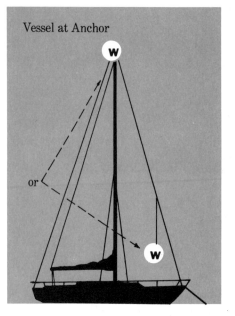

Vessel at Anchor

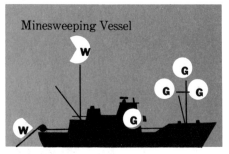

Minesweeping Vessel

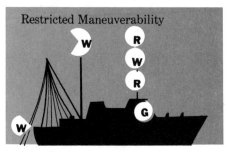

Restricted Maneuverability

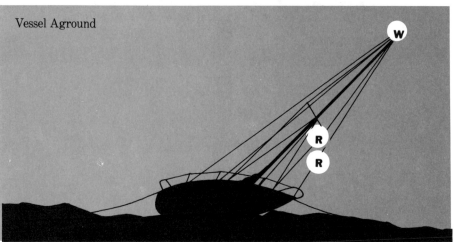

Vessel Aground

Maneuvering in Collision Situations

If you're sailing on a course that appears to be converging with another vessel's, take careful compass or relative bearings on her every few minutes, increasing their frequency as the gap narrows. If the bearings move forward, she'll cross ahead of you; aft, she'll cross behind you. But if they don't change, you're on a collision course. *You must take immediate action.* Slow down or speed up and take more bearings. Better yet, turn radically toward her wake, let her pass ahead, then turn back on your original course. Whatever you do, you can't afford to wait until the last moment.

Converging courses are especially hard to judge if the other boat is at a distance and going much faster than you are. Large commercial vessels offer a particular challenge because while they *seem* to be moving slowly, they're actually going twice or three times your speed. Once you spot a tanker or freighter, assign a crew member with good eyesight and judgment to lookout duty. Nothing should distract this person from looking at

and taking bearings on the ship until it's *clearly* ahead. Unless you're absolutely sure that you'll cross its bow at least 1 mile ahead, alter course so it crosses your bow. Chances are that it's on autopilot with the deck watch preoccupied with various chores. If the wind were to die out or your engine to poop out, there would be nothing to stop him from running you down.

If your boat is on a bow-to-bow reciprocal course with another vessel, alter course hard to starboard — at least 20°. "Show him your port side." The closer the boats are to each other, the greater the alteration should be. If the other boat confusedly alters course to *his* port, into your new course, you can steer hard to port for a starboard side to starboard side passing, you can stop and let him pass, or you can keep going to starboard. Watch him like a hawk. In this situation, taking bearings won't tell you much about the chances of evading collision.

When passing a ship or a tow, stay well away. A tug's large wake can easily pull a small boat into the tow line or

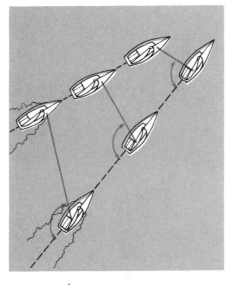

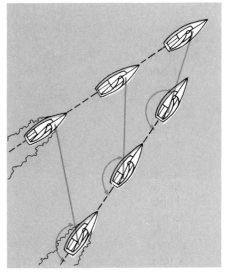

Bearings taken on a boat on a converging course indicate whether a collision is imminent. If the bearings don't change, be wary; if they move forward, the other boat will pass ahead; if they move aft, you'll pass ahead.

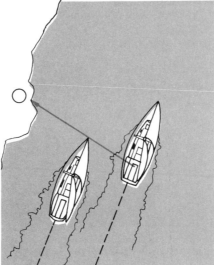

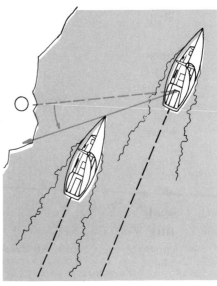

Convergence may also be gauged by judging the other boat's relationship to the land behind. If the land seems to be moving ahead of her, you're going faster; if it seems to be falling back, she's going faster. This is called "making and losing land."

Navigation Lights

a barge. Never attempt to sail across a tow line; it's shallower than you think.

Exercise extreme caution when passing any boat in a narrow channel, especially if a crosswind is blowing. Observe the "intent-agreement" rule to the letter; that way you'll be certain that the other skipper won't make any careless course alteration into your side.

At night, judging the other boat's position, course, and intentions is especially difficult since you have only her lights to go by. You may not be able to distinguish them from her cabin lights or flashlights, or high waves may obscure them.

You must identify the other vessel as soon as possible. If she shows range lights, she's a large power vessel moving faster than first appears. If you see a yellow towing light and a string of lights trailing after, she's a tug pulling a tow. If the red-white-red line of lights is visible, her maneuverability is severely restricted. A single masthead light indicates a boat under powr — if it's high up, she's probably a sailing auxiliary, which means she's slow. If you don't see any masthead lights, that means only one thing: she's a sailboat under sail, and her maneuverability and crew's visibility probably are limited.

If the only sidelight you see is her red light, and you are meeting, alter your course (if necessary) to "show her your red" and pass port side to port side. If you see her green light, make whatever adjustments you must make to clear her at a safe distance, preferably port side to port side but, if necessary, starboard side to starboard side. If both sidelights are visible, she's heading directly at you on a collision course. Alter course hard to starboard until you see only her red light, sail on a little farther to be safe, then turn back to your original course. If you see a white light down low, it's probably a sternlight.

Since red and green have about 25 percent less range than white, don't be at all surprised if you see masthead lights, sternlights, and ranges well before the sidelights appear, especially on large ships. If you can't see the sidelights, study the relationship between the masthead light and the range light, if the other vessel is a big powerboat. If they're in line, she's heading at you; if the range light is to the right of the masthead light, she's heading to your port; if the range light is to the left, she's heading to your starboard. If neither light is visible, she's powering away from you. Since many collisions and near-collisions involve large power vessels and smaller boats, don't allow a pair of range lights to appear on the horizon without analyzing which way the ship under them is sailing.

Always keep a lookout, but don't assume that the other crew sees you. Make your boat as visible as possible. At night, shine navigation lights in the proper combination. Someone who does see you will be able to predict your future position if you steer a steady course at a steady speed. In fog, use a radar reflector, but don't assume that you will appear on every ship's radar scope. The ship's long deck, islands, and larger boats may screen you, as may rain or rough waves. At close ranges, a ship's radar may not notice you because she is rolling. A radar detector on your boat may have picked her up before she has "seen" you. When near another vessel whose intentions are not clear, call her over VHF/FM radio channel 6 or 16 (or 13 if she's a ship) and notify her of your position and course.

If a collision seems likely and the other crew obviously doesn't know you're there, do everything you can to make your boat visible. Carry a bright hand-held light to shine on your sails or at the oncoming vessel's bridge. If that doesn't do any good, fire off flares or turn on a strobe light to attract the other crew's attention.

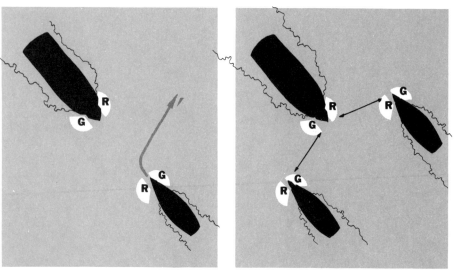

(Left) Meeting another boat bow to bow, turn sharply to starboard to "show her your red." (Right) You're safe if both boats' red or green lights are turned toward each other. When altering course try to minimize all ambiguity even if you must slow down, stop, or circle around.

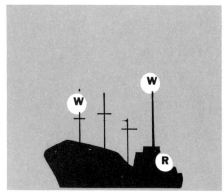 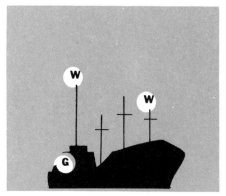

The relationship between the masthead and range lights on a big power vessel will indicate her heading. if the range light is to starboard (left), she's heading to your port; if to port (right), she's heading to your starboard. Keep a sharp lookout until she's passed.

Part III
NAVIGATION

Chapter 9
Navigation Aids

"The lonely sea" becomes much safer if you know where you are on it. The sailor uses many navigation aids to help him plot (chart) his position, including buoys, lighthouses, landmarks, charts, the sky, and the sea itself. When the ancient Phoenicians first ventured across the Mediterranean Sea, they were guided by the stars. Modern sailors still find it easier to steer by (aim at) stars — especially the fixed North Star — than to squint at a compass when sailing at night. In the Pacific, for centuries Polynesians have navigated with amazing accuracy over distances as great as 2000 miles without the use of compasses or charts. They use the stars, and they know how to interpret changes in wave shape and height. When the long swell generated by the trade wind in the open ocean begins to shorten and steepen, or when it sweeps along in a slightly altered direction, a native navigator knows that an island lies just over the horizon. A modern navigator, too, can read the water; when big, stable waves turn into many stubby breakers, he knows that shoal water approaches.

Navigation is the art and science of finding your current position and planning what course you will sail to reach your destination. It includes three disciplines: piloting, celestial navigation, and electronic navigation. Piloting is the skill most used by the average sailor as well as the foundation for the other two disciplines, so it receives much of the attention in this part. We'll introduce the tools and concepts of celestial navigation at the end of chapter 12. Electronic navigation (including Loran-C, radar, and satellite navigation) will be covered in considerable detail in chapter 13.

Even more important to the average sailor are the skills of alongshore *piloting*. When seafaring began in Sumeria and Mesopotamia around 3500 B.C., sailors' ambitions were as modest as their ships were small. They rarely went out of sight of land, and at night they pulled their reed-and-cedar boats up on the beach or anchored in quiet coves. Their only piloting aids were familiar landmarks, the temperature and humidity differences between winds from varying directions, and poles for measuring water depth. Today our dependence on visible reference points and markers is just as great as it was 5000 years ago, even though we have much more sophisticated ways to determine wind direction and water depth, and with the flick of a switch can find our position using space-age electronic devices.

Besides natural landmarks and water depth, the reference points used to find your position when sailing along shore are buoys, lighthouses, and radio transmissions, known collectively as aids to navigation. They are used in close conjunction with charts and the magnetic compass. We will discuss buoys, lighthouses, and charts in this chapter, and then go on to other piloting aids and their use.

This lovely old lighthouse guided mariners through Chesapeake Bay's Hooper Strait before being moved to the Chesapeake Bay Maritime Museum at St. Michael's, Maryland.

Buoys: The Federal System

The most common aid to navigation is the buoy. Some 25,000 unlighted and lighted buoys are installed and maintained by the U.S. Coast Guard, and many others are supervised by state agencies, towns, and yacht clubs. With minor exceptions that we'll describe later on, they are all in conformance with the U.S. federal buoyage system based on the international *lateral system*. It's called the lateral system because the buoys mark the sides of channels passing safely around rocks, shoal water, and other hazards. In European and other countries, buoys usually are laid out according to the *cardinal system*, in which the buoy's shape and color indicate the compass direction to the hazard.

In sailor's parlance, buoys are "left to starboard" or "left to port." To leave a buoy to starboard, keep it on your starboard, or right-hand, side as you pass it. To leave it to port, keep it on your port, or left-hand side. (Some sailors say "Keep the buoy on your starboard [port] hand.") Buoys work somewhat like the curb of a road, except that they don't mark every foot along a channel's edge. As you run down a channel, keep in mind imaginary lines extending between buoys on the side. Try to stay near the center of the channel unless going around a bend (where the water is often deepest toward the outside) or when encountering other boats (when the Rules of the Road prefer that you stay to the right). Since they are anchored, buoys may shift position as the tide rises and falls, or may even drag, so don't assume that one is located exactly where the chart says it is.

Stay away from the buoys; they are made of steel and are very heavy. When yawing about in a swift current, a buoy can be a powerful projectile that can hole a boat. It is illegal to tie up to a buoy or to deface it in any way.

Five creeks and bays here branch off the Choptank River, which cuts into Maryland's Eastern shore. Although the buoyage system looks complicated from above, on the water a pilot who keeps track of the numbers and characteristics won't get lost. Cans and nuns numbered in the teens line the main channel, which starts off the chart to the left. Two cans numbered 1 (A and B) are at the mouths of the Northwestern creeks, a nun 2 (C) marks the entrance to Lecompte Bay, and red flashers (D and E) announce Island and La Trappe Creeks.

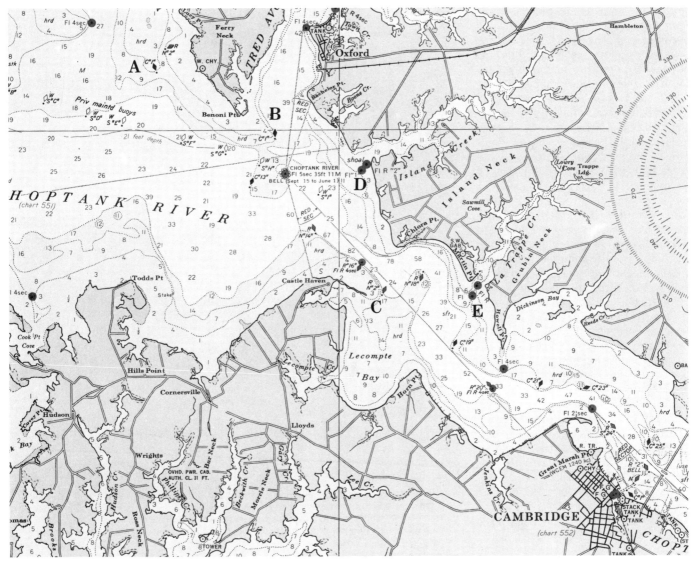

Buoys: The Federal System

Buoy Characteristics

In the federal system, buoys have distinctive colors, shapes, and other characteristics that help the sailor determine the location of the channel. Since it is redundant, the system allows you to identify a buoy with only one characteristic.

Color: "Red Right Returning"

The most important characteristic is the buoy's color. Some buoys are red, some are green or black, and others have red, green, black, white, or orange stripes. "Red Right Returning" is the essential rule of thumb for using the federal system. This means that when entering one body of water from a larger body of water (say, when returning to a harbor from a bay or sound), *always* leave the red buoys to starboard (keep them on the starboard hand). Green or black buoys will be left to port (kept on the port hand). When leaving the smaller body of water, therefore, the rule is "Green (Black) Right Leaving."

An important note: Port-side buoys were painted black until 1983, when green became the official color under an international agreement. For several years after 1983 you may see both green and black buoys marking the port side of a channel when entering. In some cases the changeover was anticipated and completed before 1983 — daymarks (channel indicators posted on stakes) changed color beginning in the 1970s — but the changeover should be complete in 1989.

Determining whether you are returning or leaving generally is fairly easy, but if you have doubts, study the chart and ask yourself which body of water is most protected by land, is farthest from the sea (or lake), and provides the safest anchorage. The answer to each question will be the body of water that you're entering, with red buoys left to starboard.

Where there is no channel, the Coast Guard arbitrarily lays out red buoys closer to the seashore. Therefore boats are "entering" as they proceed South along the Atlantic Coast, North and West along the Gulf Coast, and North along the Pacific Coast. Great Lakes buoys are laid out under the assumption that boats enter at lake outlets, so a boat heading West on Lakes Ontario and Erie, North on Lake Huron, West on Lake Superior, and South on Lake Michigan will leave red buoys to starboard. On the Mississippi and Ohio Rivers, buoys are laid out assuming that boats enter at the river mouth, so a boat heading North up the Mississippi will carry red buoys to starboard.

Numbers

An official numbering policy helps clarify the entering and leaving problem. Each channel buoy has a number, and numbers increase as the harbor is entered. Green (black) buoys carry odd numbers and red buoys carry even numbers. Thus the outermost buoys in a channel are green (black) buoy number 1 and red buoy number 2. If you get lost, simply find two green (black) or two red buoys. The direction in which the buoy numbers increase is the direction in which you enter the harbor. Numbers are painted or taped on with red or green reflectors.

Unlighted Buoys

The most common buoys are nuns and cans.

Cans are flat-topped, carry odd numbers, and are painted green or black. One or two lifting rings may be welded to the tops of cans. Cans always mark the left-hand side of a channel when entering. On the chart, a can is indicated by a green (black) diamond, the letter "C," and the number.

Nuns have pointed tops (like a nun's cowl), carry even numbers, and are painted red. A lifting ring is welded to the top. Nuns are always left to starboard when entering. The chart symbol is a red diamond, "R," "N," and the number.

Telling a can from a nun may be a problem on a hazy day or when the sun is low on the horizon, when you can't distinguish the colors. Look carefully at the shape; even at a distance the can's flat top looks different from the

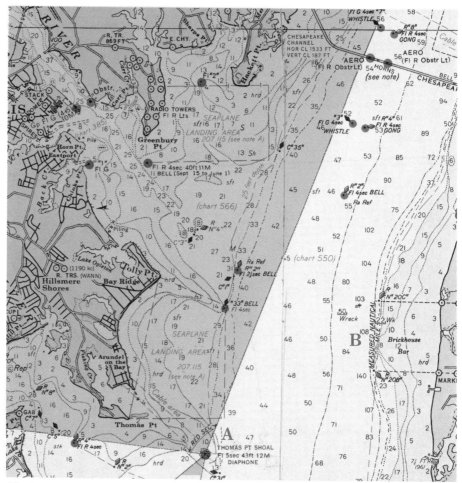

The buoy numbers increase "entering" Northbound on Chesapeake Bay, red to the right and green to the left, while buoys to the side mark entrances to bays and rivers. The Thomas Point lighthouse (A) guards a dangerous shoal and its red sectors (shaded) warn pilots when they stray too near the Western shore. If you see a white 5-second flasher, you're in the main channel. A measured mile runs between ranges on the Eastern shore (B).

nun's point. At night, when both color and shape may be indistinguishable, you can identify a buoy by shining a flashlight at it. If the number can't be made out, its red (for a nun) or green (for a can) reflector will help.

Junction buoys are a hybrid between cans and nuns. A junction buoy marks a rock or other obstruction in a channel, or indicates the preferred course where two or more channels meet. Either can- or nun-shaped, junction buoys are painted with red and green (black) horizontal stripes. If the buoy is shaped like a can and the top stripe is green (black), you should leave it to port when entering. You *may* leave it to starboard, but it's safer to leave it to port. Likewise, a nun-shaped junction buoy whose top stripe is red should be left to starboard. These buoys may carry letters, not numbers. The chart symbol for a junction buoy that is unlighted is a red diamond, "RG," and the letter if it's treated like a nun, or a green (black) diamond, "GR" and the letter if it's treated like a can.

Can, nun, and junction buoys are the most frequently encountered aids to navigation. Several others are used in special situations:

Midchannel (fairway) buoys mark the center of a channel, indicate safe water, and may be left on either hand (although since the Rules of the Road prefer a boat to go down the starboard side of a channel, they should be left to port). As of 1983 new midchannel buoys have red-and-white vertical stripes and may be lettered. If unlighted, they are spherical; if lighted, they have tall frameworks. Their chart symbol is a white diamond divided vertically by a line and "RW" plus the letter. The old fairway buoys, gradually being replaced, are can-shaped with black-and-white vertical stripes (left to port when entering) and nun-shaped with red-and-white vertical stripes (left to starboard).

Quarantine anchorage buoys are yellow and are shown on charts by a white diamond and the letter "Y." They show where to anchor while awaiting health officials.

Anchorage buoys indicate areas set aside for anchoring. The buoys are white and are shown on charts by a white diamond and the letter "W."

Fish net area buoys warn of the existence of nets. Black-and-white banded, they are indicated on charts by a black-and-white diamond and "BW."

Dredging buoys are placed near dredging operations. The buoy is white with a green top, and is shown on a chart by "GW" and a white diamond with a horizontal line.

Special-purpose buoys have orange-and-white bands and are indicated by a white diamond with a horizontal line and "W Or." But under the new rule these buoys will be yellow and have yellow lights.

Danger buoys are white with orange bands at the top and bottom, and are shown on a chart by an orange diamond with no letters. Under the new rule these buoys will be yellow and have yellow lights.

Isolated danger buoys are anchored near isolated wrecks, rocks, and other hazards. They come in several different shapes, but they all are black with one or more broad horizontal red stripes and have two black balls at the top. A light on this buoy is group-flashing white with two flashes.

Anchorage area buoys are white with orange bands at the top and bottom with an orange diamond enclosing an orange cross. They have no chart symbol. Under the new rule these buoys will be yellow and have yellow lights.

Except for the can and the nun, which are numbered, all of the above buoys may carry letters.

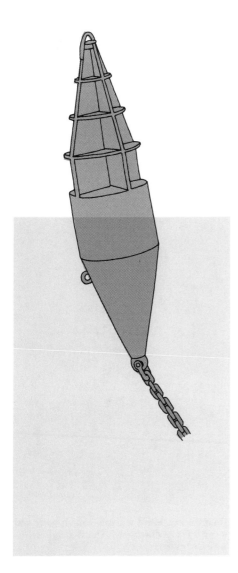
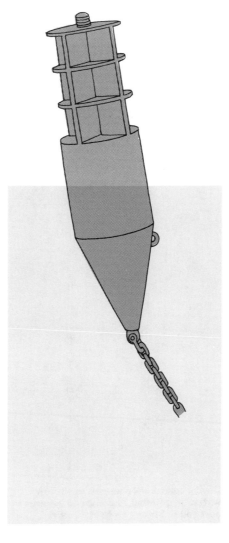

A nun (far left) is red and has a pointed top, a red reflector, and an even number. A can is green or black and has a flat top, a green reflector, and an odd number. On entering, leave nuns and other red buoys to starboard, cans and other green buoys to port. The buoy's skeleton may be visible, as shown here, or plated over.

NOTE: For more details about buoys and their chart symbols see the color pages in this chapter.

Buoys: The Federal System

Daybeacons

The oldest and simplest marker is a daybeacon, a stick pounded into the mud or sand and identified with some distinguishing mark. Their distinguishing characteristics are plaques called "daymarks," whose shape, color and identifying number indicate whether they should be treated like cans, nuns, junction buoys, or midchannel fairway buoys.

A triangular red daymark with a reflective red border and an even number is left to starboard on entering. On the chart, it is shown by a red triangle and "R."

A square green daymark with a reflective green border and an odd number is left to port, like a can. Its symbol is a green square and "G." (This is phasing out a black square with a green border and a white square with a green border.)

A square daymark with a green reflective green border and a green band above a red band may be left to either side, but preferably to port. On the chart, it is indicated by a white square and "GR."

A triangular daymark with a red reflective border and a red band above a green band may be left to either side, but preferably to starboard. Its symbol is a white triangle and "RG."

A white-bordered octagon enclosing red-and-white vertical stripes is a midchannel fairway indicator. A white square and "RW" mark it on the chart.

Lighted Buoys

A buoy isn't any help unless you know where it is, so in poor visibility, buoys at key turns in the channel must make themselves noticed. That's why many green (black), red, and junction buoys carry flashing lights in several colors and patterns, and also why some are equipped with sound-making devices.

Lighted buoys consist of a frame enclosing a light, and sometimes a bell or whistle, all supported by a floating base holding batteries. The lights usually switch on automatically at dusk or when fog sweeps in. Like nuns and cans, red and green (black) lighted buoys are numbered according to the channel's sequence. Many carry radar reflectors (as do some unlighted buoys) secured to the frame. If so, "Ra ref" is printed next to the chart symbol. Regardless of their color and light characteristics, all lighted buoys have the same shape.

Light Characteristics

The light's color and phase characteristic — the rhythm with which it flashes — identify it at night. With three colors (red, green, and white) and five phase characteristics to choose from, there are 15 possible light characteristics, but the Coast Guard has several guidelines that impose order on a potentially confusing situation, keeping buoy identification fairly simple.

The light's *color* indicates the buoy's color and therefore the hand on which it should be kept when entering or leaving a channel. The *phase characteristic* changes from light to light to minimize the chances of misidentification and confusion.

Color

Green lights are used on green (black) buoys that *must* be left to port when entering, and on those junction buoys with green (black) top stripes that *should* be left to port. If you see a green light, leave it to port when entering.

Red lights go on red buoys that *must* be left to starboard when enter-

Daybeacons mark channels in shallow water. On entering, leave green squares to port and red triangles to starboard.

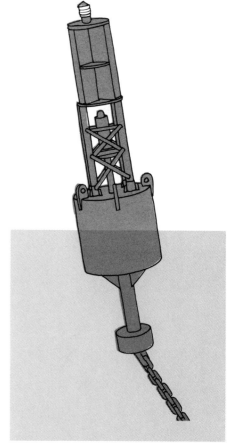

On entering, leave a green light to port and a red light to starboard. This is a lighted whistle buoy.

ing and on those junction buoys with red top stripes that *should* be left to starboard. Leave red lights to starboard when entering.

White lights used to go on either red or black buoys marking dangerous or important turns in a channel or marking the outer entrance to the channel. White was chosen over the other colors for this purpose because its range of visibility is greater. However, under the international agreement that went into effect in 1983, white lights have entirely different purposes. They now are used only on midchannel fairway buoys and with only one phase characteristic: short-long-short-long, and so on. This is Morse Code for the letter "A." The chart symbol for a lighted fairway buoy is "RW Mo (A)," showing that it is red-and-white striped and flashes Morse Code "A."

Phase Characteristics

The following phase characteristics are used only on red and green (black)

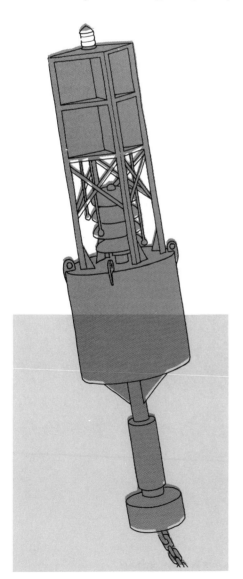

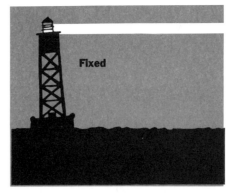

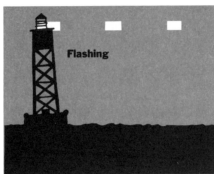

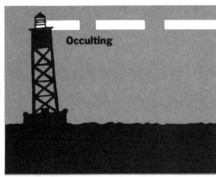

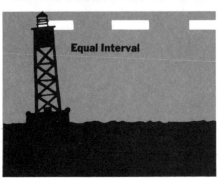

(Left) This is a lighted gong buoy, with several tones sounded by clappers. A bell buoy has only one tone. **(Above)** Five phase characteristics are available for use on red and green (black) lighted buoys.

channel side buoys with red and green lights:

Fixed, a steady light, shown on the chart as "F."

Flashing, at intervals of 2.5, 4, or 6 seconds with a chart symbol "Fl" and the interval of darkness between flashes.

Occulting, which differs from flashing in that the periods of light are longer than the periods of darkness. The symbol is "Occ" plus the darkness interval between flashes.

Quick Flashing, rapid flashing, at least once a second. The chart symbol is "Qk Fl."

Equal Interval, flashing with equal periods of light and darkness, indicated on the chart by "Eq Int."

The chart shows a red or green (black) diamond connected to a purple circle (the symbol for a light) and the color of the light. For example, "F R" indicates a fixed red light and "Fl G 4 sec" a green flashing light with a 4-second period of darkness between flashes.

Those phase characteristics apply only to side channel markers. A lighted junction buoy with a red or green light has only one characteristic under the new rule. This is an irregular series of flashes called *Composite Group Flashing* (2+1). The pattern is this: two quick flashes, a short moment of darkness, one quick flash, a long moment of darkness, two quick flashes, and so on. The chart symbol is "CGp Fl" and the color. This new junction buoy light replaces Interrupted Quick Flashing: six quick flashes, three seconds of darkness, six quick flashes, and so on. Its symbol has been "I Qk Fl" plus the light color.

How to Identify Phase Characteristics

To identify the phase characteristic or rhythm of a light, you can use a stopwatch if there is a red light available; otherwise you will quickly lose your night vision. Better, practice counting seconds, using "thousand" or "elephant." Start the count when the light goes off and end it when the light comes back on. Repeat the count until you're absolutely sure of it. To avoid

Buoys

Western Rivers and Intracoastal Waterway Aids to Navigation

Although "Red Right Returning" remains the dominant rule, the constricted waterways of the "Western rivers" — the Mississippi and its tributaries, the Red River, the upper Atchafalaya River, and other rivers so designated by the Coast Guard — and of the Intracoastal Waterway are subject to special buoyage systems and rules. On the Western rivers, buoys and daymarks have slightly different color schemes from the ones in the federal system described above. Only lighted buoys are numbered, and the numbers indicate mileage upstream from a charted reference point. Special marks called ranges are posted on banks and shore to indicate channels (when two ranges of the same color scheme line up, the observer is in the channel).

The buoys and daymarks on the Intracoastal Waterway (ICW, sometimes called the inland waterway) comply

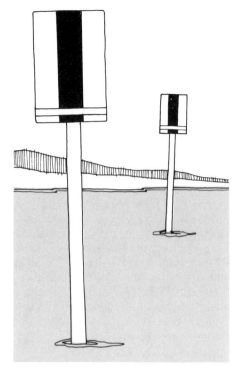

A range daymark is used to indicate the channel on the Intracoastal Waterway and Western Rivers.

double vision, don't stare at the buoy; rather, keep your eyes moving so you see it out of the corner of your eye. Don't panic if a phase characteristic seems wrong or the light doesn't seem to be where it belongs. Land, another boat, or waves may be obscuring it. Slow down, rest your eyes, and then look back.

From year to year the Coast Guard may move buoys or change their light characteristics. Only an up-to-date chart (supplemented by information found in the Coast Guard *Local Notice to Mariners*) will keep you abreast of any alterations.

Minor Lights

Lights on daybeacons (poles stuck in the bottom) are called minor lights. Found usually on lakes, rivers, and the Intracoastal Waterway, they have the same characteristics that a lighted buoy would have in the same position.

Sound Buoys

The presence of some important buoys is emphasized by sound makers. There are four kinds of sound buoys all of which may be lighted.

Bells have a single bell against which four clappers swing, banging out the same tone as the buoy rolls with the waves. Some bells are run automatically by an internal mechanism.

Gongs have two, three, or four bells, each with its own clapper and unique tone. Where bells ring monotones, gongs ring changes.

Whistles create a moanlike sigh as air is forced up through a pipe when the buoy rolls.

Horns are electrically powered so they work in smooth water; their sound is more abrupt than the whistle's moan.

All four are clearly labeled in capital letters on charts and are usually placed in a way that minimizes the possiblity of confusion — for instance, with a whistle buoy separating two bell buoys. In fog, although the sounds may be clear, you may have difficulty tracking them down as they reverberate through the damp air.

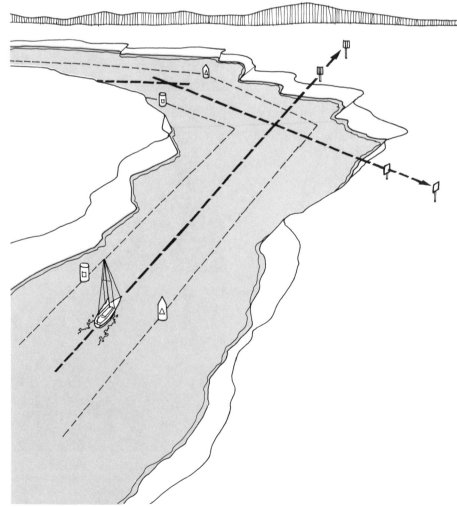

When daymarks are lined up in a range, the observer is in the channel.

with the federal system except that a *yellow triangle* indicates that the buoy must be left to starboard and a *yellow square* shows that it must be left to port. As long as you know which way you're going on the Intracoastal Waterway, regardless of temporary meanders, you'll be safe if you follow the yellow brick road: triangles to starboard and squares to port when heading toward Florida and New Orleans; squares to starboard and triangles to port when heading toward New Jersey. This is a new system that went into effect in 1988 and should be fully implemented by 1991. It replaces a more complicated system in which lateral ICW aids to navigation (buoys and daymarks) carried yellow stripes or borders, while "dual-purpose" aids (buoys and daymarks that marked the ICW and other bodies of water the ICW passes through) carried squares and triangles. Nonlateral system ICW aids (including ranges) continue to have yellow stripes in the new system.

Like the Western rivers, the ICW has ranges, each of which carries the distinctive yellow marker.

Uniform State Waterway Marking System

The federal lateral system of buoyage is enforced by the U.S. Coast Guard only on waters subject to federal jurisdiction — coastal waters, waters that can be reached from the sea, and any river or lake not lying entirely within the boundaries of one state. That jurisdiction includes an immense amount of navigable water, but excludes many boating areas. These small bodies of water are covered by state buoyage systems that have been standardized in the Uniform State Waterway Marking System.

"Red Right Returning" — the foundation of the lateral system — still applies in most USWMS waters, where you will find small black cans with odd numbers and small red cones with even numbers. But the USWMS also includes the *cardinal system* which, instead of using buoys to mark the sides of channels, uses them to indicate the compass direction to an ob-

struction. Buoys in this system have three different color schemes:

A black-topped white buoy indicates that boats should pass to the North and East of its location. Its light (if it has one) is quick-flashing white; it may have a white reflector.

A red-topped white buoy warns boats to pass to the South and West of its position. It may also have a white quick-flashing light and a white reflector.

A red-and-white vertically striped buoy indicates that boats should not pass between it and the shore, or between it and a reef or other obstruction.

In this system, numbers on buoys increase and letters proceed in alphabetical order going upstream.

Black buoys use only green lights and red buoys red ones, either flashing or, to indicate caution, quick-flashing.

Other state markers may have written warnings or speed limits, all posted on white buoys with two orange bands.

Other Systems

Until relatively recently there was no standardized international buoyage system — in fact more than 30 systems were in use around the world as late as 1976. In 1980 national maritime agencies agreed to standardize their rules, and there are now two systems either in effect or going into effect. Labeled Rule A and Rule B, they differ in one big respect: under Rule A (in Europe, Australia, New Zealand, Africa, the Persian Gulf, and parts of Asia), red buoys are left to *port* on entering. Under Rule B (in the Americas, Japan, Korea, and the Philippines), red is left to *starboard*. Each rule includes a lateral system for use in well-defined channels, a cardinal system that identifies hazards using the cardinal points of the compass (North, East, South, and West), a safe water system that specifies midchannel markers, and a list of special buoys.

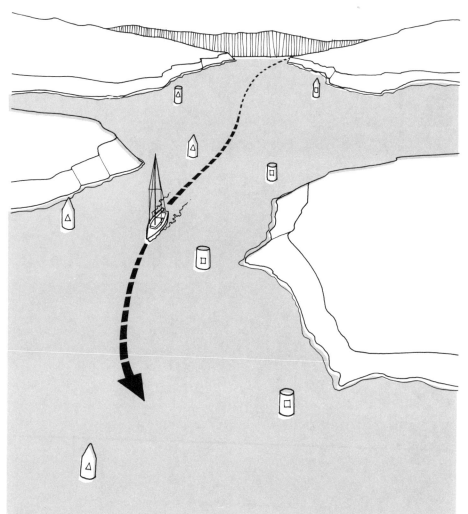

On the Intracoastal Waterway, aids to navigation are arranged so that red buoys (such as nuns) carry yellow triangles and are left to starboard heading from New Jersey toward Texas, and green buoys (such as cans) carry yellow squares and are left to port.

Lighthouses

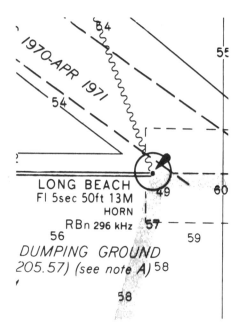

DUMPING GROUND 205.57) (see note A)

This lighthouse flashes a white light every 5 seconds and the light has a nominal range of 13 nautical miles. The lighthouse is 50 feet above mean low water, sounds a horn in fog, and has a radio beacon transmitting over a frequency of 296 kHz. (Below) Lighthouses use ten light phase characteristics.

No land-based object is more symbolic of the sea and ships than the lighthouse, the tower of stone capped by a glass house with a bright light sweeping over the far horizon to embrace and comfort lost sailors. As the sea became commercialized after the 16th century, shipping companies and governments built lights on cliffs, points of land, rocks, and islets to warn ships away from reefs and the shore. Soon these led to extensive systems of lights that could lead merchantmen from harbor to harbor. When there was no land to support the light, it was placed on lightships moored to great anchors far offshore. Now these offshore lights and radio beacons are placed on large buoys or towers. The last lightship, off Nantucket Island, Massachusetts, was finally replaced by a buoy in the mid-1980s.

Like lighted buoys, lighthouses may have red, green, or white lights. Because their range of visibility is so great, the beams of several lighthouses may be seen simultaneously from the deck of a boat sailing in popular boating areas. To avoid confusion, the Coast Guard uses a wider variety of light characteristics on lighthouses than it does on buoys, sometimes using two colors in the same light.

Light Characteristics

As with buoys, the light characteristics of lighthouses are clearly shown on charts. In addition, a government publication called the *Light List* provides light characteristics as well as many other data about lighthouses not given on the chart.

On charts, lighthouses are indicated in two ways. If it is *on shore* the lighthouse's symbol is a red exclamation mark emanating from a black dot, and if *offshore* on a built-up underwater foundation its symbol is a red exclamation mark emanating from a black dot within an irregular circle that looks like the outline of a daisy. This circle indicates rip-rap, or rocks and piles extending beyond the lighthouse's base.

The most important light characteristics and symbols for lighthouses are:

Flashing lights show a single flash at regular intervals with the period of light always being shorter than the period of darkness. White, red, or green lights may be used singly or together in alternating sequence. On a chart, the label "Fl 8sec" indicates a white light flashing every 8 seconds. "Alt Fl R & G 10sec" means that red and green flashes alternate every 10 seconds. Sometimes high-visibility strobes are used in flashing white lights.

Occulting lights show a flash at intervals with the period of light *longer* than the period of darkness. White, green, or red lights are used singly or in alternating sequence. "Occ G 4sec" means a green light is off for 4 seconds; "Alt Occ W & R 7sec" means that white and red lights alternate every 7 seconds.

Fixed lights remain illuminated. Sometimes a lighthouse will show a flashing or fixed white or green light

Flashing

Occulting

Fixed

Equal Interval

over safe water and also show a fixed red light over dangerously shoal water. The red light is called the red sector of the lighthouse. "F" or "FW" indicates fixed white, "FG" and "FR" fixed green and red.

Equal Interval lights are illuminated for periods equal to the time of darkness. White only, their label is "E Int" with a time in seconds indicating the sum of the lighted and dark times; one-half that time is the length of the flash.

Group Flashing is the term for a light that flashes twice or more in regular intervals. "Gp Fl (2) 5sec" means that every 5 seconds there are two white flashes. In an alternating group flashing light, for example "Alt Gp Fl R & G (2) 6sec," the lights alternate in color. Here every 6 seconds there is a group of one red flash and one green flash.

Composite Group Flashing lights are white. Their groups are not the same size. For example, "C Gp Fl (1+2) 8sec" is a white light flashing in this phase sequence: flash, 8-second interval, two flashes, 8-second interval, flash, and so on.

Fixed and Flashing lights have a fixed light broken regularly by a brighter light. "F Fl 10sec" describes a white light interrupted every 10 seconds by a brighter white flash. "Alt FR FlG 14sec" is an alternating fixed flashing light whose red fixed light is broken every 14 seconds by a green flash.

Fixed and Group Flashing lights have a fixed light interrupted regularly by groups of two or more flashing lights. "FR Gp Fl R (3) 10sec" describes a red fixed light broken every 10 seconds by a group of three red flashing lights. Usually these lights are alternating, with two different colors, for instance "Alt FG Gp Fl (2) 15sec" describes a fixed green light interrupted every 15 seconds by a group of two white lights.

Group Occulting lights are white and consist of groups of two or more occulting lights (lights that are illuminated longer than they are dark). The chart label is "Gp Occ."

Composite Group Occulting lights are white only. Their groups have different combinations of flashes. For instance, "C Gp Occ (1+3)" describes a composite group occulting light with a sequence of one flash and another of three flashes.

All this seems pretty complicated on paper, but what it means is that at night, every lighthouse you see will have a distinctive light characteristic and there will be little chance of confusion.

Other Characteristics

Besides their light characteristics, chart labels and listings in the *Light List* include other significant data about lighthouses. The word "HORN" shows that the lighthouse has a foghorn that starts automatically in poor visibility. The phase characteristic of the horn is not shown on the chart, but it is given in the *Light List* and some local pilot or tide books. Some lighthouses may use bells, sirens, dual-tone diaphones, or even cannon during fog. A type of horn called a diaphragm horn has two or three pitches. Use extreme caution when piloting by these sounds, since they may be distorted or even masked by the fog, clouds, or the lighthouse itself.

A purple circle around the lighthouse symbol on the chart indicates

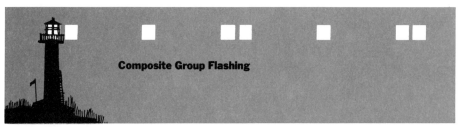

Group Flashing

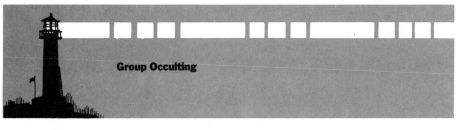

Composite Group Flashing

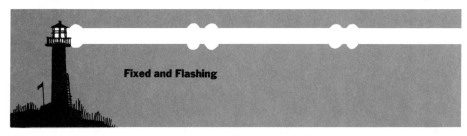

Fixed and Flashing

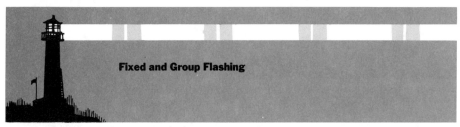

Fixed and Group Flashing

Group Occulting

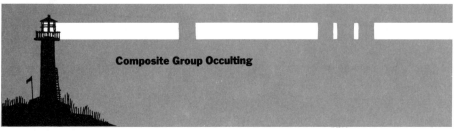

Composite Group Occulting

Lighthouses

that the tower contains a radio beacon, which can be a navigation aid. The label gives the frequency and the characteristics of the beacon, but not the intervals at which the signal is sent. The latter information is listed in the *Light List* and in other publications. Signals are either continuous or are transmitted every 6 minutes starting on the hour or 1, 2, 3, 4, or 5 minutes after the hour. The signals are in Morse Code.

For example, the Point Judith, Rhode Island, lighthouse is labeled as follows:

Gp Occ (1+2) 15sec
HORN
R Bn 325 ꞏꞏꞏꞏ & ⎯

This means that the light is white group occulting (intervals of light longer than intervals of darkness), with one flash alternating every 15 seconds with two flashes. There is a fog horn on the light. A radio beacon sends out a signal on a frequency of 325 kHz, and the signal "PJ" (dot-dash-dash-dot, dot-dash-dash-dash) is repeated for 50 seconds, after which a long dash is transmitted for 10 seconds. (For more on radio beacons, see Chapter 13.)

Range of Visibility

Two other numbers are included in the lighthouse label, one in feet and the other in miles. These are the height in feet of the light itself above mean high water (the average level of high tide) or above mean lake level, and the nominal visibility in miles (the distance from which the light can be seen over a straight line). In coastal areas the nominal visibility is in nautical miles; it's in statute miles on lakes.

The *nominal range* of visibility is determined solely by the brightness of the bulb and the clarity of the light lens. Red and green lights have a nominal range 25 percent less than a white light of the same wattage.

More important than the nominal range is the *geographical range* of visibility, which is the distance at which you can actually see the light. Geo-

graphical range takes into account the light's nominal range — its brightness — and the effect of the curvature of the earth. Another way to describe geographical range is to say that it is the distance to the horizon from the top of the lighthouse. The taller the lighthouse, the wider is its horizon — and the greater the distance over which it can be seen.

All you need to know to calculate geographical range is the lighthouse's

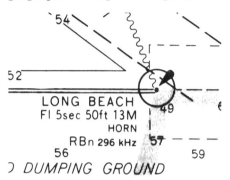

Using the table below, the pilot determines that the geographical range of the 50-foot Long Beach light is 8.1 miles, well under its 13-mile nominal range.

height above sea level, and that information is given right on the chart. You can enter that number into Table 1, or you can use it in one of these formulas:

Geographical range (nautical mi.) =
$1.144 \sqrt{\text{lighthouse height}}$
Geographical range (statute mi.) =
$1.317 \sqrt{\text{lighthouse height}}$
Light range $= 1.144 \sqrt{65} = 9.2$ miles

Just as long as the bulb is bright enough to have a nominal range of 9.2 miles, in clear weather anybody within 9.2 miles of the lighthouse should see its light.

Of course a pilot standing on the bridge of a big ocean liner will see the light long before a helmsman in a 30-foot yacht. Range of visibility is a combination of two geographical ranges — that of the observer and that of the object being observed. So to figure how close you must be to see a lighthouse's flash on a clear night, you must also calculate your own geographical range — the distance to your own horizon. You use exactly the same

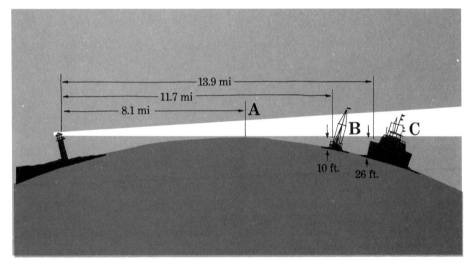

At water level (A) the light is visible up to only 8.1 miles away due to the earth's curvature. To determine geographical range from greater heights, use the table and add the ranges of the light and the observer. A sailor 10 feet up (B) can see the light from 11.7 miles; if the nominal range were equally great, somebody 26 feet up (C) could see the light from 13.9 miles.

Geographical Ranges of Visibility in Nautical Miles

Height (Feet)	Visibility (Nautical Miles)	Height (Feet)	Visibility (Nautical Miles)	Height (Feet)	Visibility (Nautical Miles)
6	2.8	55	8.5	110	12
10	3.6	60	8.9	120	12.6
15	4.4	65	9.2	130	13.1
20	5.1	70	9.6	140	13.6
26	5.8	75	9.9	150	14.1
30	6.3	80	10.3	160	14.5
36	6.9	85	10.6	170	14.9
40	7.2	90	10.9	180	15.4
46	7.8	95	11.2	190	15.8
50	8.1	100	11.5	200	16.2

Note: To find range in statute miles, multiply range in nautical miles by 1.15.

table or formula. Let's say that a sailor 6 feet tall is standing on a deck 5 feet above water searching the horizon for a light. Since his height of eye is 11 feet,

$$\text{Observer range} = 1.144 \sqrt{11} = 3.8$$

So he can see objects almost 4 miles away.

The range of visibility is the sum of the two ranges. If the light's range is 9.2 miles and the observer's range is 3.8 miles, the geographical range is 13 miles. What that means is that on a clear night, anybody whose head is 11 feet above water should be able to see this light from a distance of 13 miles — assuming of course that the light is bright enough to shine that far. If the light's nominal range is less than 13 miles, then the observer will have to get closer; if it's more, then somebody standing higher off the water should be able to see the light from farther off. The nominal range is the one of the brightest flash. If a lighthouse has alternating white and red (or green) lights, the white light will be seen farther than the other lights. This explains why you sometimes see a white flash long before the red or green flash appears.

How to Use the Range of Visibility

Because a lighthouse's light is so prominent, it can be your most important aid when sailing at night. Most boating areas contain a network of lighthouses whose lights' geographical ranges of visibility overlap in pairs or trios. You can use them like stepping stones to get to your destination. In unfamiliar waters, a good pilot may calculate the ranges of visibility for all the lighthouses near his route, and using a drawing compass, draw them to scale on the chart so he can anticipate new lights as he progresses down the course. Additionally, the horizon line around the lighthouse formed by its range coupled with your range can be used as a circle of position to help you plot your position. We'll say more about this helpful piloting technique in chapter 12.

Visibility Problems

So far we've assumed ideal visibility, but changing atmospheric conditions can play tricks with the light's range of visibility. A dense fog or heavy rain may severely shorten it. On the other hand a light overcast or thin fog may lengthen it by enhancing the light's loom — its reflection by the atmosphere. On cloudy nights just before the arrival of a warm front, when humidity rinses the air of dust and the blanket of clouds acts like a mirror, the loom may appear several minutes before the actual geographical range is reached.

Rarely, a light may disappear due to a power failure or some other accident. Many lighthouses have backup lights that switch on when the primary lights die. Described in the *Light List*, these emergency lights may have shorter nominal ranges and characteristics different from the primary lights.

Light Towers

Light towers are offshore structures that look much like oil rigs, and they have the same light characteristics as lighthouses. They are shown on charts by red exclamation marks without the daisy-shaped line that identifies offshore lighthouses. Often a mooring buoy is anchored near the tower for use by supply boats. The chart symbol for this buoy is a small black boat hull with a white circle superimposed on its side.

Daytime Identification

Identifying lighthouses is usually much easier at night than during the day, particularly if you're trying to pick out the tower against a built-up background. Lighthouses are sometimes painted with black, red, or white stripes to distinguish them from neighboring buildings, but nearby abandoned lighthouses may be confused with an active light. Light towers and offshore lighthouses are much more readily identified because they usually stand solitary in the sea. One's first view of a light tower may in fact be unsettlingly clear, since a black platform blinking a piercing strobe light from atop four skeleton legs may seem more like a monster from *War of the Worlds* than an aid to navigation. Except in fog and rain, light towers may be seen by day a long way out toward the limit of their geographical range of visibility. Onshore lighthouses, however, are hard to pick out of their surroundings until the observer is within about 5 miles.

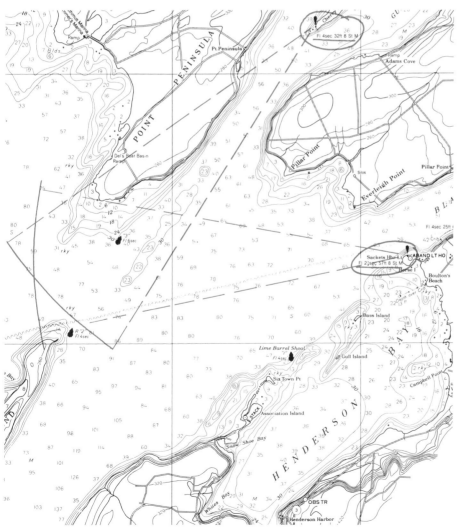

Before entering an unfamiliar channel at night, draw arcs of visibility around lighthouses to help you determine distance from shore. Calculate in statute miles when using a Great Lakes chart like this one of Eastern Lake Ontario.

Charts

As the waters of the earth were explored they were mapped, and as they were sounded, dredged, channeled, and dotted with aids to navigation they were charted. A chart is a miniaturized overhead view of the sea, a lake, or a river and its shores, emphasizing natural and artificial obstructions to safe sailing and anything that the sailor can use to find his way. Charts are for seamen what topographical maps are for hunters, trail guides are for hikers, and road maps are for drivers.

The first charts showed little detail, but what they did contain was enough to make them state secrets. Eventually enough was known about the New World, the East Indies, and other treasure grounds for each maritime nation to have its own charts. Understandings soon developed about ways to recreate the three-dimensional global sphere on a two-dimensional piece of paper, and to locate places with cross references called latitude and longitude. Hydrographic survey ships examined the seas and harbors of the world, and their reports, combined with data sent by merchant and naval vessels, became the authorities for sailing instructions and new charts.

Chart Projections

While his reliance upon his chart must be implicit, every pilot must be aware that certain distortions are inevitable whenever the surface of a round object like the globe is projected onto a flat surface like a map sheet. If you've ever tried to flatten an orange peel, you know how difficult this problem is and how many ways there are to solve it. Although its effect on the average sailor covering short distances is minor, chart distortion influences how a pilot does his job.

The solution to the projection problem has taken a variety of forms, all of which have at least one thing in common: in each, a grid of imaginary lines called meridians of longitude (running from the North Pole to the South Pole) and parallels of latitude (circling around the earth East to West) is assumed to exist so the navigator or pilot has a frame of reference. Each projection, however, arranges these lines in different ways.

The simplest and most popular projection of round globe upon flat paper was devised in 1568 by a Flemish geographer named Gerhard Kremer, better known by the Latin form of his name, Gerardus Mercator. On his projection, the meridians of longitude run exactly parallel to each other up and down the chart sheet, and the parallels of latitude cross them at right angles. Obviously this is a major distortion, since on a globe meridians actually converge like seams between orange

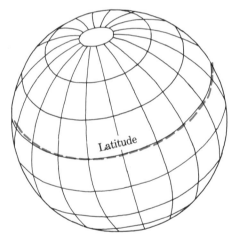
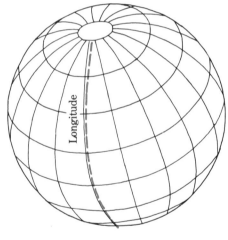

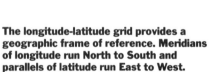
The longitude-latitude grid provides a geographic frame of reference. Meridians of longitude run North to South and parallels of latitude run East to West.

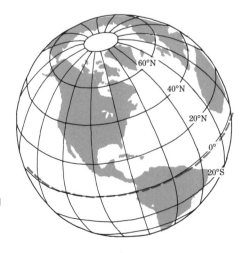
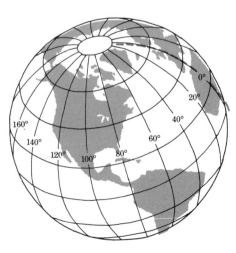
Longitude is reckoned in degrees West and East of the prime meridian, or 0°, and latitude in degrees North and South of the Equator.

slices as they approach the poles. But by assuming that meridians are parallel, Mercator greatly simplified navigation and piloting. His rectilinear grid allowed short courses to be plotted not in complicated curved lines but in straight lines.

The distortion on a *Mercator Projection* map is greatest near the poles, less in the temperate zones, and nonexistent on the Equator. This is because "North" and "South" are not pinpoints, as on the globe, but general areas above and below the sheet. On this world shaped like a beer can, each degree between meridians represents exactly the same distance. But on a globe, 1° equals 60 miles at the Equator and 0 miles at the poles. One result of this distortion is that extreme Northern and Southern areas are shown larger than they are in reality. For example, Greenland shows up much bigger than South America, whereas South America is actually about eight times larger than Greenland. If you were sailing far North and far South, these misrepresentations might mis-

lead you badly, but since most boating is done between about 40° North and 40° South, the distortion is relatively small and unimportant.

Another effect that has considerably more impact on the average pleasure sailor is that the parallels of latitude must also be distorted in order to keep them parallel and running at right angles to the meridians. Mercator did this by gradually narrowing the distance covered by 1° of latitude, working North and South from the Equator. Like a degree of longitude 1° of latitude equals 60 miles near the Equator. Since 1° equals 60 minutes, the rule of thumb is "a mile a minute." Farther North or South, a Mercator degree of latitude is smaller than a global degree of latitude. Since the latitude increments on the sides of the chart are used to measure the length of courses that have been plotted, the pilot must be careful to use increments exactly East or West of his charted position. If you use the latitude scale South of the position, the measured distance will be less than

the actual distance; if you use the one to the North, the measured distance will be greater. (You could use the bar scale printed on the chart, but it's only the average of the latitude increments on the side.) As we'll see in chapters 11 and 12, accurately measuring the distance you have run is very important, and using the proper scale is the first step.

The Mercator Projection is used on almost all the charts carried by salt-water sailors. Yet there is one type of sailing where its distortions can cause big errors. This is long-distance sailing toward the East or the West. You can sail the straight-line course between your departure and destination — but what looks like a straight line on the Mercator Projection chart is a long curved line in reality. A course plotted as a straight line on a globe would be about 12 percent shorter. This course is curved on a Mercator chart, and is called a "Great Circle" course. To plot Great Circle courses, navigators use special charts drawn to the *Gnomonic Projection*, whose meridians of longi-

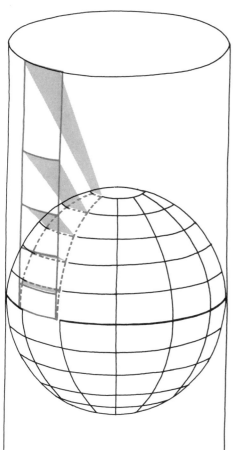

Transfering the grid from a globe to a sheet of paper inevitably leads to distortions. The Mercator Projection presents a world shaped like a beer can, with equidistant meridians of longitude and a varying latitude scale, and shows Northern and Southern land masses larger than they really are. It is used on most salt-water charts.

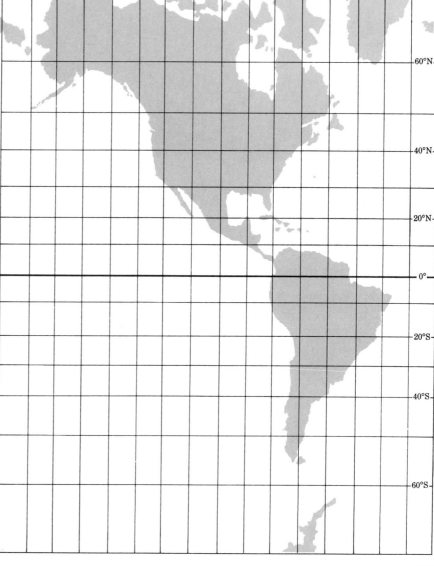

Charts

tude and parallels of latitude are curved, and which best represents the earth's actual shape. While more complicated to use than the rectilinear grid on the Mercator Projection, the Gnomonic Projection is much preferred for long-distance sailing.

On Great Lakes charts, a third projection — called Polyconic — is used. Where the Mercator Projection shows the earth as a cylinder, the *Polyconic Projection* shows it as a series of cones whose points are above the poles. A steep, tall cone is tangent to the earth around the Equator; progressively shallower and lower cones are tangent

and cover areas working toward each pole. There is less distortion with this projection because the meridians of longitude converge toward each other, with the center meridian on the chart or map are vertical and ones on either side leaning toward it, and the parallels of latitude are concave. Of course this is much more representative of the shapes of the lines on the global graticule than the Mercator Projection, but the grid is less simple. The distance covered by a minute or a degree of latitude is the same anywhere up and down the side scales of the chart, so measuring distance with these scales is easier than on the Mercator Projection. (Distances are in *statute, or land, miles*, on Great Lakes charts.) But because the meridians of longitude converge toward the middle on a Polyconic chart, laying off a straight-line West-East or East-West course may be difficult, for it will cross each meridian at a slightly different angle — much the way a Great Circle course curves across the rectilinear grid of a Mercator chart. For ex-

ample, the charted magnetic course from one end of Lake Superior to the other varies 4° over almost 300 miles in several small stages. A navigator taking that route would have to plot a series of alterations in course.

Chart Scale

Different charts cover different size areas in varying detail. The amount of land and water and the degree of detail are indicated by the chart's scale shown in a ratio in its upper left-hand corner (under a label indicating the projection being used). Charts and maps are referred to as being "small scale" or "large scale" — *the larger the second number in the ratio, the smaller the scale and the more territory is covered.* Using atlas maps as an example, a map of the world may have a scale of 1 : 75,000,000, meaning that 1 inch represents 75 million inches, or 1183.7 miles. That is an extremely small scale. In the same atlas a map of the United States has a scale of 1 : 12,038,400, or 1 inch represents 190 miles. That scale is larger than the

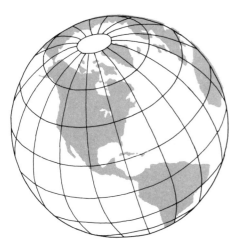

The Gnomonic Projection is truer to reality but its curved grid lines are difficult to work with when navigating. This projection is used on many offshore salt water charts.

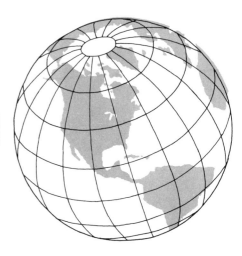

The Polyconic Projection shows the earth as a side of a cone. The center meridian and parallels of latitude are straight on this projection, which is used on most Great Lakes charts.

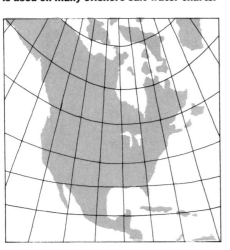

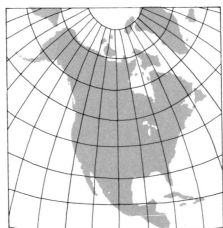

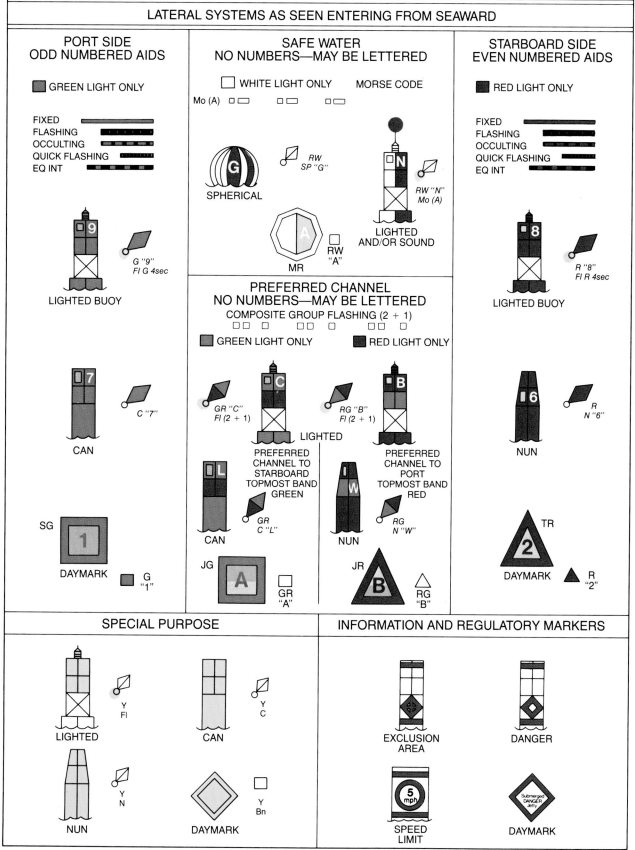

LATERAL SYSTEMS AS SEEN ENTERING FROM SEAWARD

PORT SIDE
ODD NUMBERED AIDS

GREEN LIGHT ONLY

FIXED
FLASHING
OCCULTING
QUICK FLASHING
EQ INT

9

G "9"
Fl G 4sec

LIGHTED BUOY

7

C "7"

CAN

SG

1

DAYMARK

G "1"

SAFE WATER
NO NUMBERS—MAY BE LETTERED

WHITE LIGHT ONLY   MORSE CODE

Mo (A)

G
SPHERICAL

RW SP "G"

RW "A"
MR

N

RW "N"
Mo (A)

LIGHTED
AND/OR SOUND

PREFERRED CHANNEL
NO NUMBERS—MAY BE LETTERED
COMPOSITE GROUP FLASHING (2 + 1)

GREEN LIGHT ONLY   RED LIGHT ONLY

C

GR "C"
Fl (2 + 1)

LIGHTED

B

RG "B"
Fl (2 + 1)

PREFERRED
CHANNEL TO
STARBOARD
TOPMOST BAND
GREEN

L

GR C "L"

CAN

JG

A

GR "A"

PREFERRED
CHANNEL TO
PORT
TOPMOST BAND
RED

W

RG N "W"

NUN

JR

B

RG "B"

STARBOARD SIDE
EVEN NUMBERED AIDS

RED LIGHT ONLY

FIXED
FLASHING
OCCULTING
QUICK FLASHING
EQ INT

8

R "8"
Fl R 4sec

LIGHTED BUOY

6

R N "6"

NUN

TR

2

DAYMARK

R "2"

SPECIAL PURPOSE

LIGHTED

Y Fl

CAN

Y C

NUN

Y N

DAYMARK

Y Bn

INFORMATION AND REGULATORY MARKERS

EXCLUSION
AREA

DANGER

5 mph

SPEED
LIMIT

Submerged
DANGER
Jetty

DAYMARK

NOTE: Green is replacing black on buoys to be left to port when entering. Other buoyage changes are noted in chapter 9.

AIDS TO NAVIGATION ON THE INTRACOASTAL WATERWAY

AS SEEN ENTERING FROM NORTH AND EAST—PROCEEDING TO SOUTH AND WEST

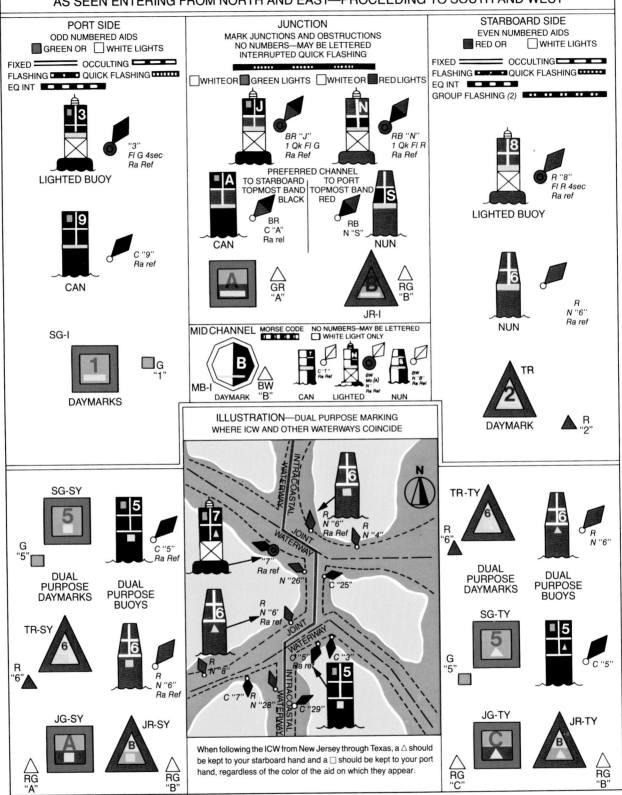

PORT SIDE
ODD NUMBERED AIDS
GREEN OR WHITE LIGHTS

FIXED ══════ OCCULTING
FLASHING ▪▪▪▪ QUICK FLASHING
EQ INT

"3" Fl G 4sec Ra Ref
LIGHTED BUOY

C "9" Ra ref
CAN

SG-I

G "1"
DAYMARKS

JUNCTION
**MARK JUNCTIONS AND OBSTRUCTIONS
NO NUMBERS—MAY BE LETTERED
INTERRUPTED QUICK FLASHING**

WHITE OR GREEN LIGHTS   WHITE OR RED LIGHTS

BR "J" 1 Qk Fl G Ra Ref

RB "N" 1 Qk Fl R Ra Ref

PREFERRED CHANNEL
TO STARBOARD TOPMOST BAND BLACK
TO PORT TOPMOST BAND RED

BR C "A" Ra rel
CAN

RB N "S"
NUN

A   GR "A"

B   RG "B"
JR-I

MID CHANNEL
MORSE CODE
NO NUMBERS—MAY BE LETTERED
WHITE LIGHT ONLY

B
MB-I DAYMARK

BW "B" DAYMARK

C "T" Ra Ref CAN

BW Mo (A) N "N" Ra Ref LIGHTED

BW N "B" Ra Ref NUN

STARBOARD SIDE
EVEN NUMBERED AIDS
RED OR WHITE LIGHTS

FIXED ══════ OCCULTING
FLASHING ▪▪▪▪ QUICK FLASHING
EQ INT
GROUP FLASHING (2)

R "8" Fl R 4sec Ra ref
LIGHTED BUOY

R N "6" Ra ref
NUN

TR

2

R "2"
DAYMARK

ILLUSTRATION—DUAL PURPOSE MARKING
WHERE ICW AND OTHER WATERWAYS COINCIDE

INTRACOASTAL WATERWAY

N

6   R N "6" Ra Ref   R N "4"

JOINT WATERWAY

7 "7" Ra ref   N "26"

C "25"

6   R N "6' Ra ref

JOINT WATERWAY

O "5" Ra ref   C "3"

R N "8"

5

C "7"   R N "28"   C "29"

INTRACOASTAL WATERWAY

When following the ICW from New Jersey through Texas, a △ should be kept to your starboard hand and a □ should be kept to your port hand, regardless of the color of the aid on which they appear.

SG-SY

5   5
G "5"   C "5" Ra Ref

DUAL PURPOSE DAYMARKS   DUAL PURPOSE BUOYS

TR-SY
6   R "6"   6   R N "6" Ra Ref

JG-SY
A   RG "A"

JR-SY
B   RG "B"

TR-TY
6   R "6"   6   R N "6"

DUAL PURPOSE DAYMARKS   DUAL PURPOSE BUOYS

SG-TY
5   G "5"   5   C "5"

JG-TY
C   RG "C"

JR-TY
B   RG "B"

NOTE: Green is replacing black on buoys to be left to port when entering. Other buoyage changes are noted in chapter 9.

AIDS TO NAVIGATION ON WESTERN RIVERS

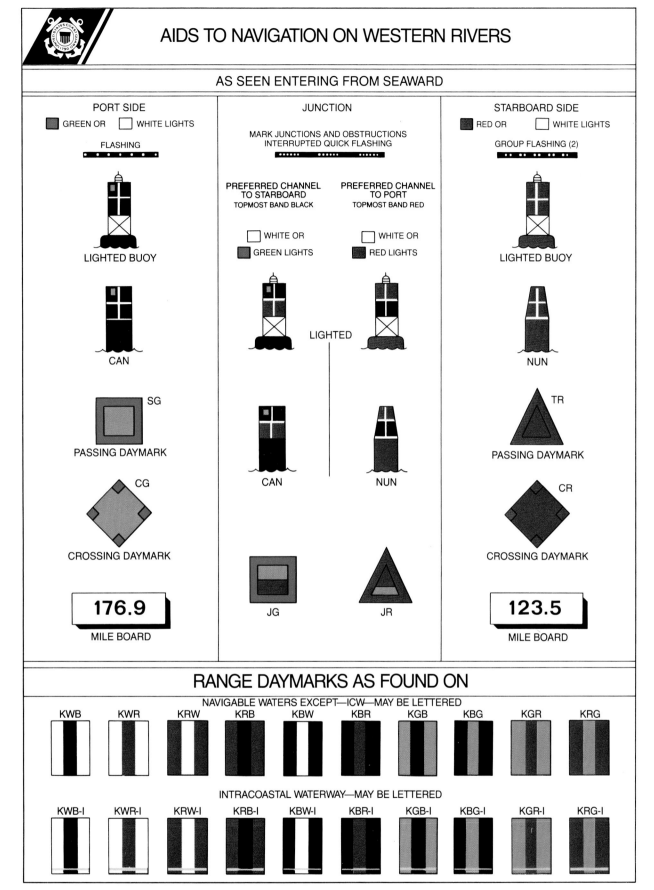

AS SEEN ENTERING FROM SEAWARD

PORT SIDE
GREEN OR — WHITE LIGHTS

FLASHING

LIGHTED BUOY

CAN

PASSING DAYMARK — SG

CROSSING DAYMARK — CG

176.9
MILE BOARD

JUNCTION
MARK JUNCTIONS AND OBSTRUCTIONS
INTERRUPTED QUICK FLASHING

PREFERRED CHANNEL TO STARBOARD
TOPMOST BAND BLACK

WHITE OR
GREEN LIGHTS

PREFERRED CHANNEL TO PORT
TOPMOST BAND RED

WHITE OR
RED LIGHTS

LIGHTED

CAN — NUN

JG — JR

STARBOARD SIDE
RED OR — WHITE LIGHTS

GROUP FLASHING (2)

LIGHTED BUOY

NUN

PASSING DAYMARK — TR

CROSSING DAYMARK — CR

123.5
MILE BOARD

RANGE DAYMARKS AS FOUND ON

NAVIGABLE WATERS EXCEPT—ICW—MAY BE LETTERED

KWB   KWR   KRW   KRB   KBW   KBR   KGB   KBG   KGR   KRG

INTRACOASTAL WATERWAY—MAY BE LETTERED

KWB-I   KWR-I   KRW-I   KRB-I   KBW-I   KBR-I   KGB-I   KBG-I   KGR-I   KRG-I

NOTE: Green is replacing black on buoys to be left to port when entering. Other buoyage changes are noted in chapter 9.

UNIFORM STATE WATERWAY MARKING SYSTEM

AIDS TO NAVIGATION

PORT (left) SIDE

COLOR — Black
NUMBERS — Odd
LIGHTS — Flashing green
REFLECTORS — Green

THE LATERAL SYSTEM—In well-defined channels and narrow waterways, USWMS aids to navigation normally are solid-colored buoys. Though a can and a nun are illustrated here, SHAPES may vary. COLOR is the significant feature. When proceeding UPSTREAM or toward the head of navigation, BLACK BUOYS ← mark the *left* side of the channel and must be kept on the left (port) hand. RED BUOYS → mark the *right* side of the channel and must be kept on the right (starboard) side. This conforms with practice on other federal waterways. On waters having no well-defined inlet or outlet, arbitrary assumptions may be made. Inquire in the locality for further information and charts when available.

STARBOARD (right) SIDE

COLOR — Red
NUMBERS — Even
LIGHTS — Flashing red
REFLECTORS — Red

Note: In some areas red buoys may be of ''can'' shape.

THE CARDINAL SYSTEM—Used where there is no well-defined channel or where an obstruction may be approached from more than one direction.

BLACK-TOPPED WHITE BUOY indicates boat should pass to NORTH or EAST of it. Reflector or light, if used, is white, the light quick-flashing.

RED-TOPPED WHITE BUOY indicates boat should pass to SOUTH or WEST of it. Reflector or light, if used, is white, the light quick-flashing.

RED-AND-WHITE VERTICALLY STRIPED BUOY indicates boat should not pass between buoy and nearest shore. Used when reef or obstruction requires boat to go *outside* buoy (away from shore). White stripes are twice the width of red stripes. Reflector or light, if used, is white, the light quick-flashing.

MOORING BUOY—White with horizontal blue band. If lighted, shows slow-flashing light unless it constitutes an obstruction at night, when light would be quick-flashing.

NOTE—The use of lights, reflectors, numbers and letters on USWMS aids is discretionary.

LIGHTS—On solid-colored (red or black) buoys, lights when used are flashing, occulting, or equal interval. For ordinary purposes, *slow-flashing* (not more than 30 per minute). *Quick-flashing* (not less than 60 per minute) used at turns, constrictions, or obstructions to indicate *caution*.

REFLECTORS—On lateral-type buoys, *red* reflectors or retro-reflective materials are used on solid-red buoys, *green* reflectors on solid-black buoys, *white* on all others including regulatory markers (except that *orange* may be used on orange portions of markers).

NUMBERS—*White* on red or black backgrounds. *Black* on white backgrounds. Numbers increase in an upstream direction.

LETTERS—When used on regulatory and white-and-red striped obstruction markers, letters are in alphabetical sequence in an upstream direction. (Letters I and O omitted.)

UNIFORM STATE REGULATORY MARKERS

Diamond shape warns of DANGER! Suggested wording for specific dangers: ROCK (illustrated), DAM, SNAG, DREDGE, WINGDAM, FERRY CABLE, MARINE CONSTRUCTION, etc.

Circle marks CONTROLLED AREA "as illustrated." Suggested wording to control or prohibit boating activities: 5 MPH (illustrated), NO FISHING, NO SKI, NO SWIM, NO SCUBA, NO PROP BOATS, SKI ONLY, FISHING ONLY, SKIN DIVERS ONLY, etc.

SWIM AREA

Diamond shape with cross means BOATS KEEP OUT! Explanatory reasons may be indicated outside the crossed diamond shape, for example SWIM AREA (illustrated), DAM, WATERFALL, RAPIDS, DOMESTIC WATER, etc.

Square or rectangle gives INFORMATION, names, activities. May give place names, distances, arrows indicating directions, availability of gas, oil, groceries, marine repairs, etc.

REGULATORY MARKERS are *white* with *international orange* geometric shapes. Buoys may be used as regulatory markers. Such buoys are *white* with two horizontal bands of *international orange*—one at the top, another just above the waterline. Geometric shapes, colored *international orange*, are placed on the white body of the buoy between the orange bands. When square or rectangular *signs* are displayed on structures as regulatory markers, they are *white* with *international orange* borders. Diamond and circular shapes, when used, are centered on the signboard.

NOTE: Green is replacing black on buoys to be left to port when entering. Other buoyage changes are noted in chapter 9.

other map's scale. And a map of the Great Lakes has a scale of 1 : 2,977,920, or 1 inch represents 47 miles — the largest scale of the three. When the second number in the ratio is relatively small, less area is covered, but in more detail.

Types of Charts

The National Ocean Service (a division of the National Oceanic and Atmospheric Administration) publishes several types of charts and a chart catalog for American coastal, waterway, and lake areas. There is considerable overlap between these charts.

The sailing chart has the smallest scale and covers the largest area, and therefore is used when sailing between distant ports and approaching land from the sea. A typical sailing chart is number 13003, "Cape Sable to Cape Hatteras," and covers the huge area between Cape Hatteras, North Carolina, and Nova Scotia. Its scale is 1 : 1,200,000, or 1 inch = 19 miles. This chart is useless for navigating in or

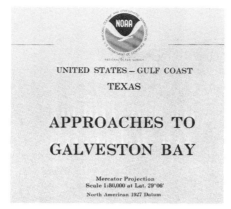

UNITED STATES — GULF COAST

TEXAS

APPROACHES TO GALVESTON BAY

Mercator Projection
Scale 1:80,000 at Lat. 29°06'
North American 1927 Datum

Covering a relatively small area, a coast chart has a relatively large scale between 1:150,000 and 1:50,000.

CHESAPEAKE BAY

CHOPTANK RIVER
AND
HERRING BAY

Mercator Projection
Scale 1:40,000 at Lat. 38°38'

The smallest area and the largest scale (1:50,000 and larger) are on a harbor chart, which also shows the greatest detail.

The shortest East-West track is plotted as a straight line on a globe or Gnomonic Projection (below), but on a Mercator Projection it is an arc called the great circle, which is 12 percent shorter than the straight line track.

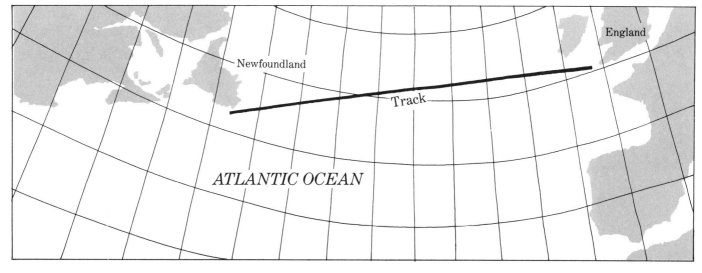

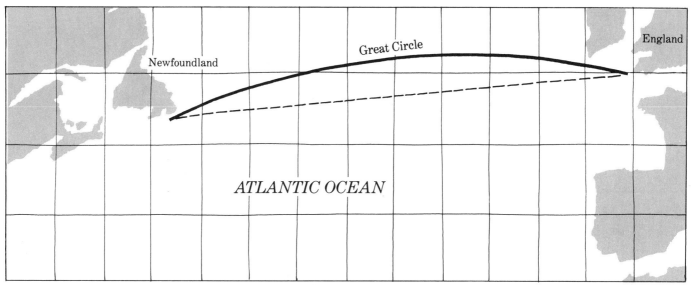

Charts

around Long Island Sound, Chesapeake Bay, or any other body of water along this coastline — but it will help a navigator on the open ocean. The largest scale on a sailing chart is 1 : 600,000 (1 inch = 10 miles).

The general chart has a larger scale, so covers smaller areas, than the sailing chart. With scales ranging from 1 : 150,000 to 1 : 600,000 (1 inch = 2.4 miles to 1 inch = 10 miles), general charts can show the most important buoys and landmarks at the entrances to major bays, and so are helpful when making approaches from seaward. There are nine general charts covering the large area included in sailing chart 13003, among them chart 1220 ("Cape May to Cape Hatteras").

Coast charts are larger in scale than sailing and general charts and show much more detail, such as reefs, shoals, and the buoys that mark channels around them. Coast charts may be the most useful charts for most pleasure sailors because they cover relatively large areas in considerable detail. Their scale varies from 1 : 150,000 to 1 : 50,000 (1 inch = 2.4 miles to 1 inch = 0.8 mile) and they cover areas from 7600 down to 850 square miles. In the area covered by sailing chart 13003 there are 31 coast charts — for example, two for Long Island Sound.

Harbor charts provide the greatest detail. With a scale of 1 : 50,000 (1 inch = 0.8 mile) and larger, they cover small waterways, harbors, and islands. Unlike the other charts, harbor charts do not necessarily overlap each other; their job is to show how to get into a harbor once you have used the sailing, general, and coast charts to get to it. There are 135 harbor charts for the area covered by sailing chart 13003.

Small-craft charts differ from the others because they come in small booklets rather than on large sheets. Compilations of harbor charts and portions of coast charts that cover certain popular bodies of water, they have the added advantage of containing other valuable information, such as tide tables and lists of marinas. Because they duplicate already-existing charts, the National Ocean Service began to eliminate some small-craft charts in 1983, citing budgetary exigencies.

Buying Charts

The National Ocean Service has an inventory of more than 900 charts and sells about 10 million individual charts annually. To find out which ones you need, look at the NOS *Nautical Chart Catalog* for your area. Catalog 1 includes the Atlantic and Gulf Coasts, Puerto Rico, and the Virgin Islands. Catalog 2 covers the Pacific Coast plus Hawaii, Guam, and Samoa. Catalog 3 is for Alaska. And Catalog 4 lists all charts available for the Great Lakes and adjacent waterways. These catalogs are available at no cost from: Distribution Branch (N/CG33), National Ocean Service, Riverdale, MD 20737-1199 (tel. 301/436-6990). These catalogs list all authorized chart agents, which include many marine equipment stores.

How many charts should you purchase? Enough to cover your anticipated cruising area with some spillover into adjacent areas. You should carry aboard a harbor chart or a small-craft chart covering every harbor that you might enter. Also take along a harbor chart for one or two ports that have yards with marine railways, even if you don't plan on calling there. Some day a leak or other major emergency may force you in, most likely in difficult weather. And carry the coast charts covering the area and surrounding waters, plus relevant general charts. Sailing charts won't be of much help unless you're planning a long offshore passage.

The NOS chart catalogs clearly show the coverage and publication number of each chart. Chart prices increased from $5 each in 1983 to $13 each in 1988. They will probably increase more as the government continues to withdraw subsidies for what was traditionally (and rightly) regarded as a public service for all mariners. Reasonably complete coverage of a well-charted boating area

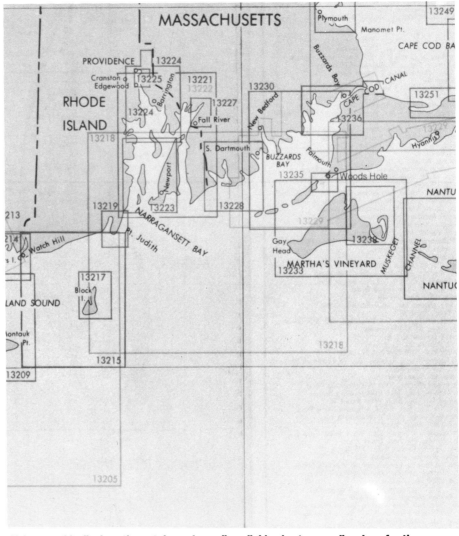

Using graphic displays the catalogs show all available charts as well as how far they overlap. The catalogs must not be used for navigation, since they show no detail.

about 100 miles across might cost $130. This price alone should encourage navigators to keep charts dry, unwrinkled, and clean. Be sure to buy the latest edition so you'll be up to date on changes in buoy locations, shoals, and landmarks.

A way to save money on charts while also gaining considerable convenience is to buy bound collections of charts for limited geographical areas, for example the collections in the *Chart Kit* series. However, don't rely on sketches and small chart segments printed in cruising guides; they don't show anywhere near enough detail for reliable navigation. The National Ocean Service publishes about 450 new editions of charts annually, on which are noted changes in the characteristics of aids to navigation and alterations in channels or shorelines. The edition number and date of each chart are clearly printed on the bottom left-hand corner of the chart sheet and on the cover of a small-craft chart. You may not need to buy each new edition of harbor charts for your home port and other waters that you know well — marking changes on your original chart should suffice — but always use the most recent edition when entering unfamiliar waters. Coast charts, showing relatively large areas, should be replaced automatically by new editions as they are published and the old charts taken ashore. Since few coast charts are usually carried, the cost is minimal.

Other Charts

Canadian publications: charts, chart catalogues, tide tables, light lists, and sailing directions for Canadian waters are available from Hydrographic Chart Distribution Office, Department of Fisheries and the Environment, P.O. Box 8080, 1675 Russell Rd., Ottawa, Ontario K1G 3H6 (tel. 613/998-4931). Publications for the Pacific and Arctic are available from Canadian Hydrographic Service, Department of Fisheries and the Environment, 512 Federal Building, Victoria, B.C. (tel. 604/388-3830). Canadian canal regulations, lists of radio aids, and navigation rules are available from Printing and Publishing Supply Services Canada, Ottawa, Ontario K1A 0S9. Payment must be in Canadian dollars. Most of these publications are also available from dealers authorized by the Canadian Hydrographic Service. Canada's weekly *Notice to Mariners* is available free from Director, Aids and Waterways, Canadian Coast Guard, Department of Transport, Ottawa, Ontario K1A 0N7.

Other foreign waters: Defense Mapping Agency, Office of Distribution Services, Attn. DOA, 6500 Brookes Lane, Washington, DC 20315-0010 (tel. 800/826-0342).

Tennessee Valley: Tennessee Valley Authority, Maps and Engineering Section, 416 Union Ave., Knoxville, TN 37902.

Mississippi River System Charts, published by the Army Corps of Engineers and available from the following district offices: Lower Mississippi to Ohio River, Vicksburg District, P.O. Box 60, Vicksburg, MI 39180; Middle and Upper Mississippi, Illinois Waterway to Lake Michigan, Chicago District, 219 S. Dearborn St., Chicago, IL 60604; Ohio River, Ohio River Division, P.O. Box 1159, Cincinnati, OH 45201; Missouri River, Omaha District, 6014 U.S. Post Office and Courthouse, Omaha, NB 68102.

Government agencies and private publishers also produce many specialized collections of charts for local use. Among these are NOS Recreational Craft Charts for the Great Lakes and adjoining waters; *Chart Kits*, which combine small- and large-scale charts for areas as large as New England; and many annual almanacs that combine tide tables, advertising, and redrawn charts of harbors. Privately published bound collections of charts may seem to be — and often are —convenient to use. They may also be out of date or leave out substantial areas. Redrawn charts *are not* to be substituted for the originals.

Stowing and Using Charts

Chart sheets can be as large as 36 by 54 inches, so stowing them and laying them out for use can be a big problem. They can be rolled up and secured in a dry locker, or folded and kept under bunk mattresses. Some boats have large chart tables that will hold a dozen or more folded charts. When folding, make sure the creases don't cross especially difficult channels or important aids to navigation.

Use a soft-lead pencil when plotting courses on the chart, and make only the marks that you need. Erase the marks later on so they won't confuse you the next time you use the chart. Although they're made of heavy paper, charts will crumble and mildew when damp. They can blow overboard. If you're sailing shorthanded and have to bring the chart on deck so the helmsman or sheet trimmer can also navigate, make sure the chart is weighted down — and not with a cushion, winch handle, or other object that somebody is likely to pick up in a hurry. It takes a second for a chart to go over the side, leaving you not only embarrassed, but perhaps in a dangerous bind. Whenever possible, keep charts below where they belong.

Notice to Mariners

New editions of charts are published relatively infrequently, but the Coast Guard, other agencies, and Mother Nature herself are constantly at work. Their labors are reported in two periodicals called *Notice to Mariners*. The nationwide edition, *Notice to Mariners*, includes portions of charts showing important changes. These portions may be cut out and glued directly on the original chart, saving the cost of a new edition. This weekly publication is free to people who can claim a need, from Defense Mapping Agency, Office of Distribution Services, 6500 Brookes Lane, Washington, DC 20315-0010.

Local Notice to Mariners is published in ten editions, each covering a Coast Guard district. Free subscriptions are available from local district headquarters, listed in appendix II.

In addition, emergencies such as drifting buoys and extinguished lights may be announced over National Weather Service VHF/FM (Very High Frequency) marine radio bands.

Non-Paper Charts

New technology has come up with alternatives to paper charts. Charts have been printed on tiny microfiches that can be examined on electronic readers on the chart table. Chart data have also been programmed onto software that allow charts to be displayed on personal computers. An advantage of the second system is that read-outs from electronic instruments can be fed into the computer so the display on the monitor shows the boat's position and course, Loran-C waypoints, and other plotted information. Since these systems are dependent on the boat's electrical system, which is never 100-percent reliable, they must be backed up by an inventory of paper charts.

Charts

What Charts Show

Using a large variety of symbols, labels, and colors, charts provide a two-dimensional overhead view of a body of water and any shorelines, islands, reefs, aids to navigation, and other natural and man-made hazards and landmarks. National Ocean Service chart 1 ("Nautical Chart Symbols and Abbreviations"), a small pamphlet available from the NOS and its authorized chart agents, shows and identifies more than 800 symbols and labels. Here we'll look at some of the more important data provided by a nautical chart, using as our example NOS chart 13218 ("Martha's Vineyard to Block Island").

The chart is clearly labeled in its upper left-hand corner:

UNITED STATES-EAST COAST
MASSACHUSETTS-RHODE ISLAND
MARTHA'S VINEYARD
TO
BLOCK ISLAND

There is no question as to which country, region, states, and local area this chart covers. In this corner we are also given the chart number and the name of its publisher, shown in the NOAA seal. A note next to the chart number says that lines used for Loran-C electronic navigation are printed on the chart.

Immediately below the label is some extremely important information. This chart is made with a Mercator Projection at a scale of 1 : 80,000 (1 inch = 1.3 miles) — it is a coast chart. It was based mainly on data assembled in 1927, which, as charts go, is relatively recent. And all soundings are in feet (instead of fathoms). This last news is so important that it is repeated in purple letters above the label. "At Mean Low Water" means that soundings (depths of water) show the water at its *average* most shallow level — *not* its extreme most shallow level. There-

On every coast chart one corner includes a considerable amount of valuable information about the chart and the area it covers.

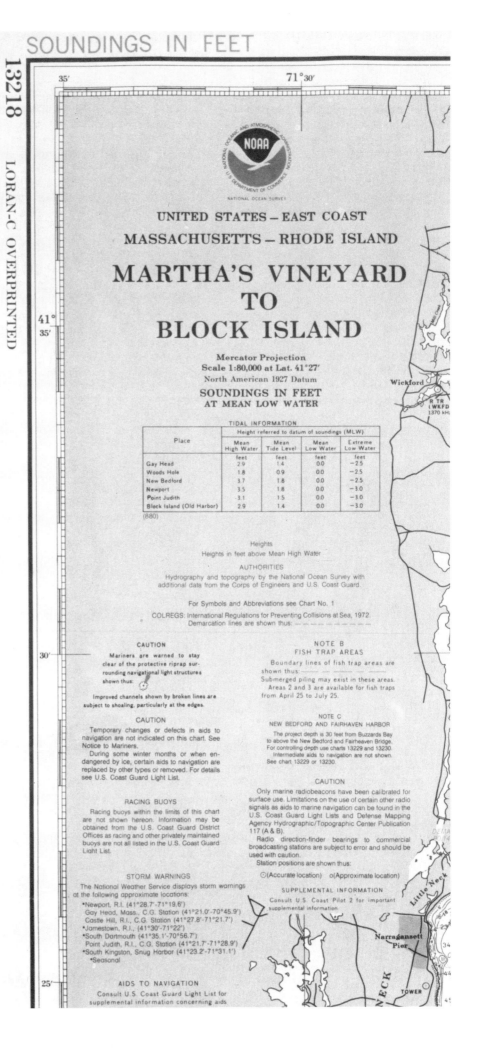

SOUNDINGS IN FEET

13218   LORAN-C OVERPRINTED

UNITED STATES — EAST COAST
MASSACHUSETTS — RHODE ISLAND

MARTHA'S VINEYARD TO BLOCK ISLAND

Mercator Projection
Scale 1:80,000 at Lat. 41°27'
North American 1927 Datum

SOUNDINGS IN FEET
AT MEAN LOW WATER

TIDAL INFORMATION

Place	Mean High Water	Mean Tide Level	Mean Low Water	Extreme Low Water
	feet	feet	feet	feet
Gay Head	2.9	1.4	0.0	-2.5
Woods Hole	1.8	0.9	0.0	-2.5
New Bedford	3.7	1.8	0.0	-2.5
Newport	3.5	1.8	0.0	-3.0
Point Judith	3.1	1.5	0.0	-3.0
Block Island (Old Harbor)	2.9	1.4	0.0	-3.0

(880)

Heights

Heights in feet above Mean High Water

AUTHORITIES

Hydrography and topography by the National Ocean Survey with additional data from the Corps of Engineers and U.S. Coast Guard.

For Symbols and Abbreviations see Chart No. 1

COLREGS: International Regulations for Preventing Collisions at Sea, 1972.
Demarcation lines are shown thus:

CAUTION

Mariners are warned to stay clear of the protective riprap surrounding navigational light structures shown thus:

Improved channels shown by broken lines are subject to shoaling, particularly at the edges.

CAUTION

Temporary changes or defects in aids to navigation are not indicated on this chart. See Notice to Mariners.

During some winter months or when endangered by ice, certain aids to navigation are replaced by other types or removed. For details see U.S. Coast Guard Light List.

RACING BUOYS

Racing buoys within the limits of this chart are not shown hereon. Information may be obtained from the U.S. Coast Guard District Offices as racing and other privately maintained buoys are not all listed in the U.S. Coast Guard Light List.

STORM WARNINGS

The National Weather Service displays storm warnings at the following approximate locations:
*Newport, R.I. (41°28.7'-71°19.6')
Gay Head, Mass., C.G. Station (41°21.0'-70°45.9')
Castle Hill, R.I., C.G. Station (41°27.8'-71°21.7')
*Jamestown, R.I., (41°30'-71°22')
*South Dartmouth (41°35.1'-70°56.7')
Point Judith, R.I., C.G. Station (41°21.7'-71°28.9')
*South Kingston, Snug Harbor (41°23.2'-71°31.1')
*Seasonal

AIDS TO NAVIGATION

Consult U.S. Coast Guard Light List for supplemental information concerning aids

NOTE B
FISH TRAP AREAS

Boundary lines of fish trap areas are shown thus:
Submerged piling may exist in these areas. Areas 2 and 3 are available for fish traps from April 25 to July 25.

NOTE C
NEW BEDFORD AND FAIRHAVEN HARBOR

The project depth is 30 feet from Buzzards Bay to above the New Bedford and Fairheaven Bridge. For controlling depth use charts 13229 and 13230. Intermediate aids to navigation are not shown. See chart 13229 or 13230.

CAUTION

Only marine radiobeacons have been calibrated for surface use. Limitations on the use of certain other radio signals as aids to marine navigation can be found in the U.S. Coast Guard Light Lists and Defense Mapping Agency Hydrographic/Topographic Center Publication 117 (A & B).

Radio direction-finder bearings to commercial broadcasting stations are subject to error and should be used with caution.

Station positions are shown thus:

⊙(Accurate location) o(Approximate location)

SUPPLEMENTAL INFORMATION

Consult U.S. Coast Pilot 2 for important supplemental information.

fore the water will be shallower than the chart indicates at spring (full- and new-moon) tides.

Next comes a table that summarizes water depths at six points on the chart and a note telling how heights of landmarks, lighthouses, and shoreline features are calculated. We then learn who is responsible for the chart. A note shows the symbol for the demarcation line between international and inland waters for determining applicability of the Rules of the Road. Below the label are two columns of information about hazards, storm warnings, aids to navigation, and calibration of radio beacons.

All this information does not always go in the upper left-hand corner, but it can be found on all coast charts and some harbor charts.

On the top center of chart 13218 is an illustration showing adjoining harbor and coast charts. Next to it is a list of Loran stations and rates. And above it is a scale in nautical miles and yards that is the average scale for this chart. A small label in the margin above the

latitude scale gives the number assigned to a previous edition of this chart when it was published by another government agency.

The chart number and name, and the advice that soundings are in feet and that Loran-C lines are printed on the chart, are all repeated at the bottom of the sheet, as are the nautical mile and yard scales. Over the chart number on the lower left-hand corner are printed the number and date of this edition of the chart.

There are definite limits of a coast chart. On it safe water beyond 30 feet in depth is white. Elsewhere the water is light blue. This does not mean that it is shallower than 30 feet. What light blue does indicate is that anybody entering those areas must switch from this coast chart to one of the harbor charts shown in the illustration in the top center section of chart 13218. There is too much detail in Narragansett Bay to be covered adequately by a small-scale coast chart. Note also a printed description of a nearby NOAA National Weather Service VHF sta-

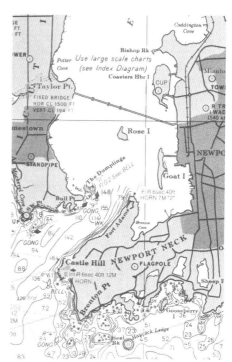

When a chart cannot give details the area is shown in light blue and the pilot is referred to a chart with a larger scale (above). Chart 13218 displays a local chart catalog (below).

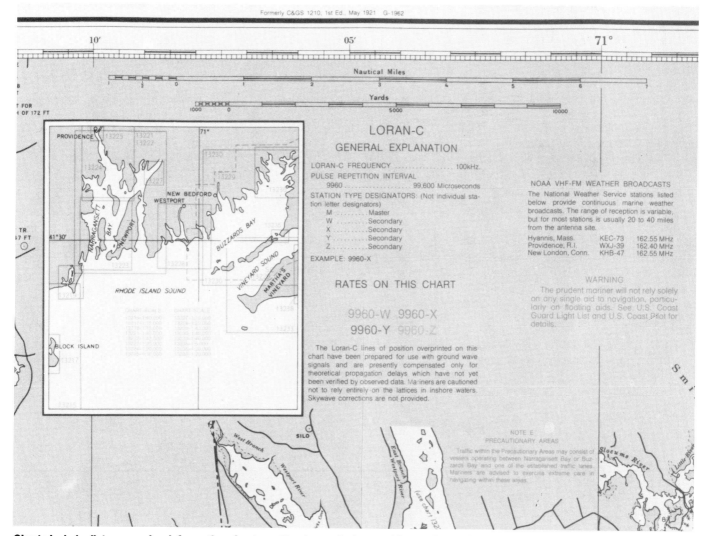

Charts include distance scales, information about weather transmissions and Loran electronic navigation, and clear warnings against becoming too dependent on individual aids to navigation.

Charts

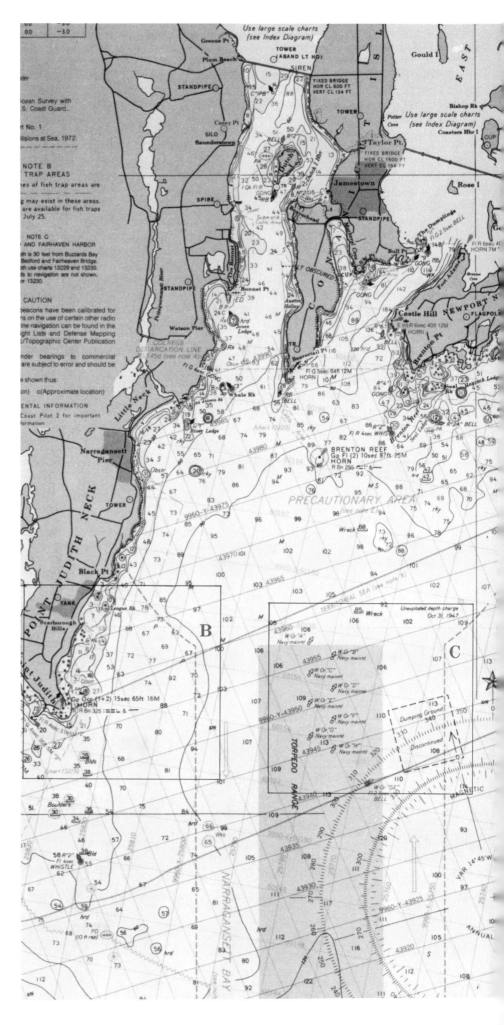

tion. Such a label will be found somewhere on any chart of an area covered by an NWS station.

Note how major landmarks — a flagpole, the Northwesternmost of four spires, five radio towers, a standpipe, two towers, a cupola, and two bridges — are identified. Each is visible from the water. Also note how roads, urban areas, piers, and railways are shown. All of these may help you find your position.

The ink colors used on charts have been selected to provide the greatest contrast and visibility, particularly under the red lights usually used by navigators to preserve their night vision. The National Ocean Service uses six colors in several tints: gold for land, white for deep water, blue for shallow water, green for land exposed at low tide and submerged at high tide, black for lettering and black buoys, and purple for caution and red buoys. Purple is used on the traffic separation zone for ships entering Narragansett Bay — inbound ships to the East side of the purple separation zone, outbound ships to the West side. On the chart is a reference, "see Note D." Note D describes the traffic separation zone. Under red lights, these light-purple shades and letters appear more brightly. A dotted black circle around a presumed danger area shows where an unexploded depth charge has sat for many years. This cautionary advice should not deter any yachtsman from sailing in this area; neither should the stark identifying label "TORPEDO RANGE," which only describes a training area for navy officer candidates.

Notes such as Note D are usually not found next to the objects they describe but are printed on gold land masses. In this case, although the Narragansett Bay traffic separation zone is on the left side of the chart, Note D is printed on Martha's Vineyard (see page 217). Just below is a note "AN-

Listed in NOS chart 1, chart symbols show hazards and reference points. The next four pages illustrate some of the more important symbols.

A

The entrance to the Sakonnet River is hazardous. Cormorant Rock surfaces at low tide (dots in broken line — shown green on a chart), and near it is another rock that is awash, or just under the surface (+ with dots). The most important landmarks are the silo and radio towers (with fixed red lights) on Sachuest Point, the abandoned lighthouse off Sakonnet Point, and the flashing 4-second light in the 30-foot tower at the end of the Sakonnet Point breakwater (solid line East of bell R "2A"). The cove North of Sachuest Point is a questionable anchorage, since its bottom is sticky (*stk*) — you may not recover your anchor — but the rocky bottom (*rky*) of Sachuest Bay probably is no better. Bell R "2" off Sakonnet marks a dangerous shoal.

B

Point Judith is surrounded by submerged rocks (+) and rocks visible at low tide (*). Mud banks (behind dotted and scalloped lines) extend from shore. A partially submerged wreck (hull) lies approximately (PA) where shown. To its North lies an obstruction 3 feet down — the dotted circle indicates it's a hazard to navigation. A sewer pipe extends from shore. Though only the lighthouse guards this dangerous point, the pilot can use the gas or water tank on shore as a navigation aid and the town (shaded area) as a guidemark.

C

The buoys maintained by the U.S. Navy have no navigational significance since their colors do not conform to the federal system. The wreck's depth of 85 feet has been determined by a sweep with a wire sounder (upturned bracket), and the early date near the depth charge indicates that it's not a hazard. Since the garbage dumping ground is no longer used no barges will be stationed over it.

Charts

lines labeled with numbers are part of the Loran electronic navigation system.

Dotted purple lines define areas where caution should be exercised.

The gray line labeled "TERRITORIAL SEA (see Note X)" marks the junction between the American territorial sea and a contiguous zone — a distinction important in maritime law.

Finally, there are several circles that look like the faces of compasses scattered across the chart. These are called *compass roses*, and they will play an important role in our discussion of the marine compass in chapter 7. Suffice it to say here that the outer of the two rings represents true, or geographical, directions; the star indicates true North. And the inner ring on the rose shows magnetic directions — the compass face as it is affected by the earth's magnetic field. The label inside the rose gives the difference in degrees between true and magnetic directions. By using the compass rose on the chart and the compass in his boat, the sailor has a constant reference point with which he can translate actual courses and bearings onto his miniaturized paper "sea," use them to calculate his position, and then convert them back to help him guide his yacht safely. Without a compass, a compass rose, and a chart, the sailor in unfamiliar waters is lost.

CHORAGE AREAS" that identifies three assigned general anchorages that are labeled on the chart and that conform to Coast Guard Regulation 110.140. Below that is "Note A," which is also mentioned in a purple rectangle on the chart around Noman's Land, where anchoring is prohibited.

The black contour lines around the island and its shoals indicate how quickly the land surfaces from a depth of about 90 feet. The blue area is shallower than 30 feet — note the "30" in the broken contour line just below the island — and contour lines with differing dot and dash characteristics within the blue area come at intervals of 10 feet, judging from the soundings either side of them.

Contour intervals differ from chart to chart. Contour lines showing elevations of land on shore are drawn on harbor charts, whose large scale encourages such detail. Also note how much attention is given to the type of bottom, information that will help you select a place to anchor since mud and sand bottoms are more secure than rocky ones.

The spider's web of lines and dashes on a chart is bewildering to new sailors. Here is a brief guide:

Black straight lines running across and up the sheet either parallel or at right angles are meridians of longitude and parallels of latitude. Their scales along the border identify them. For example, the Gay Head Lighthouse is at Longitude 69° 50' 10" West and Latitude 41° 20' 5" North (in practice, the seconds are not recorded).

Black curved lines, usually irregular and sometimes dashed, are underwater contour lines joining points of the same depth.

Fine blue, gray, yellow, and purple

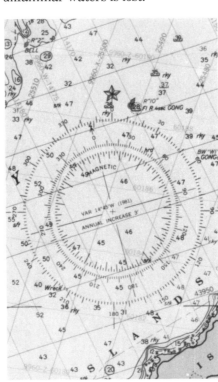

A chart's compass rose shows true North and degrees (outer ring), magnetic North and degrees (inner ring), and the variation between the two.

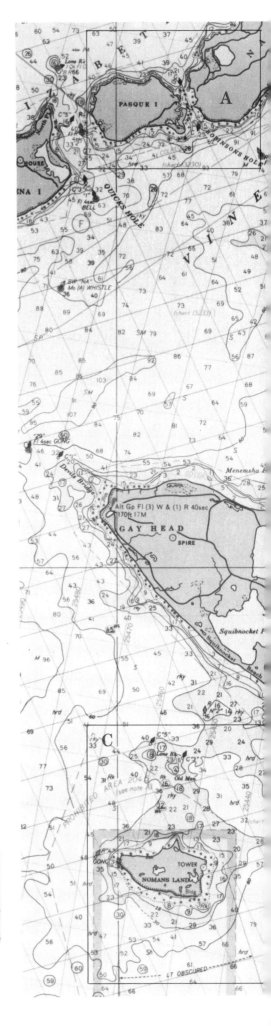

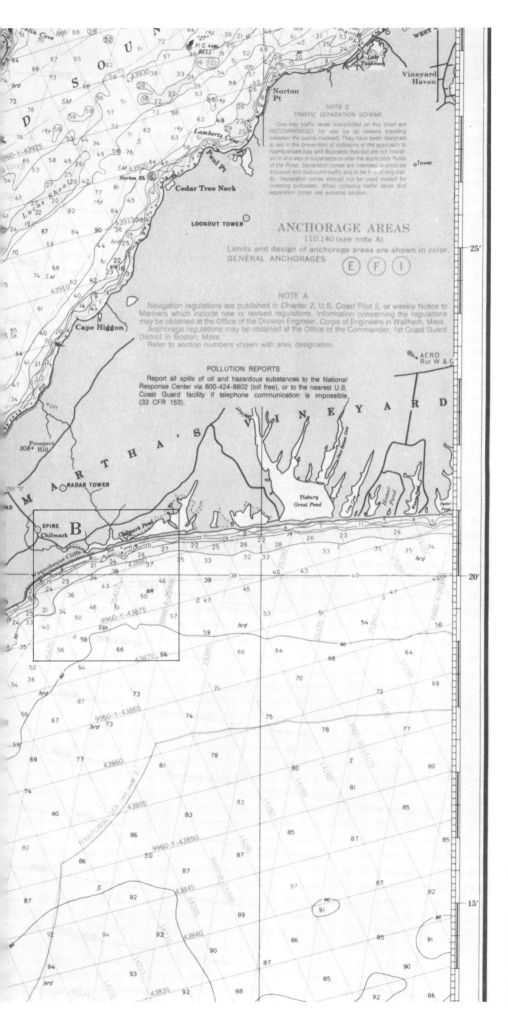

A

You'll need a larger-scale chart to determine if Robinson's Hole is navigable by a deep boat. Since it and Quicks Hole connect two bodies of water, expect the tide to run fast through them.

B

Labeled fine lines are Loran time difference (TD) lines, heavy straight ones are meridians and parallels, and heavy irregular ones are depth contours.

C

Steep cliffs (vertical lines) run along the South shore of Noman's Land. The island obscures the Gay Head lighthouse's light, and this might confuse a pilot who hasn't studied the chart. The island is in a prohibited area where anchoring is not allowed. The naming of rocks ("Lone Rk" and "Old Man") suggests that they have been hazards for many generations and the pilot should be extra alert.

Other Helpful Publications

Informative government and privately published books and manuals cover every major sailing area. The most helpful and thorough are the government *United States Coast Pilot*, *Tide Tables*, and *Tidal Current Tables*. Most cruising guides, almanacs, and local tide tables are based on these three publications, which are published by the National Ocean Service and sold by NOS authorized agents and by Distribution Branch (N/CG33), National Ocean Service, Riverdale, MD 20737-1199 (tel. 301/436-6990).

There are nine volumes in the *United States Coast Pilot* series. These books describe the navigation regulations, channels, anchorages, ports, weather, and hazards of almost all the waters covered by NOS charts. The *Coast Pilot* is, in a way, a written commentary on the charts. Free annual supplements are published each year:

Number 1, Eastport to Cape Cod
Number 2, Cape Cod to Sandy Hook
Number 3, Sandy Hook to Cape Henry
Number 4, Cape Henry to Key West
Number 5, Gulf of Mexico, Puerto Rico, and Virgin Islands
Number 6, Great Lakes and the St. Lawrence River
Number 7, California, Oregon, Washington, and Hawaii
Number 8, Dixon Entrance to Cape Spencer
Number 9, Cape Spencer to Beaufort Sea

The National Ocean Service's two complementary tide table publications are *Tide Tables* and *Tidal Current Tables*. *Tide Tables* comes in four volumes (East Coast of North and South America, West Coast of North and South America, Europe / West Coast of Africa, and Central Pacific / Western Pacific / Indian Oceans) and lists predicted times of high and low tide for a given year for all important harbors and many intermediate harbors. *Tidal Current Tables*, on the other hand, lists times of slack water (when there is no tidal current) and times and velocity of maximum flood and ebb tide currents. There are two volumes in the *Tidal Current Tables* set: East Coast of North America and West Coast of North America / Asia. *Tide Tables* and *Tidal Current Tables* are good *only* for the year shown on the cover; outdated volumes should be discarded.

Other tide and current information published by the NOS includes *Tidal Current Charts* showing direction and velocity of current, for each hour of the tidal cycle, on the following bodies of water: Boston Harbor, Narragansett Bay to Nantucket Sound, Narragansett Bay, Long Island and Block Island Sounds, New York Harbor, Delaware Bay and River, Upper Chesapeake Bay, Charleston (S.C.) Harbor, San Francisco Bay, Southern Puget Sound, and Northern Puget Sound. Using the *Tide Tables* and a *Tidal Current Chart*, the navigator can take advantage of favorable currents and avoid contrary ones — no small consideration when the tide may flow almost as rapidly as the boat sails.

All aids to navigation are described in words in the *United States Coast Guard Light List*, which is available in six volumes from the Superintendent of Documents, U.S. Government Printing Office, Washington, DC 20402, and can often be found at NOS chart sales agents. The *Light List* provides some information not usually given on charts, for example, the characteristics of seasonal buoys, lighthouse emergency lights, and fog signals. The volumes in the series are:

Volume I, Atlantic Coast, from Maine to Ocean City Inlet, Maryland
Volume II, Atlantic Coast, from Ocean City Inlet to Little River, South Carolina
Volume III, Atlantic and Gulf Coasts, from Little River to Econfina River, Florida, plus Puerto Rico, Virgin Islands, and Guantanamo Bay, Cuba
Volume IV, Gulf Coast, from Econfina River to Rio Grande, Texas
Volume V, Mississippi River system
Volume VI, Pacific Coast and Pacific islands
Volume VII, Great Lakes

```
                    POLLOCK RIP CHANNEL, MASSACHUSETTS, 1982                          31

                 F-Flood, Dir. 035° True    E-Ebb, Dir. 225° True

              JULY                                      AUGUST

     Slack     Maximum      Slack     Maximum      Slack     Maximum      Slack     Maximum
     Water     Current      Water     Current      Water     Current      Water     Current
     Time    Time   Vel.    Time    Time   Vel.    Time    Time   Vel.    Time    Time   Vel.
 Day                    Day                    Day                    Day
     h.m.    h.m.  knots    h.m.    h.m.  knots    h.m.    h.m.  knots    h.m.    h.m.  knots

  1          0256   2.0F  16         0125   1.9F   1         0410   2.1F  16         0316   2.0F
 Th  0552    0847   1.5E   F  0452   0727   1.7E  Su  0708   1005   1.5E   M  0633   0910   1.6E
     1145    1520   2.0F      1034   1350   1.8F      1300   1630   1.8F      1221   1545   1.7F
     1811    2115   1.7E      1713   1953   1.8E      1917   2216   1.7E      1846   2132   1.7E
                             2306
  2          0352   2.1F  17         0226   1.9F   2         0455   2.1F  17  0045   0421   2.1F
  F  0647    0944   1.6E  Sa  0551   0825   1.7E   M  0756   1050   1.6E  Tu  0733   1014   1.6E
     1240    1611   1.9F      1134   1450   1.8F      1347   1713   1.9F      1322   1646   1.8F
     1901    2204   1.7E      1807   2050   1.8E      2002   2259   1.7E      1944   2232   1.8E
  3  0104    0439   2.1F  18  0002   0326   2.0F   3  0201   0538   2.2F  18  0143   0518   2.2F
 Sa  0737    1033   1.6E  Su  0649   0926   1.7E  Tu  0839   1131   1.6E   W  0828   1112   1.7E
     1329    1658   1.9F      1233   1549   1.8F      1429   1754   1.9F      1419   1742   1.9F
     1946    2247   1.7E      1901   2145   1.9E      2043   2338   1.8E      2038   2328   1.9E
  4  0148    0524   2.2F  19  0058   0427   2.1F   4  0240   0617   2.2F  19  0238   0612   2.3F
```

The *Tidal Current Tables* (above) shows times of slack water and maximum current, which are more helpful to sailors than times of high and low tide. They also list the current direction.

CURRENT TABLE
POLLOCK RIP CHANNEL, MASS.

Day of Month	Day of Week	MARCH CURRENT TURNS				Day of Month	Day of Week	APRIL CURRENT TURNS			
		NORTHEAST Flood Starts		SOUTHWEST Ebb Starts				NORTHEAST Flood Starts		SOUTHWEST Ebb Starts	
		a. m.	p. m.	a. m.	p. m.			a. m.	p. m.	a. m.	p. m.
1	W	7 21	7 49	1 33	2 06	1	S	9 04	9 49	3 12	3 58
2	T	8 18	8 52	2 29	3 08	2	S	10 15	11 01	4 20	5 06
3	F	9 22	10 01	3 30	4 15	3	M	11 25	.....	5 27	6 09
4	S	10 30	11 11	4 35	5 22	4	T	12 06	12 30	6 31	7 07
5	S	11 38		5 41	6 26	5	W	1 05	1 27	7 28	8 01

Based on the *Tidal Current Tables*, this commercial tide book provides most of the same information but is easier to use. During summer, be sure to add an hour for daylight time.

The *Light List* supplements charts. It is no substitute for an up-to-date nautical chart.

A special chart combining maps and weather data is published by the Defense Mapping Agency. Called a *Pilot Chart*, it comes in editions for each of the world's major seas and oceans, and is issued monthly to account for seasonal weather changes. Each pilot chart graphically describes the normal wind direction and strength, the frequency of gales and calms, the average water temperature, usual wave heights, and current direction and velocity for 300-mile squares of ocean. The scale is too small for coastal cruising, but anybody planning a long offshore passage would purchase a pilot chart for the month of the voyage. On the back of each sheet is an illustrated essay about some marine topic, for example, seamanship or sea animals. Pilot charts are available from Defense Mapping Agency, Office of Distribution Services, 6500 Brookes Lane, Washington, DC 20315-0010.

Nongovernmental Publications

The publications described above are published by several branches of the United States government. In addition, nonofficial publishers have produced a whole library of books that will help the pleasure sailor get more out of his boat with safety and enjoyment. Many of these books fall under the generic label "cruising guide"; they are guidebooks to popular sailing areas like Southern California, Chesapeake Bay, and the New England coast, and focus on problems special to sailors. Some offer helpful advice on navigation and local weather patterns. These books, as well as many technical and nontechnical volumes about boating, are available from your local bookstore or chandlery. Read the book review section in your favorite national boating magazine in order to keep up with new publications.

---

5. VINEYARD SOUND AND BUZZARDS BAY

Vineyard, is a prominent high bluff. It is marked by **Gay Head Light** (41°20.9′ N., 70°50.1′W.), 170 feet above the water, shown from a 51-foot red brick tower on top of the head. A lighted gong buoy is 1.6 miles northwestward of the light.

Devils Bridge is a reef making off 0.8 mile northwestward of Gay Head. The reef has a depth of 2 feet about 0.4 mile offshore and 17 feet at its end, which is marked by a buoy.

Nomans Land, about 5.5 miles southward of Gay Head, is a prominent, high, and rocky island. Except for a small section on its northwestern side, the shore consists of clay and gravel cliffs 10 to 18 feet high with boulders lining the shores. In the interior of the island are many hills, the highest over 100 feet high, with considerable marshy area between the hills. A **danger zone** surrounds Nomans Land (See **204.5**, chapter 2, for limits and

on Juniper Point, a standpipe 2.2 miles of Nobska Point, a water tower and s town, the cupola of the Woods Hole O ic Institution, and the buildings of t Marine Fisheries Service and the Marin Laboratory.

Channels.–Woods Hole Passage, a d tion through the northern part of W connects Vineyard Sound and Great H Buzzards Bay, and consists of **The Strai** channel known as the **Branch** at the we The Strait, and **Broadway**, the souther to The Strait from Vineyard Sound. In the controlling depths were 8 feet midchannel) in The Strait, 11 feet in and 6 feet (12 feet at midchannel) in The northerly entrance from Great H The Strait is preferred over Broadw

---

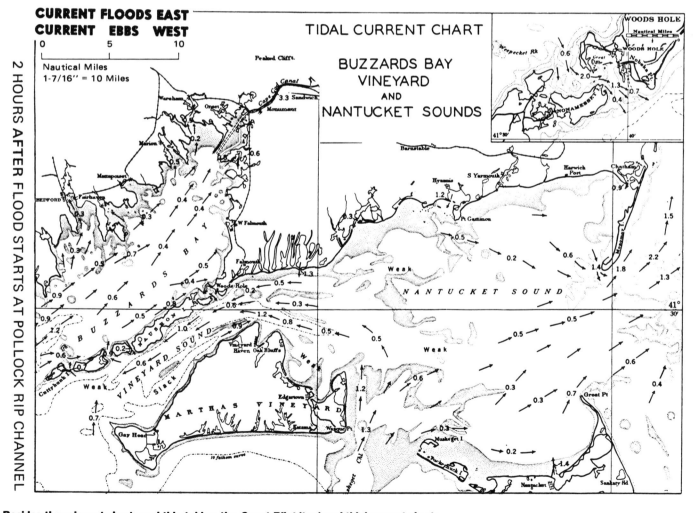

CURRENT FLOODS EAST
CURRENT EBBS WEST

2 HOURS AFTER FLOOD STARTS AT POLLOCK RIP CHANNEL

Nautical Miles
1-7/16″ = 10 Miles

TIDAL CURRENT CHART

BUZZARDS BAY
VINEYARD
AND
NANTUCKET SOUNDS

WOODS HOLE

Besides the relevant charts and tide tables, the *Coast Pilot* (top) and tidal current charts are your most helpful guides to a boating area. The current charts are coordinated with times of tide change at reference stations. In areas like this one, where the currents can run as fast as 5 knots, it's foolish to set a course without taking tidal current into account.

Chapter 10
The Magnetic Compass

Any system of navigation without instruments must depend primarily — in many cases entirely — upon dead reckoning; upon the navigator's estimate from hour to hour of the direction and distance he has traveled from his point of departure.
— *J. H. Parry,* Discovery of the Sea

Dead Reckoning

Dead reckoning has nothing to do with death. "Dead" stands for "ded," which is an abbreviation of "deduced." In his definitive *The Mariner's Dictionary*, Gershom Bradford defines dead reckoning as "the calculation necessary to ascertain the ship's whereabouts by using the courses steered and the distances run." The only improvement on that definition that we can make is to say that it is the calculation *absolutely* necessary to ascertain the ship's whereabouts without the use of electronic instruments.

The dead reckoning plot — the charted summary of dead reckoning positions during a passage — is simply called "the D.R." The D.R. is the *sine qua non* both of piloting (navigation within sight of land or aids to navigation) and of celestial navigation (navigation far offshore using star and sun sights). If you know how fast you're sailing, what direction you're moving in, and how long you've been underway, you should be able to keep a D.R. plot and, with it, chart your position with considerable accuracy. There are variables, of course: the actual heading or speed may be slightly different from what you estimated; the wind or current may hold you back, push you forward, or set you off course; or your compass may be inaccurate. But conscientious helmsmanship and a detailed record of heading and speed kept in a log book and plotted on a chart produce a D.R. that may be as accurate as a position based on sextant sights of several stars or on calculations by a $5000 computerized electronic navigational device. In chapter 11 we'll see how positions are plotted. Here we'll look at the key to the D.R.: the simple magnetic compass.

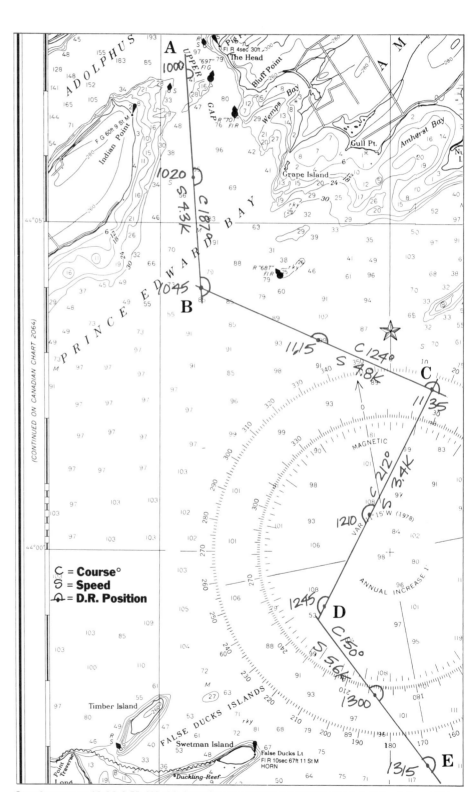

C = **Course°**
S = **Speed**
A = **D.R. Position**

Starting out at 10:00 A.M. (A) this boat beats against a variable wind, tacking frequently to take advantage of shifts. Carefully noting course and speed on the chart, the pilot keeps a dead reckoning plot of her progress by updating distance run on a given course. If the compass were wrong this D.R. plot would be worthless.

Magnetic North and the First Compass

For millennia before the development of the magnetic compass, seamen everywhere used natural phenomena as fixed references against which they measured their courses. The ancient wind rose indicated wind direction for early Greek seamen, and Polynesians navigated by wave size and direction. After long study, mariners realized that the firmament moved above their heads in repeatable patterns, and that certain constellations were reliable guides in certain seasons of the year. Seamen eventually came to depend on a star that never seemed to disappear or waver throughout the year: Polaris,

the North Star. Actually the North Star is not exactly stationary, since it lies about 2½° off to the side of the North Pole. But few helmsmen can steer to within 2° of a course, even with modern instruments. So for many centuries courses were determined, sailed, and recorded in reference to this one fixed star. As long as a mariner could see Polaris and knew what the relative angle of his course should be to it, he could find his way to his destination.

No one knows when exactly, but sometime before the 11th century A.D. seamen began to measure their progress against another, but much less tangible, constant — the earth's magnetic field. A rock called lodestone, found in a region of Asia Minor known as Magnesia, had long been known to have special properties that we now call magnetism. Samples of lodestone attracted or repelled each other, depending on which end was placed next to which. Experiments must have taken place, and by the 11th century lodestone was used to help guide sail-

ing ships. A piece of the rock or a sliver of iron that had been rubbed on lodestone was placed on one end of a stick of wood in a pool of water. The stick then automatically rotated until the end supporting the rock or iron pointed approximately at the North Star.

This invention was revolutionary. With something on board that always points in the same direction regardless of the boat's heading, the wind direction, the amount of visibility, and almost all other factors, a seaman has a constant, fixed reference point. If you left, say, the North Coast of Africa headed toward Sicily, and if you knew that Sicily was North of you, all you had to do was sail in the direction that the needle pointed. You would know that was North, even if clouds obscured Polaris, the sun, and the constellations, and even if you were unsure of the wind's direction. And if you knew that Italy was somewhere to the right of Sicily, you would steer to the right of the needle.

Since the horizon forms a circle around a boat, the angles from the

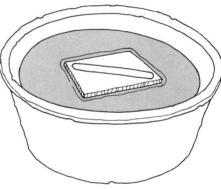

(Left) The earth's magnet field works as though a huge bar magnet lay at the core at a slight angle to the global axis, with its upper tip under magnetic North, slightly to the side of true North (star). (Above) A primitive compass was a stick floating in a bowl of water and supporting a piece of magnetized material pointing at magnetic North.

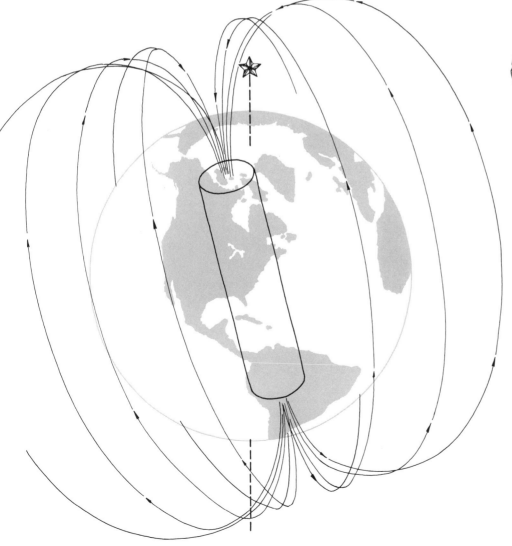

Magnetic North and True North

needle to these landmarks could be measured in fixed intervals, like slices in a pie, called compass points, of which the most important are the four cardinal points (North, East, South, and West) and the four intercardinal points (Northeast, Southeast, Southwest, and Northwest). The gaps between these eight points eventually were subdivided, making a total of 128. These were marked on the side of the compass for easy reference, and were finally placed on a circular card that also contained the magnetized needle itself. Finally, the angles were broken down by degrees, of which there are 360 in a circle, and marked on the compass card.

The needle does not point exactly at the North Pole. This is because it is attracted to a locus of magnetism called magnetic North, which is slightly to the side of the true North Pole. The earth's magnetic field has two areas, magnetic North and magnetic South, that are regions of magnetism. The magnetic loci wander around in these regions. If there were an actual geographical point called the magnetic North Pole, in 1970 it would have been located at about 76° North, 101° West, on Prince of Wales Island, north of Canada's mainland. In 1970 the needle on every accurate compass in the world pointed at that spot.

Therefore this wonderful device called the magnetic compass points to a North that is different from the North that Mercator put on the top of his charts. The meridians of longitude on a Mercator Projection chart run straight up and down, parallel to the chart sheet's side edges. But the imaginary lines that aim toward magnetic North run at angles to the chart's edges. True North is geographical North; it is the North Pole and lies almost directly under the North Star. It is true because it is constant and exact. Magnetic North, on the other hand, lies to the side of the top of the world, where it wanders around with the small annual changes in the earth's magnetic field.

Almost everywhere on earth the bearings to true and magnetic North are different. This angle is called "variation."

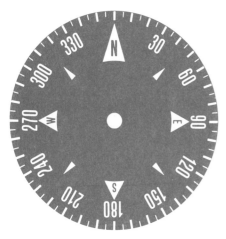

The compass card is divided into 360° at regular, clearly marked intervals between the four cardinal points (above), and it only shows direction to and relative to magnetic North (right).

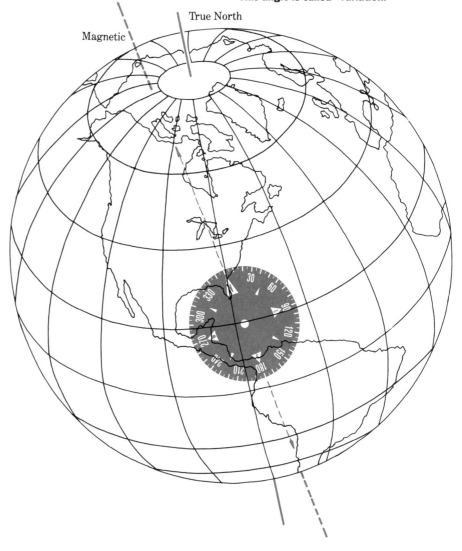

Variation

Almost everywhere on the globe there is an angular difference between the bearing (direction) to true North and the bearing to magnetic North, and this angle is called variation. There is no variation on a line that runs from the North Pole through magnetic North, Lake Superior, Havana, Cuba, and on South; neither is there variation on a line on the exact opposite side of the globe. But there is variation everywhere else, where true and magnetic Norths do not line up on the same meridian of longitude. Variation is given in compass degrees East and West. In 1983, the variation at San Francisco was 163° 31′ East—which means that the bearing to magnetic North was 16° 31′ East of the bearing to true North. At Annapolis, it was 8° 08′ West. The amount and direction of variation change slightly from year to year as the earth's magnetic field shifts. When it was first located in 1831, the magnetic North Pole was located at approximately 71° North, 97° West, or about 150 miles South of its 1970 location. In most areas variation changes by about 1 minute annually, and this shift is indicated on chart compass roses along with a datum variation.

The chart compass rose is a graphic representation of two truths, one of which — that there is one true direction against which all others are measured — has been imposed by geographers to help us understand our planet — and the other of which — magnetism — has been imposed by our planet on geographers. The outer ring on the rose reflects the first truth. The star over 0° represents true North and the 360° in the compass circle are broken down into 1°, 5°, and 10° increments. A line drawn between 0° and 180° parallels all meridians, or lines of longitude, thanks to the distortion of the Mercator Projection and to geographers' decision that all meridians meet at the North and South Poles. The inner ring reflects the second truth. It mimics the outer, true ring but is tilted the same angle as the local variation. This is the rose's magnetic ring. True North is not important on a boat unless you're steering by (aiming at) the North Star, or are using a small-scale chart that does not include magnetic roses because its coverage extends over many different variations. Some navigators plot courses and bearings on chart in true degrees after converting them from magnetic degrees, using a system that we'll describe later. But most prefer to use magnetic degrees in all calculations because those are what the boat's compass uses. The only North that means anything on deck is magnetic North; true North is irrelevant.

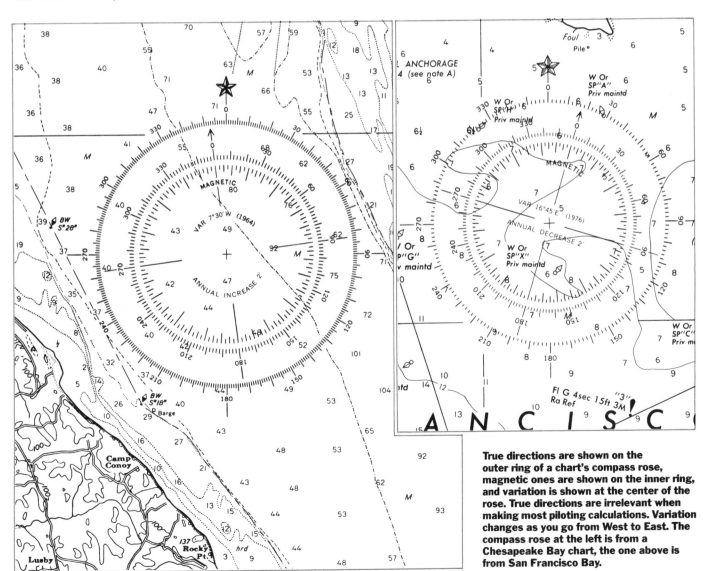

True directions are shown on the outer ring of a chart's compass rose, magnetic ones are shown on the inner ring, and variation is shown at the center of the rose. True directions are irrelevant when making most piloting calculations. Variation changes as you go from West to East. The compass rose at the left is from a Chesapeake Bay chart, the one above is from San Francisco Bay.

225

Parts of the Compass

The magnetic compass has changed considerably since the 11th century. Its heart is the aluminum compass card, a black circle around whose perimeter degrees are marked in even increments. The larger the card, the more degrees are shown. On the average 4- or 5-inch compass used in pleasure boats, degrees are shown only in 5° increments, and labels are printed at 30° intervals (30, 60, E, 120, etc.). Any more information might confuse the helmsman. The cardinal points are abbreviated: "N" for North, "E" for East, and so on. Intercardinal points — "NE," "SE," "SW," and "NW" — are sometimes shown at the 45° intervals of Northeast, Southeast, Southwest, and Northwest. Before navy usage of degrees became popular after World War II, cards were marked with more points. There are 32 points at $11\frac{1}{4}°$ intervals, each of which contains a half-point and two quarter-points at intervals of $2^{13}/_{16}°$. Oldtime sailormen "boxed the compass" by memorizing all 128 points. "Northeast by East" (written "NE × E") meant as much to them as 56° does to us. "South by West one-half West" ("SxW½W") was how they indicated 197°. The half-points and quarter-points have little use today (though they're fun to learn), but the 32 "whole" compass points can come in handy. Since we have no trouble with the cardinal and intercardinal points (North, Southwest, etc.), using the compass points in between should come easily, if we remember that a North Northeast (NNE) wind is between Northeast and North and that an East Northeast (ENE) wind is between Northeast and East. Table 1 is a conversion table for the 32 points.

At the exact center of the card is a short vertical stick called the pivot post, which is used to help align the compass and to take bearings. On a ring around the card, but not touching it, are several other posts called lubber's lines. The number varies depending on the compass, but there is always one at the forward side and there are two opposite each other at the left and right sides. The boat's heading or course is the number on the card next to the forward lubber's line. On sailboat compasses there may be two other lubber's lines halfway between the side lines and the forward one. If the boat is headed due North, these intermediate lubber's lines will be over 45° (Northeast) and 315° (Northwest), and the side lubber's lines will be over 90° (East) and 270° (West). The intermediate lines are helpful when the helmsman sits to the side of the compass, and when calculating wind direction, as most sailboats sail close-hauled at an angle of about 45° to the true wind.

The side lubber's lines may also be used as guides by helmsmen sitting either side of the compass, but their main job is to help determine when an object is dead (directly) abeam. When the object, the side lubber's line, and the pivot post are aligned, the object is abeam.

So the compass dial stays level and can be read even when the boat is heeling or rolling, it is supported by gimbals. Picture a performing seal that balances a stationary ball on its nose while it does flips and somersaults and you have an idea of the relationship between a pitching, rocking boat and her gimballed compass. To dampen the motion of the gimbals, the compass dome is filled with a liquid — mineral oil or some other non-freezing solution. Rapid changes in temperature or air pressure will cause the liquid to expand or compress, leaving an air bubble under the dome that greatly obstructs visibility. For this reason good compasses are built with rubber expansion chambers in their base to compensate for changes in the liquid's

Anatomy of a Typical Marine Compass

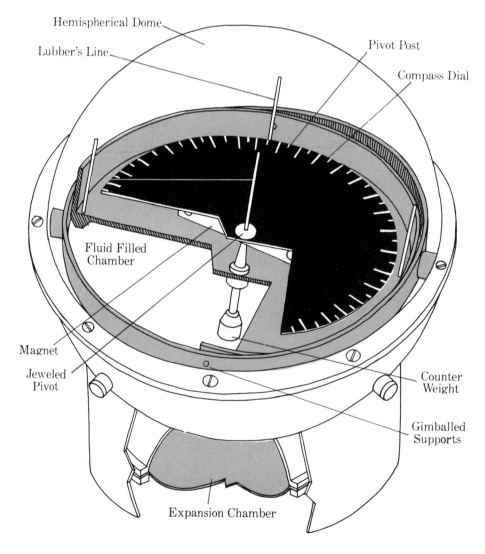

Hemispherical Dome

Lubber's Line

Pivot Post

Compass Dial

Fluid Filled Chamber

Magnet

Jeweled Pivot

Counter Weight

Gimballed Supports

Expansion Chamber

density. An air bubble indicates that the compass is leaking oil and should be refilled through the plug on its bottom. Do not fill the compass with water, which may cause rust.

The hemispherical plastic dome protects the compass and magnifies the compass card. (The card on a 4-inch compass may actually be as small as 2 inches.) The dome should be kept out of the sun when not in use, otherwise it may yellow. When cleaning a compass dome, do not use an abrasive, such as sandpaper, cleaning powder, or a knife, which may scratch the surface irreparably.

The business part of a compass is out of sight. This is the set of magnets glued under the compass card, surrounding the jeweled pivot that supports the center of the card. There usually are four sliver-shaped magnets whose combined force has a North-seeking component and a South-seeking component that line up with the earth's magnetic field. The magnets must be carefully placed for the forces to be accurately aligned. With the de-

velopment of very lightweight metals, the weight of these magnets — and therefore of the card — has been reduced considerably, thereby minimizing the friction between the card and the jeweled pivot. This is important for the seaman because the spin of a turning boat (transmitted through the pivot) has much less effect on the alignment of the card than previously. In older compasses the card would "lay," or spin slightly as the boat turned

Degrees are typically shown in 5° increments with heavier lines every 10° and labeled at 30° intervals. Large compasses show individual degrees, but still accentuate the primary reference points.

and continue to spin after she settled down on a new course. The newer, lighter, almost friction-free cards are more independent of the boat's motion. Any jerky motions they may have are dampened by the oil under the dome and a counterweight under the pivot.

Fluxgate Compass

A new type of compass, called the fluxgate, also orients itself to the earth's magnetic field but otherwise works very differently. It has no moving parts, and its readout is digital. To give accurate readings, it must be perfectly level. Fluxgate hand bearing compasses (used to take magnetic bearings on aids to navigation and other objects) must be held absolutely parallel to the horizon, and fluxgate built-in compasses must be gimballed.

A big advantage of this type of compass is that, unlike a normal magnetic compass where the sensor (the magnets under the card) is integral to the readout (the card itself), the fluxgate sensor can be distant from the readout. You can place the sensor anywhere in the boat to get it away from deviation-producing objects like the engine, and then connect it to remote readouts and electronic instruments in the cockpit and navigation station.

Table 1. Compass Points to Degrees

NORTH (N), 0°
North by East (N × E), 011° 15′
North Northeast (NNE), 022° 30′
Northeast by North (NE × N), 033° 45′
Northeast (NE), 045°
Northeast by East (NE × E), 056° 15′
East Northeast (ENE), 067° 30′
East by North (E × N), 078° 45′
EAST (E), 090°
East by South (E × S), 101° 15′
East Southeast (ESE), 112° 30′
Southeast by East (SE × E), 123° 45′
Southeast (SE), 135°
Southeast by South (SE × S), 146° 15′
South Southeast (SSE), 157° 30′
South by East (S × E), 168° 45′
SOUTH (S), 180°
South by West (S × W), 191° 15′
South Southwest (SSW), 202° 30′
Southwest by South (SW × S), 213° 45′
Southwest (SW), 225°
Southwest by West (SW × W), 236° 15′
West Southwest (WSW), 247° 30′
West by South (W × S), 258° 45′
WEST (W), 270°
West by North (W × N), 281° 15′
West Northwest (WNW), 292° 30′
Northwest by West (NW × W), 303° 45′
Northwest (NW), 315°
Northwest by North (NW × N), 326° 15′
North Northwest (NNW), 337° 30′
North by West (N × W), 348° 45′
NORTH (N), 360°

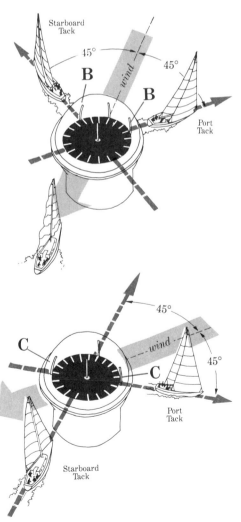

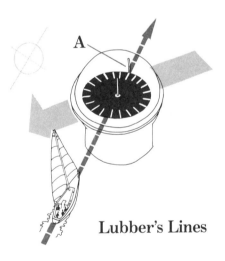

Lubber's Lines

Forward lubber's lines (A) indicate the course that your boat is sailing.

Intermediate lubber's lines (B) can be used to estimate tacking angles. For instance, if your boat is luffed directly into the wind, the intermediate lubber's lines will indicate the courses on starboard and port tack.

Side lubber's lines (C) are used for beam sightings, as a reference when steering from the side of the compass, and to estimate the heading on an opposite tack when beating to windward, as shown.

Compass Types

The hemispherically domed compass seen on most boats larger than about 15 feet is installed in a base called a binnacle, which may be secured in a pedestal to which the steering wheel is attached, in the boat's deck, or in the after side of the cabin. Wherever it's located, the compass should always be clearly visible to the helmsman in his normal steering positions. Large domed compasses have hoods that protect them from sun and spray. Compasses used on cruising boats are equipped with red electric lights for illumination during night sailing, since white lights spoil night vision.

Small boats often carry compasses with low, flat domes, which, while they

Fluxgate compasses, like this hand bearing compass, give a digital readout but must be held perfectly level to the horizon.

don't magnify the compass card as much as hemispherical domes do, offer little obstruction to feet and gear.

Hand bearing compasses are small, portable compasses used specifically for taking bearings (determining directions to objects). Some aren't much larger than ice-hockey pucks; others are attached to handles. Both kinds can be used as emergency steering compasses.

Installation

The most important consideration when installing a compass is that it be clearly visible to the helmsman. Place it securely in front of the helmsman's normal station in a site where it will not be screened by cushions, legs, or charts. This may mean that the compass will not be on the centerline. If this is the case, make sure that the line between the pivot post and the forward lubber's line is exactly parallel with the centerline; otherwise the course shown on the compass will be different from the direction in which the bow is heading.

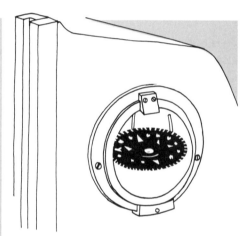

Since a pedestal would get in the way of the tiller, boats without steering wheels often have their compasses recessed in the bulkhead on the aft side of the cabin. Taking accurate bearings over a bulkhead-mounted compass may be difficult.

Compasses may be recessed in the deck to allow the helmsman and crew to see them easily from either side. They should be placed out of the way of normal traffic so people don't trip over them. Integral red lights make them useful for night steering.

A binnacle and steering pedestal should be sturdy and have a grab rail (so crewmembers don't use the compass for support) as well as a hood to protect the dome from sun rays. Insert the largest compass that can fit in the binnacle.

Deviation

Once you've decided where to install the compass, begin to correct any errors. One type of compass error, variation, cannot be corrected except on charts or when magnetic headings are changed to true headings. The other error, deviation, is local and can be corrected or compensated for. Deviation is caused by metal objects in or around the compass that alter the effects of the earth's force field on the card magnets.

Zeroing-In

The first step in correcting deviation in a new compass is to neutralize the effects of any binnacle compensators, which are small magnets adjustable by screws. Sometimes compasses are delivered with the compensators exerting some pull on the card magnets, throwing them off alignment. Zeroing-in identifies and corrects any misalignment:

1. Ashore, well away from any magnetic, iron, or steel object (including your wristwatch or beltbuckle), screw the compass to a straight board with nonmagnetic (bronze or stainless-steel) screws. The edge of the board should exactly parallel the centerline of the compass (the imaginary line running from the pivot post to the forward lubber's line). Turn the board until the lubber's line is at North. Slide a large book or another straight board against the compass board.

2. Holding the book in place with one hand, move the compass board away, rotate it 180°, and slide it back against the book. The lubber's line should be at South. If it's not at South, make a mental note of the error. For instance, if the lubber's line is at 172°, remember that the error is 8° East.

3. With a bronze or other nonferrous screwdriver, adjust the compensators until you find the one that most greatly affects the card with the compass in North-South alignment. On most compasses, if there are two compensators they are labeled "North-

South" and "East-West." With the lubber's line at the inaccurate South mark, remove one-half of the error. In this case, turn the "North-South" screw until the lubber's line is at 176°.

4. Realign the compass board and book as in (1) above, but this time with the lubber's line at South. Then reverse the board as in (2) above. If the lubber's line is exactly at North, the compass is zeroed-in on the North-South axis. If not, remove one-half of

the error as in (3) above and reverse the board. Keep repeating these steps until there is no error at either North or South. If you can't eliminate all error, either the compass is defective or a magnetic object nearby is affecting the compass.

5. Repeat steps (1) through (4) for East-West alignment using the other screw.

If there is no error, the compensators were neutralized at the factory.

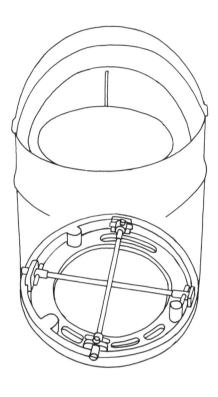

Magnetic compensators or adjusters are turned with screws to make compass corrections on the North-South and East-West axes. Use a bronze screwdriver when adjusting.

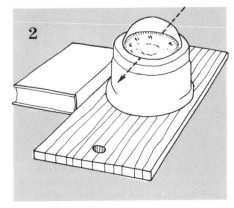

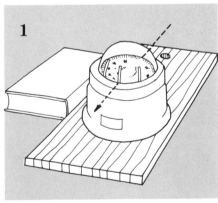

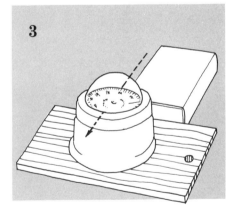

To zero-in a compass, screw it to a straight board and align the forward lubber's line with North (1). Using a book as a stationary reference, turn the board; if the lubber's line is not at South, take out one-half the error with the compensator (2). Repeat steps until all error is removed, then turn the board and book on the East-West axis and repeat the process (3).

Deviation

Swinging Ship

After the compass is zeroed-in, reinstall it in the boat, which herself may have a magnetic field that causes deviation. The first job is to find out how much deviation there may be. Next, the deviation should be eliminated or reduced by moving equipment or adjusting the compensators. And third, if the deviation is not entirely removed, it must be recorded on tables called deviation tables, which the navigator will use when correcting compass courses and bearings.

"Swinging ship" is the technique used to determine deviation. We recommend that you hire a professional compass adjustor to swing ship, adjust the compass, and make out deviation tables, since your safety depends on the accuracy of your compass. But in case you want to try to adjust your own compass, here's how you swing ship:

1. Using a large-scale harbor chart, identify several ranges. These should be shoreside landmarks in North-South and East-West alignments. One range might be a radio tower behind a flagpole; another could be a lighthouse in front of a water tower; a third could be the end of a pier ahead of a fuel tank. At least one range should be suitable for testing Easterly and Westerly bearings, and another one should work for Northerly and Southerly bearings. The goal here is to estimate what the effect of the hull, engine, and fittings are on the compass at the four cardinal point headings. (Unless it's directly above or below the compass, a magnetic or steel object will have different effects on different headings.)

2. On the chart, draw lines through the ranges and calculate bearings and

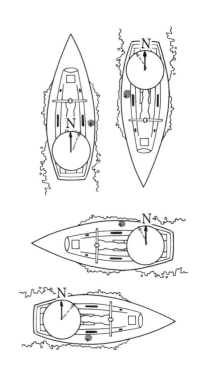

A metal object to one side of the compass will cause different amounts of deviation on different headings.

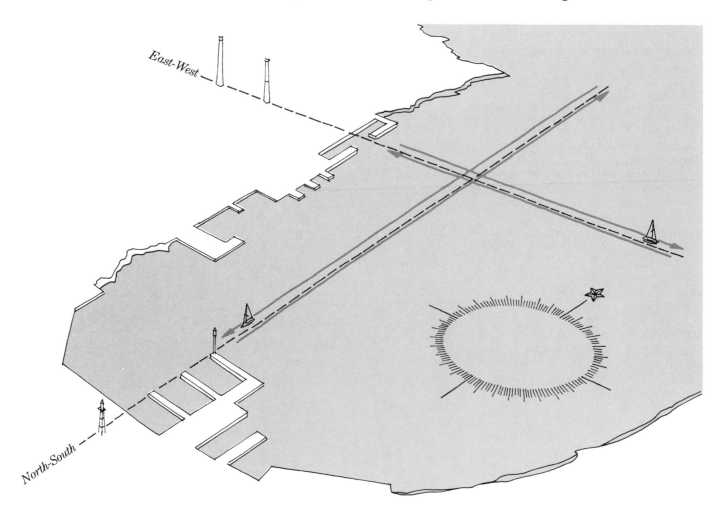

Swing ship by running up and down ranges on the East-West and North-South axes, comparing compass and charted headings. Repeat the exercise under different conditions and with electronics on. If you have any doubts, hire a professional compass adjustor.

reciprocal bearings. Get under way.

3. Slowly sail down the range lines, first toward the ranges and then away from them. While the helmsman keeps the boat accurately on the range lines, one crew member studies the compass and writes down any deviations from the calculated headings.

4. Using a nonmetalic screwdriver on the compensators, try to remove the error one-half at a time for those headings closest to North, South, East, and West. (This system is effective primarily for cardinal headings.)

5. If deviation cannot be compensated, if it is considerably greater on one heading than on another, if it is greater than 3° for intercardinal headings (Northeast, Southeast, Southwest, and Northwest), or if you have any doubts about the effectiveness of your work, *hire a compass adjuster to compensate your compass.*

Deviation can vary as conditions change, so run down the ranges at various angles of heel and with the electronics (lights, radio, and so on) switched on. You may find that the deviation will differ considerably. If there is minor deviation, move any magnetic or steel objects near the compass. With all her gear, a sailboat creates her own magnetic field that will rarely be in alignment with the earth's. Sometimes one or more large metal objects — say, a stove or the engine — will create deviation on one heading that will be nonexistent on another. But more frequently, deviation is caused by a metal object (such as a beer can, tool, or knife) lying unnoticed near the compass. If the metal object cannot be moved, a commercial demagnetizer (available from electronic supply stores) can be used to neutralize it. Sometimes electric wires create a small, local magnetic field that causes compass deviation. If so, twist the positive and ground wires around each other to neutralize their effects.

Sun Azimuths

Instead of using ranges or known bearings to landmarks, professional compass adjusters frequently compare compass bearings with sun azimuths, or bearings to the sun. The celestial position of the sun and bearings to it from most points on the earth can be calculated from tables in the *Nautical Almanac,* an annual publication used by celestial navigators. All the adjustor needs to know is the exact time and the boat's position. Azimuths are computed in true, rather than magnetic, degrees. To convert a true bearing to a magnetic bearing, subtract any Easterly variation or add any Westerly variation. The sun's magnetic bearing can be found by aiming the boat at it when it is low on the horizon and reading the degree mark directly under the pivot point's shadow. Since this is the reciprocal of the actual magnetic bearing, add 180° and compare the sum with the computed magnetic bearing.

Pelorus Bearings

A special sighting instrument called a pelorus can be useful when checking for deviation. It's like a handbearing compass except that the card is not magnetized and can be turned manually, and that an adjustable sighting arm is located around the perimeter. With the pelorus, a navigator or compass adjuster can take highly accurate relative bearings to objects without using an uncompensated handbearing compass.

First, turn the rose until the number under the forward lubber's line is the same as the boat's course. Then adjust the sighting arm to take a bearing on a charted object, read the bearing, and compare it with the bearing computed on the chart. The difference is the amount of deviation.

When to Swing Ship

Deviation should be checked for at least every 2 years and whenever your boat has been altered. Magnetism is a curious phenomenon. For instance, a boat's own magnetic field may be altered simply by lying in an East-West plane during winter lay-up. Or the compass may suddenly go out of compensation if it is mishandled. It's a good idea to use a pelorus to establish a thorough set of ranges at intervals of about 20°, and then check your compass against those ranges soon after launching each year. (Make sure the ranges themselves haven't been altered or removed.) And don't forget that your boat's own magnetic field — the source of deviation — may change anytime you replace or install equipment.

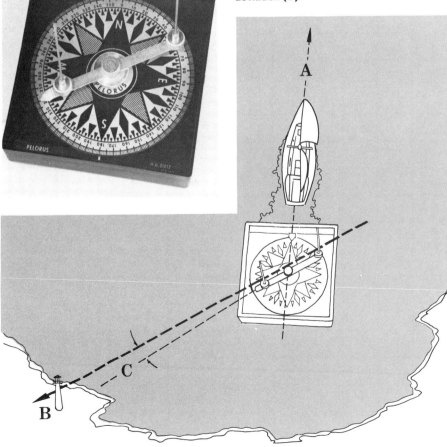

A pelorus is a hand-held device for taking relative bearings (left). To use it when swinging ship, put the forward pointer on the course (A) and sight a charted object (B). If the bearing is different from the charted bearing, the difference is the deviation (C).

Deviation

Deviation Tables

If the compass adjustor is unable to compensate the compass using the internal compensators or any external magnets that he may install near the compass, he will draw up a deviation table. This is a list of deviation errors for headings at 15° increments. The table should be clearly posted near the navigator's station and any deviation will be added to or subtracted from calculated magnetic courses to produce accurate compass courses.

The important course — the one that is steered — is the *compass course*. Before it is given to the helmsman, it must be cleared of any errors, the most important of which is deviation.

To use a deviation table when converting magnetic to compass courses:

1. Locate the desired magnetic course in the table, say, 45°.

2. In the table, determine the deviation for that course, interpolating if necessary. Assume it's 2° West.

3. If the deviation is Westerly, add it to the magnetic course; if Easterly, subtract. The compass course, then, is 47°.

Sometimes the navigator must convert compass courses to magnetic courses. For instance, the helmsman is

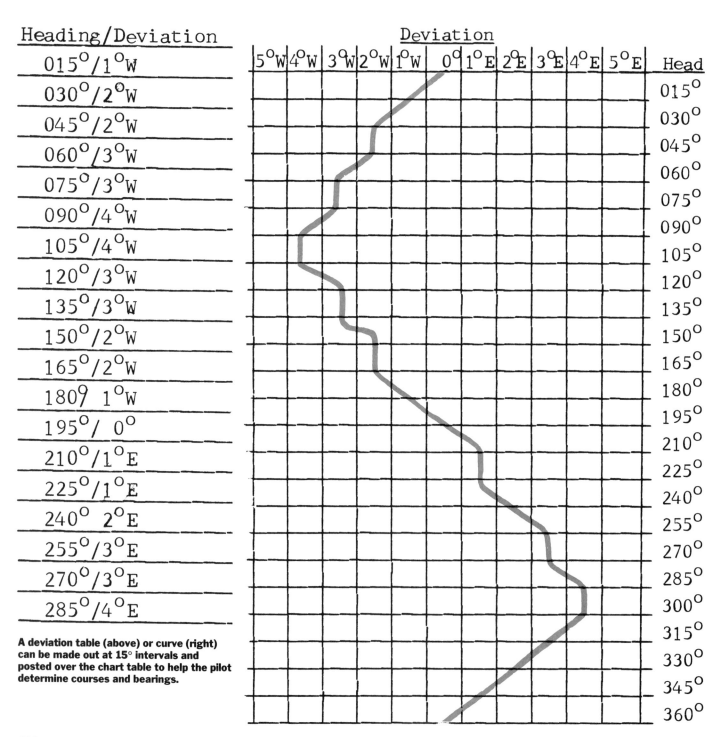

Heading/Deviation

Heading/Deviation
015°/1°W
030°/2°W
045°/2°W
060°/3°W
075°/3°W
090°/4°W
105°/4°W
120°/3°W
135°/3°W
150°/2°W
165°/2°W
180°/ 1°W
195°/ 0°
210°/1°E
225°/1°E
240° 2°E
255°/3°E
270°/3°E
285°/4°E

A deviation table (above) or curve (right) can be made out at 15° intervals and posted over the chart table to help the pilot determine courses and bearings.

steering 220° and sees a buoy that bears 015° and tells the navigator, who now wants to record the bearing on the chart. The most important thing to remember here is that the amount and direction of deviation are determined by the *course*, not by the bearing. So the deviation to be cranked into the calculation is 2° East, the deviation for a heading of 220°, and not 1°, West, the deviation for one of 015°.

1. First, the navigator converts compass degrees to magnetic degrees. When going in this direction, the rule is add Easterly, subtract Westerly error. Adding 2° to 220°, he arrives at a magnetic course of 222°.

2. He goes through the same steps to calculate the magnetic bearing to the buoy: 015° + 2° = 017°.

A deviation table may also be arranged graphically in a series of curves, with the course on one axis and the deviation on the other axis. While more sophisticated than a tabular deviation table, a deviation curve can be subject to misinterpretation; finding the deviation on one axis while keeping one's eyes focused on the course on the other axis can be extremely difficult in a tossing boat.

Another way to record deviation is to place a mock compass card inside another, larger card. The outer one represents the correct magnetic compass, the inner one the boat's deviated compass. Every 15° on the inner card, draw lines to the appropriate non-deviated number on the outer card. A glance at either ring will lead your eye quickly to the other number.

Once you have a deviation table, whether made out by yourself or by a compass adjustor, keep the original and one photocopy on board — one to be used and the other to be held in reserve. If the deviation is affected by heel angle or by electronic instruments in operation, make up separate deviation tables or cards clearly identified by their special application.

Deviation tables and curves only show the amount of deviation, but a deviation rose makes it easy to determine the course to be steered without making calculations. Glue one compass rose inside another and draw lines from the uncorrected magnetic courses on the inner ring to the corrected compass courses on the outer one. For example, steer 063° to make good 060° and 277° to make good 270°.

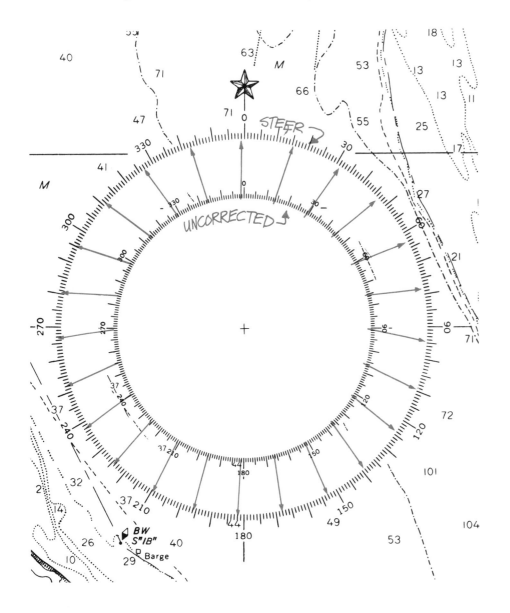

Correcting Compass Error

When we convert compass courses to magnetic courses using a deviation table, we are *correcting* a compass, and when we convert from magnetic to compass we are said to be *uncorrecting*. The most correct course or heading is the true one, the next most correct is the magnetic course (after taking account of variation), and then comes the least correct course — the compass course, determined after adding or subtracting deviation. As we work away from true toward compass, we are uncorrecting. As we work back toward true, we are correcting.

Anybody doing celestial navigation uses true bearings and directions and later converts them into magnetic. And small-scale charts require calculations in true degrees for the simple reason that they do not have magnetic roses. With those few exceptions, true degrees and the true compass rose are abstractions for the navigator.

Still, correcting and uncorrecting to and from true degrees is sometimes necessary, and there are several important rules of thumb. We've already mentioned two of them:

1. *When correcting (from compass to magnetic to true).* Easterly errors are added, Westerly errors are subtracted.

2. *When uncorrecting (from true to magnetic to compass).* Easterly errors are subtracted, Westerly errors are added.

Many navigators remember these rules in a bit of doggerel:

> *Correcting add East,*
> *Uncorrecting East is least.*

Earlier we converted both ways using variation and deviation errors. Here's another example:

On NOS chart number 5142 ("San Pedro Channel"), the course from the middle entrance of San Pedro Bay to the Fl 4sec whistle buoy is 147°T (true). There is no magnetic rose, but we know that the local variation is 14° 40′ East. Our boat has 4° West deviation on this course. What compass course should we pass up to the

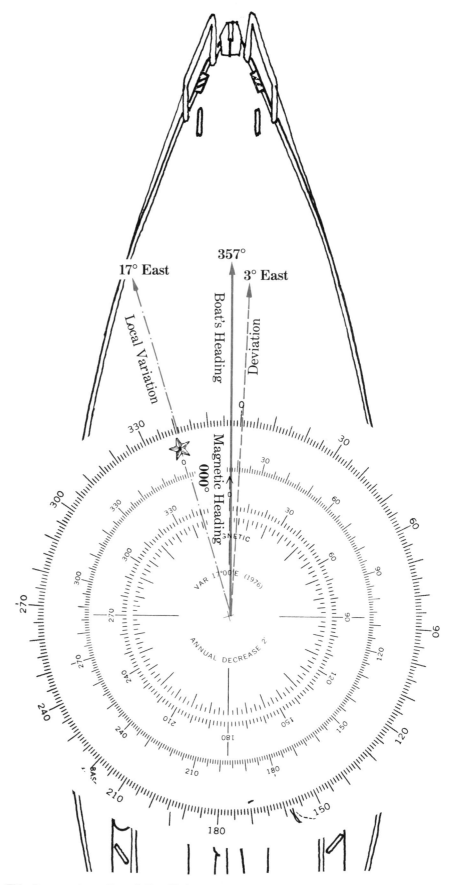

This diagram shows the relationship between true ("most correct"), magnetic ("less correct"), and compass ("least correct") degrees. The inner ring shows magnetic, the middle true, and the outer compass. The local variation is 17°, which means that the earth's magnetic field pulls magnetic headings 17° East (right) of true headings. The compass deviation at this heading is 3° East, which means that the boat's own magnetic field pulls compass headings 3° East (right) of magnetic headings. Therefore, when the compass reads 357°, the boat is sailing on courses of 000° magnetic and 017° true. These calculations may be done mathematically following the rules of thumb "correcting (toward true) add East" and "uncorrecting (toward compass) East is least."

helmsman?

First we must determine which of the two rules of thumb applies. We are converting from true to compass course, which means that we are un-correcting — working away from the most correct course. "Uncorrecting East is least." So we subtract Easterly variation.

Because degrees and minutes are computed in multiples of 60, we cannot use an electronic decimal calculator to solve this problem unless we convert minutes into fractions of degrees. The number to be subtracted is 14° 40'. Since 40 is two-thirds or .67 of 60, the calculator equivalent is 14.67. To solve this problem with a calculator:

$$\begin{array}{r} 147.00°\ \text{T (true course)} \\ -\ \ 14.67°\ \text{variation} \\ \hline 132.33°\ \text{M (magnetic course)} \end{array}$$

To solve without using a calculator, convert 147° to a more usable number, 146° 60'. Then:

$$\begin{array}{r} 146°\ 60'\ \text{T} \\ -\ \ 14°\ 40'\ \text{variation} \\ \hline 132°\ 20'\ \text{M (magnetic course)} \end{array}$$

Next the magnetic course must be uncorrected with the deviation. Which rule applies? We're still uncorrecting, working away from true, so "Uncorrecting East is least" is our guide. The deviation is Westerly, and therefore is *added*:

$$\begin{array}{r} 132.33°\ \text{M (magnetic course)} \\ +\ \ 4.00°\ \text{deviation on this course} \\ \hline 136.33°\ \text{M (compass course)} \end{array}$$

Without the calculator:

$$\begin{array}{r} +\ 132°\ 20'\ \text{M (magnetic course)} \\ +\ \ \ 4°\ 00'\ \text{deviation} \\ \hline 136°\ 20'\ \text{M (compass course)} \end{array}$$

Communicating a Course Change

The navigator then says to the helmsman "Steer one-three-six." The helmsman repeats "One-three-six," and alters course. When the course is reached, the helmsman says "One-three-six," and centers the helm. The navigator repeats, "One-three-six" in acknowledgment, and notes the time (using the 24-hour clock format), the

speed, and the course in the log book: "1525, San Pedro Entrance, 6 knots, assume 136° M for Fl 4 sec whistle." This means that at 3:25 P.M. the boat cleared the entrance, and at a speed of 6 knots, changed to a course of 136° headed toward the whistle buoy.

To some, the verbal repetitions of the course and the written log entry may seem unduly militaristic and formal, but with so many checks and double-checks there is no way that the helmsman could assume the wrong course. After a while these acknowl-edgments become almost second nature.

The "Timid Virgins" Rule

We have just followed a logical pro-cess that is summarized in the non-sense statement "Timid Virgins Make Dull Companions." The first letters of each word stand for True, Variation, Magnetic, Deviation, and Compass,

Using the rules of thumb, a course of 147° true is converted to 132° magnetic and, most useful, to 136° compass.

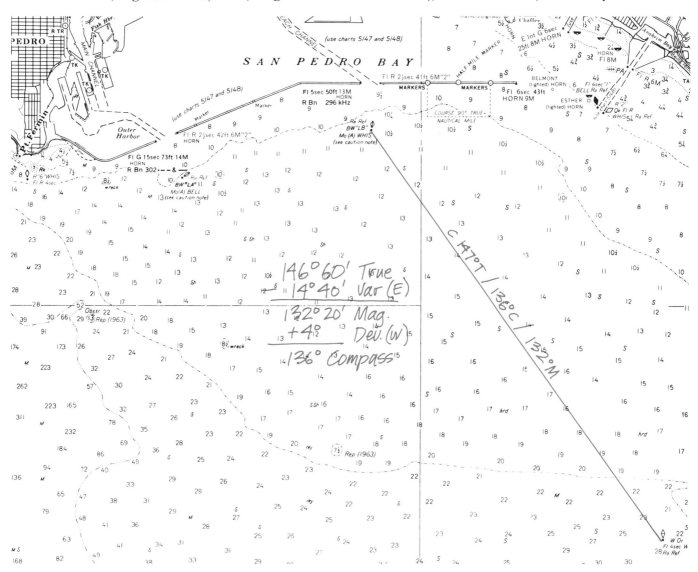

Correcting Compass Error

which we calculated in that order:

"*T*imid" = 147° true course

"*V*irgins" = 14° 40′ East variation

"*M*ake" = 132° 20′ magnetic course (true° − variation° = magnetic°)

"*D*ull" = 4° West deviation

"*C*ompanions" = 136° 20′ compass course (magnetic° + deviation° = compass°)

The letters are reversed for correcting, leaving the saying "*C*ompanions *D*ull *M*ake *V*irgins *T*imid."

The logical order is:

"*C*ompanions" = compass course

"*D*ull" = deviation (add if East, subtract if West)

"*M*ake" = magnetic course (compass° ± deviation° = magnetic°)

"*V*irgins" = variation (add if East, subtract if West)

"*T*imid" = true (magnetic° ± variation° = true°)

Remember that when correcting — working from compass to magnetic to true — "Correcting add East."

These mnemonic devices can be both helpful and confusing. Navigators who make these calculations repeatedly don't need them, and those who make them irregularly often get them mixed up. Printed below is a flow chart that may be more helpful. You can photocopy it and use it as a worksheet, filling in the blanks with the relevant numbers.

To keep the rules of thumb about adding and subtracting straight, enter the courses on this flow chart. The number at the end of row 2 will be the true or compass course.

CORRECTING (Compass to Magnetic to True)

1. "Companions"   **"Dull"**   **"Make"**

Compass Course ___°
+ Deviation East _____°
or
− Deviation West _____°
= Magnetic Course ___°

2. "Make"   **"Virgins"**   **"Timid"**

Magnetic Course ___°
+ Variation East _____°
or
− Variation West _____°
= True Course ___°

"CORRECTING ADD EAST"

UNCORRECTING (True to Magnetic to Compass)

1. "Timid"   **"Virgins"**   **"Make"**

True Course ___°
− Variation East _____°
or
+ Variation West _____°
= Magnetic Course ___°

2. "Make"   **"Dull"**   **"Companions"**

Magnetic Course ___°
− Deviation East _____°
or
+ Deviation West _____°
= Compass Course ___°

"UNCORRECTING EAST IS LEAST"

Using the Compass

Steering by the Compass

To steer by the compass, turn the boat until the desired course is directly under the forward lubber's line. The compass card will appear to move as the boat turns, but actually the card is stationary and the lubber's lines are in motion. Once she's on course, the boat will unavoidably make minor swings to either side as she heels, pitches, rolls, and is nudged by waves. To compensate for these swings, bring her back to course by pushing the tiller in the opposite direction or turning the steering wheel in the same direction. If you are sitting to the side and can't read the number under the forward lubber's line easily, use a side lubber's line after subtracting or adding 90° or 45° from or to the compass course.

Do not stare at the compass; the lubber's line and card will quickly mesmerize and desensitize you and you'll lose all feel for the boat and probably wander far off course anyway. Rather, glance periodically at the compass and try to sensitize your body to the tug of the helm and the angle of the wind when the boat is on course. Very few helmsmen are good enough to keep a boat to within ±2° of a course; in rough weather, ±5° or 10° may be acceptable. If conditions force the boat off course for more than a few minutes, notify the navigator. The helmsman should not make arbitrary course changes, no matter how good the reasons for them may be, without consulting with the navigator, checking the chart, or evaluating the consequences of the change. This is especially true in unfamiliar, tricky waters and in periods of limited visibility.

Every boat has her own unique steering characteristics. Dinghies and light-displacement larger boats will readily wander off course — and by the same token, may be easily brought back to course with a minor helm change. Heavy boats with long keels have excellent directional stability, which means that it will take a lot to force them off course. This also means that a heavy boat must usually be oversteered to initiate a course change, and must also be checked before she has reached the new course so she does not keep swinging. Only experience will tell how quickly or slowly she will maneuver. Remember that no boat can be steered unless she has steerageway. Slow-moving boats steer ponderously; rapidly moving boats usually steer relatively quickly. So don't expect her to respond promptly if she's just drifting along at 2 knots.

Taking Compass Bearings

One of the essential skills of piloting is taking accurate compass bearings on landmarks and aids to navigation in order to find a line of position. The most reliable way to take a bearing is to aim the boat right at the object and then to read the heading under the forward lubber's line. Since this usually heads her far off course, most sailors take bearings over the compass.

To take a bearing using a built-in compass, stand behind it facing the object — a buoy, a landmark, or an-

3/10	1525, San Pedro Entr.
	6K, assume 136°M
	for Fl 4 sec. whist.
	1625, Fl 4 sec. whist.
	abeam, assume 170°M
	for Newport Beach.

Log all the necessary information when recording bearings. The last number here is the reading on the boat's distance log connected to the speedometer.

other boat. Close one eye and extend a hand sideways, little finger down and flat, over the compass dome, pointing at the object. This sighting hand should be directly over the pivot post. Now read the bearing on the compass card on the far side of the pivot post and under your little finger. With practice you should be able to cut a bearing (as this procedure is called) with an accuracy of ±2°. If a lubber's line lies under your sighting hand at a 90° or 45° angle to the boat's heading, the accuracy should be even better. Remember that the bearing is the compass direction *toward* the object sighted. The reciprocal bearing, which is 180° different, is the compass direction *from* the object.

When cutting bearings:

1. Be sure that your views of the compass and the object you are sighting are unobstructed.

2. Remove your watch or other ferrous or magnetic object.

3. Keep your "cutting" hand straight and vertical.

4. Before reading the compass, sight down your hand to guarantee that it's aimed directly at the object.

5. Take three bearings and average them. In rough or foggy weather, you may have to discard any bearings widely different from the average. Reliable bearings will fall within 5° of each other.

6. To avoid memory lapses, remember the bearing in a three-digit number (35° should be remembered as "zero-three-five degrees") followed by the name of the object ("red nun number 4," "nearest tower," "large black bell," and so on). Keep reciting the bearing and the object's name until they're written down.

7. When recording bearings in the ship's log or a notebook, include the time of the sighting and the reading of the distance log, a mechanical device like an automobile's mileage gauge. The log entry might read, "1135 hours, Annapolis entrance black flasher number 1 bears 330°, log 221.4 miles."

Bearings may also be taken with special hand bearing compasses, which usually are easy to use but which may not be compensated. If there is any error, be sure to correct it before logging the bearing.

In the next chapter we'll show how the line of position that extends from the boat to the sighted object is used to estimate the boat's position, and how two or more lines of position fix her position when they are crossed on a chart.

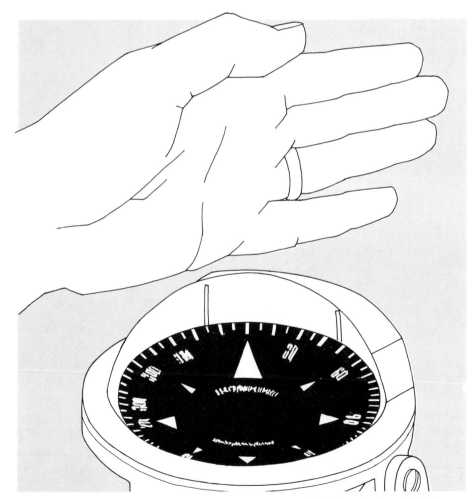

Steer at the object or use a hand bearing compass when taking important or difficult bearings. Otherwise, cut bearings over the cockpit compass using the edge of your hand. Take three bearings, average them (throwing out erratic ones), and remember them with care. Most piloting errors are caused by sloppy memories and poor communication, not lack of technique.

Chapter 11
Plotting and Position Finding

Piloting is the art and science of finding your boat's position and calculating safe courses near land using the navigation aids and tools we described earlier: buoys, lighthouses, charts, and the magnetic compass. In this chapter we'll see how these and other aids and tools help the pilot accomplish three important tasks — plotting the dead reckoning position, calculating courses to be sailed, and plotting estimated and fixed positions. In chapter 12 we will examine some advanced plotting techniques based on those three.

The pilot's main responsibility is to know his position while keeping his boat off the shore — "the bricks," "the flats," or "the beach," depending on local geology. Among the piloting tricks favored by oldtime sailors in a fog was "potato navigation," where a crew member keeps heaving potatoes ahead. When you don't hear a splash, turn *quickly*. Some boats still use sounding poles slightly longer than the keel is deep. When it touches bottom, alter course. While each of these techniques can be effective, most sailors would prefer to know that land is looming well before it can be reached with a potato or a stick, and so they rely on somewhat more sophisticated tools and skills.

This comfortable navigator's station has a large chart table, plenty of storage space for charts, books, and instruments, and a padded chair whose angle can be adjusted when the boat heels. For a plotter the navigator uses a draftsman's drawing machine screwed to the table. The instruments include a compass, a simple Loran receiver (white box), read-outs for depth sounder, boat speed, and wind direction and speed instruments (round dials and rectangular box below them), and the main electrical panel (large box).

A Pilot's Tools

A pilot's basic kit, stored in a chart table or drawer, should include the following:

1. Charts for all areas you are likely to visit, including harbor charts for all ports that you might possibly call at. Include a harbor chart for each major city-port, even if you plan to avoid urban areas on your cruise. An emergency may force a change in your itinerary. Charts should be stowed flat and dry, in numerical order.

2. Government (or privately published) *Tide Tables* and *Tidal Current Tables* covering your cruising area. Make sure they're for this year. If your area is covered by a current chart, bring a copy along too.

3. The relevant editions of the *Coast Pilot* and *Light List*.

4. A copy of a "cruising guide" — a commercial guide to the region's waterways.

5. A log book (which could be a simple wire-bound notebook, one day to a page).

6. A small notebook and scratch paper.

7. Two boxes of number 2 lead pencils or several mechanical pencils, with erasers, stored so their points won't break (wrap a piece of Velcro around a pencil and glue another piece of Velcro to a bulkhead over the pilot's working area; when the pencil is not in use, stick it to the bulkhead). A pencil sharpener. A red pencil.

8. A protractor.

9. A 12-inch ruler.

10. A clipboard.

11. A stopwatch or wristwatch with stopwatch function.

12. A hand bearing compass for taking accurate bearings.

13. At least one pair of binoculars, 7 x 35 or 7 x 50. Any magnification greater than 7 restricts field of view and causes sighted objects to jump around excessively in rough weather. The second number indicates the size of lens; the larger, more expensive 50-mm lens gathers more light than the 35-mm lens. Binoculars encased in rubber may be less susceptible to damage if dropped, but all binoculars should be handled carefully with the strap around the user's neck, and should be stored, preferably in the cabin, in sturdy cases when not in use. Clean lenses with eyeglass tissue and fresh water.

14. A fine-tip pen for marking changes to aids to navigation on charts.

15. A small electronic calculator, preferably one programmed with trigonometric functions. At the least it should be able to solve square-root problems. Some manufacturers market programmed (or programmable) calculators specifically for navigators and pilots. Stow the calculator in a box or plastic bag with a gel sack to absorb moisture.

16. A pair of 5-inch dividers for measuring distances. Dividers are similar to a drawing compass except that both legs are pointed. (A drawing compass can be used, but the pencil may mark up the chart unnecessarily.) There are various types of dividers — some with adjustable cross-arms, others whose legs cross so the instrument can be adjusted with one hand. The 5-inch dimension indi-

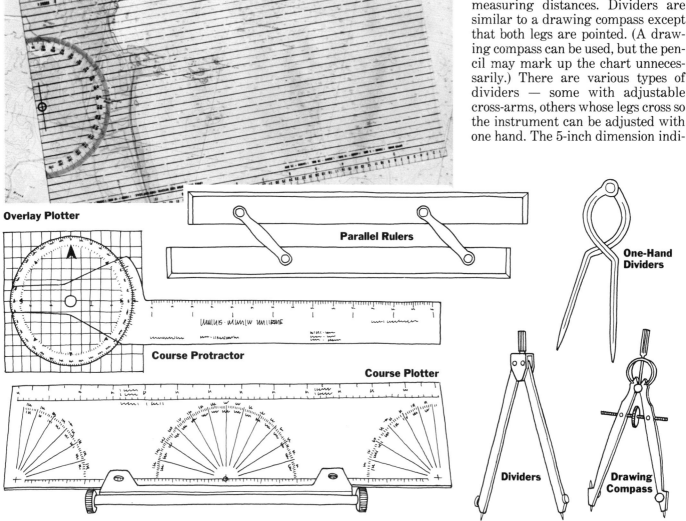

Overlay Plotter

Parallel Rulers

Course Protractor

Course Plotter

One-Hand Dividers

Dividers

Drawing Compass

A Pilot's Tools

cates the spread between the legs when they're fully extended. Larger dividers may be desired for plotting long passages between navigation aids, smaller ones for cruises in well-marked areas. A drawing compass.

17. A plotter, used to transfer bearings or courses from a compass rose to another portion of the chart, and to calculate magnetic or true bearings and courses. A plotter essentially allows the pilot to draw parallel lines. If the compass rose is in the lower right-hand corner of the chart and a course line or a bearing is in the upper left-hand corner, the pilot uses the course

plotter to duplicate the line or bearing over the compass rose. Most plotters are first lined up alongside the line and are then slid across the chart with their edges remaining parallel to the line.

One plotter, called parallel rulers, consists of two plastic or wood straightedges linked and held parallel by metal hinges. After the original alignment is made, the rulers are "walked" across the chart by alternately spreading and bringing together the straightedges, always keeping one edge immobile while the other edge is moved. The surface under the chart must be absolutely flat and the pilot must have plenty of elbow room so that the rulers can be walked across the sheet without losing parallelism. Some navigators prefer to use two draftsman's right triangles instead of parallel rulers, sliding the triangles in turns across the chart. A disadvantage with parallel rulers and triangles is that their reference point must be a compass rose on the chart, which often is far from the line to be

measured.

This problem is solved by plotters that are part straightedge, part protractor. The protractor is laid over a parallel of latitude or a meridian of longitude — which on Mercator charts run exactly East-West and North-South — in order to determine true directions or bearings. One such plotter, called a course protractor, consists of a plastic arm one end of which pivots on the center of a 360° protractor. Some course protractors are equipped with two compass roses, one for true directions and the other for magnetic directions, and the variation is adjusted with a screw. A course plotter also has a protractor, but it covers an arc of only 180° and is drawn onto a transparent ruler.

Every pilot and navigator prefers one type of plotter and swears by it with the faith of a convert, deriding all others. But given time you can learn to use all types equally well.

Those are instruments and tools found in most well-equipped pilots' kits. The following equipment found

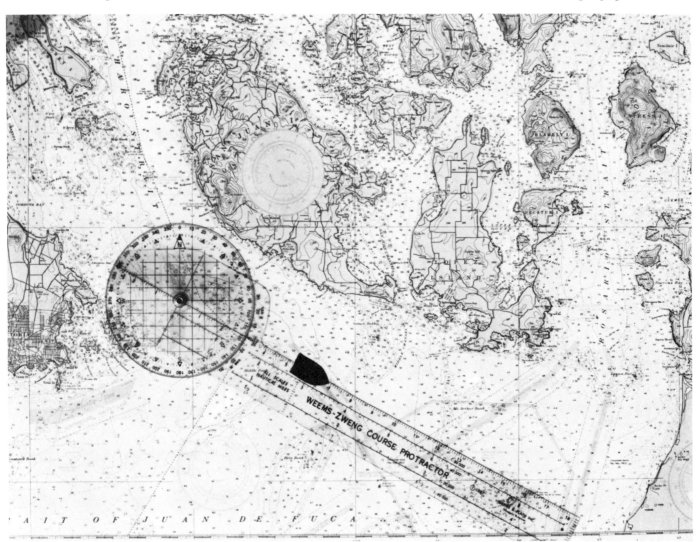

The course protractor is laid over the latitude-longitude grid rather than the compass rose. You must adjust either the protractor or your calculations for variation.

elsewhere in the boat will also help produce accurate D.R. plots and fixes:

1. A compensated magnetic compass must be on board, preferably at the helmsman's station, with a deviation table if necessary.

2. A reliable sounding device used to determine the depth of water under the hull to compare with depths shown on a chart. Today the most commonly used sounder is electronic and shows depths in graphic or digital displays. We'll describe electronic depth sounders in chapter 13, where we'll also show how to use depths in piloting.

3. An electronic speedometer, preferably with an odometer, or distance-run indicator, although later in this chapter we'll show how to estimate speed without a speedometer.

4. A reliable, accurate timepiece.

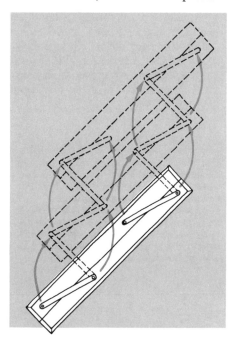

Parallel rulers are "walked" across the chart to determine parallel lines.

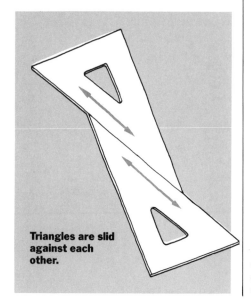

Triangles are slid against each other.

Magnetic or True?

Once he has chosen his tools, every new navigator must make an important decision about using them. Should calculations be made in true degrees or in magnetic degrees? There are good arguments on both sides, with all authorities agreeing that once you choose a style, you should stick with it. The experts who recommend making all calculations in true degrees generally are offshore celestial navigators who use true when computing azimuths before eventually "uncorrecting" (see chapter 10) from true to magnetic to come up with a compass course. You may choose to use true

degrees for other reasons: if you are using small-scale charts that do not have magnetic roses due to the frequent changes in variation; if you do celestial navigation as well as coastal piloting; or if you enjoy the challenge of "correcting" and "uncorrecting" as well as the convenience of using the latitude-longitude grid as a reference for your course protractor.

On the other hand, few pilots ever take a sun sight, and the only bearings they take are over the card in a magnetic compass. Most plotters work as well (if not better) with the compass rose as with the grid. And most important, if a pilot uses magnetic degrees, he'll be computing in the same language that the helmsman uses. Piloting is complicated enough without two meanings of the word "degree." So we recommend using magnetic degrees, especially to beginning and novice pilots who are facing plenty of other new problems. The one irreducible constant on a boat is that "North" on the compass card will aim at magnetic North. So why not use terminology directed the same way?

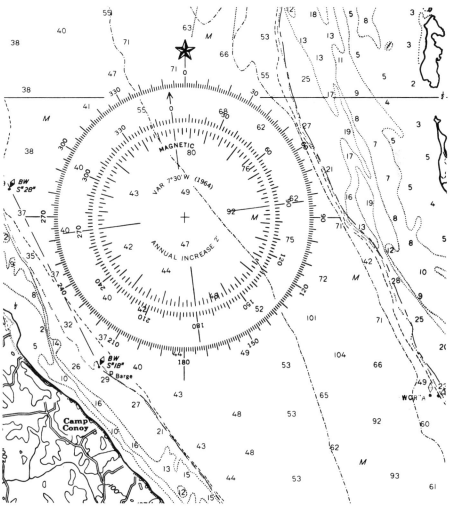

The chart's compass rose shows true directions on the outer circle and magnetic ones on the inner, and the variation is clearly labeled. It's all too easy to use the wrong circle when you're tired or distracted, so double check your calculations.

S.O.P. (Standard Operating Procedure)

Although most of us take to the sea to shed shoreside routines, we must accept the fact that system and procedure play an important role in piloting. In the short run, taking every step the same way and with the same routine will save time and worry (especially when exhaustion crimps the memory); in the long run, establishing and following a piloting S.O.P. will save mistakes, and perhaps a disaster. We provided a good example of this a moment ago: if a pilot sometimes uses magnetic degrees and sometimes uses true degrees, he's inviting confusion.

As a rule of thumb, never make a calculation without consciously considering all relevant factors: variation, deviation, tide and current, leeway (side-slippage), the skill of the helmsman, the eyesight of the person who took the bearing, the possibility of confusion between sighted objects. When providing a course for a helmsman, explain the factors that went into your calculations; otherwise he may think it is his responsibility to compensate for, say, leeway and arbitrarily alter course.

Instructions and reports about courses and bearings must be clearly enunciated by the speaker and acknowledged by the listener. Don't try to talk into the wind. More boats have gotten into trouble due to poor communications than to bad piloting.

Checking and plotting the dead reckoning position regularly is an important S.O.P. In fine weather and open, familiar waters, every 60 minutes may be sufficiently frequent, but if the conditions are difficult and the waters unfamiliar, you should check at 30-minute or even 15-minute intervals. Of course, the faster you're sailing and the more ground you're covering, the more frequently should you check. Calculations should be done on paper, preferably in a special notebook reserved for them, and positions should be clearly marked with a pencil on the chart along with the times.

Course changes and the appearance or passing of key buoys or landmarks should be noted in the log book. If you make a mistake in the log or when doing calculations, don't erase them or throw the paper away. Just cross them out with a line so they are still legible; your "mistake" may turn out to be correct. Keep in mind the slight chance that you (or somebody else, in case you are incapacitated) may have to backtrack through your plot and calculations if the boat gets lost.

In addition, describe in the log any unusual or potentially dangerous occurrences in the unlikely event that you're involved in a Coast Guard inquiry, and log all radio transmissions.

Night sailing especially requires a routine. The skipper or pilot may ask to be awakened whenever another boat is nearby or when the course or wind changes. The request should be in writing in the log book. And the pilot should be careful to brief the crew about upcoming course changes, especially in restricted visibility. The navigator's job is a specialized one, but not so sacred that he or she should feel above explaining it to his shipmates.

The Logbook

The logbook is the boat's diary. It's a written record of the boat's progress and events, with notations for courses, speeds, and other important navigation information. By referring to this written record, the navigator can double-check calculations as well as backtrack out of difficult positions. The log is a handy place to record weather observations such as barometer readings and wind directions and velocities so the crew can keep track of and anticipate long-term weather developments. The logbook also serves as a communication medium between sailors standing different watches who may not have another opportunity to alert their shipmates to problems such as damaged gear and nearby ships. In legal proceedings, the log is an official document admissible as evidence. Finally, the log is where the crew can make observations about informal events on board, for example a good joke or a tasty meal.

This is a page from a logbook the author designed, called *The Norton Sailor's Log* (New York: W.W. Norton, 1987). Note the columns for specific navigational information and weather, the blank column for data of temporary concern, the large spaces for weather and comments, and the easily read graph form for recording barometer readings.

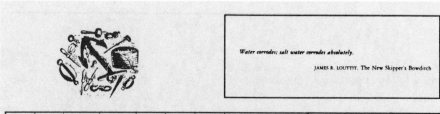

The D.R.

As we saw at the beginning of chapter 10, "dead reckoning" is "deduced reckoning" — "dead" standing for "ded." The dead reckoning (or D.R.) position is where the pilot thinks the boat is located based *solely* on her distance run over a known course. The dead reckoning plot, often simply called "the D.R.," shows a boat's progress from dead reckoning position to dead reckoning position. No bearings — either compass or radio — are required for a D.R. If there is a single bearing on a charted object, the resulting position is called an *estimated position*, and if there are two or more bear-ings, where they cross is called a *fix*. A fix is the most reliable of the three positions. Some authorities define D.R. position as any position other than a fix, thereby including what we are calling estimated position and D.R. position under the same heading. On the other hand, other authorities think it important to distinguish posi-tions plotted with no bearings from positions plotted with one bearing, and we agree. Later we'll look more closely at the estimated position and the fix.

While the fix and the estimated po-sition are potentially more reliable than the D.R. position, the last has the unique virtue of being derived solely from data available on the boat her-self, right in front of the pilot's eyes: course, speed, and the time she's been sailing. It's that simple. While you can always estimate the effects of tidal current, waves, or leeway, the chances of that estimate's being entirely accu-rate are extremely unlikely, so save it until you can plot an estimated posi-tion or a fix. The D.R. plot traces your progress through the water until an estimated position or fix allows you to plot your progress over the ground. While a fix is more definite, it also must always await the opportunity to take accurate bearings. Until that opportunity appears, rely on your D.R.

Distance Run

To compute a distance run, you need to know how fast the boat has been going and for how long. If your boat has a speedometer with a distance-run dial — like an automobile's odometer — then the job is done for you: just read the dial when you start out and read it again when you want to know where you are. But if your boat does not have a distance-run dial, or if the one you have is inaccurate (you should test it from time to time), you must keep careful track of speed and time in order to find out how far you've gone.

When you start out or pass a charted object or make a fix, note and log the time. When you want to make a D.R. plot, note the time again and factor it against the speed. Since knots are

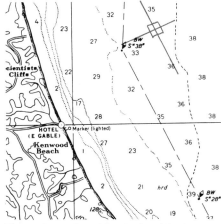

The estimated position (square) is the crossing of a single bearing and the dead reckoning plot.

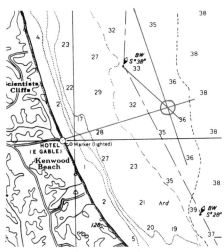

The fix (circle) is the crossing of two or more bearings. It is the most reliable position.

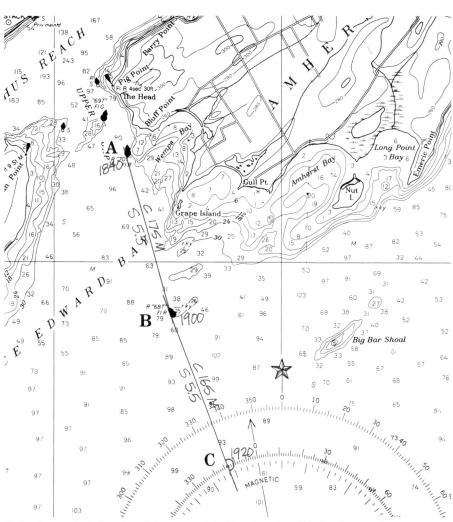

A simple way to determine distance run is to time how long it takes to run a known distance between two charted objects (A and B) and then plot the D.R. (C) at the same time interval using the same distance. Changing current, wind, or sea conditions will lead to inaccuracies, however.

The D.R.

based on 1-hour increments (a knot is 1 nautical mile per hour), these calculations will be simple if the time intervals are hourly or half-hourly, although the mathematics needed to convert minutes into fractions of an hour are not very complicated. You also need to know your average speed during that time interval, and that calculation may itself be fairly complex.

Determining Speed

The average speed used by the pilot is often the helmsman's averaging of the readings on the boat's speedometer. But sometimes the boat may not have a speedometer, or if she does, it may not be trustworthy. (Speedometers are usually less accurate at very low and very high speeds than at moderate speeds of between 3 and 10 knots, and like any electronic device they are vulnerable to malfunctions.)

There are several ways to estimate speed without using a speedometer. In chapter 1 we suggested one: since displacement boats are trapped in the hollow of a single wave when sailing at hull speed, slower speeds may be estimated by counting the number of wave crests between the bow and stern. If there are two crests, she is moving at approximately one-half hull speed; if three, about one-third hull speed; and so on.

A helmsman who knows his boat well can estimate speed about as accurately as a speedometer once he has a frame of reference. We started the 1972 Transatlantic Race from Bermuda to Spain with a broken speedometer. On the second day we measured *Dyna*'s speed by timing how quickly she passed objects in the wa-

ter, and soon the helmsmen's estimates of speed were so accurate that our D.R. was extremely close to positions determined by the sextant. Here's the system we used when we first estimated her speed:

If you know how long it takes for a boat to sail a known distance, you can quickly determine her speed through the water using the Speed/Time/Distance formula. To find speed in knots **(S)**, multiply distance in nautical miles **(D)** by 60, and divide the product by time in minutes **(T)**; or

$$S = \frac{60 \times D}{T}$$

Let's say that your boat is 30 feet long. When her bow is directly alongside (next to) a buoy, the stopwatch is started. As soon as the buoy is alongside the stern, the watch is stopped. It takes this boat 3 seconds to clear the buoy. The problem can be stated this way: "If it takes 3 seconds for a boat to go 30 feet, how fast is she sailing?" Here's the solution:

T (time)
= 3 seconds = 3/60 minute = .05 minute
D (Distance) = 30 feet
= 30/6076 (nautical mile) = .005 nautical mile

Therefore,

$$S = \frac{60 \times .005}{.05} = \frac{.3}{.05} = 6 \text{ knots}$$

Of course any measured distance may be used to determine speed. You may run between two buoys or a lighthouse and a buoy, or you may set up ranges using landmarks on shore so long as the landmarks are also charted. It's best to use fixed objects, since buoys may drag or, in deep water, swing about on their anchor rodes.

You may also use the logarithmic scale on the nautical chart to solve for speed when running over measured distances. Place one divider point on miles run and the other on minutes run, then place the right point on 60. The left point will show the speed. If the distance is in statute miles, the speed will be in miles per hour, and if the distance is in nautical miles, the speed is in knots (*not* "knots per hour,"

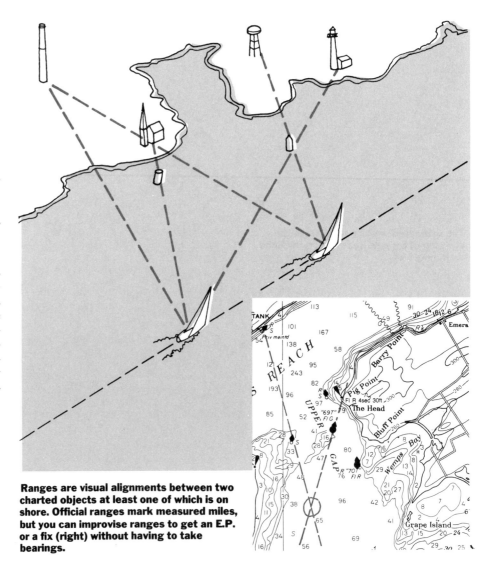

Ranges are visual alignments between two charted objects at least one of which is on shore. Official ranges mark measured miles, but you can improvise ranges to get an E.P. or a fix (right) without having to take bearings.

which is the nautical equivalent to "miles per hour per hour").

The Coast Guard and other agencies have erected ranges to indicate measured miles at various places along the coastline. The ranges and the true course along the measured mile are clearly shown on charts. When running a measured mile, start the stopwatch when the first ranges are in line and stop it when the second ranges line up. Be sure to sail the indicated course (after uncorrecting) in order not to go too far. If it takes 4 minutes 22 seconds to run the measured mile, calculate speed as follows (after converting seconds into decimals):

$$S = \frac{60 \times 1}{4.37} = 13.7 \text{ knots}$$

Measured miles and other fairly long known distances can be helpful in other ways. Sailboats without speedometers can run them under various points of sail to allow their crews time to get used to the feel of sailing at known speeds. And auxiliary sailboats and powerboats can run them at several R.P.M. settings to provide data for a speed table. Combined with fuel consumption figures — which can usually be calculated with an accurate fuel gauge — you can determine optimum fuel-efficient cruising speeds. In every boat there is a point at which increased throttle only brings a small jump in speed along with a large leap in fuel consumption.

Add any favorable current (in knots) or subtract any contrary current to find the speed made good. We'll say more about current in the next chapter.

Determining Distance

Once you know your boat's speed and the time she's been underway, you can move on to calculate the distance run. Once again, the Speed/Time/Distance formula can be used, this time solving for distance. Let's assume that our boat has been averaging 5.5 knots for 35 minutes. How far has she gone? Using the formula

$$D = \frac{S \times T}{60}$$

we enter these values: speed (S) = 5.5 and time (T) = 35. Therefore

$$D = \frac{5.5 \times 35}{60} = \frac{192.5}{60} = 3.2 \text{ miles}$$

Or you can use the logarithmic scale printed on most NOS charts. Place one divider point on 60 and the other on 5.5, then lift the dividers and place the right leg on 35. The number under the other point will be the distance run, 3.2.

Course

For the D.R. you must be able to chart the direction in which the boat has sailed since the last plot or fix. Since no boat stays precisely on course for very long, this is necessarily an average of all the small meanders. Only the helmsman can tell you what that average is. Unfortunately the human desire to please often gets in the way of an honest report, and the helmsman may simply parrot back the course that the pilot told him to steer. This course may not be the accurate average because of helmsman error, wind shifts, obstructions, or other factors. The skipper and navigator must strongly encourage helmsmen to be truthful in their reports; a 6° mistake by a helmsman will cause the D.R. to be inaccurate at a rate of 10 percent, or 1 mile every 10 miles.

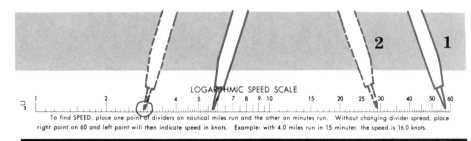

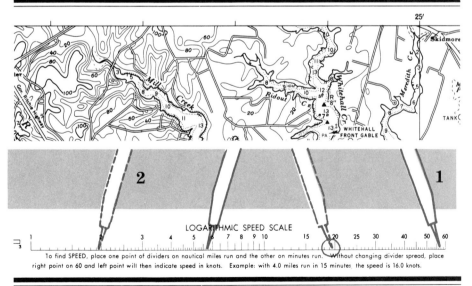

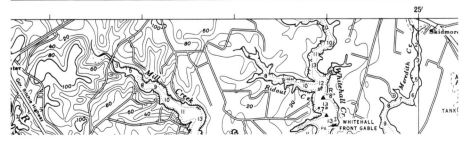

The chart's logarithmic scale can be used with dividers to solve for speed, distance, or time underway. The instructions for determining speed are printed under the scale. To solve for distance, place one point on 60 and the other on the number corresponding to speed, then move the right point to the time interval. To solve for time, place one point on 60 and the other on speed, then move the left point to the distance.

The D.R.

Plotting

With the distance and course now known, the navigator can begin to plot the D.R. Once he knows the course since the last D.R. or fix, the pilot corrects it to magnetic degrees (if there is a deviation table). The calculation should be done in writing and be clearly labeled. Then he plots the course on the chart. If using parallel rulers, he lays one straightedge over the course on the compass rose nearest to his position — being careful to use the inner, magnetic rose. Then he "walks" the rulers across the chart until a straightedge lies over the last position. He draws a fine line from the position approximately the distance the boat has run.

If he's using a course protractor, the navigator makes certain that the correct amount of variation has been added or subtracted before turning the arm to the desired course. Then he aligns the protractor with a meridian of longitude or a parallel of latitude (on Great Lakes Polyconic projections, do not use any meridians other than the center one), with the arm over the last position, and draws the line.

Plotted courses are labeled with the direction in degrees and the average speed. The direction goes above the line, the speed below. For example, the helmsman reports an average course of 165° and an average speed of 5.5 knots. The pilot converts the compass degrees to magnetic, if necessary. (If there is no deviation table, the compass course is the same as magnetic.) The label reads:

$$\frac{C\ 165\ M}{S\ 5.5}$$

"C" stands for course, "M" for magnetic, "S" for speed. Degrees and knots are not marked. If there is deviation, and for some reason the compass course is given instead of the magnetic course — perhaps because the pilot hasn't the time to correct from compass to magnetic — "C" replaces "M." Likewise, if true degrees are used, "T" replaces "M."

Now we know the direction of the course line and can plot the distance run, 3.2 miles. Two scales are available on the chart. One is the marginal scale, which shows the average of all distance scales on the chart. Place the right leg of the dividers on 3 and the left leg on the .8 point on the tenths scale, to the left of 1. The dividers now span 3.2 miles at the chart's average scale. Lift the dividers and place one leg at the departure point and the

other leg on the course line, making a small prick in the paper. Remove the dividers. Make a pencil dot over the prick and enclose it in a half-circle arcing above the line. Label the arc with the time in the 24-hour clock, without the word "hours."

The other and more accurate scale available is the latitude scale on the sides of the chart. Be sure to use the latitude *directly alongside* the course line you are measuring because on

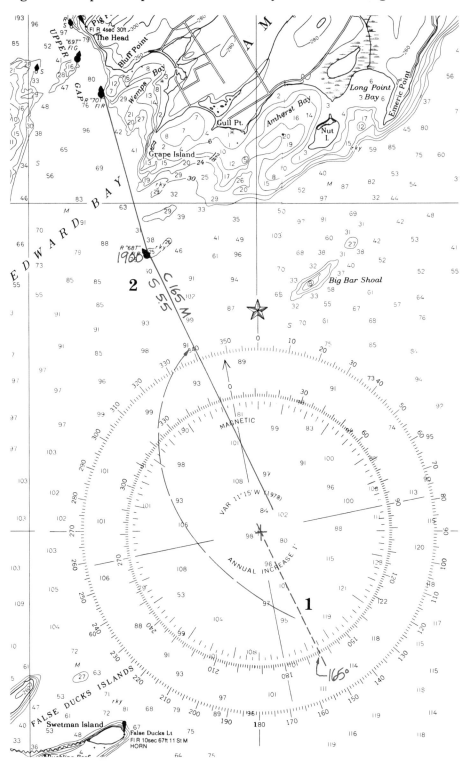

To plot a course, (1) using the plotter find the compass direction on the rose and (2) transfer it as a parallel line running through the departure point, labeling it. Reverse the steps to find the direction of a course already plotted.

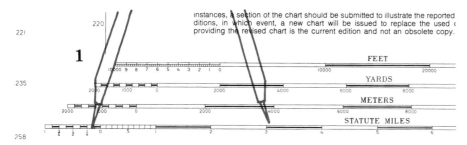

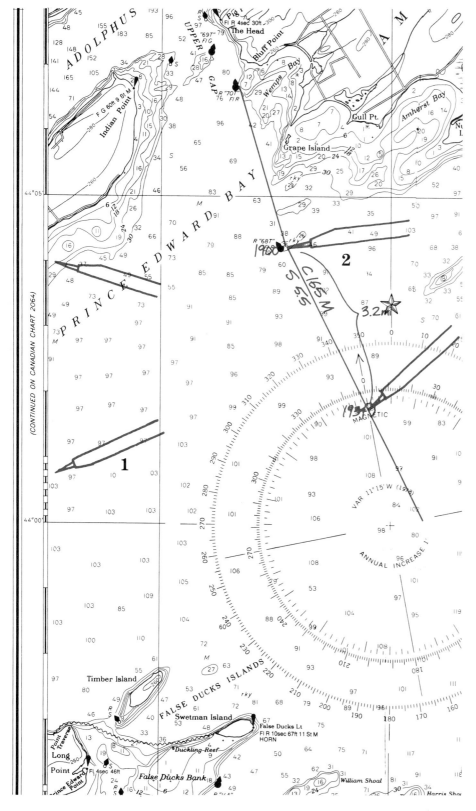

To plot the distance on a plotted course, (1) spread the dividers over the distance using the chart's marginal scale (top) or the latitude scale (side) and (2) transfer the distance to the chart with one leg on the departure point. Label the D.R.

Mercator and Polyconic charts latitude increments vary.

If the distance measured is greater than the span of the dividers, set the dividers at 5 or 10 miles and "walk off" the distance, keeping track mentally. The last bit may be less than the 5- or 10-mile increment, so may be measured on the mileage scale.

Now print "D" and the distance to the right of the "S" notation below the course line.

A D.R. plot will look like this:

$$\frac{C\ 165\ M}{S\ 5.5\qquad D\ 3.2}$$

Special Techniques

A few tricks make the D.R. calculations more versatile or even a little faster. Soon you may be developing your own shortcuts.

The 6-Minute Rule — The main problem when calculating distance run is that you usually must use time intervals of less than an hour. Since time is not figured in units of 100, or decimals, and since we were taught in grade school to calculate in decimals, finding out how much distance you've sailed in 18 or 36 minutes, say, requires some mental gymnastics that a navigator may be too relaxed, tired, or busy to perform accurately.

As it turns out, 0.1 hour is 6 minutes. So whatever distance a boat covers in 6 minutes is equal to 0.1 or one-tenth her speed. Thus a 5-knot boat covers 0.5 nautical miles in 6 minutes and 3 nautical miles in 36 minutes. And a 7-knot boat makes 0.7 miles in 6 minutes and 2.1 miles in 18 minutes.

The Rule of Threes—This rule of thumb allows quick computation of approximate distances run in yards. You must know the speed in knots (not MPH); the speed must be a multiple of 3. Here's the rule: to calculate how far the boat will go in 3 minutes, add two zeroes to the speed. For example, in 3 minutes a boat making 3 knots will go 300 yards; a boat making 6 knots will go 600 yards; and a boat making 9 knots will go 900 yards. Since scales showing yards are printed on NOS charts, this information can be used in plotting. plotting.

Statute miles are used on lake charts, like the one of Eastern Lake Ontario in our examples, while nautical miles (1.15 statute mile) are used on salt-water charts.

The D.R.

The Yards-per-Minute Rule — At certain speeds, boats cover easily remembered distances each minute. These are:

At 3 knots, 100 yards per minute (1/20 or 0.05 mile)
At 6 knots, 200 yards per minute (1/10 or 0.1 mile)
At 9 knots, 300 yards per minute (3/20 or 0.15 mile)
At 12 knots, 400 yards per minute (1/5 or 0.20 mile)
At 15 knots, 500 yards per minute (1/4 or 0.25 mile)

Occasionally a navigator must calculate how fast to go to reach his destination. For example, he may want to arrive at a channel before the tide becomes unfavorable, or at a canal lock before it closes. In those cases he wants to know how fast he should sail (or how slowly, for sometimes he may slow down in order not to reach his destination too early). The 6-Minute Rule and the Yards-per-Minute Rule can be used to solve this problem, since if the distance to be sailed is known, the navigator can factor in the time available in order to find the required speed. For instance, in 48 minutes the tide becomes favorable at a narrow channel 5.5 miles ahead. Using the 6-Minute Rule to determine how fast he should sail to get there exactly at the tide change, the navigator first divides 48 by 6 to get 8, which he divides into 5.5. The result, 0.7, is the distance he must cover every 6 minutes, or 0.1 hour. To find the optimum speed, then, he multiplies 0.7 by 10. The boat should average 7 knots. If she averages 8 knots, she'll get there too early and be set back by contrary current; if she averages only 6 knots, she'll arrive too late to take full advantage of the favorable current. You may also use the Speed/Time/Distance formula, solving for Speed (S) as shown above.

"Running Out Your Time"

Sometimes you'll need to know how long it will take to cover a known distance at a known speed. Our old friend the Speed/Time/Distance formula can be used to solve this problem. To find time in minutes **(T)**, multiply distance in nautical or statute miles **(D)** by 60 and then divide by speed in knots or miles per hour **(S)**; or

$$T = \frac{60 \times D}{S}$$

For example, heading out of a Maine harbor in a dense fog, the navigator takes his departure from (passes) a buoy at 1032 hours and sets a course for another buoy 4.1 miles distant. Anticipating that he'll never be able to see the second buoy through the peasoup fog, he wants to know how long it will take to reach the buoy at a speed of 6.3 knots. Using the Speed/Time/Distance formula to solve for time, **S** = 6.3 and **D** = 4.1. So

$$T = \frac{60 \times 4.1}{6.3} = \frac{246}{6.3} = 39 \text{ minutes}$$

Adding 39 minutes to 1032 hours, he determines that the boat will pass the second buoy at 1111 hours, or 11:11

A.M., when he will "run out his time."

The chart's logarithmic scale can also be used to solve for time. Place the right divider leg on 60 and the left one on the speed, then pick up the dividers and place the left leg on the distance. The right leg will now be on the amount of time needed to cover the distance.

Experienced navigators use stopwatches when running out their time in poor visibility, when an error of a few seconds can be dangerous.

Speed/Time/Distance Calculators

If you lack the interest or mathematical confidence needed to tackle these relatively simple formulas, buy a Speed/Time/Distance calculator at your chandlery. This is nothing more than an old-fashioned circular slide rule that includes a lot of helpful information besides Speed/Time/Distance solutions.

In addition, some electronic calculators have been programmed to solve these problems with the push of a couple of buttons.

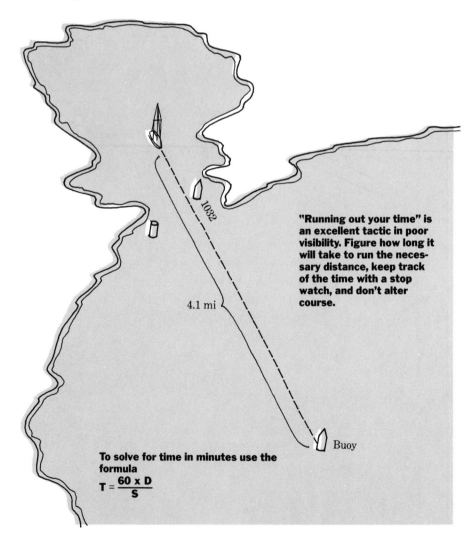

1032

4.1 mi

"Running out your time" is an excellent tactic in poor visibility. Figure how long it will take to run the necessary distance, keep track of the time with a stop watch, and don't alter course.

Buoy

To solve for time in minutes use the formula
$$T = \frac{60 \times D}{S}$$

Precalculating the Course

cause it's based on the only known indicators sitting right there in front of the navigator's eyes: the boat's course and the boat's distance run. The estimated position (abbreviated E.P.) is a kind of continuous check on the D.R. until a fix can be taken. And all courses and positions are plotted relative to the TR, the straight line between the departure and destination.

The calculated course is a combination of several factors. The most im-

portant, of course, is the TR, or the rhumb line to the destination. Once that is calculated and written down, all forces affecting the boat's progress to the destination are analyzed and

The D.R. plot is a pictorial account of the boat's progress between fixes based on regular D.R. and E.P. determinations.

When the navigator works at figuring a course, he has one important goal in mind: to get to the destination as quickly and as safely as possible. Sometimes this calculation is extremely easy. On the chart, the navigator lays the edge of the plotter along the imaginary line that runs from the point of departure to the destination, and using the chart rose, computes its magnetic angle. This rhumb-line course is called the intended track, or track line (abbreviated TR). The navigator tells the helmsman to sail the TR and, presumably, the boat eventually reaches her destination without deviating from it.

That, at least, is what happens in the best of all possible worlds when the helmsman steers with pinpoint precision and when there are no natural forces pushing the boat to one side or another of her TR. But as you can probably guess, this is rarely the case. Waves, wind, tidal current, leeway, and helmsman error can pull or push the boat far off the TR. Very rarely can a TR longer than 5 miles be set without some compensation for one or more of these forces.

Besides establishing the TR — the direct course from departure to destination — the navigator has four other jobs:

1. He must precalculate a compass course that takes natural forces and errors into account.
2. While the boat is underway, he must plot a D.R. based solely on speed and heading.
3. He must *estimate the boat's position* based on the best available evidence, which usually means a single bearing.
4. And when possible, he must *fix the boat's position* with two or more bearings.

This seems complicated, but actually it's quite simple. Between fixes — the most reliable type of position determination — the navigator keeps track of the boat's position using the D.R. and estimated positions. As we saw earlier, the D.R. is important be-

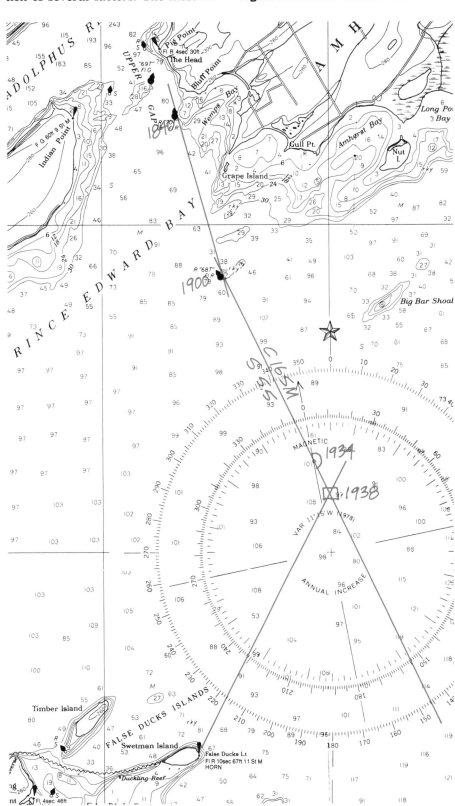

Precalculating The Course

added to or subtracted from the TR. The major forces are relatively simple to calculate. Sometimes they take the form of an angle and at other times they are shown as vectors, or force arrows.

Leeway is side-slippage. While keels, centerboards, and rudders absorb or redirect most of the side force, there usually is some leeway. It ranges between 2° for highly efficient racing boats sailing in smooth water to 20° for cruising sailboats beating into a gale. If leeway is to port, it is subtracted from the TR; if to starboard, it is added to it.

Helmsman error may be minimal with an America's Cup-winning skipper, but most of us are not that competent. If the helmsman is distracted by talking, eating, sightseeing, or daydreaming, the boat will wander and her meandering wake will tell the navigator that the calculated course is not being sailed. Perhaps a gentle reminder will bring the helmsman back to his responsibilities; maybe somebody else should steer. If factors other than boredom are driving the boat off course, a good helmsman will report them to the navigator. For example, in addition to leeway, most boats are pushed about 10° below course when a strong wind and large sea are abeam. If the navigator has not compensated for this large side force, and said so, he should be notified immediately. Helmsman error can be to either side of the TR.

Current takes two forms, tidal and wind-driven, and both are present on almost all bodies of salt water and on some large lakes. Unlike leeway and helmsman error, current can set the boat forward and backward as well as to the side. Because current calculation is complicated and involves forces not intrinsic to the boat herself, we'll examine it at length in chapter 9.

The navigator reduces these errors to degrees and applies them to the TR. For example,
TR = 168°
Predicted leeway = 3° to starboard
Predicted helmsman error = 4° to port
Predicted current effect = 4° to starboard
The total effect, then, is 3° to starboard, which is added to the TR (a port effect is subtracted). The effective course is 171°, so to compensate the pilot orders a compass course 3° the other side of the TR, or 165°. He knows full well that while this course seems to aim the boat to port of her destination, the various forces involved will take her to her destination. Another way of saying this is that her course through the water will be 165° and that other forces will take her on a course over the ground of 168°. This course over the ground is called the

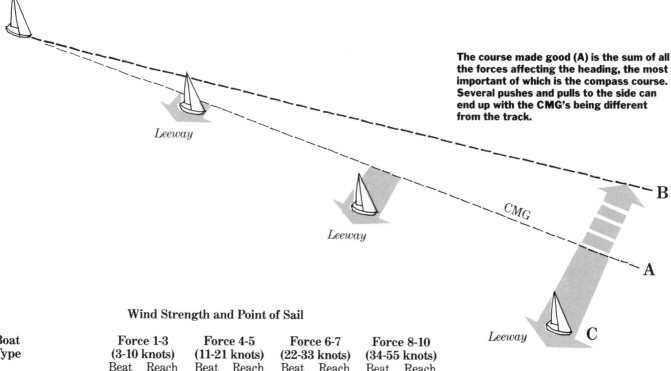

The course made good (A) is the sum of all the forces affecting the heading, the most important of which is the compass course. Several pushes and pulls to the side can end up with the CMG's being different from the track.

The boat will make leeway (C) at an angle determined by her type and the conditions.

To make good the desired course, compensate for leeway by steering to the other side (B).

Wind Strength and Point of Sail

Boat Type	Force 1-3 (3-10 knots)		Force 4-5 (11-21 knots)		Force 6-7 (22-33 knots)		Force 8-10 (34-55 knots)	
	Beat	Reach	Beat	Reach	Beat	Reach	Beat	Reach
1. Shallow-keel cruising sailboat	10°	5°	8°	4°	12°	10°	20°	12°
2. Deep-keel racer-cruiser sailboat	6°	4°	4°	2°	6°	4°	12°	6°
3. Large cruising sailboat								
Under power	4°	2°	6°	4°	10°	8°	20°	12°
Under sail	10°	4°	8°	4°	12°	12°	20°	15°

Approximate leeway angles (including surface drift) for various types of boats. (Partially derived from Bruce Fraser, *Weekend Navigator*, published by John de Graff, Inc., 1981.) "Beat" indicates close-hauled or close-reaching course. "Reach" indicates beam or broad reach. Leeway on runs is negligible.

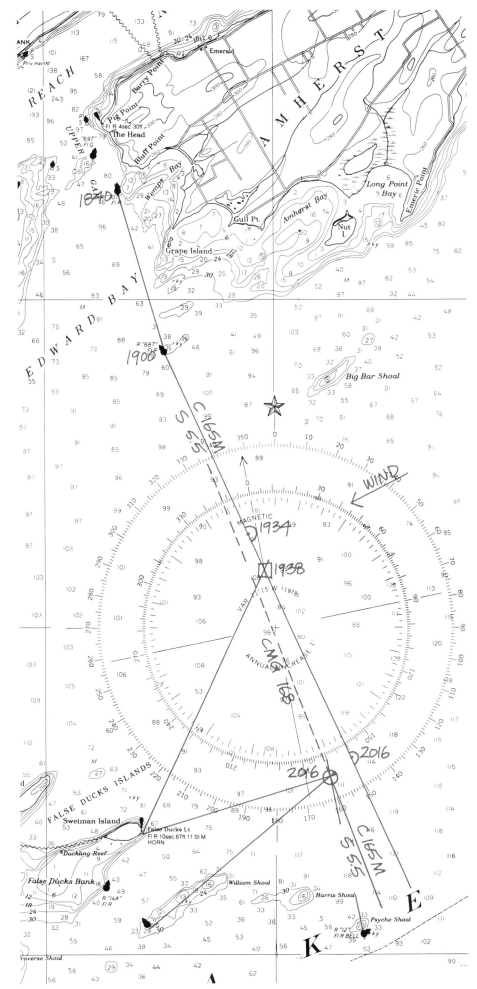

course made good, or CMG.

Updating the D.R.

Having calculated the compass course (or course through the water) that, combined with the forces and errors, will result in a course made good (or course over the ground) identical to the TR, the navigator now must start to keep track of the boat's position. Until he can take a fix, the D.R. is the most reliable and important plot. In our example, the D.R. should be on a line running at 165°, 3° to the left of the TR, even though the navigator is fairly sure that the various side forces are pushing her along on the TR. The navigator regularly brings the line up to date using the distance run since the last plot.

Anticipating helmsman error, current, and leeway with a total effect of 3° to starboard, the pilot orders a compass course of 165°, or 3° to port of the track of 168°. He updates the D.R. and takes an E.P., using the compass course until he can get a fix (A). The fix shows that his predictions were correct and that the course made good was 168°. From this new point of departure, the course remains 165° because the side effects still apply.

Estimating Positions Using One Line of Position

From time to time a navigator may come across evidence indicating that the boat is or is not on the D.R. Of course he knows full well that she should *not* be on the D.R. since forces and errors are pushing the boat to one side. But he cannot estimate the correct position until he has sound evidence. It's not enough that he has *predicted* leeway, steering, and current forces. There must be *evidence* that those predictions are true.

The best evidence to use in estimating a position is a compass bearing on a charted object, such as a buoy or a lighthouse. This bearing is called a line of position (LOP), which means that the boat is somewhere on the line or bearing. The *American Practical Navigator* defines a line of position as "a line . . . on some point of which the vessel may be presumed to be located, as a result of observation or measurement." Being on a line of position is like standing on a long road that has no identifiable cross streets: you know you're somewhere on the road, but not whether you're at its beginning, its middle, or its end. Once you discover a cross street, you're on the equivalent of two lines of position, and so are *fixed*, assuming that this intersection is mapped.

An LOP can be straight — typically, a compass bearing to or from a buoy, lighthouse, or charted landmark, or a range between two charted landmarks. An LOP can also be curved — a circle of known distance from an object — and therefore called a circle of position (see chapter 12). In each case the LOP must be based on an angular or distance measurement from a charted object. An LOP is labeled

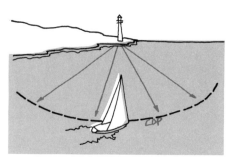

A circle of position (COP) is an arc that has a known radius from a charted object. Arc B, with a radius of 4.5 miles, is a COP in the chart segment below.

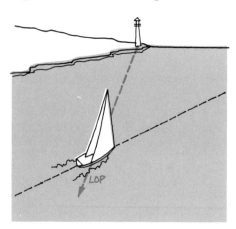

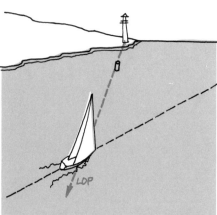

A line of position (LOP) is a single compass bearing or range line to a charted object. On the chart segment (right) line A is an LOP.

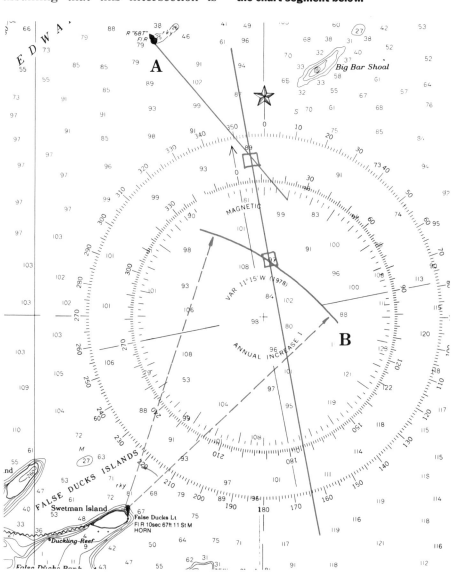

with the time of sighting above the drawn line and with the magnetic bearing below the line. Don't draw the line all the way across the chart; simply indicate clearly what object the LOP is based on and make the line long enough to cross your probable position.

After taking the bearing and marking it with a short line on the chart, update the D.R. plot. Sometimes the bearing and the D.R. position intersect. If so, draw a small square around the intersection to indicate an estimated position (E.P.). Conceivably, the boat is on the LOP either above or below the D.R., but the rule of thumb is to locate estimated positions as near as possible to dead reckoning positions.

If the LOP crosses the D.R. line behind or ahead of the D.R. position, once again the E.P. square is drawn where the LOP is closest to the D.R. position. To find the E.P., place the protractor base line over the LOP and slide it back and forth until the vertical 90° line passes through the D.R.

Mark the LOP at that place and draw the square around it.

The E.P. is not a fix! Keep making the D.R. plot along the original D.R. line. The E.P. is not entirely reliable mainly because a single LOP is not reliable. Even with an accuracy of ±5°, which is fairly good in many conditions, an LOP only indicates an area of location. Of course this can be valuable because an LOP shows that you are *not* in every other area on the

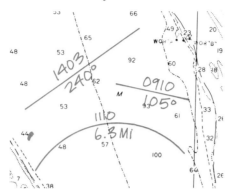

LOPs and COPs are labeled or if the charted object is clearly indicated, they are left without labels.

chart, and when a navigator is close to land in poor visibility, he's eager to avoid large portions of sea and land. But continue to base your piloting decisions on your D.R. using the E.P. as a guide until you can take a fix.

Whatever the evidence and its effect on the estimated position, the navigator is faced with a dilemma if the E.P. is far off the track. Should he change the compass course? Or should he stay with the original compass course and keep the D.R. and mark E.P.s based on this evidence? In difficult conditions, with strong winds and currents and limited visibility, the navigator should stick to his guns and his original course, meanwhile keeping an E.P. plot based on the new data, keeping the D.R., and hoping for a fix soon. In placid conditions on short passages the navigator may feel safe altering the compass course based on the E.P.

The E.P.'s Value

Too many navigators forget that the E.P. can be an extremely helpful tool. Maybe this is because they place so much faith (too much, sometimes) in the accuracy of fixes. It's much wiser to treat a fix not as a pinpoint but as an area of position.

While the area of possible error in an E.P. is greater than that in a good fix, an E.P. has two real advantages. First, it can help a navigator find out where the boat is *not*, and finding out where you are not is at least half of navigating. Second, since only one object and bearing are required, there are many more potential E.P.s than fixes, which need at least two objects and bearings.

No matter how many bearings you take, try to use lighthouses and other permanently fixed objects. Buoy locations can be shifted by the Coast Guard or by tidal currents.

If the D.R. and the E.P. coincide, simply draw a box and label it with the time (A). If the E.P. falls ahead of or behind the D.R., draw a box around the LOP where it is closest to the D.R. position (B); this will be where a line from the D.R. meets the LOP at a right angle. Here the LOPs are not labeled since the charted object is clear.

Fixing Positions Using Lines of Position

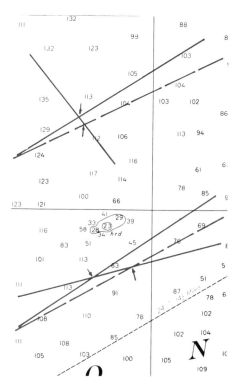

If the estimated position is where you think you *might* be based on one piece of evidence, a fix is where you almost *certainly* are, based on two or more pieces of evidence. The fix is a position that is almost absolutely certain. If your boat is tied up to a wharf that is clearly shown on a chart, her position is fixed. If she's anchored next to a lighthouse, her position is fixed. If she's sailing by a light tower, her position is fixed. And if she's located where reliable bearings can be taken on the wharf, the lighthouse, and the light tower, she is fixed where those lines cross. She is *not* considered fixed when lying near a nun or can, because buoys can drift; but she may be considered fixed where lines of position to three buoys cross at a pinpoint, because it's unlikely that all three buoys have drifted far. The most common type of fix is a position derived from two or more reliable lines of position or circles of position, based on bearings to or distances from charted objects, or on bearings to radio stations, or on signals sent between Loran stations. (We'll discuss circles of position in chapter 12 and electronic navigation in chapter 13.)

Bearings used to compute a fix should be taken as near to simultaneously as possible over the cockpit compass or with a hand bearing compass. In rough weather or poor visibility, cutting a bearing over a compass may be inaccurate by as much as ±10° and even in ideal conditions a 5-inch compass cannot be read more accurately than ±2°. A hand bearing compass (with its own deviation table) should be used when taking important "make or break" bearings. If a hand bearing compass is not aboard, take the bearing by steering directly at the object (sighting it down the centerline) and reading the heading on the cockpit compass's forward lubber's line.

Bearings should be as broad as possible, since narrow intersections can cause large errors. If two bearings are taken, they should cross at an angle no narrower than about 30°; 90° is the optimum angle of intersection. Three bearings should cross at 60° angles and at no less than 30°. Given a choice, it's always safer to use two excellent bearings crossing at right angles than three unreliable bearings crossing at shallow angles.

Ideally, three or more bearings should intersect at a point, but usually they form a small triangle (sometimes

When two LOPs cross at near-right angles (top), an error makes little difference, but shallow angles can lead to large errors.

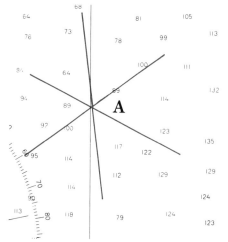

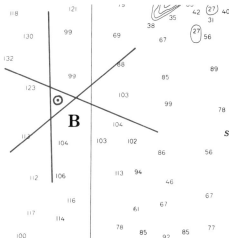

Rarely will three bearings intersect at a point (A). More likely they will outline a triangle called a cocked hat (B). If the hat is small and the bearings are equally reliable, draw the fix circle in the middle.

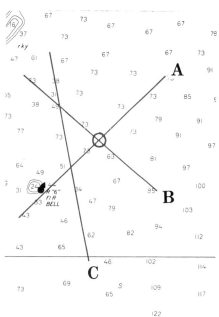

If the cocked hat is large, throw out the least reliable bearing (C).

called a "cocked hat"). If the triangle is larger than about ½ mile (or about 1 mile in rough conditions, when scalpel-sharp bearings are hard to come by), the bearings should be considered untrustworthy and taken again. If the triangle remains large, consider it an area of uncertainty rather than a fix. Plot the course using the two most reliable bearings rather than the center, as you would with a small triangle of intersection.

If you're fairly sure where you are before taking bearings, it's best to pick out the objects on the chart that will give you the best angles and then take the bearings. Sometimes you'll even be able to predict the bearings. But if you're not at all sure of your position, it's better to look around and find objects that make good angles, take bearings, then locate them and plot the LOPs on the chart.

The label for a fix is a circle around a dot, with the time of the fix using the 24-hour clock. If the fix is based partly or wholly on radio bearings, write "RDF Fix" next to the circle and time; it it's based on Loran readings, write "LFix."

The Running Fix

The standard fix that we have just described is based on two or more near-simultaneous bearings. Quite frequently, though, only one object is in sight to take a bearing on; in that case the navigator uses a technique called "advancing the bearing" to take a special type of fix called the running fix. What he does is take successive bearings on the same object, then move them along his track so that, in effect, LOPs from the same object are crossed with each other. Though not as reliable as the standard fix, the running fix is still valuable.

To advance a bearing after plotting it on a chart, draw a line parallel to it through the boat's D.R. track, making the distance between the first LOP and the advanced LOP equal to the distance run. Label the advanced LOP with the times both of the original bearing (for ready reference) and of the advancement, and with the compass bearing in degrees. When advancing a bearing for a running fix, be sure to compute any course changes and current effects as you calculate.

Simply advancing the LOP provides a bearing for a new E.P. on the D.R. track. To turn this E.P. into a running fix, take another bearing on the original object and cross it with the advanced LOP. Circle the intersection and label it "R Fix." Alternatively, cross the advanced LOP with a bearing on a second charted object; again label the intersection "R Fix."

Circles of position (covered in chapter 12) show distances from charted objects and may also be advanced to make a running fix.

In all cases, a running fix's accuracy lies somewhere between the near-certainty of a standard fix and the mixed reliability of an estimated position. Use it if you must, but use it with caution.

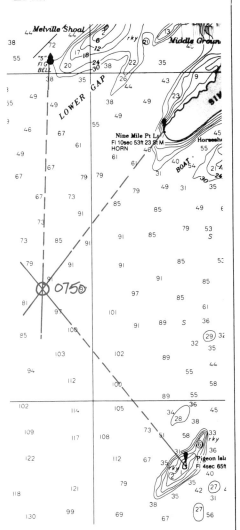

Lable the fix with a circle and the time.

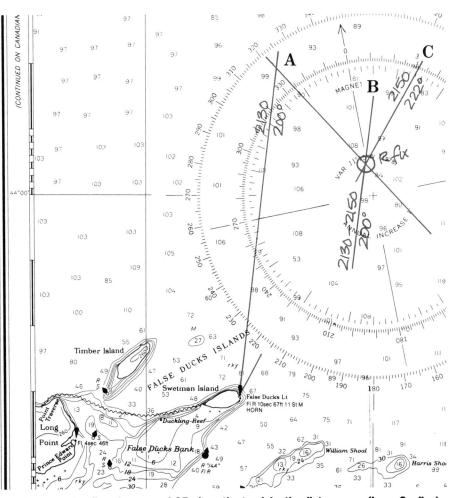

To take a running fix, advance an LOP along the track by the distance run (here, 2 miles) and take another bearing either on the same object or on another object. Here, A is the first bearing, B is the advanced bearing, and C is the new bearing.

255

Piloting on Indirect Courses

So far we've been talking about direct courses from departure to destination. Sometimes, however, the wind isn't very cooperative. You may have to beat to windward to your destination on a series of legs, and at no time will you be sailing right at your destination. There are also times when a strong following wind or sea makes running dead before it dangerous; in those conditions it may be safer to sail or power with wind and waves coming slightly over the quarter on a broad reach, jibing from time to time to stay near the rhumb line.

Keeping track of position on such indirect courses is no different from normal piloting, so long as the plot is updated at every tack or jibe. In undemanding conditions, keeping a D.R. plot and figuring an estimated position (E.P.) just before each tack or jibe should be sufficient. When estimating leeway and helmsman error, remember that both are greatest when close-hauled or in waves. However, if the visibility is limited, the wind and sea are fierce, or the waters are dangerous, do not alter course until you have made a reliable fix, if at all possible.

If fixes are impossible, limit the variables by sailing an equal time or distance on each tack so you stay roughly the same distance from the rhumb line on either side. Unfortunately this works only when the destination is dead to windward and the rhumb line bisects the tacking angle.

Sail the Longest Leg First

If the course is indirect but not a dead beat to windward (either because the wind is slightly off to one side or because the waves run at an angle), the boat will sail on one tack longer than she sails on the other. A sound rule of thumb for this situation is to sail the longest tack first. This will take you closest to your destination and will minimize the effects of a shift in wind or wave direction. An important exception to this rule is to take the shortest tack earliest if it presents a good opportunity for a fix in poor visibility, for knowing where you are is a

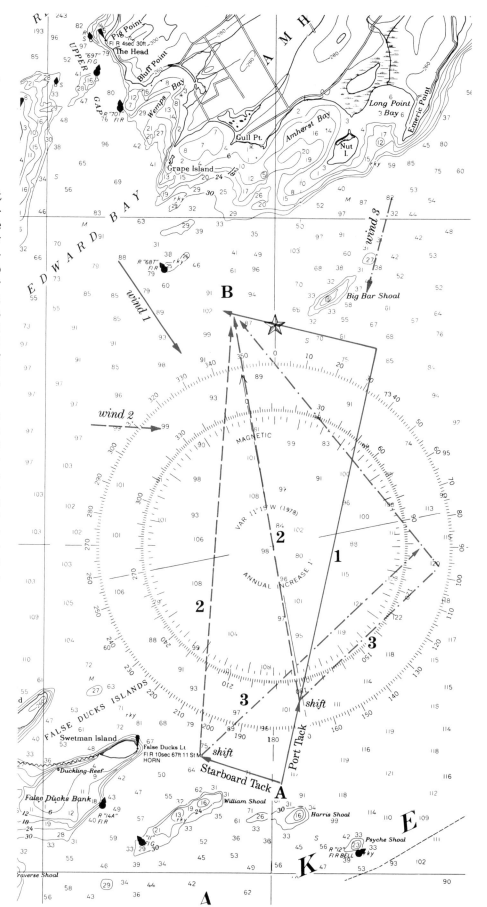

The main reason to sail the longest leg of an indirect course first is that it puts you in the best position to take advantage of wind shifts. Here, to get to B from A, the boat first sails on a long port tack. If the wind backs (shifts counterclockwise) she is lifted up to the mark and sails the shortest possible distance. If it veers (shifts clockwise), she tacks on the header and again sails the shortest distance. A boat starting out on starboard tack, however, will sail the same distance only if the wind does not shift; otherwise, she will waste all the distance she covers on starboard tack before the shift.

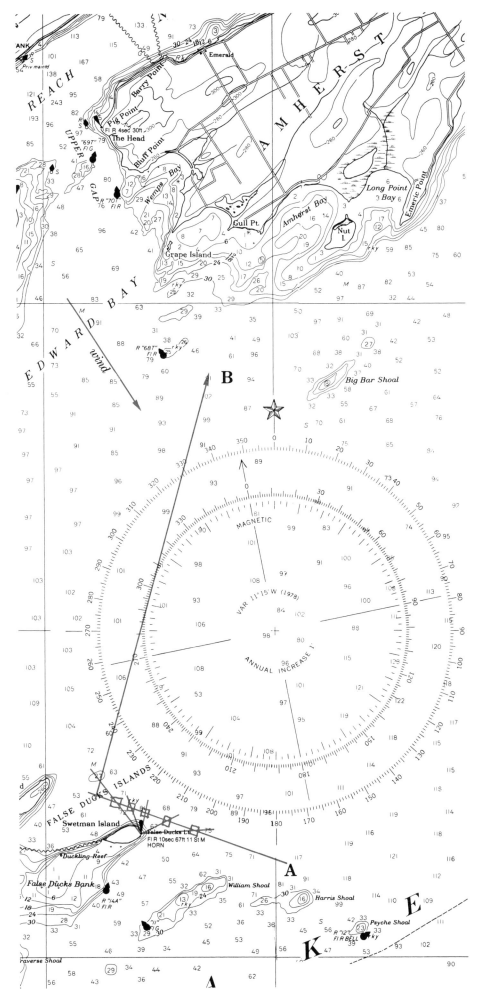

higher priority than sailing an efficient course.

Calculating Distance Run on Indirect Courses

Obviously an indirect course is longer than a rhumb line. An electronic calculator programmed with trigonometric functions can solve two formulas to find distance sailed when tacking upwind or when sailing an indirect course downwind (also called tacking downwind).

First, to find the distance traveled when sailing dead to windward, when the rhumb line bisects the tacking angle:

$$D = \frac{200\,(\sin \text{ angle of attack})}{(\sin \text{ tacking angle})}$$

where **D** = a percentage to be multiplied against the rhumb line distance to find distance sailed; tacking angle = angle between port and starboard tacks (usually 75° to 95°); and angle of attack = the angle to the true wind, or one-half the tacking angle. A tacking angle of 90° increases the distance sailed by about 45 percent of the rhumb-line distance.

Tacking downwind — or sailing an indirect course when running — also increases the distance sailed. The following formula determines actual distance sailed if the wind is the exact reciprocal of the course:

$$D = \frac{2 \times DL \times \sin A}{\sin (2A)}$$

where **D** = the distance sailed in miles; **DL** = the rhumb-line distance; and **A** = the angle between the rhumb-line course and the actual course.

The second formula may be helpful to racing sailors who want to know if heading up from a dead run to a broad reach will increase speed sufficiently to compensate for the added distance sailed. A dead run is the slowest point of downwind sailing, as well as the most dangerous in heavy weather with the constant threat of an accidental jibe.

The exception to the rule of sailing the longest leg first is when it violates the rule of always sailing toward bright aids to navigation in poor visibility. In fog or rain, sail toward a lighthouse even if it is on the shorter leg.

Review Quiz

Solve plotting problems on the charts printed here using a plotter on the compass roses and dividers on the latitude scale on the left margin. Courses and bearings are in magnetic degrees, distances are in nautical miles, and speeds are in knots. Solutions may be found after the Index.

1. What is the magnetic course from False Ducks Lt. (on Swetman Island) to buoy R"70T" FlR (off Bluff Point)?

A. 358°

B. 009°

C. 189°

2. A boat runs from False Ducks Lt. to buoy "70T" FlR and then back to False Ducks Lt. On the first run she averages 5.5 knots and reaches the buoy in 1 hour 50 minutes; she makes the second run in 2 hours 15 minutes. What is the approximate distance between the two objects? What is the average speed on the second run?

A. 11 miles; 5 knots

B. 10 miles; 4.4 knots

3. A boat on a course of 176° passes buoy R"70T" FlR at 1842 hours (6:42 P.M.). At 1900 hours, she passes buoy R"68T" FlR. What is her average speed?

A. 8.7 knots

B. 5.5 knots

C. Not enough information is available

4. In a fog, a boat making 4 knots on a course of 345° passes buoy R"68T" FlR at 1003 hours (10:03 A.M.). At what time should she pass the buoy off Indian Point?

A. 1103 hours

B. 1054 hours

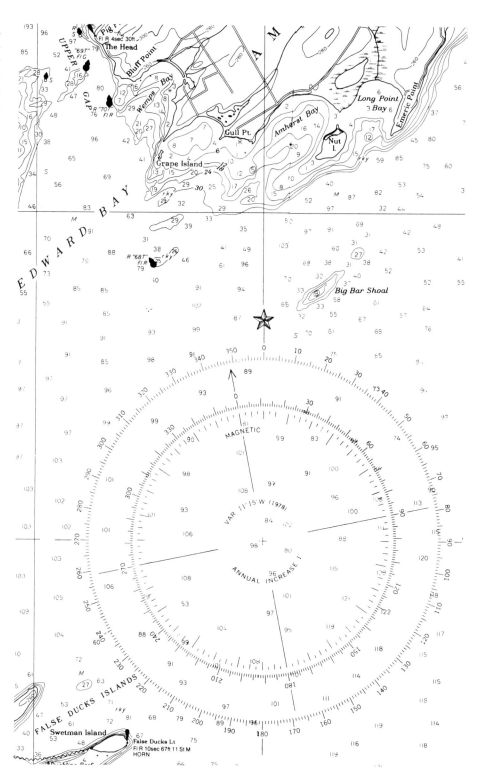

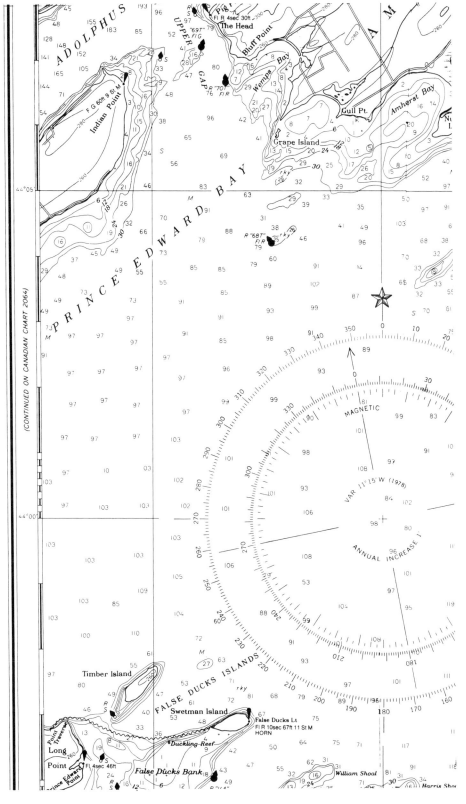

5. A shallow-draft cruising sailboat under sail passes buoy "69T" FlG on a course of 180°, which will take her 1 mile East of Swetman Island. However, a 25-knot East wind quickly comes up. How much leeway, and in which direction, should her navigator anticipate? What course should be sailed to compensate for leeway so she sails East of Swetman Island?

A. 10-12° leeway to the West; compensated course 168°

B. 10-12° leeway to the East; no compensation

6. What type of position is shown at "1934" on page 247? What type would it be if there were an LOP to False Ducks Lt.? If there were an LOP to False Ducks and another LOP to Indian Point Lt.?

A. An estimated position, a fix, and a dead reckoning position

B. A dead reckoning position, a fix, and an estimated position

C. A dead reckoning position, an estimated position, and a fix

7. From R"68T" FlR, your boat sails at 6 knots on a course of 230°. At 1400, False Ducks Lt. bears 180°. At 1412 hours, it bears 160°. How could you fix her position without taking another bearing? From this position, what are the bearing and range to the Fl 4sec lighthouse on Prince Edward Point?

A. This position can only be estimated; bearing 205°, range 6.2 miles

B. With a running fix; bearing 195°, range 4.5 miles

8. Beating into a South-Southeast wind (compass direction 158°), you sail out of Upper Gap late in the afternoon. Your destination is False Ducks Lt. Which tack should you sail on first?

A. It doesn't matter

B. Starboard tack

C. Port tack

Chapter 12
Special Piloting Techniques

Anybody who has sailed through a thick fog, across a swift tidal current, or along a rocky, irregular shoreline guarded by few aids to navigation knows the meaning of the word "anxiety." From moment to moment, a pilot in these tricky situations may not know where he is, much less where his course will take him. While many of us go to sea in quest of adventure, there are times when we would prefer less of it, thank you, and more certainty.

It's in times like these when a good pilot earns his keep. He must stay calm while examining all available evidence, carefully figuring his calculations, and attempting to reduce each of the many variables down to the narrow edge of probability. He must keep up the dead reckoning plot assiduously and not turn down any chance for getting a fix. While he should present a mien of confident optimism to his shipmates, he must be honest with them about their dilemma. False pretense and idle egotism have no place on board when the navigation becomes uncertain. It is much healthier for a pilot to admit a mistake and turn the boat around than allow false pride to run her up on a reef.

This chapter will describe some special skills that the pilot can use when poor visibility, rough weather, or a paucity of aids to navigation gets in the way of making optimum pinpoint fixes. We'll show several ways to estimate and fix your position using only one buoy, and how to calculate course alterations to avoid hazards ahead or to compensate for currents. Finally, we'll provide some hints and guidelines for safe piloting.

A circle of position, linking points equidistant from a charted object, is one of the ingredients of a successful fix using only one aid to navigation. Be sure to use the scale at the same latitude as the D.R. position.

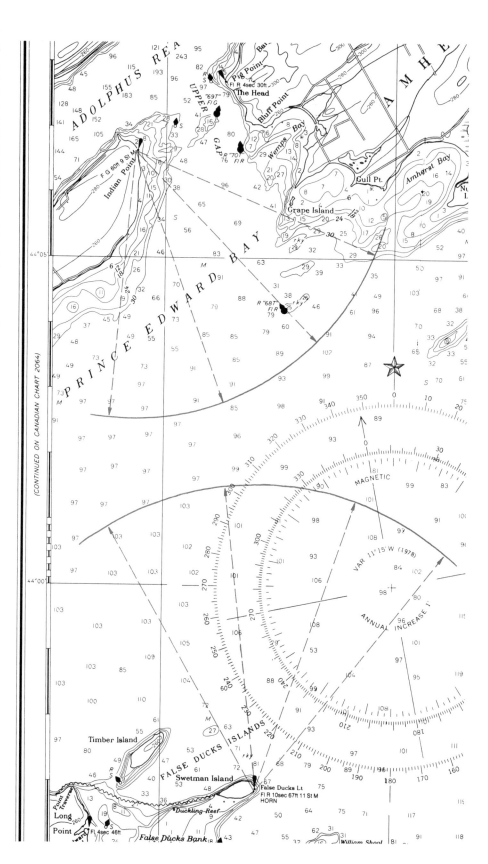

Position Finding with One Aid: Distance Off

We saw in chapter 11 how to make a running fix by using two bearings on the same object, advancing the first LOP along the boat's track until it intercepts the second. There are several other ingenious ways to find your position using only one aid or landmark. They fall under the general category of *distance off*. By using simple trigonometry (in almost every case, already precalculated), you can convert a single bearing and your distance run into a number that shows how far offshore you are sailing — that's the distance off part — and more important, into a reliable estimated position or fix. The feature common to all these techniques is the concept of the circle of position.

Circle of Position (COP)

In chapter 11 we described lines of position (LOP) — bearings to or from charted objects. An LOP, as the name suggests, is a straight line. A circle of position (COP) is a circle, and every object on its circumference is equidistant from the center of the circle.

Using any of the techniques described below, determine the distance off from the sighted object either by taking a series of bearings on it, by measuring a vertical angle with a sextant, or by some other means. The distance off is the radius of the circle of position. Spread your drawing compass a distance equal to the distance off on the chart's side latitude scale exactly left or right of the object. Then place the point of the compass on the object and draw an arc of the COP near your D.R. position. If you are completely lost you may have to draw the entire circle, or at least an arc sufficiently long to cover the body of water.

Doubling the Relative Bow Bearing

This method for finding distance off and making a one-aid fix requires you to take two bearings on the aid as you approach it on a steady course. These are *relative* bearings — angles between the bow and the aid — so you can use a pelorus or the side lubber's lines on any accurate compass. At the moment that the second bearing is exactly twice the first bearing, the distance off (from the boat to the sighted object) equals the distance run between the times of the two bearings. This is because the distance run, the distance off, and the distance from the object to the boat at the moment of the first bearing form three sides of an isosceles triangle, whose two equal sides are the distance off and the distance run.

The easiest pair of relative bearings to work with is 45° and 90°, since they can readily be taken using the two side lubber's lines on the normal sailboat compass. When the aid bears 45° off the bow, start your stopwatch or read the log. When the object is dead abeam at 90° relative, stop the watch and, using the Speed/Time/Distance formula (see chapter 11), calculate the distance run or read the log. At that moment the boat is on a circle of position from the object, its radius equal to the distance run. Where the COP crosses the D.R. track, you have an estimated position. A 45°/90° combination is called a "bow and beam" bearing.

To fix your position using this method, take a compass bearing on the object when the bearing is doubled. That compass bearing forms a line of position. Where the LOP and the COP cross, you have a fix.

When taking the first bearing, make it as wide as possible — preferably between 30° and 45° (meaning that the second bearing will be 60° to 90°). Any error will have a greater effect if the relative angle is shallow.

Predicting Distance Off

A serious drawback of most doubled bearings is that they only tell you distance off at the time of the second bearing. Quite frequently you want to be able to predict distance off when the sighted object is abeam. This may be because you're worried about approaching it too closely; many light-

The simplest way to determine distance off and a COP is to double the relative bow bearing. When the second bearing (2) is twice the first one (1), the boat's distance from the object (B) equals the distance run between the two bearings (A). Where the COP crosses the D.R., there is an estimated position (box). As you run between the bearings don't alter course, but be sure to factor in current when making your calculations for distance run. "Bow and beam bearings" taken over the 45° and 90° lubber's lines are the easiest combination to use, but 40°/80°, 35°/70°, and many other pairs also work.

Position Finding With One Aid: Distance Off

houses stand on rocky points of land that should be given a wide berth (passed at a distance). Or you may want to take a departure from the aid (log it when it's abeam as the start of a passage). Certain combinations of relative bearings (including a few doubled bearings) can be used to predict distance off when the object is abeam. In each case the distance off is equal to the distance run between each of these two bearings; you need not compute distance run between the second bearing and when the object is abeam. Again, don't alter course between bearings. As listed by Frederick

Graves in his fine book *Piloting*, these pairs are:

20°/30°, 22°/34°, 25°/41°, 26½°/45°, 27°/46°, 29°/51°
32°/59°, 35°/67°, 37°/72°
40°/79°, 43°/86°, 44°/88°, 45°/90°

Two helpful rules of thumb called the $^{7}/_{10}$ Rule and the $^{7}/_{8}$ Rule can also be used to predict distance off when the sighted object is abeam.

In the $^{7}/_{10}$ **Rule,** if the first relative bearing is 22½° and the second is 45°, the distance off when the object is abeam is $^{7}/_{10}$ (0.7) the distance run between the first two bearings.

In the $^{7}/_{8}$ **Rule,** the two bearings are 30° and 60°. When the object is abeam, the distance off is $^{7}/_{8}$ (0.875) the distance run.

Relative Stern Bearings

So far we've been talking about bow bearings made while the boat is approaching a charted object, like a buoy, a lighthouse, a water tower, or a large smokestack. Bow bearings allow you both to calculate your present distance

off (at the time of the second bearing) and to predict your distance off when the object will be abeam.

There may be times when you must calculate distance off by taking two bearings on an object you are passing or have already passed. For example, a landmark may be obscured by a hill as you approach it but be visible once it's abaft the beam. Or you may want to plot a series of estimated positions or fixes while the landmark is visible, before you sail off into a fog. To figure distance off an object you have passed, take relative stern bearings using any of the techniques already described *except* that instead of doubling a bearing you halve it. The first bearing will be the broader one. When the relative bearing to the object is exactly one-half the first bearing, compute the distance run and the distance off — which will apply to the moment when the first bearing was taken. Using paired bearings or the $^{7}/_{10}$ or $^{7}/_{8}$ Rules, you can work backward to find out how far off the object you were when it was dead abeam, at a relative bearing of 90°.

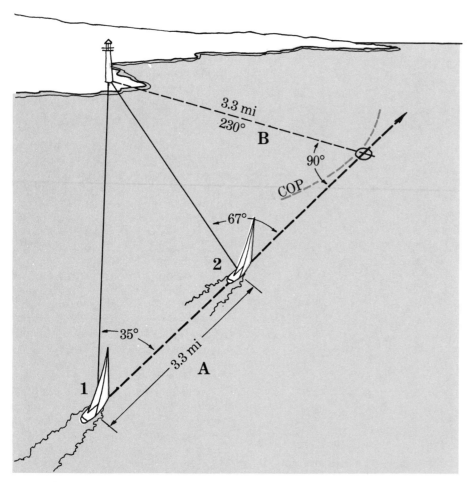

Several pairs of relative bearings listed in the text can be used to predict distance off when the charted object will be abeam. Here, the distance run between the first and second bearings (A) equals the eventual distance off (B). There is an E.P. where the COP crosses the D.R. If the pilot were to take a compass bearing on the object when abeam, the intersection of the LOP and the COP would be a fix (circle).

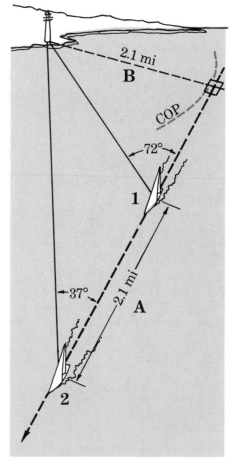

Paired stern bearings can be used to determine distance off at a previous time. Take the broadest bearing first. The distance run between the two bearings (A) equals the previous distance off (B).

Bobbing the Horizon

As we saw in chapter 9 in the section on lighthouses, if you know the height of an object and your own height above the water, you can calculate the range of visibility between you and it. In the case of lighthouses this method is used to determine how far away the light's flash can be seen. To review, calculate range of visibility using these steps:

1. Find the object's height. Lighthouse heights are shown on the chart and in the *Light List*. To find its range of visibility in nautical miles, use the table in chapter 9 or this formula:

Geographical range (nautical mi.) =

$1.144\sqrt{\text{lighthouse height}}$

To find its range in statute miles, use the table or this formula:

Geographical range (statute mi.) =

$1.317\sqrt{\text{lighthouse height}}$

2. Next, determine the height of your eye above the water, and using the table or either formula, determine your own range of visibility.

3. Finally, add the two ranges of visibility to come up with the mileage you must be from the object to first see it.

That total, the geographical range of visibility, is bounded by a big COP around the object. To see if you are on that COP, use a technique called bobbing the horizon. If the light or top of the lighthouse or light tower is visible on the horizon, stand or sit in the position used in step 2 above. Then bob your head down a foot or so. If the object disappears, then it's likely that the boat is on the COP whose radius is the range of visibility. If the object stays in sight, you're inside the COP.

Lighthouses showing alternating lights of different colors can have two ranges of visibility — one for a white light and another, 25 percent shorter in radius, for a green or red light.

Using the Sextant to Determine Distance Off

Used in celestial navigation, the sextant can be a handy tool when piloting, and especially for determining distance off a tall object by measuring its vertical angle. A sextant is an adjustable sighting device used to determine angles to elevated objects — usually the sun and the stars, but also to the tops of lighthouses and tall buildings of known height. Since the sextant can't be used unless there is a clear horizon line, the system we will describe is helpful only in daytime and good visibility.

First off, you must know the height of the sighted object. The *Light List* and the chart show the heights above mean high water of lighthouses and some other objects, such as bridge spans. The U.S. *Coast Pilot* provides the heights of these and other objects from base to top — you must add the distance from mean high water to the base. Read this number carefully. Often the height shown is not the height of the top of the lighthouse itself but that of its light, which may be several feet below the structure's top.

Using the sextant, find the vertical angle between the top of the object and the high-water mark on shore (which usually is indicated by a change of color or a line of weed). Do not correct the sight for "dip," or height of eye. Read the angle on the sextant. Then enter the corrected angle into the following formula to determine distance off in nautical miles:

Distance off in nautical miles =

$\dfrac{\text{object height} \times 0.566}{\text{corrected angle in minutes}}$

To convert to statute miles, multiply by 1.15.

This technique can be used to determine your distance from *any* object of a known height — another boat's mast, a skyscraper, a church steeple, or a bridge span. Tall objects have wider ranges of visibility than short ones.

Besides measuring vertical angles, a sextant can be used to measure the included horizontal angle between two visible objects. Once you know the horizontal angle, you can draw a circle of position whose circumference passes through both objects and your own position. Hold the sextant on its side and adjust it. Read the angle. Using the plotter or a protractor, duplicate the angle on the chart, one side passing through each object and then draw a COP through it with a drawing compass. (Later we'll see how this COP and the sextant can be used to help you stay away from rocks or shoals.)

Both uses of the sextant — determining a COP with vertical and horizontal angles — may be less accurate than taking bearings, although they

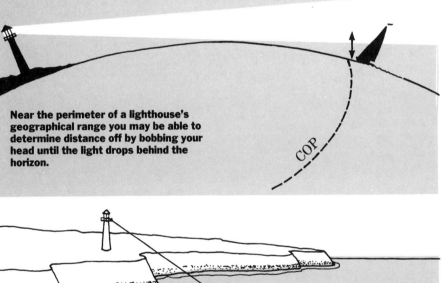

Near the perimeter of a lighthouse's geographical range you may be able to determine distance off by bobbing your head until the light drops behind the horizon.

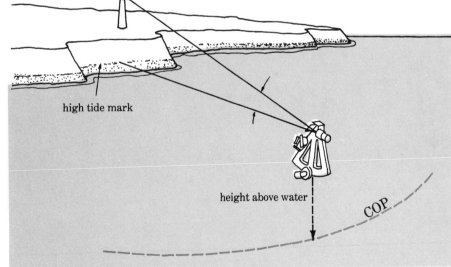

high tide mark

height above water

A sextant sight on an object of known height can provide distance off. Measure the angle between the high tide mark and the object's top and be sure to compensate for your height of eye with the "dip" correction.

Position Finding With One Aid: Distance Off

may also be quicker. Pilots will find taking bearings more reliable, but pilots who own sextants will find the sextant-sighting system more fun.

Estimating Distance Off

Besides calculating distance off and circles of position using bearings and angles, you can *estimate* them quickly and with reasonable accuracy using several techniques demanding almost no mathematical figuring.

Sound can be used in two ways. When near a bluff or cliff in limited visibility, blow a horn and time how long it takes for the echo to return.

Divide the interval by 10; the quotient is your distance to the hill in nautical miles. And when you see a lightning flash or a cannon's smoke, start counting seconds. The time interval until you hear the thunder or boom is divided by 5, and the quotient is the distance to the lightning or cannon in nautical miles. Unfortunately neither way is reliable in fog, which diffuses noises in unpredictable patterns.

The eyeblink method exploits the fact that almost everybody's arm is 10 times longer than the span between his eyes. Stretch out your right arm and raise a finger (or hold a pencil or stick). Then, closing your left eye, line the finger up against a tree or landmark on shore. Now open your left eye and close your right eye. Estimate the number of feet, yards, or miles your finger has apparently moved and multiply that number by 10. The product is the distance off in the same units.

Counting trees can give a rough estimate of distance offshore. In this technique, passed along by Hewitt

Schlereth in his book *Commonsense Coastal Navigation*, you look at the shore with your naked eye. If you can count individual trees, you're about 1 nautical mile offshore. If you can count windows on waterfront houses, the distance off is about 2 nautical miles. And if you can see the junction line between land and water, you're about 3 nautical miles away.

The hand-span method of determining distance off is used when you can see two objects on shore that are a known distance apart — such as a lighthouse and a water tower shown on the same chart. Hold your hand up with the palm facing shore and move it toward or away from your face until it covers the ground between the two objects. (You may have to spread or fold down some fingers). Now measure the span of your hand covering the ground as well as the distance from your face to your hand. The ratio of the two distances is equal to the ratio of the distance between the two objects to the distance off. Use this formula to calculate distance off:

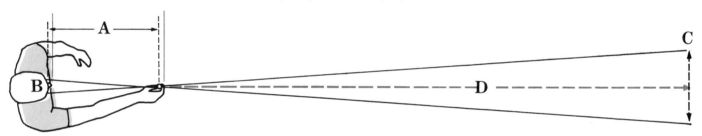

To estimate distance off, stretch out your hand (A), blink your eyes (B), and estimate how far the object has apparently moved (C). The distance off (D) is 10 times that distance.

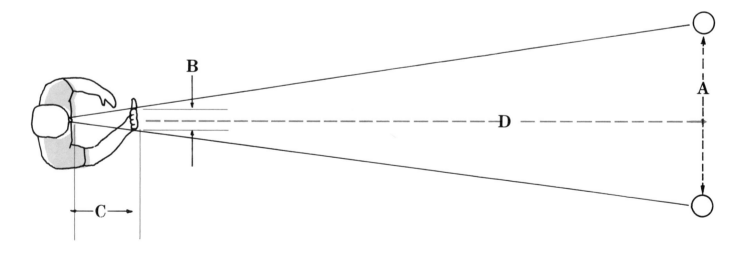

If you know the distance between two objects on the shore (A), hold your hand until it covers them (B). Multiply the ground distance by the distance to your hand (C) and divide by your hand's width to determine distance off.

Distance off =

$$\frac{\text{(face to hand)} \times \text{(ground distance)}}{\text{hand span}}$$

For example, if the hand span is 6 inches, the face-to-hand distance is 9 inches, and the ground distance between objects is 2 miles, the solution is:

$$\text{Distance off} = \frac{9 \times 2}{6} = 3 \text{ miles}$$

(Another interesting hand-span trick that has nothing to do with finding distance will tell you how much more daylight you'll have to get where you're going. Hold your hand sideways at arm's length with the thumb tucked in, and estimate the number of palm widths between the horizon and the sun. Each palm width represents an hour until sundown. Add about half an hour for dusk if you're sailing in temperate latitudes.)

While not as reliable as taking bearings or using a sextant, these "quick and dirty" tricks will keep you from piling up on shore, and perhaps equally important, they're enjoyable to use.

Uses for Distance Off and Circles of Position

As we've already suggested, there are three important uses for circles of position. Before we move on, let's review and elaborate on them.

First, by calculating distance off using relative bow or stern bearings or sextant angles, you can plot an estimated position. The circle of position is considered a single bearing, and the E.P. is where it crosses the track nearest to the D.R. position.

Second, by combining a circle of position with a line of position that is a compass bearing to the same charted object, you can plot a fix where the COP and the LOP cross. Therefore by using a series of bearings on a single charted navigation aid you can keep a careful plot as you pass it. This will be extremely helpful when sailing along a lonely, rocky shore in unpredictable currents, for rarely are such places guarded by more than one or two aids.

Third, distance off and COPs can keep you from getting too close to shore. Some people are naturally able to judge distance accurately; most people are not and need all the help they can get.

You can make a fix using only one aid by drawing a COP based on bow and beam bearings (A) or bobbing the horizon (B), and crossing it with an LOP to the same charted object.

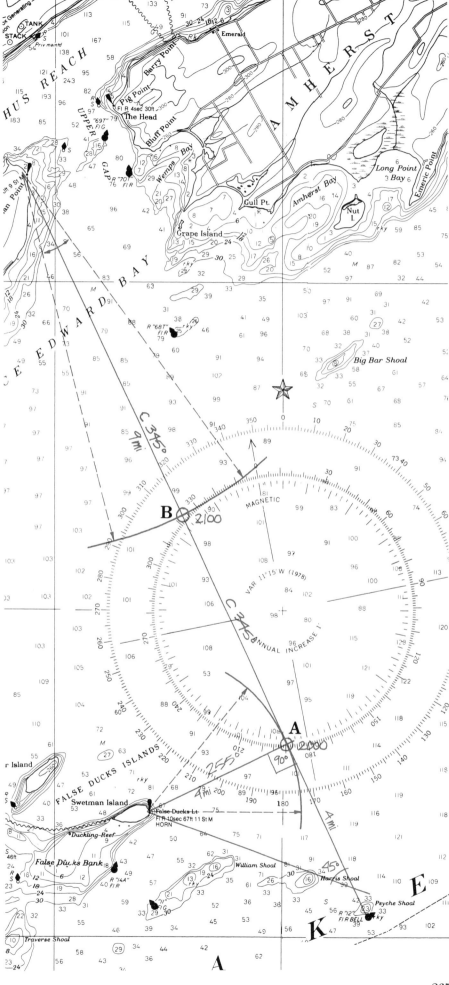

265

Danger Bearings and Circles

When sailing near shore, the pilot may precalculate and plot lines and circles of position to help him stay outside rocks and other hazards. These LOPs and COPs are called danger bearings and circles. When plotted against highly visible landmarks, they can be used the way a driver uses the center line in a road.

Danger Bearings

Sometimes an aid to navigation may include a danger bearing. For instance, the angle where a lighthouse's white or green sector ends and its red sector begins is a danger bearing. On one side a boat is safe; on the other side she's in shoal water. Another kind of danger bearing is a range, two or more daybeacons and/or landmarks that, when aligned one behind the other, indicate a safe course. If the boat swings either side of the range, she's in danger.

When approaching a hazard such as a reef or sunken boat, the pilot should plot a danger bearing to an adjacent charted object or to the edge of the hazard itself. The bearing is the minimum safe course that avoids the hazard — an LOP that, assuming the boat stays on it or to the safe side, will take her clear. Once the pilot has identified the danger bearing, this safe LOP, he should plot it on the chart and mark its dangerous side with hachures using a red pencil. If the danger is to starboard of the bearing, he writes "NLT" and the bearing on the LOP. This means that the bearing to the charted object must be no less than the one marked. For example, "NLT 072" means that the boat is in danger if the bearing to the object is 071° or less,

which would indicate that she was in dangerous waters. But if the danger is to port, "NMT" and the bearing are written on the LOP — indicating that the bearing to the charted object should not be greater. Thus "NMT 072°" means that the boat is at risk if the object bears 073° or more. If the boat is exactly on the danger bearing, she is safe.

Now the pilot must pass this information up to the helmsman using the simplest, least ambiguous language possible. If the danger bearing is 072° and he has written "NLT 072°" on the chart, he can say, "Don't let the bearing to that buoy get below 072°," or, better, "We're safe if that buoy bears more than 072°." Still, "below" and "more" could be interpreted two ways. The pilot may *want* "below" to mean "between 000° and 071°," but the helmsman steering a boat on port tack may think "below" means "to leeward" — or 073° to 360°.

Better yet, the pilot should give the helmsman a safe course that will skirt the danger. Or if trustworthy land-

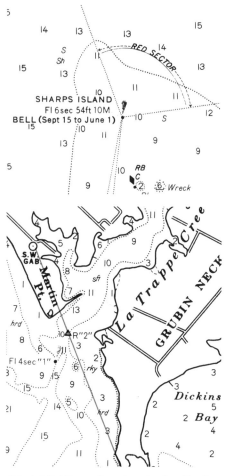

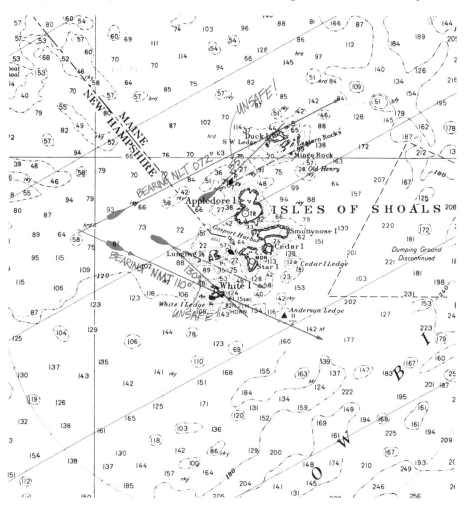

(Top) A lighthouse's red sector is a fixed light shining over shoal water and other areas off the main channel. (Above) Compass courses can be misleading when approaching a shoal so find two charted objects that when aligned serve as a range to guide you into the channel.

Lacking a range, set a course around a hazard but also establish danger bearings — courses or bearings that provide the minimum safe berth. If a bearing labeled "NLT" decreases or one labeled "NMT" increases, you are being sucked toward the hazard. Danger bearings are particularly helpful at night, when it's difficult to estimate distance off.

marks can be lined up in a range, he can say, "Keep that church steeple in front of that water tank." When there is no tidal current or leeway shoving the boat toward the hazard, the pilot can simply tell the helmsman to head right at a single buoy or landmark. However, this instruction invites disaster if there is any chance that the boat will be swept toward the shoal or reef, for the helmsman will obediently continue to steer toward the object, ignoring the rapidly approaching hazard.

Whatever instructions the pilot gives, he should go on deck and explain the situation to the helmsman, pointing out the hazard and any buoys or landmarks, and asking if there will be any difficulty sailing the safe course. It's all well and good for a pilot to tell a helmsman to steer 072°, but if the boat can't sail that course because it means running dead before the wind in a dangerously wild sea or because she's close-hauled and must pinch to make it, then the pilot should know enough to give other instructions. Boats have been lost because the pilots buried their heads in the charts and lost touch with the situation on deck.

Danger Circles

If you can enclose a hazard in a danger circle and then find a way to stay outside it, you'll keep out of trouble. This is where the sextant can be handy. First, draw an arc around the hazard with a drawing compass. Then using the plotter or a protractor, plot bearings from various points on the circumference to landmarks or buoys that the circle passes through and calculate the included angle. Shade the hazard with red hachures and label the circle "NMT" and the minimum safe included angle between the objects. Set the sextant to the angle and take horizontal sights as you sail by the hazard. Whenever the angle between the two objects is greater than the computed angle, you're inside the danger circle. Whenever it's smaller, you're outside it. If you don't have a sextant, use relative bearings sighted through a pelorus or an improvised viewfinder, or take compass bearings.

Another way to make sure you're safe is to locate an object on or near the center of the plotted danger circle, such as a daybeacon or an oyster stake, and keep it dead abeam. By doing this, you'll sail around the circumference of the circle.

The Rule of 60 for Making Course Alterations

A pilot frequently must calculate a safe course around a hazard that lies at a distance dead ahead. An interesting method called the Rule of 60 computes the necessary course alteration with good accuracy. You must know how far ahead the hazard lies as well as how far to one side you want to leave it. The formula is:

Course alteration =
$$\frac{60 \times \text{desired distance off}}{\text{distance ahead}}$$

For example, sailing on a course of 185°, the boat is headed right at a reef 12 miles ahead. The safest passage around the reef is 4 miles from its center. So,

Course alteration =
$$\frac{60 \times 4}{12} = 20° \text{ course alteration}$$

So the safe course around the reef is either 165° or 205° — both 20° either side of the present course.

The Rule of 60 works only when short distances are involved, and even then it may not be perfectly accurate. However, even if it is off by a couple of degrees, it provides an extremely quick solution to one of piloting's most difficult problems.

The Rule of 60 is both easy to use and quite accurate for determining course alterations to avoid approaching hazards or to compensate for leeway or current. The answer is the course change in degrees.

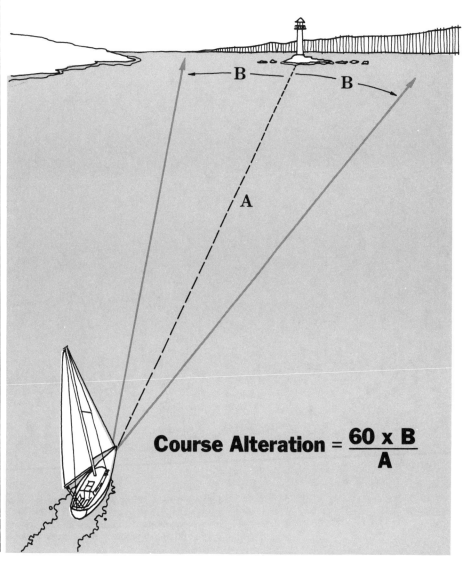

Course Alteration = $\dfrac{60 \times B}{A}$

Piloting with Soundings

We've seen how position determination depends on reference to visible, charted objects using the magnetic compass and up-to-date charts. Nautical charts also contain information about objects invisible from the boat but that can be verified, measured, or identified using electronic equipment. Among these are radio beacons, which become "visible" through the eye of the radio direction finder and the Loran receiving set. We'll look more closely at these navigational aids in chapter 10. Another important but invisible set of data printed on charts is soundings, or water depth. Charts show soundings in either feet or fathoms (multiples of 6 feet), with the scale clearly indicated on the chart border. In tidal areas the soundings are at mean low water (MLW), which is the average depth at low tide, exclusive of spring and neap tides. The National Ocean Survey *Tide Tables* and privately published publications derived from it show the range between mean low water and mean high water and the range for spring and neap tides for every day of the year, and most charts show tidal ranges for a few places in the area they cover. Therefore you can convert the charted depth to depths for times other than that of MLW.

On charts, soundings are printed at intervals, and dashed or dotted contour lines are drawn to make it easier to distinguish areas of relatively shallow water from those of deep water. Bodies of especially shallow water are shaded light blue. The delineations for these contour lines and shaded areas vary from chart to chart and area to area. Using these aids, the navigator can easily reduce hundreds of individual soundings into several relatively clear blocks of water, some safe and some dangerous.

Sounding Instruments

The navigator's other aid besides the chart is his boat's sounding instrument. Until about 30 years ago most soundings were made with *lead lines*. These are long lengths of narrow-diameter rope with a lead weight at one end and marked at regular intervals with leather, rag, or painted indicators using a variety of colors or numbers to show depth. Nowadays numbered plastic tags are available to be secured to the line at fathom or foot intervals. The traditional sounding lead had on its bottom some soft tallow to pick up a small sample of the sea's floor. An experienced fisherman would know not only the depth of water near his home port but also the location of spots with mud, sand, rock, or weedy bottom. (Astonished by his skipper's skill at navigating by sounding lead, a mate once smeared some shore dirt from his boots onto the tal-

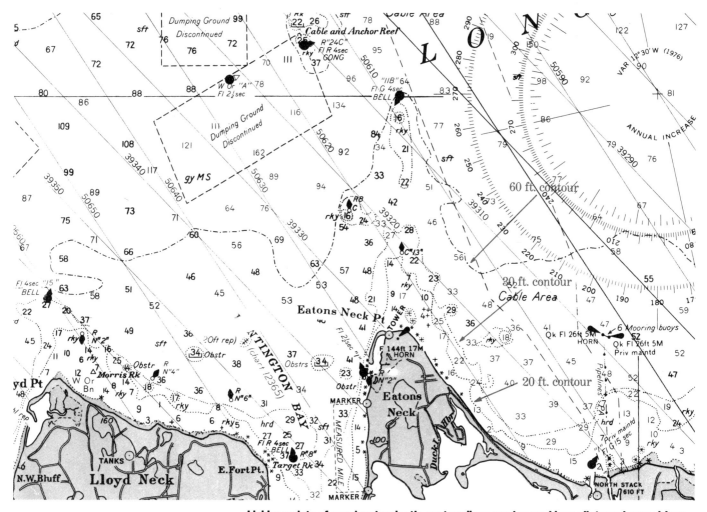

Linking points of equal water depth, contour lines can be used by a pilot much as a driver uses a road's centerline and curbs. On this chart, where soundings are in feet below mean low water, dashed and dotted lines mark 60-foot, 30-foot, and 20-foot contours. Using his chart and depth sounder the pilot can follow the contour lines around hazards and into harbors.

low and showed it to the old man, who, after inspecting it carefully, announced that the nearby island had sunk and they were fogbound over one of its hills.)

To use the lead line, stand on the bow (with the boat going slow ahead) and heave the lead forward. Let the line run out. When the bow passes near the line, pull until the line is vertical and read the tag nearest the water. Be sure to retrieve the line before it tangles in

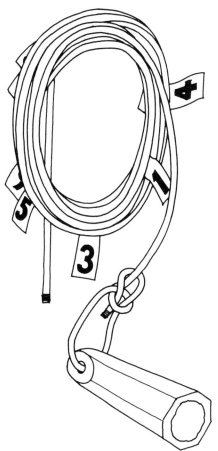

Determining depth with a lead line or depth sounder (above), the pilot slowly feels his way along contour lines staying in safe water while navigating around hazards (right above). Depth soundings can also be used to estimate positions when fog shrouds buoys over shoaling areas (right below).

the propeller or rudder. Before heaving the lead again, coil the line carefully.

Obviously, this is a fairly slow procedure that would be difficult to repeat more than once every minute or so. Today, electronic depth sounders are much faster, and in most cases more accurate. The *depth sounder* is sometimes called a "Fathometer" after the trade name of the first of its type, developed by the Raytheon Company, or an "echo sounder," which accurately describes how it works. A sound signal is sent out through a transducer installed in the boat's bottom. It travels through the water until it bounces off an object, and its echo is received by a hydrophone located near the transducer. An instrument converts the time lag between the sending and reception of the signal into an easily understood indicator. In older depth sounders, a blip of light is shown on a graduated scale. In newer instruments, the depth is shown in numbers. Sometimes a switch allows a choice between feet and fathoms, and there

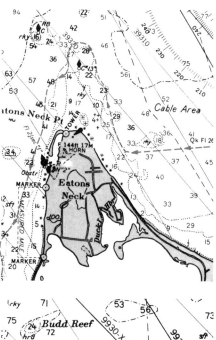

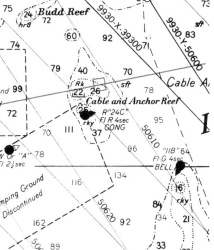

may be an alarm that goes off when the sounding is less than a specified depth, say, 8 feet. When reading the depth sounder, add the depth of your boat's bilge since the number shows only the distance from the transducer to the bottom.

The depth sounder provides a continuous readout of soundings with an accuracy of ±5 percent. Because its signals are echoed by any object underneath, the depth sounder will momentarily pick up a large fish or school of fish. You will be more than mildly surprised the first time a tuna triggers a 15-foot spot in water that your chart shows is 100 feet deep, but you'll become accustomed to such fluctuations — almost.

Using the Depth Sounder in Piloting

The depth of the water below is one more piece of information that a good pilot uses to find his position. In clear weather, other data — bearings particularly — will be more important, but when the visibility clamps down to less than 100 yards, the pilot can't rely on his long-range eyesight to check on his D.R. plot. Rarely will the sounder provide information that will allow you to pinpoint your position, since it shows gradual trends as the water deepens or shoals, allowing you to estimate your position with less rather than more reliability. But where the water depth changes drastically, usually near rocky shores, you can use the sounder's reading much like a single bearing on a landmark to provide a good E.P.

Because water depth may vary on several sides of a deep channel or hazard, you can judge which way you are approaching by the sounder's reading. There are times, too, when you can "follow" a contour line clearly shown on a chart right around a hazard and into a harbor without ever seeing a buoy or land. When sailing along a contour line, keep the speed down and post one crew member to watch the screen (or heave the lead) and another to keep a lookout. It's all too easy to become mesmerized by the sounder and lose touch with other aids.

Most important, the sounder helps the pilot fulfill his main responsibility, which is to keep the boat in navigable water. While most soundings won't tell you exactly where you are, they're very good guides for finding out where you are *not*, which is in water shallower than your keel.

Tide and Current

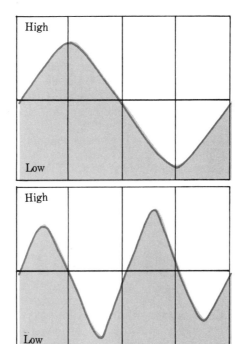

Tide (the rise and fall of water) and current (the horizontal motion of water due mainly to tidal changes) are key considerations for any pilot on salt water. It's important to be able to predict tide changes and current direction and velocity. Remember, though, that tide tables are only *predictions* of tidal behavior. Due to local conditions, tides may be higher or lower and currents may be faster or slower than predicted. Rarely do they stick exactly to schedule.

Government tide publications use Standard Time. Be sure to add an hour for Daylight Saving Time to syn-

There is one tide change a day in a diurnal schedule (top), and there are two (with tides at different levels) in a semidiurnal system (above).

chronize the tables with your watch.

Determining Tide Levels

Tides change on a semi-diurnal (twice-a-day) or diurnal (once-a-day) schedule in relatively regular patterns. It all depends on the relative position of the moon and the local geography. Whatever the schedule, it is described in the National Ocean Survey publication *Tide Tables* (one book each for the East and West coasts of the Americas, for Europe and West Africa, and for the Indian and Pacific Oceans). *Tide Tables* provides the time and range of high and low tides for every day of the year for thousands of locations. In each case the point of reference is called the datum level. Presently the datum level is soundings at mean low water (the average of low tides other than spring and neap tides) but it is gradually being changed by the Coast Guard to mean lower low water (the average of the *lower* of the two low tides), which most accurately reflects the most extreme low tide levels.

A tide table shows times of high and low tide. here, the second low tide on July 18 is at 3:16 P.M., according to the table. Adding an hour for Daylight Saving Time, change that to 4:16 or 1616 hours. The height, or range between low and high tides, is listed under high tide.

Day of Month	Day of Week	JULY HIGH a.m.	Ht.	JULY HIGH p.m.	Ht.	JULY LOW a.m.	JULY LOW p.m.	Day of Month	Day of Week	AUGUST HIGH a.m.	Ht.	AUGUST HIGH p.m.	Ht.	AUGUST LOW a.m.	AUGUST LOW p.m.
1	S	8 20	6.3	8 36	7.2	2 14	2 23	1	T	9 24	6.4	9 37	7.2	3 19	3 29
2	S	9 08	6.3	9 21	7.2	3 03	3 11	2	W	10 03	6.6	10 16	7.2	4 01	4 11
3	M	9 51	6.4	10 03	7.3	3 46	3 55	3	T	10 42	6.7	10 54	7.2	4 37	4 49
4	T	10 32	6.5	10 41	7.3	4 27	4 36	4	F	11 17	6.9	11 30	7.2	5 14	5 26
5	W	11 09	6.6	11 20	7.2	5 05	5 14	5	S	11 53	6.9	.....	...	5 48	6 03
6	T	11 47	6.7	11 56	7.2	5 43	5 52	6	S	12 06	7.2	12 28	7.0	6 24	6 40
7	F	.....	...	12 22	6.7	6 18	6 30	7	M	12 41	7.1	1 05	7.1	6 59	7 18
8	S	12 33	7.1	12 59	6.8	6 54	7 07	8	T	1 20	6.9	1 45	7.1	7 35	7 58
9	S	1 10	7.0	1 38	6.8	7 31	7 47	9	W	2 03	6.8	2 27	7.1	8 13	8 45
10	M	1 51	6.9	2 19	6.8	8 08	8 29	10	T	2 49	6.6	3 14	7.1	9 01	9 38
11	T	2 32	6.7	3 01	6.9	8 48	9 19	11	F	3 41	6.4	4 09	7.1	9 51	10 37
12	W	3 19	6.5	3 49	6.9	9 33	10 10	12	S	4 40	6.2	5 08	7.1	10 49	11 41
13	T	4 10	6.4	4 42	7.0	10 24	11 06	13	S	5 45	6.2	6 13	7.2	11 55	.....
14	F	5 06	6.3	5 38	7.1	11 19	.....	14	M	6 50	6.4	7 15	7.4	12 44	1 01
15	S	6 08	6.3	6 36	7.3	12 06	12 19	15	T	7 53	6.6	8 17	7.6	1 46	2 04
16	S	7 10	6.4	7 35	7.5	1 06	1 19	16	W	8 51	7.0	9 15	7.8	2 44	3 03
17	M	8 09	6.6	8 33	7.8	2 06	2 20	17	T	9 47	7.3	10 11	7.9	3 39	4 01
18	T	9 07	6.9	9 29	8.0	3 02	3 16	18	F	10 40	7.6	11 03	7.9	4 32	4 54
19	W	10 04	7.2	10 24	8.1	3 58	4 12	19	S	11 31	7.7	11 55	7.8	5 22	5 46
20	T	10 58	7.4	11 18	8.1	4 50	5 08	20	S	.....	...	12 22	7.7	6 12	6 38
21	F	11 51	7.5	.....	...	5 42	6 03	21	M	12 45	7.5	1 12	7.6	7 02	7 31
22	S	12 12	7.9	12 43	7.6	6 33	6 57	22	T	1 36	7.2	2 03	7.4	7 52	8 23
23	S	1 05	7.7	1 36	7.5	7 26	7 55	23	W	2 29	6.8	2 55	7.2	8 43	9 20
24	M	2 01	7.3	2 32	7.4	8 19	8 50	24	T	3 25	6.4	3 50	6.9	9 37	10 18
25	T	2 56	6.9	3 28	7.2	9 14	9 50	25	F	4 22	6.1	4 46	6.7	10 34	11 15
26	W	3 57	6.5	4 25	7.0	10 11	10 50	26	S	5 21	6.0	5 45	6.6	11 32	.....
27	T	4 56	6.2	5 24	6.9	11 07	11 51	27	S	6 19	6.0	6 42	6.6	12 14	12 30
28	F	5 57	6.1	6 21	6.9	.....	12 07	28	M	7 14	6.1	7 35	6.8	1 09	1 23
29	S	6 56	6.0	7 16	6.9	12 49	1 03	29	T	8 04	6.3	8 22	6.9	1 59	2 14
30	S	7 49	6.1	8 07	7.0	1 44	1 56	30	W	8 51	6.5	9 05	7.0	2 45	2 59
31	M	8 39	6.3	8 55	7.1	2 34	2 47	31	T	9 31	6.8	9 47	7.2	3 26	3 42

When tides exceed average rise in height, expect a corresponding drop in low tide. Add one hour for Daylight Saving Time   Average Rise and Fall 6.7 ft.

Tides are rarely the same from change to change, since the rapidly varying orbit of the moon, whose gravitational pull is mainly responsible for the tides, pulls the mound of water that is the tide wave along under it. In a semidiurnal tidal pattern one tide will be higher and lower than the other by different amounts: the more overhead the moon is situated, the greater the range will be. Another big effect on tide levels is the relative position of the moon and the sun, which has some gravitational pull that augments the moon's pull when they're in alignment at full and new moons and reduces it when they're at right angles to each other in midphase between full and new moons. The higher than average tides that occur when they are aligned are called spring tides, and the lower than average tides at midphase are called neap tides.

The *Tide Tables* say when the tide is high and low, and what the level is at those times. They don't tell you what the level is at other times, but there are ways to predict intermediate levels.

As a rule of thumb, the amount of rise and fall over a period of time is directly proportional to the total rise and fall and the entire duration of the tidal change: if the duration is 6 hours, the tide has risen (or fallen) $1/6$ of its total range after 1 hour, $1/3$ after 2 hours, $1/2$ after 3 hours, $2/3$ after 4 hours, and $1/6$ after 5 hours. Most semidiurnal tides change approximately every 6 hours 15 minutes. Since diurnal tides change about every 12 hours 30 minutes, halve the figures in this rule of thumb to estimate tide rise and fall during a once-daily tide.

The table at the left provides all or most of the information you'll need. Given a choice, buy the most complete tide table, as information like range and duration will come in handy when

TIME FROM THE NEAREST HIGH WATER OR LOW WATER

A — Duration of rise or fall, see footnote.

h.m.	h.m.	h.m.	h.m.	h.m.	h.m.	h.m.	h.m.	h.m.	h.m.	h.m.	h.m.	h.m.	h.m.	h.m.	h.m.
4 00	0 08	0 16	0 24	0 32	0 40	0 48	0 56	1 04	1 12	1 20	1 28	1 36	1 44	1 52	2 00
4 20	0 09	0 17	0 26	0 35	0 43	0 52	1 01	1 09	1 18	1 27	1 35	1 44	1 53	2 01	2 10
4 40	0 09	0 19	0 28	0 37	0 47	0 56	1 05	1 15	1 24	1 33	1 43	1 52	2 01	2 11	2 20
5 00	0 10	0 20	0 30	0 40	0 50	1 00	1 10	1 20	1 30	1 40	1 50	2 00	2 10	2 20	2 30
5 20	0 11	0 21	0 32	0 43	0 53	1 04	1 15	1 25	1 36	1 47	1 57	2 08	2 19	2 29	2 40
5 40	0 11	0 23	0 34	0 45	0 57	1 08	1 19	1 31	1 42	1 53	2 05	2 16	2 27	2 39	2 50
6 00	0 12	0 24	0 36	**B** 1 00	1 12	1 24	1 36	1 48	2 00	2 12	2 24	2 36	2 48	3 00	
6 20	0 13	0 25	0 38	1 03	1 16	1 29	1 41	1 54	2 07	2 19	2 32	2 45	2 57	3 10	
6 40	0 13	0 27	0 40	0 53	1 07	1 20	1 33	1 47	2 00	2 13	2 27	2 40	2 53	3 07	3 20
7 00	0 14	0 28	0 42	0 55	1 10	1 24	1 38	1 52	2 06	2 20	2 34	2 48	3 02	3 16	3 30
7 20	0 15	0 29	0 44	0 59	1 13	1 28	1 43	1 57	2 12	2 27	2 41	2 56	3 11	3 25	3 40
7 40	0 15	0 31	0 46	1 01	1 17	1 32	1 47	2 03	2 18	2 33	2 49	3 04	3 19	3 35	3 50
8 00	0 16	0 32	0 48	1 04	1 20	1 36	1 52	2 08	2 24	2 40	2 56	3 12	3 28	3 44	4 00
8 20	0 17	0 33	0 50	1 07	1 23	1 40	1 57	2 13	2 30	2 47	3 03	3 20	3 37	3 53	4 10
8 40	0 17	0 35	0 52	1 09	1 27	1 44	2 01	2 19	2 36	2 53	3 11	3 28	3 45	4 03	4 20
9 00	0 18	0 36	0 54	1 12	1 30	1 48	2 06	2 24	2 42	3 00	3 18	3 36	3 54	4 12	4 30
9 20	0 19	0 37	0 56	1 15	1 33	1 52	2 11	2 29	2 48	3 07	3 25	3 44	4 03	4 21	4 40
9 40	0 19	0 39	0 58	1 17	1 37	1 56	2 15	2 35	2 54	3 13	3 33	3 52	4 11	4 31	4 50
10 00	0 20	0 40	1 00	1 20	1 40	2 00	2 20	2 40	3 00	3 20	3 40	4 00	4 20	4 40	5 00
10 20	0 21	0 41	1 02	1 23	1 43	2 04	2 25	2 45	3 06	3 27	3 47	4 08	4 29	4 49	5 10
10 40	0 21	0 43	1 04	1 25	1 47	2 08	2 29	2 51	3 12	3 33	3 55	4 16	4 37	4 59	5 20

CORRECTION TO HEIGHT

C — Range of tide, see footnote.

Ft.	Ft.	Ft.	Ft.	Ft.	Ft.	Ft.	Ft.	Ft.	Ft.	Ft.	Ft.	Ft.	Ft.	Ft.	Ft.
0.5	0.0	0.0	0.0	0.0	0.0	0.0	0.1	0.1	0.1	0.1	0.1	0.2	0.2	0.2	0.2
1.0	0.0	0.0	0.0	0.0	0.1	0.1	0.1	0.2	0.2	0.2	0.3	0.3	0.4	0.4	0.5
1.5	0.0	0.0	0.0	0.1	0.1	0.1	0.2	0.2	0.3	0.4	0.4	0.5	0.6	0.7	0.8
2.0	0.0	0.0	0.1	0.1	0.1	0.2	0.3	0.3	0.4	0.5	0.6	0.7	0.8	0.9	1.0
2.5	0.0	0.0	0.1	0.1	0.2	0.2	0.3	0.4	0.5	0.6	0.7	0.9	1.0	1.1	1.2
3.0	0.0	0.0	0.1	0.1	0.2	0.3	0.4	0.5	0.6	0.8	0.9	1.0	1.2	1.3	1.5
3.5	0.0	0.0	0.1	0.2	0.2	0.3	0.4	0.6	0.7	0.9	1.0	1.2	1.4	1.6	1.8
4.0	0.0	0.0	0.1	0.2	0.3	0.4	0.5	0.7	0.8	1.0	1.2	1.4	1.6	1.8	2.0
4.5	0.0	0.0	0.1	0.2	0.4	0.6	0.7	0.9	1.1	1.3	1.6	1.8	2.0	2.2	
5.0	0.0	0.1	0.1	0.2	0.5	0.6	0.8	1.0	1.2	1.5	1.7	2.0	2.2	2.5	
5.5	0.0	0.1	0.1	0.2	0.4	0.5	0.7	0.9	1.1	1.4	1.6	1.9	2.2	2.5	2.8
6.0	0.0	0.1	0.1	0.3	0.4	0.6	0.8	1.0	1.2	1.5	1.8	2.1	2.4	2.7	3.0
6.5	0.0	0.1	0.2	0.3	0.4	0.6	0.8	1.1	1.3	1.6	1.9	2.2	2.6	2.9	3.2
7.0	0.0	0.1	0.2	0.3	0.5	0.7	0.9	1.2	1.4	1.8	2.1	2.4	2.8	3.1	3.5
7.5	0.0	0.1	0.2	0.3	0.5	0.7	1.0	1.2	1.5	1.9	2.2	2.6	3.0	3.4	3.8
8.0	0.0	0.1	0.2	0.3	0.5	0.8	1.0	1.3	1.6	2.0	2.4	2.8	3.2	3.6	4.0
8.5	0.0	0.1	0.2	0.4	0.6	0.8	1.1	1.4	1.8	2.1	2.5	2.9	3.4	3.8	4.2
9.0	0.0	0.1	0.2	0.4	0.6	0.9	1.2	1.5	1.9	2.2	2.7	3.1	3.6	4.0	4.5
9.5	0.0	0.1	0.2	0.4	0.6	0.9	1.2	1.6	2.0	2.4	2.8	3.3	3.8	4.3	4.8
10.0	0.0	0.1	0.2	0.4	0.7	1.0	1.3	1.7	2.1	2.5	3.0	3.5	4.0	4.5	5.0
10.5	0.0	0.1	0.3	0.5	0.7	1.0	1.3	1.7	2.2	2.6	3.1	3.6	4.2	4.7	5.2
11.0	0.0	0.1	0.3	0.5	0.7	1.1	1.4	1.8	2.3	2.8	3.3	3.8	4.4	4.9	5.5
11.5	0.0	0.1	0.3	0.5	0.8	1.1	1.5	1.9	2.4	2.9	3.4	4.0	4.6	5.1	5.8
12.0	0.0	0.1	0.3	0.5	0.8	1.1	1.5	2.0	2.5	3.0	3.6	4.1	4.8	5.4	6.0
12.5	0.0	0.1	0.3	0.5	0.8	1.2	1.6	2.1	2.6	3.1	3.7	4.3	5.0	5.6	6.2
13.0	0.0	0.1	0.3	0.6	0.9	1.2	1.7	2.2	2.7	3.2	3.9	4.5	5.1	5.8	6.5
13.5	0.0	0.1	0.3	0.6	0.9	1.3	1.7	2.2	2.8	3.4	4.0	4.7	5.3	6.0	6.8
14.0	0.0	0.2	0.3	0.6	0.9	1.3	1.8	2.3	2.9	3.5	4.2	4.8	5.5	6.3	7.0
14.5	0.0	0.2	0.4	0.6	1.0	1.4	1.9	2.4	3.0	3.6	4.3	5.0	5.7	6.5	7.2
15.0	0.0	0.2	0.4	0.6	1.0	1.4	1.9	2.5	3.1	3.8	4.4	5.2	5.9	6.7	7.5
15.5	0.0	0.2	0.4	0.7	1.0	1.5	2.0	2.6	3.2	3.9	4.6	5.4	6.1	6.9	7.8
16.0	0.0	0.2	0.4	0.7	1.1	1.5	2.1	2.6	3.3	4.0	4.7	5.5	6.3	7.2	8.0
16.5	0.0	0.2	0.4	0.7	1.1	1.6	2.1	2.7	3.4	4.1	4.9	5.7	6.5	7.4	8.2
17.0	0.0	0.2	0.4	0.7	1.1	1.6	2.2	2.8	3.5	4.2	5.0	5.9	6.7	7.6	8.5
17.5	0.0	0.2	0.4	0.8	1.2	1.7	2.2	2.9	3.6	4.4	5.2	6.0	6.9	7.8	8.8
18.0	0.0	0.2	0.4	0.8	1.2	1.7	2.3	3.0	3.7	4.5	5.3	6.2	7.1	8.1	9.0
18.5	0.1	0.2	0.5	0.8	1.2	1.8	2.4	3.1	3.8	4.6	5.5	6.4	7.3	8.3	9.2
19.0	0.1	0.2	0.5	0.8	1.3	1.8	2.4	3.1	3.9	4.8	5.6	6.6	7.5	8.5	9.5
19.5	0.1	0.2	0.5	0.8	1.3	1.9	2.5	3.2	4.0	4.9	5.8	6.7	7.7	8.7	9.8
20.0	0.1	0.2	0.5	0.9	1.3	1.9	2.6	3.3	4.1	5.0	5.9	6.9	7.9	9.0	10.0

(**D** appears at the intersection within the CORRECTION TO HEIGHT table.)

To estimate depths for times between low and high tides, first find the time closest to the interval between low and high (A), then go across that row until you reach the column under the number closest to the interval between the desired time and the nearest tide change (B). Run down this column to the row headed by the number most closely corresponding to the tide range (C). The intersection between the row and column (D) is the height above mean low water at the desired time. If the day's tide range is greater than the average range (printed on the tide table and chart), you must subtract their difference from MLW before adding the number at the intersection; if less than the average range, add the difference to MLW.

Tide and Current

you're predicting intermediate water levels.

Determining Tidal Currents

Not only are water levels subject to calculation and prediction, but tidal current — the speed and direction of the water flooding in and ebbing out — must be considered when planning a course. The slower the boat, the more current affects her progress, yet even high-speed powerboats can be delayed or thrown off course by strong contrary or side currents. A tidal stream as slow as 1 knot can double the size of wind-driven waves if current and wind are contrary, and 2- or 3-knot currents running against a Force 7 wind can set up mammoth breaking waves. So it's valuable and sometimes vital to be able to predict the direction and speed of any upcoming tidal currents.

Some general principles apply about currents. They tend to run swiftest in constricted channels between two large bodies of water. Still water does *not* run deep; current is most rapid in deep channels, not shallow areas. When going around a bend, currents usually run swiftest on the outside of the turn and most slowly on the inside. And current may be created or accelerated by strong, steady winds. The greatest current of all is the Gulf Stream, which acts as a kind of drain for immense quantities of water shoved into the Gulf of Mexico by the Atlantic's trade winds.

Two government publications cover tidal currents. One is the NOS *Tidal Current Tables* for each year in two volumes, one for the Atlantic Coast (including the Gulf of Mexico) and the other for the Pacific Coast. Here are listed times of slack water and of maximum current and speed of maximum current for several reference stations and thousands of subordinate stations, plus several very helpful tables describing rotary tidal currents on large bodies of water, and currents in the Gulf Stream and other tricky areas. Other helpful NOS publications are the various *Tidal Current Charts*, which use force arrows to show current for various stages of the tide in many important boating areas. Since these charts cover rather large areas, what they gain in graphic clarity they may lose in detail. But using the *Tidal Current Tables*, a chart, and a pencil, you should be able to draw vectors representing the direction and force of local tidal currents.

Once again, don't expect these tables and charts to be perfectly accurate. Onshore winds may shorten the duration of the ebb (outgoing tide) and weaken ebb currents, while lengthening and strengthening the flood. The best indication of tidal current is not an entry in the *Tidal Current Ta-*

The Tidal Current Tables shows when the flood or ebb current starts to flow at the end of slack water (A), as well as the time and velocity of maximum current (B and C). The true directions of the current are shown at the top of the page (D). Again, add an hour for Daylight Saving Time.

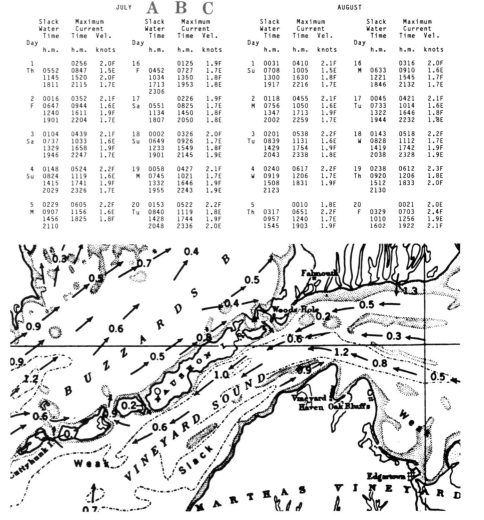

You can draw your own current charts or use ones published for a few areas. Here, using the current wisely can add up to 1.5 knot in speed if you run with the current on the North side of Naushon Island rather than run into the 1-knot flow on the South side. Remember, however, that all tide tables and charts aren't much more than highly educated guesses at tidal activity. Pay as much attention to local indicators as you do to the printed publications.

POLLOCK RIP CHANNEL, MASSACHUSETTS, 1982

D F-Flood, Dir. 035° True   E-Ebb, Dir. 225° True

JULY **A B C**   AUGUST

Day	Slack Water Time h.m.	Maximum Current Time h.m.	Vel. knots	Day	Slack Water Time h.m.	Maximum Current Time h.m.	Vel. knots	Day	Slack Water Time h.m.	Maximum Current Time h.m.	Vel. knots	Day	Slack Water Time h.m.	Maximum Current Time h.m.	Vel. knots
1 Th	0552 1145 1811	0256 0847 1520 2115	2.0F 1.5E 2.0F 1.7E	16 F	0452 1034 1713 2306	0125 0727 1350 1953	1.9F 1.7E 1.8F 1.8E	1 Su	0708 1300 1917	0410 1005 1630 2216	2.1F 1.5E 1.8F 1.7E	16 M	0633 1221 1846	0316 0910 1545 2132	2.0F 1.6E 1.7F 1.7E
2 F	0016 0647 1240 1901	0352 0944 1611 2204	2.1F 1.6E 1.9F 1.7E	17 Sa	0551 1134 1807	0226 0825 1450 2050	1.9F 1.7E 1.8F 1.8E	2 M	0118 0756 1347 2002	0455 1050 1713 2259	2.1F 1.6E 1.9F 1.7E	17 Tu	0045 0733 1322 1944	0421 1014 1646 2232	2.1F 1.6E 1.8F 1.8E
3 Sa	0104 0737 1329 1946	0439 1033 1658 2247	2.1F 1.6E 1.9F 1.7E	18 Su	0002 0649 1233 1901	0326 0926 1549 2145	2.0F 1.7E 1.8F 1.9E	3 Tu	0201 0839 1429 2043	0538 1131 1754 2338	2.2F 1.6E 1.9F 1.8E	18 W	0143 0828 1419 2038	0518 1112 1742 2328	2.2F 1.7E 1.9F 1.9E
4 Su	0148 0824 1415 2029	0524 1119 1741 2326	2.2F 1.6E 1.9F 1.7E	19 M	0058 0745 1332 1955	0427 1021 1646 2243	2.1F 1.7E 1.9F 1.9E	4 W	0240 0919 1508 2123	0617 1206 1831	2.2F 1.7E 1.9F	19 Th	0238 0920 1512 2130	0612 1206 1833	2.3F 1.8E 2.0F
5 M	0229 0907 1456 2110	0605 1156 1825	2.2F 1.6E 1.8F	20 Tu	0153 0840 1428 2048	0522 1119 1744 2336	2.2F 1.8E 1.9F 2.0E	5 Th	0317 0957 1545	0651 1240 1903	1.8E 2.2F 1.7E 1.9F	20 F	0329 1010 1602	0021 0703 1256 1922	2.0E 2.4F 1.9E 2.1F

bles but a buoy leaning downstream, ripples streaming off a pier's piling, or the way your own boat is held stern to the wind when she's at anchor. Careful piloting is an excellent test of current. If a fix puts you 2 miles ahead of (beyond) your D.R. position after an hour of sailing, you have 2 knots of favorable current even if the *Tidal Current Tables* say otherwise.

Slack Water

The times of high and low tide given in the *Tide Tables* indicate when the water level has reached its apex and nadir. However, the *Tidal Current Tables* refer to another time that is much more important when using currents. This is the time of slack water, when the current is flowing at a speed of 0.5 knot or less. Oddly enough, the times of high or low and slack water aren't aways coincidental. The water may keep flowing into an area even when the rise has stopped, since it may be moving along to another body of water.

Then, too, slack water varies in duration. In places where the maximum current is weak it lasts for quite a while, but where the maximum current runs strong slack water is short-lived. If the maximum current is 1-3 knots, slack water lasts for 2 hours down to 38 minutes — one-half before and one-half after the time given in the tables. With maximum currents of 4-6 knots, slack water lasts for 29 down to 19 minutes. A 10-knot current has only 11 minutes of slack water between the end of the flood and the start of the ebb, and vice versa.

Predicting Tidal Currents

Experienced sailors always calculate tidal current predictions before they set their itinerary through an area where the waters run swift, for there's a lot to lose and gain. A 3-knot head (contrary) current will cut a 6-knot boat's speed by 50 percent; a 3-knot favorable current, on the other hand, will increase her speed by 50 percent. Few cruising sailboats are so fast that their pilots can choose courses without taking current into account. Often, a 1- or 2-hour delay in getting under way in the morning may actually get you to your destination earlier if it means avoiding a head current.

The *Tidal Current Tables* provide considerable information for thousands of channels, harbors, and other waters that is used with data given for a relatively few reference stations. Each listing gives time differences to be added to or subtracted from the

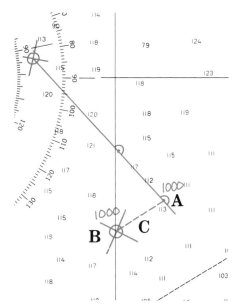

A reliable way to determine set and drift is to keep a careful D.R. plot and compare it with a series of reliable fixes. The differences between a D.R. (A) and a fix made at the same time (B) should be the result of current (C). Some Loran navigational devices programmed to calculate speed and course over the ground show tidal effect.

reference station's times for maximum flood and ebb and slack water (called "minimum before flood" and "minimum before ebb"); the true directions in which maximum currents flow; and a factor "speed ratio" to be multiplied against the reference station's current speeds to determine local current velocities.

To translate these numbers and directions into helpful piloting aids, first try to visualize the relationship between the current and the boat's course. It might help to sketch the course on a sheet of paper and then draw vectors, or force arrows, at the appropriate relative angles (after converting the true directions listed in the *Tidal Current Tables* to magnetic directions). Use these rules of thumb to determine the current's effect on the boat:

1. When a current is running within 20° of parallel to the boat's course, it affects only her speed. A head current decreases her speed made good over the bottom by a number equal to its velocity. A stern current increases her

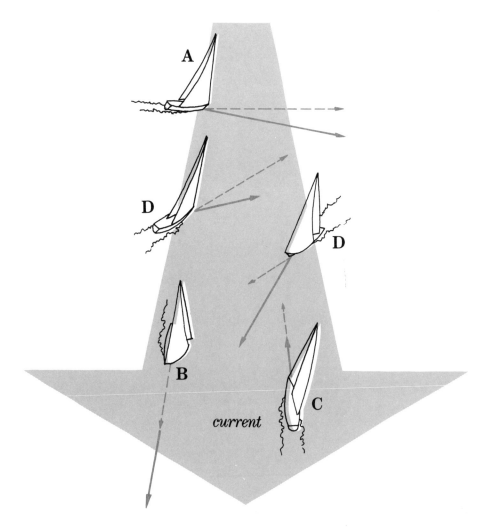

A beam current (A) affects only the course made good over the ground, and bow and stern currents (B and C) only the speed made good. Currents at a 45° angle to the bow and stern (D) affect course and speed, one-half their velocity for each.

Tide and Current

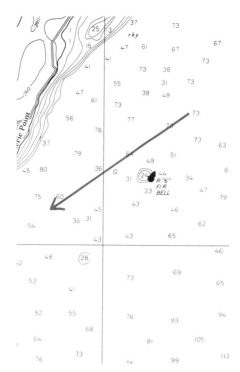

speed made good also by its own velocity.

2. When a current is beam-on (from the side), it affects only the course made good. A beam current pushes a boat to the side at a rate equal to the current's velocity.

3. A current at a 45° angle to the course affects the boat in two ways: one-half its force increases or decreases the speed made good over the bottom, and the other one-half pushes the boat to the side.

The current velocity is called *drift* and the direction it runs in is called *set*. A force arrow will have a length equal

The length and compass or true direction of a vector (force arrow) indicates the current's drift and set. When drawing vectors, always use the same scale.

to the drift in knots, and its direction will represent the set. Since the effect of drift and set is measured in terms of the length of time that the current strikes the boat, the first thing you do when planning a course is calculate how many hours you will be underway between your departure and destination. Start by figuring how long the passage would take with no current: divide the distance by your anticipated speed; the quotient is the passage time in hours.

If the vectors indicate that the current will be *contrary* all the way, multiply its velocity by the passage time and add the product to the passage time. What you're doing is calculating how much you will be set back for the duration of the passage. If the current is *favorable*, subtract the product from the passage time. Here you're figuring how much you will be advanced for the duration of the passage.

A simpler way to predict the current's effect on speed is to subtract (or add) average current velocity from (or to) your anticipated speed to find a

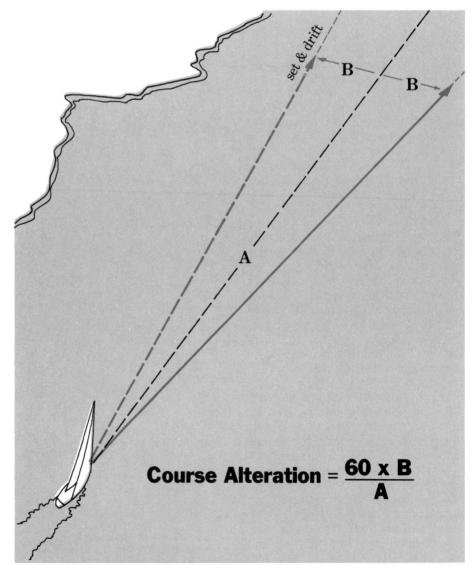

Once you have predicted the total set and drift for a leg or passage (B) you know how far you should head on the other side of the rhumb line (A) to compensate. Determine the course alteration in degrees using the Rule of 60.

$$\text{Course Alteration} = \frac{60 \times B}{A}$$

speed made good over the bottom, and then divide that speed into the distance to find your passage time.

With a *beam current*, multiply the average velocity by the passage time to see how far the boat will be pushed to one side during the trip. An accurate course, then, will be sailed toward a point that same distance up current.

Using the Rule of 60 formula presented earlier for calculating course alternations around an object dead ahead, you can figure exactly how far to compensate. This formula is:

$$\text{Course alteration} = \frac{60 \times \text{desired distance change}}{\text{distance ahead}}$$

If the Current Changes Direction

Those predictions are fairly easy to make if the current runs consistently in the same direction. But what if the tide changes during the passage or you alter course?

If these changes are predictable, break your long passage down into a series of short legs and precalculate the set, drift, passage time, and course alteration for each. If the tide changes halfway across, at midpassage, you may well find that the flood and the ebb cancel each other out so the rhumb-line (straight) course can be sailed without corrections. On the other hand you may not be able to anticipate set and drift with 100 percent accuracy. The *Tidal Current Tables* predictions may not be fulfilled due to weather conditions, or you may sail slower or have to alter course for a new destination. If that's the case, don't alter course until you're quite sure of your position. Wait for a reliable estimated position or fix. Then try to estimate the actual set and drift and make your calculations for the next leg or legs.

Wind-Driven Current

The wind blows the water surface to leeward at rates that might affect accurate piloting. Any wind-driven current will run at a slight angle to the right of the direction in which the wind is blowing (for instance, an East wind will create a current flowing Northwest). A 10-knot wind may create 0.2-knot current, a 20-knot wind a 0.3-knot current, a 30-knot wind a 0.4-knot current, and a 40-knot wind a 0.5-knot current. In areas with weak tides, such as Chesapeake Bay, most currents are wind-driven. On tideless lakes, strong wind-driven currents called seiches may develop. The effect of wind-driven current is figured like that of tidal current.

A Calculator Solution to Current Problems

What we have done using the Rule of 60 and some simple math can also be accomplished slightly more accurately with a calculator programmed with trigonometric functions using the following formula:

$$\text{Magnetic course} = RL - \arcsin \frac{\text{drift} \times \sin{(\text{set} - RL)}}{\text{boat speed}}$$

Where RL is the rhumb-line direct course in magnetic degrees, set is in magnetic degrees, and drift and boat speed are in knots or miles per hour.

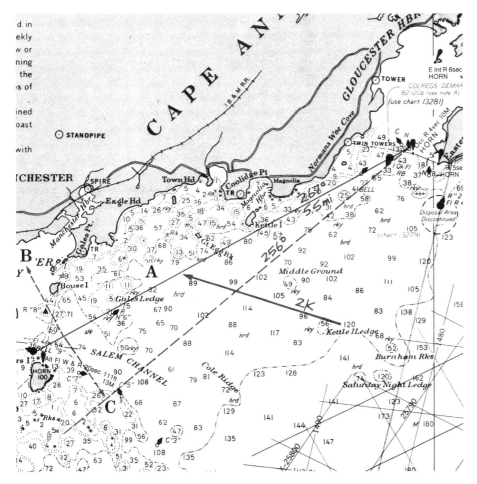

In this example, the pilot estimates that at 4.5 knots, with one-half the 2-knot 45° current working in his favor, it will take 1 hour to sail from Gloucester to the Salem Channel bell buoy. Since the other one-half of the curent's velocity will push the boat to starboard at a drift of 1 knot (B), he must set a course that takes him 1 mile to port through the water (C). The rhumb line is 5.5 miles long (A). How many degrees should he alter course? Using the Rule of 60, Course Alteration = 60 x 1 mile ÷ 5.5 miles = 11°. The rhumb line course is 267°, so he alters course 11° to port to 256°.

Hints for Sailing in Current

Try to maximize the amount of time you sail in favorable stern currents and minimize the time you sail in unfavorable bow currents. This may mean getting under way earlier or later than you would normally wish, but you'll end up saving time in the end. Remember, too, that currents tend to run faster in deep water and around points of land than in shallow water and in shallow indentations in the shore. A few hours spent studying a *Tidal Current Chart* will be extremely edifying.

In rough weather, a current contrary to the wind, even if on your stern, will slow you down because of the large breaking seas it creates. You will sail faster, safer, and more comfortably in a current running with the waves.

If you have a choice, save your fastest point of sail (almost always a reach) for sailing into an unfavorable current and your slowest point of sail (normally a run) for going with a favorable current.

When sailing in a beam current, steer by a range on the shoreline. This might be two buildings or big trees in alignment. When the range is steady, you know you're steering in a way that compensates for the current. If the near object moves up-current, you're being set down; if it moves down-current, you're overcompensating.

Backeddies, or local countercurrents, may form off piers or wharfs or inside indentations in the shore. They will set your boat contrary to the normal current.

In tide races, where extremely swift-moving currents meet each other or slow-moving water at an angle, choppy waves, whirlpools, or large slicks caused by upwellings may appear. Except in small boats these are not to be feared, but they can make steering difficult and roll the boat uncomfortably for a few moments.

When beating in a beam current on the leeward side, pushing the boat upwind, you'll make the best speed over the ground if you foot (sail fast without pinching).

Contrary to some popular beliefs, if

A range between two fixed objects in alignment will tell you if you are being carried to one side or the other. If the two objects stay aligned, you are correctly compensating for the current no matter what your heading may be.

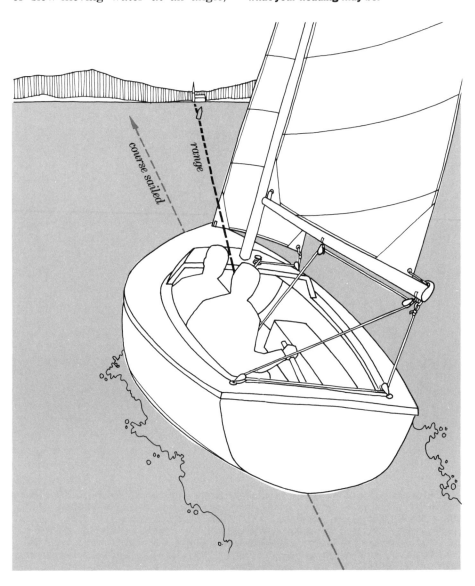

Currents alongshore may turn back on themselves in backeddies. If you play them right you can turn a contrary current into a favorable one.

you're beating into a head current there's no advantage to pinching up so the current hits the bow on its leeward side. Called "lee bowing the current," all this does is slow you down since the boat will be carried downcurrent no matter what her heading is. A much more effective way of handling a head current is to foot and sail fast so you get out of it as soon as possible.

Keep your eye out for any indicator of current velocity and direction — a lobster buoy, a drifting object, or the water around an oyster stake or piling all will signal water motion.

When sailing on a long leg in current, take advantage of every opportunity to take a bearing to estimate your position, or two or more bearings to fix it. A fix is the best possible measure of the current's set and drift. Between fixes, keep a careful D.R. plot.

Reaching a Surprise Destination

Sometimes a pilot will get a fix and find himself located far from his D.R. position for no apparent reason. His first reaction should be to get another fix immediately; if it confirms the first one, he has some backtracking to do, since the discrepancy must be explained and understood. Among the errors he could have made are that he forgot to account for deviation, leeway, or helmsman error, or one of those was larger or smaller than anticipated. More likely than not, when he calculated the course he either overcompensated or undercompensated for current.

To help analyze the error or errors, first calculate how far off the D.R. actually is. Measure the distance and magnetic direction from the D.R. position to the fix and compute the drift and set since the last fix. If they are large (2 knots and more than 10 degrees) and the visibility is poor or night is approaching, the wisest thing to do is to slow down or stop (by heaving-to, as described in chapter 3) while you and your shipmates try to solve the problem. Look around the compass for a piece of metal, double-check your course and current calculations, and try to reconstruct the events since the last fix — perhaps one helmsman wandered way off course while trying to put on foul-weather gear or identify a passing boat. In the short run these meanders are easily corrected, but if their cause is serious, in the long run they can be dangerous.

Guidelines for Safe Piloting

First and foremost, don't make assumptions and don't cut corners when the visibility is poor or the sea is rough. Observe all buoys, giving them a wide berth. Stay well outside shoal areas.

If at all possible make the most difficult passage on a reach, when you have speed, comfort, and maneuverability. Try to avoid beating out of a small harbor with few aids to navigation. Sailing close-hauled and tacking require much more concentration than reaching and running — concentration that should be available for piloting in a challenging situation.

If you have doubts about your piloting ability or the visibility, plot your course toward the most visible object available. A lighted buoy is more visible than a can or nun; a lighthouse is more visible than a lighted buoy; and in daylight a steep, rocky cliff may be more visible than a lighthouse Once you've seen the object, set your course toward another highly visible aid or landmark and leap-frog toward your destination.

Preplot your course and any alternatives, including danger bearings, danger circles, and lighthouse ranges of visibility.

In fog, use the technique of running out your time at a moderate speed: make your passage a series of short legs of precomputed duration, which you keep track of using a stopwatch and the Speed/Time/Distance formula.

When in doubt or anxiety, *stop*, rethink your assumptions, and calm down.

Alcohol and piloting or helmsmanship don't mix in challenging situations. Even a beer can scramble a pilot's calculations.

Keep a good lookout for other boats, land, and aids to navigation.

Assign the best helmsman to the wheel or tiller and the most knowledgeable, experienced pilot to the chart table. Make clear who is in charge.

Use all your senses: if you smell pine trees, you're probably approaching shore; if you see a buoy leaning, there's current flowing in the direction of the tilt; if you feel rougher water, a shoal may be approaching. The best way to tune your senses, especially that of hearing, to the surroundings is to stop the boat, quiet the sails and the crew down, and *concentrate*.

At night, avoid using white lights if at all possible; otherwise night vision will disappear and not return for 10 or 15 minutes. You need night vision to watch the water, the sails, and the sheets, and to look for buoys and lights.

Stay away from lee shores. If the wind is blowing onshore (toward the land) stay much farther offshore than you would in an offshore wind blowing toward the water. Even if you aren't in danger of being blown onto shore, the wind will be unpredictable up to a mile to windward of a lee shore as it skips up and over the water — much like wind blowing over a snow fence.

Don't panic. Keep your head. Trust your D.R. plot until an estimated position or a fix tells you otherwise. Rely on basics and your boat's S.O.P. This is why you established it to begin with.

Introduction to Celestial Navigation

Despite great advances in electronic navigation (which we will cover in the next chapter), the most reliable technique for finding your way when out of sight of land remains the skill that Americans call celestial navigation and the British call astro-navigation. This is the science of gauging your position using the sun, moon, planets, and stars as reference points. Electronics can break down, but celestial bodies are always there (albeit at times obscured by clouds and fog).

In a general book on sailing seamanship there isn't enough room to do justice to every aspect of celestial navigation. The best we can do is introduce the fundamental equipment and skills, and encourage readers to go on from there. Many planetariums, maritime museums, and colleges offer courses on the subject, and there are good instructional manuals, some of which are listed below, beginning with the shortest and simplest books and ending with ones that lean more on theory:

Mary Blewitt, *Celestial Navigation for Yachtsmen*. Clinton Corners, New York: John de Graff, 1964.

Warren Norville, *Celestial Navigation Step by Step*, 2nd edition. Camden, Maine: International Marine, 1984.

Susan P. Howell, *Practical Celestial Navigation*, 2nd edition. Mystic, Connecticut: Mystic Seaport Museum Stores, 1987.

Elbert S. Maloney, *Dutton's Navigation and Piloting*, 14th edition. Annapolis, Maryland: Naval Institute Press, 1985.

Basic Principles and Tools

The tools of celestial navigation are the sextant (which takes "sights," or vertical angles to the celestial body), the chronometer (to take the exact time of a sight), and some printed tables (for calculating the position from the sight and time).

In basic theory, celestial navigation and piloting share some common features. The navigator takes bearings on objects whose positions are known and charted. Those bearings are lines of position (LOPs), and where LOPs cross is

a fix. The difference is that where bearings in piloting are compass angles to stationary objects on or near the water's surface, bearings in celestial navigation are vertical angles to objects in the sky that are moving or appear to be in motion. Those vertical angles are measured with a sextant.

In piloting, the navigator uses a chart to locate the objects on which bearings are taken. In celestial navigation, the navigator uses printed astronomical tables that pinpoint the positions of bodies for every second of the year. To make sense of the tables, the navigator needs to know not only what the angle to a celestial body is but when the sight was taken. This is why the chronometer is needed.

To illustrate celestial's concepts, construct a simple model from an apple, a pencil, a thumbtack, and some string. Celestial navigation texts use more complicated models when teaching theory, but this will do fine for a general introduction. Anywhere on the side of the apple, push the pencil point into the core, leaving the eraser several inches above the skin.

The apple represents the globe and the eraser represents the celestial body (the sun, star, or moon). The spot where the pencil pierces the apple's skin represents what is called the celestial body's *geographical position* (G.P.), or the position on the earth's surface between the center of the earth and the celestial body.

Next, tack the end of the string to the tip of the eraser. Stretch the string

In this simple model, the apple is the globe, the pencil eraser tip is a celestial body, the string is the sight through the sextant, and the inscribed angle between the string and the surface is the altitude to the body as measured by the sextant. The G.P. is where the pencil pierces the apple and the COP is the circle defined by the altitude. For a given altitude, you're somewhere on the COP. If you know exactly when the sight was taken, you can determine the COP using tables that show the positions of the celestial body.

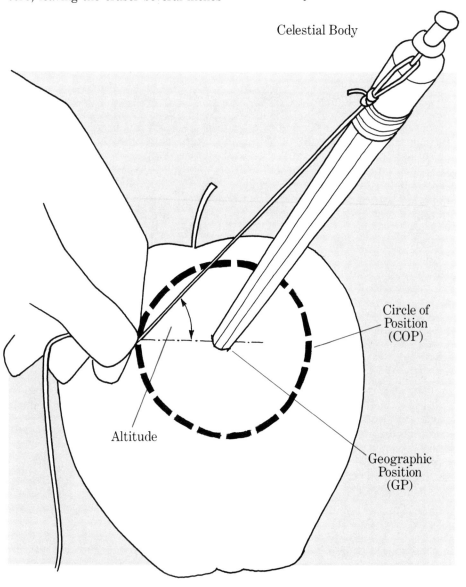

Celestial Body

Circle of Position (COP)

Geographic Position (GP)

Altitude

down to the apple and swing a circle around the G.P. That circle is a *circle of position* (COP). From every point on that circle, the altitude to the celestial body is the same. To put it another way, for a given altitude you're somewhere on a circle like this one. While a full-size COP is never straight, its radius is so great (thousands of miles in length) that the part of the circle used to plot positions on a chart is represented as a straight line of position (LOP). The bearing in true degrees from the boat on the LOP to the G.P. is called the *azimuth*.

This LOP based on a celestial sight is used just like an LOP based on a compass bearing. Cross it with the boat's track and you have an estimated position (E.P.). Cross it with another LOP from another celestial body and you have a fix. You'll also have a fix if, using the technique of the running fix described in chapter 11, you advance this LOP to cross another LOP based on a later sight on the same body.

Because it uses the dimension of altitude, celestial navigation has an ad-vantageous position-finding technique that is impossible with piloting. It's called the *noon sight*. The noon sight is used when the sun has risen as far as it will rise, which happens within a few minutes of noon local time. A noon sight gives the boat's longitude. Cross this longitude with an LOP advanced from a star or sun sight taken earlier in the day, and you have a fix.

The Sextant

The sextant measures the altitude (or vertical angle) to the celestial body, using the horizon line on the water as the base line. For calculating positions, the most reliable altitudes are between 30° and 60°. Since a clear, steady horizon is the frame of reference for taking altitudes, celestial navigation may be impossible in bad weather due either to instability because of wild rolling or to poor visibility (navigators speak of times when there is "no horizon" because it blends into the sky). While "bubble" sextants with artificial horizons may work on aircraft, the bubble may be too unstable for use on pleasure boats.

In price, new sextants range from under $100 (for small plastic ones that serve as emergency instruments in life rafts), to about $150 (for plastic, reliably accurate instruments), to well over $500 (for very high-quality precision sextants). For more on sextant selection, use, maintenance, and history, see Bruce Bauer's helpful book, *The Sextant Handbook* (Camden, Maine: International Marine, 1986).

The Chronometer

A chronometer is an extremely accurate timepiece such as a quartz crystal watch. Set it to Coordinated Universal Time, informally known as Greenwich Mean Time (GMT or Z), or the time at zero degrees longitude passing through Greenwich, England. This is the time used in the tables. Chronometers should be checked against atomic clocks or the time tick on shortwave radio stations WWV and WWVH, which can be picked up on the 15-MHz band during the day and the 5-MHz band at night. If a chronometer has an error, it usually is constant and predictable, for example two seconds a day. Don't try to correct the chronometer. That may lead to more errors. Instead, "rate" the chronometer by writing the daily error down, then compensate for it when you do the calculations. Another way to take time is to set a stopwatch off the time tick and then record the time when the sight is taken.

In practice, it's a good idea to do sights with two people, one to take the sight and read the angle off the sextant and the other to write down the time of the sight. Be accurate: an error of less than five seconds can lead to a plotting error of one mile. Take several sights and either choose the best one, throwing out the ones that fall out of a pattern, or average the readings and the times.

The Almanac and Tables

Once the sight is taken and its time (exact to the second) is noted, the navigator refers to tables in two publications, the almanac and the sight reduction tables. The data found there is used in calculations that produce a position.

The almanac is used to figure the position of the celestial body at the time of the sight and to make small corrections in the sight based on the navigator's height above the water and other factors. There are two versions of this publication, *The Nautical Almanac* and *The Air Almanac*, both of which are published in annual editions. Each publica-

A good sextant is easily adjusted and has clear altitude indicators. There should be several filters to protect the eye when taking sun sights.

Celestial Navigation

tion has tables that show the geographical positions (G.P.) of celestial bodies for every second of every day of the year covered by the edition. These positions are expressed in two measurements, declination and Greenwich hour angle (GHA). *Declination* in degrees North or South of the Equator is the same as latitude. *GHA* is the same as longitude except that it is expressed from 000° to 360° West instead of 000° to 180° East or West. For example, while Tokyo's longitude is 139° 30' East, its GHA is 221° 30'.

Sight reduction tables are then used to figure the boat's position, using as a

Although a celestial plot uses many piloting concepts and skills, running fixes play a more important role in celestial navigation than in piloting since daytime sights usually are taken only on one object (the sun).

point of reference the boat's *assumed position*, which is based on her dead reckoning or estimated position. Different types of sight reduction tables are used in the various systems of making calculations.

Calculations

Using all these data, celestial positions are worked out mathematically in several simple steps. It helps to use printed forms with blanks that are filled in. The end result is two numbers: the *azimuth*, or true bearing to the celestial body; and the *intercept*, or distance down the azimuth. The LOP is a line passing through the intercept at a right angle to the azimuth.

These calculations and, in fact, all of celestial navigation may sound complicated, and indeed they are at first. But the complications have more to do with learning the steps than with mastering astronomical theory or calculus. Much more than mathematical genius, what's needed is attention to detail. Many calculations can be done on pocket-size electronic calculators. A good survey of skills is H. Rolf Noer's *Navigator's Pocket Calculator Handbook* (Centreville, Maryland: Cornell Maritime Press, 1983). Some calculators have been programmed with sight reduction tables and the almanac. However, nobody should go far out to sea without knowing how to calculate a sight in case the computer's batteries fail.

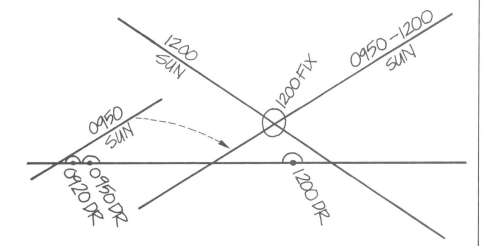

Review Quiz

Solve plotting problems on the chart here using a plotter on the compass rose and dividers on the latitude scale on the left margin. Courses and bearings are in magnetic degrees, distances are in nautical miles, and speeds are in knots. Solutions may be found after the Index.

1. You are sailing at a speed of 5 knots on a course of 180°. At 1300 hours (1 P.M.), False Ducks Lt. bears 045° off the starboard bow at 225°. At 1336 hours, the light is directly abeam at 270°. What is your position at 1336?

A. The light bears 315° and is 3 miles away

B. The light bears 270° and is 3 miles away

C. There's not enough information

2. When you stand up in a rowboat, you see the light on False Ducks lighthouse. When you sit down, the light disappears behind the horizon. Approximately what is the distance to the lighthouse?

A. 10.8 nautical miles

B. 9.4 nautical miles

C. 11 nautical miles

3. You are next to the buoy off Prince Edward Point (just above "4sec") and heading in a Northerly direction out into Prince Edward Bay. What are the approximate danger bearings for clearing Timber Island (including the buoy at the 9-foot spot)?

A. Not less than (NLT) 200° on the buoy and not more than (NMT) 230° on the Northeast tip of the island

B. NLT 020° on the buoy and NMT 045° on the tip of the island

C. 030° on the center of the island

4. The course from R "68T" FlR, South of Grape Island, to the middle of Timber Island is 210°. What approximate

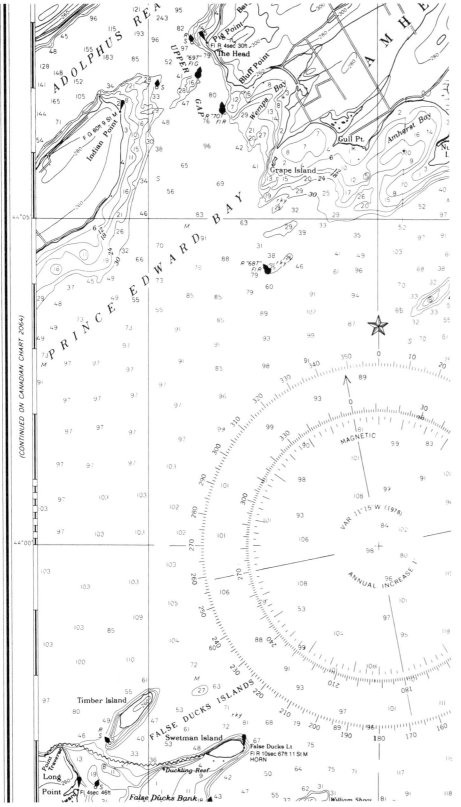

courses must the boat steer to pass by the island with a safe berth of 0.3 mile?

A. *204° to pass to the East and 216° to pass to the West*

B. *175° to pass to the East and 220° to pass to the West*

5. If you had to enter Upper Gap from Prince Edward Bay using your depth sounder to find your way, on which of the following routes would your equipment serve to best advantage?

A. *Up the middle of the channel*

B. *Up the Eastern side of the channel*

C. *Up the Western side of the channel*

6. Use the tide tables on pages 2xx-2xx to solve this problem. What will be the approximate predicted water depth on August 4 at 0814 Daylight Saving Time?

A. *3 feet above mean low water (MLW)*

B. *1.8 feet above MLW*

C. *1.8 feet below mean high water (MHW)*

7. You will need only scrap paper for this problem. You are sailing at 6 knots on a course of 045°. The current chart indicates that the tidal current's set and drift are 090° and 2 knots respectively. Estimate your approximate speed made good (SMG) and approximate course made good (CMG).

A. *SMG 4 knots, CMG 045°*

B. *SMG 5 knots, CMG 030°*

C. *SMG 7 knots, CMG 060°*

8. At night, you pass "69T" FlG, off The Head, at 2130 at a speed of 5 knots. You steer 188° in order to keep False Ducks Lt. dead ahead. A friend in another boat tells you over the VHF-FM radio that there is a current with a set of 270° and drift of 1 knot. Which course should you steer to compensate for this set and drift?

A. *200°*

B. *176°*

Chapter 13
Electronic Navigation and Radiotelephones

In this chapter, we will survey the operating principles and uses of the most popular electronic instruments used on today's boats. These include the speedometer and other performance instruments, Loran-C, radar, satellite navigation, radio direction finder, and the radiotelephone. (The depth sounder was described in chapter 12.) This chapter should not be regarded as a substitute for instrument owners' manuals, which are the best sources of information about instrument abilities and problems.

Which instruments should you carry? While computerized performance indicators probably will appeal only to racing sailors, many owners will want to have a speedometer and a wind strength and direction indicator so they can gauge performance relative to the wind strength and angle. Sailors who want quick, accurate, repeatable navigational assistance will want to have a Loran-C set. If there is considerable traffic or frequent fog, radar can provide great peace of mind. Radio direction finders, while not as accurate as Loran or radar, can be helpful if radio beacons are nearby. For sailing far out in the ocean, no electronic device backs up celestial navigation as well as a satellite navigation receiver-computer. Radiotelephones provide instant access to nearby boats, weather forecasts, shore-based telephones, and (in emergencies) the Coast Guard.

All those instruments are available and very helpful, but along with their advantages come expense and maintenance problems. The best advice is to buy only the instruments that you really need.

The accuracy, compactness, and seeming simplicity of electronics can be distracting if not downright hypnotic. It's all too easy to assume that a Loran-C receiver or an RDF is precisely correct 100 percent of the time and therefore to forget to keep a systematic dead reckoning plot. Not only do electronics make mistakes, but navigators can interpret and plot their readings erroneously. A seeming shortcut offered by the flashing numbers on a Loran-C receiver may turn out to be a very long cut indeed.

Never rely entirely on only one navigation aid or system. If the Loran or the RDF set is the belt of your vessel's navigational trousers, use the D.R. plot as suspenders. In rough weather, tide-swept waters, poor visibility, or other difficult conditions, take advantage of every possible navigation aid, electronic or visual, but consider the D.R. to be your baseline. As we saw in chapters 11 and 12, keeping an accurate plot demands time and concentration — much more than are needed to make a Loran fix. It requires accurate helmsmanship and sensitivity to the boat's performance, as well as knowledge about wind and tide. Keeping a D.R. plot forces the navigator to focus his eyes and senses not on a LED readout but on the boat herself and the weather itself. Sailing "by the numbers" is never a total substitute for alert piloting.

Performance Instruments

Devices that measure and indicate the boat's speed and the wind's strength and direction help you plan and sail safe, accurate courses. Since these devices were developed for racing boats, they are called performance instruments, but cruising sailors can also take advantage of them.

Speedometers (also called knotmeters) measure raw straight-ahead speed through the water. The paddlewheels or electronic devices that serve as sensors should be kept clean, and the instrument should occasionally be calibrated during timed runs over known distances using the Speed/Time/Distance formula described in chapter 11. If the speedometer can compute and display the average speed over a period of time ranging from a few seconds to a

view of a boat's speed than a momentary readout influenced by waves. Speedometers can be connected to **recording logs** that show the distance run in miles.

Apparent-wind indicators (AWI) indicate the direction and speed of the apparent wind. With the help of the AWI you can determine at what wind speeds and angles you should reef or shorten down to smaller sails. True-wind indicators show the direction and speed of the true wind and tell the navigator what point of sail the boat will be on when she changes course. This can be a great help if you want to avoid sailing on

Performance Instrument Package

Loran

Depth Sounder

Performance, Loran-C, and depth-sounding instruments are the electronic devices most widely used aboard boats.

slow or uncomfortable points of sail.

Velocity-made-good (VMG) indicators work off small on-board computers that calculate the boat's progress dead upwind and dead downwind when she is beating to windward or jibing downwind. Upwind, the VMG tells the crew how to balance closewindedness against straight-ahead speed; downwind, it helps the crew decide on the fastest, shortest course. A computer may be programmed to compare this information with data from a velocity prediction program (a mathematical prediction of a boat's speed and VMG for each point of sail and wind strength). The computer then calculates and displays a number that tells how efficiently the boat is being sailed.

In the late 1980s, Ockam Instruments, a marine electronics company, developed a helpful approach for using these devices called the **target speed** method. With the help of a velocity prediction program, knowledge of the boat's actual performance, and the instruments, a crew using this method can identify the most productive boat speed and VMG for each point of sail and wind strength. These are called the target speed and VMG. The crew then attempts to get the boat to match those numbers. The method provides clear points of reference where sailors would otherwise have to rely on vague "feel" to determine when their boats were sailing fast or slowly.

Radio Direction Finder (RDF)

Less accurate than Loran and radar, and (in clear weather) not as reliable as visual compass bearings, radio bearings made with a radio direction finder (RDF) are still helpful navigational aids. An RDF receiver is used to determine the direction to a radio beacon using a signal sent from that beacon. If the beacon is charted, then a line of position (LOP) can be drawn from it to the boat.

An RDF is a radio with a long-wave band (200-400 kHz) and, usually, an AM band. The major difference between it and a normal household radio is that the antenna is external and can be rotated either manually or automatically. The signal is loudest when the antenna cuts across it at right angles. When the antenna is aimed either directly at or directly away from the beacon, the signal is not received at all — this point of silence is called the null. Aiming the antenna to find the null is like pointing your hand directly at a buoy or a lighthouse, except that the "sighted" beacon may be up to 30 miles away if it's a short-range beacon located near bays and harbors, or up to 200 miles distant if it's a long-range beacon located at the entrance to a major harbor or along a coast. An RDF can also home in on the tower sending an AM radio signal or an aerobeacon, but of course you won't be able to plot an LOP unless you know the location of these beacons. NOS charts show the locations, frequencies, and Morse Code call signals of almost all marine beacons and some aerobeacons, but you probably will have to plot the position of commercial broadcast beacons using a road map.

Permanent beacons are listed and described in *Radio Navigational Aids*, Publications 117-A and 117-B of the U.S. Defense Mapping Agency Hydrographic Center. Volume 117-A lists beacons on coastal areas contiguous to the Atlantic Ocean, the Arctic Ocean, and the Mediterranean Sea; 117-B lists those fronting on the Pacific Ocean, the Bering Sea, and the Indian Ocean. The *Light List* also describes radio beacons. Temporary or permanent changes to beacons are described in *Notice to Mariners* and *Local Notice to Mariners*.

The antenna on an RDF receiver usually is a ferrite-rod type rotated

radio beacon

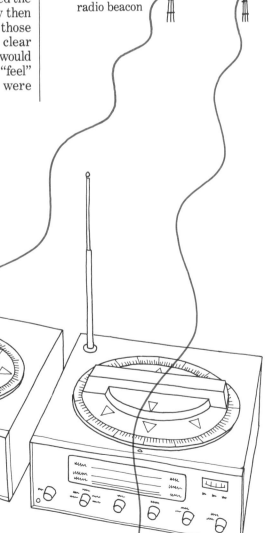

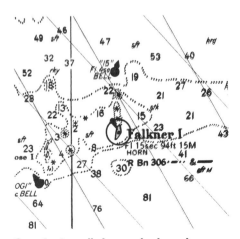

On a chart a radio beacon is shown by a circle, the letters "R Bn," the frequency, and the dot-dash identification sequence (above). Reception is weakest at the "null," when the rotating antenna points at or away from the beacon, and strongest when the antenna is at a right angle to the signal (left).

Radio Direction Finder (RDF)

around a pivot on top of the set. The signal it receives can be determined aurally. It is a characteristic Morse Code signal whose sound fades as the antenna is rotated toward the null point and strengthens as it is rotated the other way. Although the radiobeacon system is arranged so that signals with similar characteristics are usually not sent over adjacent frequencies, some people who have trouble distinguishing dots from dashes may not be able to identify the signal readily. The use of earphones may make identification of the radio signals easier, as well as protect your shipmates from the brain-numbing repetition of high-frequency dots and dashes. But the best way to identify signals and the null is to closely watch a set's signal-strength meter. This meter, which is active with each signal, is more sensitive than the audible indicator. When the meter is blank, the antenna is at the null. The signalstrength meter is especially helpful when using the RDF while a gasoline engine is running, since the ignition system will cause static. Turning an adjustment knob labeled "gain" will increase the sensitivity of the meter, while decreasing the volume will minimize the distraction of the audible signal once the signal is identified.

To operate the RDF, first look at the chart or other publication to find the frequency of a nearby beacon. Turn on the machine and tune it to that frequency. Now you must adjust the antenna to find the bearing to the beacon. Under the antenna on most RDF receivers are rotatable 360° azimuth rings over which the antenna is rotated to find either the relative bearing or the compass bearing. In each case the receiver must be securely located on deck or a cabin table with its fore-and-aft axis exactly on or parallel to the boat's centerline. You can use marks on the set and the surface underneath as reference points.

To measure the *relative bearing* to the beacon, turn the azimuth ring until 360°/0° is forward and 180° is aft. Rotate the antenna toward the beacon

until there is a null; then read the bearing on the ring. This is a relative bearing — for example, if it reads 325°, the beacon bears 035° relative off the port bow (since 360° - 325° = 035°). The moment that you have the strongest signal, shout "Mark!" to the helmsman, who should respond with his heading. Here, since the bearing is to port, subtract it from the course to determine the compass bearing. For example, with a relative bearing of 035° to port and a compass course of 135°, the compass bearing to the beacon is 100° (135° - 035° = 100°). If the bearing is to starboard, add it to the compass course to find the compass bearing.

You may also read the *compass bearing* directly on the receiver. Tell the helmsman to stay on a heading (he should shout "Mark!" when on course) and adjust the azimuth ring until the heading is forward. With the azimuth mimicking the steering compass, the antenna is right over the compass bearing to the beacon.

Why not place the RDF receiver

over, behind, or in front of the cockpit compass so the compass bearing can be read without adjusting the azimuth? The RDF should be kept several feet away from the cockpit compass since its metal components and internal magnet will cause deviation. Some RDF receivers are equipped with small antennas connected to hand bearing compasses, which may be taken on deck at the end of long cords. If the hand bearing compass mimics

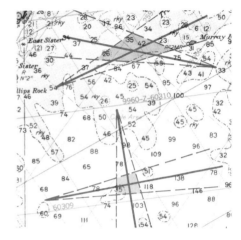

Take radio bearings at right angles to each other to minimize inaccuracies due to reception or operator error. Label the fix to show its origin.

Align the RDF on or parallel to the boat's centerline and turn the azimuth ring until the course or 360°/0° is forward. Adjust the antenna to find the null and read the compass or relative bearing to the beacon on the ring.

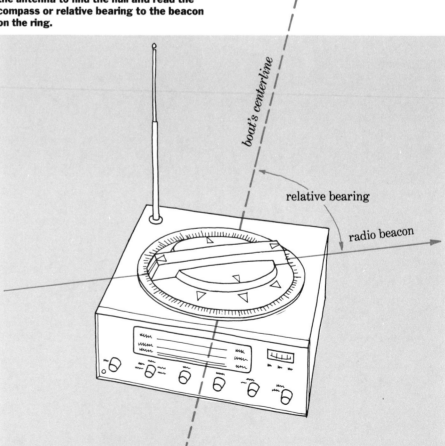

the cockpit compass, this portable feature is extremely helpful; if it does not, errors may result.

Taking an RDF bearing can be as easy as taking a compass bearing, but some problems often turn up. First, RDF bearings are rarely accurate to within 5° at distances of 150 nautical miles or less. This is because the receivers usually are not very sensitive. Operator error will increase that margin of error significantly. Because of RDF inaccuracy, fixes made with radiobeacon bearings should not be done at shallow angles; the safest fix is one made with two bearings at right angles. Even better, use a visual aid and only one radiobeacon.

Radio waves follow confused paths during the half-hour before and the half-hour after sunset and dawn due to changes in the ionosphere. Don't rely on any radio bearings taken during these times. The land can also affect radio waves, distorting them especially if they run approximately parallel to shore. Any bearing within 20° of being parallel to the shoreline is unreliable.

An RDF must be calibrated for the boat. To calibrate a receiver, sail into open water from which you can take clear visual bearings on a beacon on which you also take radio bearings. Place the receiver in its normal location and proceed to take bearings at 5° to 10° intervals as you turn the boat through 360°. Take notes of any differences between the observed compass bearings and the calculated compass bearings (based on the radio bearings), and then draw up an RDF deviation card similar to the compass deviation card. This card should indicate the number of degrees to be added to or subtracted from the relative bearing for each of 72 bearings taken at 5° intervals, or 36 bearings taken at 10° intervals.

Low-power beacons generally send out signals without pause on their own frequencies (shown on charts), but high-power beacons are often grouped in sequences on the same frequency, sending a signal for 1 minute and then standing silent for 5 or 6 minutes. The navigator has to move fast to identify the signal and then find its null. Schedules in *Radio Navigational Aids* and other publications indicate the sequence for beacon groups.

Because there is a null when either end of the antenna is aimed at a beacon, there may be times when a pilot doesn't know which side the beacon is on. The D.R. plot should offer a solution. Some RDF's have a special at-tachment called a telescoping sense antenna that indicates which way the beacon lies.

What to Look for in an RDF

An RDF should be encased in a sturdy waterproof box and should have a radiobeacon band and an AM or FM band; the more bands it has, though, the less sensitive it may be.

Sensitivity — or the ability to pick up weak signals — is measured in microvolts per meter (μV/m). The lower the number, the better. A 75-μV/m RDF should pick up a signal at the beacon's nominal range; a 40-μV/m set has a greater range.

Selectivity is the receiver's ability to pick up a signal with minimum interference from nearby signals. This is indicated by a ratio of dB (decibels) to kHz (kilohertz), with higher ratios indicating better selectivity, or ability to differentiate between several beacons. This may not be very important, since adjacent beacons of about the same power are usually placed far apart on the radio band, and beacons with the same or nearly the same frequencies are located many miles apart.

The **signal-to-noise ratio** indicates how strongly a receiver enhances a signal compared with the nonsignal noise that it also receives. This is measured in dB; the higher the dB level, the better the reception.

Automatic Radio Direction Finder (ADF)

An automatic radio direction finder (ADF) takes some of the work out of calculating radio bearings by showing the bearing on a visual display. On an ADF, the antenna may rotate mechanically or electronically. Originally developed for aircraft, the ADF is used on many yachts.

Plotting a Radio Bearing

There is almost no difference between plotting a compass bearing or fix and plotting a radio bearing or fix. The radio bearing should be labeled with the time and degrees (magnetic or true, depending on your boat's S.O.P.), and a clear sign that it is based on an RDF rather than a visual bearing, either with a brief label ("RDF Bearing") or with a line drawn to the beacon itself. A fix based wholly or partly on radio bearings should be labeled "RDF Fix."

The reason why radio bearings require special labels is that their normal unreliability demands special attention. Given a choice between making a fix based on compass bearings and one based on radio bearings, the cautious navigator will always choose the compass.

Homing-In

Since RDF beacons are often located in lighthouses and light towers at the mouths of harbors, a navigator may find his way to port in poor visibility by aiming the antenna dead ahead and steering not by the compass but by the null. Once again, the small reception error must be consciously acknowledged. Be sure to keep track of your progress, or you may run aground or even hit the lighthouse. Many years ago a steamer homing-in on the beacon on the Nantucket lightship ran the lightship down with considerable loss of life.

The most modern RDF's, like this one demonstrated by the author, are completely self-contained and easily aimed.

CHAPTER 13:
ELECTRONIC NAVIGATION
Loran

In the late 1970s an increasing number of small-craft navigators came to replace radio direction finders with Loran receivers as their standard electronic navigational devices. RDF continues to be important: it is less expensive than Loran, and because it uses flashlight batteries for a power source where Loran draws off the ship's battery, it functions independently of the vessel's electrical system. But Loran is easier to use and is far more accurate than an RDF — down to 50 feet if the station is less than 200 miles away. Many fishermen use Loran as their only navigational device to locate lobster pots even in dense fog. Loran is also considerably more versatile than RDF.

The raw data provided by Loran are numbers displayed on the instrument. These numbers are called TDs, shorthand for the time difference (or time delay) in reception of signals sent between two distant transmitters as measured in microseconds (millionths of a second). TDs are also printed as curved lines on most charts (the main exceptions are harbor and small-craft charts) at intervals of 1 to 10 microseconds. TDs falling between those printed lines are identified by interpolation. To plot a position, the navigator matches TD lines printed on the chart (or their interpolations) with the TDs displayed on the instrument. On the chart, TDs are lines of positions (LOP). Where two lines meet, there is a fix.

Loran instruments are also computers. Many of them can convert the raw data of TDs into other data, which are then analyzed by the receiver in ways that allow for numeric or graphic displays to help navigators.

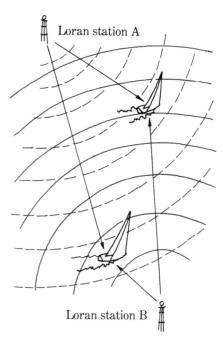

A Loran receiver is tuned to signals sent simultaneously by a pair (or pairs) of stations (above). It displays the time difference (TD) in reception and the pilot plots the position using a chart printed with corresponding TD lines (right). Loran navigation is usually extremely accurate.

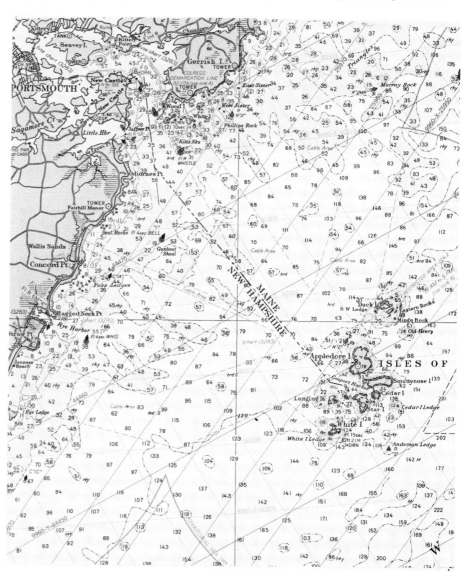

The most useful of these features is the **waypoint**, or the geographic position of any object that will help the boat reach her destination. The navigator identifies the waypoint and enters its geographic location into the set's memory. The Loran instrument can display the range (distance) and bearing from the boat to the waypoint, as well as the time to it and other information. A waypoint can be the position of a buoy, harbor, racing mark, or fishing ground. A good Loran set can be programmed with dozens of waypoints. Waypoints and their positions should be written down in a notebook in case the set's memory is erased.

The computer may also convert TDs into latitude and longitude geographic positions. Since mathematical and other errors may be involved with these conversions, TD readouts are more accurate than latitude-longitude readouts. Fixes based on TDs are easier to plot than fixes based on latitude and longitude, which must be read way out on the chart edge. Unfortunately, on most Loran-C sets waypoints must be entered using latitude and longitude, not TDs.

Other useful features found on most Loran-C sets include display of the boat's actual speed and course over the bottom; display of "cross-track error," or the variance between the charted course to the waypoint and the actual course due to current or wind; an audible "anchor watch" alarm that sounds when the boat drags beyond the anchor's original position; interface with an autopilot so the boat is steered on a precise course; interface with radar and computerized charts so waypoints are shown on radar scopes and computer screens; and interface with satellite navigation so the Loran constantly updates NAVSAT fixes.

If waypoint, course, and speed data can be shown in the cockpit on a remote display, the steerer can keep track of the boat's progress and adjust for cross-track error without having to depend on someone below to monitor the Loran set.

Loran Problems

While Loran-C is the electronic tool of choice for most navigators, it is not foolproof.

Land may bend the signals. This is why the Coast Guard usually does not allow TD lines to be printed on harbor charts (latitude-longitude readouts in these areas should not be relied on unless they have been carefully checked out). In addition, signals may be made inaccurate by precipitation, lightning, or electronic "noise" caused by fluorescent lights, television sets, and alternators. Large amounts of interference are usually indicated by visual alarms such as flashing lights, but sometimes an inaccuracy is not caught. Therefore, never rely entirely on a Loran fix. Back it up with compass bearings or depth soundings.

Errors often result when the boat is either near a transmitter or near a baseline extension, which is the imaginary line running from a master transmitter to a secondary transmitter. Baseline extensions are shown on charts. You're near a transmitter or a baseline extension if the printed TD lines on the chart near your plotted position make tight turns.

Loran today means Loran-C, the second generation of *Long Range Navigation* systems developed during World War II, although the original Loran-A system is still used in some parts of the Pacific Ocean. In Loran-C, pairs of transmission stations send out pulsed signals simultaneously over the low frequency of 100 kHz. The on-board receiver tuned to those stations receives the signals. If the boat is exactly halfway between the two stations, on what is called the center line, there will be no time difference (TD) between the reception of the two signals. If she is anywhere else between the stations, one signal will be received before the other one. The TD in microseconds will be displayed on the receiver. Using a chart on which TDs are printed, the navigator finds the line corresponding to the display on the receiver. This line is one LOP. Most of the time the receiver displays TDs for two or more sets of stations, allowing the navigator to plot several LOPs, and therefore get a fix where they cross. It takes only a minute or two to plot a fix once the receiver is warmed up.

These sets of stations are called chains. They consist of a master transmitting station and several secondary stations that exchange signals with the master station. Each chain has a specified pulse group repetition interval (GRI), or rate, identified by a

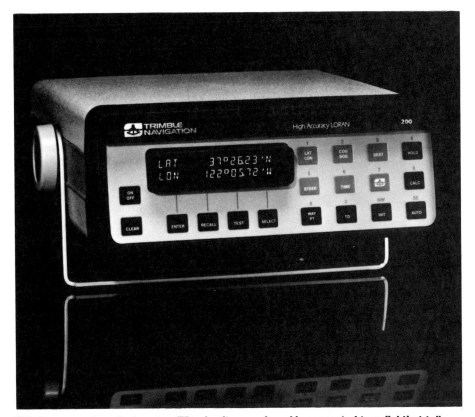

This Loran receiver displays two TDs simultaneously and is connected to a dial that tells the helmsman if he is on course. Some receivers also display latitude and longitude or range and bearing to the destination.

Loran

number that consists of the first four digits of the GRI. Letters on the rate identify signals sent by secondary stations. TD lines are curved like hyperbolas, which is why Loran is called a hyperbolic navigation system. As a result the lines of position between Loran stations on charts are actually *curves* of position. Everywhere on that curve an object is the same TD between the two stations. Where two or more curves meet, the navigator has a fix.

A Loran-C receiver is amazingly simple to operate. Turn it on, enter the GRI, and wait for the receiver to lock in on the signals. With clear signals during daytime, this should take no longer than about 3 minutes. All receivers have some sort of alarm system to indicate when reception is unreliable. When the alarm stops, simply read off the numbers. The TDs stay visible for a few seconds, allowing the navigator ample time to write them down, and repeat themselves continuously. When recording TDs, note the time of day. Keep these notes in the log book or a special notebook so you can refer back to them if plotting problems appear later on.

Loran receivers and signals can misbehave in storms, around dawn and sunset, at night, and even when fluorescent lights are turned on. The alarm system usually alerts the navigator to poor or misleading reception, but sometimes an inaccurate TD may slip through. The best protection is to keep a good D.R. plot, and to carefully record all Loran readings, inspecting for anomalies in patterns.

Land formations may limit a Loran signal's accuracy; usually this is predicted and compensated for on charts, but some navigators have noticed that an island may "bend" a signal. All the same, a fix that's accurate to at least 1500 feet or a quarter-mile can be anticipated almost all the time when there is a strong signal.

Plotting a Loran Fix

Few navigator's tasks are easier than plotting a Loran fix — indeed a problem with Loran is that many people come to rely excessively on it, forgetting other piloting skills as well as how to use their eyes, ears, and other senses. Addiction to those little LED numbers is not unlike becoming hooked by computer games.

The major complication comes when interpolating between printed Loran TDs, which may be 1, 5, or 10 microseconds apart — or 1 or more nautical miles distant on a chart. Interpolation may be done with a pair of dividers and eyeball estimates, or with Loran linear interpolators, which are small scaling graphs printed on NOS charts. (The U.S. Coast Guard also distributes plastic interpolators.) The only other tools required for plotting Loran fixes are a straight edge and a sharp pencil. As with compass bearings and radio bearings, LOPs should cross at angles greater than about 30° in order to minimize the consequences of error. Loran fixes are labeled "L Fix"; their usual reliability allows them a status greater than a radiobeacon fix or a compass fix.

Fixes may be plotted by crossing two or more LOPs. Since in most areas in North America, a Loran receiver should be able to pick up signals from at least two pairs of transmitters, there should always be at least two LOPs. Visual alarms and experience with the set will alert you to inaccurate TDs. Even if only one LOP is reliable, you still have enough information to plot an estimated position where the LOP crosses your dead reckoning track, or to make a fix by crossing the Loran LOP with a compass bearing.

What to Look for in a Loran Receiver

Even inexpensive receivers will automatically continue to track signals once they've been locked in strongly, will have an alarm system for indicating inaccurate reception and readout, and will have adjustable filters for minimizing atmospheric interference (these filters may have to be adjusted if the boat leaves the area approximately 100 miles around her home port). The receiver must be grounded, and its antenna must be professionally installed. The antenna should be located on deck out of crew traffic. Placing it at the top of the mast is a mistake, for if the boat is dismasted the antenna and the set's usefulness will be lost. To test whether the antenna or the receiver's filters need adjustment, get away from shore to a position accurately fixed by good visual bearings and turn off all instruments that might cause electronic noise. The Loran fix should be no more than 0.1 miles off your plotted position. If the discrepancy is greater, have a technician adjust the filters or examine the receiver and antenna. (On some sets, the filters can be adjusted by the crew.)

Power

A Loran-C receiver runs off the ship's batteries drawing 1½ amps — a very small power demand for most boats' electrical systems. And since much of that is used simply to light the display panel, energy can be saved by switching off or dimming the display when you're not reading it. The best economy is to establish and follow an S.O.P. that allows the receiver to be used only when necessary.

Although it operates continuously and is simple to use, Loran is limited for offshore use by its relatively short range. Its accuracy is not reliable beyond about 1200 miles. For accurate navigation along coastlines Loran is superb, but elsewhere it's either inaccurate or nonexistent.

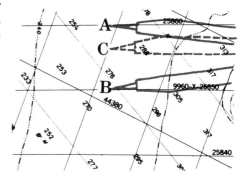

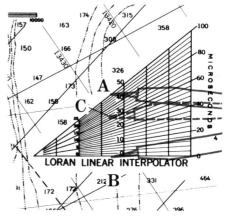

To interpolate between TDs on the chart linear interpolator, find a vertical line the same length as the interval between the TDs. With dividers estimate the distance along that line equal to the ratio between the interpolated display and the interval. Here, the display is 25856 microseconds and falls between the 25850 and 25860 TDs. Line A-B equals the interval and line B-C equals .6 the interval. Transfer B-C to the chart to plot the line of position.

Satellite Navigation

A prime benefit to mariners of the post-Sputnik era has been the use of orbiting satellites in electronic navigational systems. Generally called NAVSAT (or sometimes SATNAV), the U.S. Navy's Project Transit Navigation Satellite System was first used by submarines. Since 1967 it has become standard equipment onboard many war and commercial ships, and though it costs about four times as much as a simple Loran receiver and twice as much as a simple Omega set, a NAVSAT receiver is found in the navigation station of some offshore yachts.

NAVSAT works on a principle similar to that of celestial navigation: if you know the exact location of a celestial body and can measure your relationship to it, you can calculate your own position. In celestial navigation, the relationship is measured in angular degrees above the horizon, and a circle of position results. Cross two circles of position and you have a fix. With NAVSAT, the relationship is the distance from the boat to the satellite measured in the change in the wave length of a radio transmission between the two. This change is the Doppler shift. An example of how it works is the change in pitch of a train whistle as it approaches. With NAVSAT, the boat's receiver "hears" a satellite's radio signal (which includes the satellite's position) and, with its self-contained computer, factors the change in wave length, her speed and course, and the satellite's position, speed, and course against each other to arrive at the boat's position.

The satellite's own position is calculated and fed to the satellite by several ground tracking stations. Orbits are predictable within the limits of astronomical laws, but since the five operational satellites (as of 1982) are only 600 miles up, perturbations due to natural and gravitational irregularities are inevitable. For this reason the tracking stations calculate and predict new orbits about every 12 hours. Theoretically a vessel can make a NAVSAT fix once every 30 to 90 minutes, but orbital irregularities may stretch that interval out to 4 hours.

Once the receiver is turned on, all the navigator has to do is enter the boat's course and speed. (Known current set and drift should be factored in.) Being off 1 knot of boat speed will cause an error in the fix of 0.25 miles unless the computer is allowed to correct it — a sizeable error since NAVSAT frequently is accurate to within 100 yards if the receiver has only one frequency and 50 yards if it has two frequencies. Some advanced NAVSAT receivers can be connected to the boat's speedometer and distance log so that speed and course data can be entered automatically. So long as the boat's motion is properly entered and the angle to the satellite is between 15° and 75°, NAVSAT is just about foolproof everywhere in the world.

GPS/NAVSTAR

The U.S. Department of Defense has long been planning another satellite navigational system that, unlike NAVSAT, will be usable at any time. Called the Global Positioning System, or NAVSTAR, it will consist of 18 satellites orbiting about 11,000 miles above the earth's surface. The signals of any four of these satellites will be available at any time to allow instantaneous pinpoint navigation 24 hours a day. Like Loran-C sets, satellite navigation receivers may interface with computers that generate and display charts.

The GPS/NAVSTAR system is expected to be operational in the early 1990s.

In satellite navigation, a ground station (A) gives the satellite its position, which the satellite (B) transmits. The boat's receiver (C) picks up the signal and calculates the distance to the satellite.

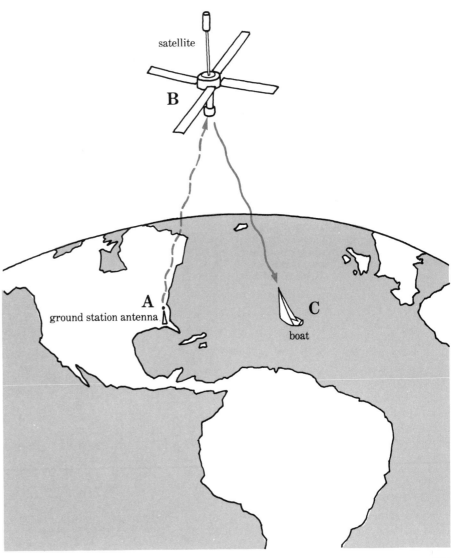

satellite

B

A
ground station antenna

C
boat

Radar

Radar scanners used to be found only on ships and large yachts, but now they appear on boats as small as 20 feet. When operated and interpreted with care, radar is a valuable navigation tool as well as a fine safety feature.

In radar, a radio pulse is transmitted through a rotating antenna called a scanner. If the pulse hits a reflective target (the best reflections are made by wide, vertical metal objects), it bounces back to be received by the scanner before another pulse is transmitted. A device in the transceiver calculates the time difference between transmission and reception and converts this infor-

mation into a visual display on a screen called a scope. The display is a point of light called a pip or blip.

The theoretical radar range in nautical miles is 1.22 times the square root of the height of the scanner, or about 5 percent greater than the geographic range of visibility. For example, a radar scanner 16 feet above the waterline has a range of almost 5 miles. Tall targets like the bridge of a large freighter may be seen beyond that range, assuming that the radar transceiver is powerful enough to send the pulses that far. Rain and other precipitation considerably shorten the range and may even make radar ineffective, and fog slightly shortens the range. The benefit of this sensitivity to precipitation is that radar is a useful detector of approaching bad weather.

Scope Displays

Three different types of scopes are found on pleasure-boat radar sets. Each is round or rectangular, with a 360° azimuth around the perimeter to indicate relative courses and bearings.

The display seen on most pleasure-boat scopes is **Relative Presentation/Ship's Head Up,** which shows the boat in the center of the scope and displays the boat's heading as a line running straight up. When the boat turns, the land is seen as moving around her; when the scope is switched to short ranges, this motion can be dizzying. Another problem is that the scope's display is oriented differently from most charts, which are North up. It takes some practice to be able to move confidently and easily from the scope to the chart and back again.

Another display, **True Presentation/North Up,** is oriented like a chart. The boat is in the center and True North is straight up.

On a **True Motion** display, True North is also straight up but the boat need not be placed at the center. True Motion displays can interface with Loran-C to display waypoints, range, and bearing on the scope.

The set's range (the mileage scale on the scope) can be quickly adjusted to change the display from long ranges

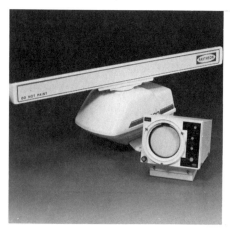

A radar set sends out pulses through a scanner (above), which then receives echoes bounced back by objects, whose locations are shown as pips on the scope (right). Clarity of reception varies with the object and the weather.

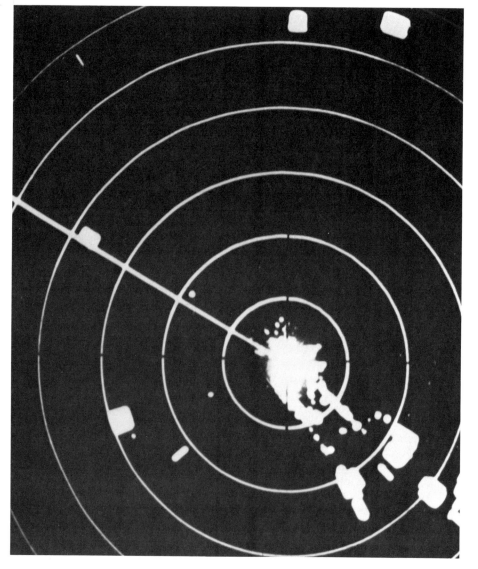

(showing large areas) to short ranges (showing small areas). A good practice is to start with a medium range like 4 or 6 miles in order to get oriented to your general position, and then to shift down to short ranges like 2 or even 0.5 miles to identify targets.

Ranges (distances) to targets in miles are calculated using fixed **range rings** and the adjustable **variable range marker** (VRM). The distances in miles between range rings and between the boat and the VRM are displayed on the scope.

Bearings to targets in degrees are taken with the adjustable **electronic bearing line** (EBL). The bearings are displayed on the scope, usually in relative degrees. To convert the relative bearing to a magnetic bearing, add it to the boat's compass course. For example, if the relative bearing is 033° and the compass course is 192°, the magnetic bearing is 225°.

Tune the set so the strongest possible signal is being used. Signal strength and reception change as the set warms up and as ranges are changed, so keep an eye on tuning gauges. Set the gain control so there is a very faint background of white dots, or "sea clutter" (the reflection off waves). If the accuracy of ranges and bearings seems in doubt, slightly reduce the gain and switch to a shorter range. If nearby targets appear fuzzy, it may be due to too short a range, sea clutter, or reflection off waves.

Precipitation can completely cloud a target. By adjusting the set's rain clutter control in order to reduce sensitivity, you can "open up" a rain squall and see inside it.

If a target appears distorted, there may be a "second trace echo," where the echo from one pulse does not return to the scanner before another pulse is transmitted. To get the timing back in sync, switch to a shorter range. Sometimes a single target appears as several evenly spaced targets on the same bearing. Called a multiple echo, this is caused by reflections between your boat and the target. The nearest target is the true one; it generally is stronger than the false targets. However, don't automatically assume that such a display always is a multiple echo. It may be a tugboat towing barges.

Another potentially misleading reflection between your boat and the target is an indirect echo, which causes a duplicate target to appear at a different bearing from the true target at about the same range. Interference may also take the form of spokes whirling around your boat. These spokes, which may also screen targets, are caused by a nearby radar with the same wavelength as yours.

A problem inherent with sailboats is a blind spot caused by a mast, boom, or other on-board reflective object that may screen targets. To check to see if your boat has built-in blind spots, go out in a light rain or moderately rough sea and adjust the rain and sea clutter controls to show some clutter, which is shown as white dots. Then turn the boat in a circle. Wherever the clutter disappears on the scope, there is a blind spot.

Radar Navigation

When sailing near buoys and distinctive landmarks, navigators with a choice of equipment often prefer to find their way with radar ranges, radar bearings, or both. Fixing your position with radar can be faster than using Loran-C or visual bearings.

To make a fix with ranges, first determine your range to each of two or more known charted objects (preferably lighthouses or headlands) using the range rings or the variable range marker (VRM). The range in miles is displayed on the scope. On the chart, spread the legs of a drawing compass to the range in miles, using the chart's mileage or latitude scale. Place the compass's sharp point on the charted object and, without changing the spread of the legs, draw an arc near your dead-reckoning position. That arc is a circle of position (COP); you are somewhere on it. Repeat these steps with another fixed charted object. Where the COPs cross is a fix.

While radar ranges generally are more accurate than radar bearings, bearing fixes can be made using the electronic bearing line (EBL) much the way that they are made with a compass or radio direction finder. Be sure to convert the relative bearing displayed on the scope to a magnetic bearing.

Range-and-bearing fixes, like the distance off fixes (see chapter 12), can be made with just one charted object. At the same time, determine both your range and relative bearing to a charted object. Convert the relative bearing to

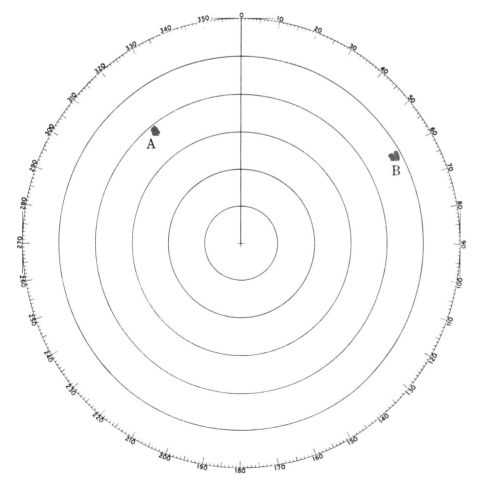

A Relative Presentation/Ship's Head Up display like this one is found on many pleasure-boat radar scopes. The observing boat is shown at the center of the scope and the line straight up is her heading. The circular range rings show distance from her at equal intervals. On most scopes, the heading in magnetic degrees, the range (or distance to the outer ring), and the interval between the rings are clearly displayed.

Radar

a magnetic one and plot it as a line of position (LOP). Lay off the range using a drawing compass and plot a circle of position (COP). Where the COP crosses the LOP is the fix.

Label these fixes "Radar fix" so you have a record of how you arrived at them in case you later discover that electronic interference or some other factor has made your instruments unreliable.

Collision Avoidance with Radar

The main reason most people outfit their boats with radar is to help them avoid collisions with other objects. While this capability is not part of navigation, it is an important aspect of good seamanship.

Identifying Targets

Accurate target identification is one of the most difficult aspects of good radar use. As we have seen, targets sometimes seem to appear and disappear, enlarge and shrink, and even multiply in number. They can also be extremely difficult to identify. Reliable target identification comes with experience, but there are some helpful rules of thumb. First we'll look at the problem. Later on we'll discuss the rules of thumb.

Radar "sees" only those objects that reflect its pulses. This means that the display on the scope can be misleading. The size of a target has little to do with its reflectibility; shape and composition are everything. Metal reflects and wood does not: at short range, a floating soft drink can may seem as large as a 20-foot wooden boat. Vertical surfaces reflect and horizontal ones do not: where a waterfront beach slopes gradually back to a hill, the radar will pick up the hill but not the beach, encouraging the navigator to plan a course that will take the boat right onto the beach. Another problem is that a large target like a ship or island screens smaller targets behind it.

Most buoys and other government aids to navigation are exceptionally reflective. Some are equipped with small radar reflectors called a *ramark*, which transmits a dot-dash signal, or a *racon*, which responds to radar pulses by transmitting its own signal in order to enhance the echo. Even buoys without these special devices reflect very well because their angular structures offer plenty of metal faces to catch and throw back pulses.

Add reflections off the water and you see a lot of pips on the scope. Which one is a target to worry about? Is it stationary or moving? If stationary, is it a buoy or a vessel dead in the water? If moving, which direction is she heading and at what speed?

The problem of identifying targets may sound simple, but it is not. The reason is that *you the observer are also moving*. In other words, the view on the scope is not the same kind of steady bird's eye view that we get when doing dead-reckoning, Loran, or any other kind of navigation.

What this means is that on a moving boat the display on the radar scope is not a true representation of reality. Things that seem to be in motion are actually dead in the water, and vice versa. If that sounds strange, compare a buoy with a boat paralleling your course at your speed. The anchored buoy appears on the scope as moving in a course opposite to yours at a speed equal to yours. Meanwhile, the moving boat seems to be stationary.

Because radar can be misleading, people who purchase radar sets should be aware that their legal or insurance liability in case of a collision may well depend on their proving that they accurately interpreted the display. According to Rule 7 of the Navigation Rules (Rules of the Road), "Proper use shall be made of radar equipment if fitted and operational, including long-range scanning to obtain early warning of risk of collision and radar plotting or equivalent systematic observation of detected objects." A radar textbook summarizes court opinions this way: "Failure to interpret correctly what your radar shows, or can be made to

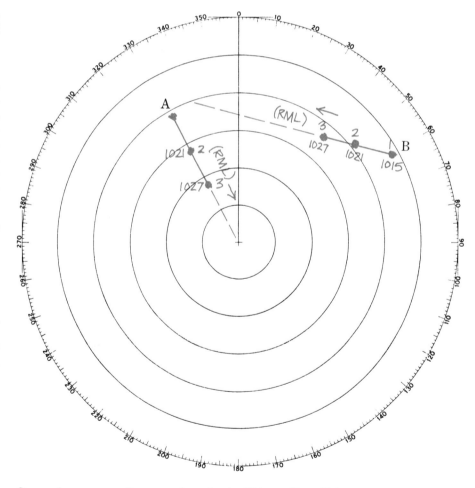

Once a pip appears on the scope, keep track of it to see if a collision threatens. Using a straight edge (like a short narrow piece of cardboard) trace the target's motion from position to position. The line that results is called the relative motion line (RML). If you do this every six minutes (which is one-tenth of an hour) you can easily convert distance into speed by multiplying by ten. Here the RML for target A indicates a collision will occur unless one of the boats turns, while the other RML shows you will clear target B.

show, is held by the courts to be culpable negligence."

So, if you have radar, use it, and use it well.

The Relative Motion Line

To identify and keep track of potentially dangerous moving targets, military and merchant mariners use a technique called Rapid Radar Plotting. Using vector analysis, the observer first determines the other vessel's true speed and course, then calculates what course or speed changes his or her own boat must make in order to avoid a collision. This work is done with grease pencil right on the scope. If you have ever used vector analysis to calculate true wind from the apparent wind, you already understand the approach. However, Rapid Radar Plotting does take special training. Your Coast Guard district headquarters should be able to provide the names and addresses of nearby schools.

There is another way to identify and avoid targets that, while less accurate than Rapid Radar Plotting, is simpler to learn and use. This is the technique of keeping track of the target's relative motion line (RML). When done with care, RML analysis and plotting may meet the requirement in Rule 7 to keep a "systematic observation of detected objects."

There are two ways to keep track of the target's RML. The "quick and dirty" method is to lay a **straight edge** on the scope along the line of the target's relative motion in order to see if the target is on a collision course with your boat. The straight edge can be a strip of paper or cardboard. When you first see the target on the scope, place a finger on its location. A couple of minutes later, place the edge of the paper on the target's new position and turn the edge until it cuts through the first position. Remove your finger. As you continue to track the target, adjust the straight edge to compensate for changes in her relative course. Back up these observations with visual bearings on the target. If you are confused by the scope, you can stop your boat in order to track the target's actual course (which unlike the RML is based solely on her speed and heading). But don't stop when you're near another moving boat, whose crew may be misled by your action.

If the straight edge aims toward the center of the scope, you and the target will collide unless one or both of you takes action. Carefully monitor the situation on the scope and on deck, and don't change course impulsively.

A more thorough way to keep track of the other vessel's relative motion is to **plot the RML**. Much the way a careful navigator plots his or her boat's progress around a dangerous headland by taking fixes on it, the radar operator takes range and bearing fixes on a nearby vessel every few minutes. The faster you and the vessel are closing on each other, the more frequent the fixes should be. Remember that the course and speed shown on the scope are relative and apparent. The other vessel's actual course and speed are different. Again, if you want to be sure of her actual course and speed, stop your boat and take radar or compass bearings on her.

Keep track of the analysis by plotting it on a standard ship's plotting sheet (available at special navigation instrument outlets) or on a sheet of paper with range rings drawn on it.

Whenever possible, back up an RML plot with visual bearings on the other vessel. If there is any chance of collision, call her on VHF/FM radiotelephone channel 6 or 16 to identify yourself and talk the situation over. Alter course with care. There are many stories of crews that turned into targets' actual courses while thinking that they were dodging them.

Here's how to keep an RML plot on a target:

1. From the center, lay out your course, mark it OC ("own course"), and note your speed.

2. Using the range and bearing to the target as shown on the scope, plot the target's position. Label it "1" and note the time.

3. At regular intervals, take new range and bearing fixes on the target and plot them, labeling them "2," "3," etc. and noting the time. Draw a line between the positions. That line is the RML. It represents the target's apparent speed and course taking into account your boat's speed and course.

4. Compare the positions. If position 2 is closer to you than position 1, you and the target are closing on each other.

5. Calculate the object's relative speed. With dividers, measure the distance the target traveled between position 1 and position 2 on the RML. With the plotting sheet's scale, estimate the distance, then estimate the object's speed. (If the plots are 6 minutes apart, simply multiply the distance by 10 to get the speed.)

6. Compare the target's relative speed with your boat's actual speed. If the target's relative speed is *greater than* your speed, the target is another vessel coming at you. If the target's rel-

ative speed is *less than* your speed, the target is another vessel headed away from you at a speed slower than yours. If the two speeds are *equal* and the two positions are on a line paralleling your course, the target actually is stationary. It may be a rock, a buoy, or a boat dead in the water. Finally, if the target's two positions are the same, it is another vessel heading on the same course as yours at the same speed as yours.

7. If the RML is aimed at you and the target is getting closer, a collision or very close call is likely. An RML pointed at you means that the bearing to the target is not changing. Either you must alter course or you must talk the situation over with the other vessel and ask her to alter course.

Radar Regulations

Each radar set must be licensed by the Federal Communications Commission and the license must be posted nearby. The FCC also requires that any repairs, failures, or unusual effects be written down in a log.

Radar Reflectors

Making sure your own boat is visible on other vessels' radar scopes is as important as spotting them on your own scope. The best reflector is a metal object with a lot of faces at sharp angles. A round aluminum mast may not provide enough reflectibility on its own, but stuff it with crumpled-up aluminum foil and it will stand out beautifully on other vessels' radar scopes.

Tests of commercial radar reflectors have shown that the best one is a simple, inexpensive folding device hung off the backstay or a flag halyard. While an electronic radar detector won't make you more visible on another vessel's scope, it may pick up her radar pulses and give enough warning to get out of the way.

Radiotelephones

Several types of radio systems are used to link one vessel to another, a vessel to the Coast Guard and the marine police, a vessel to shore, and a vessel to weather and emergency services. Among these are citizens band (CB) and ham radio, which have much wider uses ashore and which we will not discuss here. The most popular communications systems afloat are very high frequency/FM (VHF/FM) and single-sideband (SSB) radiotelephones. VHF/FM provides a sharp signal over many channels within a short range, using inexpensive transmitter-receivers. SSB is more expen-

sive and complicated to use, but has a range of up to 2000 miles — only ham radio covers longer distances, but ham requires training and licensing.

Very High Frequency / FM (VHF/FM)

As anyone who owns an AM/FM radio knows, FM (frequency modulated) stations provide by far the sharper reception. This clarity is extremely important on a boat, where radio transmissions often concern emergencies. Unfortunately the price paid for this excellent reception is a fairly wide signal. To make room for the large number of FM channels required by the growing population of sailors, the very high frequency band must be used. The higher the frequency of radio transmissions, the shorter is their range, and the 156- to 163-MHz frequencies normally used by marine VHF/FM systems have a range limited to less than about 50 miles, although a temperature inversion or other atmospheric irregularity may increase the range. Channels are

listed in *Marine Radiotelephone Users Handbook*, available from Radio Technical Commission for Maritime Services, Box 19087, Washington, DC 20036 for $7.95. Most boats need about 24 channels, including two weather channels.

Each channel serves a special purpose. Channel 16 (156.80 MHz) — the distress channel continuously monitored by the U.S. Coast Guard and other agencies — is required, for obvious reasons. It is used not only to call for help but also to initiate communications, which are then quickly switched to other channels. Channel 16 *must not* be used for prolonged conversations. Another mandatory channel is channel 6 (156.30 MHz), used for ship-to-ship communications concerning safety. Channel 22 (157.10 MHz) is reserved for nondistress communications with the Coast Guard, and therefore is recommended. Each VHF/FM transmitter-receiver should also have at least one weather channel for receiving NOAA's continuous weather broadcasts and have all three chan-

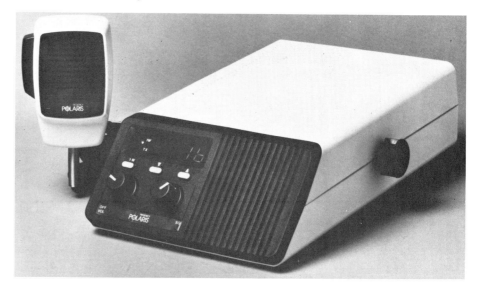

The very high frequency/FM radiotelephone is the standard tool for communicating when sailing near shore, where its limited range is not a problem.

Offshore, the single-sideband radiotelephone provides a range of 1000 miles or more. Like VHF/FM, SSB sets must be equipped with a crystal for the distress frequency.

nels if the boat normally cruises well outside her home area. In addition, a public telephone channel will connect the boat to a shoreside marine operator for making collect and credit-card telephone calls. Other channels are usually used by the local marina, yacht club, or drawbridge. You may choose channels when you purchase the receiver and readily change them later on by buying and installing new crystals. Do some research to find out which channels will cover your specific needs in your cruising area.

A valuable option when sailing in crowded waters is a scanner, which automatically receives any transmission it picks up over the channels. Without a scanner you may miss an important message or a distress signal from another boat, the Coast Guard, or the marine police.

What to Look for in a VHF/FM

Technology and advertising hype can be misleading, and a VHF/FM purchaser may end up with more or less equipment than he actually needs. A standard 25-watt set is sufficiently powerful for most needs, but the variety of antennas available presents a choice that is much less simple. The typical antenna is a wire protected by a long fiberglass whip. Generally speaking, the longer the antenna, the greater is its power — or "gain." A 4-foot antenna may have a gain of 3 dB (decibels), an 8-foot antenna 6 dB, an 18-foot antenna 9 dB. High gain tends to narrow and focus the radiation pattern of the radio waves, which increases effective range. But this arrow may be so sharp that it aims far above other boats as the transmitting vessel rolls and pitches in rough weather. The "fatness" of a low-gain transmission will cover a deeper though shorter range in the same conditions. The decision about which antenna to purchase often has more to do with the boat's size than with any other factor. An 8-foot antenna would be extremely awkward on a boat small enough to roll violently in a seaway, while it would fit nicely on a large vessel stable enough in rough weather to effectively use a high-gain antenna.

On sailboats, VHF/FM antennas are often placed at the masthead. This increases the range and locates the antenna far out of the way of crew members (who could break it simply by leaning on it), but the long cable to the antenna may lead to a power loss. More significant, the receiver will be useless if the mast breaks unless a replacement antenna can be installed on deck. There's the same risk if the permanent backstay is used as the antenna, as is also common. The best place for the antenna is far aft, where it will be out of the way of normal deck activity. Most VHF/FM equipment can be readily installed by the operator, though to be sure it's done correctly, hire a professional.

Besides permanently installed radio telephones, there are hand-held, battery-operated VHF/FM sets on the market. Though their low power means that their range is very small, these receivers are extremely convenient for use in or near port. They pro-

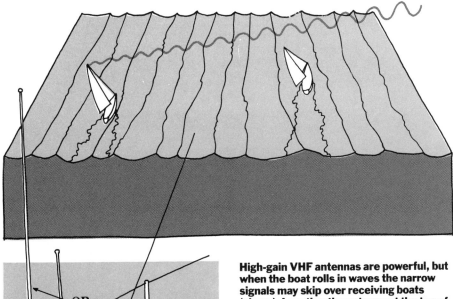

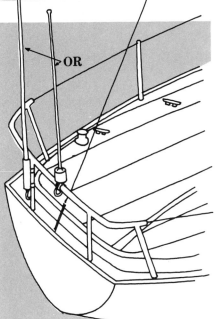

High-gain VHF antennas are powerful, but when the boat rolls in waves the narrow signals may skip over receiving boats (above). Locating the antenna at the top of the mast provides the longest range, but putting it on the after pulpit guarantees it can still be used after a dismasting (left).

Though limited in range, a hand-held VHF provides backup and contact directly from a cockpit or life raft.

Radiotelephones

vide excellent emergency backup for built-in receivers.

Licensing

The Federal Communications Commission requires that all marine-band equipment and operators be licensed. The equipment license is issued in the names of the owner and the vessel; therefore a new license must be obtained when the boat is sold or when the owner moves the radio to a new boat. The license provides a call sign, which should be used at the beginning and end of all transmissions. Equipment licenses are issued by the FCC, P.O. Box 1040, Gettysburg, PA 17325. Any U.S. or foreign citizen may obtain an equipment license; a corporation requires a special license. The license is good for 5 years, and it must be conspicuously displayed near the radio.

All that is required for a lifetime restricted operator's permit is a declaration that the applicant is at least 14 years old, can receive and transmit messages in English and keep a log in English or a foreign language, and is familiar with relevant regulations. A nonrestricted permit is required for at least one crew member onboard a boat carrying six or more people for hire. This permit requires a simple test. Somebody with a permit of either type must be aboard when the receiver is being used. Operators' permits are issued by the FCC, P.O. Box 1050, Gettysburg, PA 17325.

Transmitting Regulations

Although marine radio frequencies are often the nautical equivalent of the backyard fence, the system is not intended for gossip and chitchat. Transmissions should not be made unless necessary; in particular, *channel 16 must be reserved for initiating calls and for distress calls.* Certain FCC regulations govern marine-band transmissions. In summary, these regulations say the following:

1. Any transmissions (made or overheard) concerning marine safety — including distress calls — must be logged, and the log entries must be signed.

2. Profanity may not be used during transmissions.

3. Attempts to contact another boat over channel 16 may take no longer than 30 seconds and be repeated no more frequently than every 2 minutes. After the third failed attempt, a delay of 15 minutes (or 3 minutes, if transmissions from other boats will not be interrupted) must ensue before another try is made.

4. Once contact is successfully completed on channel 16, you must switch to another channel within 2 minutes.

5. Transmissions must be made with the minimum necessary power. (A switch on VHF/FM sets allows power reduction from 25 watts to 1 watt.)

6. Conversations must be as brief as possible, and messages must be truthful.

7. Identification using the boat's name and her call sign is required by all parties at the beginning and the end of a conversation, but not at the

The navigator's station in the 62-foot *Falcon II* is a pilot's dream. Above the 5-foot wide chart table are almost a dozen instruments, including a NAVSAT with printed read-out (left), a course recorder (white screen), an automatic direction finder (top center), and a 55-channel VHF/FM (right). She also carries a radar set and a weatherfax receiver.

start and end of each exchange during the conversation. In any case, the parties must identify themselves at least once every 15 minutes.

8. Overheard information is considered secret and may not be divulged — except, of course, in cases of emergency. A radiotelephone channel works like a big telephone party line and, by law, the privacy of exchanges must be respected.

Violations of these and other regulations can lead to warnings, revocations of licenses, and fines of up to $10,000.

Making a Call

To contact another boat, first turn on the VHF/FM set and turn to channel 16. When the frequency is clear of all other conversations, state the following message into the microphone.

"[Boat called], this is [sending boat and call sign]. Over." State the boats' names slowly and accurately. Use the military alphabet when saying the call sign (for example, WS 3838 is "Whiskey Sierra three-eight-three-eight"). Since "nine" and "five" can

sound alike, say "niner" for "nine."

The contacted boat should respond: "[Sending boat], this is [boat called and call sign]. Over." Then the sending boat names a channel to switch to. This channel usually is 68, 69, 70, 71, 72, or 78. When the two boats are on that channel, the conversation resumes.

To end a conversation, say "out" in place of "over."

To contact a shore station, such as the marine operator, say the name of the station instead of the name of a boat. Marine operators are often exceptionally cheerful, competent, and concerned people who will go to great lengths to help a caller. Their primary job is to connect you to shore telephone lines so you can place a call to a home or office, but they may also be ready and willing to help in other ways too.

When you place a call through a marine operator, you will be required to charge it to your telephone credit card or home phone, or to call collect. We don't recommend using credit cards, since somebody overhearing

the conversation may unscrupulously write down the number and use it himself.

You'll save considerable time if you prearrange times and channels for transmissions with another boat. That way, both crews will be sure to have their radiotelephones ready so nobody will hog a channel trying to place a call to a boat whose radio is off.

Procedures for distress calls are described in chapter 16.

Single-Sideband (SSB)

Although single-sideband (SSB) radiotelephones are licensed like VHF/FM equipment and their use and rules of operation are the same, they are quite different in other ways. A high-frequency (12- to 22-MHz), high-power (75- to 150-watt) system, SSB is much better suited for offshore use than its very-high-freqency, low-power, limited-range cousin. Since its 1000+-mile range is dependent on sky waves, SSB is sensitive to atmospheric and ionospheric interference. At a given time one frequency may be more effective than the others that are available. The higher frequencies generally filter out static better than the lower frequencies. SSB antennas are large and complicated; they and the receivers must be installed and tuned by professionals. An SSB station license will be approved only if the boat also has a VHF/FM receiver.

The name "single-sideband" is derived from the way in which the radio waves are transmitted, which in turn is a variation on AM (amplitude modulation) transmission. An AM signal includes a "carrier" on which two bands that contain the same information are transported. Since these bands lie either side of the carrier, they are called sidebands; old AM radiotelephones were called "double-sidebands." SSB replaced AM in the early 1970s, suppressing the carrier, eliminating one of the sidebands, and focusing all the saved energy into the remaining single sideband. The resulting signal is narrower and takes up less space — allowing more channels to be utilized.

Operating an SSB radiotelephone is more difficult than handling a VHF/FM. Propagation tables ease the chore of selecting the right channel for the conditions, but the operator's experience and "touch" are equally important.

Every SSB receiver must have the distress frequency, 2182 kHz; 1670 kHz is used to contact the U.S. Coast Guard.

Part IV
SELF-SUFFICIENCY

Chapter 14
Anchoring

Whether you're "dropping the hook" for a brief lunch stop in a quiet cove or for several months in a tropical port, anchoring is perhaps the quintessential seaman's act, for it combines careful planning, sensitivity to weather and current, knowledge of your equipment, and continuous watchfulness. Here we'll describe the different types of anchors and how to use them so that you stay in one place.

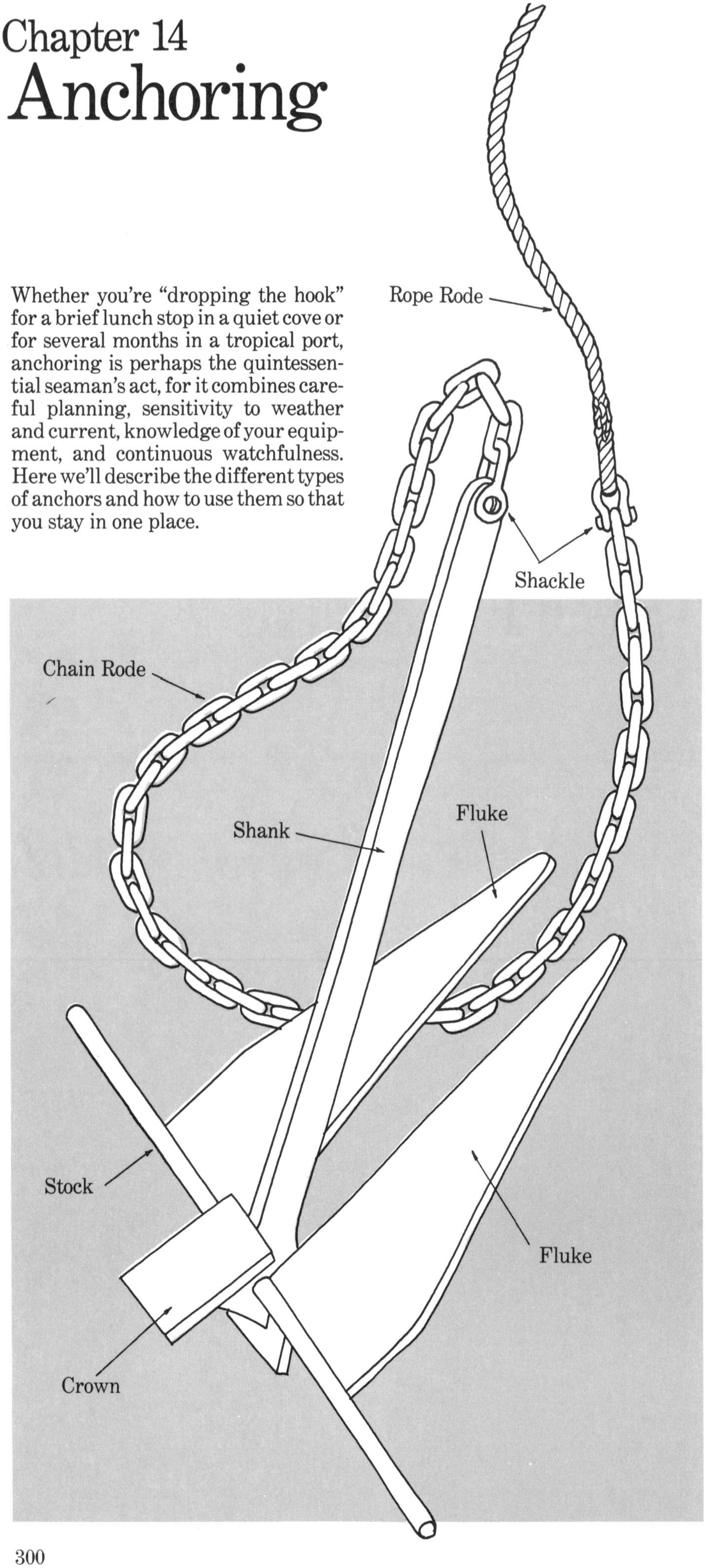

Rope Rode

Shackle

Chain Rode

Shank

Fluke

Fluke

Stock

Crown

Ground Tackle

The equipment used when anchoring, called ground tackle, is divided into two categories: anchors themselves and the anchor rode — the rope and chain that links them with the boat.

Anchors

While they differ in many respects, almost all anchors have four things in common. First and most obviously, they are nonbuoyant and made of either galvanized or stronger high-tensile steel. Second, they have one or more points called flukes that dig into the bottom or hook on rocks. Third, they have a long arm called a shank running between the flukes and the rode; the length and angle of the shank combine to help the flukes dig in. And fourth, they have some device that keeps the flukes from twisting out of the bottom when the boat swings from one side to the other on the rode; on some anchors a horizontal bar called a stock holds the flukes in, and on others the shank swivels over the flukes.

While it would take a book to describe all the different anchors that seamen have tried, we can list the most successful and popular pleasure-boat anchors under three categories: the yachtsman's, the plow, and the lightweight or Danforth.

The **yachtsman's anchor** (also called the fisherman type, the Admiralty type, and the Herreshoff anchor) is the heaviest, the most awkward to handle, and in some conditions the most reliable of the three. Called a nonburying anchor since its success depends as much on its sheer weight as on how far its flukes dig in, it is especially effective on rocky or coral bottoms where the wide flukes easily grab and hold. But because they don't bury very deeply, the yachtsman's anchor may be less effective than the others in mud. Many long-distance cruising sailors carry a yachtsman's anchor disassembled in two or three pieces. It can be assembled within about 10 minutes for use on rocky bottoms or to supplement other anchors in storms. A 35-foot racer-cruiser would carry a 35-pound yachtsman's anchor.

The **plow anchor** (known also by the trade name CQR — "secure") is less awkward to handle than the yachtsman's, and because it is more effective in the soft bottoms found in most cruising areas, it can be lighter too. The average 35-footer would be equipped with a plow weighing at least 18 pounds. The plow gets its name from its plowlike appearance. It's a burying anchor but can hook well on rocks or coral. The sturdy shank lies about parallel to the bottom, so that when the boat pulls back on it, the plow automatically digs in. A swivel allows the shank to swing over, which means that a pull is exerted on the fluke even if the boat is way off to one side. If the wind or current changes and the yacht swings 180°, the rode will spin the anchor. In soft mud the fluke may rotate without breaking the bottom's surface, but in a hard bottom, such as gravely mud or sand, the anchor may break out. As soon as the boat has settled down in her new position, however, the rode will pull the shank, which will drive the fluke back into the bottom. Many experienced sailors consider the plow to be the ideal all-purpose anchor for boats larger than 30 feet. Although it may not be best in any bottom, it still holds well in all of them, whether rock, mud, sand, or weed. More compact than the yachtsman's anchor, the plow still is awkward to handle; most of its weight is in the fluke, which flops about clumsily when the anchor is being lifted. It's best stowed on a bowsprit or on the bow, with the fluke hanging out. That way, too, it can be quickly dropped simply by untying a couple of lashings of light line.

The **lightweight anchor** is the most popular of them all. It usually is known as the Danforth anchor after the company that invented it, though somewhat similar anchors are made by other firms. Like the plow, it's a burying anchor; its sharp, wide flukes dig in deep under the pull of the shank and rode, and a pipelike stock behind the flukes keeps it from capsizing and breaking out when the boat goes off to one side or the other. If the boat changes position 180°, the lightweight anchor might spin under thin mud, but it's more likely to break out and then reset itself in the new direction. Because it buries so well, this anchor needn't be very heavy. If made of high-tensile steel, which permits very sharp points on the flukes, it can be as light as 12 pounds for use on the normal 35-foot cruiser-racer — 6 pounds lighter than the same boat's plow anchor. Though lighter and easier to handle, the Danforth may be awkward to stow because it has many projecting corners to catch jib sheets and ankles. While special deck stowage brackets are available, many sailors prefer to keep their lightweight anchors in plastic laundry baskets when not in use, or to lash them to the deck with light line and then cover the flukes and stock with the coiled anchor rode. Because of its light weight it may skip across a hard or weedy bottom before it finally comes to a patch of soft ground. Rocks, clam shells, or hard

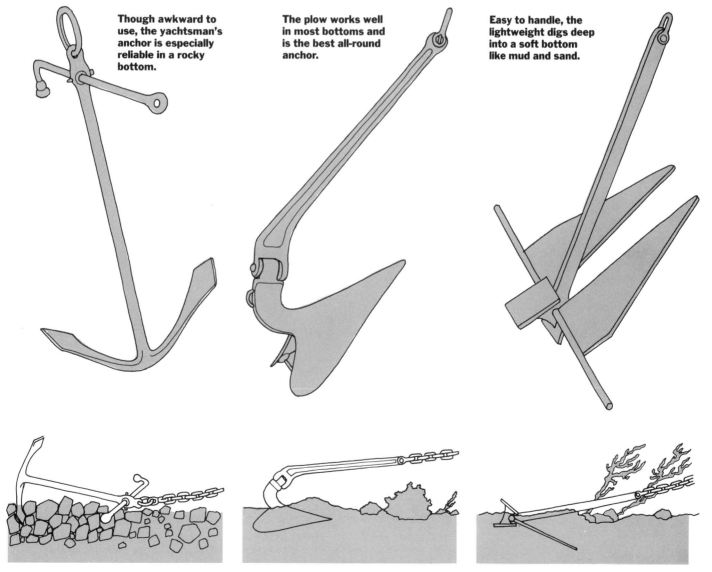

Though awkward to use, the yachtsman's anchor is especially reliable in a rocky bottom.

The plow works well in most bottoms and is the best all-round anchor.

Easy to handle, the lightweight digs deep into a soft bottom like mud and sand.

301

Ground Tackle

mud may jam in the hinge of the shank or on the tips of the flukes themselves, making it hard for the anchor to dig in or be raised. For every sailor who swears by his plow anchor, there is at least one who would use nothing other than a lightweight — this may have as much to do with the type of bottom as anything else. The lightweight anchor is widely thought to be superior in sand and mud but not as good on a rocky or coral bottom. And its lightweight characteristics make it less clumsy to handle on deck. Still, we think the plow (and especially the CQR type of plow) is your choice if you carry only one anchor.

These three anchors — the yachtsman's, the plow, and the lightweight — are popular among pleasure sailors because they hold well in almost all bottoms and usually can be broken out and weighed (retrieved) simply by sailing or powering several feet in the direction opposite to the one in which they are dug in. Of the three, the plow and particularly the lightweight are found on most boats because of their relatively low weight and ease of handling. In addition, a few other types of anchors are used on some pleasure boats.

The **Bruce anchor** is the first new idea in anchor design to appear since the Danforth. Developed for securing oil rigs in the North Sea, this English-built anchor is unique in that it has no moving parts. Its fluke looks like a large three-fingered claw suspended under the shank like a plow's fluke. This anchor is said to be effective on short scope (when the rode is let out less than usual), especially in mud and sand. Only recently introduced to the market (which for good reasons is wary about innovations in such an important area), the Bruce anchor may catch on.

The **mushroom anchor** looks just like its namesake. It holds well in mud or sand once it is set, but may be hard to break out and retrieve. Another disadvantage for yacht use is that with its long shank and heavy end, it's awkward to handle. Mushrooms often are used on moorings.

The **Northill anchor** is the oldest type other than the yachtsman's and plow. Light in weight, it is a deep burying type and stows a bit more easily than the lightweight Danforth and, like the Danforth, has earned a reputation for being a good anchor for soft sand and mud bottoms.

The **grapnel anchor** is light and has four sharp, arrowlike flukes that dig well into weed and grass.

Anchor Rode

The anchor is one part of ground tackle. The other is the rode. The rode must perform three jobs simultane-

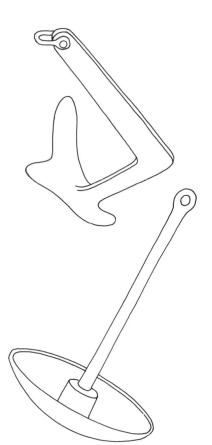

The Bruce (top) and mushroom (above) anchors have many adherents — the Bruce as a mediumweight anchor for normal use and the mushroom as a permanent anchor for a mooring.

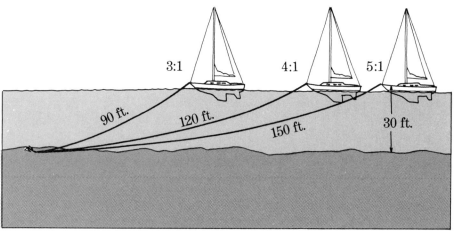

Scope is the ratio between the amount of rode let out and the depth of the water (plus the freeboard, or topside height). The higher the ratio, the more parallel the rode lies to the bottom, increasing horizontal pull on the anchor.

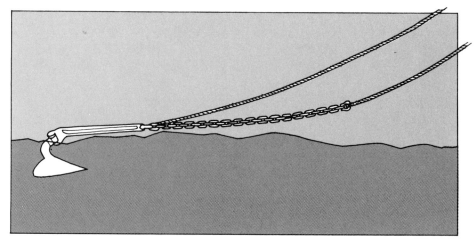

A rode that is all-chain or part-chain will sag more than a rope rode, thereby creating horizontal pull without having high scope ratios. Chain will not be chafed by a rocky bottom, as will happen with a rope rode.

ously. First, of course, it links the anchor to the boat and so must be strong and long enough for expected loads and water depths. (As a rule of thumb, find the deepest harbor you may anchor in and multiply its high-tide depth by eight to determine how long the rode should be.) Second, the rode must absorb the sudden shocks of a boat jerking in rough weather — otherwise the anchor will be pulled right out of the bottom. Third, the rode should allow the pull on the anchor's shank to be as close to horizontal (parallel to the bottom) as possible.

Using nylon line in the rode satisfies the first two requirements quite well. The strongest and stretchiest synthetic line, nylon also is more resistant to chafe than its cousin Dacron. Although the rode should be large and strong enough to take the load, you should not buy a rode that is too large, otherwise it won't stretch sufficiently to absorb the shocks. Stretch is a function of the rope's size and the load's weight; under a given load, a small line will stretch more than a large one.

Another way of making this important point is to say that a rode too big for your boat won't stretch enough to be safe — jerks on it will be transmitted to the anchor and break it out. So resist the temptation to play it safe by going a size or two larger than the rope that just meets your boat's load requirements. And don't use any other rope than nylon on your rode. Dacron will chafe and won't stretch, polypropylene floats and is impossible to hold tight, and manila and cotton are too weak and will rot.

Nylon's elasticity allows it to meet the third requirement reasonably well. It's important to keep the pull horizontal so that the flukes continue to dig in. Once the pull becomes vertical, the shank lifts and may not be resisted by the flukes. By letting out a lot of rode — many times more than the actual depth of the water — you let the boat fall back far from the anchor. This decreases the rode's angle to the bottom and also increases the shock absorption, since there is now more rode available to stretch. The ratio between the amount of rode let out and the bottom depth is called *scope*. In light winds, the rode may not straighten out with a scope as low as 3 : 1 (for example, 30 feet of rode let out in 10 feet of water), but stronger winds may demand a scope of 7 : 1 (70 feet of rode) or more. We'll say more about scope later on.

A heavier rode would sag. Therefore, its pull on the anchor would be more horizontal, and it would dig the flukes in rather than pull them up. For this reason, plenty of chain should always be used in a rode left unattended. Another advantage of chain is that, unlike rope, it won't be cut or abraded by rocks. The rule of thumb is that the weight of the chain should be the same as the weight of the anchor. As Table 2 shows, the lead, or the chain between the rope rode and anchor, should be between 6 and 50 feet in length depending on the boat's length and the anchor's weight.

If your rode doesn't have a length of chain near the bottom, or if there isn't enough chain, you can increase the sag by running a weight down the rode. The weight could be another anchor, a lead pig, or a heavy tool. Snap a snatch block over the rode and attach a long control line. Then shackle or lash the weight to the block. Let the block run down the line until you think it's about 10 feet from the set anchor, then cleat the control line.

If 6 feet of chain is helpful, then a rode made up entirely of chain should be even more seaworthy. Many long-distance voyagers in boats of all sizes as well as owners of big yachts prefer an all-chain rode to a nylon and chain one. While it won't stretch, a chain rode is so heavy that it will take a hurricane to straighten it out. There are, however, problems with an all-chain rode. Chain is much more awkward to handle than rope. Rope can be coiled on deck and stowed either there or below, or it can be passed through a hole to a small locker below. You can winch a rope rode up using a standard sheet or halyard winch, and it may be cleated on a normal horn cleat. The only maintenance you need to perform on nylon is to hose it off periodically with fresh water and check for chafe. On the other hand chain is extremely heavy. It must be stowed below in a special chain locker (which should be toward the middle of the boat to keep weight out of the bow). From time to time it must be regalvanized to avoid rust. To pull it up, you need a special wildcat on a windlass, and while it can be cleated on a large horn cleat, it should be secured either on the wind-

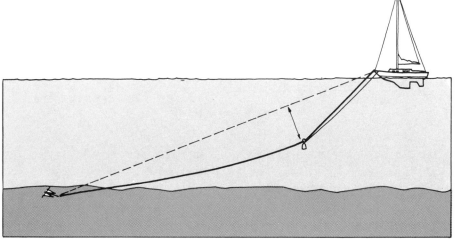

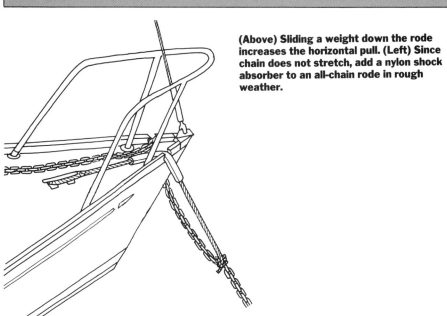

(Above) Sliding a weight down the rode increases the horizontal pull. (Left) Since chain does not stretch, add a nylon shock absorber to an all-chain rode in rough weather.

Ground Tackle

lass or in a special chain grabber.

Another disadvantage of an all-chain rode is that since it doesn't stretch, the boat absorbs heavy shock loads. In strong winds you can rig a nylon shock absorber to ease some of this load. Using 3/8-inch nylon line, tie a rolling hitch around the chain. Cleat the nylon about 6 feet from the hitch and let out about 8 feet of chain. The shock load will now be entirely on the stretchy line.

Choosing Ground Tackle

The average cruiser-racer sailing in normal conditions and anchoring in relatively soft bottoms will get by perfectly well with a nylon and chain rode and either a plow or a lightweight anchor of suitable size. If you usually anchor just for a swim, lunch, or overnight stay, one anchor should be sufficient; carry a long line that can be used as a backup rode in case your primary rode chafes badly. But if you do a lot of anchoring, have a backup anchor as well. Many people take a plow and a lighter Danforth, which is

Table 1. Minimum Horizontal Loads on Anchored Boats (in pounds)

Boat Length	Boat Beam	Approximate Wind Speed		
		15 knots	30 knots	42 knots
20'	7'	90	360	720
30'	9'	175	700	1400
35'	10'	225	900	1800
40'	11'	300	1200	2400
50'	13'	400	1600	3200
60'	15'	500	2000	4000

NOTE: Loads increase with beam. To calculate the load at 60 knots, multiply the load at 30 knots by 4. Source: the American Boat and Yacht Council's table of Typical Design Horizontal Loads.

Table 2. Anchor and Rode Selection Guide

Working Anchor (Wind to 30 knots)

Boat Length	Anchor (pounds)				Rode (diameter)		Lead Range
	Light-weight	Plow	Bruce	Yachts-man's	Nylon	Chain	Chain
20'	5	15	11	25	3/8"	1/4"	6'-33'
30'	12	20	17	35	7/16"	1/4"	16'-46'
35'	12	25	22	45	1/2"	5/16"	11'-40'
40'	20	35	33	55	1/2"	5/16"	18'-48'
50'	35	45	44	75	5/8"	3/8"	21'-46'
60'	60	60	66	100	3/4"	7/16"	27'-44'

NOTE: These are minimum figures for boats of moderate displacement and beam. Go up at least one size for storm anchors or if your boat is especially heavy or wide. The two figures in the right-hand column show the range in length of the lead, or the chain inserted between a rope rode and the anchor. The lower number shows the length for the lightest anchor in the row, the higher number the length for the heaviest anchor. The chain's weight should equal the anchor's weight. The lightweight anchor used in these calculations is a Danforth Hi-Tensile, the plow is a CQR, the yachtsman's anchor is the Herreshoff type. Nylon line is twisted three-stranded, and chain is Proof Coil hot galvanized. Source: Earl Hinz, *The Complete Book of Anchoring and Mooring* (Centreville, Maryland: Cornell Maritime Press, 1986).

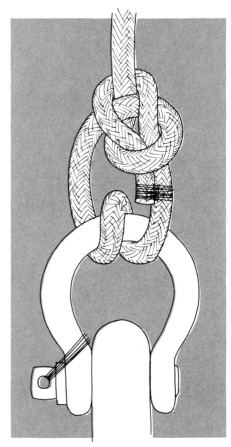

If you anticipate switching the rode, tie it to the anchor or chain. The fisherman's bend (top) is more secure than the bowline (bottom). Secure the bitter end by tucking it under a strand of laid line or seizing it to braided line with twine.

more convenient for "lunch hook" service when stopping just for a couple of hours. If you have two anchors, you should also have two rodes of equal length and strength. Someday you may have to set both anchors in a storm, or a rode may break, or one anchor may be so inextricably tangled in an underwater cable or rock that you won't be able to recover it and will have to cut the rode. If you anticipate anchoring in coral or rock and leaving the boat unattended for lengths of time, buy a yachtsman's anchor too.

The size of ground tackle that you use is determined by two factors: the manufacturers' recommendations (based on their own tests) and the horizontal loads imposed by your boat. These loads are a function of the boat's resistance, which depends on her displacement and the area she presents to wind and waves. A 25-foot-long catboat with 12 feet of beam may provide more resistance than a 30-foot-long sloop 10 feet in beam. Various agencies have developed load predictions based on average-size boats — for in-

stance, 35-footers with 10-foot beams. Many boats built in the late 1970s and the 1980s are wider for their length, so owners should use Table 1, typical horizontal loads, with care. These are *minimum* loads. If your boat is especially heavy or beamy, use the load for the next higher size. These figures are in pounds and can be used to determine which size of anchor, rope, and chain will provide safe ground tackle for calm conditions (lunch hook), normal conditions (working anchor), and storms (storm anchor). These figures may be used to choose equipment from manufacturers' catalogs. A rough guide is found in Table 2, which is *minimum estimated figures.*

Splices and Shackles

The weak link in any ground tackle is the attachment point between the rode and the anchor or between the nylon and the chain. Braided line should be tied using the anchor bend, and its bitter end should be seized (sewn) securely to the standing part to make absolutely sure it won't back out

of the knot. With laid line, finish the bend by sticking the bitter end between strands, or eye-splice it carefully around a stout metal or plastic thimble, which will keep the eye from being chafed. Don't splice the line directly into the anchor or chain, for this will prohibit shifting the rode to another anchor; always secure the eye to the anchor or chain with a large bronze or galvanized steel shackle. While initially stronger, a stainless-steel shackle will be considerably weakened if it is bent or dented — strong likelihoods considering the hard use an anchor gets. In addition, if the shackle is badly bent you may have to cut it off with a hacksaw, which works much better in soft metals than in stainless.

Tighten the shackle's screw pin *hard* using a pair of pliers or a marlinspike. Then "mouse" it to the shackle using several turns of galvanized, rust-resistant wire or strong synthetic cord (marline will rot). In general, *do everything you can* to guarantee that the shackle, knot, and splice will not work loose when they're out of sight underwater.

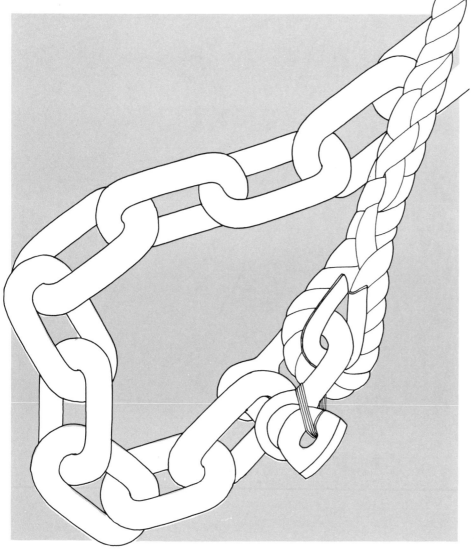

Since it weakens line less than a knot, an eye splice is best for semi-permanent connections. Insert a thimble in the eye to protect the line. Just in case you do have to disconnect the rode, use a sturdy shackle whose threads have been greased to prevent freezing up. Tighten the shackle pin and mouse it with wire or light line.

Ground Tackle

Deck Equipment

One important concern with ground tackle is its handling on board. Be sure that the chocks the rode passes through are smooth and direct the line or chain with a minimum amount of chafe. If you have a choice, purchase the largest ones available that will fit on the bow, one on either side of the stem. Many boats are equipped with short bowsprits or rollers over which the shank may be secured to allow the anchor to be stowed ready for immediate lowering. Be sure that the roller is firmly bolted to the bowsprit or bow.

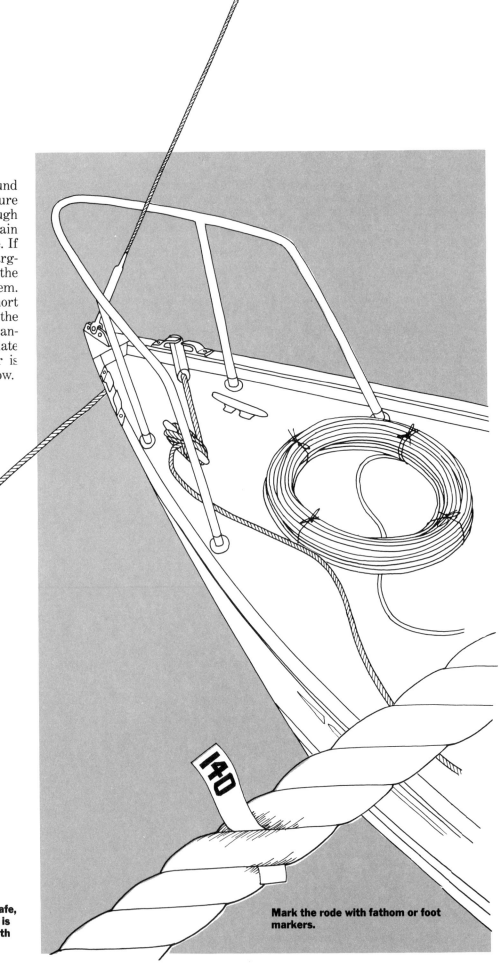

Deck gear includes wide chocks, hose wrapped around the rode to prevent chafe, and large angled cleats. When the rode is not in use, coil it in big loops secured with several short lengths of line or tape.

Mark the rode with fathom or foot markers.

Nylon anchor rodes are cleated on large through-bolted cleats abaft the chocks. Often the lead is fairest when the rode crosses the deck to the cleat on the side opposite the chock. The cleats must be angled so the rode doesn't jam. On a windlass, the wildcat notches must match the size of the chain links; otherwise the chain will slip while it's being retrieved or when the boat tugs on the rode. Some windlasses have drums for rope rodes.

As the rode and anchor come aboard, be sure to hose off or brush off any mud that comes along. If the mud gets on deck, it will foul up your shoes and clothes, and perhaps the sails as well. Even worse, if it gets below it will make a terrible stink before it dries, and then flake off and clog the limber holes, which allow water to pass from between frames back to the bilge pump.

The bitter end of the rode must be secured before you drop anchor. It's embarassing as well as unseamanlike to let the whole rode slip overboard. If you stow the anchor and rode on deck or in a portable container such as a laundry basket, tie the bitter end around the mast with a bowline. If the rode is stowed in a chain locker below, tie the bitter end to a padeye bolted to the locker or to a strong beam. Don't shackle chain to the boat; in an emergency you may have to let the chain go, and it's much quicker to cut a short length of line than to undo a shackle. The rode may kink, so from time to time untie the bitter end, shake out the twists, recoil it, and then resecure it.

Additional Equipment and Chafe

You will want to know exactly how much rode you have paid out, so mark the line or chain. You could paint chain links in color patterns — for instance, using white, red, and yellow paint you can make marks representing 1 to 100 fathoms (6 to 600 feet). Paint doesn't adhere well to rope; there you may sew on markers, either in color patterns or with depths written directly on the markers. Some hardware manufacturers make small fabric flags that can be sewn to braided line or twisted between strands at every fathom.

Once a year, cut the nylon rode just above the splice or knot and redo it. If the line or chain is worn in any area toward the end, turn it end for end — with the old bottom now at the top — to spread the wear. To minimize chafe, wrap rubber garden hose (a piece about 2 feet long that is slit from end to end) around the vulnerable part of the rode, or place a thick rag or a piece of leather between the line and the chock or other chafe point. Since nylon is elastic, check for wear 2 feet either side of the fitting that is causing chafe. While at anchor in rough weather, let out or pull in the rode 1 or 2 feet every few hours to keep chafe from being dangerously localized.

Sometimes an anchor may be bent between rocks or under some other underwater obstruction. If the damage seems to affect the anchor's basic design and holding ability, take the hook to a welder and have him straighten it out (this may weaken it, however).

This plow anchor is stowed in its own bowsprit. To drop it, just pull the pin over the shank and loosen the windlass brake. The windlass takes both chain and rope. The large bow chock provides a fair lead, but since it is not open at the top the docking line must be threaded through rather than quickly dropped in. The U-bracket in the pulpit provides a fair lead for hauling in anchor rode hand-over-hand. This boat is equipped with a roller-furling jib, whose taped turnbuckle has been slightly abraded by the anchor rode.

How to Anchor

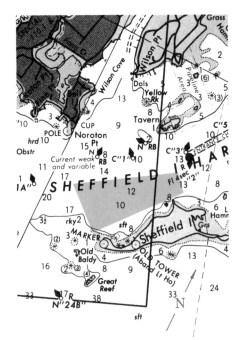

Anchoring properly requires you to do more than simply heave the hook overboard. It takes careful planning, some teamwork, and a lot of concentration.

Choosing an Anchorage

The first problem is to make sure that you anchor in the right place. In most sailing areas you have a wide choice of possible anchorages — but on a given day some may be safer than others. Have an anchorage in mind as your destination when you get under way in the morning, but also check the chart for one or two fallbacks in case the weather deteriorates or your plans change. Often a local "cruising guide" will help you choose an anchorage that is safe, convenient, and charming.

The first requirement of any anchorage is that it be *safe* in the existing and anticipated conditions. Few harbors are so snug that they offer protection from strong winds in all directions, so you usually must try to match the anchorage to what you think the weather might be. Listen to the National Weather Service forecasts on your VHF/FM radio, watch the sky, and be sensitive to the wind's puffs and shifts. A protected anchorage is one lying just to leeward of the shore. Obviously, an offshore wind is safer than an onshore wind, so at almost all costs do not anchor off a potential lee shore (the only exception to this rule is when an onshore wind is extremely light). By "on-shore" we mean blowing anywhere between 30° and 90° to the shore. If you can get a point of land, an exposed reef, or even a shallow underwater sand bar between you and the wind, you'll be a whole lot safer than if the wind and waves come at you unimpeded. So if the forecast is for rain squalls and a strong clearing Northwest wind, don't anchor with land to the South and East and open water to the North and West.

Two other safety factors to be considered when choosing an anchorage are the holding ground and the anticipated crowds. Given a choice between a rocky bottom and a mud bottom —

When the wind is in the prevailing Southwest, the shaded area is an ideal anchorage since it is protected by Sheffield Island and its reef and is well out of the channel marked by the buoys. But it's no place to anchor in a strong North wind.

you can read this right on the chart — any crew with only a lightweight Danforth anchor to use should choose the mud bottom. Avoid weed and kelp whenever possible, no matter what type of anchor you're carrying. And carefully examine the chart for any underwater snags, such as cables or sunken boats. You may be able to grab them tightly, but you may also never see your anchor again.

Crowded harbors are dangerous harbors, especially if a squall comes up in the night. Chances are that one boat out of ten will drag her anchor and be blown right down onto your boat when the wind shifts at 2 in the morning. Rarely will you be able to have sufficiently safe scope in a crowded harbor, which means that you might end up in that 10 percent casualty list.

While studying the chart, try to anticipate tidal flow in and around possible anchorages. While current deep in harbors usually is weak, it may flow at oblique angles near the mouth, leaving anchored boats lying with their

There is an abundance of anchorages in this Maine bay. A offers shelter except in a Northeasterly, B is well protected to the North, C is sheltered from all directions except the South once you get in close to Cranberry Island, and D would be a good anchorage in an East wind. Besides protection from the wind, the skipper takes tidal current, water depth, and possible crowding into consideration when choosing his anchorage for the night.

bows into the current but their sides to the wind. Try to anchor where the current runs either in one direction or its opposite direction, rather than erratically. A line of white foam indicates a tide rip or tide line on either side of which currents run in different directions. Veer (let) out enough rode for the deepest possible depth, which can be predicted by adding the local tidal range (found in tide books) to the water depth at low tide (shown on charts).

Convenience and comfort are two other important considerations. You don't want to anchor so far out that you're faced with a 30-minute row just to get ashore. Neither do you want to be located right next to a channel used by ferryboats.

Special Anchorages

The U.S. Coast Guard sets aside areas called special anchorages for mooring and anchoring. While the holding ground may be no better in a special anchorage than in some isolated cove (it may actually be worse in fact, since the bottom may be littered with old anchors and rodes waiting to trip your own hook), there are advantages to using one, if only because you don't have to set out an anchor light to warn off moving vessels. Moorings and launch service may be available (at a fee) from a local marina or yacht club. And there generally are services, such as fuel docks, laundries, and grocery stores, just in from the nearby shore. Most moorings in special anchorages are extremely secure and well cared for — a plus in a hard blow — and the few dollars' rent for the night is more than adequately compensated for by increased peace of mind. (Be wary, though, about picking up a free mooring early in the afternoon, for its owner may return from his daysail with little charity in his heart. Don't leave the boat until you're sure the mooring is safely yours for the night.)

Approaching the Anchorage

If the anchorage is unfamiliar, approach it cautiously, and with the chart in hand. Be alert to the confusing effects of a change in scale from a relatively small-scale coast chart to a large-scale harbor chart. What seemed like a short distance on the former can turn into a long one on the latter. As you enter the harbor, work to orient yourself visually to the buoys and landmarks shown on the chart. Study the landscape and try to judge how the wind and water will flow around it. For example, a steep bluff to windward may create violent williwaws (strong gusts spilling off its banks), causing your boat to sail around at anchor and perhaps break the hook out. Check the water depth on the chart and your depth sounder (if you have one). A gradual shoaling means there are no especially tricky tidal currents to worry about, but a steep shoaling suggests that current may be a factor later on.

Try to locate a suitable square area about ¼ mile on each side where the water is reasonably shallow (30 feet down to about 6 feet more than your boat's draft at low tide) and where there aren't too many other boats. If your potential neighbors are bunched in one part of the anchorage, try to figure out why — perhaps there's less wind or a softer bottom there, or perhaps they're friends who want to anchor near each other. If the weather is problematical, try to project a disaster scene on your mental movie screen. When the squall comes, how will all those boats lie to it? Where will the gusts come from? Which boat is likely to drag first? What's the quickest way out of the anchorage if you have to leave?

While an anchorage may initially look mobbed, a patient study often reveals a hole. However, before dropping the hook there try to find out if other skippers have avoided it for a reason, like a bottom covered with weed or fouled with old anchor chains.

Anchoring Etiquette

Having blocked out a safe anchorage area, cruise around it for a few minutes with your senses open. Without being hypercritical, evaluate your neighbors. A big powerboat with closed windows probably has her air-conditioning on, which means her noisy generator will run all night. A boat smothered by children won't be any quieter. Any boat with a general atmosphere of being unkempt may well be the one most likely to drag, either because the wrong anchor is down or because her crew didn't set it properly.

The fundamental etiquette in anchoring is first come, first served. If boats swing together, the blame is on the vessel that anchored later. Yet it seems that no matter how much elbow room you have when you drop your hook, the neighborhood gets crowded when the wind or current changes direction. This is because the boats have varying amounts of rode veered out, and they swing on radiuses of different lengths. Whether they become uncomfortably (or dangerously) close neighbors depends on the amount of forethought their crews exert when choosing where to drop anchor.

The first step in anticipating how everybody will behave when the wind shifts is to look carefully at the boats that are already anchored. Your main concern is with their swinging room, which is how much space they will take up if the wind shifts. Obviously, long boats take up more room than short ones, but factors other than length count, too. Boats with large rigs usually will lie fairly steadily to the wind, while those with small rigs may be more influenced by the current. Light boats with high freeboard and the mast well aft may sail around their anchors with the unpredictability of puppies dancing on a leash.

You can guess other boats' swinging room by looking closely at their anchor rodes for evidence of the kind of ground tackle they have down and the amount of rode their crews have veered out.

The steeper the angle there is between the rode and the water, the less scope there is and (presumably) the more weight is down below the water. A boat lying to an all-chain rode, two anchors, or a rope rode with a lot of chain near the anchor should have quite a bit less scope than another boat lying to an all-rope rode, and the rode will come out of the water almost vertically. On the other hand, an all-rope rode should come out of the water at a very shallow angle. If you think that the other boat has an all-rope down but not enough scope, anchor upwind of her so she doesn't drag down on you in the middle of the night.

By now you have narrowed your sights down to a box of water about 100 feet to a side. The last step in determining where to drop the hook is to estimate your own swinging room. For people who feed on numbers, there is a simple formula for calculating a boat's maximum swinging radius:

$$\text{swinging radius} = \\ \text{length} + \sqrt{(\text{rode})^2 - (\text{depth}) + \text{freeboard}^2}$$

First, take the footage of rode let out and square it. Second, add the water depth at the anchor to the freeboard of the bow and square the sum. Third, from the result in the first step subtract the result in the second step. Fourth, calculate the square root of the remainder and add it to the boat's total length, including projections astern (for example a dinghy). The result is the swinging room with the rode fully extended. (This formula finds the length of the horizontal top leg of a right triangle whose vertical leg is the water depth plus the boat's freeboard and whose hypotenuse is the length of the rode.)

Don't anchor where anchoring is not allowed, for example in a channel (unless an emergency forces you to anchor there). When you drop the hook in an area that is not marked "special anchorage" on the chart, Rule 30 in the Rules of the Road specifies that you warn off other boats by displaying a 360° all-round white light at night. Either hang it off the headstay or turn on the all-round light at the top of the

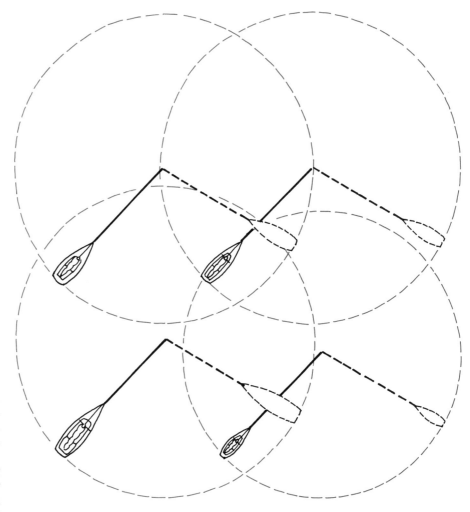

When the wind shifts in a crowded anchorage, boats on long scope will swing near or into each other. Using all-chain rodes, two anchors, or moorings permits less scope and may eliminate this problem; otherwise, choose a less crowded anchorage if you anticipate a major wind shift.

mast. (Do not use a strobe light, which people will interpret as signaling an emergency.) During the day, the rules say, a black ball must be hung over the foredeck.

This survey can be conducted under either sail or power. In fact, successfully anchoring under sail alone is a soul-satisfying mark of good seamanship. But if you do approach under sail, get your big genoa jib down to improve your visibility and be ready to switch on the engine, if your boat has one. Remember, too, to keep up steerageway by reaching back and forth rather than trying to beat into the wind. By definition a good anchorage is fairly calm, so you may have to work hard to keep her sailing comfortably under mainsail alone. Though less challenging to seamanship than anchoring under sail, anchoring under power is safer and more reliable.

Preparing to Anchor

While the skipper is choosing a spot for anchoring, one or two crew members should be on the foredeck preparing the ground tackle. On some boats, everything may already be almost ready, with the anchor lying over the stem or on a bowsprit and the rode led below to the chain locker. Just check that the rode is clear to run without snagging (pulling out about 50 feet), untie the lashings holding the anchor down, and cleat the rode taut to keep the hook from dropping over until you need it. If the rode is all-chain, lead it over the wildcat with the windlass brake on.

Otherwise the anchor and rode must be led properly under the lifelines and through the chock. Bring the ground tackle on deck (if necessary), and tie the rode's bitter end to the mast with a bowline. Then carry the anchor forward, slip it under the lifelines or pulpit (a restraining assembly of pipes on the bow), and either leave it there or, if it might bang against the hull, pull it back aft *over* the lifelines and pulpit. Inspect the shackles. Take a wrap of the chain or nylon around a cleat to keep the anchor from sliding overboard. Now carefully run down the

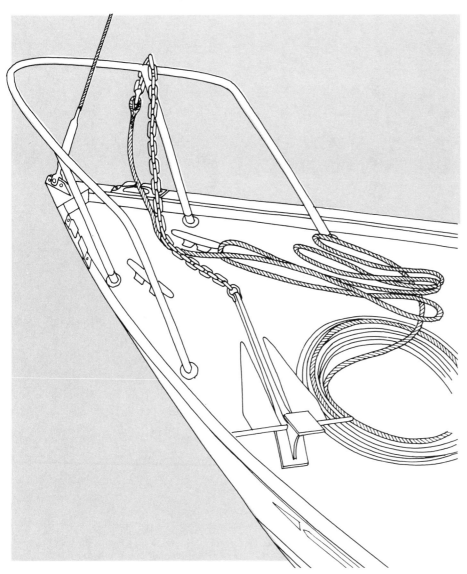

Before anchoring, pull the jib aft and out of the way, rig the anchor, and fake out sufficient line, leaving the rest of the coil ready to let out if you need it.

How to Anchor

rode to make sure that it's not tangled: pull out about 50 feet of it and then fake it in long loops on deck with the part near the anchor lying on top.

Once the skipper knows where he wants to anchor, he should notify the foredeck crew and everybody else on deck, pointing to the spot and announcing the water depth. If it's very deep, more rode must be pulled off the coil or out of the locker or container.

Dropping the Anchor

As the boat shoots into the wind toward the chosen spot (or, in a calm, into the current), the foredeck crew gets ready to drop the hook. The boat slows and stops — the best indication is a range on shore or a floating object (such as spit) on the water nearby. With the engine in slow reverse or the mainsail backed (pushed out against the wind), the boat begins to make sternway (sail backward). Only then does the skipper order the anchor dropped; it's his decision (in fact he may decide to move elsewhere, perhaps because another boat is too close).

When anchoring in very deep water, just before dropping the anchor fix the boat's position on the chart using bearings, Loran-C, or radar. Ninety percent of the time this fix won't be needed, but someday when you're having trouble getting the anchor up because you don't know where it is and what direction its flukes are dug in, you will want to be able to return to this exact position. Another way to locate the anchor is to tie a buoy to it with a long length of line. To retrieve the anchor, power to the buoy and pull straight up on the line.

On the skipper's command or hand signal, the foredeck crew drops the anchor over (it may have to be thrown to clear the topsides). With an all-rope rode, veer out about 10 feet of rode for every foot of water depth at high tide plus the boat's freeboard height. That's a scope of 10 : 1. With an all-rope rode that has at least 12 feet of chain, the initial scope can be about 7 : 1. With an all-chain rode, it can be about 4 : 1. In strong winds or rough seas, the scope should be higher. The goal here is to make the rode lie at a shallow angle to the bottom so the flukes dig in rather than lift up.

Then back the boat down *hard* against the rode. If there is any time a cruising boat needs a reverse gear, it's now. The foredeck crew snubs the rode on the cleat or windlass drum (if the rode is rope) or tightens the brake on the windlass wildcat (if it is chain). If the bow suddenly dips and swings toward the anchor, the anchor is dug in.

You can "read" the anchor by putting your fingertips on the rode. If the fibers stretch and compress in rhythm with the boat's surges, or if the chain is quiet, the hook is set. But if the fibers or chain are jerking back and forth, the anchor is dragging across the bottom. Veer out more rode until the hook digs in. If that doesn't work after a couple of minutes, pull up the anchor, clean off any rocks or shells that might have been picked up, then try again. If the anchor is clean, consider trying another spot.

In light and moderate conditions, once you are *sure* the anchor is dug in securely, you may shorten the scope slightly (to about 7 : 1 for an all-rope rode and about 5 : 1 for rope and chain) to decrease your swinging room in a crowded area. But keep your initial scope if the wind and waves are high, or if the conditions seem to be deteriorating.

The scope recommended here may seem high, but it is based on much experience. Earl Hinz, in his excellent *Complete Book of Anchoring and Mooring*, argues persuasively that the angle between the rode and the bottom should be 8° or less. "Scope is the ultimate secret to successful anchoring,"

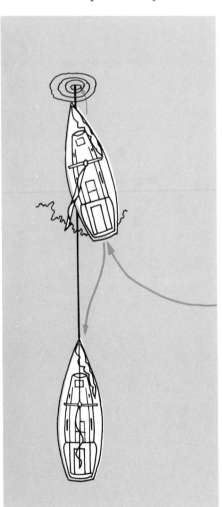

Drop the anchor when the boat begins to make sternway. Light-displacement, highsided boats may swing to one side, so try to steer the bow back into the wind.

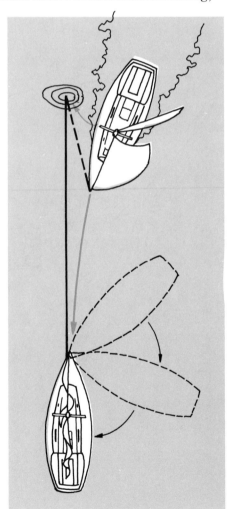

Anchoring under sail in light air, you may drop the hook on a run to dig it in quickly without losing steerageway.

he asserts, "and it is highly dependent on the materials with which the rode is made. An all-rope rode at short scope seriously impairs an anchor's holding power. Not until the scope reaches 10 : 1 is the all-rope rode anchor able to realize a significant part of its holding power." That's a large swinging radius, and one very good reason for shackling at least two fathoms (12 feet) of chain between the anchor and the bottom of the rope rode.

Once the right scope is veered out and the anchor is securely dug in, fix the boat's position with bearings or electronic devices. Alternatively, establish a range at a right angle to the boat (for example a house behind a wharf). A fix, bearing, or range will help you determine, during periodic inspections, if she is dragging. At night, try to find a lighthouse, street lamp, or other fixed light on shore to use as a guide. Many Loran-C sets have anchor watch alarms that sound when the boat moves away from a position programmed into the machine.

Aft, the skipper should find a range ashore, say, between two large trees, while he steers her backward with her bow in the wind. When the anchor grabs, the bow will make a quick nod and swing toward it. That's when the engine should go into neutral or the sail should be allowed to luff. The skipper studies the range: if the boat springs forward, the anchor is safely in, for the moment at least. But if she slides backward, the hook is dragging.

The first thing to do if the anchor is dragging is to increase the scope, but if scope of even 7 : 1 is ineffective, then the anchor has probably picked up a shell or some weed, and it must be retrieved and cleaned off before you try again in another spot. But more often the anchor catches within a few seconds and its flukes dig safely in. After a few minutes of watchful waiting, more rode should be let out — the amount depending on the weather and sea conditions. In calm weather, 6 : 1 is safe for plows and lightweights, 5 : 1 for yachtsman's anchors. In very rough weather, 10 : 1 and 7 : 1 may be needed. In between, throw out enough

rode so there is a shallow angle between it and the water — perhaps 30° if the sea is smooth and shallower as it gets rougher. *When in doubt, let more rode out.* In tidal areas calculate scope using high-tide depths.

If you're anchoring under sail using the method we've just described, you'll quickly lose steerageway as the boat shoots into the wind toward the spot —which of course leaves you extremely vulnerable and makes it hard to sail away if at the last minute you decide to anchor elsewhere. So in light winds (when this is most likely to happen) you may want to try to drop the anchor on a run dead before the wind. Instead of shooting up to the spot, run down to it at about 2 knots. Drop the anchor over, let out enough rode for 6 : 1 scope, and cleat the rode securely. When the anchor grabs it will grab hard, and the bow will swing right up into the wind — help it along with the helm while leaving the main sheet eased entirely. Once she's headed into the wind's eye, find a range and feel the rode as we have described.

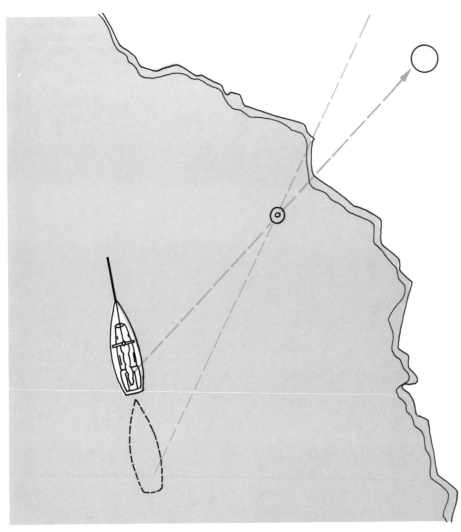

Once the anchor is dug in, find ranges or take bearings so you have references to check to see if you're dragging. One range should include a lighted object to allow nighttime reference.

How to Anchor

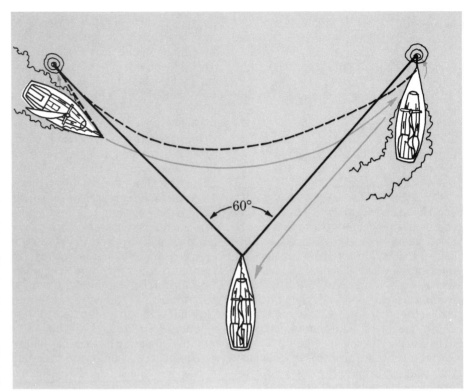

Cleaning Up

Once you're sure the anchor is safely dug in, take two or three bearings on some prominent landmarks, including at least one that will be lit at night, and write them down on a piece of paper on the chart table. Check these bearings every few minutes for an hour or so. Later you'll refer to them if you wake up at night with normal skipper's anxiety (some skippers even switch on the cockpit compass light before they go to bed in order to facilitate taking night bearings). Leave the applicable harbor and coast charts open on the chart table for quick reference, and make sure some flashlights are handy in case you have to set sail in the dark. While everybody's starting to relax, point out the boat's position to one or two trusted crew members who may have to take charge if you're not around for some reason.

Douse and furl the sails, tying them securely with sail ties. You may bag the jib, but keep the luff hanked to the headstay. When the muddy anchor comes up in the morning, you'll want to lift the jib clear of the deck. Leave the main halyard shackled onto the sail and pull it and the other halyards away from the mast so they don't clank. Keep the sheets rigged — once again, you may have to make a quick getaway under sail in case the weather worsens, the wind shifts, or the anchor drags. Finally, the skipper should personally inspect the foredeck to make sure the anchor rode is properly cleated and coiled and that any necessary chafing gear is installed.

Is all this nit-picking preparation for emergencies absolutely necessary? Only one time in a hundred — but that's the one time when you'll be lost if you haven't done it.

Using Two Anchors, and Other Techniques

Another level of security is provided by using two anchors on two rodes laid at an angle to the bow so they don't drag into each other. To drop two anchors, set one to port of where the boat should lie, then sail or power across

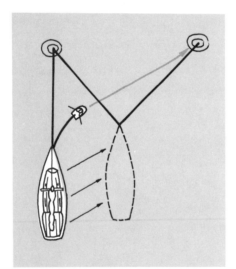

Setting two anchors allows you to use less scope with increased security against dragging and swinging. You can set them under sail (above) or with a dinghy or other boat (left), keeping an angle of 60° between the rodes. Or you can set them bow and stern (below).

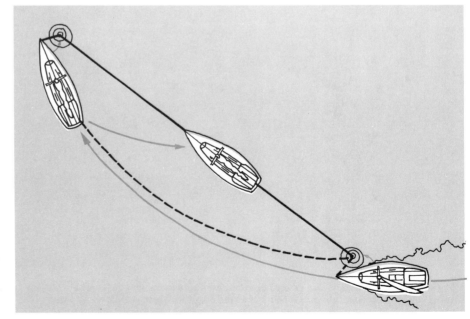

the wind, letting out rode (keeping it clear of the propeller), to a spot the same distance to starboard of the intended position. Drop the second anchor there, then let the boat fall downwind as you pay out both rodes until she hangs balanced between them. The included angle should be between about 60° and 90°, the wider angles preferred. In calm weather the second anchor may be run out in a dinghy or other small boat. Because each anchor carries half the boat's load, the two-anchor system requires less scope than a single anchor. This is a superior way to prepare for a coming storm.

In narrow anchorages where there is little room to swing when anchored it may be necessary to anchor bow and stern with two anchors. Drop one over the stern and dig it in as you power upwind until the scope is about 8 : 1. Drop the other anchor over the bow and fall back with the wind until the boat is halfway between, with 4 : 1 scope on both rodes, the after rode cleated on the stern and the forward one on the bow. Besides security, an advantage of using two anchors is that they form a bridle that keeps the boat from sailing around at anchor. The wind resistance of sailboat spars and hulls produces aerodynamic forces that can push a yacht over a long, never-ending course downwind of its anchor.

In some deep harbors — especially in Europe — yachts use anchors to help them moor next to wharves. They approach the wharf slowly, drop the anchor over the bow, and then swing and back their transoms up to the wharf, paying out rode. The anchor rode secures the bow, and stern lines keep the stern from swinging. Crews board and leave the yachts over wooden walkways that run from the wharves to the yachts' afterdecks. Anchors may also be used to keep yachts from blowing down onto piers or floats in rough weather. The anchor is run out in a small boat and dropped abeam of the yacht.

Sometimes several boats will hang off a single anchor in temporary or overnight "rafts." The center boat, usually the largest one, drops her heaviest anchor. When it's firmly dug in, the other boats tie up on either side, using fenders and full sets of spring, bow, and stern lines to keep the boats from sliding forward and aft, and the masts from tangling if the boats should roll. Obviously the scope should be greater than if a single boat were anchored. Every boat must be prepared to leave the raft quickly if the anchor drags, and overnight raft-ups should be limited to two or three boats.

If you're sailing singlehanded or shorthanded and plan to anchor, you can drop the hook without going onto the foredeck. Before entering the anchorage, heave-to, lead the rode properly through the chock, carry the anchor aft outside the pulpit, lifelines, and all rigging, and lay it in the cockpit. Cleat the rode on the foredeck so there's sufficient scope for the anchorage. When you've found your spot, either shoot into the wind or run downwind to get to it, and drop the anchor from the cockpit. Then go onto the foredeck and adjust the rode. Anchoring singlehanded under sail may be difficult in restricted quarters, since the boat may yaw around considerably before you can get back aft to douse the mainsail.

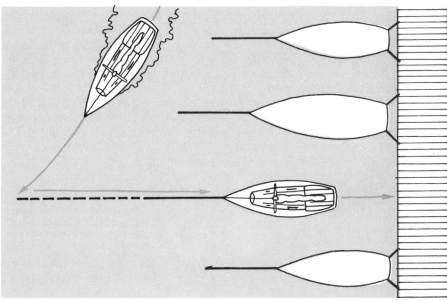

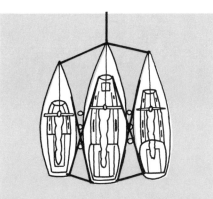

(Above) Tying up stern-to involves dropping the anchor before backing into the wharf. (Left) Rafting-up requires one heavy anchor and full sets of docking lines so the rigs don't tangle.

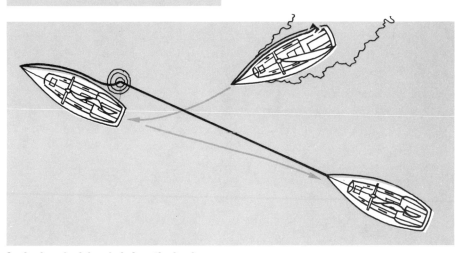

Anchoring singlehanded, drop the hook from the cockpit and be sure the rode is free to run out.

Kedging Off

Kedging Off

If you have run aground, you can often use the anchor to pull yourself off into deeper water. This is called kedging off.

First, carefully study your situation and decide which is the best route off. You may want to back off, simply reversing the path that led you to the shoal spot. Before pulling the anchor out, try to back off in reverse gear while heeling the boat to one side with crew weight or rocking the boat from side to side to break the bottom's suction on the keel. If this doesn't work within about 1 minute, put the engine back into neutral since the propeller may kick up sand that will be pulled into the cooling system.

Now row out an anchor in a dinghy or swim it out. If you plan to back off, place it well astern at a scope of about 5 : 1, lead the rode to a cockpit sheet winch, and winch her off backward with the helm centered so the rudder's resistance is as low as possible. Be absolutely sure that the rode is clear of the propeller before you shift into gear.

Backing off may not be feasible — for instance, you may not want to risk banging the rudder into any rocks lying astern. You may pull the boat off bow first if she's sitting on a small shoal spot or, more likely, you may try to spin her on her keel until she's aimed back toward safe water. Spinning is especially effective with modern boats whose short fin keels make excellent pivots and offer little resistance.

Run out the anchor to deep water just abaft the beam, at a relative angle of about 100° off the bow, and lead the rode through a sturdy block shackled to the stem near the jib tack fitting. Do *not* lead it through the bow chock, which will badly chafe any line led at broad angles. Then lead the line to the windlass or to the most powerful sheet winch, running it through turning blocks if necessary to make a fair lead to the winch. Grind the winch to pull the bow toward the anchor. When the bow is pointed directly at the anchor, try to power off the shoal spot. If you're still stuck, weigh and reset the anchor and pull the boat around some more. The keel should shave off several inches of mud or sand as it turns, which might help.

Warning: Kedging-off places immense strains on ground tackle, and nylon rodes may be stretched to the breaking point. Never stand over or behind a rode while kedging off. The backlash of a broken rode may cause serious injury.

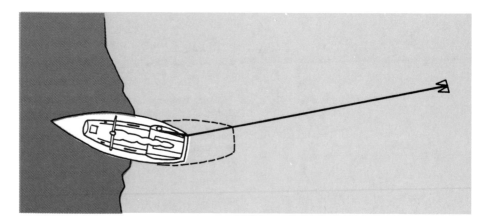

If you run aground and can't sail off, first try to kedge off stern-first, leading the rode to a powerful sheet winch.

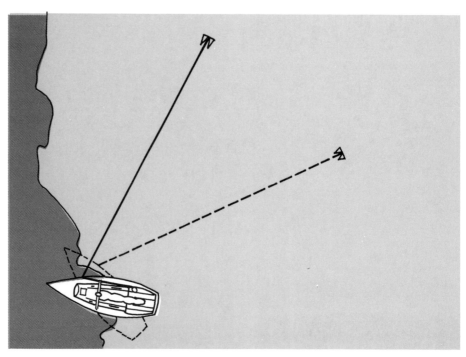

A fin-keel boat may often be spun off by leading the rode through a block on the bow, resetting the anchor if necessary.

Weighing Anchor

Raising the anchor involves even less planning than dropping it. The crew member on the foredeck hauls in the rode as the helmsman steers the boat — in slow forward gear — directly toward the anchor. From time to time the foredeck crew points in the direction the helmsman should steer, since the anchor rode is hidden from the view of those in the cockpit. When the bow is directly over the anchor, the crew says or signals "Straight up and down!" and the helmsman shifts into neutral gear as the taut rode is cleated on the bow cleat. When the foredeck crew signals that the line is secure, the engine is put back into forward gear and the throttle is pushed forward slightly. Moving forward, the boat pulls the rode, the anchor shank, and the flukes up. After a momentary hesitation caused by the resistance of the anchor in the bottom, the boat accelerates, dragging the anchor along. The foredeck crew signals that the hook is off the bottom (which usually is apparent anyway since the bow will bob), the clutch goes back into neutral, and the crew pulls in the rode. When the anchor breaks the surface, if it's clean the crew hauls it up on deck, but if it's dirty he may signal to have the engine shifted into forward gear so the bow wave scours the chain and hook. If mud still sticks on, he cleats the rode and knocks the material free with a mop handle or boathook or scrubs it with a long-handled scrub brush. He may also bounce the anchor up and down by hauling on the rode, being careful not to pull the sharp flukes into the topsides (looping the bight of a line under the flukes helps keep them from spinning against the sides). Before the anchor is pulled on deck, sails should be tied up onto the pulpit or dragged well aft to keep them away from muddy water. Then any remaining mud is scrubbed off on deck, the rode is untied from the mast and coiled, and the ground tackle is left to dry on deck before it is taken below. Remember to finish the coil off by tying three or four light lines around it with bow knots or by taping it.

The anchor may be weighed while under sail if the harbor is not crowded and if the hook breaks out quickly. Otherwise, the boat may not gain steerageway and may bang into neighbors or may not be able to pull the flukes out.

If It Doesn't Break Out

Sometimes an anchor will become stuck in very thick mud, behind a rock, or under an obstruction like a cable or a length of chain. Simply pulling on the rode in the direction away from the flukes will not be sufficient, so you must use some special techniques.

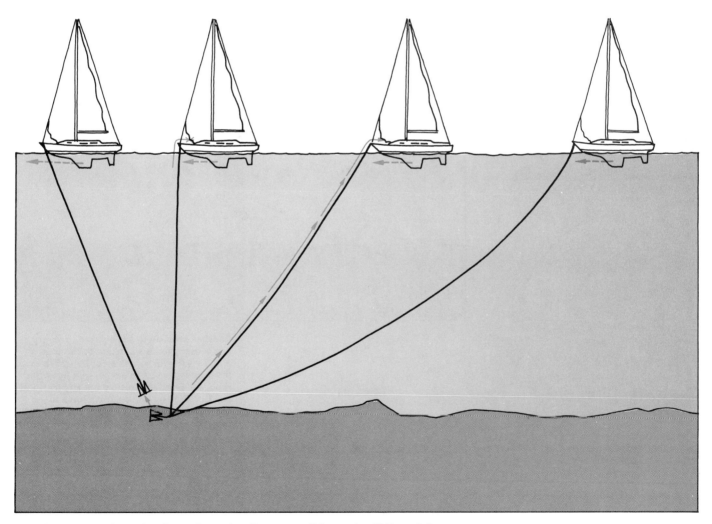

Use the boat's motion to break out the anchor. Power or sail forward until the rode is straight up and down, cleat the rode, and head in the direction opposite to the one in which the flukes are dug to pry the anchor out.

Weighing Anchor

Such problems often can be anticipated. A bottom marked "Co." or "Rk." may well be a maze of coral ledges and cracks that can snag flukes, and as we said earlier, a special anchorage may cover a rat's nest of old rodes and anchors. If you're anchoring in such places, first rig a trip line — a long length of strong nylon tied to the crown (the point where the shank meets the flukes). You can let the trip line out with the rode, but at some risk of tangles. Better, tie the other end to a buoyant object, such as cushion, a fender, or a block of foam. The distance from the buoy to the anchor should be a bit greater than the water depth. Coil up any excess line and tie it to the buoy so it won't foul your propeller.

When you've reached your spot for anchoring, throw out the buoy and trip line when the boat begins to gather sternway, and then drop the anchor. Later, if the anchor doesn't break out, let out enough rode so you're sure the shank is lying on the bottom, then pull up the trip line from a dinghy or some other boat. Alternatively, you can buoy the rode itself by tying it to a buoyant object. Cast it off and sail over to the trip line and pick it up.

Some anchors are made so the rode itself can serve as a trip line. The shank is cut away to allow the shackle at the end of the rode to slide all the way down to the crown, so after you sail beyond the anchor a vertical pull will lift the crown rather then the shank. Some ingenious sailors produce the same effect on normal anchors by tying or shackling the rode to the crown itself and then passing it through a wire loop at the end of the shank. A horizontal pull drags the shank back, but a quick, hard, vertical jerk will break the wire and allow the hook to be pulled forward by the crown. Be sure to use rust-resistant stainless-steel or galvanized wire if you use this system.

Sometimes you may have to move the obstruction itself. More often than not it's a chain rode leading to a mooring or another anchored boat, or some

By pulling the opposite way on the rode, an anchor with an open shank can be slid out backward.

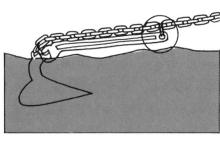

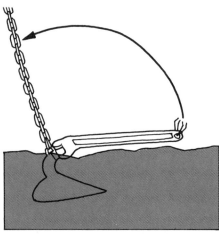

If you anticipate having a problem breaking the anchor loose, secure the rode to the crown and through a shank wire that holds when the anchor is set. To break the anchor out, pull up on the rode, break the wire, and slide the flukes out the other way.

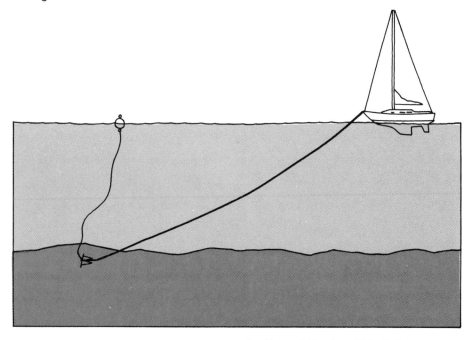

Another solution to anticipated recovery problems is to tie a trip line to the crown and buoy it with a cushion or buoy. When it's time to leave the anchorage, buoy the rode, sail or power over to the trip line, and pull the hook up before going back to recover the rode.

chain that has been discarded. Once you've located the obstruction, fish for it with a grapnel or lightweight anchor, or if one of its ends is visible, loop a length of chain around it and slide the loop down to the obstruction. Then pull up and retract your own anchor. Be patient; in a crowded harbor you may have to lift many chains.

Making a Mooring

You can construct your own mooring for use in your home harbor using a heavy object (many people use old engine blocks), a big anchor, or two smaller anchors. In each case the mooring rode should be attached below with a swivel, which will keep it from twisting and kinking. Make sure the swivel's own breaking strength is at least double the load that your boat will put on a storm anchor in a gale. The swivel should be chained to an engine block, shackled to one anchor, or shackled to the middle of a chain bridle running between two anchors. Since you won't be carrying this ground tackle on board, you don't have

to worry about convenience: make the rode and fittings as heavy and as strong as you can, and hold them up with a foam buoy attached to a strong mooring pendant that will fit through the chock and around the bow cleat.

The main advantages of a mooring are that it is more secure than any anchor you could carry on board, and that you can safely use it with scope of 2 : 1 or even less. This reduced swinging room allows many more moored boats to use a harbor than could be accommodated if they were anchored with scope of 4 : 1.

Hints on Anchoring

Safe anchoring depends as much on cautious, alert seamanship as it does on strong ground tackle. While you should have an anchor big enough for your boat (plus some), a nylon rode long and stretchy enough for the anticipated water depth and strains, and sufficient chain to keep the rode low to the bottom — while your equipment must be right, the way you use it must be sound. Use all your senses to de-

termine if the hook is holding: bearings on landmarks, the sound of waves splashing dead on the bow and on the sides, the bounce-bounce as her stem rises and falls when she's secure and when she's dragging.

If there are three irreducible rules of thumb for safe anchoring they are: avoid lee shores like the plague; don't anchor too close to other boats; and when in doubt, let out more rode. All too many sailors can tell you hair-raising stories about boats dragging down on them and, eventually, onto shore in the midst of a predawn thunder squall. It is land, not the sea, that is a ship's greatest enemy, and if you plan to avoid a run-in with land, choose and use your ground tackle wisely.

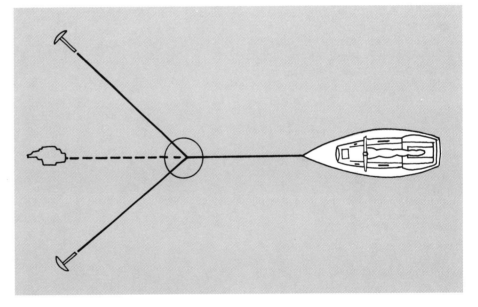

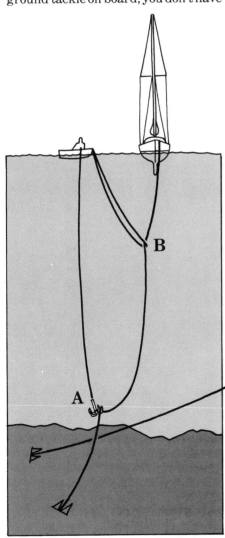

To recover your rode from under another, fish with a grapnel (A) or pull the other rode up with a weighted line (B).

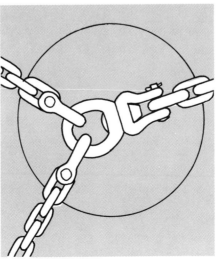

(Above) A mooring secured to two mushroom anchors or a single weight requires less scope than a normal anchoring system. (Left) The mooring line should be connected to a strong swivel to minimize twisting.

319

Chapter 15
Sailing in Heavy Weather

When the wind strengthens to Force 6 (22-27 knots) and above and waves build to 6 feet and higher, it definitely is heavy weather. Depowering the sails (as described in chapter 3) is not enough to keep your boat in balance and control. Now you're in a whole different category of sailing where survival and relative comfort are more important considerations than speed. Everything is different in heavy weather, and every job is more difficult. Big waves complicate steering, strains on your body and the rig become almost intolerable, commands are inaudible in the shrieking wind, and even simple chores like going forward to lower a jib or cooking become major challenges. For beginning sailors, willingly venturing out into rough weather is a risk to be avoided. But as you gain experience and confidence you should not automatically decide to stay ashore just because the wind is piping up into the 20s — get a good crew together, take a deep breath, and head out there. The more you sail in heavy weather, the more you'll learn about your boat (and each boat has her own special handling characteristics) and the more confident you'll feel. Someday the knowledge that you can survive it will help you get through a squall or storm.

In this chapter we'll tell how to prepare yourself, your crew, and your boat for heavy weather, and how to shorten sail and steer in rough seas when you find it. We'll go on to describe ways to handle sudden thunder squalls and big gales.

The 48-footer *Toscana*, with the author at the helm, plows into a wave in a Force 8 gale. Her mainsail is double-reefed, her storm spinnaker trimmed forward near the shrouds to keep it flat and stable. Crewmembers that are not lashing the jib down or trimming sheets are far aft to help push the stern and rudder low in the water. This combination of refined technique and brute force usually is required in heavy weather.

Crew Preparation

In cold gales, the crew will be especially thankful to have warm clothes, plenty of rest, and a settled stomach. Here the author steers down the face of a huge wave during the 1979 Fastnet Race storm. The air and water temperatures were in the 60's; the wind speed was slowly dropping from a peak around 60 knots.

If strong winds and rough seas appear, each crew member should use clothing and personal safety equipment described in chapters 6 and 7. These include good foul-weather gear, a life jacket, a pocket knife, and (in a larger boat) a safety harness to be hooked onto a jackline or other suitable fitting. Before it gets rough, sailors who are prone to seasickness should watch their diet and take medication that they know works for them (this is not a time to experiment with new pills).

While some organization is required at all times, clear crew structure is especially important in rough weather, where good teamwork and quick, decisive action are fundamental to safety. The skipper must lay out the chain of command and specify who should perform such duties as sail handling, steering, cooking, and navigating. Assign duties appropriate to the crew members' strengths and weaknesses. For example, the cook should have an iron stomach, and the winch grinders should be muscular.

Many skippers are surprised to discover that in heavy weather the most qualified steerer for even large boats may well be a good dinghy sailor. This is because the typical dinghy sailor has had more experience with survival conditions than most big-boat sailors. While dinghies can be overpowered in winds as light as 15 knots, which blow frequently, most big boats don't get out of control until the wind is over 25, which happens rarely in most areas.

Watch Systems

During the day in heavy weather and whenever the boat is sailing for more than 24 hours, spread the personnel load and keep people rested by breaking the crew up into subcrews called watches, which change at regular intervals. Each watch should have its own organization. The head, called the watch captain, should be the most experienced, knowledgeable sailor regardless of his or her age, familiarity with the boat, and relationship to the boat's owner. Besides being an experienced sailor, a good watch captain also

is a strong, decisive leader. While individual watch members must be prepared to perform any necessary task, the watch captain should appoint them to specific jobs (such as navigating, setting sails, cooking, and steering in bad weather) according to their own skills and aptitudes.

There is a well-tested set routine to the change of the watch. The members of the new, oncoming watch are roused by the offgoing watch in time for them to get dressed, have a cup of coffee or a snack, and get on deck with a few minutes left over so they can get a feel for the conditions, develop night vision, and be briefed by the offgoing watch about the boat's position, nearby vessels, the weather, and the status of the running rigging. All this should take 20-30 minutes in bad weather (when foul-weather gear and safety harnesses must be put on) and 10-15 minutes in good weather. You don't do the other watch a favor by letting them sleep a little longer if it means that they have to rush to get on deck in time. It is rude to your shipmates to be late getting on deck. It is dangerous *and* rude for the offgoing watch to leave important chores (like changing sails) to the oncoming watch, whose coordination and alertness will revive slowly.

Regardless of the weather, as soon as the new watch is settled down they should inspect the sails and recoil and recleat all halyards and sheets to make sure there are no kinks in the lines.

The more difficult the conditions are,

the shorter are the watches and the fewer the people who are on deck. There should always be some people assigned to be on call ready to come on deck. They may be the next watch according to the schedule, or they may be people who for one reason or another don't stand scheduled watches, for example a full-time cook or navigator, whose duties keep them below most of the time. In difficult conditions, the on-call watch should sleep in their foul-weather gear and safety harnesses so they can spring up on deck immediately.

Many watch systems have been tried. Here's a sample of four of the more successful ones. Our example is a six-person crew, but these systems can be adjusted for bigger or smaller crews.

1. **Two three-person watches.** This system provides a relatively large crew on deck to trim sails. They can stand watches 4 hours on deck and 4 hours off deck (called "4-on/4-off"). Daily they "dog the watch" (stand 2-on/2-off) so they aren't on deck at the same time each day. The traditional "dog watches" are 1600-1800 and 1800-2000 hours in the 24-hour clock that's used afloat, or 4-6 and 6-8 P.M. At night or in rough weather, when sailors tire quickly, the watches can be 3 hours on/3 hours off. An alternative in good weather is to stand 6 hours each in the morning and afternoon watches to allow the off-watch more bunk time, and then 4 hours in each of the night watches.

2. **The Swedish watch system** also

Crew Preparation

splits the crew in half, but automatically dogs and adjusts the lengths of watches to the time of day. The schedule of watch duration, beginning at 1900 hours (7 P.M.) and ending at the same time the next day is 5 hours, 4 hours, 4 hours, 5 hours, 6 hours. The shortest watches are between 0000 and 0800 hours (midnight-8 A.M.). The longest is in the afternoon.

3. **Three two-person watches** standing 2-on/4-off or 3-on/6-off. Splitting the crew into thirds is a good system for bad weather since it keeps a minimum number of people on deck for relatively short periods. It's also good for long passages when not much sail handling is called for.

4. **Three-person watches with hourly changes.** In this relatively new watch system, the crew is not broken into distinct watches. Instead, each hour one of the three sailors on deck goes below, awakens a replacement, and goes to bed when relieved. An advantage here is that since only one person is changing clothes at a time, there is no crowding below. Another advantage is that since personnel on deck are constantly changing, the crew gets acquainted with more people than they would with traditional systems.

Getting used to any watch system on a boat sailing 24 hours a day takes a while. By the third day, everybody should be getting more sleep than they normally get at home; by the seventh day, they feel more rested and healthy than ever.

Hand Signals

Heavy weather is so noisy that verbal communication is often impossible. The following hand signals are a good substitute. They should be agreed on and rehearsed by the crew.

Point toward somebody holding a line ("trim"). Point away from her or him ("ease").

Point down ("douse the sail"). Point up ("hoist the sail"). Open palm ("stop temporarily"). Circle with index finger and thumb ("stop and cleat the line").

Boat Preparation

One skipper whose sloop was caught in a North Atlantic gale later reported that the boat rolled and pitched so violently that every unsecured object in the cabin became a dangerous missile. "Even cottage cheese was lethal," he said. Even in small boats the gear must be stowed to keep it in one place not only when the boat is level but also when she rolls or pitches at steep angles. Be especially alert to heavy objects such as fuel tanks, tackle boxes, tools, cutlery, pots and pans, batteries, radios, and canned goods. If possible, stow them low in the cabin or cockpit, in sturdy drawers or lashed down with strong, light line. The best drawers are either self-locking when they close or have strong latches. Refrigerator lids must be locked or lashed down. Storage batteries must be tightly secured with metal straps or lashings; if they capsize, acid will leak out, mix with bilge water, create noxious fumes, and stain or eat away almost anything it touches.

Most sailors have something other than capsizes in mind when they buy their boats, but a cautious "worst case" psychology will force them to inquire, for instance, whether the stove will fall out of its supports if the boat rolls upside down. Almost all keel sailboats will right themselves after a severe knockdown (a rollover beyond 90°), but much damage may occur below. If the hatches, ports, and stowage compartments are not securely shut in rough weather, spray or even solid water will come below. Every boat must have at least one big manual pump — an electric pump is not reliable in emergencies because the batteries or wiring may short out. A mesh screen secured across the pump intake will prevent matches, tea bags, and other gurry from clogging the mechanism. Larger boats have self-bailing cockpits whose sole is above the water level so that water automatically drains out through scuppers (drain holes). All boats should carry sturdy buckets for bailing in emergencies.

Shortening Sail

When the wind blows so hard that flattening the sails, easing down the traveler, luffing, and other depowering techniques aren't sufficient, you must make the sail plan smaller by reefing or setting smaller sails.

Reefing

All racer-cruisers and some daysailers can be reefed by lowering the mainsail (or, infrequently, the jib) a few feet and securing excess sail cloth out of the wind. The normal mainsail can be reefed twice, with each reef decreasing the exposed sail area by about 15 percent. Racing boats may be equipped with another, very small reef at the bottom called a flattening reef; by taking this reef in, you flatten the mainsail while decreasing its area only slightly. And boats heading far offshore may have a third deep reef that, when tied in, reduces the sail to less than half its original size.

When Should You Reef?

Like depowering, reefing should be done when the boat heels too far and goes out of balance. Try to keep the angle of heel less than 25° if your boat is a beamy racer-cruiser, 30° if she's a narrow keel boat, and 15° if she's a centerboard daysailer. The optimum angle of heel varies from boat to boat, at least when you're concerned about sailing fast. In heavy conditions, when you may not be worried about speed, find the heel angle that is both comfortable and allows the boat to sail in balance at a moderate rate. A reliable maxim is "When in doubt, reef her." If the boat is hard to steer, heeling sharply, and pounding wildly into waves, tie in a reef.

Reefing Equipment

There are two types of reefing systems, tied-in reefing and roller reefing. **Tie-in reefing** is by far the most common system because it is faster and more efficient. It's also called jiffy reefing (because it's quick) and slab reefing (because the sail is tied down in lines, or slabs). To tie in a reef, you must have a mainsail equipped with two cringles (reinforced metal eyes) at equal heights on the leech and luff and, running between them, a row of grommets (small metal eyes).

The *leech cringle* is pulled down to the boom by a line called the leech line (or, traditionally, the earing). This line should be Dacron of a fairly large diameter; it takes a heavy load and should be easy to grasp. The line is led through a block in or on the boom so that when the cringle is pulled all the way down, the line hauls it both aft and down. So it can be adjusted, the line is led forward inside or outside the boom to a winch, often through a series of blocks down to the deck and aft to the cockpit, where it can be easily trimmed or eased.

The *luff cringle* is pulled down to the boom's gooseneck (the fitting holding the boom to the mast) by hauling down either on a luff line (another sturdy Dacron line), which is then cleated, or on the cringle itself with your hands as the sail is lowered, in which case the cringle is secured on a metal hook.

The *grommets* are used only to secure the unused sail area; all the major loads are taken by the leech and luff cringles. Once the leech and luff are pulled down and secured, pass light ¼-inch line though the grommets and around the boom to gather the excess sail.

Other than a flattening reef, which is tied in only at the leech and has no grommets, each mainsail reef has the same equipment. However, there may be only one or two leech lines, so you may have to switch lines as you tie in additional reefs. If there is a line for each reef, simply pull it down on top of the previous, lower reef. Any boat heading offshore should be equipped with at least two leech lines.

Jibs may be reefed using the tie-in system if they have cringles and grommets. The sail is lowered until the luff cringle is hooked into the jib tack fitting, and a new jib sheet is led to the upper leech cringle. The excess sail is bunched up inside lacings passed through the grommets.

Roller reefing accomplishes the same purpose without having to use cringles, grommets, lines, and hooks. The boom is turned using a special crank inserted at the gooseneck, rolling up the sail. Once extremely popular, roller reefing is rarely used on boats built since 1970. New, stronger sail fabrics allow tie-in reefing without any stretch in the sail, and tie-in reefing is much faster than roller reefing anyway. Another form of roller reefing is used on mainsails and jibs with roller-furling equipment on the luff. Unfortunately a partially rolled-up sail may be too full and baggy for use in heavy weather.

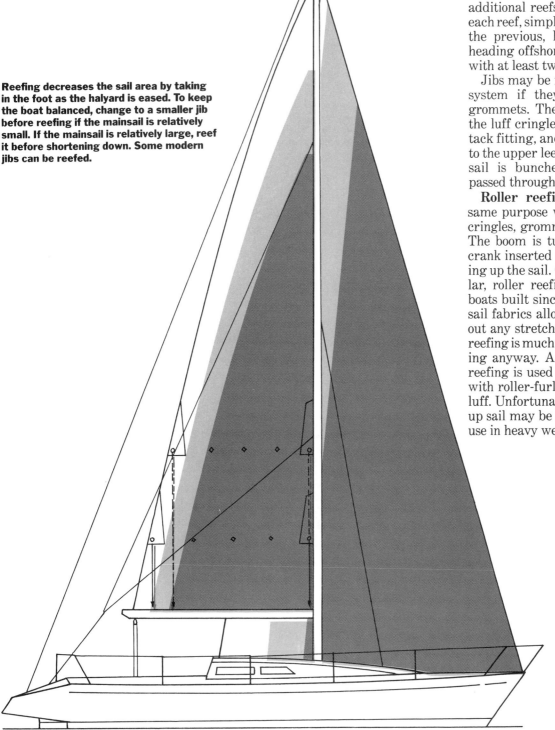

Reefing decreases the sail area by taking in the foot as the halyard is eased. To keep the boat balanced, change to a smaller jib before reefing if the mainsail is relatively small. If the mainsail is relatively large, reef it before shortening down. Some modern jibs can be reefed.

Shortening Sail

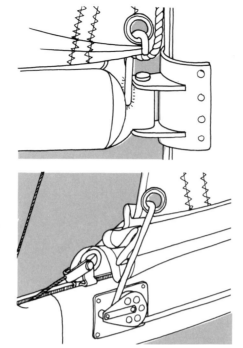

How to Reef

A reef may be tied in singlehanded, but the job's usually faster and safer if two crew members do it. One is stationed at the main halyard, the other at the leech line winch or cleat.

First, decrease the downward pull on the main boom by easing the main sheet and boom vang. This permits the boom to rise up to the leech cringle as the line is tightened, saving time and strain on the leech. Tighten the topping lift to hold the boom up during the next step.

Then the main halyard is lowered so

Hook the luff cringle under the tack hook (top) before tensioning the leech cringle with the reefing line (above). The line should pull the cringle out and down with equal tension.

the luff cringle can be pulled down to the gooseneck or secured under the hook — this step will be quick if there is a paint, tape, or wire reference mark on the halyard so you know exactly how far to lower it. The sailor cleats the halyard and pulls the luff cringle down and secures it. The halyard is then tightened until there is a crease running from the tack to the head.

As soon as the main halyard is tightened and cleated, the other crew member hauls down on the leech line, using the winch if necessary, until the leech cringle is lying on the boom. You may have to luff the mainsail.

When the leech line is cleated, you may trim the sheet, tighten the vang, slacken the topping lift, and using a long length of light line passed through the grommets and around the boom, neaten up.

To roll in a reef, ease the main sheet and vang, tighten the topping lift, and easing the halyard, turn the boom with the crank until enough sail area has been rolled up.

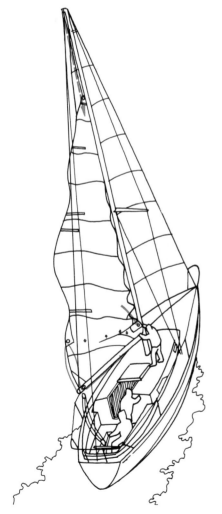

Tying in a reef, first tighten the topping lift, ease the main sheet, and lower the halyard until the cringle is at the tack.

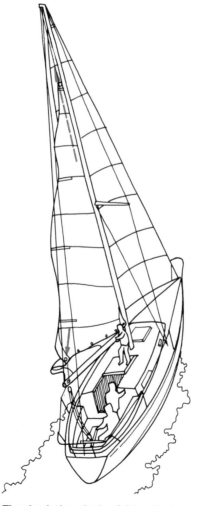

Then hook the cringle, tighten the halyard and begin to pull the flapping leech and the boom end toward each other with the leech reefing line.

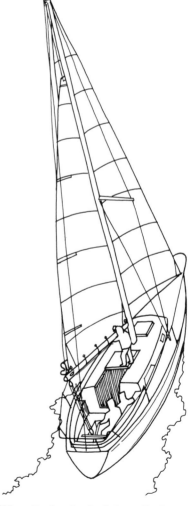

When the leech cringle is on the boom, ease the topping lift, trim the sheet, and tie up the loose sail with light line.

Storm Sails

A racer-cruiser's sail inventory should include one relatively small jib for fresh winds, but if she's heading offshore or sails in areas known for heavy weather, she should also have a provision for shortening down to a very small sail plan. This may be accomplished by tying in a third reef in the mainsail and reefing the small jib. Otherwise she should have, and be prepared to set, storm sails.

The **storm trysail** is set on the mainmast. Although it may not be smaller than the regular mainsail after the last reef is taken in, it has one big advantage for heavy-weather sailing: it's set without a boom, which in rough seas can whack crew members and standing rigging with dangerous violence. The storm trysail is hoisted on the main halyard after the mainsail is lowered, its luff secured to the mast with slides or slugs just like the mainsail's luff. Its tack is shackled or tied to the gooseneck, and its clew is controlled by a sheet led through a snatch

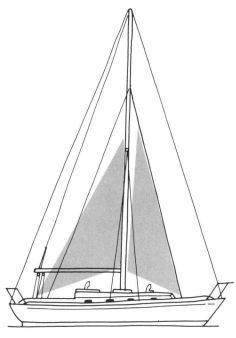

Storm sails should be carried as near to the center of lateral resistance as possible so the boat is kept in balance.

block on the leeward rail to a cockpit winch. Adjust the lead fore and aft much as you would a jib lead until the trysail luffs near its head at the same time as near its tack. Before setting the trysail, furl the mainsail securely on the boom and then lower the aft end of the boom onto the deck and tie it there.

The **storm jib** is a tiny jib usually set on the headstay but sometimes set on an inner stay called the forestay. Experienced seamen prefer to carry their storm sails as close to the mast as possible to keep the center of effort of the sail plan over the center of lateral resistance of the hull and help the boat to balance well.

Under storm sails a boat can reach comfortably in strong winds or can heave-to with the jib backed (trimmed to windward). She can sail under one of the storm sails alone, although lowering the trysail removes considerable fore-and-aft support from the mast, which may wobble and go out of column with only the jib set. Tensioning running backstays will keep the mast from pumping (throbbing back and forth); temporary running backstays may be rigged by leading the shackle end of a spare jib or spinnaker halyard aft under a spreader to an attachment point amidships and then tightening the halyard.

Sailing in Large Waves

"It wasn't the wind; it was the waves!" many survivors of storms have reported about the greatest threat they encountered. Since salt and fresh water weigh more than 60 pounds per cubic foot, a large breaking wave can heave more than 20,000 pounds of water at a boat at a speed of 30 knots. Like a swimmer on a surf beach, a skipper should do his best to minimize the effect of these waves or to dodge the most violent ones. Sailing or powering into them at high speeds can be dangerous. The bow may plunge into the faces of the waves and water will sweep over the deck into the cockpit. Or the boat may fly up and over the crest to smash down — literally, "fall off a wave" — with a crash that can dent or fracture the boat's bottom and heave the crew around with rib-cracking violence.

Having broken a shroud in a Gulf Stream gale, the 72-foot ketch *Windward Passage* jogs along under staysail and storm trysail, which is trimmed to the deck.

Boat Handling

Waves on the Bow

Try to keep the speed down when heading into large waves, especially on light flat-bottomed planing boats that will pound down onto waves like a springboard diver doing a belly flop. Heavier boats with sharp bows and round shapes will land with a squish rather than a splat, yet they still can fall off waves with dangerous consequences. The helmsman should be constantly looking ahead for especially steep and breaking waves, which usually come in groups of three. When you see a steep wave, try to steer around it; if you can't avoid it, slow down and steer through it where it is least steep.

Changing course upwind may be very difficult in slow boats when a heavy sea is running, particularly in a tacking sailboat. As the boat heads up toward the eye of the wind, a wave may strike her bow and slow her down, perhaps cancelling out the way (momentum) she carries out of the old tack and leaving her hanging head-to-wind and dead in the water. The next wave might smash her and spin her either way, or force her backward. Sternway (sailing backward) in these conditions is very dangerous because the rudder may be forced hard over and either jam or break. When you tack in a rough sea, head off slightly to increase speed and then come around in a relatively flat spot of water. After the boat falls off on the new tack, be careful not to point too close to the wind until the speed has built up.

Changing course in these conditions may be complicted if the sea and the wind aren't exactly parallel. Usually the waves run with the wind, but the wind may shift and the "new sea", as

(Left) A confused sea can cause severe pitching upwind, so try to steer around bad waves. (Below) Broaching is most likely to happen off the wind in gusty winds. Decrease heeling force by luffing the sails or shortening sail.

sailors call it, may take a while to replace the old one. For a period of time the sea may be extremely confused, with waves coming from both directions meeting to form small breakers. Such a mixed sea may toss a boat around uncomfortably or even dangerously. If the wind happens to decrease (and it often does so during a major wind shift), the sails may not steady a sailboat and she may slat (rock violently). Strains on rigging, gear, and crew may actually be greater in slatting conditions than in a strong wind. To steady the boat's motion you may have to increase speed or alter course to find a more favorable angle to the confused sea. The agitation will eventually die (sooner in deep water than in shallow), leaving a single wave train running with the wind.

Waves on the Stern: Pitchpoling and Broaching

Running with steep waves presents other dangers, the greatest of which is called *pitchpoling*. As a boat accelerates down the face of a steep wave she may develop so much momentum that instead of leveling off in the trough, she plunges bow-first into the back of the next wave and literally somersaults over her stem, her mast being flung forward and down like a falling pole. The forces created by this somersault are immense.

Pitchpoling is possible in especially steep, short waves — waves with high crests and narrow troughs that provide small landing platforms. These typically arrive early in a storm before the waves have aged and lengthened out, and in shallow water. The boats most vulnerable to pitchpoling are light, fast boats with narrow bows that slice into the backs of waves. Heavy boats do not accelerate sufficiently to be driven into the next wave, and wide-bowed boats are so buoyant in their forward sections that they cannot submarine.

Another risk of running before steep waves is *broaching*. When a boat accelerates down a wave she may go out of her normal trim: the bow will drop and the stern will lift, moving the center of lateral resistance forward (see chapter 3). This throws the boat out of balance and creates weather helm; she will want to round up. An alert helmsman will anticipate and catch this change in balance and head off slightly, for if the boat allowed to head up as she races down the wave's face, she may suddenly come beam-to the wave, which could break over and down on her.

The first step toward controlling broaching is to keep the boat from rounding up by compensating for sudden bursts of weather helm. The second step is to keep the boat from heeling, because heeling (like pitching) throws a boat out of balance and creates weather helm. Experienced helmsmen steer downwind in rough seas concentrating not on the compass but on the spatial relationship between the foredeck and the horizon. If the foredeck is parallel to the horizon the boat is not heeling, but if it's at an angle to the horizon she's heeling and out of balance.

Within those two guidelines, the helmsman should steer much the way a surfer aims down a breaking wave. Steer partly across it and look ahead for a flat spot on one side or the other of the next wave and head for it. This flat spot serves as a runway on which the boat levels out like a decelerating airplane.

The speed of a light sail or powerboat may double as she surfs down the face of a large wave, and as the speed increases, the boat's tolerance of helmsman error decreases. Mariners talk of "forgiving" and "unforgiving" boats, of "seakindly" and "unseakindly" hulls. A forgiving, seakindly vessel will almost make her own way through rough weather, tolerating all but the most flagrant mistakes at the helm. But an unforgiving, unseakindly boat — like a sportscar in the hands of a beginning driver — can be a dangerous weapon if her helmsman does not respond *instantly* to changes in speed, course, and balance. Generally speaking, heavy, round-bilged boats whose bow sections and stern sections have the same shape are forgiving. Because of their weight, they accelerate slowly and have low maximum speeds; their symmetrical shapes keep them in balance no matter what their angle of heel or bow-down pitch. On the other hand, light flat-bottomed boats with narrow, fine bows and wide sterns tend to be unforgiving in rough seas.

As when sailing into big waves, the safest thing to do if your boat threatens to go out of control when running in rough weather is slow down. Keep steerageway on — at least 3 knots — but shorten sail to keep her from accelerating wildly.

Jibes

An accidental jibe is a constant worry on any sailboat running before a strong wind and steep seas. A boom slamming across without warning can smash unwary sailors with terrible violence or cut through steel stays like a scythe through wheat. The best protection against an accidental jibe is a helmsman who doesn't allow the boat to sail by the lee — the feel of the wind on the neck and ears is the most reliable guide, not the compass. The boom should be held to leeward by a tackle or a line called a preventer, which restrains the spar from swinging across. The preventer leads from the boom to the deck, then back to the cockpit for ready adjustment. On a run the preventer also holds the boom down, but when the sail is trimmed closer on a reach, a boom vang should be led from the boom to the base of the mast. The boom vang keeps the boom from lifting, which would spoil the sail's shape and allow the boom to rise uncontrollably in the middle of the jibe and perhaps hang on the backstay.

Even an intentional jibe in heavy weather can be risky. The boom will slam across no matter how hard the sheet is trimmed in, and unless the helmsman heads off quickly as the sheet is eased on the new tack, the boat may broach. Everybody on deck should be wary of the boom as it passes, ducking heads a foot or two. Sometimes jibing will seem much too risky, and the only alternative is to tack. Do so gradually to build up sufficient headway to carry the boat through the eye of the wind; otherwise she'll hang in irons at the mercy of the waves.

When jibing intentionally in strong winds, do so when sailing fast down the face of a wave rather than when climbing slowly up the back of one. The apparent wind will be less and the boom will bang across with less force. Trim the mainsheet as much as you can without creating excessive weather helm; after the jibe, ease the sheet out quickly. Don't worry about the jib sheets — they can be straightened out after the jibe. (When it's blowing this hard, you may well be running under reefed mainsail alone, anyway.)

Sailing when only a racing boat would be carrying a spinnaker (here a narrow, flat one), this helmsman has excellent control. His eyes are focused on the foredeck, and he steers the boat level by gauging the angle between the deck and the horizon. Though the wind is in the 30s and the sea is very rough, she seems very stable. The mainsail has been roller-reefed to about one-half its size, and a preventer (dark line) holds the boom out. The crew's weight is concentrated way aft. The object dragging in the water is a reaching strut used on the after guy on reaches.

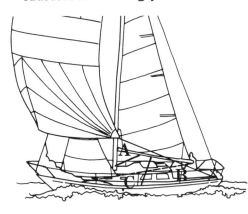

A vang (A) keeps a boom from lifting, a preventer (B) holds it out, and a combination vang-preventer (C) holds it both down and out.

Squalls

Heavy weather generally appears in either a local, fast-moving, and unpredictable squall or a large, relatively well-anticipated gale created by a depression. For most sailors, squalls are more dangerous than gales because they spring up so rapidly and because, in a given summer, there may be ten squalls for every one gale. Toweringly fierce and black, kicking up steep waves with 50-knot gusts, then flattening those same waves with hammers of rain before sweeping on — a thunder squall can pass in 20 minutes and scatter whole fleets of boats across large bodies of water. Squalls are not to be taken for granted.

The calling card of a squall is a steep pile of dark cumulonimbus clouds that overlies a thick swirl of dark-gray clouds — the kind that announces the imminent arrival of witches and extraterrestrial beings in a Hollywood film.

The distance in miles to the approaching storm may be estimated by timing the interval between the sighting of lightning and the sound of the thunderclap and dividing by five. Squalls move at very high speeds — as rapidly as 30 or 40 knots over the ground and water — so don't waste too much time in timing thunderclaps. The barometer isn't much help when predicting squalls since their tightly packed structure means that the atmospheric pressure changes very abruptly, almost at the edge of the squall line itself.

The National Weather Service weather radio system is intended to be sufficiently flexible to warn mariners about squalls. Sometimes, however, the squalls move or develop too rapidly or locally for the government forecasters to catch up with. If the mid-afternoon sky is black and if the VHF/FM weather station in your area is broadcasting forecasts for continuing fair weather, trust your own eyesight and judgment, not that of a forecaster isolated somewhere in an airport or midtown skyscraper.

Thunder squalls may come at night if the evening temperature and humidity are sufficiently high. Usually, however, both drop at sunset, thereby reducing the violence in the weather battle, unless a front is approaching. Most dangerous squalls occur during the day and especially in the afternoon, after the air temperature has peaked.

When you see a black cloud approaching, take a moment to analyze it. The sharper, darker, and lower the front edge of the cloud, the more trouble you can expect. Another cause for alarm is the existence of rapid vertical turbulence between layers in the cloud. These alone should stimulate you to prepare for the worst, but if weather forecasts announce a "thunderstorm warning," meaning that squalls are likely, or a "thunderstorm watch," meaning that they are possible, you can be sure that trouble is at your doorstep.

Preparing for a Squall

Your first step is to plot your position as accurately as possible using every available aid. If you're near a harbor and if you're *certain* you can reach it before the squall hits, you may want to run for it. It's often hard to know which direction a squall's gusts will blow from, and getting close to land may invite being thrown up onto a lee shore. If you have any doubts about your chances of reaching a safe harbor before the squall hits, stay offshore as far away from all land as possible.

Whether or not you decide to head for shore, make your vessel safe for rough weather. Here are some important tasks:

1. Provide each crew member with a safety harness and/or life jacket and be certain he knows how to use the equipment.

2. If you plan to sail through the squall, set a small jib and take two reefs in the mainsail; make sure halyards and sheets are properly coiled and free to run without kinks.

3. Dog (bolt down) all hatches and ports.

4. Tightly secure deck gear, personal items, food, dishes, and other objects

When the sky suddenly turns dark and threatening, start preparing for a squall: hand out safety harnesses, shorten down and reef, secure hatches and gear, decide on your strategy, and double-check your position.

in lockers, which must be shut.

5. Inform your crew of your strategy for handling the squall, and make sure that at least one crew member besides yourself knows how to operate essential equipment; don't overdramatize the situation, but don't underestimate it either.

6. If there are young children on board, make sure someone is firmly in charge of them; when the squall first hits, they should be below, but if the situation on deck warrants it, you may later allow them on deck to watch the spectacle — and a rousing thunder squall is one of God's wonders.

7. Double-check your position.

8. Assign the most experienced helmsman to the helm — this person may not necessarily be the skipper.

9. Visually inspect all sail-handling gear; when the air begins to chill, put on your foul-weather gear and safety harness, and instruct your crew to follow your example.

By now you should see the danger under the black cloud — either an equal-

When a squall threatens, prepare the boat as you try to sail away from the storm. Unless you can get into a harbor immediately, stay well away from land so you're not blown ashore.

ly dark line of wind (broken, perhaps, by white spray), or, if rain comes first, a dense white fog. Either should be racing toward you extremely rapidly.

A thunder squall may hit first with a sudden gust of wind knocking the boat well over on her side. If the gusts are preceded by rain, be prepared for a long bash. According to the old mariner's saying:

> When the wind before the rain,
> Let your topsails draw again;
> When the rain before the wind,
> Topsail sheets and halyards mind.

And remember, too:

> The sharper the blast,
> The sooner it's past.

Thus the rainless first blast may well be the last one, but a gust on the heels of a downpour and a building breeze most likely will be the first of many.

If you must luff your sails in this first gust, go ahead and do it, but don't let the mainsail flog violently or a batten will break and rip the cloth. You may have to douse the sails; don't worry too much about a neat furl, but do make sure that the sails won't blow off the boom or foredeck and that there are no lines dragging overboard to tangle in the propeller in case you use the engine. If the mainsail is down and the boat is rolling violently, dropping the boom and lashing it on deck may save a cracked head.

Lightning

While lightning rarely hits boats, when it does it can cause considerable damage. Crews should not become fatalistic about being fried; instead, they should take precautions. Get down below; if you must be out in the open, stay out of the water. Don't simultaneously touch two objects that can conduct electricity, for example a stay and the mast. And don't panic and make navigation and seamanship mistakes that can cause more damage than the lightning itself will probably produce.

If lightning does strike, it probably will damage the boat and her equipment more than it will the crew. Holes have been blown in hulls, antennas have been melted, electronic instruments have been blown up, and compasses have lost their magnetism. The best protection (but not a 100-percent guarantee against damage) is a good grounding system. A simple ground from the mast or shrouds to the keel bolts is standard on most boats. The mast will attract the energy from direct hits and transfer it to the water through the ground. If lightning strikes and you are not shocked, don't

move; the position you're in has been proved safe.

The American Boat and Yacht Council recommends the following special ground system for boats sailing in areas where lightning is a recurring problem. First, install a lightning rod at the top of the mast. Second, run a number 8-17 AWG copper electric conductor wire from the lightning rod to a submerged metal ground whose area is at least 1 square foot (a plate on the keel or a metal centerboard should do). Third, run conductor wire to the ground from on-deck metal objects (for example stanchions and winches) and from below-deck metal objects that lie within 6 feet of stays, the mast, or some other lightning conductor (for example the galley stove and water tanks). Fourth, bond through-hull and through-deck metal objects (for example chain plates and engine controls) to the nearest metal conductor at the place where the objects pass through the boat, and also ground the objects. Though this system is no insurance policy against damage, it may minimize it.

If your boat is hit by lightning, immediately inspect her for damage and her instruments for inaccuracies. You or your insurance company should hire a professional surveyor and a professional compass adjustor. For more on lightning ground systems and other boat construction standards, contact the American Boat and Yacht Council, 405 Headquarters Drive, Suite 3, Millersville, MD 21108.

In the Squall

Other than the strong wind, your main problem will be poor visibility, for thick rain or hail may make it impossible even to see the bow of the boat and strong wind and spray will sting your eyes shut. Keep as good a lookout as possible as you sail away from land and narrow channels, where boats may be bunched dangerously as they try to make harbor. If you do come across another boat, don't automatically assume that her crew has her completely under control or is alert to the niceties of the Rules of the Road — give her a wide berth.

In the noisy confusion and poor visibility of a squall it's very easy to lose track of your position and heading. In fact you may not be able to read the compass from more than a foot away. Try to gauge your changing relationship to aids to navigation and your heading relative to the shore. If at all possible, sail a course parallel to the shoreline or angled out from it slightly. If your boat is equipped with a Loran

Gales

Gales are depressions so wind circulates around them predictably. When your back is to the wind your extended left hand will point at the center of the storm.

receiver, turn it on (if there is no lightning) and find a time difference line that takes you safely along or away from shore. A crew member posted in the companionway can watch the receiver's display and tell the helmsman when he's wandering to one side or the other of the line.

After the Squall

The storm should pass after an exciting 15-30 minutes, leaving in its wake cool air, sunshine, and decks scrubbed clean by rainfall. There may be a fresh Northwest wind or there may be a flat calm. If you're sure that another squall is not looming on the horizon, open the hatches to air the cabin out and get up more sail. Pump out the bilge — water may have seeped below — and check the halyards and sheets for chafe. Then plot your position and have something warm to drink.

Gales

A gale that is part of a large weather system is usually (but not always) predictable. The forecasts broadcast over VHF/FM frequencies often are quite accurate, as can be your own observations of the sky and the barometer. Far at sea, an indication of an approaching gale is a ground swell (long waves) running across the waves caused by the local or prevailing wind. A depression may wander from its predicted course and catch you unawares. No matter what the forecast is, if the wind begins to rise quickly, start preparing for heavy weather. You may not easily notice an increasing wind when you're sailing on a broad reach or run, since the boat's speed effectively decreases the true wind, but it will be painfully obvious on a beam or close reach or a beat.

Preparing for a Gale

Get ready for a gale much as you would prepare for a squall, but with the knowledge that the rough weather will last much longer than 30 minutes; some gales may blow for as long as 3 days. The checklist for squall preparation should be followed, with these additions:

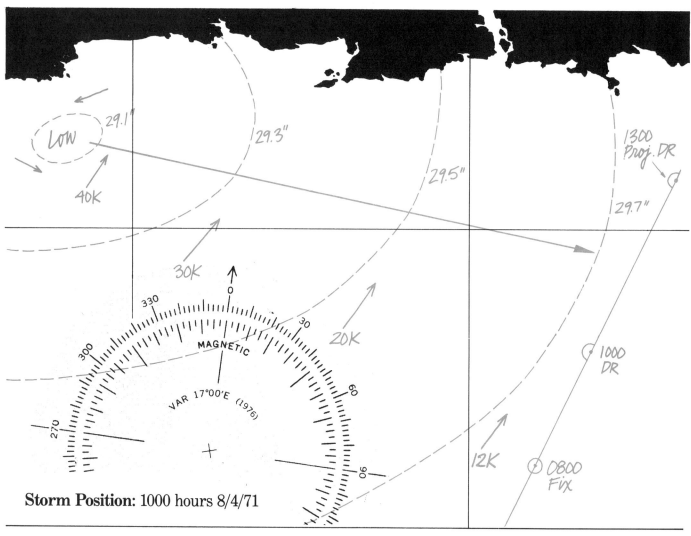

Storm Position: 1000 hours 8/4/71

From a variety of sources you can compile enough information to draw a rough weather map showing a storm, the wind and isobars around it, and its possible track.

1. Cover all large windows with storm shutters — wooden or plastic coverings screwed to the cabin over windows to protect the glass from shattering in breaking waves; cover *all* the windows on all sides of the cabin, no matter what the wind direction.

2. Do your cooking before the seas get rough, and fill Thermos bottles with hot drinks, soup, and stew; cooking in a gale is extremely unpleasant and can be dangerous (if you must cook when the boat is rolling and pitching, wear your foul-weather gear to protect your body from spilled hot food).

3. Establish a watch schedule and assign helmsmen — only the best helmsmen should steer.

4. Stow all unnecessary sails well out of the way and pull the storm sails out so they're accessible; check the slides and hanks on the storm sails — their seizings (lashings) may have rotted.

5. If there are few grabrails below or on deck, rig lines between sturdy attachment points to facilitate moving around.

6. If you have any longstanding worries about your equipment, end them now either by replacing the weak fitting or fixing it (if you have time).

7. Keep crew morale up, but not at the level of euphoric exuberance; cautious optimism is the best state of mind.

8. Decide on some hand signals to use on deck in case verbal communication is impossible.

9. Most important, if you can't reach a safe harbor, head offshore.

Try to predict the path of the gale and how it will affect you. With your back to the wind, extend your left hand to point at the center of the depression; then using your own barometer and any barometer readings from other sources (weather broadcasts may provide them), sketch a weather map showing the approaching storm and your position. Estimate the storm's rate of advance and its force. A shallow depression with a minimum atmospheric pressure of 30 inches (1016 millibars) that is moving relatively slowly at 15 knots will probably have Force 5 to Force 7 (17- to 33-knot)

winds that shift gradually. But a deep depression with a pressure of 29 inches (984 millibars) that's racing over the ground at 30 knots will contain Force 8-10 (34- to 55-knot) winds that shift drastically.

The danger of the storm will depend on how it hits you. If its backside just grazes you, consider yourself lucky. But if its front side, called the "dangerous semicircle," hits you squarely, then you will have major problems. On your sketch, draw the wind arrows as they circulate counterclockwise around the storm, then plot the route of fastest escape. If the storm aims to catch you in the maw of its dangerous semicircle, you must try to get as far from the center of the depression as you can by sailing as fast as possible at a right angle to the storm's track. This means sailing either on a starboard-tack close reach to get to the left of the approaching depression or on a port-tack run or broad reach to get to the right of it. With a storm approaching from the West, this means sailing South or North — whichever takes you

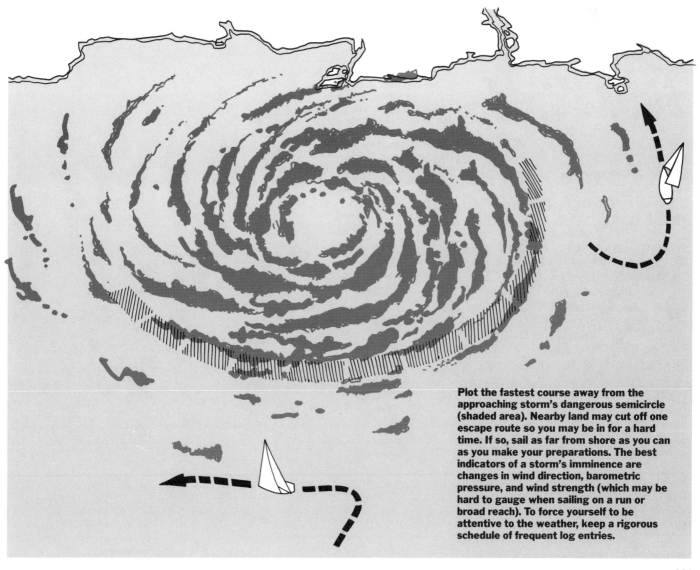

Plot the fastest course away from the approaching storm's dangerous semicircle (shaded area). Nearby land may cut off one escape route so you may be in for a hard time. If so, sail as far from shore as you can as you make your preparations. The best indicators of a storm's imminence are changes in wind direction, barometric pressure, and wind strength (which may be hard to gauge when sailing on a run or broad reach). To force yourself to be attentive to the weather, keep a rigorous schedule of frequent log entries.

Gales

fastest away from the path of the gale. If the barometer rises, you're succeeding; if it falls rapidly, however, you're either sailing toward the center or are being enveloped by the gale. Obviously, a fast boat will get out of the way of a depression more quickly than a slow boat, but if the storm is moving at 30 knots, even a 10-knot boat has little chance of avoiding it completely.

An important factor in storm strategy is the direction to the nearest shore. If the storm is coming at you from land and there's plenty of open sea around you, there are few limitations (unless the gale blows for several days). More likely, you may be trapped against a lee shore if you sail too far in one direction. On your sketch of the storm be sure to include any nearby land as well as shoals over which large waves may break.

If you have serious worries, call the Coast Guard on VHF/FM channel 16, describe your situation, and schedule status reports.

Storm Tactics

The best storm strategy is to get to a safe, protected harbor and tie up to a secure mooring or anchor with a lot of scope (preferably using two anchors). But if you can't dodge a gale that way or by sailing around it, you must sail through it under shortened canvas or storm sails. Sometimes it's blowing too hard to sail toward your destination, and you must change your priorities to concentrate on survival, or at the least, comfort. Over the years sailors have evolved three tactics for surviving a bad storm: running before it, heaving-to, and lying ahull.

Running before it on a run or broad reach has been called an "active" storm tactic because the boat is steered. Just enough sail is carried to create steerageway when the boat is sailing "uphill" on the backs of waves — 3 knots should be sufficient. She may surf down the wave faces at much higher speeds. In breaking seas, the speed should be higher to keep her from being pooped (smashed on the stern by breakers, which might cause damage

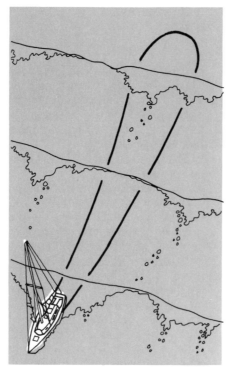

Run before a gale towing warps or (better yet) a drogue to slow the boat down. The best drogues, like the Galerider, are made of heavy mesh.

or fill the cockpit). In extremely heavy weather, when no sail can be carried, just the windage of the rig and hull may pull her along too rapidly at the risk of pitchpoling. Then you'll have to tow a drogue to create resistance and slow her down. A drogue is a sturdy parachute-shaped object towed at the end of the anchor rode or other heavy line from a large cockpit winch or cleat. The best drogues are made of heavy mesh, which provides enough water re-

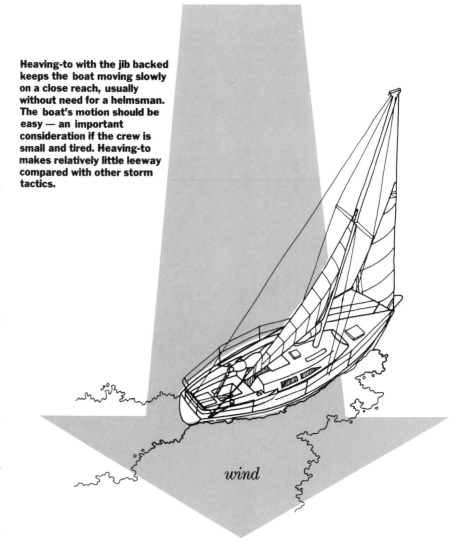

Heaving-to with the jib backed keeps the boat moving slowly on a close reach, usually without need for a helmsman. The boat's motion should be easy — an important consideration if the crew is small and tired. Heaving-to makes relatively little leeway compared with other storm tactics.

wind

sistance to slow the boat yet is fairly easy to retrieve. Adjust the length of the line so the drogue digs in deepest when you're surfing down the face of a wave. If you don't have a drogue, tow long bights of line called "warps" or anything else that will create drag.

The two main problems with running before it are that it demands constant, careful steering and that it may take a boat downwind toward a leeward shore.

Heaving-to keeps the boat more or less in the same place and does not require a helmsman. To heave-to, back the jib (trim it to windward) and adjust the main sheet (or storm trysail sheet) and the helm until she's just making headway at about 2 knots. Normally the helm is lashed all the way to leeward. Though some of the wind's force is translated into forward drive, most of it is sideways and causes leeway. The boat will sail herself in a series of swoops, coming off to about 60° to the apparent wind and then coming up to about 40°, all the while making about 1 knot of leeway. She will be heeled enough to steady her motion and going fast enough to avoid being trapped by steep waves. The crew may rest and eat without having to bother with the helm (though a lookout should be kept and the running rigging should be checked periodically for chafe). A disadvantage of heaving-to is that it may leave a boat vulnerable to breaking waves; when the seas break, to dodge them you may have to steer the boat with storm sails trimmed to leeward, sailing about 60° to the wind at approximately 4 knots. It may also be difficult to find the right angle for the sails and helm so the boat can sail herself slowly — every boat balances differently at varying angles of heel, and when the boat swoops down she may heel so far that she rounds up head-to-wind before the backed jib can check her. So before you have to heave-to in a gale, try it in a fresh wind on a clear day. (As we pointed out in chapter 3, heaving-to is an easy way to stop a boat in all conditions, even for a lunch break in light air.)

Lying ahull, like heaving-to a passive tactic, leaves the boat lying across the wind and seas under bare poles (with no sail set) with the bow aimed at about 50° to the wind. Many skippers lie ahull with a sea anchor set. This is a small, sturdy fabric parachute set at the end of a long line. A light trip line is run to the parachute to collapse it when the sea anchor is retrieved. Nylon parachute sea anchors are available from marine equipment suppliers, or you may use surplus navy cargo parachutes. A 9-foot-diameter parachute is suitable for a boat displacing 20,000 pounds or less. Lacking a parachute, you can make a sea anchor from fenders lashed together or to sails in their bags. The goal is to have a buoyant object dragging in the water several dozen feet to windward, leaving the boat angled across the waves and sliding downwind, with little or no forward motion. As the boat makes leeway, she leaves a slick that smooths the water to windward. The angle the sea anchor line makes to the boat is critical. If it's cleated on the bow, the boat will simply stream with her bow dead into the wind and seas, making a very small slick. Every boat will lie to a sea anchor differently as conditions change, so you must be able to adjust the line angle. Instead of leading the line directly to a cleat, tie it to a bowline in the middle of a second, shorter line that is then rigged as a bridle — one end cleated at the bow and the other led to a cockpit winch. To decrease the angle and bring the bow closer to the wind, ease out the bridle on the winch; to increase the angle and bring her side across the seas, trim the bridle on the winch. Larry Pardey, who describes lying to a sea anchor in *Seraffyn's Oriental Adventure*, suggests dropping paper towels into the water to windward to estimate the size of the slick and whether the boat is making headway. Lying ahull, a boat may make 2 or 3 knots of leeway. That's 48-72 miles a day, so this is not a tactic to use when lying near a lee shore.

Each of these three storm tactics has its proponents and detractors. The best advice we can give is to be prepared to use all three, run before it until your helmsmen wear out or you're within 50 miles of a lee shore, and use the passive tactics of heaving-to or lying ahull to allow you to rest and to keep her more or less in one place. If you're lucky, you'll never be caught by any weather worse than a sudden squall and not have to use any of these techniques for surviving a gale, but you should try them out.

Lying ahull leaves the boat sliding sideways and creating a slick to windward. Some boats can lie ahull without help, but many need a sea anchor let out at the end of an adjustable bridle.

wind

Chapter 16
Emergencies

An essential part of good seamanship concerns how to avoid emergencies and then, if they do happen, how to deal with them. In chapter 7 we looked at personal safety concerns for individual crew members. Here we will discuss situations that may put the boat and the whole crew in jeopardy. While every sailor hopes such emergencies will not occur, hope alone will not prevent them from happening. "Man marks the earth with ruin," Lord Byron wrote, "his control stops at the shore." Humans cannot control the sea, but we can improve our own skills and equipment so that the tragedies of the past are not repeated in the future.

The Float Plan

An important safety practice is to make sure that other people know where you are on the water. Before heading out, leave a float plan with a friend, relative, yacht club, or marina. A float plan is an itinerary of your planned trip that includes telephone numbers where you can be reached and the times when you plan to check in. If you change your schedule later on, check in and alter the float plan. Instruct your contact at home to notify the Coast Guard if you do not call or appear on schedule.

Avoiding Emergencies

"Why did all those people get into such terrible trouble?" As the author of *"Fastnet, Force 10"*, a book about the 1979 Fastnet Race, the most murderous storm in the history of pleasure boating, I'm often asked that question. It's a weighty one. Fifteen sailors died, 24 yachts were abandoned, and five yachts sank in a vicious gale in the waters between Ireland and England on August 13, 1979. It was the worst single disaster in the history of pleasure sailing. I sailed in the race, and while the boat I was in suffered no major damage, I would not want to go through a storm like that one again.

What happened? There are several answers. Some of the boats in the race were not fit for storm conditions. Yet not every boat that got into trouble was poorly designed or built. Crew injuries, gear damage, poor seamanship, and bad luck all played their parts. The importance of each factor varied from boat to boat. This section is based on close studies of these factors in the Fastnet storm and other catastrophes. We all can learn from the experiences of every sailor caught out in unsafe weather.

"Formula for Disaster"

Seven factors appear time and again in major emergencies involving sailboats. Often only three or four of them are at play, but there are some catastrophes where all seven can be found. These seven factors have been called "the formula for disaster."

Factor 1. A rushed, ill-considered departure is first on the list because it turns up in almost every bad accident. While the demands of jobs, families, and racing schedules often dictate when we go out on the water, none of these imperatives bears any relation to the schedule that counts the most in good seamanship. That schedule is nature's cycle of good and bad weather.

Every sailor should be able to identify the sailing conditions in which she or he is comfortable, and say *"No!"* when that

His 34-foot sloop lying disabled in 50-knot winds and 30-foot breaking waves, a sailor prepares to jump overboard so he can be rescued by a military helicopter during the 1979 Fastnet Race storm.

comfort zone is exceeded. Skiers do this when they read signs posted at the tops of trails. A black diamond on a sign indicates an expert trail that may be too demanding for the average recreational skier. While nobody posts "expert" signs over sailing areas, each sailor should be able to recognize his or her "black diamond" conditions by looking at the waves, feeling the wind, and reading a weather map.

Factor 2. The route is dangerous because it passes through predictably risky waters. This doesn't automatically mean deep water. It can be more hair-raising to sail a 20-foot daysailer through a narrow channel crowded with high-speed powerboats than to pound into a Gulf Stream gale in a 40-foot cruising boat. Sometimes a route suddenly becomes dangerous because conditions change. For example, you may choose a route because the tidal current is favorable there, but you'll wish you were somewhere else when the wind shifts dead ahead and kicks up steep waves as it blows against the contrary current.

Other dangerous routes take a boat away from protected waters, toward a lee shore, through areas of unpredictable currents, far from visible aids to navigation, and into waters frequented by sudden storms.

Factor 3. The route has no alternatives. Many crews have gotten into serious trouble because they set courses far from intermediate harbors of refuge. Plan ahead for times when you will need to find nearby shelter in order to deal with a small problem (such as a torn sail or a tired crew) that, if not addressed, may lead to emergencies.

Factor 4. The crew is unprepared. Poor crew preparation can take several forms. Sailors who come aboard without foul-weather gear and warm clothes are candidates for hypothermia. Some people do not have the basic sailing skills and experience to handle themselves and the boat. However, old salts can be just as vulnerable if they don't know where to find and how to use equipment that will help them get out of a jam. Crews who are not drilled in such procedures as bending on storm sails and handling crew-overboard recoveries will always be at least two steps behind.

Factor 5. The boat is unprepared. Major damage can occur because the crew, when preparing the boat, did not have the healthy caution that accompanies a "worst-case" state of mind. The results can be dangerous. To cite a few simple examples, when charts are missing, boats can't find refuge; when flashlights don't have batteries, nobody on deck can see at night; when knives are dull, lines can't be cut; when life jackets are waterlogged, they won't provide buoyancy; when the boat's batteries aren't tied down, they may capsize and leak noxious acid into the bilge and force the crew on deck.

Factor 6. The crew panics after an injury. A shipmate's injury or illness always threatens to distract the crew from good seamanship. In order to get the injured person to assistance, people may make impulsive, wrong decisions that risk the boat and her whole crew, like sailing toward a lee shore in a gale or abandoning ship when the boat is safe. Even when the injury or illness is treated competently on board, crew discipline can break down unless the skipper and watch captains assert strong leadership. The hard truth that the health of the individual must sometimes give way to the good of the whole may seem out of place in a pastime that usually is relaxed and enjoyable, but there are times when it must be the governing principle.

Factor 7. The command structure is unclear. Vague, weak leadership can cause low morale and lead to mistakes. Poor leadership results when skippers suffering from false pride cannot bring themselves to identify and admit their limitations. There are times when special skills are needed, for example in electronic navigation and steering in rough seas. If a clear line of authority has not been established, there will be a leadership vacuum should the skipper be incapacitated. A good skipper will recognize when to hand over responsibility to qualified crew members. Assigning a chain of command may sound too "navy" for people who think of sailing as an escape from hard discipline and structure, but it's necessary.

An Example

Those are the seven factors. Here's an extreme example of how all seven can come together.

Despite pessimistic weather forecasts and a falling barometer, a boat sets out on an overnight delivery trip because the skipper has a business meeting the next day (Factor 1). The first part of the chosen route is across a patch of shoal water that is notoriously rough in even a capful of wind (Factor 2). While beating off a lee shore (Factor 3), she is caught by a building wind that quickly develops into a gale. The crew, who were up partying the night before, collapse in seasickness and exhaustion (Factor 4). The main halyard (which the skipper has been meaning to replace for weeks) snaps and the main boom falls, hits the skipper in the head, and knocks him out (Factor 5). Because the skipper did not designate a second in command (Factor 7), the crew spends an hour arguing about what to do next (Factor 6). They finally decide to get the injured man ashore and head into a tricky harbor for which there is no chart on board since the owner never anticipated calling there (Factor 4 again). From there on, blind luck is their only salvation. It is poor seamanship to have to fall back on luck.

Four Rules of Preparation

The lessons of the formula for disaster can be boiled down to four rules of preparation for emergency-free sailing. Each of these rules covers a small family of concerns on sailboats of all types. Write down step-by-step standard operating procedures (SOPs, or what the Navy calls billets) to cover equipment and job assignments. Type the SOPs in duplicate and bind both sets in brightly colored notebooks. Put one notebook in

Preparation

the chart table and the other in the emergency pack described below under Rule 1.

In an emergency, turn to the relevant SOP and read it out loud to the assembled crew. If the reading does anything, it will calm the crew by forcing them to focus on specifics.

Rule 1. Prepare the Boat

With a worst-case state of mind, inspect your boat and gear. Look at furnishings and equipment below, asking, "What will happen when the boat is rolled over?" From that point of view, you'll find yourself being seriously concerned about many gear items you might otherwise take for granted. For example, lash down batteries, examine the bolts holding down the toilet, make sure the galley stove won't fall out of its gimbals, and see to it that electronic instruments are secured and lockers and

drawers won't fly open.

Look at safety equipment, asking, "Can we get to it fast in an emergency? Will it work?" Check that safety gear is aboard, accessible, and in good shape. Fire extinguishers must be charged and handy to the cook. Flares must be dry and easy to locate, the life raft should have received its annual checkup from a certified inspector, and safety harnesses, flashlights, foul-weather gear, emergency rations, heaving lines, crew-overboard gear, and other important equipment must be ready for use. Set aside emergency gear in a waterproof sack (available from camping supply stores). This gear includes flares, the emergency position indicating radio beacon (EPIRB), emergency rations, a knife, rope, tape, and other gear you would need if you had to abandon ship.

On an overhead drawing of the boat, such as the designer's accommodation plan, chart the location of all important gear, and post the drawing over the chart table.

Finally, examine the hull and rig, asking, "Will they work in rough weather?" A boat heading out into the ocean must be designed and built with the heavy loads and special needs of seagoing in mind. If you are headed far offshore, pay special attention to having ample ventilation, powerful bilge pumps, strong storm sails, and sturdy steering gear, spars, and rigging. The hull should have a range of positive stability (the heel angle at which the boat will continue to reright herself when knocked over) of at least 120°.

For detailed recommendations on the design, construction, and rigging of oceangoing boats, you may want to consult a book written by members of the Technical Committee of the Cruising Club of America and edited by myself, titled *Desirable and Undesirable Characteristics of Offshore Yachts* (New York: W. W. Norton, 1987).

In their concern about big equipment, sailors often ignore the small items that hold all these pieces (and many others) together. In other words, don't lose your kingdom for the want of a horseshoe nail. Nautical horseshoe nails are shackles and clevis pins, cotter pins, and other fastenings.

One last concern: make sure all your sails go up and down easily without special treatment or magical incantations. When you want to set and douse them, things should happen *fast*.

Rule 2. Prepare the Crew

Introduce the crew to the workings of the sailing gear, engine, plumbing, pumping, and electronic equipment.

They must be shown safety gear and given the opportunity to practice with it in emergency drills.

Hold a crew meeting for assigning jobs and establishing the chain of command. If the boat will be out overnight or longer, make up and post watch schedules (described in chapter 15), and insist that people stick to them so there are no misunderstandings. Be explicit about rules for personal safety devices. On well-managed boats far from assistance, safety harnesses are usually worn at night and in rough weather.

Assign priorities and tasks for preparing for heavy weather, among them pumping bilges, getting rest, and cooking food and heating hot water before the sea gets too rough for working at the stove. In rough weather, shorten watches and make them smaller in order that as few people as necessary are exposed to the elements.

Make sure everybody has proper clothing and personal gear, including nonslip shoes, foul-weather gear, and warm clothes for damp, cool weather.

Rule 3. Choose a Safe Route

When you plan your cruise or voyage, be sure to identify and be prepared to enter backup ports between your departure point and ultimate destination. You'll need plenty of charts plus relevant tide tables, cruising guides, *Light Lists* and *Coast Pilots*. On the charts locate and mark especially risky or crowded areas such as race courses, shoals, tide races, and narrow channels. Also mark highly visible landmarks and aids to navigation. In poor visibility, you'll want to be able to avoid the risky spots while steering for the highly visible ones. You may want to highlight potentially dangerous areas on the chart using an indelible pen with purple ink, which is visible under the red light used in the navigator's station to preserve the navigator's night vision.

Rule 4. Prepare for Emergencies

Your goal is to be able to solve a life- or boat-threatening problem quickly and efficiently, without crew panic. Practice crew-overboard rescue with everybody taking different roles. Demonstrate how to light a flare, work the fire extinguisher, operate the bilge pumps, go aloft in the bosun's chair or sling, and start the engine with the hand crank. After you have refined your techniques, write down the steps in the emergency SOP book so a newcomer can read them.

Running Aground

Running aground can be a minor annoyance, a catastrophe, or something in between depending on the situation. When a centerboarder runs up on a shallow sand or mud bottom, it's no problem: raise the centerboard, turn the boat around, and sail back the way you came. If the centerboarder fetches up hard on gravel, however, the centerboard trunk may be jammed and you may not be able to raise or lower the appendage. If she bangs into a rock, the centerboard or rudder may be bent or broken. Running aground in a keel boat presents a more difficult problem, since the keel cannot be raised. If the tide is flooding, you'll eventually float off. Otherwise you must kedge off with the anchor (as described in chapter 14), sail or power off, arrange for a tow — or wait for the tide to change.

You may be able to sail or power off, but first you must decrease the boat's draft by heeling her. Move the crew as far to leeward as possible and trim the sails. If that doesn't heel her sufficiently, run a halyard out to an anchor or boat and pull hard. Sometimes rocking the hull back and forth will break the suction of the bottom on the keel. You may even be able to shove her off with the spinnaker pole, or by jumping overboard and putting your shoulder to her bow. Be aggressive and don't give up until you're absolutely sure she's stuck.

If you must wait for the tide to flood and lift you off, and if there's an onshore wind, set out an anchor in deeper water to restrain the boat from being blown farther up the shore. You can use this anchor to pull yourself off when the water rises. If the shoal will dry out (be exposed) at low tide, hang fenders along the low side to protect it from scratching. Then sit and wait.

In a strong onshore wind, try to arrange a tow off as soon as you can. You may have to call the Coast Guard or use one of the emergency signals described later in this chapter.

If you ran aground at high speed, the impact may have loosened the keel bolts and she may be leaking. So check the bilges right away, and if you find water seeping (or, God forbid, pouring) in, start pumping.

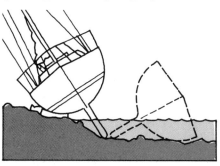

A grounded boat should be allowed to lie on the side away from the water, otherwise she may be flooded by incoming tide.

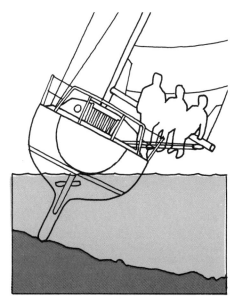

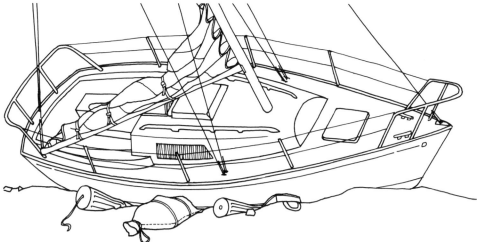

Lay fenders, cushions, and other protection between the hull and the bottom to keep the topsides from being badly scratched. Put out an anchor and wait for the tide to rise unless a strong onshore wind is blowing, when you must call for help.

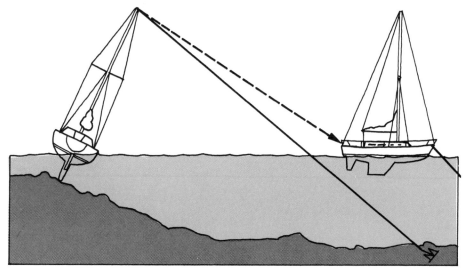

(Left above) If barely aground, heel the boat and try to spin her away from the shore by backing the jib or kedging off. (Left) To induce heel lead the main halyard to an anchor or moored boat and heave in on it.

337

Towing

There may be times when you must request or accept a tow from another boat, for example, if you're hard aground, if your boat is leaking badly, or if the engine has broken down and another emergency requires that you get to shore quickly. One reason that does *not* justify an emergency tow is running out of gasoline or diesel fuel when there's plenty of wind to sail home. Of the many thousands of missions conducted each year by the U.S. Coast Guard, all too many are to "rescue" crews that have panicked simply because their fuel tanks have run dry. In fact the huge expense of these needless missions is gradually causing the Coast Guard to pass its free search-and-rescue operations on to commercial towing and salvage companies that charge for their services.

But there are times when a tow is appropriate. In any situation when a boat offers a tow, before passing her your line, tactfully ask her crew if they will charge for their service. They may be insulted (in which case apologize). Then again, this question may save you a lot of money. If a Coast Guard vessel arrives, she'll give you a tow unless a commercial vessel is available. Under present policy, a Coast Guard vessel may even drop a tow when a nonofficial, commercial boat shows up. To protect yourself from salvage claims that might leave the boat in the hands of the towing crew, stay on board. Under salvage law an abandoned boat could be claimed by whoever boards her unless the abandoning crew leaves a specific written warning that they intend to return. And instead of taking a tow line from the other vessel, pass your own line; this certifies that you are volunteering to be towed.

The tow line should be strong and long; the anchor rode is ideal. Secure it to the strongest object forward, such as a through-bolted bow cleat or the mast. With large strains (such as when being hauled off a shoal), secure the line forward and then pull the excess aft to the largest sheet winch. Take several wraps and grind most of the stretch out of the line to take some of the load off the cleat or mast. The tow line must be led through a chock at the stem, using chafing gear if necessary (see chapter 5), but if the chock makes for an unfair lead, rig a block as a fairlead. Start with the line short, then lengthen it as you increase speed.

Before getting under way, tell the tow boat's skipper how fast your boat will safely go, and if she's aground, how deeply into the bottom she's imbedded. If he appears to be careless and unseamanlike, you may decide to cast off the tow and fend for yourself — he could get you into more trouble than

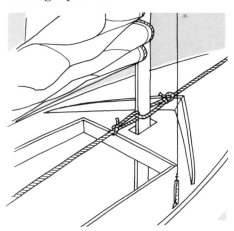

Tie the lines of towed and towing small boats through each other at the mast using bowlines.

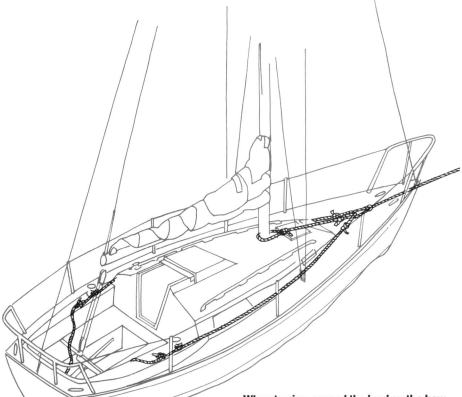

When towing, spread the load on the bow cleat by leading backup lines to winches and the mast (do not use the mast if it is stepped on deck).

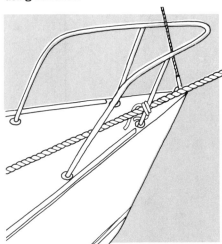

If there is no bow chock or if the towing line is too big for the chock, rig a temporary fairlead for the towing line with a short line through a stanchion base.

you're in right now. But if you do decide to be towed off, agree on hand signals or a VHF/FM channel to be used to transmit instructions.

The tow should start slowly and gradually pull the stretch out of the line. *Stay away from the tow line when it's under a load.* If it snaps, its backlash could break your leg.

When being towed off a shoal, gauge your progress against a range of trees or buildings on shore. If she doesn't move after a few minutes, try pulling her the other way; be cautious about pulling her off backward since the rudder might break. Don't force her. If she doesn't want to come off, she *won't* come off until the tide is higher.

Once under way on a tow, find a safe speed where the two boats are in wave troughs and on crests at the same time. The helmsman on the towed boat should keep the tow line from rubbing against the headstay and the boat from wandering out to the sides of the wake. If another boat wants a tow, take her line and secure it where your own tow line is cleated. If your tow line

is tied around the mast with a bowline, tie her line through the bowline (not around the mast) with another bowline. This way, when the tow has reached hull speed most surges or stops will be absorbed by the two lines and not by your mast.

A swamped boat full of water must be towed in a different way, described later in the section on capsizing.

Keep the tow line long with the towed boat riding easily in the trough of her wave (A) and not climbing up it (B). Steer carefully and use hand signals between the two boats.

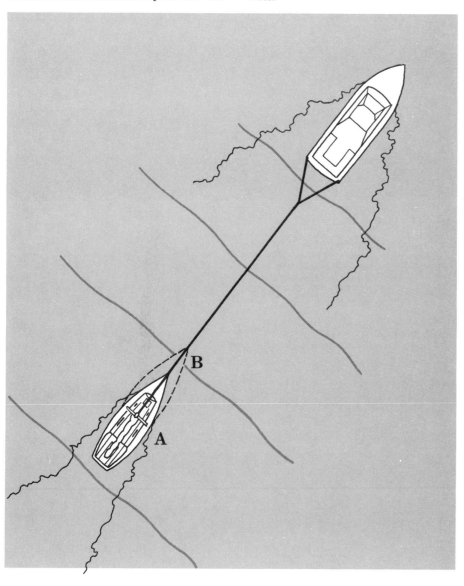

Steering Failure

If the tiller, wheel, or steering cable breaks, you'll have to make emergency repairs. You might be able to fix the cable with wire clamps and splice the tiller with a piece of hardwood or stainless-steel tubing, but replacing a broken steering wheel and its gear is a more difficult proposition. Most sailboats equipped with wheels also have an emergency tiller that can be installed on the rudder post; be sure you know how it works before heading out.

Replacing a broken steering mechanism is one thing, but jury-rigging a damaged rudder can be very difficult. If the rudder post breaks or the rud-

der hits a floating object and falls apart, you've lost the major component of the steering gear. An emergency rudder for a small boat can be fashioned out of an oar lashed at its middle to the transom. An oar is too weak for a boat larger than about 20 feet, but applying the same principle will lead to a long "tiller" created from a spinnaker pole or other long metal tube and, at its end, a "rudder" made of plywood sheets screwed with sheet-metal screws to the pole. The hinge could be a lashing on the transom, but on larger boats a one-point pivot will create large bending forces that will

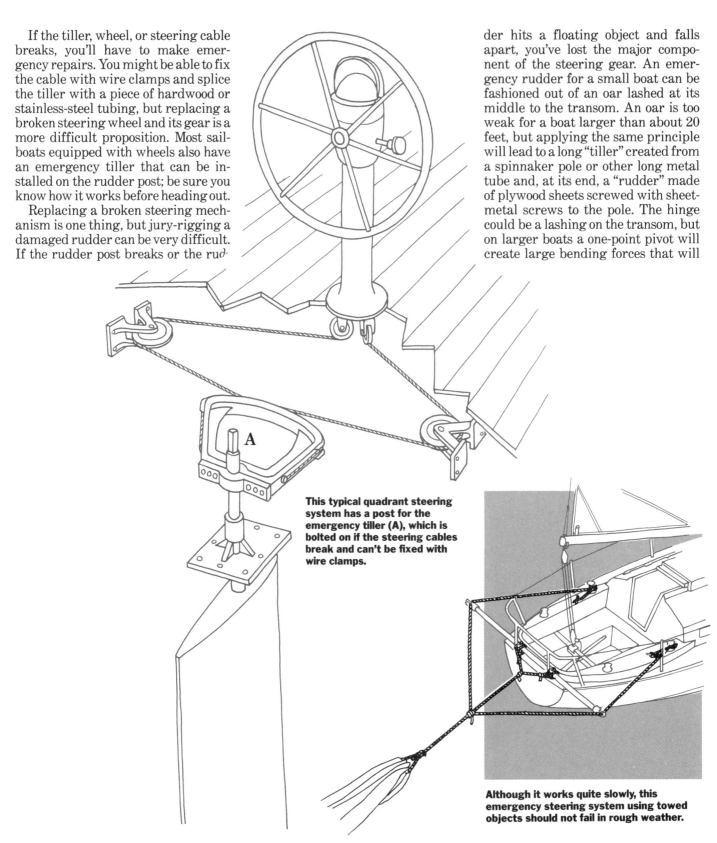

This typical quadrant steering system has a post for the emergency tiller (A), which is bolted on if the steering cables break and can't be fixed with wire clamps.

Although it works quite slowly, this emergency steering system using towed objects should not fail in rough weather.

quickly break the pole "tiller." To provide some give in the system, hang the pole at the fulcrum several feet above deck from a line suspended from the backstay.

Lacking a long pole to use as a "tiller," drag a bucket, fender, or other large object astern from lines leading from the corners of the transom. Pulling the object to port will slowly force the boat to head to port, and the same to starboard.

Of course, a rudderless sailboat can always be steered with her sails either with or without emergency equipment. As we explained in chapter 3, by adjusting the fore-and-aft location of the sail plan's center of effort, a crew can create weather or lee helm. Since most sailboats are designed and built to have a few degrees of weather helm, self-steering may require moving the center of effort well forward by reefing the mainsail, lowering the mizzen (if there is one), or setting a small jib and trimming it to windward inside a larger jib. Tacking or jibing under a self-steering rig may not be possible.

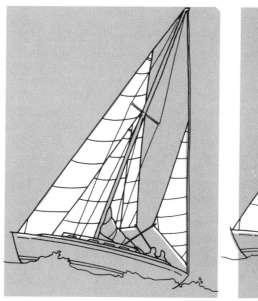

Either alone or in combination with an emergency system, steering with the sails should aim the boat generally in the right direction. Rig sails as far aft and forward as possible so that small trim changes are effective. "Jib and jigger" works best on a divided rig (right); a temporary mizzen can be rigged by hanging a small jib off a sloop's backstay (left).

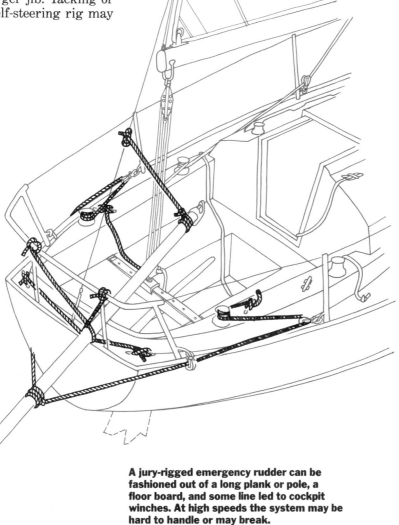

A jury-rigged emergency rudder can be fashioned out of a long plank or pole, a floor board, and some line led to cockpit winches. At high speeds the system may be hard to handle or may break.

Dismasting

Although ocean racers often suffer mast failures due to hard use of extremely slender spars, the normal cruiser-racer's mast should outlive its owner — assuming that its owner treats it with reasonable care. There are two common causes of dismasting. One is allowing the mast to bend too far, either sideways (due to poor tuning; see chapter 16) or fore and aft (see chapter 3). If the mast is not straight, it goes out of column and loses much of its built-in strength. The second, and by far most frequent, cause of mast failure is a broken fitting — a collapsed spreader, a snapped shroud, or a parted turnbuckle.

The crew's first response to a dismasting will be confused shock, but as soon as they recover they must spring to the broken spar and keep it from holing the hull. In rough weather, the mast will be jackknifed over the leeward rail and every wave will slam the boat down onto it. If possible, drag the mess back on board. Otherwise you'll have to pull or cut the sails off, cut the halyards, pull the cotter and clevis pins out of any remaining turnbuckles, and let the top part of the mast sink. In the next chapter we'll show how to rig the cotter pins so they can be pulled out quickly in emergencies; if you can't remove them, cut the turnbuckles or shrouds with a sturdy hacksaw or heavy bolt cutters (which should be carried on any boat heading offshore). However you do it, clear the broken mast away from the topsides before they are punctured.

Bent when the boat capsized and it hit the water, this mast could be supported laterally by leading a wire halyard from the base of the spreaders to a handy billy on the starboard rail.

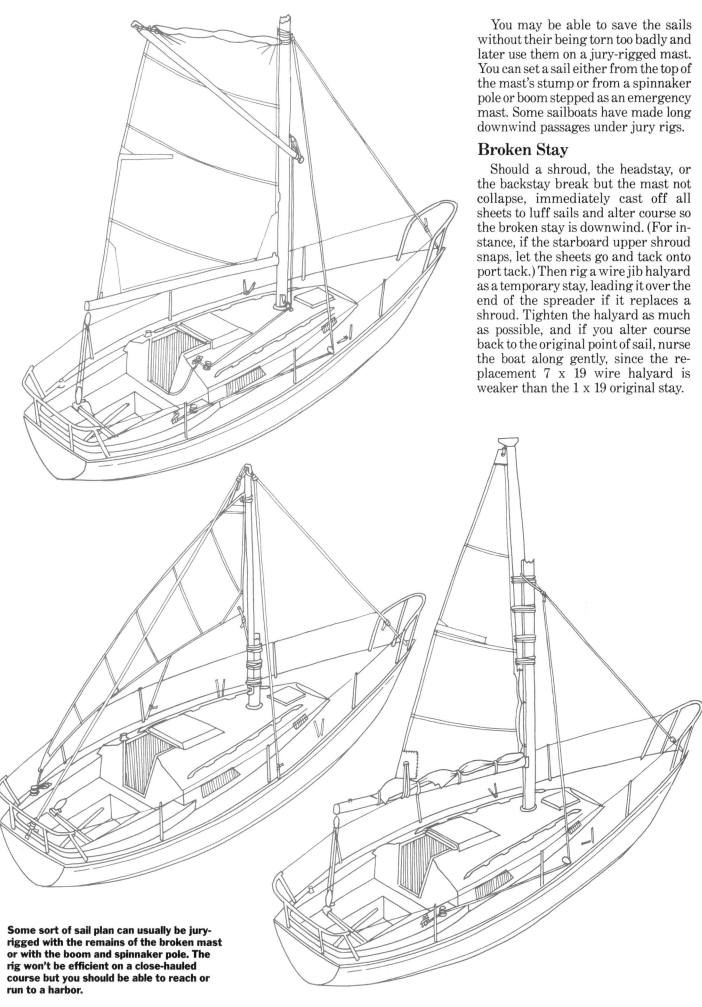

You may be able to save the sails without their being torn too badly and later use them on a jury-rigged mast. You can set a sail either from the top of the mast's stump or from a spinnaker pole or boom stepped as an emergency mast. Some sailboats have made long downwind passages under jury rigs.

Broken Stay

Should a shroud, the headstay, or the backstay break but the mast not collapse, immediately cast off all sheets to luff sails and alter course so the broken stay is downwind. (For instance, if the starboard upper shroud snaps, let the sheets go and tack onto port tack.) Then rig a wire jib halyard as a temporary stay, leading it over the end of the spreader if it replaces a shroud. Tighten the halyard as much as possible, and if you alter course back to the original point of sail, nurse the boat along gently, since the replacement 7 x 19 wire halyard is weaker than the 1 x 19 original stay.

Some sort of sail plan can usually be jury-rigged with the remains of the broken mast or with the boom and spinnaker pole. The rig won't be efficient on a close-hauled course but you should be able to reach or run to a harbor.

Capsize

All kinds of boats can capsize, but this accident occurs most often when dinghies and other small centerboarders are overloaded or are hit by a sudden gust of wind just after a tack, a jibe, or some other course alteration and the crew is unable to hike out or cast off sheets. If you do capsize in one of these boats, you can count on her staying afloat; unless they are holed or float away, built-in flotation tanks or blocks of foam should keep her buoyant with the rail above the water. Lasers and other boats with a small cockpit (or no cockpit at all) can be righted immediately. Swim around the boat or climb over the windward rail and pull down on or stand on the centerboard to lever the hull back upright. Make sure the sheets are cast off; otherwise she can tip right over again once the sails are filled. Climb back aboard and sail off. (If there's enough wind to capsize a small boat, you must wear a life jacket.)

If the boat can't be righted, either because she has swamped (is full of water) or because you're too tired to pull her up, don't leave the boat. *Stay with the capsized boat with your life jacket on and wait for rescue.* Some open daysailers may be bailed out after being swamped, but many must be towed to shore. When the tow boat comes alongside, get the sails down and secured, tie the tow line to the mast, and as the boats gather way, hang off the transom. Water will flow aft and over the stern, and soon you may be able to hail the powerboat, stop the tow, and bail out the rest. Great strains are put on a hull and rig when a swamped boat is towed, so try to make the tow as short as possible.

A dinghy that has turtled (turned completely over) may resist righting by her crew. In that case you may have to swim — cautiously — under the boat, lower the sails, and hand the main halyard to a powerboat crew, who can pull the mast up.

When a catamaran capsizes, she very likely will turtle unless the crew is very quick. Many catamarans are rigged with special righting lines under trampoline decks. If they capsize, but don't turtle, the crew can pull back and down on the line to bring the raised hull down to the water. Proponents of large cruising multihulls, especially trimarans, point out that though they may capsize more readily than monohull racer-cruisers, these craft won't sink. After capsizing in one of these boats, a crew may cut a hole in the exposed bottom of the center hull and climb below to wait for rescue. Following several well-publicized capsizes by trimarans, a few ingenious designers began to develop self-righting systems using gin poles and counterweights, but as yet they have not

(Above) If your dinghy can't be righted, or if you're too tired, stay with her and await rescue. (Right) Otherwise, stand on the centerboard and lever her back upright. Be sure to free all sheets first so that the sails do not fill when the boat becomes upright.

been successfully tested in rough seas.

Boats with keels can capsize and survive. In the infamous 1979 Fastnet Race, about one-third of the boats caught in a Force 10 gale rolled over between 90° and 180°, and many stayed turtled for a minute or more. Breaking seas were responsible for most of these capsizes. Typically, a boat would surf down the face of a wave, spin out of control, and broach with her side exposed to the next breaker, which would heave her over on the other side, or in extreme cases throw her upside-down. All but five of these 100 or so boats recovered and were sailed or towed to port, but only after the crews spent hours bailing out tons of water. Nineteen crews came to believe either that their boats were sinking or that the mass of broken, loose fixtures and fittings flying around in the cabins would injure them or destroy the hulls, so they abandoned ship. Yet a total of five men later died in or near their life rafts as the yachts they had abandoned survived the gale.

While it is extremely unlikely that your racer-cruiser will capsize in heavy weather, you should take certain precautions to minimize the chances of a rollover. Exhaustive tests with models indicate that a boat is less likely to stay upright if dismasted than if her rig is still standing, so do everything you can to keep her mast up. Steer carefully in breaking seas if you're running before it. If not, choose the best passive storm tactic, either heaving-to or lying ahull, for your boat in the prevailing conditions. If there's any chance of a capsize, seal off the cabin and any lockers accessible from deck. Install shutters over the windows. Make sure that all fittings and equipment, including radios, the stove, and batteries, are securely installed or stowed.

Life Rafts

Any boat heading offshore in the open waters of large lakes or seas should carry a life raft with a *tested* capacity equal to or greater than the size of the crew (the manufacturer's claimed capacity may be overly optimistic). The raft should be equipped with a first-aid kit, emergency rations, a sharp knife with a ground-down point, a sea anchor, a canopy to protect the crew, sturdy rope hand-holds, a strong painter, a blanket or cloth to insulate the crew from the cold rubber bottom, and if you're heading far offshore, an emergency position-indicating radio beacon (EPIRB, described later in this chapter). Have your life raft thoroughly inspected by a professional every year. If the inflation system malfunctions, the painter breaks, or the raft falls apart, nobody may be saved.

A packed life raft is both bulky and heavy, so it's usually hard to find a secure, accessible stowage location for one on a small boat. Many skippers lash the packed raft on deck amidships, so that if inflated it will lie in the lee of the hull. If stowed and inflated on the afterdeck, the life raft will have little protection to windward and blow away when it goes into the water. If you stow a life raft in a plastic cannister, make sure there are handles so it may be carried.

As the 1979 Fastnet Race experience suggests, don't place all your faith in a life raft. It may capsize or fall apart, unless it has a canopy it offers little or no shelter, and it may be difficult to spot from a search plane or boat. Some of these faults have been corrected: a noncapsizeable life raft is now on the market, and a raft carrying a functioning EPIRB can be located extremely quickly. In a few well-known cases crews have survived in rafts for several weeks. Still, we emphasize that while a life raft may sometimes be necessary, often it may only *seem* to be necessary. The best rule of thumb is not to get into the raft until your yacht goes down, for a floating boat is the best life raft of all.

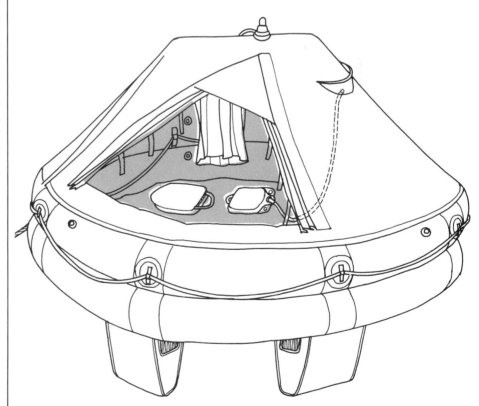

You may never use it, but your peace of mind will be secure if your life raft is well-equipped with emergency gear, has a canopy, and is large enough for you and your crew. Have it inspected annually and replace worn or rotted parts.

Sinking

A considerable amount of water can be taken aboard a keel boat before she sinks — much more, in fact, than is needed just to fill the bilges. If the boat is so low that water is splashing over the rails, she's probably going down, but keep pumping and bailing until then.

Often the amount of water in the cabin after a capsize or a holing may cause a crew to panic and abandon a boat that is later found safely afloat. Perception has a great deal to do with your faith in the vessel. While a heavy-displacement boat with deep bilges can take a considerable amount of water aboard before it is even visible above the cabin sole (floor), in a light-displacement boat with a shallow bilge and no sump (recessed area to hold bilge water), almost every drop that comes aboard as spray or rain will be noticed.

Minor Leaks

Still, you may be taking on more water than the conditions warrant. If so, first inspect the through-hull fittings. Some of these are intake and outlet holes for water and waste that are opened and closed with sea cocks (valves controlled by levers or faucet-type handles). The fitting may be corroded or cracked, the hull around it may have opened up slightly, or the tube or pipe led to the fitting may be loose. Another through-hull fitting to inspect is the speedometer sensor stuck through the bottom of the boat. Look, too, at the stuffing box, which keeps water from coming in through the rudder post and may be loose, and the engine's exhaust system, which may be cracked. The exhaust pipe should have a loop to keep sea water from backing into the engine and corroding it. Perhaps the loop is leaking.

Spray and solid water may be coming down through the hatches, the partners (the deck hole around the mast), and fastenings for deck fittings, such as cleats. If so, replace the rubber gasket inside the hatch, fit a new, tight rubber boot around the mast at the partners, or coat the screws and bolts with sealant.

If a leak continues after you've attended to all those areas, pull up the cabin floorboards and pump and sponge out the bilge until it's perfectly dry. Water may be seeping in around the keel bolts, which might have been loosened if you ran aground.

Another source of relatively minor leaks is the wooden or foam core in the hull. Water may enter the core under the bilge, and when the boat heels, travel up the sides and seep into a locker or (if you're really unlucky) a bunk. Such a mysterious leak may take a long time to track down and fix.

If the boat has a centerboard, there may be a leak around the pin or in the centerboard trunk (case) where the appendage touches. Tighten the pin or seal it with a washer.

Leaks can occur around bolts holding the keel to the hull (A), along the rail and in the foam core (B), around windows, hatches, and the partners (C, D, and E), and at through-hull fittings (F).

Major Leaks and Holes

Except perhaps for a broken through-hull fitting, none of the leaks described above will sink a boat quickly. But a broken hatch or window or a hole in the hull can be fatal. To cover the hole above the waterline, nail, screw, or tie on sheets of plywood that support bunk mattresses. Repairing a holed hull is more difficult. A good temporary patch can be made by tying a sail or a mattress over the outside of the hole with lines that pass under the boat. Then plug the hole from the inside with cushions, sail bags, clothing, or some other object. If possible, heel the boat so the hole is above water.

If the hole cannot be located, the only solution is to keep pumping and bailing until you reach a boatyard. Use the boat's own bilge pumps; sometimes the freshwater pumps in sinks can be adapted to pump out the bilge too. Somebody should be delegated to keep the bilge free of small objects that might clog the pumps. Most bilges are divided into compartments by the frames used to keep the hull rigid. Small holes in the frames called limber holes allow water to pass to the sump, or lowest point in the bilge, where the pump's intake is normally located. The limber holes may be clogged with paint, dirt, fastenings, fiberglass resin, or other gurry. A limber hole chain — a light chain that runs fore and aft through all the limber holes — can be pulled to clear the limber holes. In boats not equipped with limber hole chains, clean out these small drains with a marlinspike or a screwdriver.

The Coast Guard has high-speed engine-powered pumps that it can drop to you from an airplane or helicopter or bring out in a boat.

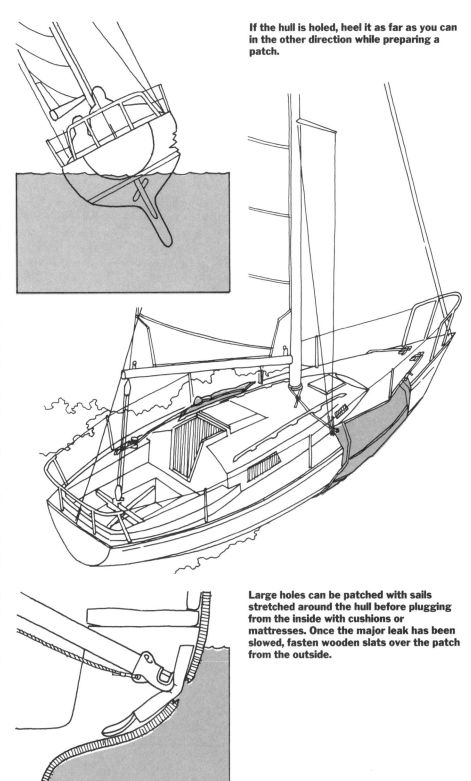

If the hull is holed, heel it as far as you can in the other direction while preparing a patch.

Large holes can be patched with sails stretched around the hull before plugging from the inside with cushions or mattresses. Once the major leak has been slowed, fasten wooden slats over the patch from the outside.

Fire

Besides sinking, the greatest danger to any vessel is fire. One reason why most racer-cruisers now carry diesel engines, even though they're heavier and more expensive than gasoline engines, is that diesel fuel is noncombustible except at very high temperatures. Yet there are still several opportunities for a fire to break out on board any boat.

Fire Extinguishers

The Coast Guard requires almost every boat with an engine to carry at least one approved Type B fire extinguisher. The only exception to this rule is an open outboard engine-powered boat smaller than 26 feet. A Type B extinguisher is designed to put out liquid fuel fires involving gasoline, diesel fuel, and some cooking fuels (although small fires on alcohol stoves can be put out with water). For more information about other Coast Guard fire extinguisher requirements, which vary with the size of the boat, see appendix I.

Obviously a boat's fire extinguishers should be within arm's reach of anybody working at the galley stove or on the engine, but not where you must reach through flames to get to them. All extinguishers should be checked, and if necessary, charged at least once a year.

Fighting Fires

Small alcohol fires and wood and fabric fires should be immediately drenched with water. Many cooks using alcohol stoves keep a pot of water handy in case there's a fire or flare-up.

A fire involving liquefied cooking gas should first be dealt with by turning off the fuel supply from the tank. The shutoff valve should be near the stove but neither behind it nor in a location that will require reaching through flames. Once the fuel supply is cut off, let the fire burn itself out. You may have to soak nearby wooden or fabric surfaces with water to keep the fire from spreading.

Gasoline, diesel oil, or grease fires should be attacked with a Type B extinguisher. Do not use water, which will only spread the flames.

Engine fires are fought with a Type B extinguisher aimed through the smallest possible access hole to the engine compartment so the extinguisher does not blast the flame into the rest of the boat. Turn off the engine before using the extinguisher.

Electrical fires should be fought with a Type C fire extinguisher designed specifically for this purpose, although a heavy dousing with water may work if a Type C extinguisher is not available.

To use a fire extinguisher properly, aim at the base of the flame, with a sweeping motion if it's spread out. Of the four kinds of Type B extinguishers (identified on the label), dry chemicals are effective for 5-15 feet from the nozzle, Halon 1211 for 9-15 feet, Halon 1301 up to 6 feet, and carbon dioxide up to 3 feet. A major advantage of a carbon dioxide extinguisher is that it does not leave a residue or harm the workings of engines.

"Sniffers" and Blowers

While not active fire-fighters, sniffer-type alarm systems are superb fire-prevention aids for boats with heaver-than-air stove fuels (like propane) or with gasoline engines. Fumes from these fuels may settle in the bilge and be unnoticed by crew members unless the sniffer alarm goes off. An open flame may ignite the fumes with the force of a bomb.

For the same reason, the engine's blower helps vent fumes through ducts required on most boats by the Coast Guard.

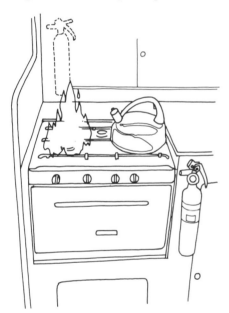

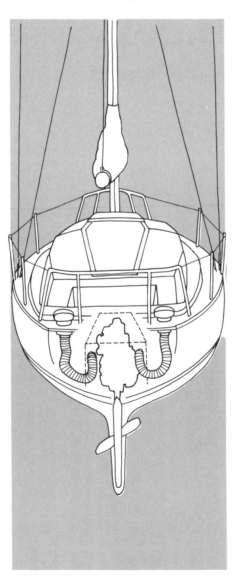

(Above) Locate an approved fire extinguisher near the stove but not where the cook must reach through flames to get to it. When cooking with alcohol fuel, keep a pot of water handy to douse a flare-up. (Right) A boat with a gasoline engine *must* have a bilge blower; one with a diesel fuel engine and a heavier-than-air cooking *should* have one.

Distress Signaling

The Coast Guard and the Rules of the Road require that certain equipment and signals be used by distressed mariners when attracting attention. Before using any of them, the skipper must honestly ask himself whether a life-threatening emergency actually exists on board. Can the boat make her way to port under sail if the engine has been disabled, or under jib alone if the mainsail has blown out? Does the crew's scalded hand actually require medical attention? Are we in truly great danger because the electronic navigation devices have shorted out? All too often skippers and crews panic when confronted with unexpected, minor breakdowns which their state of mind quickly converts into major disasters. Obviously a severe head injury to a crew member or a major hole below the waterline or a broken mast is an emergency, but each demands different levels of attention: the head wound should be treated immediately, while the holed boat may be able to make her way to harbor and the dismasted boat's crew can anchor and clean up. Coast Guard and private search-and-rescue missions are expensive, time-consuming, and frequently dangerous. Even the act of coming alongside a disabled boat in a rough sea can do considerable damage to the rescuing craft and her crew. If, as we said earlier, the boat is the best life raft, then self-help is usually the best kind of rescue.

Yet there are times when a seaman cannot save himself. To summon assistance he uses one or several kinds of carefully prescribed distress signals.

Approved and Recognized Distress Signals

The U.S. Coast Guard rules establish the minimum legal requirements for distress signals on all boats in U.S. waters. Here is a summary. See appendix I for a more detailed list.

With the exceptions of rowboats, boats smaller than 16 feet, boats participating in races, and open engineless sailboats smaller than 26 feet, all pleasure boats must carry day and night distress signals. The excepted boats must carry night signals when out at night. Acceptable *day signals* include three orange smoke signals and a flag with a black square and black circle on an orange field. Acceptable *night signals* include a bright flashlight signaling SOS (dot-dot-dot, dash-dash-dash, dot-dot-dot). Acceptable *day and night signals* meeting both requirements are three Coast Guard-approved red flares that are either handheld or capable of being fired into the sky. (Note: In some states, flare guns must be registered as firearms.)

The best flares are parachute flares; because they descend slowly, they are visible longer than other flares. The best parachute flares are the ones made to the standards of the international Safety of Life at Sea Convention (abbreviated SOLAS).

Do not use distress signals in jest. By law, they may be displayed only when a life is in danger.

Flares may lose their power with age and dampness. One way to check that flares are in operating condition is to test one flare from a set during the annual July 4th celebration. Another is to have a group test along with other boat-owners after receiving permission from your local Coast Guard district headquarters.

The International and Inland Rules of the Road include the following as acceptable distress signals: continuous sounding of a foghorn; firing a gun or other explosive device; rockets throwing stars of any color and fired at short intervals; a rocket parachute flare or a red hand flare; orange smoke; flames (such as a fire in a bucket); a square flag above or below a ball; code flags "NC"; S-O-S sent by any means; "Mayday" spoken over a radio telephone; and a person slowly and repeatedly raising arms outstretched to his side.

Unofficial but widely recognized distress signals include: waving an orange or orange-red flag; flying the national flag or yacht ensign upside-down; a rapidly flashing strobe light; and dye marker in the water.

Stow distress signals in dry, accessible, and clearly marked lockers in the cabin near the companionway. Since flares can absorb moisture, replace them periodically. Make sure everybody on board knows how to work a flare before heading out on a long passage. When sailing at night, have a very bright battery-operated flashlight handy to shine on your sails if another vessel approaches.

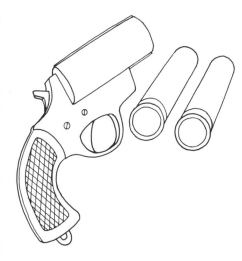

Boats larger than 16 feet are required to carry official distress signals such as flares fired by guns.

Accepted unofficial distress signals include flying the national flag upside down and showing a strobe light.

Waving arms, throwing dye marker in the water, and waving an orange flag are other distress signals.

Distress Calling

Distress Transmissions

Most distress signals are sent out over VHF/FM channel 16. When sending a call for aid, you must make clear who and where you are, and what kind of help you require. This is the procedure:

1. Press the alarm signal on the transmitter (if it has one) for 30-60 seconds. This will alert people monitoring channel 16 that a distress call is imminent.

2. Say "Mayday" three times, then the name of your boat three times. Give your VHF/FM call sign (printed on the license). Report your position either as a bearing and distance from a charted object or as latitude and longitude.

3. Describe your situation briefly; for example, "Dismasted and drifting at 2 knots onto Catalina Island 3 miles downwind. Require tow."

4. Describe the boat, emphasizing her rig, length, and color. Say how many people are aboard. Finally, repeat her name and call signal.

Keep repeating steps 1 through 4 until somebody acknowledges your call.

You or the official supervising channel 16 may order radio silence by all other stations with the words "Silence Mayday." ("Silence" is given the French pronunciation, "seelonce.")

Other stations may tell each other to clear the channel of all nonrelated communication with the words "Silence Distress."

The end of radio silence is announced by the operator with the words "Silence Fini" ("seelonce fee-nee" — silence ended).

Crews hearing the original call should immediately determine if they can help by plotting their and the distressed boat's positions. If they *cannot* help, they say nothing. If they *can* help the boat, they address the distressed boat by name, give their own boats' names and call signs, acknowledge the distress call, say they are proceeding toward her, and give course, speed, and estimated time of arrival.

If a crew can help by relaying the Mayday message, it prefaces the message by announcing "Mayday Relay."

Mayday distress calls must not be made unless there is a legitimate emergency threatening the boat or her crew. *It is illegal to knowingly transmit a fraudulent or false distress signal.*

If you require assistance but are not distressed, preface your call by saying "Pan-Pan" three times (pronounced "pahn-pahn").

Phonetic Alphabet

A	Alfa	**I**	India	**R**	Romeo
B	Bravo	**J**	Juliet	**S**	Sierra
C	Charlie	**K**	Kilo	**T**	Tango
D	Delta	**L**	Lima	**U**	Uniform
E	Echo	**M**	Mike	**V**	Victor
F	Foxtrot	**N**	November	**W**	Whiskey
G	Golf	**O**	Oscar	**X**	X-Ray
H	Hotel	**P**	Papa	**Y**	Yankee
		Q	Quebec	**Z**	Zulu

Morse Code

A	•—	I	••	R	•—•
B	—•••	J	•———	S	•••
C	—•—•	K	—•—	T	—
D	—••	L	•—••	U	••—
E	•	M	——	V	•••—
F	••—•	N	—•	W	•——
G	——•	O	———	X	—••—
H	••••	P	•——•	Y	—•——
		Q	——•—	Z	——••

To make radio transmissions absolutely clear you may have to use the phonetic alphabet when spelling words or names (right). Morse Code may also come in handy during transmissions or when trying to identify radio beacons (right below).

EPIRB

Another way to call for help — and the only way to do it automatically when you get into trouble — is to use an emergency position-indicating radio beacon (EPIRB). An EPIRB is a small buoyant radio transmitter that sends out a signal that the receiver can home in on. A Class A EPIRB will activate itself automatically when it turns upright. This type could be connected to a horseshoe life ring or a life raft; when the ring or raft go into the water, the transmitter rights itself and starts to send out a signal. A Class B EPIRB must be turned on manually.

Both the Class A and the Class B EPIRBs send out two signals. One is at 121.5 MHz, the aeronautical emergency frequency that all aircraft flying over water are required to monitor except when the crews are busy with other duties. Having received an EPIRB signal, the aircraft's navigator can home in on it with his radio direction finder, plot the position of the transmitter, and relay the position to nearby ships. By international agreement, certain U.S. and Soviet satellites can receive EPIRB signals and automatically transmit the sending vessel's position to shore facilities. Interestingly enough, the first use of this system involved a capsized American trimaran whose signal was picked up by a Soviet satellite, which transmitted her coordinates to an air force base in Illinois. A day later the trimaran was found in the Western Atlantic by a Coast Guard cutter, a Canadian air force plane, and a tanker, and her three crew members were efficiently rescued. At least 300 lives have been saved with the help of this system since that first rescue in 1982.

Unfortunately, many Class A and B EPIRB distress transmissions are not picked up, and some that are picked up give ambiguous positions. These problems should be solved by a new class of EPIRB operating on a special search and rescue frequency of 406 MHz. These EPIRBs should be approved for sale by the U.S. Federal Communications Commission in 1990.

Many false alarms have resulted when owners have tested their EPIRBs carelessly. Use the following test suggested by *Practical Sailor*, a boating magazine that is one of the best sources of information on the selection, maintenance, and operation of sailing gear.

First, tune an FM radio to 99.5 MHz and place it a few inches from the EPIRB antenna. Then, in the first 5 minutes of the hour (the time reserved for testing) turn on a Class B EPIRB's test switch or dip the bottom of a Class A EPIRB into water. You should hear a signal on the radio. Tests may run only one second, so quickly turn off the switch or pull the EPIRB out of the water. Test the device monthly, and replace its batteries before the expiration date.

RADIO LOG

DATE	TIME	VESSEL	CALL	MESSAGE
11/8/82	1415	R.H. DANA	KX1111	SOS. Fire. Pos 6mi E of Miami
	1416	called R.H. DANA	11	Acknowledge SOS
	1417	called USCG	16	Report SOS and Dana Pos.
	1420	USCG		Informs standing by Dana. No help needed.
	1440	R.H. Dana	KX1111	Informs fire out — no injury
		Jane Walsh 11/8/82		

The Coast Guard requires that every radio transmission concerning safety be summarized in the log book, with the time and the signature of the operator. In addition, log any repairs done on the radiotelephone.

An EPIRB is an automatic radio transmitter whose signal can be homed in on by aircraft, vessels, or satellites. It should be carried on a boat sailing offshore and located in a readily accessible spot so it can be activated on short notice. An EPIRB may also be carried in a life raft's emergency pack.

Helicopter Evacuation

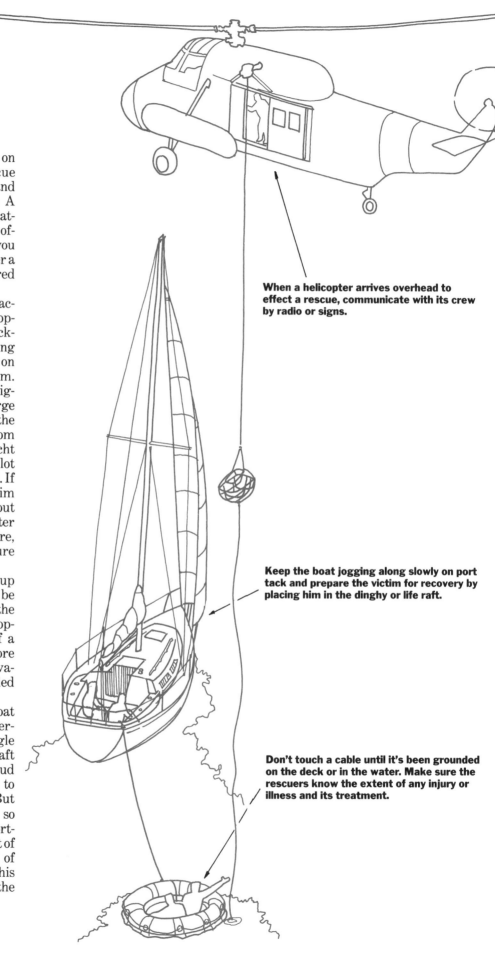

The Coast Guard relies heavily on helicopters for search-and-rescue missions because they're faster and have greater range than a cutter. A helicopter may drop a pump, an inflatable dinghy, or even a Coast Guard officer or enlisted person to help you with your problem. It may also lower a seat or basket to pick up an injured crew member.

If somebody on board must be evacuated and you see or hear the helicopter approaching, first clear the cockpit and deck of all unnecessary rigging and gear, then bring the casualty on deck. Put a life jacket on the victim. Using the VHF/FM radio, hand signals, or messages written on large sheets of paper, ask the pilot if the rescue is to be made from deck or from a life raft. If the boat is a sailing yacht and her rigging is in the way, the pilot may be chary about a deck retrieval. If so, inflate the life raft, put the victim and another person in it, and let it out at the end of a long line. The helicopter will drop a sling or a basket on a wire, usually with a man who will secure the victim before he is pulled up.

Whether the victim is picked up from the deck or from the life raft, be extremely careful when handling the equipment dropped from the helicopter. Any metal cable will give off a strong shock if it's touched before being grounded on deck or in the water. A rope, however, may be handled as it drops, but don't cleat it.

During the rescue, keep the boat moving on port tack so there is steerageway at the most comfortable angle to the wind and seas. The downdraft from the helicopter rotor will be loud and powerful, making it difficult to stand and to have conversations. But the typical helicopter rescue is so quick this discomfort will be short-lived. Tape or pin a detailed account of the victim's injury or illness, and of any treatment you've given, to his clothes so that doctors ashore know the background.

When a helicopter arrives overhead to effect a rescue, communicate with its crew by radio or signs.

Keep the boat jogging along slowly on port tack and prepare the victim for recovery by placing him in the dinghy or life raft.

Don't touch a cable until it's been grounded on the deck or in the water. Make sure the rescuers know the extent of any injury or illness and its treatment.

Preparing for Emergencies

While you can't anticipate emergencies, you certainly can prepare for them. All emergency equipment should be in good condition and easily retrievable from storage lockers. You may decide to put all flares, the EPIRB, the bolt cutters, and a set of tools in one clearly marked emergency locker. Or you may mark all emergency gear with a red stripe.

No matter where it's located, your crew should be able to find and use it as well as you do. Before a cruise, gather everybody together in the cockpit, tell them how to deal with certain emergencies, and show them how to use the gear. At the very minimum, everybody on board should know how to use the fire extinguisher.

Many emergencies occur because people don't know how to use the boat's basic equipment. Nobody should be allowed to cook until he's been shown how to turn on and light the stove and turn off the shutoff valve on the gas line.

The skipper should also assign a chain of command. He needn't be brusque about it; saying "Jim's in charge if I'm taking a nap" will be enough. In the Fastnet Race gale that we described, many accidents occurred after skippers were lost or incapacitated, sometimes because it was unclear who among the remaining crew was in charge. Good leadership and clear authority are important in emergencies, whether on land or at sea.

If you're a crew member new to the boat and the skipper doesn't say where the emergency gear is and how he plans to retrieve someone who's fallen overboard, don't be afraid to ask. Keep asking until you get a tour of the boat and perhaps a long disquisition about man overboard procedures. A good skipper will be glad that you've asked, a bad one may call you a landlubber. But there's absolutely nothing landlubbery about being concerned over boating safety.

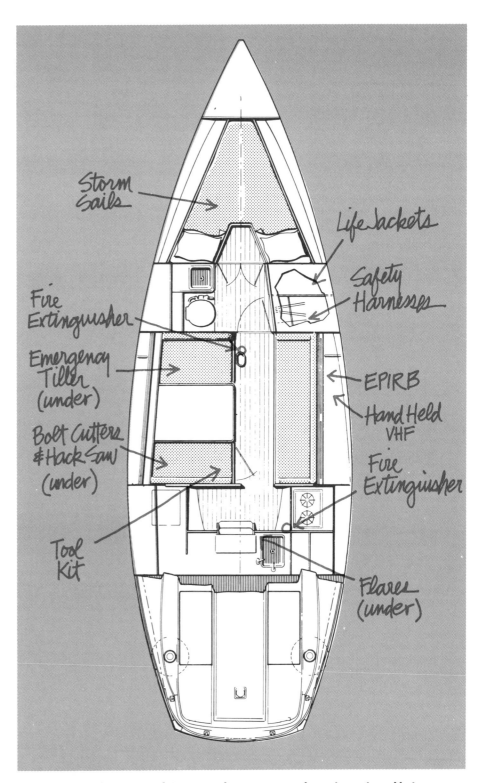

Storm Sails

Life Jackets

Safety Harnesses

Fire Extinguisher

Emergency Tiller (under)

Bolt Cutters & Hack Saw (under)

Tool Kit

EPIRB

Hand Held VHF

Fire Extinguisher

Flares (under)

You may know where your safety gear and emergency equipment are stowed but your crew may not. Locate them on a plan of the boat and post it on a bulkhead. Before getting under way, talk through all emergency procedures, show how to use flares and the life raft, and take newcomers on a thorough tour of the boat.

Chapter 17
Equipment and Maintenance

Above all, seamanship is the art of being self-sufficient on a boat. In this last chapter we'll look more closely at how to keep sails, rigging, the hull, and the engine in good condition, and we'll suggest tools that will help. This will be an overview that may help you get through a day's hard passage in a strong wind or a long summer cruise without having to face a major repair job. For more detailed information, consult your sailmaker and boatbuilder, and read the engine manual.

Running Rigging

Chafe is the main cause of broken sheets and halyards, so keep your eye peeled for unfair leads, broken fibers or wire strands, and worn or flat spots on lines. Turn sheets end-for-end once a year so the strains imposed by knots and blocks are equally distributed. When you buy new sheets, make sure they're long enough to do the job and have enough line left over so they'll still do even if they're broken near the working end. Spinnaker sheets should be twice the length of the boat and genoa sheets should be 1½ times its length.

If the block is too small for the sheet, the line will chafe. Make sure, too, that the block swivels enough so the lead is fair. During the off-season, disassemble the blocks and clean off any salt deposits or dirt with a rag dampened with solvent. Then rub a little light waterproof lubricant on the center pin (heavy grease will clog it and light oil will wear off quickly) before reassembling the block. This goes for halyard sheaves and blocks up the mast too. If the mast is pulled in the off-season, examine all its fittings. A worn main halyard sheave (or loose strands on the halyard itself) indicates that the lead may not be fair. At the least, replace the sheave; you may also have to angle it slightly to improve the lead. Sometime in midsummer have a couple of friends hoist you aloft on a bosun's chair; spray some oil or silicone into the sheaves and blocks, and check that the fittings and their fastenings are

secure. Down on deck, keep a spray can of oil or silicone handy for frequent squirts into blocks, shackles, and other moving fittings. Bearing surfaces on the traveler car and the spinnaker pole slide should be given a light coating of lubricant every few times that they're used. Keep a rag handy to clean up any excess lubricant before it drips onto the deck or sails.

Winches

A couple of times every sailing season, pull the drums off the winches, clean off the old lubricant with a paper towel soaked with solvent, re-

pack the roller bearings with light grease, and spray the pawls (which prevent backward rotation) with oil. Be careful not to use too much lubricant, which might gum up the bearings and make the winch hard to turn.

Steering System

Grease the system regularly using the grease cap located on or near the rudder post. Examine and lubricate the blocks for the steering cables, replacing them if they're cracked or loose, and make sure the cables themselves are tight and not frayed. Tighten the stuffing box around the rudder

Keep winch pawls (top) and bearings (bottom) free of caked salt and lubricated with light oil and grease.

Swiveling turning blocks provide a fair lead no matter where the line is led. Wash out salt deposits with fresh water and spray light oil on the pins and swivels. Bearing surfaces like those on spinnaker pole cars and tracks (top left) should be greased lightly.

post where it enters the hull, and replace the gasket if it leaks.

Standing Rigging

The mast must be straight athwartships when you're sailing close-hauled in about 12 knots of wind. Tuning the mast (adjusting the rigging so the mast is straight) is done before and while you are underway. After the mast is stepped, tighten the shrouds and stays so it is straight when you look up the track or groove on its aft side. To make sure it's not tilted to one side, use the main halyard as a reference. Lower the halyard so it's taut when the shackle is on the chain plate (deck eye) of the starboard upper shroud. Then without adjusting the halyard, take it over to the port side, and if the shackle does not lie against the chain plate, you know the mast is canted. Keep adjusting the shrouds until the halyard measurement shows the mast is straight.

Now go sailing in a moderate wind in smooth seas. Look up the mast track on both tacks. If the tip of the mast falls off, the upper shroud is too loose; if it cants to windward, the upper's too tight or the lower shroud running halfway up is too loose. On boats with two sets of spreaders, the intermediate shroud running from the tip of the lower spreader to the base of the upper spreader controls the upper part of the mast along with the upper shroud, complicating mast tuning. An overly tight intermediate can lead to mast failure in rough seas since, because it is shorter, it stretches less than the upper shroud and may pull the mast to windward while the top sags off.

Do not adjust the shrouds when they're to windward. Tack, pull the cotter pins out of the appropriate leeward turnbuckle (or loosen the locknuts), and using a wrench, a screwdriver, or a marlinspike, tighten or loosen the turnbuckle two or three turns. Then tack back and look at the mast. Keep going through these steps until the spar is straight. With a simple, one-spreader rig tuning can be quite quick, but it becomes increasingly complicated with more complex rigs, so be patient. Once the mast is straight in moderate winds, check it in other conditions.

Fore-and-aft tuning affects the mast's rake, which in turn affects the boat's balance. To increase weather helm, unwind the headstay's turnbuckle several turns and tighten the backstay's turnbuckle; to reduce weather helm, do the opposite. If you tune in light winds, you probably will be tempted to rake the mast aft, since modern boats with small mainsails and large jibs tend not to develop optimum weather helm of about 3° until they are heeled more than 10°. However, enough rake to provide weather helm in light air may give you too much helm in moderate winds. Instead of raking the mast aft, try to induce weather helm by pulling the traveler car up until the main boom is over the centerline.

Mast bend, which can flatten a mainsail (see chapter 3), is caused by pulling the top of the mast back with the permanent backstay and either pulling the middle of the mast forward with the jackstay (running from the mast to the foredeck) or pushing it forward with a tightly trimmed or vanged main boom. Wooden wedges called blocks may be put in the partners behind the mast (to bend it forward) or ahead of the mast (to straighten it). On some boats the main limit on mast bend is the after lower shroud, which runs from the base of the lower spreader to the deck aft of the upper shroud. However, on many modern reader-cruisers and all racing boats there is no after lower shroud, so crews must be extremely careful not to overbend the mast. If your boat has a flexible mast and powerful hydraulic equipment with which to bend it, we strongly recommend that you go sailing with your sailmaker or boatbuilder to get sound professional advice on handling this equipment without breaking the spar.

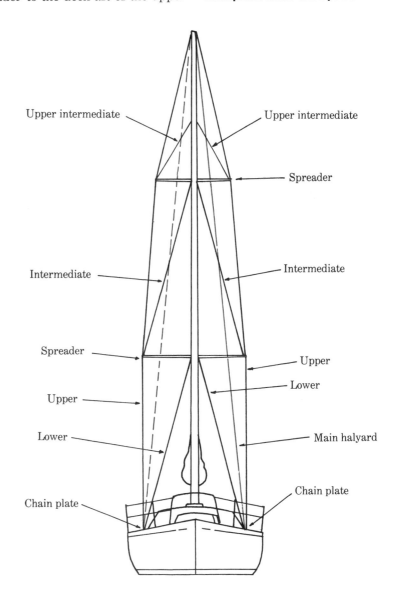

This double-spreader rig is held up by four shrouds. To check if a mast is tilted, lower the main halyard to one chain plate, cleat the halyard, and take the shackle over to the other chain plate. It should touch the chain plates at the same point.

Upper intermediate

Upper intermediate

Spreader

Intermediate

Intermediate

Spreader

Upper

Upper

Lower

Lower

Main halyard

Chain plate

Chain plate

Stays and Their Equipment

A stay is no stronger than the spreader, turnbuckle, and tang that are attached to it. Make sure the upper and intermediate shrouds are secured in the ends of spreaders with a pin or wire, and that the spreader tips are taped or padded with leather to protect any sails that brush against them.

Turnbuckles must be hefty enough for the load, with a large safety factor. Ones with open barrels that allow you to see the threads are preferable to close-barreled fittings. Turnbuckles that are locked with cotter pins are more secure than those with locknuts, which can vibrate loose unless they're glued down with silicone sealer.

The turnbuckle-to-stay connection must be perfectly straight yet have sufficient give so the turnbuckle doesn't bend if pressure is put on it. The only way to meet both requirements is to rig toggles between the stay's eye and the turnbuckle and between the turnbuckle and the deck.

Tangs are the metal plates on the mast to which stays and turnbuckles are connected. They must be aimed along the line of the stay, and their eyes should not be worn. If there is any wear or elongation in a tang, replace it immediately.

The terminals (ends) of stays usually are Tru-Lock swages applied under extremely high pressure. Check them for kinks or cracks and spread silicone sealer over any gaps between them and the wire so water doesn't get in and corrode from the inside out. A strong mechanical fitting called a Norseman terminal may also be used at the end of a stay or to repair broken stays. Cautious offshore skippers carry a length of 1 x 19 wire with a Tru-Lock swage at one end and several Norseman fittings, just in case they have to rig an emergency stay.

The windward stay and its fittings must be allowed to find their own ideal position and angle to take the load of the mast. And on the leeward side, the toggles and connecting pins must be allowed to turn as a shroud swings loosely, for otherwise the stay itself will bend, kink, and lose strength. The undisputed expert on sailboat rigging, Roderick Stephens, Jr. (of the yacht design firm of Sparkman & Stephens), strongly recommends that all moving parts in a stay system be lubricated with a coating of anhydrous lanolin, which can be purchased at pharmacies. He also advises rubbing lanolin into the turnbuckle threads to keep them from freezing up.

Never secure a line under load to a turnbuckle or toggle, or the fitting may bend.

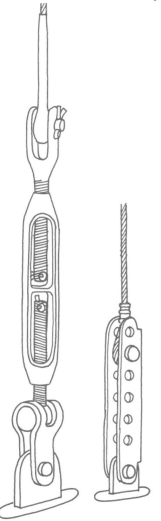

(Left) A turnbuckle must have a toggle so it can find its own angle without bending. (Right) Stays on small boats connect to simple hole-and-pin adjusters.

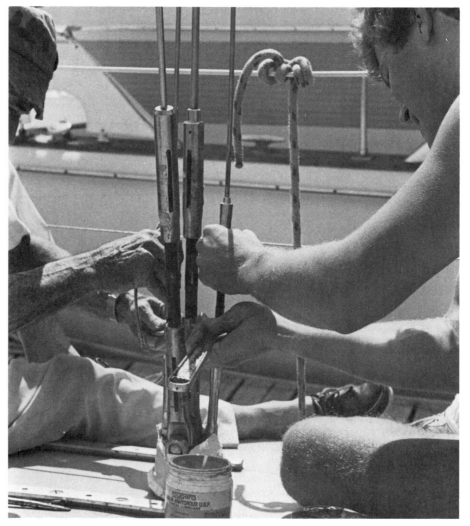

Lubricating the threads with anhydrous lanolin, and keeping a careful count of turns, these seamen tighten shroud turnbuckles using a wrench and spike. The stays are low-stretch rods, which are favored by serious racing sailors.

How to Use A Cotter Pin

Cotter pins hold the rig together. They keep a turnbuckle from unwinding, a shackle from opening, and a center pin from pulling out of a block. Either because they're small and inexpensive, or because they don't appear to take a load, they are often taken for granted.

The standard straight cotter pin that looks like a bobby pin should fit snugly into the hole in the fitting. On the other side, it should project a distance one-half the width of the fitting — just enough so that it can be locked in place simply by spreading the two sides about 20°. You may have

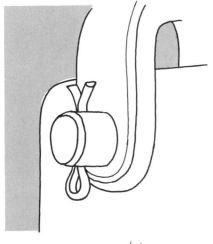

to cut the pin to get the ideal length.

Why should it be so short? So it can be easily removed with one sharp tug on the head with a pair of pliers. If the pin is longer, you'll have to double it back on the fitting to get it out of the way, and pulling a doubled-back pin will take much too long — say, when clearing away a broken mast.

Once you've found or made a cotter pin the right length, file off any sharp edges, stick it through the hole in the fitting, and with the tip of a screwdriver, gently spread the sides about 20°. Put a drop of silicone sealer on the pin to hold it in place, and then take two wraps of duct tape or plastic tape around it. According to Rod Stephens, who should know, that's how to rig a cotter pin correctly.

Some people cover turnbuckles with plastic boots to protect sails from cotter pins, but while that goal may be satisfied, they're also hiding the turnbuckles from a critical eye. It's much safer to use a couple of wraps of good tape over the pins (as well as over locknuts). You'll have to replace the tape from time to time, which provides a good excuse for a thorough inspection.

Besides straight cotter pins, circular cotter pins are available and frequently come as standard equipment. They do not project from the fitting, and they're easy to install — which, unfortunately, also means that they come undone easily. A capsize, vibration, or a chafing sail or line can unscrew one of these little pins with amazing efficiency. If you use them, tape them carefully.

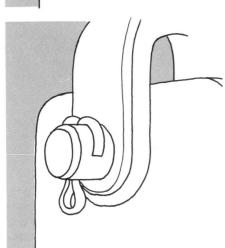

A cotter pin should project one-half the fitting's width and be bent back only slightly (top). If doubled back on itself, it will be almost impossible to remove in an emergency (above). Hold the pin in place with sealer and tape it.

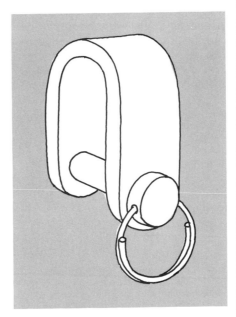

Circular cotter pins, called "ring-dings," are easy to install and do not have sharp edges, but they may bend or be shaken loose.

Going Aloft

The only way to inspect or repair rigging, lights, and other gear on the mast above the deck is to go aloft on a seat supported by a halyard. With the proper equipment and technique, going aloft should not be a problem at anchor or the dock, or even when under way in smooth water. Only in big emergencies should anyone go aloft in rough conditions, when wild swinging can cause seasickness and severe injuries.

The seat is called the "bosun's chair." The bosun (derived from "boatswain") is the crew member assigned to do maintenance. The traditional bosun's chair was a wooden slat, but today it's

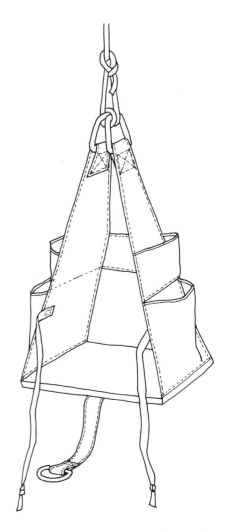

A good bosun's sling has side pockets and a strap to secure the seated sailor. Use two halyards, preferably tied to the sling.

Going Aloft

more likely to be a diaperlike Dacron sling, which is more comfortable and less easy to fall out of. Buy the sling from a reputable manufacturer.

The person going aloft in the sling or chair should wear long pants, since legs will rub against the mast and halyards. He or she should also wear a safety harness or short tether to secure to the mast or stays to stop swinging when the boat rolls and serve as a backup support should the halyard break. Tools, fittings, oil, and tape are carried in pouches in the chair or in a canvas bag dangling from the seat. Items that will be used often should be tied to the chair with light lines.

One or more crew members can pull the halyard with the aid of a winch or electric anchor windlass. Alternatively, the person can haul him- or herself up with a tackle. In both cases, attach two halyards (a primary and a backup) to the chair. Use a wire, Dacron, or other low-stretch halyard; with a nylon line, the person will bounce unsteadily as the line stretches and compresses. On some boats there is a special line for pulling crew aloft called the gantline. Rigged outside the mast through a large block at the masthead, the gantline also serves as a backup main halyard.

Don't secure the halyard to the chair with a snap shackle, which can open if its pin or its lanyard are rubbed against the mast. Instead, tie the chair on with a fisherman's bend in the end of a rope halyard or a length of heavy line passed through the eye in the end of a wire halyard. A screw-in shackle is suitable. If there's absolutely no way to avoid using a snap shackle, wrap the pin and lanyard with several tight layers of tape.

Lead the halyard to the biggest cockpit winch or the windlass. The winch should be well away from the mast so the haulers won't be hit by objects accidentally dropped by the person aloft. Use blocks to make the lead fair, with the line coming up to the winch drum at an angle so there are no overrides. Attach a long line to the bottom of the chair and lead it through a block on deck well away from the mast and from there back to the cockpit; this is a downhaul to hold the person away from the mast if he or she swings about as the boat rolls in waves.

Here's how to pull a person up. With one person tailing on the primary halyard from a position that allows a clear view aloft, and with another person grinding on the winch, steadily haul on the halyard. Pause every few feet to tension and cleat the backup halyard on its own winch. When the boat rolls, stop hauling and take a strain on the downhaul. To avoid confusion, communications should be only between the tailer and the person aloft, and every command should be acknowledged.

The person going up may be able to help by pulling on the halyard, but he or she should concentrate on not banging into the mast or tangling in the rigging. Whenever there's a pause to do some work, loop the tether around the mast. In the unlikely event that the two halyards fail, there will be a back-up to break the fall to the deck.

When the person aloft is at the desired height, cleat the halyards. Label the cleat in some way (for example by wrapping sail stops around it) to remind other people not to touch the halyard. Avoid walking under the person aloft.

To lower the person, sit behind the winch with your feet braced against it, facing the mast. Take all but three or four turns off the winch. With large-diameter rope you may need three turns; with wire or small-diameter rope you'll need more turns. Working your arms in a motion like a long, steady swimming stroke, let the halyard out so the person comes down in a slow but continuous drop. Short bites are no good because the person drops in uncomfortable jerks. If necessary, brake the halyard by pushing the sole of your foot against the turns on the winch. Let off the backup halyard to keep up with the primary halyard.

The person going up can also pull him- or herself aloft. The advantage is that you are free to adjust your position without assistance. You'll need a sturdy 3 : 1 or 4 : 1 block and tackle with enough line in it so the blocks can be spread at least one-half the length of the mast; if the normal line in the tackle is too short, temporarily replace it with a jib or spinnaker sheet (don't use a stretchy nylon anchor rode). Secure the tackle between the chair and the two halyards using screw shackles or lines. If the tackle has a cam cleat, put it at the bottom end, near the chair.

Pull the halyards until the top tackle block is as far aloft as possible when the chair is a couple of feet above the deck. Carefully cleat the halyards, put on the tether line or safety harness, gather your tools and fittings, and get into the chair. Then slowly pull yourself up with the tail of the tackle. When you stop, secure the hauling part of the line around the tackle parts with two double half-hitches (don't trust the cam cleat to do all the work) and hook onto the mast with the harness. When coming down, slow your descent by snubbing the line around your back or the tackle.

Pulling a crewmember aloft, lead the halyard to the biggest winch through one or more turning blocks. Nobody except the person aloft should give instructions. Additional gear can be hauled aloft in a bucket hooked to another halyard. Lowering, let the line out with a smooth, easy motion to minimize jerking aloft.

The Hull and Interior

If the boat is to remain in the water for extended periods of time, her bottom must be painted with an antifouling paint known to be effective in her local waters. Some of these paints can be easily applied with a roller. Just who does the painting may depend on where you store your boat during the off-season, since many boatyards do not allow owners to paint or do other work below the deck or the waterline. Some bottom paints require special preparation and are quite expensive. If you intend to race, spend some time smoothing the bottom with special wet sandpaper, starting with a rough grade and working down to smooth grades.

Even if your boat has antifouling paint, take a swim every week or so and scrub the bottom and propeller off with a scrub brush. Oil, pollution, and weeds tend to cake up along the waterline, especially if it's not painted with antifouling paint.

The topsides can be cleaned with nonabrasive powders, such as Bon Ami, or special fiberglass cleansers, and then polished. After a while any fiberglass hull's gel coat will start to fade and craze, and the only solution is to paint it. Modern polyurethane paints will provide a longlasting, glossy finish; they should be applied by professionals.

While the boat is out of the water, examine the keel, rudder, and the outside of through-hull fittings for cracks and loose fits.

On deck, the stanchions and lifelines should be inspected regularly because the vibration and friction they are subject to may loosen set screws and locknuts on turnbuckles. If there is a gangway (opening) in the lifelines, make sure the hooks used to open and shut it are not bent; tape them when the gangway is closed.

Down below, inspect the fuel line to the stove for cracks and kinks, and make certain the shutoff valve works easily. If you anticipate cooking while under sail, rig a strong strap that can be snapped around the cook's waist to keep him safely in the galley even in rough weather. In the same conditions, people may want to sleep in bunks on the windward side. To restrain them, rig 8-inch-high wooden bunk boards that can be quickly installed, or Dacron straps hung from lines.

Locker doors and drawers must stay closed when on the windward side. Magnetized latches aren't strong enough. Install positive snap latches accessible through finger holes. Stow tools and other heavy objects as low as possible, and put emergency gear in a special clearly marked locker.

If salt water gets below, wipe it off with a rag damp with fresh water. Keep water off the electrical panel, but if you can't, spray it with silicone before it gets too wet and shorts out.

Many racer-cruisers are delivered without any grab rails or ventilation ducts. Buy and bolt in enough grab rails to allow a crewmember to go forward to the mast both on deck and below. The best ventilation duct is the Dorade vent, another idea of Rod Stephens's. A rubber or plastic cowl is screwed into a box that contains a baffle to restrict water, but not air, from getting below (unless there's considerable solid water on deck). The head (marine bathroom) should have a vent, and there should be at least two more in the main cabin. In hot weather, a cloth air scoop may be hung through the forward cabin's hatch.

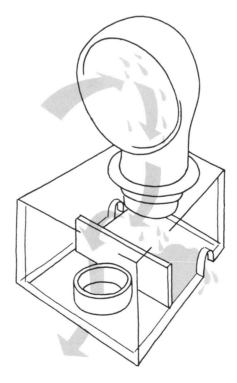

A Dorade vent allows air below while its baffle blocks incoming spray. In rough water, however, turn the cowl aft.

The Engine

The best guide to engine upkeep is the owner's manual, which describes scheduled maintenance, troubleshooting, and minor repairs that can be performed by owners. However, there are some rules of thumb for maintaining the diesel engines found in the vast majority of cruising boats and the small gasoline engines used in outboard-powered boats.

Use clean fuel. According to one diesel equipment manufacturer, 90 percent of engine troubles are caused by dirt or water in the fuel. There should be two fuel filters. One is a sedimenter-type filter for separating out water. It is located between the on-board tank and the pump that lifts fuel from the tank. Drain the bowl on this filter periodically. The other filter, between the lift pump and injection pump, has a fine-mesh paper filter for catching dirt. Clean this filter regularly. A related fuel problem is an air lock caused by air bubbles in the line. It will cause the engine to stop suddenly. Remove an air lock by opening petcocks in the fuel line

The Engine

and hand-pumping fuel through until no bubbles show.

Use the right oil. High-speed modern diesels depend on good lubrication. According to Nigel Calder, in his book *Marine Diesel Engines*, 58 percent of bearing failures are due to dirty oil or lack of oil. Use the correct grade of oil, and change the oil on schedule. Run your engine regularly and at fairly high speeds to keep oil circulating. The pleasure of handling a boat under sail often distracts sailors from this duty.

Run at reasonable temperatures. When you start the engine, look over the stern at the exhaust to see if cooling water is splashing out. If it is not, or if the engine temperature gauge reads high, shut off the engine and inspect the cooling system. The filter on the water pump may be clogged with weed, or the blades on the impeller that pulls water into the cooling system may be broken or fouled with weed or plastic bags sucked from the water.

Keep water from backing into the engine. There should be a loop in the exhaust pipe to stop this from happening, but even if there is a loop a big following wave may shove water up the pipe. A pine plug on the end of a lanyard can be inserted in the pipe, but remember to pull it out before starting up.

Keep the battery charged. Make sure its connections are tight and clean. Cruising boats should carry two or more heavy-duty batteries with a master switch that allows one or all to be used. By using one battery for just lights and electronics and reserving another to start the engine, you will always be able to get the engine going; once the engine is running, all the batteries can be charged. A testing system (either a voltmeter or a lamp connected to a wire) measures engine charge and traces down juice-draining short circuits.

In gasoline engines use clean spark plugs. Carry the proper size wrench to remove the plug, an emery board to clean the points, and some spare plugs. Also be sure to use the correct oil-gas mixture to keep the engine properly lubricated.

Through-Hull Fittings

Drains, intakes, and other through-hull fittings can cause serious problems if they malfunction. You must be able to shut them off quickly with sea cocks, which should be greased and marked at open and closed positions. Ideally, any pipe leading overboard will loop above the waterline so that water does not siphon back, but this isn't always the case.

Keep sea cocks lubricated, and shut them off when you leave the boat. If a hose breaks when a sea cock is open, the boat may sink.

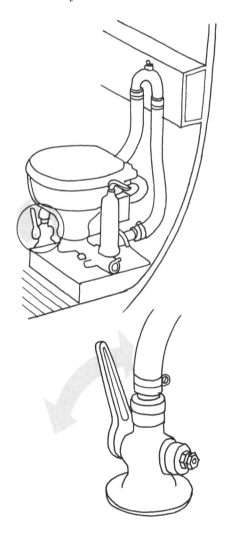

Loops above the waterline keep water from siphoning in through water intakes and drains. A sea cock must be installed near the hull to cut off all flow should the pipe leak or the hull settle.

Winterizing

Many of the maintenance problems surrounding boats can be pinpointed during the end-of-season haul-out, when the boat is prepared for the winter. This is the time when a careful inspection will reveal the ravages of a long summer. It's also the time to prepare the boat for what might be an even more brutal winter ashore in a Northern boating area.

The first job after your boat is hauled — on a trailer or on a boatyard's crane — is to clean her as thoroughly as possible. Start with the underbody. With a high-powered hose, a scrub brush, and (if necessary) a putty knife, get all the marine growth off before it dries and cakes onto the paint. Wear your foul-weather jacket, pants, and boots for this wet, messy job. Once the growth is completely removed and the underbody and waterline are dry, give them a thorough sanding with rough sandpaper to smooth the paint and knock off any loose chips in preparation for next spring's painting.

Remove sails from the spars and lockers below, and take them home or to the sailmaker's for repair and cleaning. Also take along cushions, awnings, and other fabric objects; wipe them off with a sponge and store them in a cool, dry part of the house. That's where the sails should also be stored after being washed and folded.

If the mast and rigging are pulled out of the boat, lay them on sawhorses and inspect them carefully, looking for cracks, loose fastenings, and enlarged screw holes. If you cannot replace or repair these items now, tag them and make a note to look at them in the spring (or next month, if you're lucky enough to live in Florida or California). Remove every moving fitting from the deck and cockpit and inspect it for wear and damage.

Below, wipe down the cabin with a damp rag, for any salt left behind will breed a generation of mildew. Clean out the toilet and sinks, remove the door to the head so it will be ventilated, and thoroughly pump out and clean the bilge. Electronic instruments are sensitive to condensation caused by the extreme rise and fall of temperature and humidity that come with winter, so take them home. Any paper items — books, toilet paper, notepads — should be taken off so they don't mildew and rot. Anchors and rodes should be washed off, dried, and put below.

Drain all water lines with the same care with which you would drain pipes in a house before a freeze. If you think that water remains in a U-joint or other low spot, pour a cup of vodka into the line. Regular antifreeze is poisonous, and vodka's relatively mild taste will not offend anybody but teetotalers on your first cruise next spring.

Carefully follow manufacturer's instructions for winterizing the engine. For safety reasons, empty all gasoline tanks; a diesel tank should be left topped-off so there's no space for condensation to occur. Batteries may either be taken home or left on board with their cables disconnected.

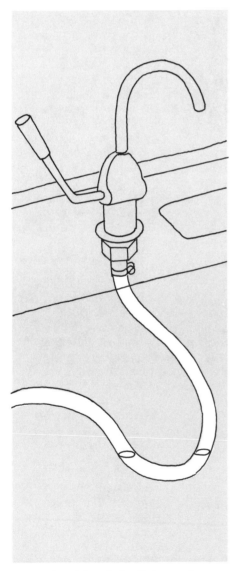

When winterizing, drain all pipes and pour some vodka anti-freeze into U-joints where moisture might collect.

Tools, Tape, and Lubricants

Every valve, screw, and nut on board should be adjustable by a wrench or screwdriver in the tool chest. Don't rely on pliers, since they provide limited grip and can mangle a recalcitrant nut. "Vice grips," or adjustable locking pliers, are powerful and useful tools, as are crescent wrenches, but every boat larger than 25 feet deserves a birthday present of a set of socket wrenches. (Before you make this sizable investment, check whether your fittings are secured with metric- or English-gauge fastenings.) If you have a choice, use Phillips-head screws — the ones with the cross-shaped slots. They retain their integrity longer than most slot-headed screws.

A heavy hammer or small sledge is a handy tool to have. You will drive few nails but you will have to loosen many corroded fittings or spring several cleats from hardened glue or putty. A wood chisel is also helpful.

Have on hand a good supply of stainless-steel and bronze wood, sheet metal, and machine screws (with the right-size nuts for the latter). Secure them tightly in plastic jars (carefully labeled) stored in a sturdy, water-resistant box, like an old-fashioned leather shaving kit. Before buying the extra fastenings, see what gauge and length are needed for your most important fittings.

A strong hacksaw, bolt cutters, and a small ax will help clear broken rigging away. Store them in a waterproof bag with other emergency equipment.

If your pocketbook can stand it and if you sail on salt water, buy one each of the most important tools in noncorroding bronze. Otherwise inspect your steel tools for corrosion and give them a light coating of lanolin or Vasoline.

Along with the tools, have a variety of lubricants in cans, tubes, and spray dispensers. Silicone sprays are especially useful since they can lubricate without leaving a greasy film. Lanolin is an excellent lubricant as well.

In another container have a variety of rolls of tape. Duct tape — the wide, silver tape used by appliance repair-

men — is remarkably strong. Electrician's tape is stretchy and strong, and comes in many colors, which may be handy when you must label different wires or lines.

Spare line can be classified as a tool — especially the strong light line that serves a wide variety of needs. Marline is one of these, and there are strong nylon braids and shock cords as small as ¼ inch in diameter that will do many jobs. Make sure, too, that there is at least one sharp sailor's knife on board to cut these lines.

An excellent way to protect yourself against crippling breakdowns is to standardize your fittings and fastenings so that backup parts can be versatile. Few problems can be more irritating than trying to turn a Phillips-head screw with a slot-head screwdriver, or wondering how to replace a broken main halyard shackle with a spare shackle half its strength. If every screw and shackle has five uses, then you not only need many fewer spare parts but also are secure in knowing that you're entirely self-sufficient.

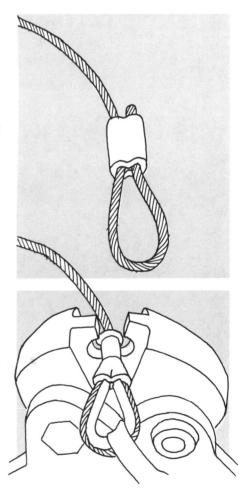

Using a Nico press tool to make eyes or splice wire together, you can fashion emergency stays out of spare halyards and odd lengths of wire rope. Be sure the sleeves are the right size for the wire.

361

Chapter 18
Traditions and Courtesies

The pastime and sport of pleasure sailing, traditionally called "yachting," is more than 300 years old. That's far older than football, golf, tennis, and almost every other outdoor sport. In all those years, sailors have developed many traditions that not only add a touch of ceremony but also provide guidelines for courteous behavior on crowded waterways. Although nobody has to subscribe to these traditions and courtesies to sail a boat competently, they do make sailing more meaningful and enjoyable.

In this final chapter we will describe the most important traditions and courtesies of pleasure boating, including its etiquette, flags, uniforms, and history.

Sailing Etiquette

There are two fundamental principles of sailing etiquette: privacy and mutual aid. Sailors must respect each other's rights to privacy and quiet. Yet at the same time, sailors must always be ready to come to each other's assistance. When these two principles come into conflict, as they occasionally do,

something has to give. Usually it's privacy. As with farmers and other battlers against the elements, there is a commond bond among true seafarers that inevitably brings them together in mutual support no matter what individualistic motives drove them to sea in the first place.

Courtesies at Rest

As we saw in chapter 8, "The Rules of the Road," and chapter 14, "Anchoring," there are important safety reasons for keeping away from other boats. But collision should not be the only concern.

When moored, anchored, or docked, don't infringe on other boats' air and physical space. Here's the rule of thumb for when you are anchored: the longer you have to run your engine or your charcoal grill, the more numerous are your children, the louder is your voice, or the more you want to play your radio (in short, the more disruptive you are), then the farther downwind you should be from your neighbors. This basic tactfulness isn't any different

from simple courteous behavior ashore, where the golden rule "do unto others as you would have them do unto you" works so well.

In the marina (just as at home), don't impose on your neighbors' privacy and patience any more than you have to. If you must cross their boats, walk across their yards (their foredecks), not through their living rooms (their cockpits). Rig your docking lines so you can adjust them yourself on your own boat without having to crawl about on a neighbor's deck. When finished with equipment belonging to the marina and intended for common use, put it back where it belongs. Do not leave hoses, electrical cords, and docking lines strewn around.

Just part of the problem in today's crowded marinas is keeping boats from banging into each other. Sailors have a right to privacy that is best honored by observing several basic rules of nautical etiquette. Yet balance privacy against the rule of coming to other crews' assistance in emergencies.

363

Under Way

Sailors who like to party should not assume that everybody else does, too. Many people go out in boats in order to find a place for quiet reflection that is rarely available on shore. There is an etiquette to determining whether a neighbor is open to an invitation to socialize. Go over to the other boat and stop about 6 feet away. Engage in some wheel-greasing small talk (compliments about the boat's design and appearance are always welcome). Judge from the tenor of the conversation whether an invitation would be welcome. If you do ask the other people over to your boat, don't be offended if they express their need for solitude by politely turning you down.

While it is not a breach of courtesy to reject a social invitation, no true sailor will turn away a request for advice concerning weather, navigation, or anchoring, or help with rigging, the engine, and first aid.

When you do go aboard another boat, your hosts may solicit your opinions about her. This is tricky territory. No matter how strongly the owner protests that your most frank and objective evaluation will be welcome, treat the situation as delicately as you would a parent's request for an opinion about his or her children. Most boatowners believe in their heart of hearts that their boats are beyond criticism, and those few who believe otherwise do not want their doubts echoed by a stranger.

Courtesies Under Way

When you're under way, your behavior should be guided by respect for the letter of the law combined with sensitivity to other people's concerns. Leaving a float plan (a copy of your planned itinerary) with friends may save needless worry on their part. If they notice that you're not on schedule, they could save your life by notifying the Coast Guard. There are times when attentiveness to other people's problems is heightened by self-interest. For example when sailing near boats that are fishing, you should pass well upwind of them not only to avoid scaring away the fish but also to avoid tangling your boat in their lines. Observe speed limits posted in harbors because it's the law and because you don't want to collide with another boat whose crew is distracted by your unexpectedly high speed.

While the Navigation Rules are explicit about the obligations of most sorts of boats, nowhere is it written that a racing sailboat has the right of way over a nonracing sailboat. All the same, cruising and daysailing sailors usually are pleased to relinquish the right of way temporarily if they are asked to in a nice way. Waving fists and shrieking "We're racing!" can be counterproductive.

Racing boats are not hard to identify. They do not fly the national flag, they are sailing in clusters toward or away from powerboats flying a blue flag with "RC" (for race committee), and they are being sailed with great intensity (if

As a matter of courtesy and common sense, daysailers and cruisers should avoid interfering with racing boats, which stand out because they are sailed with great intensity in large groups.

most of the crew is looking at the sails, she's probably racing).

Flag Etiquette

Flag etiquette is the correct use of flags that are flown on or around boats. These flags include the ensign (the national flag), the burgee (the flag of a boating organization the boat's owner is a member of), and the private signal (the owner's unique identifying flag).

The Ensigns

For most people on boats, flag etiquette begins and ends with the problem of which ensign, or national flag, to fly and where to fly it. Sailors and all other boating people who are U.S. citizens may choose between two flags. One is the usual 50-star national flag known as the ensign. The other is a special flag called the yacht ensign that, in place of the 50 stars standing for the states, has a fouled anchor on a field of 13 stars.

Why are there two national flags? In the early to mid-19th century, when pleasure boating got its start and the first yacht clubs were founded, most yachts looked like commercial ships. Since ships had to pay local duties when they entered harbors, their skippers would try to convince customs officials that they were pleasure sailors. Naturally, the officials ignored those claims and collected fees, not just from commercial vessels but from all entering boats, including yachts. To deal with this problem, the American and British governments approved special national flags to be flown only from yachts. In the United States, this special flag was designed by the officers of the New York Yacht Club in 1848. It remains a legal national flag for pleasure boats.

By law, the only pleasure boats required to fly the yacht ensign in U.S. waters are ones that are documented, or registered with the federal government and not a state. Every other U.S. boat may fly either the yacht ensign or the standard national ensign (except in foreign waters, where a U.S-registered boat may fly only the 50-star flag). However, many yacht clubs require members to fly the yacht ensign.

The size of the ensign is determined by the size of the boat that flies it. On the fly (the flag's horizontal measurement) there must be a minimum of 1 inch per 1 foot of the boat's overall length. The hoist (vertical measurement) must be two-thirds the length of the fly.

The ensign or yacht ensign may be flown from either of two locations. One is a flagstaff on the stern. Wooden staffs of various lengths are available at many marine equipment outlets. Choose a staff that flies the flag free of the boat's equipment.

Either ensign may also be flown from the leech of the aftermost sail. On a boat with a Bermudian (Marconi) rig, the flag should be sewn to the sail two-thirds of the way up from the clew. On a gaff-rigged boat, it should be sewn to the leech right below the gaff. The problem with flying the flag from the leech of the mainsail on a typical Bermudian-rigged sloop is that there is usually a permanent backstay or a main boom topping lift (or both) to foul and fray the ensign. Since it is disrespectful to the national flag to allow it to be tattered, this form of display is best left to gaff-rigged boats, most of which do not have permanent backstays and topping lifts.

Whichever ensign is used, fly it from morning colors (8 A.M.) to evening colors (sunset) whether you are under way or not under way. There are three exceptions to this rule. First, the flag is not flown from a stern staff on a boat sailing in a race. Second, the flag need not be flown when sailing offshore on the high seas. Third, the flag is flown while entering or leaving a port, even at night, and then is lowered after anchoring or leaving the port.

At morning colors, the ensign is hoisted rapidly before other flags. At evening colors, the ensign is lowered slowly and with ceremony after other flags.

The ensign is used to salute dignitaries by dipping (lowering). It is dipped when passing ships in the U.S. and foreign navies; when passing another yacht (with the most junior skipper initiating); when anchoring, mooring, or docking near a senior flag officer (commodore, vice commodore, rear commodore) in the skipper's yacht club; and when a senior flag officer anchors, moors, or docks nearby. After the ship or yacht being saluted returns the salute, the flag is hoisted again.

With its fouled anchor, the yacht ensign is the traditional national flag for pleasure boats, although the regular ensign may be flown. Except when the boat is racing, fly the ensign from 8 A.M. to sunset on the stern or from the leech of the aftermost sail.

Flag Etiquette

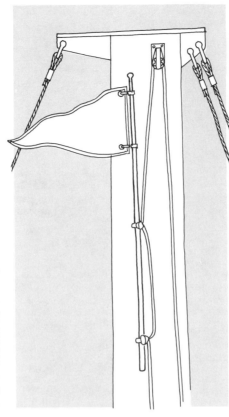

The Burgee

The burgee is a small swallow-tailed flag displaying the symbol of the owner's yacht club or other sailing organization. Although it may be flown day and night, many owners lower it when they leave the boat in order to save wear and tear.

The burgee should be flown from the top of the forwardmost mast. The flag is carried on a small pole called a pig stick, hoisted on a halyard called a flag halyard. If the halyard and its cheek block at the top of the mast are strong, they can also be used to haul up the mainsail if the main halyard breaks.

Traditionally, the yacht club burgee is flown at the masthead on a pig stick hoisted on a small halyard (top), but it may be flown from the starboard spreader or (if the owner's private signal is at the masthead) on a bow staff. The USPS burgee is flown from the starboard spreader. On boats with permanent backstays, the ensign is flown from the stern.

The pig stick is a wooden or aluminum rod with a swivel for attaching the flag and two eyes for securing the halyard. One eye is partway up the stick and is used for the part of the halyard that pulls up; the other eye is at the bottom of the stick and is used for the part that pulls down. Tie both ends of the flag halyard together to make it a continuous loop. Then tie it to the pig stick eyes with bowlines, leaving a little slack in the line between the eyes. Hoist the stick quickly but carefully so it doesn't foul in the rigging; it's best to pull the stick up on the leeward side when sailing on a reach. Then tension the part of the halyard that pulls down to keep the stick steady. Don't cleat the halyard on the mast; otherwise the rope will clang unmercifully as the pig stick sways aloft.

Carrying the burgee at the masthead is impossible or very difficult on the many modern boats that have masthead radio antennas and wind-direction indicators, which may be knocked off by the burgee. In that case, many conscientious owners fly the burgee from the lowest starboard spreader on a flag halyard. While this practice is decried by purists, it is a reasonable adaptation of an old and good tradition to new practicalities.

Alternatively, you can use an especially long pigstick (which is difficult to keep vertical), rearrange the equipment aloft (which may be impractical), or fly the burgee from a bow staff on top of the forward pulpit (which is lower and less visible than the masthead).

The burgee's dimensions are, on the fly, approximately .5 inch for each foot between the water and the top of the tallest mast; and on the hoist, two-thirds the length of the fly.

The U.S. Power Squadrons prefers that the organization's burgee, called the USPS ensign, be flown from the starboard spreader. The "blue ensign" of the U.S. Coast Guard Auxiliary is flown day and night from the top of the mainmast.

The Private Signal

A private signal is a small, custom-designed flag that carries symbols standing for the owner. For example a man named Page with a boat named *Pageant* has a private signal that shows a ceremonial trumpet. Yacht club yearbooks may include pictures of private signals to help people identify a boat and her owner from a distance. The signal is sized according to the rule for burgees. It may be flown day and night or only when the owner is aboard. On a single-masted boat that flies the burgee on a bow staff, the private signal is carried at the top of the mast. On a single-masted boat without a bow staff, the private signal is flown at the top of the mast when under way and the burgee is flown at the masthead at anchor. On a double-masted boat, the private signal is flown at the top of the aftermost mast.

Since the private signal follows the owner, not the boat, when he or she is not on board the signal should not be flown.

Flagpoles

On yacht club and other waterfront flagpoles, the ensign is flown from a gaff below the yacht club's burgee, which is flown from the top of the flagpole. While this arrangement may appear to be disrespectful, it reflects traditional usage on gaff-rigged sailing vessels where the ensign is flown off the gaff and the burgee or private signal of the owner is flown at the masthead.

Half-Masting

The ensign is half-masted (hauled down halfway and left there) from 8 A.M. to 12 noon on Memorial Day and other days of mourning. It is full-masted (hoisted all the way) before half-masting as well as before being lowered all the way.

When a member of a yacht club dies, the only burgees half-masted in mourning are those at the clubhouse and on the late member's boat, where the private signal also is half-masted.

Other Flags

The **union jack** is a rectangular blue flag with 50 stars. This flag is flown from a short spar on the bow called a jackstaff. Naval vessels fly it whenever they are at anchor between 8 A.M. and sunset. Pleasure boats fly it only when at anchor on Sundays and holidays and when dressing ship.

A **courtesy flag** is the flag of the host country that is flown in the starboard rigging of a visiting vessel after *pratique* (health and customs clearance) has been issued. Port officials have been known to take great offense at a visiting vessel that does not fly the courtesy flag. This flag should be .5 inch on the fly for every foot of overall length.

A boat used to start and finish races flies a blue **race committee flag**, which shows a fouled anchor between the letters "R" and "C." If you see this flag and are not racing, stand well clear.

Many yacht clubs and boating organizations issue a distinctive **officer's flag** for each club official. Flag routines vary from club to club, but typically the flags of the commodore, vice commodore, and rear commodore are flown day and night in place of the burgee on a single-masted boat and in place of the private signal on a yawl, ketch, or schooner. The fleet captain, whose job is to organize a fleet of boats for a cruise or race, flies a distinctive flag from the bowstaff of the boat in which she or he is working.

Flags signaling **owner absent** (blue flag) and **guest present** in absence of owner (blue with white stripe) may be flown from the lower starboard spreader. The size of these flags is determined the same way as that of the courtesy flag.

On large yachts with professional crews, **meal pennants** announce that the owner (white flag) or the paid crew (red flag) is eating. The owner's flag is flown from the lower starboard spreader, the crew's flag from the lower port spreader. The owner and guests board the boat on the starboard side, with the owner boarding first and leaving last. The paid crew boards on the port side.

(Top to bottom) The race committee, guest present, and owner absent flags.

Clothing

Code Flags

Even in this day of radiotelephones, signalling with code flags still occurs. Each flag stands for a letter of the alphabet, a number, or a repetition of a letter or number. Many flags also have special meanings depending on the circumstances. For example, the red "B" flag generally signals "dangerous cargo," but in a race it indicates that a crew believes that another crew has violated the racing rules.

Between colors on the Fourth of July and other days specified by authorities, pleasure boats not under sail **dress ship** by hanging code flags from their masts in lines stretching from the water below the bow to the water below the stern. Only code flags are used in the hoist; the ensign, burgee, private signal, and union jack fly in their usual places. A recommended flag sequence that produces a colorful display is: AB2, UJ1, KE3, GH6, IV5, FL4, DM7, PO, Third Repeater, RN, First Repeater, ST Zero, CX9, WQ8, ZY, Second Repeater.

Clothing

Any sort of clothing will do in a boat so long as it is appropriate for the weather, but there are some traditional outfits for various occasions.

Daytime Clothing

When many people think of sailing, one of the first things to come to mind is a version of the naval officer's hat called a "yachtsman's cap." When worn without any other formal clothing, it's meant to tell the world that the wearer is a capable, nautical character.

What that cap actually communicates will vary with the part of the world that is looking at it and its wearer, but to many experienced sailors it means only one thing: *rookie*. Even mild physical labor on a sailboat may be impossible when this hat is worn. It will flop over your eyes and eventually fall right off. As we will see in a moment, this hat is best suited for wear on formal occasions.

For normal activity in a boat or around a yacht club or marina, the only uniform needed is an outfit consisting

Boats dress ship on special days.

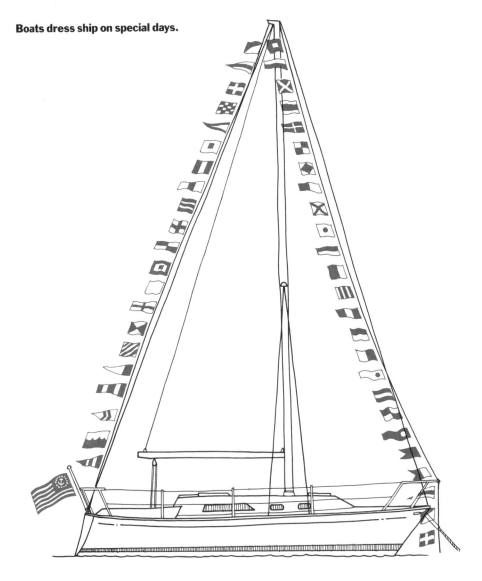

of comfortable shirt and pants and a fisherman's or other wide-brimmed hat for keeping off the sun. Long or short sleeves and pants legs are appropriate depending on the weather, but skimpy clothing (tank tops, for example) is often frowned upon in waterfront restaurants and stores. A shirt with a collar and without a slogan or picture is more formal than a collarless T-shirt, and it will keep your neck from getting sunburned, too. While there is no written protocol concerning colors, many sailors favor khaki or Breton red pants and navy blue shirts.

Semiformal Dress

The jacket for semiformal dress most commonly worn by sailors, both male and female, is the blue blazer. A descendant of the first uniforms used in the British Royal Navy, it is standard dress at yacht club functions and other boat-related gatherings. At relatively informal occasions, it may be worn with an open-collared shirt over trousers or a skirt. At more formal occasions, the blazer is worn over gray trousers or

The blue blazer is standard wear at such sailors' functions as awards ceremonies. If made of synthetic materials, it will survive a stay in a crowded onboard locker without wrinkling.

skirt, white dress shirt, and the official tie or scarf of a boating organization. A blazer pocket patch may carry the insignia of the wearer's primary boating organization.

Formal Dress

The yachtsman's cap, so inappropriate on the deck of a boat that is under way, does find its place in formal uniforms prescribed by yacht clubs, Power Squadrons, and other boating organizations. These hats and the uniform jackets carry the insignia of rank of the wearer. The uniforms are either navy blue or white. For men, the least formal uniform, called service dress, is a double-breasted jacket worn under the hat and over a waistcoat of the same color and navy blue, gray, white, or khaki trousers and the organization's tie. The most formal uniform, the full-dress mess jacket, is a sailor's tuxedo worn over a black bow tie. Women wear comparable formal outfits with their insignia of rank.

A sensible sailing outfit includes sunglasses, a brimmed hat, and loose-fitting clothes. A shirt collar protects the neck from the sun.

Yachting History

Yachting History

While men and women have been sailing for thousands of years, the idea of going to sea for pleasure is fairly new. The first systematic pleasure sailing took place in the Netherlands in the 16th century. The word "yacht" is derived from the Dutch word *jaght*, meaning "fast in pursuit." A *jaght schip* was a quick, maneuverable boat. In 1660, when King Charles II left Amsterdam after a long exile to return to Great Britain, the Dutch presented him with one of their fast boats. Before long, his brother James (the future King James II) also had a boat. The inevitable occurred, and the first yacht race recorded in history was sailed on May 21, 1661 (Charles won). Of Charles it was said that "two leagues' travel at sea was more pleasure to him than 20 by land." He bought more than 25 luxurious yachts during his 25-year reign and encouraged much experimentation with rigs and hulls. His biggest mistake was to make fun of the first Western multihulled sailboat, a catamaran named *Innovation* built by Sir William Petty. It wasn't until after 1970 that multihulls were taken seriously by large numbers of sailors.

Like horse racing, sailing came to be known as a "sport of kings" thanks to its royal sponsor. But commoners also took to the water. The first yacht club was the Water Club of the Harbour of Cork, founded in Ireland in 1720. While the members occasionally sailed their yachts in choreographed processions, the club was mostly a social organization. One club rule said that if members talked about sailing during banquets they would be fined.

The most prestigious of the early English yacht clubs was the Royal Yacht Squadron, founded in 1815. Seeing itself partly as a mutual aid society, it issued a book describing flag signals members could use in order to attract assistance when they were in distress.

The America's Cup

There is some dispute about the identity of the first U.S. yacht club; good cases have been made that clubs were

The most famous pleasure boat in history probably is the schooner *America*, which in 1851 won the trophy that came to be named after her and that is still being raced for.

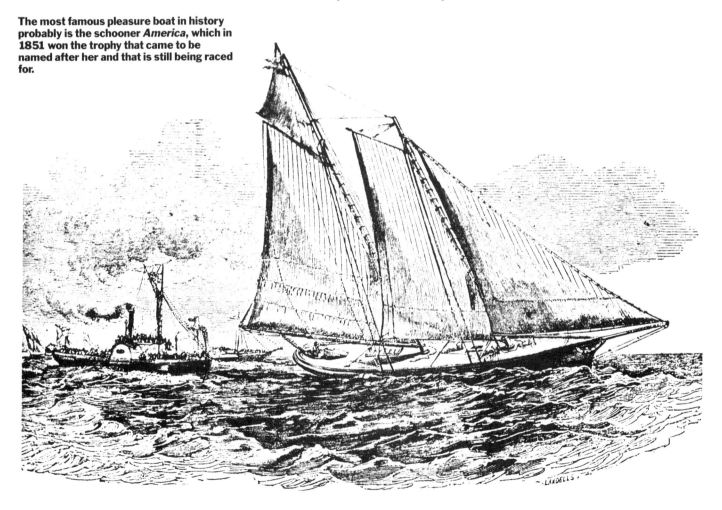

founded in Detroit, Boston, and New Orleans in the 1830s. But it took a New York yacht to spur the growth of the sport in America. The yacht was the 101-foot schooner *America*, owned by a syndicate of members of the New York Yacht Club (founded in 1844). On August 22, 1851, she won a race off Cowes, England, and with it a trophy called the Squadron Cup. The syndicate gave the trophy to the New York Yacht Club for use in international competition. It

soon came to be called the America's Cup, and in 24 matches between 1870 and 1980 the club's boats successfully defended it against challenges from Britain, Canada, Australia, France, Sweden, and Italy.

The greatest boat in America's Cup competition was the 1903 winner, *Reliance*. At 143 feet from bow to stern she was the largest singlemasted sailboat ever built. *Reliance* was designed and built by a man who stands next to Alex-

ander Graham Bell and Thomas Edison in the pantheon of American technological geniuses. This was Nathanael G. Herreshoff, the great "Captain Nat" of Bristol, Rhode Island. Other than the sailboard and the winged keel, there are few concepts in sailing today that he did not think up or develop in his long lifetime between 1848 and 1938.

The America's Cup, the oldest trophy for regular international competition, finally changed hands in 1983, when *Australia II* with her innovative winged keel took it to Australia. Four years later, the cup was taken back to the U.S. by *Stars & Stripes*, from the San Diego Yacht Club.

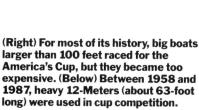

(Right) For most of its history, big boats larger than 100 feet raced for the America's Cup, but they became too expensive. **(Below)** Between 1958 and 1987, heavy 12-Meters (about 63-foot long) were used in cup competition.

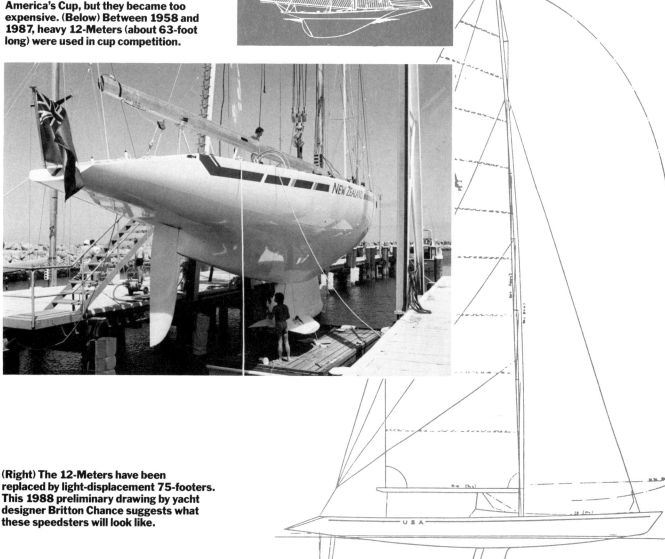

(Right) The 12-Meters have been replaced by light-displacement 75-footers. This 1988 preliminary drawing by yacht designer Britton Chance suggests what these speedsters will look like.

Sailing Today

Joshua Slocum's *Spray*

The Second Golden Age of Sail

Racing has often been the laboratory where yacht designers work out their ideas. Some of the most important technological advances were first tried on the race course. And yet for most people the story of pleasure sailing is cruising and daysailing in relatively small boats. One of the most famous of these boats was *Spray*, a tubby 36-foot converted fishing sloop a grizzled sea captain named Joshua Slocum sailed around the world between 1895 and 1898. His book about this, the first singlehanded circumnavigation, *Sailing Alone Around the World*, has inspired generations of cruising sailors.

Slocum was a professional seaman, as were the men who sailed the huge boats that raced for the America's Cup, so for many people the word "yachting" meant paid sailors at the beck and call of rich owners. One of those owners, J. P. Morgan, was said to have advised an acquaintance who wanted to buy a yacht: "If you have to ask how much it costs, you can't afford it." Even though Morgan might well have been saying

that pleasure sailing offers emotional rewards that far outweigh its financial cost, there seemed to be a barrier of wealth and snobbery surrounding the pastime.

For average people to come to believe that the sea could be their playground, there needed to be more encouraging and specifically practical advice than Morgan gave. This advice has long been provided by the editors and writers of boating magazines. Early on, the most important of them was Thomas Fleming Day, the son of a paleontologist. He became the editor of the boating magazine *The Rudder* in 1890 and spent 26 years assuring people of the radical idea that they could go out there in small boats without spending a fortune. "Small vessels are safer than large," he wrote, "providing they are properly designed, strongly built, thoroughly equipped, and skillfully manned." Good seamanship was simple. He declared that its backbone was "confidence in yourself, confidence in your craft, confidence in your crew." Confidence was important because, to Day,

Boats made of fiberglass have been the mainstays of the great boom in sailing. This husky-looking but fast Valiant 40 is owned by Scott and Kitty Kuhner, who earlier sailed around the world in a 30-footer.

The dream of sailing is expressed in many forms. Among them are (top to bottom) commercially sponsored professional racing in high-tech catamarans, amateur racing in one-design classes like this Soling, and young Tania Aebi's singlehanded circumnavigation.

the only damage occurring on a boat at sea would be self-inflicted. To him, the sea (which he called "our Great Green Mother") was benevolent. "The danger of the sea forj generations has been preached by the ignorant," he enthusiastically wrote.

Day went overboard here. As anybody who has been in a bad storm knows, there are times when there's nothing a crew can do to help themselves, and at those times the sea seems very murderous indeed. Yet the conviction that our own confidence and abilities will fend off the sea's power lies at the very heart of the pastime of amateur sailing and motivates the writing of books like this one. Nobody would go sailing for pleasure without sharing at least some of Day's demythologization of the sea.

Inspired by Tom Day and other writers and sailors, people began to go out there in increasing numbers at the same time that the great golden age of commercial sailing was drawing to a close. It is no exaggeration to say that the rush of amateur, pleasure-seeking men and women to the sea has created a Second Golden Age of Sail.

As if in direct response, the boating industry developed a way to build boats out of materials like fiberglass and aluminum that require little of the time- and cash-absorbing maintenance work that old wooden boats did. Fiberglass construction also allowed the cost of building a boat to drop, since many hulls could be taken off one mold. By the 1980s, almost every sailboat was built of fiberglass or a combination of it and space-age, strong, lightweight materials.

And yet, for all the talk about conquering the sea, there were indications that the sea could still fight back. In August 1979, in the famous Fastnet Race, a terrible storm struck a fleet of 303 boats racing between England and Ireland, and 15 sailors died. This tragedy stimulated a healthy reevaluation of safety equipment and boat design, as well as some second thoughts about the kind of optimism Tom Day had propounded.

Small Boats

For decades sailors came into the sport and learned their skills in small one-design centerboard racing boats. But today most new sailors are introduced to the sport in cruising boats and large one-design keel boats. This does not mean that small-boat sailing is dead. New types of small boats appeared after 1960, most notably sailboards and catamarans, and older de-

signs that have been around for many decades (including the Snipe, Thistle, and Lightning) have, if anything, gained in popularity since they made the transition from wooden hulls and cotton sails to fiberglass hulls and Dacron sails.

One of the strengths of sailing as a whole and small-boat sailing in particular is its remarkable diversity. In almost every sailing area, people can choose a boat that suits their athletic ability, skills, and ambitions. From beginners competing in local fleets to experts traveling around the world for competition, there literally are different boats for different folks. At the 1984 Los Angeles Olympics, where U.S. sailors won gold or silver medals in each of the seven classes, one of the gold medalists was a young man from Seattle named Carl Buchan and another was his father, Bill, who at 49 was at the age that would have disqualified him from top-flight competition in most other sports.

Much international racing at the America's Cup and other regattas has acquired some of the characteristics of professionalism, with athletes who train as intensely as track stars. The difference is that most top sailors, unlike most top runners, continue to be traditional amateur athletes competing for the fun of it all.

The Dream

There are other things that do not change. The sea is one of them. The human passion to cross the sea is another. In 1985 a 19-year-old woman, Tania Aebi, set out alone from New York City in a 26-foot sloop to sail around the world. She could have been criticized on several grounds, among them that sailing alone without a steady lookout is potentially dangerous, and that she had not yet acquired the skills needed to sail offshore. Both criticisms still stand. But through experience and study, she acquired the necessary navigation and sailing skills, and she accomplished her goal in 27 months.

To point out this accomplishment is not to denigrate the voyages of more experienced, knowledgeable sailors who have followed the same precepts of cautious seamanship propounded in this book. It is only to say that while skill and preparation must play their part, what motivates all sailors is the same wonderous dream that has attracted people (you and me among them) to the pastime in the first place.

Epilogue

Throughout this book we've suggested a truth that some might think ironical: to enjoy sailing, the most individualistic of all sports, you must try to standardize your techniques and your equipment and do every job the same way, time after time. Always screw in shackle pins from right to left. Always use either magnetic or true degrees. Always acknowledge a command. Always take every opportunity to fix your position. Always stop the boat's forward motion when a crewmember falls overboard. Always gauge the boat's performance by her balance. With repetition come good habits, with good habits comes good seamanship, with good seamanship comes security, and with security comes...enjoyment.

And after all, isn't that what we're looking for in the first place?

Appendix I
Required Equipment

Throughout the text we have referred to or summarized Coast Guard regulations concerning safety equipment and navigation lights. Below is a list of equipment that pleasure boats must carry. If you are unsure whether your boat meets Coast Guard regulations, get in touch with your local Coast Guard Auxiliary and request a free courtesy examination. The Auxiliary will also recommend some equipment not required by the Coast Guard but that any sensible skipper should carry when he gets under way.

Life Jackets (Personal Flotation Devices)

The Coast Guard's regulations on life jackets (also called personal flotation devices, or PFDs) are specific as to the type and number to be carried on boats of various sizes. In chapter 7, we explored the advantages and disadvantages of each type. Here is a summary of the regulations.

In 1988, the Coast Guard gave new names to the five types of PFDs. They are: Off-Shore Life Jacket (formerly Type I); Near-Shore Life Vest (formerly Type II); Flotation Aid (formerly Type III); Throwable Device (formerly Type IV); Special Use Device (formerly Type V). To save space, we will use the old "type" designations.

Boats smaller than 16 feet and canoes and kayaks must carry one Coast Guard-approved PFD of suitable size for each crew member. Types I, II, III and IV (see below) qualify. Sailboards, rowing sculls, and racing shells and kayaks are exempted (but state laws may remove this exemption).

Boats 16 feet or longer must carry one Coast Guard-approved PFD of suitable size for each crew member. Types I, II, and III apply. In addition, except for canoes and kayaks these boats must also carry at least one Type IV PFD.

All life jackets of Types I, II, III, and V must be readily accessible and of a suitable size for the wearer. All Type IV PFDs must be immediately available.

Type I is designed to turn an un- conscious person from face-down to face-up and maintain him in that position. It provides the greatest buoyancy and safety, and comes in two sizes, Adult (for persons weighing 90 pounds or more) and Child (for persons weighing less than 90 pounds).

Type II contains less flotation than Type I and will not turn as many people as the Type I jacket. It comes in three sizes: Adult (more than 90 pounds), Child Medium (50-90 pounds), and Child Small (either less than 50 pounds or less than 30 pounds).

Type III is similar to Type II in performance but is more comfortable to wear. Neither of these two jackets should allow the wearer to turn face-down.

Type IV is not a life jacket but rather a throwable life ring or cushion.

Type V PFDs are approved for restricted use only.

Each approved PFD is clearly labeled with the Coast Guard type to which it conforms, its approval number, and its capacity. The Coast Guard requires that all PFDs be kept "in serviceable condition."

Sound Signals

Boats smaller than 16 feet: None required.

Boats between 16 and 39 feet: A relatively high-pitched whistle or horn.

Boats 39 feet and larger: A whistle or horn with a range of at least ½ mile (39-55 feet) to 2 miles (large vessels), with pitch decreasing on larger boats; and a bell.

Visual Distress Signals

Day and night distress signals must be carried on all pleasure boats with the following exceptions, which need not carry day signals but which must carry night signals if they are underway after sunset: boats smaller than 16 feet; boats participating in races or marine parades; open sailboats smaller than 26 feet that do not have engines; and manually propelled boats.

All other pleasure boats must carry day signals and night signals, or signals approved for use at day and at night. The following signals are approved. They are clearly labeled, and they must be stowed where they are readily available to the crew.

Day signals only: Floating orange smoke signals (3 must be carried); hand-held orange smoke signals (3); orange flag with black square and circle (1).

Night signals only: Electric distress light, such as a bright flashlight (1).

Combination day and night signals: Self-contained rocket-propelled parachute red flare signals (3); aerial pyrotechnic red flare signals (3); hand-held red flare signals (3, must carry a date of manufacture of October 1, 1980, or later); pistol-projected parachute red flare signals (3, the pistol may be subject to state or local firearms laws).

You may not display any of these signals except when "assistance is needed because of immediate or potential danger to the persons aboard."

Fire Extinguishers

All boats equipped with motors must carry at least one fire extinguisher, with the exception of boats smaller than 26 feet equipped with outboard engines which do not have compartments in which fumes can be trapped. These compartments include a cabin, a permanently installed fuel tank, an enclosed section under seats where a portable fuel tank is stored, and a double bottom not sealed to the hull and not completely filled with flotation material. All other powered boats must carry fire extinguishers:

Boats smaller than 26 feet: 1 B-I extinguisher (see below).

Boats between 26 and 39 feet: 2 B-I extinguishers or 1 B-II extinguisher.

Boats between 39 feet and 65 feet: 3 B-I extinguishers, or 1 B-II and 1 B-I extinguishers.

If a fixed extinguishing system is installed in her engine room, a 26- to 39-foot boat must carry at least 1 B-I extinguisher, and a 39- to 65-foot boat must carry 2 B-I extinguishers or 1 B-II extinguisher.

The letter in the classification refers to the type of fire the extinguisher is designed to put out:

"A" is for combustible solids.

"B" is for flammable and combustible liquids.

"C" is for electrical fires.

Different types of extinguishants are used. The Roman numeral following the letter indicates the amount of extinguishant that is contained:

B-I extinguishers contain at least 1¼ gallons of foam, 4 pounds of carbon dioxide, 2 pounds of dry chemical, or 2½ pounds of Halon.

B-II extinguishers contain at least 2½ gallons of foam, 15 pounds of carbon dioxide, 10 pounds of dry chemical, or 10 pounds of Halon.

Only foam, carbon dioxide, dry chemical, and Halon fire extinguishers meet Coast Guard requirements; other extinguishants create toxic gases.

Backfire Flame Control

All boats with gasoline inboard engines must be equipped with a backfire flame arrestor.

Ventilation

Except for open boats, all boats equipped with gasoline inboard or outboard engines must be suitably ventilated. An open boat is defined as one with as least 15 square inches of open area directly exposed to the atmosphere for each cubic foot of engine or fuel tank compartment area and with no long or narrow unventilated spaces accessible from these compartments. If a portable fuel tank is enclosed in a compartment, the boat is not considered open.

The federal requirement is met with metal or plastic ducts running from the bilge to cowl vents on deck. On boats built after July 31, 1980, the ducts must be at least 2 inches in diameter and 3 square inches in area, and the vents must be at least 3 square inches in area. Vents operate in pairs: one faces forward to suck in air and pass it below; the other faces aft to allow fumes to blow overboard. (Louvers may be used in place of cowl vents.) The lower ends of the duct must be placed sufficiently low in the bilge to pick up fumes, but not so low that they are plugged by bilge water. The size of the cowls and ducts is determined by the volume of the compartment to be ventilated. For example, if the compartment contains 12 cubic feet, the duct must be at least 2½ inches in diameter and the cowl must be 5 square inches in area; if 20 cubic feet, 3¼ inches and 8 square inches; if 30 cubic feet, 4 inches and 13 square inches; and if 39 cubic feet, 4½ inches

and 16 square inches.

The engine compartments in gasoline-powered inboard boats built after July 31, 1980, must also be ventilated by an exhaust blower, which must be run for at least 4 minutes before you turn on the ignition. A sign to that effect must be posted near the blower switch.

Older boats do not have to have blowers, and there are no federal regulations concerning their duct size. Still, the Coast Guard considers 2 inches to be the minimum diameter and expects the ventilation system to meet the standards imposed on newer boats.

Navigation Lights

The Inland and International Rules of the Road specify certain combinations of navigation lights for every type of boat, and we covered these in detail in chapter 8. To summarize:

Boats smaller than 23 feet under oars or sail must be prepared to show a white light if not carrying navigation lights.

Larger boats under sail must show red and green sidelights and a white sternlight. If smaller than 39 feet, they must carry sidelights visible 1 mile away and a sternlight visible 2 miles away. If larger, all three must be visible 2 miles away.

Boats under power must carry sidelights, a sternlight, and a white "masthead" light that shines through the same arc as the sidelights. If she is smaller than 39 feet, the stern and masthead lights must be visible 2 miles away and the sidelights must have a range of 1 mile. Between 39 and 65 feet, she must carry lights with longer ranges: 3 miles for the masthead light and 2 miles for the stern and sidelights.

Whether at anchor or under way, all vessels must show lights between sunset and sunrise except that anchor lights are not required in special anchorages.

Capacity Plates

The Coast Guard calculates maximum capacity for monohull rowboats and powerboats smaller than 20 feet. To minimize the chance of overloading, a plate showing the calculated capacity in persons, weight, and engine horsepower must be affixed to the hull.

Oil Discharge Placards

The Federal Water Pollution Control Act prohibits the discharge of oil or oily waste onto the water if the dis-

charge would cause a film, discoloration, or sludge. Violators are liable to a $5000 fine. A placard summarizing the law must be conspicuously posted near the engine compartment of any boat larger than 26 feet.

Marine Sanitation Devices

At the time of writing, the Coast Guard is charged with enforcing federal laws that require treatment of human waste before it is pumped overboard (in Type I and Type II marine sanitation devices) or retention of waste in holding tanks until it can be pumped out ashore (Type III MSDs). However, other responsibilities and concerns have gotten in the way and it may be that the states will take over this regulatory burden. Since many states have legislated their own anti-pollution laws, and some of these are contradictory, a boat owner may find himself in compliance with one state's law when sailing along one shoreline and in violation of another state's law when he sails across the bay or lake. The common denominator for most federal and state regulations is the holding tank used in the Type III MSD; you probably will be legal wherever you sail as long as you retain your own sewage and plan on pumping it out at a marina. Whether you may use a Y-valve so the MSD can serve both as a chemical toilet and as a holding tank will depend on your state's and neighboring states' regulations.

Numbering

Almost all boats with engines, and many sailboats as well, must be numbered and registered by the Coast Guard or a state. For more on numbering, see appendix II.

Appendix II
The Coast Guard and Other Boating Organizations

A great many government and volunteer organizations are concerned with pleasure boating in one way or another, and you should know who they are and what they do in case you have to request their aid and services.

The United States Coast Guard

A part of the U.S. Navy during wartime, the Coast Guard is an agency of the Department of Transportation during peacetime and is charged with supervising or regulating a wide variety of areas of concern to all mariners. The Coast Guard maintains aids to navigation, polices America's shoreline (most recently against illegal immigrants and drug runners), and conducts search-and-rescue missions in its own vessels and aircraft (although private agencies are gradually taking over much of that responsibility). The Coast Guard's jurisdiction includes the following areas of specific interest to pleasure sailors:

Documentation, a federal boat-registration system, is available to owners of boats measuring at least 5 net tons (usually larger than 30 feet) as an alternative to state registration. A documented boat is legally permitted to fly the yacht ensign instead of the American flag, and her title and other papers may be filed with federal officials, which may be an advantage if you cruise over a wide area and prefer not to have an official home port. For more on documentation, consult Coast Guard publication CG-177, "Yacht Admeasurement and Documentation," available from any of the Coast Guard district headquarters listed below.

Enforcement of the law is one of the Coast Guard's foremost responsibilities. Coast Guard officers and enlisted personnel do not have to obtain a search warrant in order to board your boat. You must stop when hailed and allow them to come aboard. Written warnings or, more seriously, citations and fines may be imposed if your safety and other required gear are found deficient or incomplete. If drugs or other contraband are discovered,

your boat may be impounded and you and your crew arrested. You may also be cited for careless boat handling.

Investigation of accidents may lead to penalties. The Federal Boat Safety Act of 1971 requires that after an accident, skippers must do their best to assist victims and later, if there is death or injury, file an accident report either to the state or to the Coast Guard. Penalties are: for negligence, a fine of up to $1000; for gross negligence, a fine of up to $5000 and/or 1 year in prison; for failure to render assistance, a fine of up to $1000 and/or 2 years in prison. Someone who renders assistance without objection from the individual assisted is not liable for any damage incurred.

Enforcement of the federal drunk boating law is another Coast Guard responsibility. The standard for arrest of recreational boaters is a blood alcohol content of .10 percent or more (.08 percent in Utah and .04 percent for nonrecreational boaters). Officers may also arrest people whose appearance, speech, or behavior indicates that they are intoxicated or under the influence of drugs. Operation of a boat when intoxicated can entail a civil penalty of up to $1000, a criminal penalty of up to $5000, and/or a prison sentence.

Local Notice to Mariners is a weekly newsletter sent out by each Coast Guard District announcing changes in buoyage and other aids to navigation, regattas and marine parades, and anything else that might affect safe navigation in the district's waters. Subscriptions are available from local district headquarters, listed below.

Licensing of commercial operators is required by the Federal Boat Safety Act of 1971 and other laws. There are two categories of license: one for vessels carrying more than six passengers and one for vessels carrying six or fewer passengers. (The definition of "passenger" includes a crew member who contributes food or a share of the expenses as well as a fee-paying guest.) Licenses are issued by the Marine Inspection Division of the Coast Guard. Applicants must pass an

examination concerning the Rules of the Road and marine safety, and also must be physically fit. Only motorboat operators require licenses for carrying six or fewer passengers.

Boating safety is one of the Coast Guard's biggest concerns. Its Office of Boating Safety is commanded by a rear admiral and advised by the Boating Safety Advisory Council, whose 21 members are drawn from official agencies, the marine industry, and volunteer groups. The Coast Guard distributes dozens of highly informative pamphlets and films about boat handling, communications, emergency procedures, first aid, and other important topics. These are available from the district headquarters and the U.S. Coast Guard Auxiliary.

Coast Guard District Headquarters

The Coast Guard divides its jurisdiction into ten geographical sections called districts (districts 3, 4, 6, 10, 12, 15, and 16 are no longer active). Notify your local district headquarters to report a hazard to navigation (after reporting it to the Coast Guard over VHF/FM channel 16), or to request documents or a subscription to *Local Notice to Mariners*. Here are the addresses of Coast Guard district headquarters as of fall 1988:

1st District, 408 Atlantic Ave., Boston, MA 02210-2209.

2nd District, 1420 Olive St., St. Louis, MO 63101-2378.

5th District, Federal Building, 431 Crawford St., Portsmouth, VA 23705-5004.

7th District, Federal Building, 51 S.W. 1st Ave., Miami, FL 33130-1608.

8th District, Hale Boggs Federal Building, 500 Camp St., New Orleans, LA 70130-3396.

9th District, 1240 East 9th St., Cleveland, OH 44199-2060.

11th District, Union Bank Building, 400 Oceangate, Long Beach, CA 90822-5399.

13th District, Federal Building, 915 2nd Ave., Seattle, WA 98174-1067.

14th District, Prince Kalanianaole

Federal Building, 300 Ala Moana Blvd., Honolulu, HI 96850-4982.

17th District, Box 3-5000, Juneau, AK 99802-1217.

Other Coast Guard Addresses

The mailing address of the Coast Guard's national headquarters is: Commandant, U.S. Coast Guard, Washington, DC 20593.

The United States Coast Guard Academy is a four-year college where many officers are educated and trained, much the way naval officers are trained at the U.S. Naval Academy at Annapolis. Its address is: U.S. Coast Guard Academy, New London, CT 06320.

The United States Coast Guard Auxiliary

The Coast Guard Auxiliary is a civilian organization founded in 1941 with these goals:

1. To promote safety and to effect rescues on and over the high seas and on navigable waters;

2. To promote efficiency in the operation of motorboats and yachts;

3. To foster a wider knowledge of, and better compliance with, the laws, rules, and regulations governing the operation of motorboats and yachts; and

4. To facilitate other operations of the Coast Guard.

Some 32,000 Coast Guard Auxiliarists, on their own time and in their own boats, conduct boating classes, inspect yachts when invited by their owners, and patrol popular waterways. Every year almost half a million people take Auxiliary-sponsored courses, 300,000 boats receive courtesy inspections, and more than 10,000 boats are assisted in Auxiliary operations. The Auxiliary also publishes its own manuals and distributes Coast Guard publications.

The Auxiliary probably is best known for its courtesy inspection program. After being invited aboard, an Auxiliarist will thoroughly examine your boat's safety, mechanical, and electronic equipment for conformance both with federal requirements (summarized in appendix I) and with the Auxiliary's own, more stringent guidelines. For example, while the federal life jacket regulation specifies one personal flotation device for each crew member, the Auxiliary prefers one PFD for each *bunk* — each removed from its plastic bag and ready for use. And while federal regulations don't say anything about ground tackle, to pass the Auxiliary courtesy inspection

your boat must carry an anchor (or suitable alternative) and sufficient rode. A boat that passes the inspection is given a special decal to be stuck on a window or port.

The relationship between the Auxiliary and the Coast Guard is extremely close, and each Coast Guard district headquarters has an Auxiliary director. More than 1200 Auxiliary flotillas are located around the United States; many are located on the waterfront, and their telephone numbers are listed in local directories.

The United States Power Squadrons

The U.S. Power Squadrons is a national organization composed of more than 400 local squadrons and some 65,000 members committed to the goal of encouraging and promoting "a high amateur standard of skill in the handling and navigation of yachts, power and sail. . . ." The Power Squadrons is not connected with any government agency; it is a club whose membership is by invitation only. But its programs, the best known of which is a series of instructional courses, are open to all. Each squadron must teach the basic U.S.P.S. Boating Course each year, and many also follow that with a sequence of advanced courses in seamanship, piloting, and navigation, as well as others on weather and maintenance. Despite its name, the Power Squadrons has many sailing members.

Other Government Agencies

The Federal Boat Safety Act of 1971 requires that all undocumented boats propelled by power carry numbers issued by a state agency. Some states number sailboats as well. If you're buying a new or used boat, the salesman or previous owner will tell you where to register your boat, pay the fee, and receive the numbers. Otherwise this information may be available from your city hall or police department. The numbers must be placed on either side, forward of amidships, so they are clearly visible; the registration certificate must be carried on board.

States have marine divisions with enforcement powers — some are part of the parks department; others are arms of a special watercraft division. In addition, many police departments in waterfront towns have marine divisions that place local channel buoys and speed limit signs, and that may fine or arrest reckless skippers. Police boat crews have access to VHF/FM frequencies so they may be contacted by sailors in trouble.

Besides the Coast Guard, the Army Corps of Engineers, the National Park Service, and other federal agencies supervise navigable waters in their jurisdictions. The Federal Communications Commission regulates all radio and radar transmissions.

Sailing and Yacht Clubs

These volunteer organizations serve a variety of functions. Some clubs are purely social and provide a pleasant setting (not always near the water) where sailors can gather; others have extensive waterfront facilities that include marinas, moorings, boathouses, and sailing schools; and many clubs of both types sponsor races (for more on racing, see appendix III). Since these clubs are not public accommodations — some may have exclusionary membership policies — don't expect to be welcome at one just because you like to sail and own a boat. However, you should be able to count on a yacht club to lend you a hand in an emergency. Many clubs monitor VHF/FM channel 16 and will send someone out in a launch or other powerboat to pick up an injured crewmember or tow you in if there's a rigging failure. If you are a member of another recognized yacht club that has reciprocal privileges, you may be allowed to use a club's facilities as a guest. Annual dues at yacht and sailing clubs range from less than $100 to thousands of dollars, depending on the extent of the facilities and services available.

Construction Standards

Two private agencies publish construction and rigging standards that are observed by good boatbuilders. The American Boat and Yacht Council (ABYC) is a nonprofit agency that sets and publishes recommended voluntary standards and practices for boat and equipment design, service, and repair. It also publishes *Boating Information*, a thorough bibliography of boating-related publications, films, and videos. The ABYC's address is 405 Headquarters Drive, Suite 3, Millersville, MD 21108.

The American Bureau of Shipping (ABS) has established standards for building oceangoing sailboats. These standards are described in a book, *Guide for Building and Classing Offshore Racing Yachts*, available from the ABS, 45 Eisenhower Drive, Box 910, Paramus, NJ 07653-0910.

Appendix III
Cruising and Racing

There are no public opinion polls to back up this claim, but it is a fair estimate that of every 10 people who start sailing, five hope eventually to go on a long cruise (perhaps around the world) and three hope to win a big racing championship. Of course, not all of them fulfill their ambitions; most join the remaining two sailors in pleasant daysailing with an occasional cruise or race. But dreams of great adventure live on wherever there are wind, water, and sails.

One difference between racing and cruising lies in the boats that are used. Cruising boats tend to be heavier and more commodious. Besides being more comfortable, they are easier to sail well by small crews. There are also differences in the ways cruisers and racers are sailed. Where cruising sailors set their sails to produce the most comfort in the wind gusts, racing sailors usually set enough sail to produce the best speed in the wind lulls. Most cruisers usually sail in a comfortable low or middle gear, while racers are always in a hard-driving high gear.

Here we will say a word or two about those great lures of new sailors, cruising and racing, and about how to get involved with them.

Learning How to Cruise

People who want to go cruising should first learn how to sail. The basic skills of steering, sail trimming, and boathandling must be mastered if cruising is to be more than powering around in calms with the engine on. The best way to learn how to sail is to go to sailing school, and the best boat to do that in is not a cruising boat but a small boat. Lively dinghies and keel daysailers are the most effective teachers because they reward good techniques and punish bad ones much more quickly than big boats.

Once you've learned the basic seamanship skills knocking around in small boats in a sailing school, the next step is to try cruising with a friend or in a chartered boat. Choose pleasant weather; the bad weather can wait until you're sure you like cruising without

rain, cold, and gales. Many charter companies (listed in the advertising sections in the back of boating magazines) lease boats with instructors on board who will reinforce the skills you learned in sailing school while you acquire a taste for the cruising lifestyle.

Chartering

You don't have to own a boat in order to go cruising. Many people who love cruising but who don't have the time, energy, and money to bother with boat upkeep ("messing about in boats" doesn't appeal to everybody) get their kicks through chartering (renting) a boat. For the price of the annual upkeep of a 30- to 40-footer, you should be able to charter a comparable size boat for two weeks. Instead of being confined to the same area, you can try out the exotic cruising grounds of the world like the Caribbean, Greece, Scotland, the Bahamas, Lake Huron's Georgian Bay, the Pacific Northwest, and Maine.

There are two types of charters and two types of charter operations. Boats can be chartered either with paid professional crew (typically a captain and cook) or "bare-boat," which means without paid crew. The former appeals to people who want (and can afford) some luxury, or who are uncertain of their sailing ability. The latter is attractive to people who can handle a boat alone.

Of the two types of charter operations, the simplest is the individual boat owner who cannot use his or her boat every week and wants to recoup some of the cost of purchase and maintenance. The other operation is a company that owns a fleet of boats for full-time charter duty, usually in resort areas. Fleet boats, which have to satisfy the lowest common denominator of cruising sailors, tend to be undistinguished in appearance and sailing performance. Another disadvantage is that a charter from a company is usually more expensive than a charter from a private owner, although seasonal rates vary widely. On the other hand, chartering from a fleet operator usually guarantees prompt service on the water should

you require assistance.

Boats for charter are listed in the advertising and classified sections of many boating magazines. Boat owners and bare-boat charter companies don't lease their boats out unless they are sure that the charterers are qualified sailors, for obvious reasons. Novices can always charter with a captain/instructor.

Boat Ownership

Still, many people want to have their own boats. Much has been said in these pages about the types of boats. But these and other technical concerns have rarely stopped people from making decisions about buying boats for reasons that do not involve objective criteria like dimensions. A boat may appeal because she has a special "look," a particularly handsome interior, or the capacity to be handled easily by only one or two sailors. For people who like a vessel with distinctive appearance or want to enjoy the freedom to go sailing without having to drag a football team along to trim the sails, those concerns can be crucial.

Tastes vary and (fortunately) so do the types of cruising boats, which can be small or large, simple or complicated, traditional or modern, slow or fast, under $20,000 or more than $1 million. There are cruising boats available for almost every requirement. While there is no such thing as an all-around perfect boat, there are boats that are suited to different needs and different people.

New boats have the advantage of being fresh and untried, with the latest generation of equipment, while the big advantage of used boats is their relatively low initial cost (although money will have to be spent to repair wear and tear). Before buying any boat, carefully budget for maintenance, insurance, storage, and other annual costs, which may run as high as 10 percent of the purchase price of a new boat and higher for a used boat. Anybody looking at a used boat should be alert to hidden structural problems that only a careful inspection by a professional boat surveyor will turn up. Surveyors can be found through the Yellow Pages and boat sales offices.

While personal taste in appearance is a perfectly good standard for choosing a boat for cruising near shore, it takes second place to such technical matters as strength and stability when selecting a boat for sailing offshore, where charm does not compensate for the fact that there are no tight little harbors offering escape from strong winds.

Types of Cruises

One of the pleasures of cruising is that there is no reason to feel restricted to one type of cruise. The general categories are, first, coastal (or alongshore) cruising for people who anchor at night and, second, long-distance (or ocean) cruising for those who do not. And there are categories within categories. Coastal cruisers may make anywhere between 5 and 50 miles a day, sailing between 2 and 12 hours to reach a new harbor. Shallow-draft boats can "gunkhole" in small quiet creeks and coves; deep-draft boats look for fuller waters. Occasionally, a larger coastal cruiser will sail overnight to find a new coast to cruise along. People who have never sailed for a few days without stopping have missed out on the wonderful experience of waking up on a boat that is under way. Even going out on short overnight cruises to little corners of the coastline is rewarding, for nothing quite focuses the restless mind as a maturing familiarity with a few small places.

Racing

Wherever there are sailors, there is sailboat racing. Every weekend and on many weekday evenings throughout the year, winter and summer, hundreds of thousands of sailors aged eight to 80 compete in sailboats of all sizes. You can have just as much fun banging about a lake in a dinghy or sailboard costing less than $1000 as racing on the ocean or a big lake in a $3 million, 80-foot ocean racer. Although the only

prize most racing sailors are looking for is a winning gun, there is a small and growing band of professional sailors racing for cash.

Besides offering enjoyment and an outlet for competitive spirit, racing is one of the best ways to learn steering and sail trim and to hone their boat-handling skills.

One-Design Racing

Perhaps the most popular kind of racing is one-design competition, which gets its name from the fact that all the boats in the race have the same shape and sail area, and are potentially equally fast. This leaves winning entirely up to the skipper and crew, although the hull, rigging, and sails must be carefully refined, too. One-designs sail relatively short day races lasting between 30 minutes and 3 hours.

When choosing a one-design class, first figure out how much money, time, and energy you can afford to expend, then look around for local classes that fit your requirements. If you're extremely ambitious and skilled, you might be attracted to one of the classes used in the Olympic Games, such as the Soling, Tornado, and 470. Olympic-class sailing is extremely intense and demanding, and American sailors have been quite successful at it over the years. For most people, however, an Olympic campaign would be too great a drain on financial and emotional resources, and they can usually find satisfaction in one of the non-Olympic one-design classes like the Thistle, Hobie 16, Laser, Lightning, and Etchells 22. Many one-design classes sponsor national championships, but if all you're looking for is some relatively low-key competition, almost every boating area has one or two classes that will fit the bill.

Handicap Racing

Besides one-design racing between equal boats there is also handicap racing between different types of sailboats. Some of this is between one-designs of different classes using an

arbitrary system called the Portsmouth Numbers system. But most handicap racing is between racer-cruisers, boats designed for overnight or long-distance cruising as well as for fast sailing. In this branch of the sport — often called distance racing or ocean racing — boats of all lengths between 20 feet and 80 feet can compete against each other and the handicaps are meant to equalize them. There are three popular handicapping systems

Racing success depends on mastery of many of the skills described in this book: alert boat handling, sail-trimming for the best speed, sailing the course that takes you fastest toward the mark, and weather-watching. You must also be able to sail in crowded fleets without violating the racing rules or having your sails blanketed by competitors.

Appendix III:
Cruising and Racing

(sometimes called rating rules), one for each level of intensity.

All-out ocean racers built solely for competition, with almost no cruising amenities, sail under the International Offshore Rule, a rating rule that governs most international racing. In cost, energy, and prestige, racing under the IOR is the equivalent of grand-prix auto racing.

The IOR is supervised by the Offshore Racing Council (ORC), whose headquarters are in London, England. Another rule overseen by the ORC (this one for boats that are cruised as well as raced) is the International Measurement System (IMS). The IMS encourages good cruising interiors and seaworthy hulls for ocean sailing.

The third rule is a handicapping system called the Performance Handicap Racing Fleet, which is used mainly in North America. Unlike the IOR and MHS, it assigns handicaps through committee decisions based on actual performance rather than measurements. Because it is relatively easy and inexpensive to administer, and usually provides fair handicaps, PHRF is by far the most popular of the three rules in North America.

How Races Are Conducted

Races are started between buoys or between a buoy and an official boat, called the committee boat. A series of signals indicates the time left to the start, and boats maneuver to get the best position on the line. In one-design racing and day racing between racer-cruisers, the first leg of the course usually is upwind to a buoy. The fleet of boats rounds the buoy and alters course to a downwind leg (most frequently a reach) and continues to zig-zag around buoys until it reaches the finish line. Small one-design boats may sail a course with five 1-mile legs, but racer-cruisers and America's Cup boats may cover a total of 25 miles in six legs. The winner is the first boat to finish if the boats are not racing with handicaps, or the boat with the lowest elapsed time after handicaps are computed.

Distance races are started the same way. Most are finished in the same location after the boats sail out around a buoy or island and back, but some long-distances run from one port to another — for example, from Los Angeles to Honolulu; Newport, Rhode Island, to Bermuda; Chicago to Mackinac Island, Michigan; and St. Petersburg to Ft. Lauderdale, Florida.

Although they may be run by the competitors themselves, who time their own finishes, most races are conducted by a committee from a yacht club or other organization. In many cases entrants must be paid-up members of clubs or sailing associations. Since race fleets can obstruct navigation, organizers must notify the U.S. Coast Guard well in advance. Races are announced in *Local Notice to Mariners*.

Racing Rules and Tactics

The objective in sailboat racing is no different from that of any other competition: to win, you've got to finish ahead of the other guy. Like horse racing, sailboat racing is governed by rules that keep the competitors from running into each other and taking unfair advantage, but because yacht racing involves such unpredictables as wind and tide, its rules are probably more complicated than those of any other sport. Here is a summary of the most important rules.

1. **Port-Starboard.** Like the Rules of the Road, the racing rules require a boat on port tack (with her boom on the starboard side) to give way to a boat on starboard tack.

2. **Windward-Leeward and Overtaking.** When boats are on the same tack (with booms on the same sides), a boat to windward or behind must give way to a boat to leeward or ahead. (The first provision is also part of the Rules of the Road.)

3. **Changing Tack.** A boat that is tacking or jibing must give way to a boat that is not. If you tack or jibe into a right-of-way position, you must give the give-way boat time to alter course to avoid you.

4. **Luffing before Starting.** Before starting a race, you may luff (cause to head up) a boat to windward, but you must do it slowly.

5. **Barging.** At the start, don't barge. That means don't try to squeeze between a boat close to leeward of you and a starting line mark.

6. **Over Early.** If you are over the line before the start signal, keep clear of other boats as you return to restart.

7. **Buoy Room.** When two boat lengths from a turning buoy, an obstruction, or a finish line mark, a boat must give room to pass to all other boats between her and the object.

8. **Luffing after Starting.** When another boat tries to pass to windward, the leeward boat may luff her (force her to head up to discourage her from passing) until the helmsman of the windward boat hails "mast abeam" (which means that he is even with or ahead of the leeward boat's mast). Then the leeward boat must head off to her proper course.

9. **Touching a Mark.** A boat touching a mark must reround it while keeping clear of other boats.

10. **Rule Infringement.** If you infringe a rule while racing, you must drop out of the race immediately, although some race organizers may allow you to absolve yourself by making two complete circles and others may impose a penalty on your score. Even when you have right-of-way over another boat, it is your duty to avoid collisions.

For More Information

The official national governing body of sailboat racing in the U.S. is the United States Yacht Racing Union (USYRU), Box 209, Newport, RI 02840. In Canada, the governing body is the Canadian Yachting Association (CYA), in Vanier, Ontario. These organizations publish the yacht racing rules, manage handicap systems, run educational programs, supervise training for Olympic and other international competition, and participate in other programs that concern racers and other sailors.

Appendix IV:
Children and Sailing

The best time to learn how to sail is in childhood, when the reflexes are sharp, the mind is uncluttered, and the learning curve is steep. This does not mean that young sailors should be expected to learn everything about how boats work. Aerodynamic and hydrodynamic theory is more efficiently learned when a person has studied high school science and is old enough to draw analogies between airplane wings and sails.

Although theory can wait, practice can be picked up early. Good sailing schools begin by teaching basic skills like rowing while instilling in their young pupils a respect for the sea's dangers. Next, they put children in boats small enough so the strains can be easily managed. The best boats for the first sailing experiences are singlehanders like the Optimist Pram and the Laser with the small "M" training rig. Only when he or she is sailing alone does the young sailor experience directly how all the parts of the boat interact with each other.

After children have mastered the basic skills and gained confidence on the water, they may move on to intermediate and advanced classes in singlehanded or crewed boats. While kids might enjoy informal tests of speed that are part of fun drills, serious racing should be postponed until they are in their teens, since failure in competition can discourage them from sailing at all. For advanced junior sailors, many areas have racing programs, and the United States Yacht Racing Union sponsors national championships for sailors younger than 19 years old.

Sailing Schools

Sailing is taught to children in public community programs, private sailing schools, and private clubs. In some programs, boats are provided; in others, students must bring their own boats (there is usually a lively market in used boats). A good guide to the quality of a sailing school is to see if it meets the standards set by the United States Yacht Racing Union.

First, the school must exhibit a strong concern for safety. The facility must not be under power lines that may touch the mast of a hauled-out boat. There must be first-aid supplies. The operator must closely monitor the weather and have tested routines for dealing with squalls and other emergencies. Repair and maintenance facilities must be clean and well equipped. Coast Guard-approved life jackets must be required for all sailors, at least until they are confident sailors and have demonstrated they are capable swimmers (many sailing schools require life jackets to be worn by *all* students all the time).

Second, boats must be appropriate to the purpose. The sailboats must be self-righting and self-rescuing, equipped with proper sailing and safety gear, and maintained following an established preventive maintenance program. The powerboats used by the instructors for teaching and rescue must be readily available, in good operating condition, in close communication with each other and headquarters (preferably by VHF/FM radio), able to tow capsized sailboats and return all students to shore, and equipped with safety gear and tools. No boat is to be overloaded.

Third, instructors must be trained. They should be certified by the American Red Cross and have current CPR-First Aid cards. Powerboat drivers should have appropriate licenses. In the classroom, there should be no more than 20 students per instructor. On the water, there should be no more than ten boats per team of certified instructor with two assistant instructors.

Fourth, students must be documented. Swimming ability, health restrictions, previous sailing experience, and family or neighbor telephone contacts must be recorded before the program begins. Policies for discipline must be publicized and enforced.

Children on Cruising Boats

Children can be delightful companions on cruising boats, but there are safety concerns. Here are four tips for easing them.

Teach children to swim early. The earlier they know how to swim, the more they will respect the water.

Use safety equipment. Assign life jackets and/or safety harnesses to children. Show them how to clip on to jacklines. Take the child on a tour of the boat, pointing out such danger areas as the boom, a sheet that is under load, and a spinning steering wheel.

Impose limits. Make sure the child knows who is in charge on deck, and what the boundaries of wandering are. You can impose boundaries by stringing mesh along the lifelines or requiring the child to wear a safety harness hooked to a jackline. Develop a tone of voice that says, *"Listen to me! This is serious!"*

Know where children are. Have them check in with the steerer or somebody on deck when going below. It helps to have each child wear clothing of a distinctive color.

A final safety tip that applies to all young sailors: medical research has clearly demonstrated that a child who is badly sunburned is more likely to develop skin cancer as an adult than a child who is not burned. Make sure the sailing children whom you know are properly protected with high-S.P.F. sun lotions.

Glossary of Important Sailing Terms

The sailor's language borrows heavily from many different sources, and the resulting complexity of terms can be intimidating. Here are definitions of some 500 common boating terms, many of which have multiple meanings.

A

Aback. With sails backed, or trimmed to windward.

Abaft. Behind.

Abeam. At right angles to a boat.

Aboard. On a boat.

Adrift. Unsecured.

Afloat. Floating.

Aft. Toward the stern.

After. A prefix denoting location toward the stern.

Aground. Stuck on the bottom in shallow water.

Aid to Navigation. A buoy, lighthouse, or other channel marker.

Air. Wind.

Alee. To leeward, away from the wind. "Hard a-lee" is the command for tacking.

Aloft. In the rigging above the deck.

Alongside. Beside.

Amidship(s). In the middle of the boat, where she's widest.

Angle of Attack. The angle between the sail and the apparent wind or the rudder or centerline and the water flow.

Apparent Wind. The wind felt on the moving boat.

Appendage. A rudder, keel, centerboard, or skeg.

Astern. Behind the stern.

Athwartships. Across the boat.

Auxiliary. A sailboat that has an engine.

Aweigh. Describes an anchor unhooked from the bottom.

B

Babystay. See **Jackstay**.

Back. (1) To trim a sail to windward; (2) counterclockwise shift in the wind direction.

Backstay. A stay running aft from the upper part of the mast, either permanent or running (adjustable).

Backwind. Wind flowing from a forward sail into the leeward side of an after sail.

Bail. To remove water with a bucket.

Bailers. Sluices in the bilge of a small boat to remove water when she's underway.

Balance. The degree to which all the forces on a boat are symmetrical so she sails with slight weather helm.

Ballast. Weight in the keel or on the windward side that restrains the boat from heeling too far.

Ballast-Displacement Ratio. The numerical ratio between the ballast and displacement in pounds.

Barber Hauler. A sail control used to change the athwartships lead of the jib sheet.

Barometer. An instrument that shows atmospheric pressure in inches or millibars of mercury.

Batten. A wooden or plastic slat inserted in the leech of a sail.

Beam (BM). A boat's greatest width.

Beamy. Wide.

Bear Away. To head off, away from the wind.

Bearing. The angle to an object in relative or compass degrees.

Beat. A course sailed as close to the wind as is efficiently possible, or a close-hauled course.

Below. Beneath the deck.

Bend on Sails. To install sails on the boom and headstay.

Berth. (1) A boat's position at a pier or float; (2) a "wide berth" is a large margin of safety; (3) a bed in a boat.

Bight. Any part of a line between the ends.

Bilge. The lowest part of boat's hull.

Binnacle. A support or pedestal into which a compass is secured.

Bitter End. The end of a line.

Blanket. To come between the wind and a sail so the sail is not full.

Block. A nautical pulley made up of a sheave that rotates on a sheave pin (or center pin) or on ball bearings and hung from metal or plastic sides called cheeks.

Board. (1) Abbreviation for centerboard; (2) to go on a boat; (3) a leg or part of a course.

Boat Hook. A pole with a hook on its end.

Boat Speed. Speed through the water.

Boltrope. The line along the luff and foot of a mainsail and the luff of a jib.

Boom. The spar that extends and supports the foot of a mainsail.

Boom Vang. A tackle or hydraulic system that restrains the boom from lifting.

Boot Top. The painted band on the boat's topsides just at the waterline.

Bottom. (1) The submerged land; (2) the boat's hull under the water, or underbody.

Bow. The most forward part of the boat.

Breeze. Wind or air.

Broach. To get out of control and head up sharply, usually when sailing off the wind.

Broad Off. About 45° to (the bow or stern); sometimes "broad on."

Bulkhead. A wall separating a boat's cabins that provides athwartships support for the hull.

Bunk. A bed in a boat; sometimes "berth."

Buoy. A floating object marking a channel or a mooring.

Buoyancy. The upward force that keeps a boat floating.

By the Lee. Sailing on a run with the wind coming over the quarter on the same side that the boom is trimmed, making a sudden jibe likely.

C

Cabin. A room in a boat.

Calm. Little or no wind. A "flat calm" is totally devoid of wind.

Canvas. Sails or sail area.

Capsize. To turn over.

Cardinal Points. North, East, South, and West. The intercardinal points are Northeast, Southeast, Southwest, and Northwest.

Carry Away. To break.

Cast Off. To let a line go.

Catamaran. A multihull with two hulls separated by a deck or crossbeams from which a trampoline is suspended; abbreviated "cat."

Cat Boat. A wide, shallow boat with a large mainsail and no jib.

Cat Rig. A single- or two-masted boat with no jib.

Caught Aback. With the sails backed, or trimmed to windward.

Centerboard. A retractable appendage that increases or reduces the draft and the lateral area of the underbody.

Center of Effort. The point in the sail plan that is the balance point for all the aerodynamic forces.

Center of Lateral Resistance. The point in the hull's underbody that is the balance point for all the hydrodynamic forces.

Centerline. An imaginary line that runs down the middle of the boat from bow to stern.

Chafe. Abrasion or wear.

Chain Plates. Straps on the hull to which stays are secured.

Chandlery. A marine hardware store.

Channel. Water sufficiently deep to sail in.

Chart. A nautical map.

Charter. To rent a boat.

Chine. The intersection between the topsides and the boat's bottom.

Chock. A fairlead for the anchor rode and docking lines.

Chop. Short, steep waves.

Chord. An imaginary line drawn between the luff and leech of a sail. The chord depth is an imaginary line drawn to the deepest part of the sail from the chord. The ratio of chord depth to chord length represents the sail's draft — a high ratio indicates a full sail; a low ratio, a flat sail.

Circumnavigation. A voyage around the world.

Cleat. A wooden, plastic, or metal object to which lines under strain are secured. There are two kinds of cleats, horn and quick-action.

Clevis Pin. A large pin that secures one fitting to another.

Clew. The after lower corner of a mainsail, jib, or mizzen, and either lower corner of a spinnaker.

Close-Hauled. Sailing as close to the wind as is efficient; also "beating" and "on the wind."

Coaming. A low wall around a cockpit.

Cockpit. A recessed area in the deck containing the tiller or wheel.

Coil. To arrange a line in easily manageable loops so it can be stowed.

Companionway. Steps leading down from the deck to the cabin.

Compass. A magnetized card in a glass dome that indicates the direction to magnetic North.

Compass Rose. A circle on a chart that orients it to North.

Cotter Pin. A small pin used to secure a clevis pin and to keep turnbuckles from unwinding.

Course. (1) The compass direction that is steered; (2) the sequence of buoys rounded in a race.

Cradle. A frame that supports a boat when she's hauled out of the water onto shore.

Crew. Everybody who helps sail a boat except the skipper.

Cringle. A large reinforced eye in a sail.

Cruise. Two or more days spent continuously on a boat that is underway, with stops for the night.

Cruiser-Racer. See **Racer-Cruiser.**

Cruising Boat. A boat used only for cruising.

Cunningham. A line controlling tension along a sail's luff, invented by Briggs Cunningham.

Current. Horizontal movement of the water caused by tidal change or wind.

Custom Boat. A boat built specifically for one client, as against a stock boat.

Cut. The shape or design of a sail.

Cutter. A single-masted boat that flies two jibs at a time.

D

Daggerboard. A centerboard that is retracted vertically rather than hinged.

Dampen. To cause to moderate.

Danger Sector. The fixed red part of lighthouse's light shining over shoals.

Daysailer. A boat without a cabin that is used for short sails or racing.

Dead. Exactly.

Dead-End. To secure an end of a line to an object.

Dead Reckoning (D.R.). The calculation of a boat's position based on course and distance run.

Deck. The top of a hull.

Depower. To lessen heeling forces by making sails less full or allowing them to luff.

Deviation. A compass error caused by metal objects on board.

Dinghy. A small, light sailboat or rowboat.

Displacement. A boat's weight —more accurately, the weight of the water she displaces. A "light-displacement" boat is relatively light for her length.

Displacement Boat. A relatively heavy boat that cannot plane.

Dock. (1) The water next to a float or pier; (2) to bring a boat alongside a float or pier.

Docking Line. A line securing a boat to a float or pier.

Dodger. A fold-up spray shield at the forward end of the cockpit.

Double-Bottom. A watertight compartment between the bottom and the sole, or floor.

Douse. To lower.

Downhaul. A line that holds an object down.

Downwind. Away from the direction from which the wind blows.

Draft (or Draught). (1) The distance between the waterline and the lowest part of the keel; (2) the amount and position of fullness in a sail.

Drag. (1) Resistance; (2) when an anchor breaks out and skips along the bottom.

Drift. A current's velocity.

Drifting. In a calm, to be carried by the current.

E

Earing. A reefing line led through a leech cringle.

Ease. (1) To let out (a sheet); (2) to reduce pull on (the helm).

Easy. Without undue strain, smooth.

Ebb. The dropping, outgoing tide.

Eddy. A circular current.

End-for-End. A reversal of a line.

Estimated Position (E.P.). A best estimate of a boat's position based on her dead reckoning plot and one bearing.

Eye. A loop.

Eye of the Wind. The precise wind direction.

F

Fairlead. A fitting through which a line passes so chafe is avoided.

Fairway. The middle of a channel.

Fair Wind. A reach or run.

Fake. To make large loops on deck with a line in order to eliminate kinks.

Fast. Secure.

Fastenings. The screws and bolts that hold a boat together.

Favor. To ease or help.

Feel. The helmsman's sense of how well the boat is sailing.

Fender. A rubber bumper hung between the boat and a float or pier.

Fend Off. To push off.

Fetch. (1) To sail a course that will clear a buoy or shoal, also "lay"; (2) the distance between an object and the windward shore.

Fish. To repair with turns of light line.

Fitting. A piece of a boat's gear.

Fix. A certain position based on two or more crossed bearings.

Float. A floating platform to which boats may be tied.

Flood. The rising, incoming tide.

Flotation. Foam blocks or air tanks that keep a swamped boat afloat.

Fluky. Unpredictable and weak.

Following Sea. Waves from astern.

Foot. (1) The bottom edge of a sail; (2) to steer slightly lower than close-hauled in order to increase boat speed.

Force. A measurement in the Beaufort Scale.

Fore. Prefix indicating location toward the bow.

Fore and Aft. Everywhere on the boat.

Forepeak. A stowage compartment in the bow.

Forereach. To carry way while heading almost into the wind.

Foresail. A jib.

Forestay. A stay running from the foredeck to the mast, on which a jib is set.

Foretriangle. The area bounded by the mast, foredeck, and headstay.

Forward. Toward the bow.

Foul. (1) To tangle; (2) to violate a racing rule.

Foul-Weather Gear. Water-resistant clothing and boots.

Founder. To swamp or sink.

Fractional Rig. A rig whose headstay goes partway up the mast.

Free. (1) On a broad reach or run; (2) a freeing wind is a lift, or a shift aft.

Glossary of Important Sailing Terms

Freeboard. The distance from the deck to the water, or the height of the topsides.

Fresh Air. Wind of about 16-22 knots.

Front. The approaching edge of a high-pressure or low-pressure system.

Full. (1) Not luffing; (2) with deep draft.

Full and By. Sailing close-hauled with sails full.

Full Sail. All sails set.

Furl. To roll up and secure a sail to a boom.

G

Gadget. A specialized piece of gear.

Gaff-Rigged. With a four-sided mainsail, whose top edge is supported by a spar called a gaff.

Galley. A boat's kitchen.

Gangway. An opening in the lifelines to facilitate boarding from a float or another boat.

Gear. Generic term for all equipment on a boat.

Genoa. A large jib whose clew overlaps the mast and mainsail.

Gilguy. A line or length of shock cord that holds a halyard away from the mast when the sails are not set.

Gimbals. Supports that allow a compass or stove to remain level as the boat heels.

Give. Stretch.

Give-Way Vessel. Under the Rules of the Road, the vessel that must take action to avoid the vessel that has right-of-way.

Gooseneck. The fitting securing the forward end of the boom to the mast.

Gradient. The relative proximity and barometric pressure of adjoining isobars on a weather map.

Grommet. A small metal ring set into a sail.

Ground Tackle. The anchor and anchor rode.

Gunwale. A boat's rail at the edge of the deck, pronounced "gun'l."

Gust. A strong puff of wind.

Guy. A line controlling the position of a spinnaker pole; the after guy pulls the pole back and eases it forward and the fore guy restrains it from lifting.

H

Halyard. A line or wire rope that hoists a sail and keeps it up.

Hand. (1) To lower; (2) a crew member.

Hank. A small snap hook that secures the jib luff to the headstay.

Harden Up. To head up.

Hard Over. As far as possible in one direction.

Hatch. An opening in a deck, covered by a hatch cover.

Haul. To veer, or shift direction clockwise.

Haul In. To trim.

Haul Out. To pull out of the water.

Head. (1) The top corner of a sail; (2) a boat's bathroom.

Headboard. The reinforcement in the head of a sail.

Header. A wind shift requiring the helmsman to alter course to leeward or the crew to trim sheets.

Heading. The course.

Head Off. To alter course to leeward, away from the wind; also "bear off," "bear away," and "come off."

Headroom. A cabin's height.

Headsail. A jib.

Head Sea. Waves from ahead.

Headstay. The stay running from the bow to the mast.

Head-to-Wind. With the bow heading dead into the wind.

Head Up. To alter course to windward, toward the wind; also "harden up," "come up," and "luff up."

Headway. Forward motion.

Heave. To throw.

Heave-To. To sail along slowly with the jib backed.

Heavy Air. Wind of gale force, stronger than 28 knots.

Heavy Weather. Rough seas and gale-force winds.

Heel. A boat's athwartship tip.

Helm. (1) The tiller or steering wheel; (2) the boat's tendency to head off course: with weather helm, she tends to head up, with lee helm, to head off.

Helmsman. The person who is steering.

High. (1) Several degrees more than the required course; (2) pinching, or sailing too close to the wind.

High Cut. With the clew high off the deck.

High Performance. Very fast.

Hike. To lean over the windward rail to counter the heeling forces on the sails.

Hiking Strap. A strap in the cockpit that restrains a hiking sailor's feet.

Hockle. A kink.

Holding Ground. The bottom in a harbor. Good holding ground, such as mud, grabs an anchor securely.

Hounds. The location of the jib halyard block on a mast.

House. The roof of a cabin extending above deck.

Hove-To. In the act of heaving-to.

Hull. A boat's shell, exclusive of appendages, deck, cabin, and rig.

Hull Speed. A boat's theoretical maximum speed determined by multiplying the square root of her waterline length by 1.34.

I

Inboard. In from the rail.

In Irons. Head-to-wind with no headway or sternway.

Isobar. A line on a weather map marking points of equal barometric pressure.

J

Jackstay. A stay running from the foredeck to the mast solely to support the mast; also "babystay."

Jackwire. A wire on deck onto which safety harness tethers are clipped.

Jib. A sail carried on the headstay or forestay.

Jibe. To change tacks by heading off until the sails swing across the boat.

Jiffy Reef. A reef that is tied in.

Jumper Strut. A strut sticking out from the mast near the jib halyard block (the hounds) of a fractional rig; over the strut passes the jumper stay, which when tensioned helps keep the top of the mast straight.

Jury Rig. An improvised replacement for damaged gear.

K

Kedge Off. To use an anchor to pull a grounded boat back into deep water.

Keel. A deep appendage, or fin, under the hull whose lateral area counteracts leeway forces and whose weight counteracts heeling forces — usually permanent but sometimes retractable.

Ketch. A two-masted boat whose after mast, the mizzenmast, is shorter than the forward mast, the mainmast, and is also located forward of the rudder post.

Kink. A temporary twist in a line.

Knockdown. A drastic increase in the angle of heel.

Knot. One nautical mile per hour.

L

Land Breeze. A wind blowing from the shore to the water.

Landmark. An object on the shore that can be helpful when piloting.

Lanyard. A short line.

Lash. To tie.

Launch. (1) To move a boat into the water from land; (2) a powerboat used as a ferry between land and a moored boat; also "shore boat."

Lay. To sail a course that will clear a buoy or shoal; also "fetch."

Layout. The arrangement of gear on deck or of furniture in the cabin.

Lazy. Not in use.

Lead. (1) A block for a jib sheet; (2) to pass a line through a block.

Lee. Contraction for "leeward."

Lee Bow. To have the current pushing the boat to windward.

Leech. The after edge of a mainsail, jib, or mizzen, and both side edges of a spinnaker.

Lee Helm. A boat's tendency to head off, away from the wind, unless checked by the tiller or wheel.

Lee Shore. Land onto which the wind is blowing and which is to leeward of the boat.

Leeward. Downwind.

Leeway. Side-slippage to leeward.

Leg. A part of a passage or race sailed between two buoys or aids to navigation.

Length. Length overall (L.O.A.) is the distance between the tip of the bow and the end of the stern. Length on the waterline, or waterline length (L.W.L.), is the distance between the most forward and most aft points touching the water when the boat is at rest.

Lifeline. A coated wire, supported by posts called stanchions, that encircles the deck to restrain the crew from falling overboard.

Life Raft. An inflatable boat for use in emergencies.

Lift. A wind shift allowing the helmsman to head up, or alter course to windward, or the crew to ease sheets.

Light. (1) Describes a sail that is luffing; (2) an illuminated aid to navigation or boat's navigation light.

Light Air. Wind less than 8 knots.

Light Line. Line smaller than ¼ inch in diameter.

Line. Any length of rope that has a specified use.

Loose. To let go.

Low Cut. With the clew near the deck.

Lubber's Line. A post in a compass used to determine the course or a bearing.

Luff. (1) The forward edge of a mainsail, jib, or mizzen, and the windward edge of a spinnaker; (2) bubbling or flapping in a sail when it is not trimmed far enough or is being backwinded by another sail, or when the course is too close to the wind.

Luff Curve. A convex (in a mainsail) or concave (in a jib) curve in a sail's luff to account for mast bend or headstay sag.

Lull. A relatively calm period between wind gusts.

M

Magnetic. Relative to magnetic North, as against true.

Mainmast. The mast, or the tallest of two masts.

Mainsail. The sail hoisted on the after side of the mainmast, pronounced "mains'l."

Mark. A buoy used in a race course.

Marline. A general-purpose tarred light line.

Marlinspike. A pointed tool on a sailor's knife used to pry open knots, start holes in wood, and accomplish other odd jobs.

Mast. A wooden or aluminum pole supported by standing rigging from which sails are set.

Masthead. The top of the mast.

Masthead Fly. A wind direction indicator at the masthead.

Masthead Light. A white light illuminated when powering at night, located *not* at the top of the mast but about two-thirds of the way up the mast.

Mast Step. The support for the bottom (heel or butt) of the mast.

Millibar (Mb.). A unit of atmospheric pressure, with 1 Mb. equal to 0.03 inches of mercury.

Mizzen. The small, aftermost sail on a ketch or yawl, set on the mizzenmast.

Moderate Air. Wind of about 9-15 knots.

Mooring. A permanently emplaced anchor with a pendant and buoy to which a boat may be secured.

Motion. The degree of instability of a boat's deck while she sails in waves.

Motor Sailer. An auxiliary sailboat with an especially large engine and spacious accommodations.

Multihull. A boat with two hulls (a catamaran) or three hulls (a trimaran), or one hull and an outrigger.

N

Nautical Mile. The unit of geographical distance used on salt-water charts (statute miles are used on Great Lakes charts), where 1 nautical mile = 6076 feet, or 1.15 statute mile. Therefore 1 statute mile = 0.87 nautical mile. One knot = 1 nautical mile per hour.

O

Obstruction. A buoy, vessel, shoal, or other object requiring a major course alteration to pass to one side.

Ocean Racer. A boat with minimal accommodations used for racing overnight or long distances.

Offshore. (1) Out of sight of land; (2) from the land toward the water.

Off the Wind. Reaching or running.

On Board. On a boat.

On Even Keel. Not heeling.

Onshore. From the water toward the land.

On the Beam. Abeam.

On the Bow (Stern). To one side of the bow (stern); also "off the bow (stern)."

One-Design. A racing boat, usually a daysailer, designed and built to the same specifications as all other boats in her class.

Open Boat. A boat without a deck.

Outboard. (1) Out toward and beyond the rail; (2) a nonpermanent engine mounted at the stern.

Outhaul. A sail control that secures the clew of a boomed sail, and adjusts tension along its foot.

Overhang. The distance the bow and stern extend beyond the waterline.

Overhaul. (1) To tighten a lazy (unused) line or the tail of a line in use in order to check that the lead is fair and that there is no chafe; (2) to overtake.

Overlapping. Alongside of; an overlapping jib extends aft of the luff of the mainsail, and an overlapping boat has her bow or stern alongside another boat's stern or bow.

Overnight. For two or three days.

Overpowered. Heeling too far and difficult to steer.

Overrigged. Having too much sail area, also "overcanvassed."

Overstand. To lay or fetch a buoy or shoal with room to spare.

Overtaking. Coming up from astern and about to pass.

P

Padeye. A metal loop to which blocks and shackles are secured.

Painter. A bow line on a dinghy.

Part. (1) To break; (2) one of the sections of line in a tackle.

Partners. The deck opening for the mast.

Passage. More than 6 hours spent under way.

Pay Out. To ease.

Pendant. A short length of wire or line used as an extender on a sail, halyard, or anchor rode, pronounced "pennant."

PFD. Personal Flotation Device, the official term for "life jacket."

Pier. A platform on posts that sticks out from the shore.

Piloting. Navigation within sight of land.

Pinch. To sail too close to the wind when close-hauled.

Pitchpole. To somersault.

Plane. To skip up and across the bow wave at high speed.

Planing Boat. A light boat that planes in fresh winds at speeds exceeding her theoretical hull speed.

Play. (1) To trim a sheet assiduously; (2) a loose fit.

Plot. To draw a boat's course and position on a chart.

Point. To sail close to the wind.

Points of Sail. Close-hauled, reaching, and running.

Pooped. Smashed by a wave breaking over the stern.

Port. (1) The left side, facing forward; (2) a small round window; (3) a commercial harbor.

Porthole. A small round window; also "port."

Glossary of Important Sailing Terms

Pound. To smash down heavily on waves.

Preventer. A line that restrains the boom from jibing accidentally.

Puff. A quick, local increase in wind velocity.

Pulpit. A stainless-steel guardrail around the bow or stern.

Q

Quarter. The after sections of the rails and topsides.

R

Race. (1) An especially strong, turbulent current; (2) an organized competition between boats.

Racer-Cruiser. A boat comfortable enough for cruising and fast enough for racing.

Rail. The outer edge of the deck.

Rake. The tilt of a mast.

Range. (1) The difference in water level between high and low tides; (2) the full extent of a light's visibility; (3) two objects that, when aligned, indicate a channel or the course of another vessel.

Reach. (1) To sail across the wind; (2) a channel between the mainland and an island.

Reef. (1) To decrease a sail's size; (2) a shoal composed of rocks or coral.

Reeve. To lead a line through a block or cringle.

Regatta. A series of races in which cumulative scores are kept.

Render. To run easily through a block.

Rhumb Line. The most direct course between two points.

Rig. (1) The spars, standing rigging, and sails; (2) to get a boat ready for sailing or prepare a sail or piece of gear for use.

Rigging. The gear used to support and adjust the sails: standing rigging includes the spars, stays, and turnbuckles; running rigging includes the sheets and halyards and their blocks, as well as sail controls such as the outhaul and boom vang.

Right-of-Way. The legal authority to stay on the present course.

Roach. The sail area aft of the imaginary straight line running between the head and the clew.

Rode. The anchor line.

Roller Furling. A way to stow sails by rolling them up at their luff.

Roller Reef. A reef secured by rolling the bottom of the sail around the boom.

Rudder. An underwater flap that is adjusted by the helm to steer the boat. It pivots on the rudder post.

Rules of the Road. Laws that, when observed, prevent collisions.

Run. (1) A course with the wind astern; (2) distance covered.

Running Lights. The navigation lights illuminated at night on the starboard and port sides and on the stern.

S

Safety Harness. A web or rope harness worn on the upper body and attached to the deck with a tether to prevent a sailor's falling overboard in rough conditions.

Sail Controls. Lines, tackles, and other gear used to hold a sail in position and adjust its shape, such as the sheets, traveler, outhaul, Cunningham, and boom vang.

Sail Cover. A protective cloth tied over a furled sail to protect it from ultraviolet rays and dirt.

Sail Handling. The hoisting, trimming, and dousing of sails.

Sail Ties. Straps used to secure a furled sail or to lash a doused sail on deck so it doesn't blow away; also called "stops" and "gaskets."

Schooner. A boat with two or more masts, the forwardmost of which, the foremast, is shorter than the aftermost, the mainmast.

Scope. The ratio between the amount of anchor rode let out and the depth of the water.

Scow. A fast, flat-bottomed, blunt-bowed daysailer raced on lakes.

Scull. To propel a boat by swinging the helm and rudder back and forth.

Scupper. A deck or cockpit drain.

Sea. (1) A wave; (2) a body of salt water smaller than an ocean but larger than a sound or gulf.

Sea Boot. A rubber boot with a nonslip sole.

Sea Breeze. A wind blowing from the water to warmer land, filling the space left by rising heated air.

Sea Cock. A valve opening and closing a pipe through the hull.

Sea Condition. The size and shape of the waves.

Seakindly. Comfortable in rough seas.

Sea Room. Enough distance from shore and shoals for safe sailing.

Seaway. Rough water.

Seaworthy. Able to survive heavy weather.

Secure. To fasten or cleat.

Self-Bailing. Automatically draining.

Self-Steering. Automatically steering without a helmsman.

Set. (1) To raise (a sail); (2) a current's direction.

Set Up. To rig.

Shackle. A metal hook that secures a line to a fitting, a line to a sail, or a fitting to a fitting.

Sheave. The roller in a block. It rotates on the sheave pin or center pin.

Sheer. The curve of the rail as seen from alongside.

Sheet. (1) The primary sail-control line, which pulls the sail in and out; (2) to trim.

Shifty. Frequently changing direction.

Shoal. Dangerously shallow water.

Shock Cord. Elastic line.

Shoot into the Wind. To head directly into the wind.

Shorten Down. To set a smaller sail.

Shorthanded. With a small crew.

Shroud. A side stay.

Singlehanded. Solitary.

Sisterships. Boats of the same design.

Skeg. A small, fixed fin attached to the underbody near the stern.

Skipper. The person in charge of a boat.

Slack. (1) Not moving; (2) loose; (3) to ease.

Slat. To roll in a calm with the sails slapping back and forth noisily.

Slicker. A foul-weather jacket.

Slip. A dock between two floats in a marina.

Sloop. A single-masted boat that flies one jib at a time.

Slop. A confused seaway.

Small Boat. A daysailer less than 30 feet long.

Snap Hook. A spring-loaded hook used as a hank and for other small jobs.

Snub. To wrap a line once around a winch or cleat so most of its pull is absorbed.

Sole. A cabin or cockpit floor.

Sound. To measure depth.

Spar. Any mast, boom, or spinnaker pole.

Speed Made Good. A boat's speed as measured by her progress relative to land, factoring in her speed through the water and current.

Spinnaker. A light, ballooning sail used when sailing off the wind.

Splice. To make an eye in the end of a line or link two line ends together by interweaving strands.

Spreader. An athwartships strut holding shrouds out from the mast and providing lateral support.

Stanchions. Metal posts supporting lifelines.

Stand-On Vessel. Under the Rules of the Road, the boat with right-of-way.

Starboard. The right side, facing forward.

Stay. A wire supporting the mast either from forward (headstay, forestay, and jackstay), from athwartships (shrouds), or from astern (backstay and running backstay). Upper stays providing athwartships support are called intermediate stays and those supporting the mast fore and aft over jumper struts are called jumper stays.

Staysail. A small jib tacked down partway back from the headstay.

Steer By. Use as a guide when steering.

Steerageway. Enough speed through the water to allow efficient steering.

Stem. The forward edge of the bow.

Step. To install a mast in a boat.

Stern. The aftermost part of the hull.

Stern Way. Motion astern.

Stiff. Resistant to heeling.

Stock Boat. A boat with many sisterships built by the same manufacturer from the same design, as against a custom boat.

Stop. A sail tie.

Stow. To put in the proper place.

Strong Air. Wind of about 23-27 knots.

Surf. To slide down the face of a wave.

Swamp. To be filled with water.

Swell. Long waves created by prevailing winds or a distant storm; also "groundswell."

T

Tack. (1) With the wind coming over one side or the other; (2) to change tacks by heading up until the sails swing across the boat; (3) the forward lower corner of a mainsail, jib, or mizzen, or the lower windward corner of the spinnaker.

Tack Down. To secure the sail's tack.

Tackle. A mechanical system of line (parts) and blocks that increases hauling power, pronounced "taykle."

Tail. (1) To pull on a sheet or halyard behind a winch; (2) the section of the sheet or halyard behind the winch and cleat.

Tang. A metal strap on the mast to which a stay or block is secured.

Telltale. A piece of yarn or ribbon either tied to the shrouds to help the crew determine wind direction or sewn to the sails to help them trim or steer.

Tender. Heels relatively quickly.

Thimble. A metal or plastic eye worked into an eye splice to protect the line or wire against chafe.

Three Sheets to the Wind. Drunk.

Tide. The rise and fall of water due to the moon's and sun's gravitational pull, as against current, which is the lateral motion of the water as the tides change.

Tide Rip. A line of rough water where a fast-moving tidal current meets stationary or contrary-moving water.

Tied-In Reef. A reef secured by tying cringles to the boom, as against roller reef; also called "jiffy reef" and "slab reef."

Tight Leech. A leech pulled down so hard that it forms a straight line between the head and the clew.

Toggle. A metal fitting inserted between a stay and the mast or turnbuckle, or the turnbuckle and the chain plate, to keep the turnbuckle from bending.

Topping Lift. A line or wire that holds up the boom or spinnaker pole.

Topsides. The outer sides of the hull.

Trailerable (or Trailable). Capable of being towed behind a car on a trailer.

Transom. The athwartships-running surface at the stern.

Trapeze. A wire hanging from a racing dinghy's mast, from which a crew member is suspended in order to counteract heeling forces.

Traveler. An athwartships-running track on which slides a car connected to the main sheet blocks; by adjusting the location of the car, the crew can change the mainsail's angle of attack to the wind.

Trim. (1) To pull in (a sheet); (2) the set of a sail; (3) the bow-up or bow-down attitude a boat assumes when she's at rest.

Trimaran. A multihull with three hulls.

Trip. To break loose.

True. Relative to true North, as against magnetic.

True Wind. The wind's direction and strength felt by a stationary object.

Tune. To adjust the standing rigging until the mast is straight.

Turnbuckle. A threaded fitting used to adjust a stay's length.

Twist. The amount that the leech sags off relative to the imaginary straight line between the clew and head.

Two-Block. To raise all the way.

U

Under Bare Poles. With no sails set.

Underbody. The part of the hull that is underwater.

Under Power. With the engine on.

Underrigged. With not enough sail set, also "undercanvassed."

Under Way. Moving.

Unreeve. To remove a line from a block or cringle.

Unrig. To remove or disassemble gear after it is used.

Upwind. Toward the direction from which the wind blows.

USCG. United States Coast Guard.

USYRU. United States Yacht Racing Union.

V

Vang. (1) A boom vang; (2) to pull down on the boom with a boom vang.

Variable. Unsteady in strength and direction.

Variation. The local difference in degrees between true and magnetic North.

Veer. A clockwise shift in the wind direction.

Vent. A ventilator.

Vessel. Any boat or ship.

VHF/FM. A very-high-frequency radiotelephone.

Voyage. A long passage under sail.

W

Wake. The water turbulence left behind by a moving boat.

Way. Speed.

Weather. (1) General atmospheric conditions; (2) wind; (3) upwind; (4) to survive a storm.

Weather Helm. A boat's tendency to head up, into the wind, unless checked by the tiller or wheel.

Wetted Surface. The area of the underbody and appendages.

Whisker Pole. A spar similar to a spinnaker pole used to hold out the jib when sailing wing-and-wing.

Williwaw. A violent gust of wind.

Winch. A geared drum turned by a handle used to pull halyards, sheets, and other lines under strain.

Windage. Wind resistance.

Windlass. A special type of winch used for pulling the anchor rode.

Windward. Upwind.

Wing-and-Wing. With the jib and mainsail set on opposite sides when sailing on a run or broad reach.

Wing Out. Set wing-and-wing.

Wire Rope. Stainless steel or galvanized wire used in stays, halyards, sheets, and other gear.

Working Sails. The mainsail and non-genoa jib.

Y

Yacht. A pleasure boat.

Yacht Designer. A naval architect specializing in the design of yachts.

Yaw. To sail a wildly erratic course.

Yawl. A two-masted boat whose after mast, the mizzenmast, is shorter than the forward mast, the mainmast, and is located aft of the rudder post.

Y.C. Yacht Club.

The Sailor's Library

While the best way to pick up the skills of sailing seamanship is to get out on a boat, not all knowledge comes from personal experience. Most good sailors have large libraries of magazines and books (and, increasingly, videotapes) that teach them new skills, tell them about new boats and equipment, and take them on dream cruises. Here is a survey of some of the best magazines, books, and tapes available in the summer of 1988.

An excellent bibliography of boating publications, films, and videos is *Boating Information*, produced by the American Boat and Yacht Council, 405 Headquarters Drive, Suite 3, Millersville, MD 21108. Another, briefer, bibliography is *The Source*, a free pamphlet distributed by BOAT/U.S. Foundation, 880 S. Pickett St., Alexandria, VA 22304.

Magazines

When it comes to the number and variety of periodicals, no hobby or sport can touch sailing. Here is a list of nationally distributed sailing magazines. In addition, each large boating area has at least one regional publication.

American Sailor (Box 209, Newport, RI 02840), the magazine of the United States Yacht Racing Union, concentrates on news of sailboat racing.

Cruising World (5 John Clark Rd., Middletown, RI 02840) prints instructional articles on all types of cruising, from overnighting to sailing around the world, as well as accounts of cruises and news of new boats and gear.

Motor Boating & Sailing (224 West 57th St., New York, NY 10019) focuses on powerboats but runs some instructional and feature articles of interest to sailors.

Nautical Quarterly (Pratt St., Essex, CT 06426) specializes in yachting history, marine art, good boats, and important sailing personalities; the format is beautiful.

Ocean Navigator (Box 569, Portland, ME 04112) carries instructional articles on all types of navigation, plus evaluations of gear and publications.

Practical Sailor (Box 819, Newport, RI 02840) is a nautical *Consumer Reports*. Since it does not carry advertising (unlike other boating magazines), its evaluations of equipment can be hard-hitting.

Sail (100 First Ave., Charlestown, MA 02129) has instructional articles (some aimed at beginning sailors) on daysailing, cruising, and racing, plus well-illustrated news reports and cruise accounts.

Sailing (125 E. Main St., Pt. Washington, WI 53074) specializes in large, handsome photos of boats in action; it also includes boat evaluations and sailing news.

Sailing Canada (95 Berkeley St., Toronto, Ontario M5A 2W8) is a general sailing magazine with instructional articles and news about Canadian events and developments.

Sailing World (5 John Clark Rd., Middletown, RI 02840) is aimed at ambitious, relatively advanced racing and cruising sailors. Besides racing news, "how-to" articles, and boat evaluations, it features columns by several well-known sailors.

Soundings (Pratt St., Essex, CT 06426) is a national boating newspaper, with special regional editions. Its classified sections carry thousands of listings of used boats for sale.

Woodenboat (Box 78, Brooklin, ME 04616) concentrates on traditional boats and building materials and runs occasional articles on maritime history.

The Yacht (Box 329, Newport, RI 02840) is a handsome bimonthly carrying photo essays and articles on the more lavish aspects of boating.

Yachting (Box 1200, Cos Cob, CT 06807) covers power and sail, concentrating on bigger yachts. There is some instructional and news material, plus a large brokerage section listing used boats.

Books and Videotapes

Most of the books and videos listed here have appeared since 1983, when the first edition of this book was published. Many are in print, which means that they may be ordered from a bookstore, a marine hardware store with a book department, or the Dolphin Book Club, the boating division of the Book-of-the-Month Club (Camp Hill, PA 17012). Books not in print may often be found in public libraries.

General

Brown, Bruce C. *Watershots: How to Take Better Photos On and Around the Water.* Camden, Me.: International Marine, 1988. A clear guide to using a piece of equipment found on almost every boat.

Maloney, Elbert S. *Piloting, Seamanship, and Small Boat Handling*, 58th edition. New York: Hearst Marine, 1987. Called "Chapman's" in honor of its first author, this manual is mainly for powerboaters but has good coverage of regulations.

Rousmaniere, John. *A Glossary of Modern Sailing Terms.* 2nd edition. New York: Putnam's, 1989. The language of today's sailor.

Videotapes

Rousmaniere, John. *The Annapolis Book of Seamanship Video Series.* New York: Creative Programming Inc., 1986-88. Five 60- to 90-minute instructional tapes elaborating on the lessons in this book using extensive on-the-water demonstrations. The titles released through 1988 were: "Cruising Under Sail," "Heavy Weather Sailing," "Safety at Sea," "Sailboat Navigation," and "Daysailers: Sailing and Racing."

The Rules of the Road

Tate, William H. *A Mariner's Guide to the Rules of the Road*, 2nd edition. Annapolis, Md.: Naval Institute Press, 1982. A survey that includes analyses of typical situations.

U.S. Coast Guard. *Navigation Rules: International-Inland.* The official text.

Cruising

Chace, Arthur F. *Precision Cruising.* New York: W. W. Norton, 1987. Cruising with intensity and care.

Cornell, Jimmy. *World Cruising*

Routes. Camden, Me.: International Marine, 1987.

Dashew, Steve and Linda. *Bluewater Handbook: A Guide to Cruising Seamanship*. Ojai, Cal.: Beowulf Publishing, 1984. Two circumnavigators describe important lessons learned.

Pardey, Lin and Larry. *The Capable Cruiser*. New York: W. W. Norton, 1987. An excellent guide to long-distance cruising and cruising boats.

Rousmaniere, John. *The Sailing Lifestyle*. New York: Simon & Schuster, 1985. Basic sailing, cruising, and live-aboard skills.

Boats

Brewer, Ted. *Ted Brewer Explains Yacht Design*. Camden: Me.: International Marine, 1985. A layperson's guide written by a practicing designer.

Brown, Larry. *Sailing on a Micro-Budget*. Camden, Me.: International Marine, 1984. Small cruising boats.

Duffet, John. *Boatowner's Guide to Modern Maintenance*. New York: W. W. Norton, 1985. A good survey of tools and skills.

James, Rob. *Multihulls Offshore*. New York: Dodd, Mead, 1983. Modern cruising catamarans and trimarans and their handling.

Roberts, John, and Maria Mann. *Choosing Your Boat*. New York: W. W. Norton, 1986. Whet to look for when buying a new or used boat.

Technical Committee of the Cruising Club of America. *Desirable and Undesirable Characteristics of Offshore Yachts*. John Rousmaniere, ed. New York: W. W. Norton, 1987. The design, construction, and rigging of boats for long-distance cruising.

Weather

Kotch, William J. *Weather for the Mariner*, 3rd edition. Annapolis, Md.: Naval Institute Press, 1983. How weather and meteorologists work.

Lee, Albert. *Weather Wisdom*. Garden City, N.Y.: Doubleday, 1976. The source of some of the useful rhymes used in chapter 4.

Watts, Alan. *Reading the Weather: Modern Techniques for Yachtsmen*. New York: Putnam's, 1987. *Wind and Sailing Boats: The Structure and Behaviour of the Wind as it Affects Sailing Craft*, 3rd edition. North Pomfret, Vt.: David and Charles, 1987. Two excellent books by a prominent sailing meteorologist.

Sails and Gear

Ashley, Clifford W. *The Ashley Book of Knots*. Garden City, N.Y.: Doubleday, 1944. The most complete knot book.

Brotherton, Miner. *The 12-Volt Bible for Boats*. Camden, Me.: Seven Seas, 1985. The workings of a boat's electrical systems.

Calder, Nigel. *Marine Diesel Engines: Maintenance, Troubleshooting, and Repair*. Camden, Me.: International Marine, 1987. An excellent engine manual. *Repairs at Sea*. Camden, Me.: International Marine, 1988. How to patch things up when there's no help at hand.

Hinz, Earl. *The Complete Book of Anchoring and Mooring*. Centreville, Md.: Cornell Maritime, 1986. A solid study of anchoring gear and skills.

Jarman, Colin. *The Essential Knot Book*. Camden, Me.: International Marine, 1986. Four dozen knots, splices, and whippings.

Kenny, Dick. *Looking at Sails*. Camden, Me.: International Marine, 1988. Modern sails, their trim, and their gear, all shown up close in color photographs.

Miller, Conrad, and E.S. Maloney. *Your Boat's Electrical System*, 2nd edition. New York: Hearst Marine, 1988. A thorough survey that includes many projects that owners can do themselves.

Ross, Wallace C. *Sail Power*. New York: Knopf, 1975. The most thorough guide to sails and their trim.

Navigation

Duncan, Roger F. *Sailing in the Fog*. Camden, Me.: International Marine, 1986. How to navigate in poor visibility.

Dunlap, G. D., and H. H. Shufeldt. *Dutton's Navigation & Piloting*, 14th edition. Annapolis, Md.: Naval Institute Press, 1985. The most thorough one-volume manual on navigation.

Melton, Luke. *The Complete Loran-C Handbook*. Camden, Me.: International Marine, 1986. A very thorough survey.

West, Jack. *Boatowner's Guide to Radar*. Camden, Me.: International Marine, 1988. An excellent manual on radar operation on pleasure boats.

Heavy Weather and Emergencies

Eastman, Peter F. *Advanced First Aid Afloat*, 3rd edition. Centreville, Md.: Cornell Maritime, 1988. Unlike most first aid manuals, this one takes the sailor's special problems into account.

Hinz, Earl. *Understanding Sea Anchors and Drogues*. Centreville, Md.: Cornell Maritime, 1987. The first book on these devices.

Wilkerson, James A., ed. *Medicine for Mountaineers*, 3rd edition. Seattle: The Mountaineers, 1985. A guide to emergency first aid that is organized by symptoms.

Rousmaniere, John. *"Fastnet, Force 10"*. New York: W. W. Norton, 1980. The

The Sailor's Library

story of the worst disaster in the history of pleasure sailing.

Racing

Bavier, Bob. *Keys to Racing Success.* New York: Dodd, Mead, 1982. A master skipper summarizes the essentials.

North Sails. *The North U. Fast Course* and *The North U. Smart Course.* Milford, Ct.: North Sails, 1988 and 1989. Informative manuals on sail trim and tactics used in seminars run by a noted sailmaker.

Perry, Dave. *Understanding the Yacht Racing Rules.* New York: Dodd, Mead, 1985. An exceptionally clear guide to a complicated subject.

History and Traditions

Howe, Hartley Edward. *North America's Maritime Museums: An Annotated Guide.* Facts on File, 1987. Descriptions of more than 250 ships and maritime museums open to the public.

Lord, Lindsay. *Nautical Etiquette & Customs.* 2nd edition. Centreville, Md.: Cornell Maritime, 1987. A short survey.

Rousmaniere, John. *America's Cup Book, 1851-1983, The Golden Pastime: A New History of Yachting,* and *The Low Black Schooner: Yacht America, 1851-1945.* New York: W. W. Norton, 1983, 1986, and 1987. Handsomely illustrated histories of yachting.

Solley, George C., and Eric Stein-baugh, eds. *Moods of the Sea* and *Short Stories of the Sea.* Annapolis, Md.: Naval Institute Press, 1981 and 1984. Great sea poetry and fiction.

Ten Classic Books

There is a long and honorable tradition of superb writing about pleasure boating. Here are 10 classics that belong in any serious sailor's library. Many are still in print in 1989.

Childers, Erskine. *The Riddle of the Sands.* First published in 1903. Probably the only spy story whose solution lies in a tide table. Made into a fine movie starring Michael York.

Herreshoff, L. Francis. *The Compleat Cruiser: The Art, Practice, and Enjoyment of Boating.* 1956. An eccentric narrative of a short cruise that teaches much about sailing small vessels.

Hiscock, Eric. *Around the World in Wanderer III.* 1956. A book that inspired many other people to try it, too.

Howland, Llewellyn. *Sou'West & By West of Cape Cod.* 1947. This one is about the quiet pleasures of shallow bays and soft breezes.

MacGregor, John. *The Voyage Alone in the Yawl Rob Roy.* 1867. One of the most influential sailing books in history.

Moitessier, Bernard. *The Long Way.* 1971. In 1968-69, this Frenchman, incredibly, sailed one and a half times around the world, nonstop and alone. This is his account of the voyage.

Robertson, Dougal. *Survive the Savage Sea.* 1973. A family's survival after their boat was sunk by a whale.

Slocum, Joshua. *Sailing Alone Around the World.* 1900. By turns inspiring and humorous, this account of the first singlehanded circumnavigation is the classic sailing tale.

Smeeton, Miles. *Once is Enough.* 1959. Rolled over and nearly sunk off Cape Horn. A story of extraordinary courage and endurance.

Thompson, Winfield M., and Thomas W. Lawson. *The Lawson History of the America's Cup.* 1902. A beautiful history of the cup between 1851 and 1901 that shows how it captured the public imagination.

Index

Topics of special interest are shown in bold face. For technical terms, also consult the glossary.

Index

Topics of special interest are shown in bold face. For technical terms, also consult the glossary.

Index

Topics of special interest are shown in bold face. For technical terms, also consult the glossary.

Index

Topics of special interest are shown in bold face. For technical terms, also consult the glossary.

Review Quiz Answers

Chapter 11

1. B. 009°. The direction in true degrees is 356°, and the reciprocal course is 189°.

2. B. 10 miles; 4.4 knots. Use two versions of the Speed/Time/Distance formula to solve these problems. First solve for distance, then for speed.

3. A. 8.7 knots. There are two ways to solve this problem. Each requires you to start with the distance run of 2.6 miles, which can be found with dividers on the latitude scale. The simplest way is to use the 6-minute rule: if the boat took 18 minutes to go 2.6 miles, then (dividing by 3) in 6 minutes she went 0.87 miles. Since 6 minutes is 0.1 hour, multiply 0.87 by 10 to find the speed, 8.7 knots. You could also use the Speed/Time/Distance formula to solve for speed.

4. B. 1054 hours. This is an example of running out your time. First use dividers to find the distance to the buoy, 3.4 miles. Then use the Speed/Time/Distance formula to solve for time under way: multiply 3.4 by 60, divide the product by 4 to arrive at 51 minutes, and add 51 to 1003 hours to find the arrival time.

5. A. 10-12° leeway to the West; 168° compensated course. A boat like yours will make 10-12° leeway in these conditions. Since an East wind blows from the East and pushes boats to the West, the compensation must be to the East, so subtract 12° from the original course to find the new course.

6. C. A dead reckoning position, an estimated position, and a fix. A D.R. (half-circle) has no LOPs, an E.P. (box) has one, and a fix (circle) has two or more.

7. B. With a running fix; bearing 195°, range 4.5 miles. Using a running fix, draw a line parallel to the first bearing on False Ducks Lt. through the intersection of the boat's track and the second bearing on the light.

8. C. Port tack. Since your course is to the South and the wind is from the Southeast, you will spend more time on the port tack than on the starboard tack. As a rule of thumb, sail the long-est leg first so you can be in a position to take advantage of wind shifts. In this case, another advantage of starting out on the port tack is that you will sail faster toward the long-range visibility lights on False Ducks and Prince Edward Point. These lights will provide assistance at night.

Chapter 12

1. B. 270° and 3 miles. Solve this problem using the system of doubling the relative bow bearing. In the 36 minutes between the 45° and 90° bearings, at 5 knots you travel 3 miles according to both the Speed/Time/Distance formula and the 6-Minute Rule. Since the distance run equals the distance off, you know that you are 3 miles off the light on the LOP of the beam bearing.

2. B. 9.4 nautical miles. You are bobbing the horizon. Use the formula for determining geographical range in nautical miles: multiply 1.144 times the square root of the lighthouse's height, 67 feet, to arrive at 9.36 nautical miles. This geographical range is a little more than 1.5 miles shorter than the light's nominal range of 11 miles (which is included in the chart label). From a higher platform you should be able to see the light out to its nominal range.

3. B. NLT 020° and NMT 045°. A danger bearing is a minimum bearing that guides the navigator in avoiding a hazard. Here, the bearing from the buoy off Prince Edward Point to the Timber Island buoy is about 020° and the bearing to the Northeast side of Timber Island is about 045°. If the boat ever gets into the cone between those bearings, then the boat is sailing into the area between the buoy and the island tip and risks running aground. This will be the case if the bearing to the buoy is a number lower than 020° (for example 015°) and the bearing on the island's Northeast tip is a number higher than 045° (for example 050°).

4. A. 204° to pass to the East and 216° to pass to the West. Use the Rule of 60 to calculate the necessary course alteration. Here, to clear the island by approximately 0.3 miles, the boat must alter course so she passes approximately 0.7 miles either side of the island's center. Therefore, the desired distance off is 0.7 miles. The distance ahead to the island is about 7 miles. Multiply 0.7 by 60, and divide the product by 7. The resulting course alteration to either side is 6°, which is subtracted from or added to 210° to come up with the new, safe courses.

5. C. Up the Western side. All things being equal, following a long, fairly straight contour like the 30-foot contour on the Western side is less confusing than working with no contours (as in the middle) or working with a circuitous one (as on the Eastern side).

6. B. 1.8 feet above MLW. Using the tide table, we see that the tide was low 2 hours ago at 6:14 A.M. (5:14 plus 1 hour for Daylight Saving Time), that the high-tide level will be 6.9 feet above MLW, and that the duration of rise or fall is 6 hours. Turning to the upper correction table on the opposite page, we read the line across from 6 hours (duration) to 2 hours (time from the nearest change). Then we read down the column to the line for 7.0 feet, the approximate tide range. The number at the intersection is 1.8 feet.

7. C. SMG 7 mph, CMG 060°. Current set (in contrast with wind direction) is the direction toward which the flow is moving. Here, the current is from off the boat's port quarter and is pushing the boat forward and to starboard. A vector diagram would provide the most accurate measurement, but as a rough estimate the SMG is about 7 knots and the CMG is about 060°.

8. B. 176°. Use the Rule of 60. Since the distance to the light is 10 statute miles, at a speed of 5 knots you will sail for 2 hours. Therefore the 1-knot current will push you to the west a total of 2 miles. Compensate by steering 2 miles to the East of the point. Multiply 2 (the course change in miles) by 60, then divide the product by 10 (the distance ahead). The result is 12°. Since the course change is to port, it is subtracted from 188° (the original course) to come up with 176°. If the course change were to starboard, it would be added, to come up with 200°.

Acknowledgments

This new edition and its predecessor could not have been finished without the help of many friends and colleagues. Mark Smith's contribution is obvious to anybody who turns these pages. Michael Korda and Fred Hills, of Simon and Schuster, and Timothy Seldes, my agent, arranged for the book to be written in the first place. Harvey Loomis again edited the text with a strong sense of its overall aim. The following helpfully critiqued chapters in the first edition: Dick Goennel, chapter 5; Dick McCurdy, chapters 4, 15, and 16; Bill Robinson, chapter 14; and Hewitt Schlereth, chapters 9-13.

The editors of several magazines have given me the freedom to try out ideas in their columns. Foremost among these is Doug Logan of *Sailing World*, but I am also thinking of Bernadette Brennan of *Cruising World*, Joe Gribbins of *Nautical Quarterly*, and Tim Queeney of *Ocean Navigator*. I thank Cornell Maritime Press and John de Graff Inc. for permitting me to use tables from Earl Hinz's *The Complete Book of Anchoring* and Bruce Fraser's *Weekend Navigator*, respectively.

Spencer Smith and Nancy Donaldson, my editors at the Dolphin Book Club (where I serve on the editorial committee), have kept me up to date with the best new boating books and videotapes. Nancy Fisher has helped me learn how to make my points with ever greater clarity as we have worked together on instructional tapes in *The Annapolis Book of Seamanship Video Series*.

Helpful suggestions about ways to improve on the first edition have come from many generous people, too many of them momentary acquaintances in crowded aisles at boat shows or around the coffee pots at safety-at-sea seminars. For help in improving my understanding of safety issues, I thank John Bonds, Kelsey Burr, Dick McCurdy, Wayne Williams, and others with whom I have served on panels at safety seminars.

For spiritual nourishment, intellectual stimulation, and a broader perception of what is important in life (all of which are needed by anybody taking on the responsibility of a *summa* like this book) I thank the faculty and students of Union Theological Seminary, in New York City, where I studied for and earned the degree of Master of Divinity in the years between the first and second editions. The subjects are different, but the discipline is the same.

At Simon and Schuster, Leslie Ellen, Jenny Cox, David Rosenthal, and Janet Schubert worked hard and well on the production of this complicated book.

Finally, I thank the many shipmates and skippers who have answered my questions, loaned me their boats, endured my impositions, and allowed me to learn from my mistakes.

John Rousmaniere
Stamford, Connecticut
January 14, 1989

Photo Credits

Bahamas News Bureau: 75 (bottom), 77 (top), 78, 87, 95
Peter Barlow: 115, 117, 152, 328
Diane Beeston: 326 (bottom)
Beken of Cowes: 320
Ellen Bentsen: 52, 96
Bermuda News Bureau: 16 (top left), 133 (Force 4), 325, 326 (top), 344 (bottom)
Tyler Carder: 32 (top), 100 (middle, below left and right), 282
Tim Cole: 373 (top)
Cruising World: 373 (bottom)
Christopher Cunningham: 33 (top)
Dan Devine: 34 (top)
Guy Gurney: 18 (bottom right), 240
Robert Hagan: 7 (top), 32 (middle and bottom), 34 (bottom), 171 (top)
Steve Henkel: 279, 369 (lower right)
Roger Kennedy: 381
Jim Kransberger: 364
Louis Kruk: 38

Roger Lean-Vercoe: 166
Leslie Lindman: 93
Long Beach News Bureau: 97
Frank MacLear: 146, 296
Millie Rose Madrick: 169
Wendy Morgan: 372
National Oceanographic and Atmospheric Administration: 110, 114, 123, 124, 125
Dan Nerney: Jacket (front cover and author), 362
New York Times: 122
J.H. Peterson: 77 (bottom)
Miles Quintan: 363
John Rousmaniere: (many taken on assignment for *Yachting* magazine) 18 (top), 25, 45, 51, 53, 63, 71, 73, 85, 91, 94, 98, 102, 103, 133 (Force 2 and 6), 139, 145, 146 (top), 154, 307, 354, 356
Royal Navy: 113, 334
Gail Scott Sleeman: 369 (lower left)
Jack Somer: 238
Barry Tenin: 285
West Marine Products: 178, 180, 181

The Annapolis Book of Seamanship Video Series

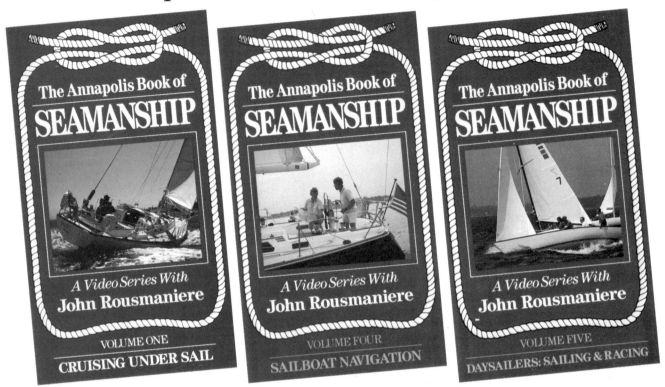

Now the information in *The Annapolis Book of Seamanship* is available in an award-winning, professionally produced video series written and hosted by John Rousmaniere. Each video features on-the-water demonstrations on board one of today's top cruising and daysailing boats. Endorsed by The Safety at Sea Committee of the U.S. Yacht Racing Union.

"Superb video. . . . Rousmaniere is a natural teacher." (George Day, editor, *Cruising World* magazine) *"These are important videos, destined to become the prime source of much sailing information for new sailors of the 'video generation.'"* (*Offshore* magazine)

Volume 1: Cruising Under Sail surveys basic sailing skills and gear, with plenty of advanced tips. An excellent refresher for the experienced skipper as well as an ideal orientation for new sailors. (72 min.)

Volume 2: Heavy Weather Sailing shows skills and equipment needed to handle tough weather. Shot in rough seas in the Caribbean. (55 minutes)

Volume 3: Safety at Sea tells how to prepare for and avoid life- and boat-threatening disasters. Careful demonstrations of crew-overboard rescues, flares, life rafts, going aloft, and safety harnesses. (94 minutes) *1988 Cindy Award winner for instructional videos.*

Volume 4: Sailboat Navigation goes step by step through basic piloting and electronic navigational skills and gear (including Loran-C, radar, and SATNAV). Shot in daylight and at night. (75 minutes)

Volume 5: Daysailers, Sailing and Racing is for small-boat sailors, whether novice crew or advanced skipper. Lessons on sail trim, steering, safety gear, and racing rules are capped by an actual closely fought race. (60 minutes)

From the reviewers:

"Will help sailors be more confident and even enjoy sailing in heavy weather . . . easy relaxed style." (Gary Jobson, ESPN sailing commentator)

"A solid 10." (*Sailing World* magazine)

"Four stars, highest rating." (*Captain's Briefing* magazine and *Video Digest* magazine)

$39.95 each, VHS or BETA

Available through marine catalogs and outlets, book clubs, and good video stores.
To order direct, call (800) 733-8862.